Computer Science
Illuminated

Fourth Edition

Computer Science
Illuminated

Fourth Edition

Nell Dale
University of Texas, Austin

John Lewis
Virginia Tech

JONES AND BARTLETT PUBLISHERS

Sudbury, Massachusetts

BOSTON   TORONTO   LONDON   SINGAPORE

World Headquarters
Jones and Bartlett Publishers
40 Tall Pine Drive
Sudbury, MA 01776
978-443-5000
info@jbpub.com
www.jbpub.com

Jones and Bartlett Publishers Canada
6339 Ormindale Way
Mississauga, Ontario L5V 1J2
Canada

Jones and Bartlett Publishers
International
Barb House, Barb Mews
London W6 7PA
United Kingdom

Jones and Bartlett's books and products are available through most bookstores and online booksellers. To contact Jones and Bartlett Publishers directly, call 800-832-0034, fax 978-443-8000, or visit our website, www.jbpub.com.

Substantial discounts on bulk quantities of Jones and Bartlett's publications are available to corporations, professional associations, and other qualified organizations. For details and specific discount information, contact the special sales department at Jones and Bartlett via the above contact information or send an email to specialsales@jbpub.com.

Amazon®, America Online®, AOL®, Apple®, Apple Macintosh®, AT&T™, BlackBerry®, BlackBerry® Pearl™, BlackBerry® Storm™, Bluetooth®, eBay®, emWave®, eNeighbor®, Epic Games UnrealScript®, FiOS®, Firefox®, HeartMath®, IBM®, iMac®, Intel®, Intel Pentium®, Internet Explorer®, iTunes®, Java™, JavaScript™, Mac OS®, Mastercard®, Microsoft®, MySpace™, Netscape Navigator®, Nintendo®, Nintendo Wii™, Nike®, Pixar®, Playstation®, PowerPoint®, Prodigy®, Software Garden®, Sony®, SpeedPass®, WalMart®, Windows®, Windows 7®, Windows Vista®, and Xbox® are trademarks or registered trademarks of America Online, Amazon.com, Apple, AT&T, Bluetooth SIG, Inc., eBay Inc., Epic Games, ExxonMobil Corporation, Healthsense, Heartmath, Intel, MasterCard, Microsoft, MySpace.com, Nintendo, Pixar, Research In Motion Limited, Software Garden, Inc., Sony, Sun Microsystems, Verizon, and WalMart Stores Inc. in the United States and other countries.

Production Credits

Chief Executive Officer: Clayton Jones
Chief Operating Officer: Don W. Jones, Jr.
President, Higher Education and Professional Publishing:
    Robert W. Holland, Jr.
V.P., Sales: William J. Kane
V.P., Design and Production: Anne Spencer
V.P., Manufacturing and Inventory Control: Therese
    Connell
Publisher: David Pallai
Acquisitions Editor: Timothy Anderson
Editorial Assistant: Melissa Potter

Production Director: Amy Rose
Associate Production Editor: Melissa Elmore
Senior Marketing Manager: Andrea DeFronzo
Composition: Northeast Compositors, Inc.
Cover and Title Page Design: Kristin E. Parker
Senior Photo Researcher and Photographer: Christine
    Myaskovsky
Cover and Title Page Image: © ImageMore/age fotostock
Printing and Binding: Courier Kendallville
Cover Printing: Courier Kendallville

Library of Congress Cataloging-in-Publication Data
Dale, Nell B.
  Computer science illuminated / Nell Dale and John Lewis. — 4th ed.
    p. cm.
  Includes bibliographical references and index.
  ISBN 978-0-7637-7646-6 (pbk.)
  1. Computer science. I. Lewis, John, 1963 II. Title.
  QA76.D285 2010
  004—dc22
                        2009033027

6048
Printed in the United States of America
13 12 11 10 09   10 9 8 7 6 5 4 3 2 1

*To my wife Sharon and my children Justin, Kayla,
Nathan, and Samantha*
—*John Lewis*

To Al, my husband and best friend
—*Nell Dale*

John Lewis, Virginia Tech

John Lewis is a leading educator and author in the field of computer science. He has written a market-leading textbook on Java™ software and program design. After earning his PhD in Computer Science, John spent fourteen years at Villanova University in Pennsylvania. He now teaches computing at Virgina Tech, his alma mater, and works on textbook projects out of his home. He has received numerous teaching awards, including the University Award for Teaching Excellence and the Goff Award for Outstanding Teaching. His professional interests include object-oriented technologies, multimedia, and software engineering. In addition to teaching and writing, John actively participates in the ACM Special Interest Group on Computer Science Education (SIGCSE) and finds time to spend with his family or in his workshop.

Nell Dale, University of Texas, Austin

Well-respected in the field of computer science education, Nell Dale has served on the faculty of the University of Texas, Austin for more than 25 years and has authored over 40 undergraduate Computer Science textbooks. After receiving her BS in Mathematics and Psychology from the University of Houston, Nell entered the University of Texas, Austin where she earned her MA in Mathematics and her PhD in Computer Science. Nell has made significant contributions to her discipline through her writing, research, and service. Nell's contributions were recognized in 1996 with the ACM SIGCSE Award for Outstanding Contributions in Computer Science Education. Nell recently retired from full-time teaching, giving her more time to write, travel, and play tennis. She currently resides in Austin, Texas.

Brief Contents

Contents

3 The Hardware Layer 90

5 The Operating Systems Layer 332

6 The Applications Layer 386

Preface

Choice of Topics

In putting together the outline of topics for this CS0 text, we used many sources. We looked at course catalogue descriptions, book outlines, and administered an email questionnaire designed to find what you, our colleagues, thought should be included in such a course. We asked you and ourselves to make the following three lists:

- Please list four topics that you feel students should master in a CS0 course if this is the only computer science course they will take during their college experience.
- Please list four topics that you would like students entering your CS1 course to have mastered.
- Please list four additional topics that you would like your CS1 students to be familiar with.

The strong consensus that emerged from the intersections of these sources formed the working outline for this book. Students who master this material before taking CS1 have a strong foundation upon which to continue in computer science. Although our intention was to write a CS0 text, our reviewers have pointed out that the material also forms a strong breadth-first background that can serve as a companion to a programming-language introduction to computer science.

Rationale for Organization

Chapter 1 of this book presents the history of hardware and software, showing how a computer system is like an onion. The computer, with its machine language, forms the heart of the onion, and layers of software and more sophisticated hardware have been added around this heart, layer by layer. First came machine language, part of the heart of this "onion." At the next layer, higher-level languages such as FORTRAN, Lisp, Pascal, C, C++, and Java™ were introduced parallel to the ever-increasing exploration of the programming process, using such tools as top-down design and object oriented design. Over time, our understanding of the role of abstract data types and their implementations matured. The operating system, with its resource-management techniques, including files on ever-larger, faster secondary storage media, developed to surround and manage these programs.

The next layer of the computer system "onion" is composed of sophisticated general-purpose and special-purpose software systems that overlay the operating system. Development of these powerful programs was stimulated by theoretical work in computer science, which make such programs possible. The final layer comprises networks and network software—that is, the tools needed for computers to communicate with one another. The Internet and the World Wide Web put the finishing touches to this layer.

As these layers have grown over time, the user has become increasingly insulated from the computer system's hardware. Each of these layers provides an abstraction of the computing system beneath it. As each layer has evolved, users of the new layer have joined with users of inner layers to create a very large work force in the high-tech sector of our economy. This book is designed to provide an overview of the layers, introducing the underlying hardware and software technologies, in order to give students an appreciation and understanding of all aspects of computing systems.

Having used history to describe the formation of the onion from the inside out, we were faced with a design choice: We could look at each layer in depth from the inside out or the outside in. The outside-in approach is very tempting. We could peel the layers off one at a time, moving from the most abstract layer to the concrete machine. However, research has shown that students understand concrete examples more easily than abstract ones even when the students themselves are abstract thinkers. Thus, we have chosen to begin with the concrete machine and examine the layers in the order in which they were created, trusting that a thorough understanding of one layer makes the transition to the next abstraction easier for the students.

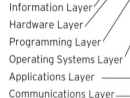

Information Layer
Hardware Layer
Programming Layer
Operating Systems Layer
Applications Layer
Communications Layer

Changes in the Fourth Edition

The early editions of a new book are like shakedown cruises of a new ship. If the design is good, only minor problems occur that need tweaking. As a book—or ship—gets older, future editions may call for a major overhaul. In planning for this revision we asked our CS education colleagues to give us feedback: What changes should be made? What kind of an overhaul is necessary? Over 30 of you, both users and nonusers, shared your ideas with us. The consensus was that the programming layer needed a major overhaul. This we have done.

In previous editions, problem solving was presented in the abstract, followed by machine language, assembly language, and high-level languages. We now believe that going from the concrete chapters in the information layer to the very abstract first chapter in the programming layer and then back to the very concrete assembly language chapter causes confusion. A better approach would be to cover machine and assembly language, followed by pseudocode, problem solving, algorithms, and abstract data types. The last chapter in this layer covers object-oriented design and high-level programming languages. This sequence makes the transition from concrete to abstract gradually.

In addition to this major revision, we have added more material on different programming languages, giving examples from Scheme and Prolog. We have added major sections on social networking and gaming; we have consolidated the sections on information and computer security into Chapter 12. Of course, all the side bars, biographies, and ethical issues have been revised and/or updated.

Synopsis

Chapter 1 lays the groundwork as described in the section explaining the rationale for this book's organization. Chapters 2 and 3 step back and examine a layer that is embodied in the physical hardware. We call the layer the *information layer*, and it reflects how data is represented in the computer. Chapter 2 covers the binary number system and its relationship to other number systems such as decimal, the one we humans use on a daily basis. Chapter 3 investigates how we take the myriad types of data we manage— numbers, text, images, audio, and video—and represent them in a computer in binary format.

Chapters 4 and 5 represent the *hardware layer*. Computer hardware includes devices such as transistors, gates, and circuits, all of which control the flow of electricity in fundamental ways. This core electronic circuitry gives rise to specialized hardware components such as the computer's Central Processing Unit (CPU) and memory. Chapter 4 covers gates and electronic circuits; Chapter 5 covers the hardware components of a computer and how they interact within a von Neumann architecture. Of course the ad that introduces Chapter 5 has been updated—and is probably out of date by the time you read this Preface!

Chapters 6 through 9 cover aspects of the *programming layer*. Chapter 6 covers the concepts of both machine language and assembly language programming using Pep/8, a simulated computer. The functionality of pseudocode is introduced as a way to write algorithms. The concepts of looping and selection are introduced here, expressed in pseudocode, and implemented in Pep/8.

Chapter 7 examines the problem-solving process, both human- and computer-related. George Polya's human problem-solving strategies guide the discussion. Top-down design is introduced as a way to design simple algorithms. We choose classic searching and sorting algorithms as the context for the discussion of algorithms. Because algorithms operate on data, we examine ways to structure data so that it can be more efficiently processed. Subalgorithm (subprogram) statements are introduced.

Chapter 8 takes a step up in abstraction and talks about abstract data types or containers: composite structures for which we know only their properties or behaviors. Lists, sorted lists, stacks, queues, binary search trees, and graphs are discussed. The discussion of subalgorithms is expanded to include reference and value parameters and parameter passing.

Chapter 9 covers the concepts of high-level programming languages. Because many prominent high-level languages include functionality associated with object-oriented programming, we detour and first present this design process. Language paradigms are discussed as well as the compilation process. Pseudocode concepts are illustrated in brief examples from four programming languages: Python, VB .NET, C++, and Java.

Chapters 10 and 11 cover the *operating system layer*. Chapter 10 discusses the resource-management responsibilities of the operating system and presents some of the basic algorithms used to implement these tasks. Chapter 11 covers file systems, including what they are and how they are managed by the operating system.

Chapters 12 through 14 cover the *application layer*. This layer is made up of the general-purpose and specialized application programs that are available for the public to use to solve programs. We divide this layer into the sub-disciplines of computer science upon which these programs are based. Chapter 12 examines information systems and information and computer security, Chapter 13 examines artificial intelligence, and Chapter 14 examines simulation, graphics, gaming, and other applications.

Chapters 15 and 16 cover the *communication layer*. Chapter 15 presents the theoretical and practical aspects of computers communicating with each other. A new section on social networking has been added to this chapter. Chapter 16 covers the World Wide Web and its influence on life today.

Chapters 2 through 16 are about what a computer can do and how it does it. Chapter 17 concludes with a discussion of the inherent limitations of computer hardware, software, and the problems that can and cannot be solved using a computer. Big-O notation is presented as a way to talk about the efficiency of algorithms so that the categories of algorithms can be discussed and the Halting problem is presented to show that some problems are unsolvable.

The first and last chapter form bookends: Chapter 1 describes what a computing system is and Chapter 17 cautions what computing systems cannot do. The chapters in between look in depth at the layers that make up a computing system.

Why Not a Language?

The original outline for this book included an Introduction to Java chapter. Some of our reviewers were ambivalent about including a language at all; others wondered why Java was included and not C++. We decided to leave the choice to the user. Introductory chapters, formatted in a manner consistent with the design of this book, are available for Java, C++, JavaScript™, Visual Basic. NET®, Python®, SQL, Ruby, Perl, Alice, and Pascal on the book's website and in hard-copy through Jones and Bartlett Publishers. Additionally, two lab manuals, one in Java and one in C++, have been written for this edition.

If the background of the students is such that they can master the introductory syntax and semantics of a language in addition to the background material in this book, just have the students download the appropriate chapter. As an alternative, one or all of these chapters can be used as enrichment for those students who have a stronger background.

Special Features

We have included three special features in this text in order to emphasize the history and breadth of computing as well as the moral obligations that come with new technology. Each chapter includes a short biography of someone who has made a significant contribution to computing as we know it. The people honored in these sections range from those who contributed to the data layer, such as George Boole and Ada Lovelace, to those who have contributed to the communication layer, such

16.2 HTML   533

Tim Berners-Lee

Tim Berners-Lee is the first holder of the 3COM (Computer Communication Compatibility) Chair at the Computer Science and Artificial Intelligence Laboratory (CSAIL) at Massachusetts Institute of Technology. He is the 3COM Founders Professor of Engineering in the School of Engineering with a joint appointment in the Department of Electrical Engineering and CSAIL at MIT. Berners-Lee is a researcher, evangelist, and visionary rather than an academician. He is Director of the World Wide Web Consortium, which coordinates Web development worldwide. The Consortium, with teams at MIT, ERCIM in France, and Keio University in Japan, aims to help the Web achieve its full potential, ensuring its stability through rapid evolution and revolutionary transformations of its usage.

How did Tim Berners-Lee arrive at this very important position? He built his first computer while Queen's College, Oxford   United

Courtesy of Le Fevre Communications/WC3

the World Wide Web. It was designed to allow people to work together by combining their knowledge in a web of hypertext documents. Berners-Lee wrote the first World Wide Web server, "httpd," and the first client, "World Wide Web," a what-you-see-is-what-you-get hypertext browser/editor. The work began in October 1990, and the program "World Wide Web" was made available within CERN in December 1990 and on the Internet at large in the summer of 1991.

Between 1991 and 1993, Berners-Lee continued working on the design of the Web, coordinating feedback from users across the Internet. His initial specifications of URLs, HTTP, and HTML were refined and discussed in larger circles as the Web technology spread. Eventually, it became apparent that the physics lab in Geneva was not the appropriate place for the task of developing and monitoring the Web. In October 1994, the World Wide Web Consortium was founded by Berners-Lee at the MIT Laboratory for Com

Used by permission of Sony Electronics Inc.

Fans Mourn the Passing of Aibo
Sadly, Sony Corporation announced the demise of Aibo, the robot dog that could learn its owner's name, show anger (eyes became red), and express happiness (eyes became green). More than 150,000 of these machines, which were the size of a toy poodle, were sold.

⚖ **ETHICAL ISSUES ▸ Blogging**   Ⓦ

Like Websites, *blogs* have become ubiquitous virtually overnight. A blog is a Weblog or online journal. Most blogs are interactive and provide for feedback from readers. Whereas most bloggers write about mundane matters, the *blogosphere* has also emerged as a viable alternative news medium. Blogs are having a growing impact, sometimes supplementing or correcting reporting of the mainstream media. In 2004, blogs quickly exposed the inauthenticity of the documents used in a *60 Minutes* story about President George W. Bush's National Guard service. Many other blogs consistently provide a unique and unconventional perspective on the local and national news.

According to the *Wall Street Journal*, the audience for alternative media is expanding: "The number of Americans reading blogs jumped 58% in 2004 to an estimated 32 million people . . . with about 11 million looking to political blogs for news during the [2004] presidential campaign." [1]

But blogs are not just for online journalists or political commentators. Their use has also grown among doctors, lawyers, and teachers. Blogs have even become popular in the classroom. Many students have their own blogs where they record their impressions about teachers or other school-related information in a diary-like format. The use of student blogs has led to a new debate about the amount of control educators should exert over online classroom activities.

Of course, the blogosphere is not without its share of controversies. One such controversy erupted in

» continued

as Doug Engelbart and Tim Berners-Lee. These biographies are designed to give the students a taste of history and introduces them to the men and women who have contributed and are contributing today to the world of computing.

Our second feature, which we call *callouts* for lack of a better word, are sidebar sections that include interesting tidbits of information from the past, the present, and the future. They are garnered from history, from today's newspapers, and from the experiences of the authors. These little vignettes are designed to amuse, to inspire, to intrigue, and, of course, to educate.

Our third feature is a section on Ethical Issues included in each chapter. These sections are designed to illustrate that along with the advantages of computing come responsibilities for the consequences of its use. Privacy, hacking, viruses, and free speech are among the topics discussed. At the end of each chapter's exercises, we include a selection of Thought Questions that cover these ethical issues as well as chapter content.

Color and Typography Are Signposts

The layers into which the book is divided are color coded within the text. The chapter openers show the onion with the outside color showing the layer. That color is repeated in bars across the top of the pages of the layer. For each chapter, there is a slide on the side of the chapter opener, which shows where the chapter is within the layer. We have said that the first and last chapter form bookends. Although they are not part of the layers of the computing onion, we have given each a color, which shows up in the onion, the slide, and the color bar. Open the book anywhere and you can immediately tell where you are within the layers of computing.

To visually separate the abstract from the concrete in the programming layer, we use different fonts for algorithms, including identifiers in running text, and program code. You know at a glance whether the discussion is at the logical (algorithmic) level or at the programming language level. In order to clarify visually the distinction between an address and the contents of an address, we color addresses in orange.

Color is especially useful in Chapter 6, Low-Level Programming Languages and Pseudocode. Instructions are color coded to differentiate the parts of an instruction. The operation code is green, the register designation is clear, and the addressing mode specifier is blue. Operands are shaded gray. As in other chapters, addresses are in orange.

Website

A companion website has been established for this text that includes a wealth of additional information, both for the students and for the instructors. Additional biographies, more information about some of the callouts, and updates that relate to ethical issues are available on the text's website. In addition, there are eLearning tools for the students that include a variety of exercises including crossword puzzles.

Answers to the exercises are available for the instructor from the textbook's catalog page at http://www. jbpub.com/catalog/9780763776466. PowerPoint® presentations and test items for each chapter are also available on the website.

Acknowledgments

Our adopters have been most helpful during this revision. To those of you who took the time to respond to our online survey: Thanks to all of you. We are grateful to the reviewers for the previous editions of the text:

Tim Bower, Kansas State University; Mikhail Brikman, Salem State College; Jacques Carette, McMaster University; Howard Francis, Pikeville College; Jim Jones, Graceland University; Murray Levy, West Los Angeles College; Lew Lowther, York University; Jeffrey McConnell, Canisius College; Richard Schlesinger, Kennesaw State University; Richard Spinello, Boston College; Herman Tavani, Rivier College; Amy Woszczynski, Kennesaw State University; C. Michael Allen, UNC—Charlotte; Lofton Bullard, Florida Atlantic University; Cerian Jones, University of Alberta; Calvin Ribbens, Virginia Tech; Susan Sells, Wichita State University; R. Mark Meyer, Canisius College; Tom Wiggen, University of North Dakota; Mary Dee Harris, Chris Edmonson-Yurkanan, Ben Kuipers, and Glenn Downing all from the University of Texas—Austin; Dave Stauffer, Penn State; John McCormick, University of Northern Iowa; Dan Joyce, Villanova University; Mike Goldwasse and Andrew Harrington at Loyola University—Chicago; and Daniel R. Collins, Mass Bay Community College.

Special thanks to Jeffrey McConnell of Canisius College, who wrote the graphics section in Chapter 14; Herman Tavani of Rivier College, who worked with us on the revision of the "Ethical Issues"; and Richard Spinello of Boston College, for his essay on the ethics of blogging.

We appreciate and thank our reviewers and colleagues that provided advice and recommendations for the content in this fourth edition:

J. Stanley Warford, Pepperdine University

Richard C. Detmer, Middle Tennessee State University

Chip Weems, University of Massachusetts—Amherst

Heather Chandler, Westwood College

Mark Holthouse, Westwood High School

Robert Vermilyer, St. Thomas Aquinas College

We also thank the many people at Jones and Bartlett Publishers who contributed so much, especially Tim Anderson, Acquisitions Editor; Melissa

Potter, Editorial Assistant; Melissa Elmore, Associate Production Editor; and Amy Rose, Production Director. A special "thank you" to Melissa Potter, who helped so much with the updates to the callouts and the ethical issues.

I must also thank my tennis buddies for keeping me fit, my bridge buddies for keeping my mind alert, my family for keeping me grounded, and my cat for waking me up in the morning.
    —ND

I'd like to thank my family for their support.
    —JL

Laying the Groundwork

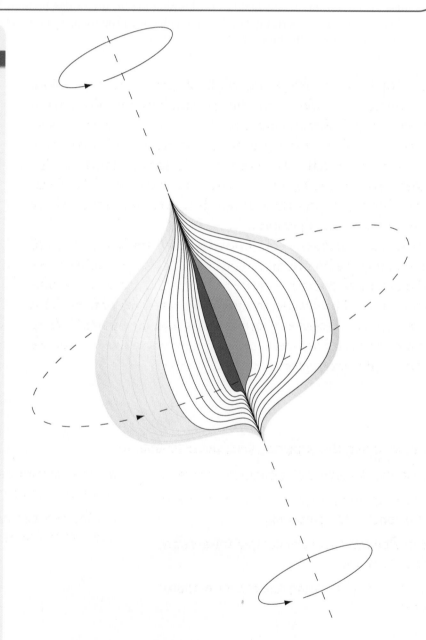

The Big Picture

This book is a tour through the world of computing. We explore how computers work—what they do and how they do it, from bottom to top, inside and out. Like an orchestra, a computer system is a collection of many different elements, which combine to form a whole that is far more than the sum of its parts. This chapter provides the big picture, giving an overview of the pieces that we slowly dissect throughout the book and putting those pieces into historical perspective.

Hardware, *software*, *programming*, *web surfing*, and *email* are probably familiar terms to you. Some of you can define these and many more computer-related terms explicitly, whereas others may have only a vague, intuitive understanding of them. This chapter gets everyone on relatively equal footing by establishing common terminology and creating the platform from which we will dive into our exploration of computing.

Goals

After studying this chapter, you should be able to:

- describe the layers of a computer system.
- describe the concept of abstraction and its relationship to computing.
- describe the history of computer hardware and software.
- describe the changing role of the computer user.
- distinguish between systems programmers and applications programmers.
- distinguish between computing as a tool and computing as a discipline.

1.1 Computing Systems

In this book we explore various aspects of computing systems. Note that we use the term "computing system," not just "computer." A computer is a device. A computing system, by contrast, is a dynamic entity, used to solve problems and interact with its environment. A computing system is composed of hardware and software, and the data that they manage. Computer hardware is the collection of physical elements that make up the machine and its related pieces: boxes, circuit boards, chips, wires, disk drives, keyboards, monitors, printers, and so on. Computer software is the collection of programs that provide the instructions that a computer carries out. And at the very heart of a computer system is the information that it manages. Without data, the hardware and software are essentially useless.

The general goals of this book are threefold:

- To give you a solid, broad understanding of how a computing system works
- To develop an appreciation for and understanding of the evolution of modern computing systems
- To give you enough information about computing so that you can decide whether you wish to pursue the subject further

The rest of this section explains how computer systems can be divided into abstract layers and how each layer plays a role. The next section puts the development of computing hardware and software into historical context. This chapter concludes with a discussion about computing as both a tool and a discipline of study.

■ Layers of a Computing System

A computing system is like an onion, made up of many layers. Each layer plays a specific role in the overall design of the system. These layers are depicted in Figure 1.1 and form the general organization of this book. This is the "big picture" that we will continually return to as we explore different aspects of computing systems.

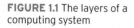

» Computing system
Computer hardware, software, and data, which interact to solve problems

» Computer hardware The physical elements of a computing system

» Computer software The programs that provide the instructions that a computer executes

FIGURE 1.1 The layers of a computing system

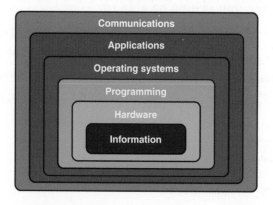

You rarely, if ever, take a bite out of an onion as you would an apple. Rather, you separate the onion into concentric rings. Likewise, in this book we explore aspects of computing one layer at a time. We peel each layer separately and explore it by itself. Each layer, in itself, is not that complicated. In fact, a computer actually does only very simple tasks—it just does them so blindingly fast that many simple tasks can be combined to accomplish larger, more complicated tasks. When the various computer layers are all brought together, each playing its own role, amazing things result from the combination of these basic ideas.

Let's discuss each of these layers briefly, and identify where in this book these ideas are explored in more detail. We essentially work our way from the inside out, which is sometimes referred to as a bottom-up approach.

The innermost layer, information, reflects the way we represent information on a computer. In many ways this is a purely conceptual level. Information on a computer is managed using binary digits, 1 and 0. So to understand computer processing, we must first understand the binary number system and its relationship to other number systems (such as the decimal system, the one humans use on a daily basis). Then we can turn our attention to how we take the myriad types of information we manage—numbers, text, images, audio, and video—and represent them in a binary format. Chapters 2 and 3 explore these issues.

The next layer, hardware, consists of the physical hardware of a computer system. Computer hardware includes devices such as gates and circuits, which control the flow of electricity in fundamental ways. This core electronic circuitry gives rise to specialized hardware components such as the computer's central processing unit (CPU) and memory. Chapters 4 and 5 of the book discuss these topics in detail.

The programming layer deals with software, the instructions used to accomplish computations and manage data. Programs can take many forms, be performed at many levels, and be implemented in many languages. Yet, despite the enormous variety of programming issues, the goal remains the same: to solve problems. Chapters 6 through 9 explore many issues related to programming and the management of data.

Every computer has an operating system (OS) to help manage the computer's resources. Operating systems, such as Windows XP, Linux, or Mac OS, help us interact with the computer system and manage the way hardware devices, programs, and data interact. Knowing what an operating system does is key to understanding the computer in general. These issues are discussed in Chapters 10 and 11.

The previous (inner) layers focus on making a computer system work. The applications layer, by contrast, focuses on using the computer to solve specific real-world problems. We run application programs to take advantage of the computer's abilities in other areas, such as helping us design a building or play a game. The spectrum of area-specific computer software tools is far-reaching and involves specific subdisciplines of computing, such as information systems, artificial intelligence, and simulation. Application systems are discussed in Chapters 12, 13, and 14.

Computers no longer exist in isolation on someone's desktop. We use computer technology to communicate, and that communication is a fundamental layer at which computing systems operate. Computers are connected into networks so that they can share information and resources. The Internet, for example, evolved into a global network, so that there is now almost no place on Earth that you cannot communicate with via computing technology. The World Wide Web makes that communication relatively easy; it has revolutionized computer use and made it accessible to the general public. Chapters 15 and 16 discuss these important issues of computing communication.

Most of this book focuses on what a computer can do and how it does it. We conclude with a discussion of what a computer *cannot* do, or at least cannot do well. Computers have inherent limitations on their ability to represent information, and they are only as good as their programming makes them. Furthermore, it turns out that some problems cannot be solved at all. Chapter 17 examines these limitations of computers.

Sometimes it is easy to get so caught up in the details that we lose perspective on the big picture. Try to keep that in mind as you progress through the information in this book. Each chapter's opening page reminds you of where we are in the various layers of a computing system. The details all contribute a specific part to a larger whole. Take each step in turn and you will be amazed at how well it all falls into place.

■ Abstraction

> **Abstraction** A mental model that removes complex details

The levels of a computing system that we just examined are examples of abstraction. An abstraction is a mental model, a way to think about something, which removes or hides complex details. An abstraction leaves only the information necessary to accomplish our goal. When we are dealing with a computer on one layer, we don't need to be thinking about the details of the other layers. For example, when we are writing a program, we don't have to concern ourselves with how the hardware carries out the instructions. Likewise, when we are running an application program, we don't have to be concerned with how that program was written.

Numerous experiments have shown that a human being can actively manage about seven (plus or minus two, depending on the person) pieces of information in short-term memory at one time. This is called Miller's law, based on the psychologist who first investigated it.[1] Other pieces of information are available to us when we need it, but when we focus on a new piece, something else falls back into secondary status.

This concept is similar to the number of balls a juggler can keep in the air at one time. Human beings can mentally juggle about seven balls at once, and when we pick up a new one, we have to drop another. Seven may seem like a small number, but the key is that each ball can represent an abstraction, or a chunk of information. That is, each ball we are juggling can represent a complex topic as long as we can think about it as one idea.

We rely on abstractions every day of our lives. For example, we don't need to know how a car works to drive one to the store. That is, we don't really need to know how the engine works in detail. You need to know only some basics about how to interact with the car: how the pedals and knobs and steering wheel work. And we don't even have to be thinking about all of those things at the same time. See Figure 1.2.

Even if we do know how an engine works, we don't have to think about it while driving. Imagine if, while driving, we had to constantly think about how the spark plugs ignite the fuel that drives the pistons that turn the crankshaft. We'd never get anywhere! A car is much too complicated for us to deal with all at once. All the technical details would be too many balls to juggle at the same time. But once we've abstracted the car down to the way we interact with it, we can deal with it as one entity. The irrelevant details are ignored, at least for the moment.

Abstract art, as the name implies, is another example of abstraction. An abstract painting represents something, but doesn't get bogged down in the details of reality. Consider the painting shown in Figure 1.3, entitled *Nude Descending a Staircase*. You can see only the basic hint of the woman or the staircase, because the artist is not interested in the details of exactly how the woman or the staircase looks. Those details are irrelevant to the effect the artist is trying to create. In fact, the realistic details would get in the way of the issues that the artist thinks are important.

Abstraction is the key to computing. The layers of a computing system embody the idea of abstraction. And abstractions keep appearing within individual layers in various ways as well. In fact, abstraction can be seen throughout the entire evolution of computing systems, which we explore in the next section.

FIGURE 1.2 A car engine and the abstraction that allows us to use it

Oil dip stick
Air cleaner
Fuse box
Battery
Radiator

Brake fluid reservoir
Engine
Windshield washer tank
Power steering fluid

1.2 The History of Computing

The historical foundation of computing goes a long way toward explaining why computing systems today are designed as they are. Think of this section as a story whose characters and events have led to the place we are now and form the foundation of the exciting future to come. We examine the history of computing hardware and software separately because each has its own impact on how computing systems evolved into the layered model we use as the outline for this book.

This history is written as a narrative, with no intent to formally define the concepts discussed. In subsequent chapters, we return to these concepts and explore them in more detail.

■ A Brief History of Computing Hardware

The devices that assist humans in various forms of computation have their roots in the ancient past and have continued to evolve throughout the present day. Let's take a brief tour through the history of computing hardware.

Early History

Many people believe that Stonehenge, the famous collection of rock monoliths in Great Britain, is an early form of calendar or astrological calculator. The *abacus*, which appeared in the sixteenth century BC, was developed as an instrument to record numeric values and on which a human can perform basic arithmetic.

In the middle of the seventeenth century, Blaise Pascal, a French mathematician, built and sold gear-driven mechanical machines, which performed whole-number addition and subtraction. Later in the seventeenth century, a German mathematician, Gottfried Wilhelm von Leibniz, built the first mechanical device designed to do all four whole-number operations: addition, subtraction, multiplication, and division. Unfortunately, the state of mechanical gears and levers at that time was such that the Leibniz machine was not very reliable.

In the late eighteenth century, Joseph Jacquard developed what became known as *Jacquard's loom*, used for weaving cloth. The loom used a series of cards with holes punched in them to specify the use of specific colored thread and therefore dictate the design that was woven into the cloth. Although not a computing device, Jacquard's loom was the first to make use of an important form of input: the punched card.

> **Beyond all dreams**
> "Who can foresee the consequences of such an invention? The Analytical Engine weaves algebraic patterns just as the Jacquard loom weaves flowers and leaves. The engine might compose elaborate and scientific pieces of music of any degree of complexity or extent."
>
> –Ada, Countess of Lovelace, 1843[2]

It wasn't until the nineteenth century that the next major step was taken, this time by a British mathematician. Charles Babbage designed what he called his *analytical engine*. His design was too complex for him to build with the technology of his day, so it was never implemented. His vision, however, included many of the important components of today's computers. Babbage's design was the first to include a memory so that intermediate values did not have to be reentered. His design also included the input of both numbers and mechanical steps, making use of punched cards similar to those used in Jacquard's loom.

Ada Augusta, Countess of Lovelace, was a very romantic figure in the history of computing. Ada, the daughter of Lord Byron (the English poet), was a skilled mathematician. She became interested in Babbage's work on the analytical engine and extended his ideas (as well as correcting some of his errors). Ada is credited with being the first programmer. The concept of the loop—a series of instructions that repeat—is attributed to her. The programming language Ada, used largely by the U.S. Department of Defense, is named for her.

During the later part of the nineteenth century and the beginning of the twentieth century, computing advances were made rapidly. William Burroughs produced and sold a mechanical adding machine. Dr. Herman Hollerith developed the first electro-mechanical tabulator, which read information from a punched card. His device revolutionized the census taken every ten years in the United States. Hollerith later formed a company known today as IBM.

In 1936, a theoretical development took place that had nothing to do with hardware per se but profoundly influenced the field of computer science. Alan M. Turing, another British mathematician, invented an abstract mathematical model called a *Turing machine*, laying the foundation for a major area of computing theory. The most prestigious award given in computer science

Stonehenge Is Still a Mystical Place

Stonehenge, a Neolithic stone structure that rises majestically out of the Salisbury Plain in England, has fascinated humans for centuries. It is believed that Stonehenge was erected over several centuries beginning in about 2180 BC. Its purpose is still a mystery, although theories abound. At the summer solstice, the rising sun appears behind one of the main stones, giving the illusion that the sun is balancing on the stone. This has led to the early theory that Stonehenge was a temple. Another theory, first suggested in the middle of the twentieth century, is that Stonehenge could have been used as an astronomical calendar, marking lunar and solar alignments. Yet a third theory is that Stonehenge was used to predict eclipses. The latest research now shows that Stonehenge was intended for and used as a cemetery.[3] Human remains, from about 3000 BC until 2500 BC when the first large stones were raised, have been found. Regardless of why it was built, there is a mystical quality about the place that defies explanation.

Courtesy of Scott Barrett

Counting Precedes Writing

It took about 4000 years to fully reduce three-dimensional tokens to written signs. It all began about 7500 BC when farmers made counters of clay in a dozen shapes to help keep track of their goods. For example, a cone stood for a small measure of grain, a sphere for a large measure of grain, and a cylinder stood for an animal. Four small measures of grain were represented by four cones. Approximately 8000 of these tokens have been found from Palestine, Anatolia, Syria, Mesopotamia, and Iran.

Approximately 3500 BC, after the rise of the city-states, administrators started using clay balls as envelopes to hold the tokens. Some of these envelopes bore impressions of the tokens they contained. The next step occurred between 3300 and 3200 BC when record keepers started just using the impression of the tokens on clay balls, dispensing with the tokens themselves. Thus it took approximately 4000 years to reduce three-dimensional tokens to written signs.

Around 3100 BC, styluses were used to draw the tokens rather than impressing the tokens on the tables. This change led to the breaking of the one-to-one correspondence between symbol and object. Ten jars of oil were represented by a jar of oil and a symbol for ten. New signs were not created to express abstract numbers, but old signs took on new meaning. For example, the cone sign, formerly representing a small measure of grain, became the symbol for "1," and the sphere (a large measure of grain) came to mean "10." Now 33 jars of oil could be represented by 10 + 10 + 10 + 1 + 1 + 1 and the symbol for "oil."

Once abstract numerals were created, the signs for goods and the signs for numbers could evolve in different ways. Thus writing derived from counting.

–Denise Schmandt-Berrerat, "Signs of Life," *Odyssey*, January/February, 2002, pages 6, 7, and 63.

Ada Lovelace, the First Programmer[4]

On December 10, 1815 (the same year that George Boole was born), a daughter—Augusta Ada Byron—was born to Anna Isabella (Annabella) Byron and George Gordon, Lord Byron. At that time in England Byron's fame derived not only from his poetry but also from his wild and scandalous behavior. The marriage was strained from the beginning, and Annabella left Byron shortly after Ada's birth. By April of 1816, the two had signed separation papers. Byron left England, never to return. Throughout the rest of his life he regretted that he was unable to see his daughter. At one point he wrote of her,

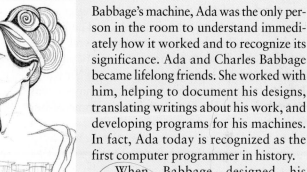

I see thee not. I hear thee not.
But none can be so wrapt in thee.

Before he died in Greece, at age 36, he exclaimed,

Oh my poor dear child! My dear Ada!
My God, could I but have seen her!

Meanwhile, Annabella, who eventually was to become a baroness in her own right, and who was educated as both a mathematician and a poet, carried on with Ada's upbringing and education. Annabella gave Ada her first instruction in mathematics, but it soon became clear that Ada was gifted in the subject and should receive more extensive tutoring. Ada received further training from Augustus DeMorgan, today famous for one of the basic theorems of Boolean algebra. By age eight, Ada had demonstrated an interest in mechanical devices and was building detailed model boats.

When she was 18, Ada visited the Mechanics Institute to hear Dr. Dionysius Lardner's lectures on the "Difference Engine," a mechanical calculating machine being built by Charles Babbage. She became so interested in the device that she arranged to be introduced to Babbage. It was said that, upon seeing Babbage's machine, Ada was the only person in the room to understand immediately how it worked and to recognize its significance. Ada and Charles Babbage became lifelong friends. She worked with him, helping to document his designs, translating writings about his work, and developing programs for his machines. In fact, Ada today is recognized as the first computer programmer in history.

When Babbage designed his Analytical Engine, Ada foresaw that it could go beyond arithmetic computations and become a general manipulator of symbols, thus having far-reaching capabilities. She even suggested that such a device eventually could be programmed with rules of harmony and composition so that it could produce "scientific" music. In effect, Ada foresaw the field of artificial intelligence more than 150 years ago.

In 1842, Babbage gave a series of lectures in Turin, Italy, on his Analytical Engine. One of the attendees was Luigi Menabrea, who was so impressed that he wrote an account of Babbage's lectures. At age 27, Ada decided to translate the account into English, with the intent to add a few of her own notes about the machine. In the end, her notes were twice as long as the original material, and the document, "The Sketch of the Analytical Engine," became the definitive work on the subject.

It is obvious from Ada's letters that her "notes" were entirely her own and that Babbage was acting as a sometimes unappreciated editor. At one point, Ada wrote to him,

I am much annoyed at your having altered my Note. You know I am always willing to make any required alterations myself, but that I cannot endure another person to meddle with my sentences.

Ada Lovelace (continued)

Ada gained the title Countess of Lovelace when she married Lord William Lovelace. The couple had three children, whose upbringing was left to Ada's mother while Ada pursued her work in mathematics. Her husband was supportive of her work, but for a woman of that day such behavior was considered almost as scandalous as some of her father's exploits.

Ada died in 1852, just one year before a working Difference Engine was built in Sweden from one of Babbage's designs. Like her father, Ada lived only to age 36, and even though they led very different lives, she undoubtedly admired him and took inspiration from his unconventional and rebellious nature. In the end, Ada asked to be buried beside him at the family's estate.

(equivalent to the Fielding Medal in mathematics or a Nobel Prize in other sciences) is the Turing Award, named for Alan Turing. A recent Broadway play deals with his life. Analysis of the capabilities of Turing machines is a part of the theoretical studies of all computer science students.

By the outbreak of World War II, several computers were under design and construction. The Harvard Mark I and the ENIAC are two of the more famous machines of the era. The ENIAC is pictured in Figure 1.4. John von Neumann, who had been a consultant on the ENIAC project, started work on another machine known as EDVAC, which was completed in 1950. In 1951, the first commercial computer, UNIVAC I, was delivered to the Bureau of the Census. The UNIVAC I was the first computer used to predict the outcome of a presidential election.

The early history that began with the abacus ended with the delivery of the UNIVAC I. With the building of that machine, the dream of a device that could rapidly manipulate numbers was realized; the search was ended. Or was it? Some experts predicted at that time that a small number of computers would be able to handle the computational needs of mankind. What they didn't realize was that the ability to perform fast calculations on large amounts of data would radically change the very nature of fields such as mathematics, physics, engineering, and economics. That is, computers made those experts' assessment of *what needed to be calculated* entirely invalid.[5]

After 1951, the story becomes one of the ever-expanding use of computers to solve problems in all areas. From that point, the search has focused not only on building faster, bigger devices, but also on developing tools that allow us to use these devices more productively. The history of computing hard-

FIGURE 1.4 The ENIAC, a World War II-era computer *U.S.*
Courtesy of Mike Muuss/U.S. Army; http://ftp.arl.army.mil/~mike/comphist/

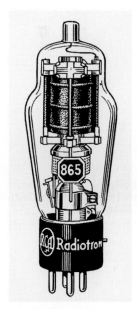

ware from this point on is categorized into several "generations" based on the technology they employed.

First Generation (1951–1959)
Commercial computers in the first generation (from approximately 1951 to 1959) were built using *vacuum tubes* to store information. A vacuum tube, shown in Figure 1.5, generated a great deal of heat and was not very reliable. The machines that used them required heavy-duty air-conditioning and frequent maintenance. They also required very large, specially built rooms.

The primary memory device of this first generation of computers was a *magnetic drum* that rotated under a read/write head. When the memory cell that was being accessed rotated under the read/write head, the data was written to or read from that place.

The input device was a card reader that read the holes punched in an IBM card (a descendant of the Hollerith card). The output device was either a punched card or a line printer. By the end of this generation, *magnetic tape drives* had been developed that were much faster than card readers. Magnetic tapes are sequential storage devices, meaning that the data on the tape must be accessed one after another in a linear fashion.

FIGURE 1.5 A vacuum tube
Reproduced by permission of University of Calgary

Storage devices external to the computer memory are called *auxiliary storage devices*. The magnetic tape was the first of these devices. Collectively, input devices, output devices, and auxiliary storage devices became known as *peripheral devices*.

Second Generation (1959–1965)

The advent of the *transistor* (for which John Bardeen, Walter H. Brattain, and William B. Shockley won a Nobel Prize) ushered in the second generation of commercial computers. The transistor replaced the vacuum tube as the main component in the hardware. The transistor, as shown in Figure 1.6, was smaller, more reliable, faster, more durable, and cheaper.

The second generation also witnessed the advent of immediate-access memory. When accessing information from a drum, the CPU had to wait for the proper place to rotate under the read/write head. The second generation used memory made from *magnetic cores*, tiny doughnut-shaped devices, each capable of storing one bit of information. These cores were strung together with wires to form cells, and cells were combined into a memory unit. Because the device was motionless and was accessed electronically, information was available instantly.

The *magnetic disk*, a new auxiliary storage device, was also developed during the second computer hardware generation. The magnetic disk is faster than magnetic tape because each data item can be accessed directly by referring to its location on the disk. Unlike a tape, which cannot access a piece of data without accessing everything on the tape that comes before it, a disk is organized so that each piece of data has its own location identifier, called an address. The read/write heads of a magnetic disk can be sent directly to the specific location on the disk where the desired information is stored.

Third Generation (1965–1971)

In the second generation, transistors and other components for the computer were assembled by hand on printed *circuit boards*. The third generation was

FIGURE 1.6 A transistor, which replaced the vacuum tube *Courtesy of Dr. Andrew Wylie*

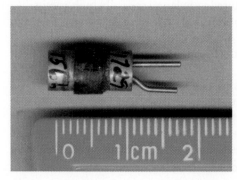

characterized by *integrated circuits* (ICs), solid pieces of silicon that contained the transistors, other components, and their connections. Integrated circuits were much smaller, cheaper, faster, and more reliable than printed circuit boards. Gordon Moore, one of the co-founders of Intel®, noted that from the time of the invention of the IC, the number of circuits that could be placed on a single integrated circuit was doubling each year. This observation became known as Moore's law.[6]

Transistors also were used for memory construction, where each transistor represented one bit of information. Integrated-circuit technology allowed memory boards to be built using transistors. Auxiliary storage devices were still needed because transistor memory was volatile; that is, the information went away when the power was turned off.

The *terminal*, an input/output device with a keyboard and screen, was introduced during this generation. The keyboard gave the user direct access to the computer, and the screen provided an immediate response.

Fourth Generation (1971–?)

Large-scale integration characterizes the fourth generation. From several thousand transistors on a silicon chip in the early 1970s, we had moved to a whole microcomputer on a chip by the middle of this decade. Main memory devices are still made almost exclusively out of chip technology. Over the previous 40 years, each generation of computer hardware had become more powerful in a smaller package at lower cost. Moore's law was modified to say that chip density was doubling every 18 months.

By the late 1970s, the phrase *personal computer* (PC) had entered the vocabulary. Microcomputers had become so cheap that almost anyone could have one, and a generation of kids grew up playing PacMan.

The fourth generation found some new names entering the commercial market. Apple®, Tandy/Radio Shack, Atari, Commodore, and Sun joined the big companies of earlier generations—IBM®, Remington Rand, NCR, DEC (Digital Equipment Corporation), Hewlett-Packard, Control Data, and Burroughs. The best-known success story of the personal computer revolution is that of Apple. Steve Wozniak, an engineer, and Steve Jobs, a high school student, created a personal computer kit and marketed it out of a garage. This was the beginning of Apple Computer, a multibillion-dollar company.

The IBM PC was introduced in 1981 and was soon followed by compatible machines manufactured by many other companies. For example, Dell and Compaq were successful in making PCs that were compatible with IBM PCs. Apple introduced its very popular Macintosh® microcomputer line in 1984.

In the mid-1980s, larger, more powerful machines were created; they were referred to as *workstations*. Workstations were generally meant for business, not personal, use. The idea was for each employee to have his or her own workstation on the desktop. These workstations were connected by cables, or *networked*, so that they could interact with one another. Workstations were made more powerful by the introduction of the RISC (reduced-instruction-set computer) architecture. Each computer was designed to understand a set of instructions, called its *machine language*. Conventional machines such as the IBM 370/168 had an instruction set containing more than 200 instructions. Instructions were fast and memory access was slow, so specialized instructions made sense. As memory access got increasingly faster, using a reduced set of instructions became attractive. Sun Microsystems introduced a workstation with a RISC chip in 1987. Its enduring popularity proved the feasibility of the RISC chip. These workstations were often called UNIX workstations because they used the UNIX operating system.

Because computers are still being made using circuit boards, we cannot mark the end of this generation. However, several things have occurred that so dramatically affected how we use machines that they certainly have ushered in a new era. Moore's law was once again restated in the following form: "Computers will either double in power at the same price or halve in cost for the same power every 18 months." [7]

From a garage to the *Fortune* 500
Boyhood friends Steve Jobs and Steve Wozniak sold their Volkswagen van and programmable calculator, respectively, to raise the money to finance their new computer company. Their first sale was 50 Apple Is, the computer that they had designed and built in a garage. In six short years Apple was listed in the *Fortune* 500, the youngest firm on this prestigious list. Jobs resigned from Apple in 1985 and founded NeXT. In 1997, Apple bought NeXT and Jobs became CEO of Apple. *Fortune* magazine listed Jobs as the Most Powerful Businessman of 2007.

Parallel Computing

Although computers that use a single primary processing unit continue to flourish, radically new machine architectures began appearing in the late 1980s. Computers that use these *parallel architectures* rely on a set of interconnected central processing units.

One class of parallel machines is organized so that the processors all share the same memory unit. In another class of machines, each central processor has its own local memory and communicates with the others over a very fast internal network.

Parallel architectures offer several ways to increase the speed of execution. For example, a given step in a program can be separated into multiple pieces, and those pieces can be executed simultaneously on several individual processors. These machines are called SIMD (single-instruction, multiple-data-stream) computers. A second class of machines can work on different parts of a program simultaneously. These machines are called MIMD (multiple-instruction, multiple-data-stream) computers.

The potential of hundreds or even thousands of processors combined in one machine is enormous, and the challenge of programming for such machines is equally daunting. Software designed for parallel machines is different from software designed for sequential machines. Programmers have to rethink the ways in which they approach problem solving and programming to exploit parallelism.

Networking

In the 1980s, the concept of a large machine with many users gave way to a network of smaller machines connected so that they can share resources such as printers, software, and data. The *Ethernet*, invented by Robert Metcalfe and David Boggs in 1973, used a cheap coaxial cable to connect the machines and a set of protocols to allow the machines to communicate with one another. By 1979, DEC, Intel, and Xerox joined to establish Ethernet as a standard.

Workstations were designed for networking, but networking personal computers didn't become practical until a more advanced Intel chip was introduced in 1985. By 1989, Novell's Netware connected PCs together with a *file server*, a PC with generous mass storage and good input/output capability. Placing data and office automation software on the server rather than each PC having its own copy allowed for a measure of central control while giving each machine a measure of autonomy. Workstations or personal computers networked together became known as LANs (local area networks).

The *Internet* as we know it today is descended from the ARPANET, a government-sponsored network begun in the late 1960s, which originally consisted of 11 nodes concentrated mainly in the Los Angeles and Boston areas. Like ARPANET and LANs, the Internet uses *packet switching*, a way for messages to share lines. The Internet, however, is made up of many different networks across the world that communicate by using a common protocol, *TCP/IP* (Transmission Control Protocol/Internet Protocol).

> **Jobs and Wozniak can't give it away**
> "So we went to Atari and said, 'Hey, we've got this amazing thing, even built with some of your parts, and what do you think about funding us? Or we'll give it to you. We just want to do it. Pay our salary, we'll come work for you.' And they said, 'No.' So then we went to Hewlett-Packard, and they said, 'Hey, we don't need you. You haven't got through college yet.'"
>
> Source: mlgnn.com/?tag=steve-jobs (accessed Sept. 14, 2009).

Paul E. Ceruzzi, in *A History of Modern Computing*, comments on the relationship between Ethernet and the Internet:

> If the Internet of the 1990s became the Information Superhighway, then Ethernet became the equally important network of local roads to feed it. As a descendent of ARPA research, the global networks we now call the Internet came into existence before the local Ethernet was invented at Xerox. But Ethernet transformed the nature of office and personal computing before the Internet had a significant effect.[8]

■ A Brief History of Computing Software

The hardware of a computer can be turned on, but it does nothing until it is directed to do so by the programs that make up the computer's software. The manner in which software evolved is crucial to understanding how software works in a modern computing system.

First-Generation Software (1951–1959)

The first programs were written using machine language, the instructions built into the electrical circuitry of a particular computer. Even the small task of adding two numbers together used three instructions written in *binary* (1s and 0s), and the programmer had to remember which combination of binary digits meant what. Programmers using machine language had to be very good with numbers and very detail oriented. It's not surprising that the first programmers were mathematicians and engineers. Nevertheless, programming in machine language is both time-consuming and prone to errors.

Because writing in machine code is so tedious, some programmers took the time to develop tools to help with the programming process. Thus the first artificial programming languages were developed. These languages, called *assembly languages*, used mnemonic codes to represent each machine-language instruction.

Because every program that is executed on a computer eventually must be in the form of the computer's machine language, the developers of assembly language also created software *translators* to translate programs written in assembly language into machine code. A program called an *assembler* reads each of the program's instructions in mnemonic form and translates it into the machine-language equivalent. These mnemonics are abbreviated and sometimes difficult to read, but they are much easier to use than long strings of binary digits.

The programmers who wrote these tools to make programming easier for others were the first *systems programmers*. So, even in first-generation software, there was the division between those programmers who wrote tools and those programmers who used the tools. The assembly language acted as a buffer between the programmer and the machine hardware. See Figure 1.7. Sometimes, when efficient code is essential, programs today may be written in assembly language. Chapter 6 explores an example of machine code and a corresponding assembly language in detail.

Second-Generation Software (1959–1965)

As hardware became more powerful, more powerful tools were needed to use it effectively. Assembly languages certainly presented a step in the right direction, but the programmer still was forced to think in terms of individual machine instructions. The second generation saw more powerful languages

FIGURE 1.7 Layers of languages at the end of the first generation

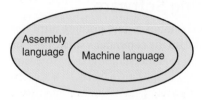

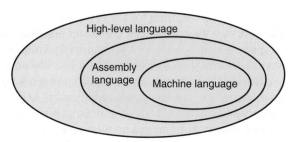

FIGURE 1.8 Layers of language at the end of the second generation

developed. These *high-level languages* allowed the programmer to write instructions using more English-like statements.

Two of the languages developed during the second generation are still used today: FORTRAN (a language designed for numerical applications) and COBOL (a language designed for business applications). FORTRAN and COBOL developed quite differently. FORTRAN started out as a simple language and grew as additional features were added to it over the years. In contrast, COBOL was designed first and then implemented. It has changed little over time.

Another language that was designed during this period that remains in use today is Lisp. Lisp differs markedly from FORTRAN and COBOL and was not widely accepted. It was used mainly in artificial intelligence applications and research. Indeed, dialects of Lisp are among the languages of choice today in artificial intelligence. Scheme, a dialect of Lisp, is used at some schools as an introductory programming language.

The introduction of high-level languages provided a vehicle for running the same program on more than one computer. Each high-level language has a translating program that goes with it, a program that takes statements written in the high-level language and converts them to the equivalent machine-code instructions. In the earliest days, the high-level language statements were often translated into an assembly language, and then the assembly-language statements were translated into machine code. A program written in FORTRAN or COBOL can be translated and run on any machine that has a translating program called a *compiler*.

At the end of the second generation, the role of the systems programmer was becoming more well-defined. Systems programmers wrote tools like assemblers and compilers; those people who used the tools to write programs were called *applications programmers*. The applications programmer was becoming even more insulated from the computer hardware as the software surrounding the hardware became more sophisticated. See Figure 1.8.

Third-Generation Software (1965–1971)

During the third generation of commercial computers, it became apparent that the human was slowing down the computing process. Computers were sitting idle while waiting for the computer operator to prepare the next job. The solution was to put the computer resources under the control of the computer—that is, to write a program that would determine which programs were run when. This kind of program is called an *operating system*.

During the first two computer software generations, utility programs had been written to handle often-needed tasks. *Loaders* loaded programs into memory and *linkers* linked pieces of large programs together. In the third generation, these utility programs were refined and put under the direction of the operating system. This group of utility programs, the operating system, and the language translators (assemblers and compilers) became known as *systems software*.

The introduction of computer terminals as input/output devices gave users ready access to computers, and advances in systems software gave machines the ability to work much faster. However, inputting and outputting data from keyboards and screens was a slow process, much slower than carrying out instructions in memory. The problem was how to make better use of the machine's greater capabilities and speed. The solution was *time sharing*—many different users, each at a terminal, communicating (inputting and outputting) with a single computer all at the same time. Controlling this process was an operating system that organized and scheduled the different jobs.

Terrorist detection software
Social network analysis provides a way of modeling how people interact using a branch of mathematics called graph theory. Graph theory maps people as nodes and their relationships as links. Today, some researchers are using this approach to build software models of terrorist networks. For example, they are trying to determine whether the chain of command in a terrorist network might have been disrupted by a particular action. When the software is given data on the number of members of a network who have been apprehended, it can estimate the probability that the network has been disrupted. This estimate may be better than one provided by human judgment.

For the user, time sharing is much like having his or her own machine. Each user is assigned a small slice of central processing time and then is put on hold while another user is serviced. Users generally aren't even aware that there are other users. However, if too many people try to use the system at the same time, there can be a noticeable wait for a job to be completed.

As part of the third generation, general-purpose application programs were being written. One example was the Statistical Package for the Social Sciences (SPSS), which was written in FORTRAN. SPSS had a special language, and users wrote instructions in that language as input to the program. This language allowed the user, who was often not a programmer, to describe some data and the statistics to be computed on that data.

At the beginning of the computer era, the computer user and the programmer were the same person. By the end of the first generation, programmers had emerged who wrote tools for other programmers to use, giving rise to the distinction between systems programmers and applications programmers. However, the programmer was still the user. In the third generation, systems programmers were writing programs—software tools—for others to use. Suddenly, there were computer users who were not programmers in the traditional sense.

The separation between the user and the hardware was growing wider. The hardware had become an even smaller part of the picture. A computer system—a combination of hardware, software, and the data managed by them—had emerged. See Figure 1.9. Although the layers of languages kept

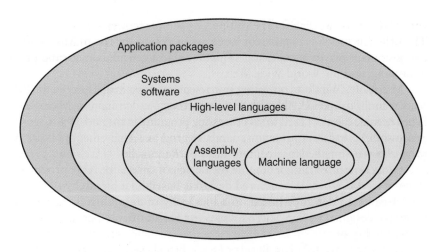

FIGURE 1.9 The layers of software surrounding the hardware continue to grow

getting deeper, programmers continued (and still continue) to use some of the very inner layers. If a small segment of code must run as quickly as possible and take up as few memory locations as possible, it may still be programmed in an assembly language or even machine code.

Fourth Generation (1971–1989)

The 1970s saw the introduction of better programming techniques called *structured programming*, a logical, disciplined approach to programming. The languages Pascal and Modula-2 were built on the principles of structured programming. BASIC, a language introduced for third-generation machines, was refined and upgraded to more-structured versions. C, a language that allows the user to intersperse assembly-language statements in a high-level program, was also introduced. C++, a structured language that allows the user access to low-level statements as well, became the language of choice in industry.

Better and more powerful operating systems were being developed, too. UNIX, developed at AT&T™ as a research tool, has become standard in many university settings. PC-DOS, developed for the IBM PC, and MS-DOS, developed for PC compatibles, became standards for personal computers. The operating system for the Macintosh introduced the concept of the mouse and the point-and-click graphical interface, thus changing computer–user interaction drastically.

High-quality, reasonably priced applications software packages became available at neighborhood stores. These programs allow the user with no computer experience to perform a specific task. Three typical kinds of application packages are *spreadsheets*, *word processors*, and *database management systems*. Lotus 1-2-3 was the first commercially successful spreadsheet that allowed a novice user to enter and analyze all kinds of data. WordPerfect was one of the first word processors, and dBase IV was a system that let the user store, organize, and retrieve data.

Fifth Generation (1990-Present)

The fifth generation is notable for three major events: the rise of Microsoft® as a dominant player in computer software, object-oriented design and programming, and the World Wide Web.

Microsoft's Windows operating system emerged as a major force in the PC market during this period. Although WordPerfect continued to improve, Microsoft's Word became the most used word processing program. In the mid-1990s, word processors, spreadsheet programs, database programs, and other application programs were bundled together into super packages called *office suites*.

Object-oriented design became the design of choice for large programming projects. Whereas structured design is based on a hierarchy of tasks, object-oriented design is based on a hierarchy of data objects. Java™, a language designed by Sun Microsystems for object-oriented programming, began to rival C++.

In 1990, Tim Berners-Lee, a British researcher at the CERN physics lab in Geneva, Switzerland, created a set of technical rules for what he hoped would be a universal Internet document center called the *World Wide Web*. Along with these rules, he created HTML, a language for formatting documents, and a rudimentary, text-only *browser*, a program that allows a user to access information from websites worldwide. In 1993, Marc Andreesen and Eric Bina released Mosaic, the first graphics-capable browser. To quote *Newsweek*: "Mosaic just may have been the most important computer application ever." [9]

There were now two giants in the browser market: Netscape Navigator® (derived from Mosaic) and Microsoft's Internet Explorer® (IE). Microsoft bundled IE with its Windows operating system, which made IE the winner in the browser wars. This bundling led to a monopoly law suit filed by the U.S. government, the 2001 settlement of which required Microsoft to be more open with its competitors. Netscape's future became uncertain after America Online® purchased it in 1998. AOL® stopped supporting Netscape products ten years later. Mozilla Firefox®, a Web browser that retained some of the flavor of Mosaic, was released in November 2004. As of March 2009, Firefox had captured more than 22% of the browser market.

Although the Internet had been around for decades, the World Wide Web made it easy to use the Internet to share information around the world (see Figure 1.10). Around 2002, the Web began changing. Social networking sites such as MySpace™, Facebook, and Twitter have become wildly popular. Online blogging has turned anyone and everyone into an author or social critic. User-generated and -edited content characterizes these new websites. For example, Wikipedia is an online encyclopedia in which anyone can enter or edit content. The term "Web 2.0" has been used by some to describe these emerging sites and uses.

The fifth generation must be characterized most of all by the changing profile of the user. The first user was the programmer who wrote programs to solve specific problems—his or her own or someone else's. Then the sys-

From computers to books

Former Microsoft executive John Wood left his job to start a nonprofit, which builds schools and libraries in the developing countries. He said, "Education is the ticket out of poverty, and it produces better family health and better treatment of woman. Every day, 250 million kids worldwide wake up with no school to go to. Two-thirds of them are girls." By April 2009, Room to Read had built 750 schools and 7000 libraries.

Source: "Newsmakers: Schools for the World," *Parade Magazine*, April 5, 2009.

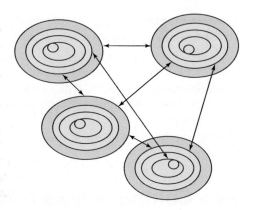

FIGURE 1.10 Sharing information on the World Wide Web

tems programmer emerged who wrote more and more complex tools for other programmers. By the early 1970s, applications programmers were using these complex tools to write applications programs for nonprogrammers to use. With the advent of the personal computer, computer games, educational programs, and user-friendly software packages, many people became computer users. With the birth and expansion of the World Wide Web, Web surfing has become the recreation of choice, so even more people have become computer users. The user is a first-grade child learning to read, a teenager downloading music, a college student writing a paper, a homemaker planning a budget, and a banker looking up a customer's loan record. The user is all of us.

In our brief history of hardware and software, we have focused our attention on traditional computers and computing systems. Paralleling this history is the growing use of integrated circuits, or chips, to run or regulate everything from toasters, to cars, to intensive care monitors, to satellites. Such computing technology is called an *embedded system*. Although these chips are not actually computers in the sense that we are going to study in this book, they are certainly a product of the technology revolution of the last 55 years.

▪ Predictions

We end this brief history of computing with a few predictions about computers that didn't come true:[10–12]

"I think there is a world market for maybe five computers."—Thomas Watson, chair of IBM, 1943.

"Where . . . the ENIAC is equipped with 18,000 vacuum tubes and weighs 30 tons, computers in the future may have only 1,000 vacuum tubes and weigh only 1.5 tons."—*Popular Mechanics*, 1949.

"I have traveled the length and breadth of this country and talked with the best people, and I can assure you that data processing is a fad that won't last out the year."—The editor in charge of business books for Prentice Hall, 1957.

"But what . . . is it good for?"—Engineer at the Advanced Computing Systems division of IBM, commenting on the microchip, 1968.

"There is no reason anyone would want a computer in their home."—Ken Olsen, president, chairman, and founder of Digital Equipment Corporation, 1977.

"$100 million is way too much to pay for Microsoft."—IBM, 1982.

"I predict the Internet . . . will go spectacularly supernova and in 1996 catastrophically collapse."—Bob Metcalfe, 3Com founder and inventor, 1995.

"Folks, the Mac platform is through—totally."—John C. Dvorak, *PC Magazine*, 1998.

1.3 Computing as a Tool and a Discipline

In the previous section on the history of computer software, we pointed out the ever-changing role of the user. At the end of the first generation, users were split into two groups: systems programmers, who developed tools to make programming easier, and applications programmers, who used those tools. Later applications programmers built large domain-specific programs such as statistical packages, word processors, spreadsheets, intelligent browsers, virtual environments, and medical diagnosis applications on top of the traditional language tools. These application programs were, in turn, used by practitioners with no computer background.

So who is using the computer as a tool? Everyone, except for those people who are creating the tools for others. For these toolmakers, either computing is a discipline (low-level tools) or the discipline of computing has made their tools possible (applications built upon applications).

A *discipline* is defined as a field of study. Peter Denning defines the discipline of computer science as "the body of knowledge and practices used by computing professionals in their work. . . . This discipline is also called computer science and engineering, computing, and informatics." [13] He continues, "The body of knowledge of computing is frequently described as the systematic study of algorithmic processes that describe and transform information: their theory, analysis, design, efficiency, implementation, and application. The fundamental question underlying all of computing is, *What can be (efficiently) automated?*"

Denning states that each practitioner must be skilled in four areas:

- *Algorithmic thinking*, in which one is able to express problems in terms of step-by-step procedures to solve them
- *Representation*, in which one is able to store data in a way that it can be processed efficiently
- *Programming*, in which one is able to combine algorithmic thinking and representation into computer software
- *Design*, in which the software serves a useful purpose

A debate has long raged about whether computing is a mathematical discipline, a scientific discipline, or an engineering discipline. Computing certainly has strong roots in mathematical logic. The theorems of Turing tell us that certain problems cannot be solved, Boolean algebra describes computer circuits, and numerical analysis plays an important role in scientific computing. Scientific disciplines attempt to understand how their systems work. The natural sciences exist to "fill in the instruction book that God forgot to leave us." [14] Thus computing is a scientific discipline as we build and test models of natural phenomena. As we design and build larger and larger computing systems, we are using techniques from engineering.

In 1989, a task force of computer science educators proposed a curriculum model that covered the subareas of computing from the three perspectives represented in our history: theory (mathematics); experimentation, called abstraction by computer scientists (sciences); and design (engineering). [15] *Theory* refers to the building of conceptual frameworks and notations for understanding relationships among objects in a domain. *Experimentation* (abstraction) refers to exploring models of systems and architectures within different application domains and determining whether the models predict new behaviors. *Design* refers to constructing computer systems that support work in different application domains.

Table 1.1 shows the topic areas outlined by the task force. Of the nine subject topic areas, six relate to understanding and building computing tools in general: Algorithms and Data Structures, Programming Languages, (Computer) Architecture, Operating Systems, Software Methodology and Engineering, and Human–Computer Communication. Not surprisingly, these are called *systems areas*. Three of the subareas relate to the computer's use as a tool: Databases and Information Retrieval, Artificial Intelligence and Robotics, and Graphics. These areas are called *applications areas*.

TABLE 1.1

Topic Areas of Computing Discipline, 1989
Algorithms and Data Structures
Programming Languages
Architecture
Operating Systems
Software Methodology and Engineering
Databases and Information Retrieval
Artificial Intelligence and Robotics
Human–Computer Communication
Graphics

Revised curriculum documents, published in 2001, reorganized and expanded the topic areas to a total of 14. Algorithms and Data Structures has been expanded and put under the title Programming Fundamentals. With the rise of the Web, networks get their own category: Net-Centric Computing. Artificial Intelligence and Robotics has been expanded to include all Intelligent Systems. Databases and Information Retrieval are now called Information Management.

The new topics include Discrete Structures, an area of mathematics that is important to computing, and Algorithms and Complexity, the formal study of algorithms rather than the study of how to write them. These would be systems areas. Computational Science includes the application of numerical techniques and simulation to fields such as molecular dynamics, celestial mechanics, economic forecasting, and bioinformatics. The last new topic is Social and Professional Issues, which relates to professionals in both systems and applications areas. Table 1.2 shows a listing of the topic areas as of 2001. The report "Computer Science Curriculum 2008: An Interim Revision of CS 2001," published in December 2008, leaves these 14 topic areas unchanged.

?

Computers go to college
The first departments of computer science were established in 1962 at Purdue and Stanford Universities. The first PhD in computer science was awarded by the University of Pennsylvania in 1965. The first curriculum effort in computer science was published by the ACM in 1968.

Source: http://www.comphist.org/ifip_report.php
(accessed April 14, 2009).

TABLE 1.2

Topic Areas of Computing Discipline, 2001
Discrete Structures
Programming Fundamentals
Algorithms and Complexity
Architecture and Organization
Operating Systems
Net-Centric Computing
Programming Languages
Human–Computer Interaction
Graphics and Visual Computing
Intelligent Systems
Information Management
Social and Professional Issues
Software Engineering
Computational Science

Research is ongoing in both systems and applications. Systems research produces better general tools; applications research produces better tools for the domain-specific applications. There is no doubt that the relationships between the people who investigate computing topics as a discipline directly affect those who use computers as a tool. Computing research fuels the applications people use daily, and the turnaround for the technology is amazingly fast. This symbiotic relationship is more dynamic in computing than in any other discipline.

In this book we explain, at an introductory level, the ideas underlying computing as a discipline. This book does not aim to make you a better user of a computer, although it should undoubtedly have that side effect. Instead, we want you to walk away with a thorough knowledge of how computer systems work, where they are now, and where they may go in the future. For this reason, we examine both systems and applications.

Summary

This book is a broad study of computer systems, including the hardware that makes up the devices, the software programs executed by the machine, and the data managed and manipulated by both. Computing systems can be divided into layers, and our organization of this book follows those layers from the inside out.

The history of computing reveals the roots from which modern computing systems grew. This history spans four generations, each characterized by the components used to build the hardware and the software tools developed to allow the programmer to make more productive use of the hardware. These tools have formed layers of software around the hardware.

Throughout the rest of this book, we examine the different layers that make up a computing system, beginning with the information layer and ending with the communication layer. Our goal is to give you an appreciation and understanding of all aspects of computing systems.

You may go on to study computer science in depth and contribute to the future of computing systems. Or you may go on to be an application specialist within other disciplines, using the computer as a tool. Whatever your future holds, given how prevalent computing systems are, a fundamental understanding of how they work is imperative.

⚖ ETHICAL ISSUES ▶ The Digital Divide ⓦ

Over the past few years, society's dependence on computer technology has increased dramatically. The ability to communicate via email and to access the Internet has become an essential part of everyday life for many Americans. The U.S. Department of Commerce says that more than 70% of U.S. households had Internet access in 2008. This means that the other 30% lacked either access to the Internet or the technological skills to use it. The term *digital divide* has come to represent this disparity between the Information Age "haves" and "have-nots."

This gap is of growing social concern. Rural communities, minority households, low-income families, and

ETHICAL ISSUES ▸ The Digital Divide, continued

people with disabilities do not have the same Internet access as the more advantaged. In terms of education, the quantity and quality of computers and Web connections in schools vary greatly across demographic regions. Programs such as the federally supported E-Rate Program, established in 1996, are responding to these inequalities within schools and libraries by providing financial discounts to needy schools.

From a global perspective, the digital divide illustrates an additional challenge that developing nations must face as they make their way into the international community. Without the necessary telecommunication infrastructures to support Internet access, emerging countries are at a serious disadvantage. Only 16% of the world's population utilizes 90% of its Internet host computers—clear evidence of this disparity.

In January 2005, Nicholas Negroponte, working with MIT, introduced the One Laptop per Child program. Believing that every child—even those in the most remote regions of the world—should have access to a computer, OLPC set out to produce an affordable laptop for children who could otherwise not afford one. OLPC designed a basic laptop that sells for less than $200, with a battery that can be charged by human power. In 2007, OLPC introduced the Give 1, Get 1 program. With a donation of $399, consumers could purchase a laptop of their own and have another sent to a child in a developing country. By January 2009, OLPC had produced and sold more than 1 million laptops.

The digital divide brings to light the serious impact that computer technology has on society, both domestic and global. It is an issue the world will undoubtedly continue to address throughout the twenty-first century.

Key Terms

Abstraction   Computer software
Computer hardware   Computing system

Exercises

For Exercises 1–10, choose from the following list of people.

  A. Leibniz
  B. Pascal
  C. Babbage
  D. Lovelace
  E. Hollerith
  F. Byron
  G. Turing
  H. Jacquard

1. What French mathematician built and sold the first gear-driven mechanical machine that did addition and subtraction?

2. Who built the first mechanical machine that did addition, subtraction, multiplication, and division?

3. Who designed the first mechanical machine that included memory?

4. Who was considered the first programmer?

5. Who proposed that a punched card be used for counting the census?

6. Who edited Babbage's work?

7. Who was Ada Lovelace's father?

8. Who would have been mentioned in the book the *Code Breakers*?

9. Who developed the concept of punched holes used in weaving cloth?

10. Who is associated with IBM?

For Exercises 11–23, match the hardware listed to the appropriate generation.
   A. First
   B. Second
   C. Third
   D. Fourth
   E. Fifth

11. Circuit boards

12. Transistor

13. Magnetic core memory

14. Card input/output

15. Parallel computing

16. Magnetic drum

17. Magnetic tape drives

18. Integrated circuits

19. Personal computer

20. Vacuum tube

21. Large-scale integration

22. Magnetic disk

23. Networking

For Exercises 24–38, match the software or software concepts listed to the appropriate generation.
   A. First
   B. Second
   C. Third
   D. Fourth
   E. Fifth

24. Assemblers

25. FORTRAN

26. Operating systems

27. Structured programming

28. Time sharing

29. HTML (for the Web)

30. Loaders

31. Spreadsheets

32. Word processors

33. Lisp

34. PC-DOS

35. Loaders/linkers bundled into an operating system

36. Java

37. SPSS

38. C++

Exercises 39–59 are short-answer questions.

39. What do we mean by the statement that "the 1980s and 1990s must be characterized by the changing profile of the *user*"?

40. Why was Mosaic important?

41. Discuss the browser wars.

42. Describe how the Web changed after 2002.

43. Of the predictions listed in this chapter on pages 23–24, which do you consider the biggest error in judgment? Explain.

44. Name the four areas in which the practitioner must be skilled.

45. Distinguish between computing as a tool and computing as a discipline.

46. Is computing a mathematical discipline, a scientific discipline, or an engineering discipline? Explain.

47. Distinguish between systems areas and applications areas in computing as a discipline.

48. Define the word *abstraction* and relate it to the drawing in Figure 1.2.

49. Compare Tables 1.1 and 1.2. Which trends do you see?

50. Define the word *protocol* and explain how it is used in computing.

51. Distinguish between machine language and assembly language.

52. Distinguish between assembly language and high-level languages.

53. FORTRAN and COBOL were two high-level languages defined during the second generation of computer software. Compare and contrast these languages in terms of their history and their purpose.

54. Distinguish between an assembler and a compiler.

55. Distinguish between a systems programmer and an applications programmer.

56. What was the rationale behind the development of operating systems?

57. What constitutes systems software?

58. What do the following pieces of software do?
    a. Loader
    b. Linker
    c. Editor
59. How was the program SPSS different from the programs that came before it?

??? Thought Questions

1. Identify five abstractions in your school environment. Indicate which details are hidden by the abstraction and how the abstraction helps manage complexity.

2. Discuss the role of *abstraction* in the history of computer software.

3. Did you have a computer in your home as you were growing up? If so, how did it influence your education to this point? If not, how did the lack of a home computer influence your education to this point?

4. The digital divide puts those who have access to technology on one side and those who do not on the other side. Do you feel that it is the right of everyone to have access to technology?

5. It will cost a great deal of money to erase the digital divide. Who do you think should be responsible for paying the cost?

6. Having access to technology is not enough; people must be taught to use the technology they have. How would you define computer literacy for each of the following groups of people?
    a. High school students in an industrialized country
    b. Kindergarten teachers in an industrialized country
    c. College graduates in an industrialized country
    d. Students in sub-Saharan Africa
    e. College graduates in sub-Saharan Africa
    f. Government officials in the Andes

The Information Layer

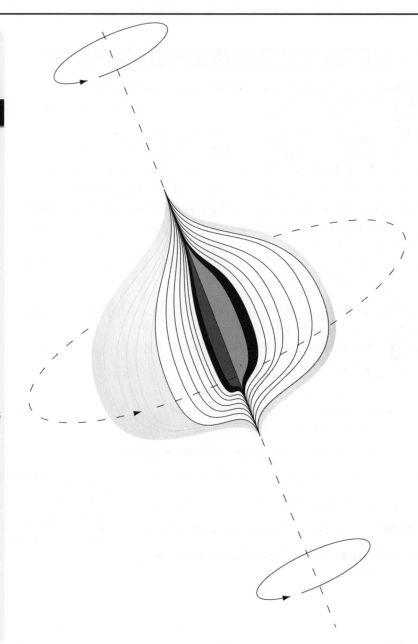

Binary Values and Number Systems

2

Now that we've established history and some common terminology in Chapter 1, our exploration of computing technology can begin in earnest. This chapter describes binary values—the way in which computer hardware represents and manages information. This chapter also puts binary values in the context of all number systems, reminding us of grade school concepts that we now take for granted. You probably already know many of the concepts about binary numbers described in this chapter, but you might not realize that you know them! The rules of all number systems are the same; it's just a matter of going back to those underlying concepts and applying them in a new base. By making sure we have an understanding of binary values, we pave the way to understanding how computing systems use the binary number system to accomplish their tasks.

Goals

After studying this chapter, you should be able to:

- distinguish among categories of numbers.
- describe positional notation.
- convert numbers in other bases to base 10.
- convert base-10 numbers to numbers in other bases.
- describe the relationship between bases 2, 8, and 16.
- explain the importance to computing of bases that are powers of 2.

2.1 Numbers and Computing

Numbers are crucial to computing. In addition to using a computer to execute numeric computations, all types of information that we store and manage using a computer are ultimately stored as numbers. At the lowest level, computers store all information using just the digits 0 and 1. So to begin our exploration of computers, we need to first begin by exploring numbers.

First, let's recall that numbers can be classified into all sorts of categories. There are natural numbers, negative numbers, rational numbers, irrational numbers, and many others that are important in mathematics but not to the understanding of computing. Let's review the relevant category definitions briefly.

First, let's define the general concept of a number: A number is a unit belonging to an abstract mathematical system and is subject to specified laws of succession, addition, and multiplication. That is, a number is a representation of a value, and certain arithmetic operations can be consistently applied to such values.

Now let's separate numbers into categories. A natural number is the number 0 or any number obtained by repeatedly adding 1 to this number. Natural numbers are the ones we use in counting. A negative number is less than zero and is opposite in sign to a positive number. An integer is any of the natural numbers or any of the negatives of these numbers. A rational number is an integer or the quotient of two integers—that is, any value that can be expressed as a fraction.

In this chapter, we focus on natural numbers and the ways that they are represented in various number systems. As part of our discussion, we establish how all number systems relate to each other. In Chapter 3, we examine the computer representation of negative and rational numbers, as well as how we use numbers to represent other forms of data such as characters and images.

Some of the material in this chapter may already be familiar to you. Certainly some of the underlying ideas should be. You probably take for granted some basic principles of numbers and arithmetic because you've become so used to them. Part of our goal in this chapter is to remind you of those underlying principles and to show you that they apply to all number systems. Then the idea that a computer uses binary values—that is, 1s and 0s—to represent information should be less mysterious.

> **Number** A unit of an abstract mathematical system subject to the laws of arithmetic

> **Natural number** The number 0 and any number obtained by repeatedly adding 1 to it

> **Negative number** A value less than 0, with a sign opposite to its positive counterpart

> **Integer** A natural number, a negative of a natural number, or zero

> **Rational number** An integer or the quotient of two integers (division by zero excluded)

2.2 Positional Notation

How many ones are there in 943? That is, how many actual things does the number 943 represent? Well, in grade school terms, you might say there are 9 hundreds plus 4 tens plus 3 ones. Or, said another way, there are 900 ones plus 40 ones plus 3 ones. So how many ones are there in 754? 700 ones plus 50 ones plus 4 ones. Right? Well, maybe. The answer depends on the *base* of the number system you are using. This answer is correct in the base-10, or decimal, number system, which is the number system humans use every day. But that answer is not correct in other number systems.

The **base** of a number system specifies the number of digits used in the system. The digits always begin with 0 and continue through one less than the base. For example, there are 2 digits in base 2: 0 and 1. There are 8 digits in base 8: 0 through 7. There are 10 digits in base 10: 0 through 9. The base also determines what the positions of digits mean. When you add 1 to the last digit in the number system, you have a carry to the digit position to the left.

Numbers are written using **positional notation**. The rightmost digit represents its value multiplied by the base to the zeroth power. The digit to the left of that one represents its value multiplied by the base to the first power. The next digit represents its value multiplied by the base to the second power. The next digit represents its value multiplied by the base to the third power, and so on. You are so familiar with positional notation that you probably don't think about it. We used it instinctively to calculate the number of ones in 943.

> **Base** The foundational value of a number system, which dictates the number of digits and the value of digit positions
>
> **Positional notation** A system of expressing numbers in which the digits are arranged in succession, the position of each digit has a place value, and the number is equal to the sum of the products of each digit by its place value[1]

$$
\begin{array}{rcrcr}
9 * 10^2 &=& 9 * & 100 &=& 900 \\
+\ 4 * 10^1 &=& 4 * & 10 &=& 40 \\
+\ 3 * 10^0 &=& 3 * & 1 &=& \underline{3} \\
& & & & & 943
\end{array}
$$

A more formal way of defining positional notation is to say that the value is represented as a polynomial in the base of the number system. But what is a polynomial? A polynomial is a sum of two or more algebraic terms, each of which consists of a constant multiplied by one or more variables raised to a nonnegative integral power. When defining positional notation, the variable is the base of the number system. Thus 943 is represented as a polynomial as follows, with x acting as the base:

$$9 * x^2 + 4 * x^1 + 3 * x^0$$

Let's express this idea formally. If a number in the base-R number system has n digits, it is represented as follows, where d_i represents the digit in the ith position in the number:

$$d_n * R^{n-1} + d_{n-1} * R^{n-2} + \cdots + d_2 * R + d_1$$

Look complicated? Let's look at a concrete example: 63578 in base 10. Here n is 5 (the number has five digits), and R is 10

The importance of zero
It is interesting to note that positional notation is only possible because of the concept of zero. Zero, which we usually take for granted, was the fundamental concept at the intersection of all branches of modern mathematics. As Georges Ifrah noted in his book, *The Universal History of Computing:* "To sum up, the vital discovery of zero gave the human mind an extraordinarily powerful potential. No other human creation has exercised such an influence on the development of mankind's intelligence."[2]

(the base). The formula says that the fifth digit (last digit on the left) is multiplied by the base to the fourth power; the fourth digit is multiplied by the base to the third power; the third digit is multiplied by the base to the second power; the second digit is multiplied by the base to the first power; and the first digit is not multiplied by anything.

$$6 * 10^4 + 3 * 10^3 + 5 * 10^2 + 7 * 10^1 + 8$$

In the previous calculation, we assumed that the number base is 10. This is a logical assumption because our number system *is* base 10. However, there is no reason why the number 943 couldn't represent a value in base 13. If so, to determine the number of ones, we would have to convert it to base 10.

$$
\begin{aligned}
9 * 13^2 &= 9 * 169 = 1521 \\
+ 4 * 13^1 &= 4 * 13 = 52 \\
+ 3 * 13^0 &= 3 * 1 = \underline{3} \\
& 1576
\end{aligned}
$$

Therefore, 943 in base 13 is equal to 1576 in base 10. Keep in mind that these two numbers have an equivalent value. That is, both represent the same number of things. If one bag contains 943 (base 13) beans and a second bag contains 1576 (base 10) beans, then both bags contain the exact same number of beans. Number systems just allow us to represent values in various ways.

Note that in base 10, the rightmost digit is the "ones" position. In base 13, the rightmost digit is also the "ones" position. In fact, this is true for any base, because anything raised to the power 0 is 1.

Why would anyone want to represent values in base 13? It isn't done very often, granted, but it is sometimes helpful to understand how it works. For example, a computing technique called *hashing* takes numbers and scrambles them, and one way to scramble numbers is to interpret them in a different base.

Other bases, such as base 2 (binary), are particularly important in computer processing. Let's explore these bases in more detail.

■ Binary, Octal, and Hexadecimal

The base-2 (binary) number system is particularly important in computing. It is also helpful to be familiar with number systems that are powers of 2, such as base 8 (octal), and base 16 (hexadecimal). Recall that the base value specifies the number of digits in the number system. Base 10 has ten digits (0–9), base 2 has two digits (0–1), and base 8 has eight digits (0–7). Therefore, the number 943 could not represent a value in any base less than base 10, because the digit 9 doesn't exist in those bases. It is, however,

The Abacus

In our brief history of computing in Chapter 1, we mentioned the abacus as an early computing device. More specifically, the abacus is a device that uses positional notation to represent a decimal number. The beads in any one column represent the digit in that column. All columns combined represent a complete number.

Photo courtesy of Theresa DiDonato

The beads above the middle bar represent units of 5 and the beads below the bar each represent 1. Beads pushed away from the middle bar do not contribute to the number. The following diagram shows the number 27,091 represented on an abacus:

Photo courtesy of Theresa DiDonato

The user performs calculations by moving the beads in specific ways to reflect the basic arith-metic operations of addition, subtraction, multiplication, and division.

Though ancient, the abacus is still used today in many Asian cultures. In stores, a checkout clerk might use an abacus instead of an electronic cash register. Although lacking some of the advantages of electronic devices, the abacus is more than sufficient for the kinds of calculations needed for basic business transactions. Skilled users of an abacus can rival anyone with a calculator in terms of both speed and accuracy.

Children in these cultures learn rote operations on the abacus, much as you were drilled in your multiplication tables. To perform an operation on a number, the user executes a series of movements using only the thumb, pointing finger, and middle finger of one hand. These movements correspond to individual digits and depend on the operation being performed. For example, to add the digit 7 to the digit 5 already showing on the abacus, the user clears the five marker (pushes it to the top), pushes 2 onto the bar from below, and increments 1 in the next column. Though this move corresponds to the basic addition operation we do on paper, the abacus user is not thinking about the mathematics. The user is conditioned to execute a specific movement when specific digits are encountered for a specific operation. When the calculation is complete, the user reads the result as shown on the abacus.

Bi-quinary Number Representation

The console of the IBM 650, a popular commercial computer in the late 1950s, allowed the operator to read the contents of memory using the bi-quinary system. This number representation system uses seven lights to represent the 10 decimal digits.

Photo courtesy of IBM Corporate Archives

Each digit is represented by two lights, one of the top two and one of the bottom five. If the upper-left light is on, the five other lights represent 0, 1, 2, 3, and 4, respectively, from top to bottom. If the upper-right light is on, the five other lights represent 5, 6, 7, 8, and 9. The following configuration represents the number 7:

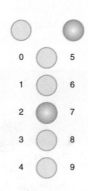

The IBM 650 was called the Ford Tri-Motor of computers: Like the Ford Tri-Motor, old IBM 650s were shipped to Latin America where they enjoyed an extended life.

a valid number in base 10 or any base higher than that. Likewise, the number 2074 is a valid number in base 8 or higher, but it simply does not exist (because it uses the digit 7) in any base lower than that.

What are the digits in bases higher than 10? We need symbols to represent the digits that correspond to the decimal values 10 and beyond. In bases higher than 10, we use letters as digits. We use the letter A to represent the number 10, B to represent 11, C to represent 12, and so forth. Therefore, the 16 digits in base 16 are:

0, 1, 2, 3, 4, 5, 6, 7, 8, 9, A, B, C, D, E, F

Let's look at values in octal, hexadecimal, and binary to see what they represent in base 10. For example, let's calculate the decimal equivalent of 754 in octal (base 8). As before, we just expand the number in its polynomial form and add up the numbers.

$$
\begin{aligned}
&\ 7 * 8^2 = 7 * 64 = 448 \\
&+ 5 * 8^1 = 5 * 8 = 40 \\
&+ 4 * 8^0 = 4 * 1 = \underline{4} \\
&492
\end{aligned}
$$

Let's convert the hexadecimal number ABC to decimal:

$$
\begin{aligned}
&\ \text{A} * 16^2 = 10 * 256 = 2560 \\
&+ \text{B} * 16^1 = 11 * 16 = 176 \\
&+ \text{C} * 16^0 = 12 * 1 = \underline{12} \\
&2748
\end{aligned}
$$

Note that we perform the exact same calculation to convert the number to base 10. We just use a base value of 16 this time, and we have to remember what the letter digits represent. After a little practice you won't find the use of letters as digits that strange.

Finally, let's convert a binary (base-2) number 1010110 to decimal. Once again, we perform the same steps—only the base value changes:

$$
\begin{aligned}
&\ 1 * 2^6 = 1 * 64 = 64 \\
&+ 0 * 2^5 = 0 * 32 = 0 \\
&+ 1 * 2^4 = 1 * 16 = 16 \\
&+ 0 * 2^3 = 0 * 8 = 0 \\
&+ 1 * 2^2 = 1 * 4 = 4 \\
&+ 1 * 2^1 = 1 * 2 = 2 \\
&+ 0 * 2^0 = 0 * 1 = \underline{0} \\
&86
\end{aligned}
$$

Recall that the digits in any number system go up to one less than the base value. To represent the base value in any base, you need two digits. A 0 in the rightmost position and a 1 in the second position represent the value of the base itself. Thus 10 is ten in base 10, 10 is eight in base 8, and 10 is sixteen in base 16. Think about it. The consistency of number systems is actually quite elegant.

Addition and subtraction of numbers in other bases are performed exactly like they are on decimal numbers.

■ Arithmetic in Other Bases

Recall the basic idea of arithmetic in decimal: 0 + 1 is 1, 1 + 1 is 2, 2 + 1 is 3, and so on. Things get interesting when you try to add two numbers whose sum is equal to or larger than the base value—for example, 1 + 9. Because there isn't a symbol for 10, we reuse the same digits and rely on position. The rightmost digit reverts to 0, and there is a carry into the next position to the left. Thus 1 + 9 equals 10 in base 10.

The rules of binary arithmetic are analogous, but we run out of digits much sooner. That is, 0 + 1 is 1, and 1 + 1 is 0 with a carry. Then the same rule is applied to every column in a larger number, and the process continues until we have no more digits to add. The example below adds the binary values 101110 and 11011. The carry value is marked above each column in color.

```
   11111      ←carry
   101110
 +  11011
  1001001
```

We can convince ourselves that this answer is correct by converting both operands to base 10, adding them, and comparing the result: 101110 is 46, 11011 is 27, and the sum is 73. Of course, 1001001 is 73 in base 10.

The subtraction facts that you learned in grade school were that 9 − 1 is 8, 8 − 1 is 7, and so on, until you try to subtract a larger digit from a smaller one, such as 0 − 1. To accomplish this feat, you have to "borrow one" from the next left digit of the number from which you are subtracting. More precisely, you borrow one power of the base. So, in base 10, when you borrow, you borrow 10. The same logic applies to binary subtraction. Every time you borrow in a binary subtraction, you borrow 2. Here are two examples with the borrowed values marked above.

```
      1                        02
    012   ← borrow           02   ← borrow
   111001                    111101
 −    110                  −    110
   110011                    110111
```

Once again, you can check the calculation by converting all values to base 10 and subtracting to see if the answers correspond.

■ Power of 2 Number Systems

Binary and octal numbers share a very special relationship: Given a number in binary, you can read it off in octal; given a number in octal, you can read it off in binary. For example, take the octal number 754. If you replace each digit with the binary representation of that digit, you have 754 in binary. That is, 7 in octal is 111 in binary, 5 in octal is 101 in binary, and 4 in octal is 100 in binary, so 754 in octal is 111101100 in binary.

To facilitate this type of conversion, the table below shows counting in binary from 0 through 10 with their octal and decimal equivalents.

Binary	Octal	Decimal
0	0	0
1	1	1
10	2	2
11	3	3
100	4	4
101	5	5
110	6	6
111	7	7
1000	10	8
1001	11	9
1010	12	10

To convert from binary to octal, you start at the rightmost binary digit and mark the digits in groups of threes. Then you convert each group of three to its octal value.

$$\underline{111} \quad \underline{101} \quad \underline{100}$$
$$7 \qquad 5 \qquad 4$$

Let's convert the binary number 1010110 to octal, and then convert that octal value to decimal. The answer should be the equivalent of 1010110 in decimal, or 86.

$$\underline{1} \quad \underline{010} \quad \underline{110}$$
$$1 \qquad 2 \qquad 6$$

$$
\begin{aligned}
 1 * 8^2 &= 1 * 64 = 64 \\
+\; 2 * 8^1 &= 2 * 8 = 16 \\
+\; 6 * 8^0 &= 6 * 1 = \underline{6} \\
& \; 86
\end{aligned}
$$

The reason that binary can be immediately converted to octal and octal to binary is that 8 is a power of 2. There is a similar relationship between binary and hexadecimal. Every hexadecimal digit can be represented in four binary digits. Let's

? Can you count to three?
Not instinctively! Cognitive psychologists have demonstrated that pre-school children do not identify more than three sets: a set of one object, a set of two objects, and a set of three or more objects (also called many). Anthropologists and linguists have determined that until some two centuries ago, numerous languages had only two or three number words: words for "single," "pair," and "many." We still have words in the English language that reflect three or more: "gang," "pile," "bunch," "flock," "herd," "school," "fleet," "pride," "pack," and "gaggle."
—Denise Schmandt-Besseerat,
One, Two … Three, Odyssey,
September/October 2002,
pages 6 and 7.

take the binary number 1010110 and convert it to hexadecimal by marking the digits from right to left in groups of four.

<u>101</u>   <u>0110</u>
 5   6

$$5 * 16^1 = 5 * 16 = 80$$
$$+\ 6 * 16^0 = 6 * \ \ 1 = \underline{\ \ 6}$$
$$86$$

Now let's convert ABC in hexadecimal to binary. It takes four binary digits to represent each hex digit. A in hexadecimal is 10 in decimal and therefore is 1010 in binary. Likewise, B in hexadecimal is 1011 in binary, and C in hexadecimal is 1100 in binary. Therefore, ABC in hexadecimal is 101010111100 in binary.

Rather than confirming that 10001001010 is 2748 in decimal directly, let's mark it off in octal and convert the octal.

<u>101</u>   <u>010</u>   <u>111</u>   <u>100</u>
 5   2   7   4

Thus 5274 in octal is 2748 in decimal.

In the next section, we show how to convert base-10 numbers to the equivalent number in another base.

■ Converting from Base 10 to Other Bases

The rules for converting base-10 numbers involve dividing by the base into which you are converting the number. From this division, you get a quotient and a remainder. The remainder becomes the next digit in the new number (going from right to left), and the quotient replaces the number to be converted. The process continues until the quotient is zero. Let's write the rules in a different form.

> WHILE (the quotient is not zero)
>   Divide the decimal number by the new base
>   Make the remainder the next digit to the left in the answer
>   Replace the decimal number with the quotient

These rules form an *algorithm* for converting from base 10 to another base. An algorithm is a logical sequence of steps that solves a problem. We have much more to say about algorithms in later chapters. Here we show one way of describing an algorithm and then apply it to perform the conversions.

The first line of the algorithm tells us to repeat the next three lines until the quotient from our division becomes zero. Let's convert the decimal number 2748 to hexadecimal. As we've seen in previous examples, the answer should be ABC.

```
    171     ← quotient
16)2748
    16
    114
    112
     28
     16
     12     ← remainder
```

The remainder (12) is the first digit in the hexadecimal answer, represented by the digit C. So the answer so far is C. Since the quotient is not zero, we divide it (171) by the new base.

```
    10      ← quotient
16)171
    16
    11      ← remainder
```

The remainder (11) is the next digit to the left in the answer, which is represented by the digit B. Now the answer so far is BC. Since the quotient is not zero, we divide it (10) by the new base.

```
     0      ← quotient
16)10
     0
    10      ← remainder
```

The remainder (10) is the next digit to the left in the answer, which is represented by the digit A. Now the answer is ABC. The quotient is zero, so we are finished, and the final answer is ABC.

■ Binary Values and Computers

Although some of the early computers were decimal machines, modern computers are binary machines. That is, numbers within the computer are represented in binary form. In fact, all information is somehow represented using binary values. The reason is that each storage location within a computer contains either a low-voltage signal or a high-voltage signal. Because each location can have only one of two states, it is logical to equate those states to 0 and 1. A low-voltage signal is equated with a 0, and a high-voltage signal is equated with a 1. In fact, you can forget about voltages and think of each storage location as containing either a 0 or a 1. Note that a storage location cannot be empty: It must contain either a 0 or a 1.

Grace Murray Hopper

From 1943 until her death on New Year's Day in 1992, Admiral Grace Murray Hopper was intimately involved with computing. In 1991, she was awarded the National Medal of Technology "for her pioneering accomplishments in the development of computer programming languages that simplified computer technology and opened the door to a significantly larger universe of users."

Admiral Hopper was born Grace Brewster Murray in New York City on December 9, 1906. She attended Vassar and received a PhD in mathematics from Yale. For the next 10 years, she taught mathematics at Vassar.

In 1943, Admiral Hopper joined the U.S. Navy and was assigned to the Bureau of Ordnance Computation Project at Harvard University as a programmer on the Mark I. After the war, she remained at Harvard as a faculty member and continued work on the Navy's Mark II and Mark III computers. She loved to tell the story of how, while she was working on the Mark II, one of the operators discovered the first computer "bug"—a moth caught in one of the relays. In 1949, she joined Eckert-Mauchly Computer Corporation and worked on the UNIVAC I.

Admiral Hopper had a working compiler in 1952, a time when the conventional wisdom was that computers could do only arithmetic. Although not on the committee that designed the computer language COBOL, she was active in its design, implementation, and use. COBOL (which stands for Common Business-Oriented Language) was developed in the early 1960s and is still widely used in business data processing.

Admiral Hopper retired from the Navy in 1966, only to be recalled within a year to full-time active duty. Her mission was to oversee the Navy's efforts to maintain uniformity in programming languages. It has been said that just as Admiral Hyman Rickover was the father of the nuclear navy, Rear Admiral Hopper was the mother of computerized data automation in the Navy. She served with the Naval Data Automation Command until she retired again in 1986 with the rank of Rear Admiral. At the time of her death, she was a senior consultant at Digital Equipment Corporation.

Admiral Hopper loved young people and enjoyed giving talks on college and university campuses. She often handed out colored wires, which she called nanoseconds because they were cut to a length of about one foot—the distance that light travels in a nanosecond (billionth of a second). Her advice to the young was, "You manage things, you lead people. We went overboard on management and forgot about the leadership."

During her lifetime, Admiral Hopper received honorary degrees from more than 40 colleges and universities. She was honored by her peers on several occasions, including the first Computer Sciences Man of the Year award given by the Data Processing Management Association, and the Contributors to Computer Science Education Award given by the Special Interest Group for Computer Science Education (SIGCSE), which is part of the ACM (Association for Computing Machinery).

Nell Dale, when notifying Admiral Hopper of the SIGCSE award, asked which of her many accomplishments she was most proud of. She answered, "All the young people I have trained over the years."

Each storage unit is called a binary digit, or bit for short. Bits are grouped together into bytes (8 bits), and bytes are grouped together into units called words. The number of bits in a word is known as the word length of the computer. For example, IBM 370 architecture in the late 1970s had half words (2 bytes or 16 bits), full words (4 bytes), and double words (8 bytes).

Modern computers are often 32-bit machines (such as Intel's Pentium® IV processor) or 64-bit machines (such as Hewlett-Packard's Alpha processors and Intel's Itanium® 2 processor). However, some microprocessors that are used in applications such as pagers are 8-bit machines. The computing machine you are using—whatever it is—is ultimately supported by the binary number system.

We have much more to explore about the relationship between computers and binary numbers. In the next chapter, we examine many kinds of data and see how they are represented in a computer. In Chapter 4, we see how to control electrical signals that represent binary values. In Chapter 6, we see how binary numbers are used to represent program commands that the computer executes.

» Binary digit A digit in the binary number system; a 0 or a 1
» Bit Binary digit
» Byte Eight binary digits
» Word A group of one or more bytes; the number of bits in a word is the word length of the computer

Summary

Numbers are written using positional notation, in which the digits are arranged in succession, the position of each digit has a place value, and the number is equal to the sum of the products of each digit by its place value. The place values are powers of the base of the number system. Thus, in the decimal number system, the place values are powers of 10; in the binary number system, the place values are powers of 2.

Arithmetic can be performed on numbers in any base represented in positional notation. The same operational rules apply to other bases as they do to base 10. Adding 1 to the largest digit in the base causes a carry into the next position.

Base 2, base 8, and base 16 are all related because these bases are powers of 2. This relationship provides a quick way to convert between numbers in these bases. Computer hardware is designed using numbers in base 2. A low-voltage signal is equated with 0, and a high-voltage signal is equated with 1.

⚖ ETHICAL ISSUES ▸ Homeland Security and Carnivore/DCS-1000   ⓦ

The Bill of Rights, Amendment IV: *The right of the people to be secure in their persons, houses, papers, and effects, against unreasonable searches and seizures, shall not be violated, and no Warrants shall issue, but upon probable cause, supported by Oath or affirmation, and particularly describing the place to be searched, and the persons or things to be seized.*

When the FBI announced plans for an Internet monitoring initiative, privacy groups and politicians were outraged. But after the attacks in New York and Pennsylvania on September 11, 2001, the new USA Patriot Act and Homeland Security Act provided support for the FBI's plan, and the agency was given the green light to hunt down criminals and terrorists.

The FBI's computer tool was initially called Carnivore, but was later given the more innocuous name DCS-1000. The tool could be installed at Internet service providers (ISPs) and could scan and collect all the data passing through each ISP's machines. Criminals of all stripes, including terrorists, have been using technology for years to plan and execute their crimes. Email, websites, banks, and phone lines are all used in the commission of crimes, and the Internet has proved to be a useful tool for those planning destructive activities.

Government and law enforcement point out that email and the Web allow criminals to circumvent the constraints of time and geography in recruiting, planning, and communicating among members. Without the use of possibly intrusive technologies such as Carnivore/DCS-1000, they argue, law keepers would stand no chance in tracking down and convicting these criminals.

Carnivore/DCS-1000's supporters also pointed out that the software was supposed to be used only against targeted suspects. So, while all data flowing through an ISP might be collected, only specific content was to be extracted. Furthermore, they argued, the FBI must seek application from a federal or state's attorney general for use of the tool, citing what will be collected and from whom. They must also show the official granting the application that other forms of surveillance have either failed or would prove too dangerous. Privacy advocates were not comforted by the government's statements about the uses to which Carnivore/DCS-1000 was put, or by assurances that proper restrictions would prevent Carnivore from being misused.

The principal concerns of privacy advocates were that Carnivore/DCS-1000 could and would be used (1) to violate individuals' privacy, (2) to violate freedom of speech, and (3) to allow the government to take over the Internet. There is a fear that use of the technology opens the door to other encroachments upon privacy.

For example, Carnivore/DCS-1000 was able to track the Web surfing habits of all customers of a given ISP. It could not only read email, but also read instant messages, track online purchases, and access anything else flowing through the ISP. To privacy groups, this was a clear violation of the Fourth Amendment.

Facing heated opposition from privacy advocates, the FBI abandoned Carnivore/DCS-1000 in 2005 in favor of an unspecified commercial software, by which means agents will eavesdrop on computer traffic during FBI investigations.

🔑 Key Terms

Base
Binary digit
Bit
Byte
Integer
Natural number

Negative number
Number
Positional notation
Rational number
Word

⌘ **Exercises**

For Exercises 1–5, match the following numbers with their definition.
- A. Number
- B. Natural number
- C. Integer number
- D. Negative number
- E. Rational number

1. A unit of an abstract mathematical system subject to the laws of arithmetic

2. A natural number, a negative of a natural number, or zero

3. The number zero and any number obtained by repeatedly adding one to it

4. An integer or the quotient of two integers (division by zero excluded)

5. A value less than zero, with a sign opposite to its positive counterpart

For Exercises 6–11, match the solution with the problem.
- A. 10001100
- B. 10011110
- C. 1101010
- D. 1100000
- E. 1010001
- F. 1111000

6. 1110011 + 11001 (binary addition)

7. 1010101 + 10101 (binary addition)

8. 1111111 + 11111 (binary addition)

9. 1111111 − 111 (binary subtraction)

10. 1100111 − 111 (binary subtraction)

11. 1010110 − 101 (binary subtraction)

For Exercises 12–17, mark the answers true or false as follows:
- A. True
- B. False

12. Binary numbers are important in computing because a binary number can be converted into every other base.

13. Binary numbers can be read off in hexadecimal but not in octal.

14. Starting from left to right, every grouping of four binary digits can be read as one hexadecimal digit.

15. A byte is made up of six binary digits.

16. Two hexadecimal digits cannot be stored in one byte.

17. Reading octal digits off as binary produces the same result whether read from right to left or from left to right.

Exercises 18–47 are problems or short-answer questions.

18. Distinguish between a natural number and a negative number.

19. Distinguish between a natural number and a rational number.

20. Label the following numbers as natural, negative, or rational.
    a. 1.333333
    b. −1/3
    c. 1066
    d. 2/5
    e. 6.2
    f. π (pi)

21. How many ones are there in 891 if it is a number in each of the following bases?
    a. Base 10
    b. Base 8
    c. Base 12
    d. Base 13
    e. Base 16

22. Express 891 as a polynomial in each of the bases in Exercise 21.

23. Convert the following numbers from the base shown to base 10.
    a. 111 (base 2)
    b. 777 (base 8)
    c. FEC (base 16)
    d. 777 (base 16)
    e. 111 (base 8)

24. Explain how base 2 and base 8 are related.

25. Explain how base 8 and base 16 are related.

26. Expand the table on page 41 to include the decimals from 11 through 16.

27. Expand the table in Exercise 26 to include hexadecimal numbers.

28. Convert the following binary numbers to octal.
    a. 111110110
    b. 1000001
    c. 10000010
    d. 1100010

29. Convert the following binary numbers to hexadecimal.
    a. 10101001
    b. 11100111

    c. 01101110

    d. 01121111

30. Convert the following hexadecimal numbers to octal.

    a. A9

    b. E7

    c. 6E

31. Convert the following octal numbers to hexadecimal.

    a. 777

    b. 605

    c. 443

    d. 521

    e. 1

32. Convert the following decimal numbers to octal.

    a. 901

    b. 321

    c. 1492

    d. 1066

    e. 2001

33. Convert the following decimal numbers to binary.

    a. 45

    b. 69

    c. 1066

    d. 99

    e. 1

34. Convert the following decimal numbers to hexadecimal.

    a. 1066

    b. 1939

    c. 1

    d. 998

    e. 43

35. If you were going to represent numbers in base 18, which symbols might you use to represent the decimal numbers 10 through 17 other than letters?

36. Convert the following decimal numbers to base 18 using the symbols you suggested in Exercise 35.

    a. 1066

    b. 99099

    c. 1

37. Perform the following octal additions.

    a. 770 + 665

    b. 101 + 707

    c. 202 + 667

38. Perform the following hexadecimal additions.
    a. 19AB6 + 43
    b. AE9 + F
    c. 1066 + ABCD

39. Perform the following octal subtractions.
    a. 1066 − 776
    b. 1234 − 765
    c. 7766 − 5544

40. Perform the following hexadecimal subtractions.
    a. ABC − 111
    b. 9988 − AB
    c. A9F8 − 1492

41. Why are binary numbers important in computing?

42. How many bits does a byte contain?

43. How many bytes are there in a 64-bit machine?

44. Why do microprocessors such as pagers have only 8-bit words?

45. Why is it important to study how to manipulate fixed-size numbers?

46. How many ones are there in the number AB98 in base 13?

47. Describe how a bi-quinary number representation works.

1. Exercise 20 asked you to classify π as one of the options. π does not belong in any of the categories named; π (and e) are transcendental numbers. Look up *transcendental numbers* in the dictionary or in an old math book and give the definition in your own words.

2. Complex numbers are another category of numbers that are not discussed in this chapter. Look up *complex numbers* in a dictionary or an old math book and give the definition in your own words.

3. Many everyday occurrences can be represented as a binary bit. For example, a door is open or closed, the stove is on or off, and the dog is asleep or awake. Could relationships be represented as a binary value? Discuss the question, giving examples.

4. Should government officials be allowed to use sophisticated technologies like Carnivore/DCS-1000 to monitor the online presence of potential personal and national security threats? Why or why not?

5. In your opinion, do technologies like Carnivore/DCS-1000 directly conflict with the Fourth Amendment right to privacy, or are they a "necessary evil" in combating the new threats faced by Americans and others around the world after the terrorist events of September 11, 2001?

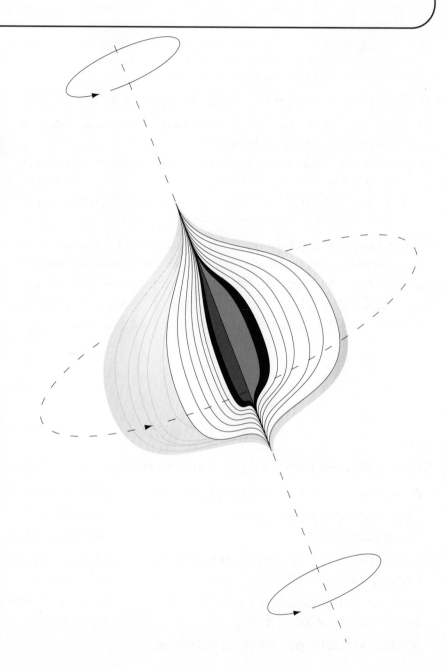

Data Representation

3

When you go on a trip, you probably follow a road map. The map is not the land over which you travel, but rather a *representation* of that land. The map has captured some of the information needed to accomplish the goal of getting from one place to another.

Likewise, the data we need to store and manage on a computer must be represented in a way that captures the essence of the information we care about, and it must do so in a form convenient for computer processing. Building on the fundamental concepts of the binary number system established in Chapter 2, this chapter explores how we represent and store the various kinds of data a computer manages.

Goals

After studying this chapter, you should be able to:

- distinguish between analog and digital data.

- explain data compression and calculate compression ratios.

- explain the binary formats for negative and floating-point values.

- describe the characteristics of the ASCII and Unicode character sets.

- perform various types of text compression.

- explain the nature of sound and its representation.

- explain how RGB values define a color.

- distinguish between raster and vector graphics.

- explain temporal and spatial video compression.

3.1 Data and Computers

Without data, computers would be useless. Every task a computer undertakes deals with managing data in some way. Therefore, our need to represent and organize data in appropriate ways is paramount.

Let's start by distinguishing the terms *data* and *information*. Although these terms are often used interchangeably, making the distinction is sometimes useful, especially in computing. Data are basic values or facts, whereas information is data that has been organized and/or processed in a way that is useful in solving some kind of problem. Data can be unstructured and lack context. Information helps us answer questions (it "informs"). This distinction, of course, is relative to the needs of the user, but it captures the essence of the role that computers play in helping us solve problems.

In this chapter, we focus on representing different types of data. In later chapters, we discuss the various ways to organize data so as to solve particular types of problems.

In the not-so-distant past, computers dealt almost exclusively with numeric and textual data. Today, however, computers are truly multimedia devices, dealing with a vast array of information categories. Computers store, present, and help us modify many different types of data:

- Numbers
- Text
- Audio
- Images and graphics
- Video

Ultimately, all of this data is stored as binary digits. Each document, picture, and sound bite is somehow represented as strings of 1s and 0s. This chapter explores each of these types of data in turn and discusses the basic ideas behind the ways in which we represent these types of data on a computer.

We can't discuss data representation without also talking about data compression—reducing the amount of space needed to store a piece of data. In the past, we needed to keep data small because of storage limitations. Today, computer storage is relatively cheap—but now we have an even more pressing reason to shrink our data: the need to share it with others. The Web and its underlying networks have inherent bandwidth restrictions that define the maximum number of bits or bytes that can be transmitted from one place to another in a fixed amount of time.

The compression ratio gives an indication of how much compression occurs. The compression ratio is the size of the compressed data divided by the size of the original data. The values could be in bits or characters (or whatever is appropriate), as long as both values measure the same thing.

≫ **Data** Basic values or facts

≫ **Information** Data that has been organized or processed in a useful manner

≫ **Multimedia** Several different media types

≫ **Data compression** Reducing the amount of space needed to store a piece of data

≫ **Bandwidth** The number of bits or bytes that can be transmitted from one place to another in a fixed amount of time

≫ **Compression ratio** The size of the compressed data divided by the size of the uncompressed data

The ratio should result in a number between 0 and 1. The closer the ratio is to zero, the tighter the compression.

A data compression technique can be lossless, which means the data can be retrieved without losing any of the original information, or it can be lossy, in which case some information is lost in the process of compaction. Although we never want to lose information, in some cases this loss is acceptable. When dealing with data representation and compression, we always face a tradeoff between accuracy and size.

■ Analog and Digital Data

The natural world, for the most part, is continuous and infinite. A number line is continuous, with values growing infinitely large and small. That is, you can always come up with a number that is larger or smaller than any given number. Likewise, the numeric space between two integers is infinite. For instance, any number can be divided in half. But the world is not just infinite in a mathematical sense. The spectrum of colors is a continuous rainbow of infinite shades. Objects in the real world move through continuous and infinite space. Theoretically, you could always close the distance between you and a wall by half, and you would never actually reach the wall.

Computers, by contrast, are finite. Computer memory and other hardware devices have only so much room to store and manipulate a certain amount of data. We always fail in our attempt to represent an infinite world on a finite machine. The goal, then, is to represent enough of the world to satisfy our computational needs and our senses of sight and sound. We want to make our representations good enough to get the job done, whatever that job might be.

Data can be represented in one of two ways: analog or digital. Analog data is a continuous representation, analogous to the actual information it represents. Digital data is a discrete representation, breaking the information up into separate elements.

A mercury thermometer is an analog device. The mercury rises in a continuous flow in the tube in direct proportion to the temperature. We calibrate and mark the tube so that we can read the current temperature, usually as an integer such as 75 degrees Fahrenheit. However, the mercury in such a thermometer is actually rising in a continuous manner between degrees. At some point in time, the temperature is actually 74.568 degrees Fahrenheit, and the mercury is accurately indicating that, even if our markings are not detailed enough to note such small changes. See Figure 3.1.

Analog data is directly proportional to the continuous, infinite world around us. Computers, therefore, cannot work well with analog data. Instead, we digitize data by breaking it into pieces and representing those

>> **Lossless compression** A data compression technique in which there is no loss of information

>> **Lossy compression** A data compression technique in which there is loss of information

>> **Analog data** A continuous representation of data

>> **Digital data** A discrete representation of data

>> **Digitize** The act of breaking information down into discrete pieces

FIGURE 3.1 A mercury thermometer continually rises in direct
proportion to the temperature

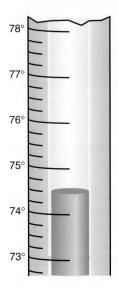

FIGURE 3.1 A mercury thermometer continually rises in direct
proportion to the temperature

pieces separately. Each of the representations discussed in this chapter takes a continuous entity and separates it into discrete elements. Those discrete elements are then individually represented using binary digits.

But why do we use the binary system? We know from Chapter 2 that binary is just one of many equivalent number systems. Couldn't we use, say, the decimal number system, with which we are already more familiar? We could. In fact, it's been done. Computers have been built that are based on other number systems. However, modern computers are designed to use and manage binary values because the devices that store and manage the data are far less expensive and far more reliable if they have to represent only one of two possible values.

Also, electronic signals are far easier to maintain if they transfer only binary data. An analog signal continually fluctuates up and down in voltage, but a digital signal has only a high or low state, corresponding to the two binary digits. See Figure 3.2.

FIGURE 3.2 An analog signal and a
digital signal

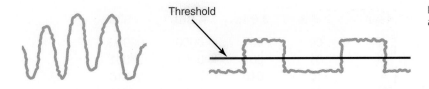

Threshold

FIGURE 3.3 Degradation of analog and digital signals

All electronic signals (both analog and digital) degrade as they move down a line. That is, the voltage of the signal fluctuates due to environmental effects. The trouble is that as soon as an analog signal degrades, information is lost. Because any voltage level within the range is valid, it's impossible to know what the original signal state was or even that it changed at all.

Digital signals, by contrast, jump sharply between two extremes—a behavior referred to as **pulse-code modulation** (PCM). A digital signal can become degraded by quite a bit before any information is lost, because any voltage value above a certain threshold is considered a high value, and any value below that threshold is considered a low value. Periodically, a digital signal is **reclocked** to regain its original shape. As long as it is reclocked before too much degradation occurs, no information is lost. Figure 3.3 shows the degradation effects of analog and digital signals.

> **Pulse-code modulation** Variation in a signal that jumps sharply between two extremes

> **Reclock** The act of reasserting an original digital signal before too much degradation occurs

■ Binary Representations

As we investigate the details of representing particular types of data, it's important to remember the inherent nature of using binary. One bit can be either 0 or 1. There are no other possibilities. Therefore, one bit can represent only two things. For example, if we wanted to classify a food as being either sweet or sour, we would need only one bit to do it. We could say that if the bit is 0, the food is sweet, and if the bit is 1, the food is sour. But if we want to have additional classifications (such as spicy), one bit is not sufficient.

To represent more than two things, we need multiple bits. Two bits can represent four things because four combinations of 0 and 1 can be made from two bits: 00, 01, 10, and 11. For instance, if we want to represent which of four possible gears a car is in (park, drive, reverse, or neutral), we need only two bits: Park could be represented by 00, drive by 01, reverse by 10, and neutral by 11. The actual mapping between bit combinations and the thing each combination represents is sometimes irrelevant (00 could be used to represent reverse, if you prefer), although sometimes the mapping can be meaningful and important, as we discuss in later sections of this chapter.

If we want to represent more than four things, we need more than two bits. For example, three bits can represent eight things because eight

FIGURE 3.4 Bit combinations

1 Bit	2 Bits	3 Bits	4 Bits	5 Bits
0	00	000	0000	00000
1	01	001	0001	00001
	10	010	0010	00010
	11	011	0011	00011
		100	0100	00100
		101	0101	00101
		110	0110	00110
		111	0111	00111
			1000	01000
			1001	01001
			1010	01010
			1011	01011
			1100	01100
			1101	01101
			1110	01110
			1111	01111
				10000
				10001
				10010
				10011
				10100
				10101
				10110
				10111
				11000
				11001
				11010
				11011
				11100
				11101
				11110
				11111

combinations of 0 and 1 can be made from three bits. Likewise, four bits can represent 16 things, five bits can represent 32 things, and so on. See Figure 3.4. In the figure, note that the bit combinations are simply counting in binary as you move down a column.

In general, n bits can represent 2^n things because 2^n combinations of 0 and 1 can be made from n bits. Every time we increase the number of available bits by 1, we double the number of things we can represent.

Let's turn the question around. How many bits do you need to represent, say, 25 unique things? Well, four bits wouldn't be enough because four bits can represent only 16 things. We would have to use at least five bits, which would allow us to represent 32 things. Given that we need to represent only 25 things, some of the bit combinations would not have a valid interpretation.

Keep in mind that even though we may technically need only a certain minimum number of bits to represent a set of items, we may allocate more than that for the storage of data. There is a minimum number of bits that a computer architecture can address and move around at one time, and it is usually a power of 2, such as 8, 16, or 32 bits. Therefore, the minimum amount of storage given to any type of data is allocated in multiples of that value.

3.2 Representing Numeric Data

Numeric values are the most prevalent type of data used in a computer system. Unlike with other types of data, there may seem to be no need to come up with a clever mapping between binary codes and numeric data. Because binary is a number system, a natural relationship exists between the numeric data and the binary values that we store to represent them. This is true, in general, for positive integer data. The basic issues regarding integer conversions were covered in Chapter 2 in the general discussion of the binary system and its equivalence to other bases. However, we have other issues regarding the representation of numeric data to consider at this point. Integers are just the beginning in terms of numeric data. This section discusses the representation of negative and noninteger values.

■ Representing Negative Values

Aren't negative numbers just numbers with a minus sign in front? Perhaps. That is certainly one valid way to think about them. Let's explore the issue of negative numbers and discuss appropriate ways to represent them on a computer.

Signed-Magnitude Representation

You have used the signed-magnitude representation of numbers since you first learned about negative numbers in grade school. In the traditional decimal system, a sign (+ or −) is placed before a number's value, although the positive sign is often assumed. The sign represents the ordering, and the digits represent the magnitude of the number. The classic number line

>> **Signed-magnitude representation** Number representation in which the sign represents the ordering of the number (negative and positive) and the value represents the magnitude

looks something like this, in which a negative sign means that the number is to the left of zero and the positive number is to the right of zero:

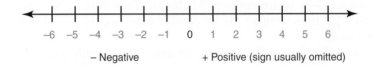

— Negative   + Positive (sign usually omitted)

Performing addition and subtraction with signed integer numbers can be described as moving a certain number of units in one direction or another. To add two numbers, you find the first number on the scale and move in the direction of the sign of the second as many units as specified. Subtraction is done in a similar way, moving along the number line as dictated by the sign and the operation. In grade school, you soon graduated to doing addition and subtraction without using the number line.

There is a problem with the signed-magnitude representation: There are two representations of zero—plus zero and minus zero. The idea of a negative zero doesn't necessarily bother us; we just ignore it. However, two representations of zero within a computer can cause unnecessary complexity, so other representations of negative numbers are used. Let's examine another alternative.

Fixed-Sized Numbers

If we allow only a fixed number of values, we can represent numbers as just integer values, where half of them represent negative numbers. The sign is determined by the magnitude of the number. For example, if the maximum number of decimal digits we can represent is two, we can let 1 through 49 be the positive numbers 1 through 49 and let 50 through 99 represent the negative numbers −50 through −1. Let's take the number line and number the negative values on the top according to this scheme:

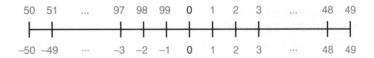

To perform addition within this scheme, you just add the numbers together and discard any carry. Adding positive numbers should be okay. Let's try adding a positive number and a negative number, a negative number and a positive number, and two negative numbers. These are shown in the following table in signed-magnitude and in this scheme (the carries are discarded):

Signed-Magnitude	New Scheme
5	5
+ − 6	+ 94
− 1	99
− 4	96
+ 6	+ 6
2	2
− 2	98
+ − 4	+ 96
− 6	94

What about subtraction, using this scheme for representing negative numbers? The key is in the relationship between addition and subtraction: $A - B = A + (-B)$. We can subtract one number from another by adding the negative of the second to the first:

Signed-Magnitude	New Scheme	Add Negative
−5	95	95
− 3	− 3 ⟹	+ 97
−8		92

In this example, we have assumed a fixed size of 100 values and kept our numbers small enough to use the number line to calculate the negative representation of a number. However, you can also use a formula to compute the negative representation:

Negative(I) = $10^k - I$, where k is the number of digits

Let's apply this formula to -3 in our two-digit representation:

$-(3) = 10^2 - 3 = 97$

What about a three-digit representation?

$-(3) = 10^3 - 3 = 997$

This representation of negative numbers is called the **ten's complement**. Although humans tend to think in terms of sign and magnitude to represent numbers, the complement strategy is actually easier in some ways when it comes to electronic calculations. Because we store everything in a modern computer in binary, we use the binary equivalent of the ten's complement, called the two's complement.

> **≫ Ten's complement** A representation of negative numbers such that the negative of I is 10 raised to k minus I

Two's Complement

Let's assume that a number must be represented in eight bits. To make it easier to look at long binary numbers, we make the number line vertical:

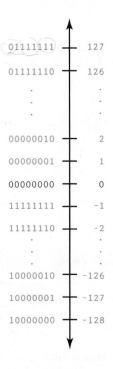

01111111	127
01111110	126
.	.
.	.
.	.
00000010	2
00000001	1
00000000	0
11111111	-1
11111110	-2
.	.
.	.
.	.
10000010	-126
10000001	-127
10000000	-128

Would the ten's complement formula work with the 10 replaced by 2? That is, could we compute the negative binary representation of a number using the formula negative$(I) = 2^k - I$? Let's try it and see:

$$-(2) = 2^8 - 2 = 128 - 2 = -126$$

Decimal 126 is octal 176, which is 1111110 in binary—but the number line has one more 1 digit to the left. What's wrong? Nothing. This is a negative number. The leftmost digit determines whether the number is negative or positive. A 0 bit in the leftmost digit says that the number is positive; a 1 bit says the number is negative. Thus, $-(2)$ is 11111110.

There is an easier way to calculate the two's complement: invert the bits and add 1. That is, take the positive value and change all the 1 bits to 0 and all the 0 bits to 1, and then add 1.

+2	=	00000010
invert		11111101
add 1		00000001
−2	=	11111110

-126

Addition and subtraction are accomplished the same way as in ten's complement arithmetic:

```
– 127   10000001
+   1   00000001
– 126   10000010
```

With this representation, the leftmost bit in a negative number is always a 1. Therefore, you can tell immediately whether a binary number in two's complement is negative or positive.

Number Overflow

Overflow occurs when the value that we compute cannot fit into the number of bits we have allocated for the result. For example, if each value is stored using eight bits, adding 127 to 3 would produce an overflow:

```
  01111111
+ 00000011
  10000010
```

In our scheme 10000010 represents −126, not +130. If we were not representing negative numbers, however, the result would be correct.

Overflow is a classic example of the type of problems we encounter by mapping an infinite world onto a finite machine. No matter how many bits we allocate for a number, there is always the potential need to represent a number that doesn't fit. How overflow problems are handled varies by computer hardware and by the differences in programming languages.

▪ Representing Real Numbers

In computing, we call all noninteger values (that can be represented) *real* values. For our purposes here, we define a real number as a value with a potential fractional part. That is, real numbers have a whole part and a fractional part, either of which may be zero. For example, some real numbers in base 10 are 104.32, 0.999999, 357.0, and 3.14159.

As we explored in Chapter 2, the digits represent values according to their position, and those position values are relative to the base. To the left of the decimal point, in base 10, we have the ones position, the tens position, the hundreds position, and so forth. These position values come from raising the base value to increasing powers (moving from the decimal point to the left). The positions to the right of the decimal point work the same way, except that the powers are negative. So the positions to the right of the decimal point are the tenths position (10^{-1} or one tenth), the hundredths position (10^{-2} or one hundredth), and so forth.

In binary, the same rules apply but the base value is 2. Since we are not working in base 10, the decimal point is referred to as a radix point, a term that can be used in any base. The positions to the right of the radix point

> ⟫ Overflow A situation where a calculated value cannot fit into the number of digits reserved for it

> ⟫ Radix point The dot that separates the whole part from the fractional part in a real number in any base

TABLE 3.1 Values in decimal notation and floating-point notation (five digits)

Real Value	Floating-Point Value
12001.00	$12001 * 10^0$
−120.01	$−12001 * 10^{-2}$
0.12000	$12000 * 10^{-5}$
−123.10	$−12310 * 10^{-2}$
155555000.00	$15555 * 10^4$

in binary are the halves position (2^{-1} or one half), the quarters position (2^{-2} or one quarter), and so forth.

How do we represent a real value in a computer? We store the value as an integer and include information showing where the radix point is. That is, any real value can be described by three properties: the sign (positive or negative one); the mantissa, which is made up of the digits in the value with the radix point assumed to be to the right; and the exponent, which determines how the radix point is shifted relative to the mantissa. A real value in base 10 can, therefore, be defined by the following formula:

sign * mantissa * 10^{exp}

The representation is called floating point because the number of digits is fixed but the radix point floats. When a value is in floating-point form, a positive exponent shifts the decimal point to the right, and a negative exponent shifts the decimal point to the left.

Let's look at how to convert a real number expressed in our usual decimal notation into floating-point notation. As an example, consider the number 148.69. The sign is positive, and two digits appear to the right of the decimal point. Thus the exponent is −2, giving us $14869 * 10^{-2}$. Table 3.1 shows other examples. For the sake of this discussion, we assume that only five digits can be represented.

How do we convert a value in floating-point form back into decimal notation? The exponent on the base tells us how many positions to move the radix point. If the exponent is negative, we move the radix point to the left. If the exponent is positive, we move the radix point to the right. Apply this scheme to the floating-point values in Table 3.1.

Notice that in the last example in Table 3.1, we lose information. Because we are storing only five digits to represent the significant digits (the mantissa), the whole part of the value is not accurately represented in floating-point notation.

Likewise, a binary floating-point value is defined by the following formula:

sign * mantissa * 2^{exp}

Note that only the base value has changed. Of course, in this scheme the mantissa would contain only binary digits. To store a floating-point number in binary on a computer, we can store the three values that define it. For example, according to one common standard, if we devote 64 bits to the storage of a floating-point value, we use 1 bit for the sign, 11 bits for the exponent, and 52 bits for the mantissa. Internally, this format is taken into account whenever the value is used in a calculation or is displayed.

But how do we get the correct value for the mantissa if the value is not a whole number? In Chapter 2, we discussed how to change a natural number from one base to another. Here we have shown how real numbers are represented in a computer, using decimal examples. We know that all values are represented in binary in the computer. How do we change the fractional part of a decimal value to binary?

To convert a whole value from base 10 to another base, we divide by the new base, recording the remainder as the next digit to the left in the result, and continuing to divide the quotient by the new base until the quotient becomes zero. Converting the fractional part is similar, but we *multiply* by the new base rather than dividing. The carry from the multiplication becomes the next digit to the right in the answer. The fractional part of the result is then multiplied by the new base. The process continues until the fractional part of the result is zero. Let's convert .75 to binary.

.75 * 2 = 1.50
.50 * 2 = 1.00

Thus .75 in decimal is .11 in binary. Let's try another example.

.435 * 2 = 0.870
.870 * 2 = 1.740
.740 * 2 = 1.480
.480 * 2 = 0.960
.960 * 2 = 1.920
.920 * 2 = 1.840
...

Thus .435 is 011011 . . . in binary. Will the fractional part ever become zero? Keep multiplying it out and see.

Now let's go through the entire conversion process by converting 20.25 in decimal to binary. First we convert 20.

$$\begin{array}{r} 10 \\ 2\overline{)20} \\ \underline{20} \\ 0 \end{array}$$

$$\begin{array}{r} 5 \\ 2\overline{)10} \\ \underline{10} \\ 0 \end{array}$$

$$2\overline{)5}$$
$$\underline{4}$$
$$1$$

$$1$$
$$2\overline{)2}$$
$$\underline{2}$$
$$0$$

$$0$$
$$2\overline{)1}$$
$$\underline{0}$$
$$1$$

20 in binary is 10100. Now we convert the fractional part:

.25 * 2 = 0.50
.50 * 2 = 1.00

Thus 20.25 in decimal is 10100.01 in binary.

> >> **Scientific notation** An alternative floating-point representation

Scientific notation is a term with which you may already be familiar, so we mention it here. Scientific notation is a form of floating-point representation in which the decimal point is kept to the right of the leftmost digit. That is, there is one whole number. In many programming languages, if you print out a large real value without specifying how to print it, the value is printed in scientific notation. Because exponents could not be printed in early machines, an "E" was used instead. For example, 12001.32708 would be written as 1.200132708E+4 in scientific notation.

3.3 **Representing Text**

A text document can be decomposed into paragraphs, sentences, words, and ultimately individual characters. To represent a text document in digital form, we simply need to be able to represent every possible character that may appear. The document is the continuous (analog) entity, and the separate characters are the discrete (digital) elements that we need to represent and store in computer memory.

At this point, we should distinguish between the basic idea of representing text and the more involved concept of word processing. When we create a document in a word processing program such as Microsoft® Word, we can specify all kinds of formatting: fonts, margins, tabs, color, and so on. Many word processors also let us add art, equations, and other elements. This extra information is stored along with the rest of the text so that the document can be displayed and printed the way you want it. The core issue, however, is the way we represent the characters themselves; therefore, those techniques remain our focus at this point.

There are a finite number of characters to represent. The general approach for representing characters is to list all of them and then assign a binary string to each character. For example, to store a particular letter, we store the appropriate bit string.

So which characters do we need to represent? The English language includes 26 letters. But uppercase and lowercase letters have to be treated separately, so that's really 52 unique characters. Punctuation characters also have to be represented, as do the numeric digits (the actual characters '0', '1', through '9'). Even the space character must have a representation. And what about languages other than English? The list of characters we may want to represent starts to grow quickly once you begin to think about it. Keep in mind that, as we discussed earlier in this chapter, the number of unique things (characters, in this case) we want to represent determines how many bits we'll need to represent any one of them.

A **character set** is simply a list of characters and the codes used to represent each one. Several character sets have been used over the years, though a few have dominated. By agreeing to use a particular character set, computer manufacturers have made the processing of text data easier. We explore two character sets in the following sections: ASCII and Unicode.

> **》 Character set** A list of the characters and the codes used to represent each one

■ The ASCII Character Set

ASCII stands for American Standard Code for Information Interchange. The ASCII character set originally used seven bits to represent each character, allowing for 128 unique characters. The eighth bit in each character byte was originally used as a *check bit*, which helped ensure proper data transmission. Later ASCII evolved so that all eight bits were used to represent a character. This eight-bit version is formally called the Latin-1 Extended ASCII character set. The extended ASCII set allows for 256 characters and includes accented letters as well as several other special symbols. Figure 3.5 shows the ASCII character set.

Character set maze
In 1960, an article in *Communications of the ACM* reported on a survey of character sets in use. Sixty distinct sets were described. Nine character sets, with differences in both content and ordering, existed in IBM's line of computers.[1]

The codes in Figure 3.5 are expressed as decimal numbers, but these values get translated to their binary equivalent for storage in the computer. Note that the ASCII characters have a distinct order based on the codes used to store them. Each character has a relative position (before or after) every other character. This property is helpful in several different ways. For example, note that both the uppercase and lowercase letters are in order. Therefore, we can use the character codes to help us put a list of words into alphabetical order.

The first 32 characters in the ASCII character chart do not have a simple character representation that you could print to the screen. These characters are reserved for special purposes, such as carriage return and tab. They are usually interpreted in special ways by whatever program is processing the data.

■ The Unicode Character Set

The extended version of the ASCII character set provides 256 characters, which is enough for English but not enough for international use. This

FIGURE 3.5 The ASCII character set

Left Digit(s)	Right Digit	0	1	2	3	4	5	6	7	8	9
0		NUL	SOH	STX	ETX	EOT	ENQ	ACK	BEL	BS	HT
1		LF	VT	FF	CR	SO	SI	DLE	DC1	DC2	DC3
2		DC4	NAK	SYN	ETB	CAN	EM	SUB	ESC	FS	GS
3		RS	US	□	!	"	#	$	%	&	'
4		(	)	*	+	,	–	.	/	0	1
5		2	3	4	5	6	7	8	9	:	;
6		<	=	>	?	@	A	B	C	D	E
7		F	G	H	I	J	K	L	M	N	O
8		P	Q	R	S	T	U	V	W	X	Y
9		Z	[	\	]	^	_	`	a	b	c
10		d	e	f	g	h	i	j	k	l	m
11		n	o	p	q	r	s	t	u	v	w
12		x	y	z	{			}	~	DEL		

limitation gave rise to the Unicode character set, which has a much stronger international influence.

The goal of the people who created Unicode is nothing less than to represent every character in every language used in the entire world, including all of the Asian ideograms. It also represents many special-purpose characters such as scientific symbols.

The Unicode character set is gaining popularity and is used by many programming languages and computer systems today. One commonly used encoding uses 16 bits per character and has ASCII as a subset. However, the character set itself is still evolving. Figure 3.6 shows a few characters currently represented in the 16-bit Unicode character encoding.

For consistency, Unicode was designed to be a superset of ASCII. That is, the first 256 characters in the Unicode character set correspond exactly

FIGURE 3.6 A few characters in the Unicode character set

Code (Hex)	Character	Source
0041	A	English (Latin)
042F	Я	Russian (Cyrillic)
0E09	ฉ	Thai
13EA	Ꮺ	Cherokee
211E	℞	Letterlike Symbols
21CC	⇌	Arrows
282F	⠯	Braille
345F	佌	Chinese/Japanese/Korean (Common)

to the extended ASCII character set, including the codes used to represent them. Therefore, programs that assume ASCII values are unaffected even if the underlying system embraces the Unicode approach.

■ Text Compression

Alphabetic information (text) is a fundamental type of data. Therefore, it is important that we find ways to store and transmit text efficiently between one computer and another. The following sections examine three types of text compression:

- Keyword encoding
- Run-length encoding
- Huffman encoding

As we discuss later in this chapter, some of the ideas underlying these text compression techniques come into play when dealing with other types of data as well.

Keyword Encoding

Consider how often you use words such as "the," "and," "which," "that," and "what." If these words took up less space (that is, had fewer characters), our documents would shrink in size. Even though the savings for each word would be small, they are used so often in a typical document that the combined savings would add up quickly.

One fairly straightforward method of text compression is keyword encoding, in which frequently used words are replaced with a single character. To decompress the document, you reverse the process: You replace the single characters with the appropriate full word.

>> Keyword encoding Replacing a frequently used word with a single character

For example, suppose we used the following chart to encode a few words:

Word	Symbol
as	^
the	~
and	+
that	$
must	&
well	%
these	#

Let's encode the following paragraph:

The human body is composed of many independent systems, such as the circulatory system, the respiratory system, and the reproductive system. Not only must all systems work independently, but they must interact and cooperate as well. Overall health is a function of the well-being of separate systems, as well as how these separate systems work in concert.

The encoded paragraph is:

The human body is composed of many independent systems, such ^ ~ circulatory system, ~ respiratory system, + ~ reproductive system. Not only & each system work independently, but they & interact + cooperate ^ %. Overall health is a function of ~ %-being of separate systems, ^ % ^ how # separate systems work in concert.

There are a total of 352 characters in the original paragraph including spaces and punctuation. The encoded paragraph contains 317 characters, resulting in a savings of 35 characters. The compression ratio for this example is 317/352 or approximately 0.9.

There are several limitations to keyword encoding. First, note that the characters we use to encode the keywords cannot be part of the original text. If, for example, the '$' was part of the original paragraph, the resulting encoding would be ambiguous. We wouldn't know whether '$' represented the word "that" or if it was the actual dollar-sign character. This limits the number of words we can encode as well as the nature of the text that we are encoding.

Also, note that the word "The" in the example is not encoded by the '~' character because the word "The" and the word "the" contain different letters. Remember, the uppercase and lowercase versions of the same letter are different characters when it comes to storing them on a computer. We would have to use a separate symbol for "The" if we wanted to encode it, or employ a more sophisticated substitution scheme.

Finally, note that we would not gain anything by encoding words such as "a" and "I" because that would simply be replacing one character for another. The longer the word, the more compression we get per word. Unfortunately, the most frequently used words are often short. Of course, some documents use certain words more frequently than others depending on the subject matter. For example, we would have realized some nice savings if we had chosen to encode the word "system" in our example, but it might not be worth encoding in a general situation.

An extension of keyword encoding is to replace specific patterns of text with special characters. The encoded patterns are generally not complete words, but rather parts of words such as common prefixes and suffixes—"ex," "ing," and "tion," for instance. An advantage of this approach is that patterns being encoded generally appear more often than

JamBayes goes commercial
INRIX Traffic Services uses a sophisticated statistical analysis technique originally developed by Microsoft Research (called JamBayes), to aggregate and enhance traffic-related information from hundreds of public and private sources, including traditional road sensors and the company's unique network of nearly 1 million GPS-enabled vehicles and cellular probes. INRIX delivers traffic information today for more than 120 markets in North America and via ARC Europe for 16 European countries.

−INRIX press release, http://www.inrix.com/ pressrelease.asp?ID=66 (accessed April 15, 2009)

whole words (because they occur in many different words). A disadvantage is that they are generally short patterns and, therefore, the replacement savings per word is small.

Run-Length Encoding

In some situations, a single character may be repeated over and over again in a long sequence. This type of repetition doesn't generally take place in English text, but often occurs in large data streams, such as DNA sequences. A text compression technique called run-length encoding capitalizes on these situations. Run-length encoding is sometimes called *recurrence coding.*

In run-length encoding, a sequence of repeated characters is replaced by a *flag character*, followed by the repeated character, followed by a single digit that indicates how many times the character is repeated. For example, consider the following string of seven repeated 'A' characters:

AAAAAAA

If we use the '*' character as our flag, this string would be encoded as

*A7

The flag character indicates that the series of three characters (including the flag) should be decoded into the appropriate repetitious string. All other text is treated regularly. Therefore, the encoded string

*n5*x9ccc*h6 some other text *k8eee

would be decoded into the following original text:

nnnnnxxxxxxxxxccchhhhhh some other text kkkkkkkkeee

The original text contains 51 characters and the encoded string contains 35 characters, giving us a compression ratio in this example of 35/51, or approximately 0.68.

In this example the three repeated 'c' characters and the three repeated 'e' characters are not encoded. Because it takes three characters to encode a repetition sequence, it is not worth it to encode strings of two or three. In fact, in the case of two repeated characters, encoding would actually make the string longer!

Given that we are using one character for the repetition count, it seems that we can't encode repetition lengths greater than nine. But keep in mind that each character is represented by a series of bits based on some character set. For example, the character '5' is represented as ASCII value 53, which in an eight-bit binary string is 00110101. So, instead of interpreting the count character as an ASCII digit, we could interpret it as a binary number. We can then have repetition counts between 0 and 255, or even between 4 and 259, because runs of three or less are not represented.

» Run-length encoding Replacing a long series of a repeated character with a count of the repetition

Huffman Encoding

Another text compression technique, called Huffman encoding, is named after its creator, Dr. David Huffman. Why should the character 'X', which is seldom used in text, take up the same number of bits as the blank, which is used very frequently? Huffman codes address this question by using variable-length bit strings to represent each character. That is, a few characters may be represented by five bits, another few by six bits, yet another few by seven bits, and so forth. This approach is contrary to the idea of a character set, in which each character is represented by a fixed-length bit string (such as 8 or 16).

The idea behind this approach is that if we use only a few bits to represent characters that appear often and reserve longer bit strings for characters that don't appear often, the overall size of the document being represented is small.

For example, suppose we use the following Huffman encoding to represent a few characters:

Huffman Code	Character
00	A
01	E
100	L
110	O
111	R
1010	B
1011	D

Then the word DOORBELL would be encoded in binary as

1011110110111101001100100

If we used a fixed-size bit string to represent each character (say, 8 bits), then the binary form of the original string would be 8 characters times 8 bits, or 64 bits. The Huffman encoding for that string is 25 bits long, giving a compression ratio of 25/64, or approximately 0.39.

What about the decoding process? When we use character sets, we just take the bits in chunks of 8 or 16 bits to see what character the chunk represents. In Huffman encoding, with its variable-length codes, it seems as if we might get confused when trying to decode a string because we don't know how many bits we should include for each character. In fact, that potential source of confusion has been eliminated by the way the codes are created.

An important characteristic of any Huffman encoding is that no bit string used to represent a character is the prefix of any other bit string used to represent a character. Therefore, as we scan from left to right across a bit string, when we find a string that corresponds to a character, that must be the character it represents. It can't be part of a larger bit string.

For example, if the bit string

1010110001111011

is created with the previous table, it must be decoded into the word BOARD. There is no other possibility.

So how is a particular set of Huffman codes created? The details of that process are a bit beyond the scope of this book, but let's discuss the underlying issue. Because Huffman codes use the shortest bit strings for the most common characters, we start with a table that lists the frequency of the characters we want to encode. Frequencies may come from counting characters in a particular document (352 E's, 248 S's, and so on) or from counting characters in a sample of text from a particular content area. A frequency table may also come from a general idea of how frequently letters occur in a particular language such as English. Using those values, we can construct a structure from which the binary codes can be read. The way the structure is created ensures that the most frequently used characters get the shortest bit strings.

3.4 Representing Audio Data

We perceive sound when a series of air compressions vibrate a membrane in our ear, which sends signals to our brain. Thus a sound is defined in nature by the wave of air that interacts with our eardrum. See Figure 3.7. To represent a sound, we must somehow represent the appropriate sound wave.

A stereo sends an electrical signal to a speaker to produce sound. This signal is an analog representation of the sound wave. The voltage in the signal varies in direct proportion to the sound wave. The speaker receives the signal and causes a membrane to vibrate, which in turn vibrates the air (creating a sound wave), which in turn vibrates the eardrum. The created sound wave should ideally be identical to the one that was captured initially, or at least good enough to please the listener.

To represent audio data on a computer, we must digitize the sound wave, somehow breaking it into discrete, manageable pieces. One way to accomplish this task is to actually digitize the analog representation of the sound. That is, we can take the electric signal that represents the sound wave and represent it as a series of discrete numeric values.

FIGURE 3.7 A sound wave vibrates our eardrums

FIGURE 3.7 A sound wave vibrates our eardrums

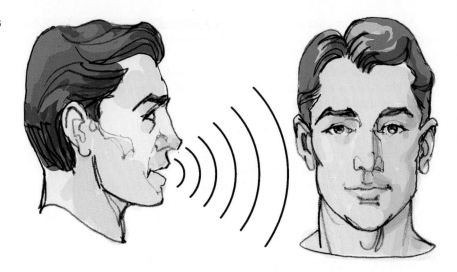

An analog signal varies in voltage continuously. To digitize the signal, we periodically measure the voltage of the signal and record the appropriate numeric value. This process is called *sampling*. Instead of a continuous signal, we end up with a series of numbers representing distinct voltage levels.

To reproduce the sound, we use the stored voltage values to create a new continuous electronic signal. The assumption is that the voltage levels in the original signal changed evenly between one stored voltage value and the next. If we take enough samples in a short period of time, that assumption is reasonable. But certainly the process of sampling can lose information, as shown in Figure 3.8.

In general, a sampling rate of around 40,000 times per second is enough to create a reasonable sound reproduction. If the sampling rate is much lower than that, the human ear begins to hear distortions. A higher

FIGURE 3.8 Sampling an audio signal

this peak value is lost

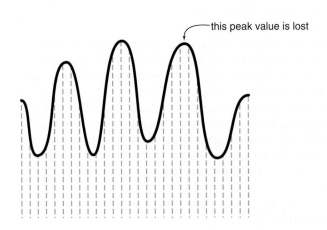

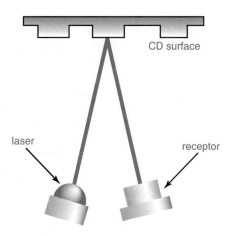

FIGURE 3.9 A CD player reading binary data

sampling rate produces better-quality sound, but after a certain point the extra data is irrelevant because the human ear can't hear the difference. The overall result is affected by many factors, including the quality of the equipment, the type of sound, and the human listener.

A vinyl record album is an analog representation of the sound wave. The needle of a record player (turntable) rides up and down in the spiral groove of the album. The rise and fall of the needle is analogous to the voltage changes of the signal that represents the sound.

In contrast, a compact disk (CD) stores audio information digitally. On the surface of the CD are microscopic pits that represent binary digits. A low-intensity laser is pointed at the disk. The laser light reflects strongly if the surface is smooth and reflects poorly if the surface is pitted. A receptor analyzes the reflection and produces the appropriate string of binary data, which represents the numeric voltage values that were stored when the signal was digitized. The signal is reproduced and sent to the speaker. See Figure 3.9.

■ Audio Formats

Over the past few years, several formats for audio data have become popular, including WAV, AU, AIFF, VQF, and MP3. All of these formats are based on the storage of voltage values sampled from analog signals, but all recognize the details of the data in different ways and all use various compression techniques to one extent or another.

Currently, the dominant format for compressing audio data is MP3. The popularity of MP3 resulted mostly because it offered a stronger compression ratio than other formats available at the time. Other formats may prove more efficient in the future, but for now MP3 is the general favorite. In mid-1999, the term "MP3" was searched for more than any other term, and it is still going strong today. Let's look at the details of the MP3 format a little more closely.

■ The MP3 Audio Format

MP3 is short for MPEG-2, audio layer 3 file. MPEG is an acronym for the Moving Picture Experts Group, which is an international committee that develops standards for digital audio and video compression.

MP3 employs both lossy and lossless compression. First, it analyzes the frequency spread and compares it to mathematical models of human psychoacoustics (the study of the interrelation between the ear and the brain). Then, it discards information that can't be heard by humans. Finally, the bit stream is compressed using a form of Huffman encoding to achieve additional compression.

Many software tools are available on the Web to help you create MP3 files. These tools generally require that the recording be stored in some other common format, such as WAV, before that data is converted into MP3 format, significantly reducing the file size.

A variety of MP3 players interpret and play MP3 files. An MP3 player can be purely software for an existing computer, or it can be a dedicated hardware device that stores and plays the files, such as the popular Apple® iPod®. Most MP3 players allow users to organize their files in several different ways and to display corresponding information and graphics during playback.

?

MGM Studios, Inc., v. Grokster, Ltd.
Since the inception of the Napster website, copyright battles involving the exchange of proprietary material over the Internet via file-sharing services have escalated. The motion picture industry had become concerned about the ease with which copyrighted movies were being freely exchanged online via P2P file-sharing systems. In 2003, Metro-Goldwyn-Mayer (MGM) Studios, along with 27 other music and motion picture studios, filed lawsuits against Grokster (which owned KaZaA) and Streamcast (which owned Morpheus). MGM alleged "contributory copyright infringement" against these services, arguing that they were legally liable for the copyrighted material exchanged on their systems. The case made it to the Supreme Court, and Grokster was eventually forced to pay $50 million to the music and recording industries, causing Grokster to shut down.

3.5 Representing Images and Graphics

Images such as photographs and graphics such as line drawings have common issues when it comes to their representation and compression. We first look at the general idea of representing color, then turn to the various techniques for digitizing and representing visual information.

■ Representing Color

Color is our perception of the various frequencies of light that reach the retinas of our eyes. Our retinas have three types of color photoreceptor cone cells that respond to different sets of frequencies. These photoreceptor categories correspond to the colors of red, green, and blue. All other colors perceptible by the human eye can be made by combining various amounts of these three colors.

In a computer, color is often expressed as an RGB (red-green-blue) value, which is actually three numbers that indicate the relative contribution of each of these three primary colors. If each number in the triple is given on a scale of 0 to 255, then 0 means no contribution of that color

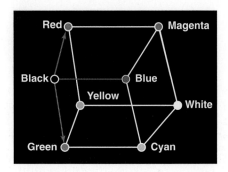

FIGURE 3.10 Three-dimensional color space

and 255 means full contribution of that color. For example, an RGB value of (255, 255, 0) maximizes the contribution of red and green and minimizes the contribution of blue, which results in a bright yellow.

The concept of RGB values gives rise to a three-dimensional "color space." Figure 3.10 shows one way to display such a color space.

The amount of data that is used to represent a color is called the *color depth*. It is usually expressed in terms of the number of bits that are used to represent the color. *HiColor* indicates a 16-bit color depth. With this scheme, 5 bits are used for each number in an RGB value and the extra bit is sometimes used to represent transparency. *TrueColor* indicates a 24-bit color depth. With this scheme, each number in an RGB value gets 8 bits, which gives the range of 0 to 255 for each. This results in the ability to represent more than 16.7 million unique colors.

The following chart shows a few TrueColor RGB values and the colors they represent:

RGB Value			Color
Red	Green	Blue	
0	0	0	black
255	255	255	white
255	255	0	yellow
255	130	255	pink
146	81	0	brown
157	95	82	purple
140	0	0	maroon

The 24-bit TrueColor values provide more colors than the human eye can distinguish. Furthermore, the monitors that display colors are restricted to a particular color depth. In older hardware in which monitor colors are reduced to, say, 256 colors, any color that is specified by a program is mapped into the closest color in the palette of colors that the hardware is capable of displaying.

FIGURE 3.11 A restricted color palette

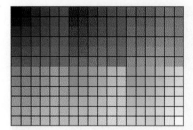

Figure 3.11 shows such a restricted color palette. When there are significant differences between the colors desired and the colors that can be displayed, the results are usually unsatisfactory. Thankfully, most modern monitors provide enough color range to greatly reduce these problems.

■ Digitized Images and Graphics

A photograph is an analog representation of an image. It is continuous across its surface, with shades of one color blending into another. Digitizing a picture is the act of representing it as a collection of individual dots called pixels, a term that stands for picture elements. Each pixel is composed of a single color. The number of pixels used to represent a picture is called the resolution. If enough pixels are used (high resolution), and are then presented in the proper order side by side, the human eye can be fooled into thinking it's viewing a continuous picture. Figure 3.12 shows a digitized picture, with a small portion of it magnified to show the individual pixels.

The storage of image information on a pixel-by-pixel basis is called a raster-graphics format. Several popular raster-graphics file formats are currently in use, including bitmap (BMP), GIF, and JPEG.

A *bitmap file* is one of the most straightforward graphic representations. In addition to a few administrative details, a bitmap file contains the

>> **Pixels** Individual dots used to represent a picture; stands for picture elements

>> **Resolution** The number of pixels used to represent a picture

>> **Raster-graphics format** Storing image information pixel by pixel

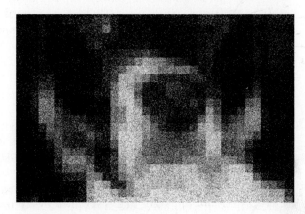

FIGURE 3.12 A digitized picture composed of many individual pixels. *Courtesy of Amy Rose*

pixel color values of the image from left to right and from top to bottom. A bitmap file supports 24-bit TrueColor, although usually the color depth can be specified to reduce the file size. Such a file may be compressed using run-length encoding.

The GIF format (Graphics Interchange Format), which was developed by CompuServe in 1987, limits the number of available colors in the image to 256. That is, a GIF image can be made up of only 256 colors, but each GIF image can be made up of a different set of 256 colors. This technique, called *indexed color*, results in smaller file sizes because there are fewer colors to reference. If even fewer colors are required, the color depth can usually be specified with fewer bits. GIF files are best used for graphics and images with few colors, and are therefore considered optimal for line art. A version of the GIF format allows for small animations to be defined by storing a series of images that a program such as a browser displays in succession.

The JPEG format is designed to exploit the nature of our eyes. Humans are more sensitive to gradual changes of brightness and color over distance than we are to rapid changes. Therefore, the data that the JPEG format stores averages out the color hues over short distances. This format is considered superior for photographic color images. A fairly complicated compression scheme can significantly reduce the resulting file sizes.

The PNG (pronounced "ping") format stands for Portable Network Graphics. The designers of the PNG format wanted to improve upon, and ultimately replace, the GIF format. PNG images can usually achieve a greater compression than GIFs, while offering a much wider range of color depths. However, PNG images do not support animation, and they are not yet as widely supported as GIFs.

■ Vector Representation of Graphics

Vector graphics is another technique for representing images. Instead of assigning colors to pixels as we do in raster graphics, a vector-graphics format describes an image in terms of lines and geometric shapes. A vector graphic is a series of commands that describe a line's direction, thickness, and color. The file sizes produced with these formats tend to be small because every pixel does not have to be accounted for. The complexity of the image, such as the number of items in the picture, determines the file size.

> ❯❯ Vector graphics Representation of an image in terms of lines and shapes

A raster graphic such as a GIF must be encoded multiple times to account for different sizes and proportions. By contrast, vector graphics can be resized mathematically, and these changes can be calculated dynamically as needed.

However, vector graphics is not good for representing real-world images. JPEG images are far superior in that regard, but vector graphics is good for line art and cartoon-style drawings.

Einstein describes the telegraph
"You see, wire telegraph is a kind of very, very long cat," explained Albert Einstein. "You pull its tail in New York and his head is meowing in Los Angeles...And radio operates exactly the same way: you send signals here, they receive them there. The only difference is that there is no cat."
    How do you think he would describe a computer?

The most popular vector-graphics format used on the Web today is called Flash. Flash images are stored in a binary format and require a special editor to create. A new vector-graphics format, called Scalable Vector Graphics (SVG), is under development. SVG is expressed in plain text. When the SVG format is finalized, it is likely to make vector graphics a popular approach for Web-based imaging.

3.6 Representing Video

Video information is one of the most complex types of information to capture, compress, and still get a result that makes sense to the human eye. Video clips contain the equivalent of many still images, each of which must be compressed. The Web is full of video clips that are choppy and hard to follow. This situation will likely improve over the next few years, depending on the evolving sophistication of video compression techniques, which are referred to as video codecs.

▪ Video Codecs

Video codec Methods used to shrink the size of a movie

Temporal compression Movie compression technique based on differences between consecutive frames

Spatial compression Movie compression technique based on the same compression techniques used for still images

Codec stands for COmpressor/DECompressor. A video codec refers to the methods used to shrink the size of a movie so that it can be played on a computer or over a network. Almost all video codecs use lossy compression to minimize the huge amounts of data associated with video. The goal, therefore, is not to lose information that affects the viewer's senses.

Most codecs are block oriented, meaning that each frame of a video is divided into rectangular blocks. The various codecs differ in how the blocks are encoded. Some video codecs are accomplished completely in software, whereas others require special hardware.

Video codecs employ two types of compression: temporal and spatial. Temporal compression looks for differences between consecutive frames. If most of an image in two frames hasn't changed, why should we waste space by duplicating all of the similar information? A *keyframe* is chosen as the basis on which to compare the differences, and its entire image is stored. For consecutive images, only the changes (called *delta frames*) are stored. Temporal compression is effective in video that changes little from frame to frame, such as a scene that contains little movement.

Spatial compression removes redundant information within a frame. This problem is essentially the same as the one we face when compressing still images. Spatial video compression often groups pixels into blocks (rectangular areas) that have the same color, such as a portion of a clear blue sky. Instead of storing each pixel, the color and the coordinates of the area are stored instead. This idea is similar to run-length encoding.

Various video codecs are popular today, including Sorenson, Cinepak, MPEG, and Real Video. The details of how these codecs represent and compress video are beyond the scope of this book.

Bob Bemer

Bob Bemer was a fixture in computing circles since 1945. His résumé reads like a list of the most influential computing companies of the last half-century. He worked for Douglas Aircraft, RKO Radio Pictures, the Rand Corporation, Lockheed Aircraft, Marquardt Aircraft, Lockheed Missiles and Space, IBM, Univac Division of Sperry Rand, Bull General Electric (Paris), GTE, Honeywell, and finally his own software company, Bob Bemer Software.

Courtesy of Bob Bemer

The predominance of aircraft manufacturers on Bemer's resume is not surprising because he studied mathematics and held a Certificate in Aeronautical Engineering from Curtiss-Wright Technical Institute (1941). In the early days of computing, aircraft manufacturers were pioneers in using computers in industry.

During his career, Bemer was active in programming language development. He developed FORTRANSIT, an early FORTRAN compiler. He was actively involved in the development of the COBOL language and the CODASYL language, an early approach to database modeling and management. In addition, he was responsible for authorizing funding for the development of SIMULA, a simulation language that introduced many object-oriented features.

Bemer was also an active participant in committees formed to bring universal standards into the new computing industry. He was U.S. representative on the IFIP Computer Vocabulary Committee, Chairman of ISO/TC97/SC5 on Common Programming Languages, and Chairman of X3/SPARC Study Group on Text Processing.

However, Bemer is best known for his work on the ASCII computer code, which is the standard internal code for 8-bit PCs today. Early on,

Bemer recognized that if computers were going to communicate with one another, they needed a standard code for transmitting textual information. Bemer made and published a survey of more than 60 different computer codes, thus demonstrating a need for a standard code. He created the program of work for the standards committee, forced the U.S. standard code to correspond to the international code, wrote the bulk of the articles published about the code, and pushed for a formal registry of ASCII-alternate symbol and control sets to accommodate other languages.

Perhaps Bemer's most important contribution is the concept of an escape character. The escape character alerts the system processing the characters that the character(s) following the escape character change the standard meaning of the characters to follow. For example, ESC (N) alerts the system that the following characters are in the Cyrillic equivalent of ASCII.

The first version of a 16-bit code called Unicode was published in October 1991. Two factors drove the need for an enlarged code: 16-bit computer architecture was becoming popular, and the expansion of the Internet and the WWW drove the need for a code that could directly include the world's alphabets. ASCII, however, has not gone away; it remains a subset of Unicode.

In May 2003, Bemer received the IEEE Computer Society's Computer Pioneer Award "for meeting the world's needs for variant character sets and other symbols, via ASCII, ASCII-alternate sets, and escape sequences."

Bob Bemer died on June 22, 2004, at his home on Possum Kingdom Lake in Texas.

–http://www.bobbemer.com/AWARD.HTM

Summary

Computers are multimedia devices that manipulate data varying in form from numbers to graphics to video. Because a computer can manipulate only binary values, all forms of data must be represented in binary form. Data is classified as being either continuous (analog) or discrete (digital).

Integer values are represented by their binary equivalent using one of several techniques for representing negative numbers, such as a signed-magnitude or two's complement. Real numbers are represented by a triple made up of the sign, the digits in the number, and an exponent that specifies the radix point.

A character set is a list of alphanumeric characters and the codes that represent each character. The most commonly used character set today is Unicode (16 bits for each character), which has ASCII as a subset. The 8-bit ASCII set is sufficient for English but not for other (or multiple) languages. There are various ways for compressing text so that it takes less space to store it or less time to transmit it from one machine to another.

Audio information is represented as digitized sound waves. Color is represented by three values that represent the contributions of red, blue, and green, respectively. Two basic techniques are used for representing pictures, bitmaps and vector graphics. Video is broken up into a series of still images, each of which is represented as a picture.

⚖ ETHICAL ISSUES ▶ Computers and Homeland Security   W

In the wake of the terrorist attacks of September 11, 2001, the USA Patriot Act was signed into law by President George W. Bush on October 26, 2001. Among other things, the Act increases the ability of law enforcement agencies to conduct electronic searches—without the owner's/occupant's knowledge or permission—of telephone, email, medical, financial, and other records. In addition, the Act relaxes restrictions on foreign intelligence gathering within the United States itself. Through an expanded use of National Security Letters (NSLs), the FBI is able to search telephone, email, and financial records with a court order; and enforcement agencies have expanded access to business, library, and financial records. Many of the Act's provisions were to end December 31, 2005, but supporters of the Act pushed to make all provisions permanent. In March 2006, most of the Patriot Act was signed into law by President Bush.

Still under debate and review are a few controversial aspects of Title II of the Act, titled "Enhanced Surveillance Procedures." Title II covers all aspects of surveillance of suspected terrorists, clandestine agents of foreign powers, as well as those who are suspected of conducting computer fraud or abuse. Two of the most controversial provisions of Title II are "sneak and peek" searches and roving wiretaps.

The "sneak and peek" provisions of the Act allowed enforcement agencies such as the FBI to search for an unspecified period of time before a search warrant was issued. In 2004, the FBI incorrectly linked the fingerprints of Brandon Mayfield, an American lawyer, to a print found near the scene of a terrorist bombing in Madrid, Spain, that killed 191 people. According to court documents, the FBI entered

» continued

Mayfield's home without his knowledge, and during a later raid, took Mayfield's computers, modem, safe deposit key, assorted papers, and his copies of the Quran. Mayfield was imprisoned without charges for a period of two weeks and then released when the FBI realized it had misidentified him. The FBI issued a rare public apology in hopes that the issue would blow over, but Mayfield pursued his case in court. On September 26, 2007, Judge Ann Aiken (Portland, Oregon), declared that the "sneak and peek" provisions of Title II violated the prohibition of unreasonable searches in the Fourth Amendment to the U.S. Constitution and were unconstitutional.

Roving wiretaps are wiretap orders that do not require the specific listing of all common carriers and third parties of a normal surveillance court order. Opponents, such as the Electronic Privacy Information Center (EPIC) and the American Civil Liberties Union (ACLU), argue that such taps are unconstitutional because they violate the particularity clause of the Fourth Amendment. Roving wiretaps, they argue, give the FBI a "blank check" to violate the communications privacy of innocent Americans. Despite such arguments, roving wiretaps were reauthorized by a bill of 2006 but were given an end date of December 31, 2009.

Key Terms

Analog data
Bandwidth
Character set
Compression ratio
Data
Data compression
Digital data
Digitize
Floating point
Huffman encoding
Information
Keyword encoding
Lossless compression
Lossy compression
Multimedia

Overflow
Pixels
Pulse-code modulation
Radix point
Raster-graphics format
Reclock
Resolution
Run-length encoding
Scientific notation
Signed-magnitude representation
Spatial compression
Temporal compression
Ten's complement
Vector graphics
Video codec

Exercises

For Exercises 1–20, mark the answers true or false as follows:
  A. True
  B. False

1. Lossless compression means the data can be retrieved without losing any of the original information.

2. A computer represents information in an analog form.

3. A computer must use the binary number system to represent information.

4. A digital signal represents one of two values at any point in time.

5. Four bits can be used to represent 32 unique things.

6. The signed-magnitude representation of numbers has two representations for zero.

7. Overflow occurs when the value that we compute cannot fit into the number of bits we have allocated for the result.

8. In the ASCII character set, no distinction is made between uppercase and lowercase letters.

9. The Unicode character set includes all of the characters in the ASCII character set.

10. Keyword encoding replaces frequently used words with a single character.

11. Run-length encoding is very good at compressing English text.

12. Huffman encoding uses variable-length binary strings to represent characters.

13. An audio signal is digitized by sampling it at regular intervals.

14. A CD stores audio information in a binary format.

15. The MP3 audio format discards information that cannot be heard by humans.

16. An RGB value represents a color using three numeric values.

17. Indexed color increases the number of colors that can be used in an image, and thus increases the file size.

18. Bitmap, GIF, and JPEG are all examples of raster-graphics formats.

19. Vector graphics represent images in terms of lines and geometric shapes.

20. A keyframe is used in temporal compression to represent the changes from one frame to another.

For Exercises 21–26, choose the correct term from the following list.
   A. Signed-magnitude representation
   B. Radix point
   C. Frequency of use
   D. Sampling
   E. Analog
   F. Digital

21. _____ data is a continuous representation of information.

22. The representation for numbers you've used since grade school is called _____.

23. If the number base is other than base 10, we call the decimal point the
    _____.

24. _____ data is a discrete representation of information.

25. Huffman codes are created based on the _____ of the character.

26. An audio signal is digitized by _____ its value at regular intervals.

Exercises 27–79 are problems or short-answer questions.

27. Why is data compression an important topic today?

28. What is the difference between lossless and lossy data compression?

29. Why do computers have difficulty with analog information?

30. Is a clock with a sweeping second hand an analog device or a digital
    device? Explain.

31. What does it mean to digitize something?

32. What is pulse-code modulation?

33. How many things can be represented with
    a. Four bits?
    b. Five bits?
    c. Six bits?
    d. Seven bits?

34. Although you have been computing simple arithmetic operations since
    the second grade, take the following quick test to confirm that you
    thoroughly understand operations on signed integers. Evaluate the
    following expressions where W is 17, X is 28, Y is −29, and Z is −13.
    a. X + Y   b. X + W   c. Z + W   d. Y + Z
    e. W − Z   f. X − W   g. Y − W   h. Z − Y

35. Use the base-10 number line to prove the solutions to the following
    operations, where A is 5 and B is −7.
    a. A + B   b. A − B   c. B + A   d. B − A

36. Given a fixed-sized number scheme where k in the formula for the
    ten's complement is 6 (see page 61), answer the following questions.
    a. How many positive integers can be represented?
    b. How many negative integers can be represented?
    c. Draw the number line showing the three smallest and largest posi-
       tive numbers, the three smallest and largest negative numbers, and
       zero.

37. Use the number line in Exercise 36(c) to calculate the following
    expressions, where A is −499999 and B is 3.
    a. A + B   b. A − B   c. B + A   d. B − A

38. Use the formula for the ten's complement to calculate the following
    numbers in the scheme described on page 61.
    a. 35768   b. −35768   c. −444455   d. −123456

39. In calculating the ten's complement in Exercise 38, did you have trouble borrowing from so many zeros? Such calculations are error prone. There is a trick that you can use that makes the calculation easier and thus less prone to errors: Subtract from all 9s and then add 1. A number subtracted from all 9s is called the nine's complement of the number.
    a. Prove that the nine's complement of a number plus one is equal to the ten's complement of the same number.
    b. Use the nine's complement plus one to calculate the values in Exercise 38(b), (c), and (d).
    c. Which did you find easier to use, the direct calculation of the ten's complement or the nine's complement plus one? Justify your answer.

40. Evaluate the following expressions, where A is 11111110 and B is 00000010, using two's complement.
    a. $A + B$ b. $A - B$ c. $B - A$ d. $-B$
    e. $-(-A)$

41. Is the two's complement of a number always a negative number? Explain.

42. Devise a number system based on base 11.
    a. Draw the number line.
    b. Show examples of addition and subtraction.
    c. Develop a representation of negative numbers based on eleven's complement.

43. Convert the rules for subtraction in a signed-magnitude system to the algorithm format.

44. Convert the following real numbers to binary (five binary places).
    a. 0.50
    b. 0.26
    c. 0.10

45. Convert the following real numbers to octal (five octal places).
    a. 0.50
    b. 0.26
    c. 0.10

46. Can fractional values be visually converted between octal and binary and back? Explain.

47. How many bits would be needed to represent a character set containing 45 characters? Why?

48. How can the decimal number 175.23 be represented as a sign, mantissa, and exponent?

49. What is the main difference between the ASCII and Unicode character sets?

50. Create a keyword encoding table that contains a few simple words. Rewrite a paragraph of your choosing using this encoding scheme. Compute the compression ratio you achieve.

51. How would the following string of characters be represented using run-length encoding? What is the compression ratio?

    AAAABBBCCCCCCCCDDDD hi there EEEEEEEEEFF

52. What does the code *X5*A9 represent using run-length encoding?

53. Given the following Huffman encoding table, decipher the bit strings that follow.

Huffman Code	Character
00	A
11	E
010	T
0110	C
0111	L
1000	S
1011	R
10010	O
10011	I
101000	N
101001	F
101010	H
101011	D

  a. 1101110001011
  b. 0110101010100101011111000
  c. 101001001010000100010000010100110110
  d. 1010001001010100010001110100011011

54. How do humans perceive sound?

55. Is a stereo speaker an analog device or a digital device? Explain.

56. What is an RGB value?

57. What does color depth indicate?

58. How does pixel resolution affect the visual impact of an image?

59. Explain temporal video compression.

60. Describe a situation in which spatial video compression would be effective.

61. Define sampling as it relates to digitizing sound waves.

62. Which produces better sound quality, higher sampling rates or lower sampling rates?

63. What is the sampling rate per second that is enough to create reasonable sound reproduction?

64. Do vinyl record albums and compact disks record sound in the same way?

65. What does an RGB value of (130, 0, 255) mean?

66. What color does an RGB value of (255, 255, 255) represent?

67. What is resolution?

68. The GIF format uses which technique?

69. What are GIF files best for?

70. How are the various video codecs alike?

71. How are the various video codecs different?

72. Name two types of video compression.

73. What do we call the perception of the various frequencies of light that reach the retinas of our eyes?

74. What is the best format for photographic color images?

75. What are the techniques called that shrink the sizes of movies?

76. What is the technique in which an application supports only a certain number of specific colors, creating a palette from which to choose?

77. What is the format that describes an image in terms of lines and geometric shapes?

78. Which format stores information on a pixel-by-pixel basis?

79. What is the difference between HiColor and TrueColor?

??? Thought Questions

1. What are some advantages of using a common (standardized) character set? What are some disadvantages?

2. When converting whole numbers from one base to another, we divide by the new base. When converting fractional parts from one base to another, we multiply by the new base. Can positional notation be used to explain these algorithms?

3. Technology is changing rapidly. What changes have occurred in data compression since this book was written?

4. Discuss the battle between national security and personal privacy. List the pros and cons of each side. Is a logical compromise possible?

5. The end date for roving wiretaps was to be December 31, 2009. Was this deadline extended or kept?

The Hardware Layer

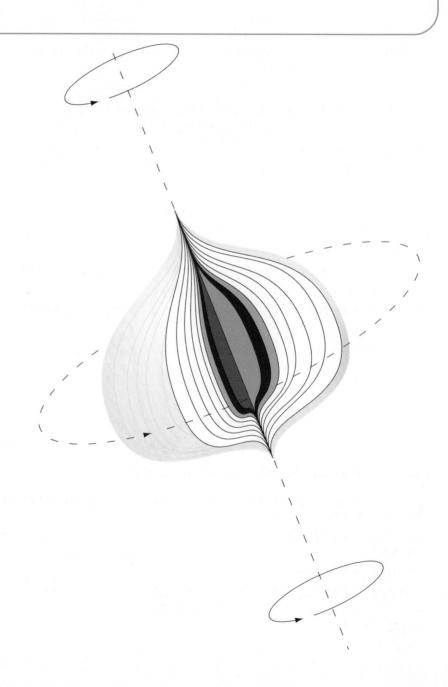

Gates and Circuits

4

Computers are electronic devices; the most fundamental hardware elements of a computer control the flow of electricity. In a very primitive sense, we use technology to harness the power of a lightning bolt, bending it to our will so that we can perform calculations and make decisions. This chapter dances the fine line between computer science and electrical engineering, examining the most basic hardware elements in a computer.

In Chapter 2, we looked at number systems in general and at the binary number system in particular. As we saw in Chapter 3, the binary number system is of special interest because it is used to represent data in a computer. In this chapter, we explore how computers use electric signals to represent and manipulate those binary values.

Goals

After studying this chapter, you should be able to:

- identify the basic gates and describe the behavior of each.
- describe how gates are implemented using transistors.
- combine basic gates into circuits.
- describe the behavior of a gate or circuit using Boolean expressions, truth tables, and logic diagrams.
- compare and contrast a half adder and a full adder.
- describe how a multiplexer works.
- explain how an S-R latch operates.
- describe the characteristics of the four generations of integrated circuits.

4.1 Computers and Electricity

Any given electronic signal has a level of voltage. As we mentioned in the last chapter, we distinguish between the two values of interest (binary 0 and 1) by the voltage level of a signal. In general, a voltage level in the range of 0 to 2 volts is considered "low" and is interpreted as a binary 0. A signal in the 2- to 5-volt range is considered "high" and is interpreted as a binary 1. Signals in a computer are constrained to be within one range or the other.

A gate is a device that performs a basic operation on electrical signals. It accepts one or more input signals and produces a single output signal. Several types of gates exist; we examine the six most fundamental types in this chapter. Each type of gate performs a particular logical function.

Gates are combined into circuits to perform more complicated tasks. For example, circuits can be designed to perform arithmetic and to store values. In a circuit, the output value of one gate often serves as the input value for one or more other gates. The flow of electricity through a circuit is controlled by the carefully designed logic of the interacting gates.

Three different, but equally powerful, notational methods are used to describe the behavior of gates and circuits:

- Boolean expressions
- Logic diagrams
- Truth tables

We examine all three types of representation during our discussion of gates and circuits.

The English mathematician George Boole invented a form of algebra in which variables and functions take on only one of two possible values (0 and 1). This algebra is appropriately called Boolean algebra. Expressions in this algebraic notation are an elegant and powerful way to demonstrate the activity of electrical circuits. Specific operations and properties in Boolean algebra allow us to define and manipulate circuit logic using a mathematical notation. Boolean expressions will come up again in our discussions of the programming layer in Chapters 6 through 9.

A logic diagram is a graphical representation of a circuit. Each type of gate is represented by a specific graphical symbol. By connecting those symbols in various ways, we can visually represent the logic of an entire circuit.

A truth table defines the function of a gate by listing all possible input combinations that the gate could encounter, along with corresponding output. We can design more complex truth tables with sufficient rows and columns to show how entire circuits perform for any set of input values.

>> **Gate** A device that performs a basic operation on electrical signals, accepting one or more input signals and producing a single output signal

>> **Circuit** A combination of interacting gates designed to accomplish a specific logical function

>> **Boolean algebra** A mathematical notation for expressing two-valued logical functions

>> **Logic diagram** A graphical representation of a circuit; each type of gate has its own symbol

>> **Truth table** A table showing all possible input values and the associated output values

George Boole[1]

Boolean algebra is named for its inventor, English mathematician George Boole, born in 1815. His father, a tradesman, began teaching him mathematics at an early age. But Boole was initially more interested in classical literature, languages, and religion—interests he maintained throughout his life. By the time he was 20, he had taught himself French, German, and Italian. He was well versed in the writings of Aristotle, Spinoza, Cicero, and Dante, and wrote several philosophical papers himself.

At 16 he took a position as a teaching assistant in a private school to help support his family. His work there plus a second teaching job left him little time to study. A few years later, he opened a school and began to learn higher mathematics on his own. In spite of his lack of formal training, his first scholarly paper was published in the *Cambridge Mathematical Journal* when he was just 24. In 1849, he was appointed professor of mathematics at Queen's College in Cork, Ireland. He became chair of mathematics and spent the rest of his career there. Boole went on to publish more than 50 papers and several major works before he died in 1864, at the peak of his career.

Boole's *The Mathematical Analysis of Logic* was published in 1847. It would eventually form the basis for the development of digital computers. In the book, Boole set forth the formal axioms of logic (much like the axioms of geometry) on which the field of symbolic logic is built. Boole drew on the symbols and operations of algebra in creating his system of logic. He associated the value 1 with the universal set (the set representing everything in the universe) and the value 0 with the empty set, and restricted his system to these quantities. He then defined operations that are analogous to subtraction, addition, and multiplication.

In 1854, Boole published *An Investigation of the Laws of Thought; on Which Are Founded the Mathematical Theories of Logic and Probabilities*. This book described theorems built on his axioms of logic and extended the algebra to show how probabilities could be computed in a logical system. Five years later, Boole published *Treatise on Differential Equations*, followed by *Treatise on the Calculus of Finite Differences*. The latter is one of the cornerstones of numerical analysis, which deals with the accuracy of computations.

Boole received little recognition and few honors for his work. Given the importance of Boolean algebra in modern technology, it is hard to believe that his system of logic was not taken seriously until the early twentieth century. George Boole was truly one of the founders of computer science.

4.2 Gates

The gates in a computer are sometimes referred to as logic gates because each performs just one logical function. That is, each gate accepts one or more input values and produces a single output value. Because we are dealing with binary information, each input and output value is either 0, corresponding to a low-voltage signal, or 1, corresponding to a high-voltage signal. The type of gate and the input values determine the output value.

Let's examine the processing of the following six types of gates. We then show how they can be combined into circuits to perform arithmetic operations.

- NOT
- AND
- OR
- XOR
- NAND
- NOR

In this book we have colorized the logic diagram symbols for each gate to help you keep track of the various types. When we examine full circuits with many gates, the colors will help you distinguish among them. In the real world, however, logic diagrams are typically black and white, and the gates are distinguished only by their shape.

What is nanoscience?
Nanoscience is the study of materials smaller than 100 nanometers—or 1/100th the width of a human hair strand. Two nanotubes—each 10 atoms wide—have been used to create a simple circuit. "They're the only thing in the world that right now has some potential of making a switch to process information that's faster than the fastest silicon transistor," said IBM's worldwide director of physical science research Tom Theis.

"If nanotechnology has the impact we think it might have, it may well cause social and industrial rearrangements not unlike the original Industrial Revolution," said Richard W. Siegel, director of Rensselaer Nanotechnology Center in Troy, New York.[2]

■ NOT Gate

A NOT gate accepts one input value and produces one output value. Figure 4.1 shows a NOT gate represented in three ways: as a Boolean expression, as its logical diagram symbol, and using a truth table. In each representation, the variable A represents the input signal, which is either 0 or 1. The variable X represents the output signal, whose value (0 or 1) is determined by the value of A.

By definition, if the input value for a NOT gate is 0, the output value is 1; if the input value is 1, the output is 0. A NOT gate is sometimes referred to as an *inverter* because it inverts the input value.

FIGURE 4.1 Representations of a NOT gate

Boolean Expression	Logic Diagram Symbol	Truth Table	
$X = A'$	A ▷∘ X	**A**	**X**
		0	1
		1	0

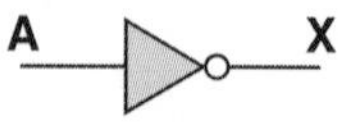

In Boolean expressions, the NOT operation is represented by the ' mark after the value being negated. Sometimes this operation is shown as a horizontal bar over the value being negated. In the Boolean expression in Figure 4.1, X is assigned the value determined by applying the NOT operation to input value A. In such an *assignment statement*, the variable on the left of the equal sign takes on the value of the expression on the right-hand side. Assignment statements are discussed further in Chapter 6.

The logic diagram symbol for a NOT gate is a triangle with a small circle (called an *inversion bubble*) on the end. The input and output are shown as lines flowing into and out of the gate. Sometimes these lines are labeled, though not always.

The truth table in Figure 4.1 shows all possible input values for a NOT gate as well as the corresponding output values. Because there is only one input signal to a NOT gate, and that signal can be only a 0 or a 1, there are only two possibilities for the column labeled A in the truth table. The column labeled X shows the output of the gate, which is the inverse of the input. Note that of the three representations, only the truth table actually defines the behavior of the gate for all situations.

These three notations are just different ways of representing the same thing. For example, the result of the Boolean expression

$0'$

is always 1, and the result of the Boolean expression

$1'$

is always 0. This behavior is consistent with the values shown in the truth table.

■ AND Gate

Figure 4.2 depicts an AND gate. Unlike a NOT gate, which accepts one input signal, an AND gate accepts two input signals. The values of both input signals determine what the output signal will be. If the two input values for an AND gate are both 1, the output is 1; otherwise, the output is 0.

FIGURE 4.2 Representations of an AND gate

Boolean Expression	Logic Diagram Symbol	Truth Table		
		A	B	X
$X = A \cdot B$		0	0	0
		0	1	0
		1	0	0
		1	1	1

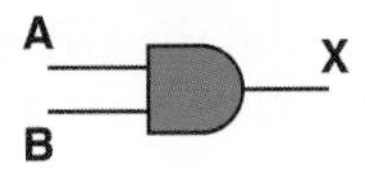

FIGURE 4.3 Representations of an OR gate

Boolean Expression	Logic Diagram Symbol	Truth Table		

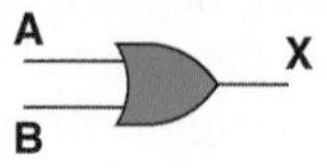

		A	B	X
$X = A + B$		0	0	0
		0	1	1
		1	0	1
		1	1	1

The AND operation in Boolean algebra is expressed using a single dot ($\cdot$). Sometimes an asterisk (*) is used to represent this operator. Often the operator itself is assumed. For example, A·B is often written AB.

Because there are two inputs and two possible values for each input, four possible combinations of 1 and 0 can be provided as input to an AND gate. Therefore, four situations can occur when the AND operator is used in a Boolean expression:

$0 \cdot 0$ equals 0
$0 \cdot 1$ equals 0
$1 \cdot 0$ equals 0
$1 \cdot 1$ equals 1

Likewise, the truth table showing the behavior of the AND gate has four rows, showing all four possible input combinations. The output column of the truth table is consistent with results of these Boolean expressions.

■ OR Gate

Figure 4.3 shows an OR gate. Like the AND gate, the OR gate has two inputs. If both input values are 0, the output value is 0; otherwise, the output is 1.

The Boolean algebra OR operation is expressed using a plus sign (+). The OR gate has two inputs, each of which can be one of two values. Thus, as with an AND gate, there are four input combinations and therefore four rows in the truth table.

■ XOR Gate

The XOR, or *exclusive* OR, gate is shown in Figure 4.4. An XOR gate produces a 0 if its two inputs are the same, and a 1 otherwise. Note the difference between the XOR gate and the OR gate; they differ in only one input situation. When both input signals are 1, the OR gate produces a 1 and the XOR produces a 0.

Sometimes the regular OR gate is referred to as the *inclusive* OR, because it produces a 1 if either or both of its inputs is a 1. The XOR

Boolean Expression	Logic Diagram Symbol	Truth Table		

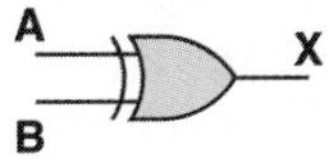

Boolean Expression | **Logic Diagram Symbol** | **Truth Table**

$X = A \oplus B$

A	B	X
0	0	0
0	1	1
1	0	1
1	1	0

FIGURE 4.4 Representations of an XOR gate

produces a 1 only if its inputs are mixed (one 1 and one 0). Think of the XOR gate as saying, "When I say *or*, I mean one or the other, not both."

The Boolean algebra symbol $\oplus$ is sometimes used to express the XOR operation. In addition, the XOR operation can be expressed using the other operators; we leave that as an exercise.

Note that the logic diagram symbol for the XOR gate is just like the symbol for an OR gate except that it has an extra curved line connecting its input signals.

■ NAND and NOR Gates

The NAND gate is shown in Figure 4.5 and the NOR gate is shown in Figure 4.6. Each accepts two input values. The NAND and NOR gates are essentially the opposites of the AND and OR gates, respectively. That is, the output of a NAND gate is the same as if you took the output of an AND gate and put it through an inverter (a NOT gate).

Boolean Expression | **Logic Diagram Symbol** | **Truth Table**

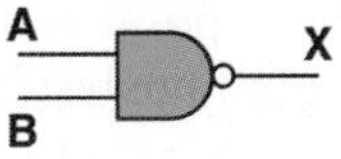

$X = (A \cdot B)'$

A	B	X
0	0	1
0	1	1
1	0	1
1	1	0

FIGURE 4.5 Representations of a NAND gate

Boolean Expression | **Logic Diagram Symbol** | **Truth Table**

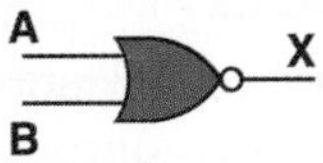

$X = (A + B)'$

A	B	X
0	0	1
0	1	0
1	0	0
1	1	0

FIGURE 4.6 Representations of a NOR gate

No specific symbols are used to express the NAND and NOR operations in Boolean algebra. Instead, we rely on their definitions to express the concepts. That is, the Boolean algebra expression for NAND is the negation of an AND operation. Likewise, the Boolean algebra expression for NOR is the negation of an OR operation.

The logic diagram symbols for the NAND and NOR gates are the same as those for the AND and OR gates except that the NAND and NOR symbols use an inversion bubble (to indicate the negation). Compare the output columns for the truth tables for the AND and NAND gates. They are opposites, when you look at them row by row. The same is true for the OR and NOR gates.

■ Review of Gate Processing

We've looked at six specific types of gates. It may seem to be a difficult task to keep them straight and remember how they all work—but that probably depends on how you think about it. We definitely don't encourage you to try to memorize truth tables. The processing of these gates can be described briefly in general terms. If you think of them in that way, you can produce the appropriate truth table any time you need it.

Let's review the processing of each gate. Some of these descriptions are stated in terms of which input values cause the gate to produce a 1 as output; in any other case, the gate produces a 0.

- A NOT gate inverts its single input value.
- An AND gate produces 1 if both input values are 1.
- An OR gate produces 1 if one or the other or both input values are 1.
- An XOR gate produces 1 if one or the other (but not both) input values are 1.
- A NAND gate produces the opposite results of an AND gate.
- A NOR gate produces the opposite results of an OR gate.

With these general processing rules in mind, all that's left is to remember the Boolean operators and the logic diagram symbols. Keep in mind that several logic diagram symbols are variations on other logic diagram symbols. Also, remember that the coloring of the gates in this book is meant to help you to keep track of the various gate types; traditionally, they are simply black-and-white diagrams.

■ Gates with More Inputs

Gates can be designed to accept three or more input values. A three-input AND gate, for example, produces an output of 1 only if all input values are 1. A three-input OR gate produces an output of 1 if any input value is 1. These definitions are consistent with the two-input versions of these gates. Figure 4.7 shows an AND gate with three input signals.

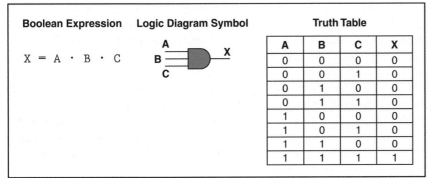

FIGURE 4.7 Representations of a three-input AND gate

There are 2^3 or 8 possible input combinations for a gate with three inputs. Recall from Chapter 3 that there are 2^n combinations of 1 and 0 for n distinct input values. This number determines how many rows appear in the truth table.

For the logic diagram symbol, we simply add a third input signal to the original symbol. For a Boolean expression, we repeat the AND operation to represent the third value.

4.3 Constructing Gates

Before we examine how gates are connected to form circuits, let's examine, at an even more basic level, how a gate is constructed to control the flow of electricity.

■ Transistors

A gate uses one or more transistors to establish how the input values map to the output value. A transistor is a device that acts, depending on the voltage level of the input signal, either as a wire that conducts electricity or as a resistor that blocks the flow of electricity. A transistor has no moving parts, yet it acts like a switch. It is made of a semiconductor material, which is neither a particularly good conductor of electricity (unlike copper) nor a particularly good insulator (unlike rubber). Usually silicon is used to create transistors.

In Chapter 1, we mentioned that the invention of transistors, which occurred in 1947 at Bell Labs, changed the face of technology, ushering in the second generation of computer hardware. Before the advent of transistors, digital circuits used vacuum tubes, which dissipated a great deal of heat and often failed, requiring replacement. Transistors are much smaller than vacuum tubes and require less energy to operate. They can switch states in a few nanoseconds. Computing, as we know it today, is largely due to the invention of the transistor.

>> Transistor A device that acts either as a wire or a resistor, depending on the voltage level of an input signal

>> Semiconductor Material such as silicon that is neither a good conductor nor a good insulator

FIGURE 4.8 The connections of a transistor

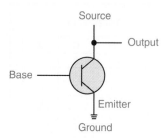

Before tackling the details of transistors, let's discuss some basic principles of electricity. An electrical signal has a source, such as a battery or an outlet in your wall. If the electrical signal is *grounded*, it is allowed to flow through an alternative route to the ground (literally), where it can do no harm. A grounded electrical signal is pulled down, or reduced, to 0 volts.

A transistor has three terminals: a source, a base, and an emitter. The emitter is typically connected to a ground wire, as shown in Figure 4.8. For computers, the source produces a high voltage value, approximately 5 volts. The base value regulates a gate that determines whether the connection between the source and ground is made. If the source signal is grounded, it is pulled down to 0 volts. If the base does not ground the source signal, it stays high.

An output line is usually connected to the source line. If the source signal is pulled to the ground by the transistor, the output signal is low, representing a binary 0. If the source signal remains high, so does the output signal, representing a binary 1.

The transistor is either on, producing a high output signal, or off, producing a low output signal. This output is determined by the base electrical signal. If the base signal is high (close to a +5 voltage), the source signal is grounded, which turns the transistor off. If the base signal is low (close to a 0 voltage), the source signal stays high, and the transistor is on.

Now let's see how a transistor is used to create various types of gates. It turns out that, because of the way a transistor works, the easiest gates to create are the NOT, NAND, and NOR gates. Figure 4.9 shows how these gates can be constructed using transistors.

The diagram for the NOT gate is essentially the same as our original transistor diagram. It takes only one transistor to create a NOT gate. The signal V_{in} represents the input signal to the NOT gate. If it is high, the source is grounded and the output signal V_{out} is low. If V_{in} is low, the source is not grounded and V_{out} is high. Thus the input signal is inverted, which is exactly what a NOT gate does.

The NAND gate requires two transistors. The input signals V_1 and V_2 represent the input to the NAND gate. If both input signals are high, the source is grounded and the output V_{out} is low. If either input signal is low,

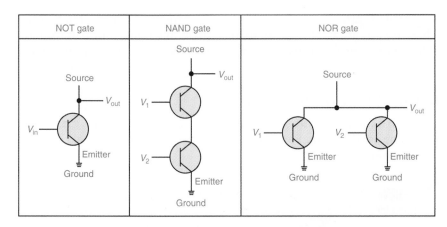

FIGURE 4.9 Constructing gates using transistors

however, one transistor or the other keeps the source signal from being grounded and the output is high. Therefore, if V_1 or V_2 or both carry a low signal (binary 0), the output is a 1. This is consistent with the processing of a NAND gate.

The construction of a NOR gate also requires two transistors. Once again, V_1 and V_2 represent the input to the gate. This time, however, the transistors are not connected in series. The source connects to each transistor separately. If either transistor allows the source signal to be grounded, the output is 0. Therefore, the output is high (binary 1) only when both V_1 and V_2 are low (binary 0), which is what we want for a NOR gate.

An AND gate produces output that is exactly opposite of the NAND output of a gate. Therefore, to construct an AND gate, we simply pass the output of a NAND gate through an inverter (a NOT gate). That's why AND gates are more complicated to construct than NAND gates: They require three transistors, two for the NAND and one for the NOT. The same reasoning can be applied to understand the relationship between NOR and OR gates.

4.4 Circuits

Now that we know how individual gates work and how they are constructed, let's examine how we combine gates to form circuits. Circuits can be classified into two general categories. In a combinational circuit, the input values explicitly determine the output. In a sequential circuit, the output is a function of the input values as well as the existing state of the circuit. Thus sequential circuits usually involve the storage of information. Most of the circuits we examine in this chapter are combinational circuits, although we briefly mention sequential memory circuits.

≫ **Combinational circuit** A circuit whose output is solely determined by its input values

≫ **Sequential circuit** A circuit whose output is a function of its input values and the current state of the circuit

As with gates, we can describe the operations of entire circuits using three notations: Boolean expressions, logic diagrams, and truth tables. These notations are different, but equally powerful, representation techniques.

■ Combinational Circuits

Gates are combined into circuits by using the output of one gate as the input for another gate. For example, consider the following logic diagram of a circuit:

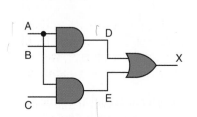

The output of the two AND gates is used as the input to the OR gate. The input value A is used as input to both AND gates. The dot indicates that two lines are connected. If the intersection of two crossing lines does not have a dot, you should think of one as "jumping over" the other without affecting each other.

What does this logic diagram mean? Well, let's work backward to see what it takes to get a particular result. For the final output X to be 1, either D must be 1 or E must be 1. For D to be 1, A and B must both be 1. For E to be 1, both A and C must be 1. Both E and D may be 1, but that isn't necessary. Examine this circuit diagram carefully; make sure that this reasoning is consistent with your understanding of the types of gates used.

Now let's represent the processing of this entire circuit using a truth table:

A	B	C	D	E	X
0	0	0	0	0	0
0	0	1	0	0	0
0	1	0	0	0	0
0	1	1	0	0	0
1	0	0	0	0	0
1	0	1	0	1	1
1	1	0	1	0	1
1	1	1	1	1	1

Because there are three inputs to this circuit, eight rows are required to describe all possible input combinations. Intermediate columns show the intermediate values (D and E) in the circuit.

Finally, let's express this same circuit using Boolean algebra. A circuit is a collection of interacting gates, so a Boolean expression to represent a circuit is a combination of the appropriate Boolean operations. We just have to put the operations together in the proper form to create a valid Boolean algebra expression. In this circuit, there are two AND expressions. The output of each AND operation is input to the OR operation. Thus this circuit is represented by the following Boolean expression (in which the AND operator is assumed):

(AB + AC)

When we write truth tables, it is often better to label columns using these kinds of Boolean expressions rather than arbitrary variables such as D, E, and X. That makes it clear what each column represents. In fact, we can use Boolean expressions to label our logic diagrams as well, eliminating the need for intermediate variables altogether.

Now let's go the other way: Let's take a Boolean expression and draw the corresponding logic diagram and truth table. Consider the following Boolean expression:

A(B + C)

In this expression, the OR operation is applied to input values B and C. The result of that operation is used as input, along with A, to an AND operation, producing the final result. The corresponding circuit diagram is

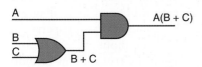

Once again, we complete our series of representations by expressing this circuit as a truth table. As in the previous example, there are three input values, so there are eight rows in the truth table:

A	B	C	B + C	A(B + C)
0	0	0	0	0
0	0	1	1	0
0	1	0	1	0
0	1	1	1	0
1	0	0	0	0
1	0	1	1	1
1	1	0	1	1
1	1	1	1	1

Pick a row from this truth table and follow the logic of the circuit diagram to make sure the final results are consistent. Try it with a few rows to get comfortable with the process of tracing the logic of a circuit.

Now compare the final result column in this truth table to the truth table for the previous example. They are identical. We have just demonstrated circuit equivalence. That is, both circuits produce exactly the same output for each input value combination.

In fact, this situation demonstrates an important property of Boolean algebra called the *distributive law:*

A(B + C) = AB + AC

That's the beauty of Boolean algebra: It allows us to apply provable mathematical principles to design logical circuits. The following chart shows a few of the properties of Boolean algebra:

<table>
<tr><th>Property</th><th>AND</th><th>OR</th></tr>
<tr><td>Commutative</td><td>AB = BA</td><td>A + B = B + A</td></tr>
<tr><td>Associative</td><td>(AB)C = A(BC)</td><td>(A + B) + C = A + (B + C)</td></tr>
<tr><td>Distributive</td><td>A(B + C) = (AB) + (AC)</td><td>A + (BC) = (A + B)(A + C)</td></tr>
<tr><td>Identity</td><td>A1 = A</td><td>A + 0 = A</td></tr>
<tr><td>Complement</td><td>A(A') = 0</td><td>A + (A') = 1</td></tr>
<tr><td>DeMorgan's law</td><td>(AB)' = A' OR B'</td><td>(A + B)' = A'B'</td></tr>
</table>

DeMorgan's Law, named for Augustus DeMorgan DeMorgan, a contemporary of George Boole, was the first professor of mathematics at the University of London in 1828, where he continued to teach for 30 years. He wrote elementary texts on arithmetic, algebra, trigonometry, and calculus as well as papers on the possibility of establishing a logical calculus and the fundamental problem of expressing thought by means of symbols. DeMorgan did not discover the law bearing his name, but he is credited with formally stating it as it is known today.[3]

▶ Circuit equivalence The same output for each corresponding input-value combination for two circuits

These properties are consistent with our understanding of gate processing as well as with the truth table and logic diagram representations. For instance, the commutative property, in plain English, says that the order of the input signals doesn't matter, which is true. (Verify it using the truth tables of individual gates.) The complement property says that if we put a signal and its inverse through an AND gate, we are guaranteed to get 0, but if we put a signal and its inverse through an OR gate, we are guaranteed to get 1.

There is one very famous—and useful—theorem in Boolean algebra called *DeMorgan's law.* This law states that the NOT operator applied to the AND of two variables is equal to the NOT applied to each of the two variables with an OR between. That is, inverting the output of an AND gate is equivalent to inverting the individual signals first and then passing them through an OR gate:

(AB)' = A' OR B'

The second part of the law states that the NOT operator applied to the OR of two variables is equal to the NOT applied to each of the two variables with an AND between. Expressed in circuit terms, this means that inverting the output of an OR gate is equivalent to inverting both signals first and then passing them through an AND gate:

$$(A + B)' = A'B'$$

DeMorgan's law and other Boolean algebra properties provide a formal mechanism for defining, managing, and evaluating logical circuit designs.

■ Adders

Perhaps the most basic operation a computer can perform is to add two numbers together. At the digital logic level, this addition is performed in binary. Chapter 2 discusses this process in depth. These types of addition operations are carried out by special circuits called, appropriately, adders.

Like addition in any base, the result of adding two binary digits could potentially produce a *carry value*. Recall that $1 + 1 = 10$ in base 2. A circuit that computes the sum of two bits and produces the correct carry bit is called a half adder.

Let's consider all possibilities when adding two binary digits A and B: If both A and B are 0, the sum is 0 and the carry is 0. If A is 0 and B is 1, the sum is 1 and the carry is 0. If A is 1 and B is 0, the sum is 1 and the carry is 0. If both A and B are 1, the sum is 0 and the carry is 1. This yields the following truth table:

>> Adder An electronic circuit that performs an addition operation on binary values

>> Half adder A circuit that computes the sum of two bits and produces the appropriate carry bit

A	B	Sum	Carry
0	0	0	0
0	1	1	0
1	0	1	0
1	1	0	1

In this case, we are actually looking for two output results, the sum and the carry. As a consequence, our circuit has two output lines.

If you compare the sum and carry columns to the output of the various gates, you see that the sum corresponds to the XOR gate and the carry corresponds to the AND gate. Thus the following circuit diagram represents a half adder:

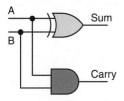

Test this diagram by assigning various combinations of input values and determining the two output values produced. Do the results follow the rules of binary arithmetic? They should. Now compare your results to the corresponding truth table. They should match the results there as well.

What about the Boolean expression for this circuit? Because the circuit produces two distinct output values, we represent it using two Boolean expressions:

$$\text{sum} = A \oplus B$$
$$\text{carry} = AB$$

Note that a half adder does not take into account a possible carry value *into* the calculation (carry-in). That is, a half adder is fine for adding two single digits, but it cannot be used as is to compute the sum of two binary values with multiple digits each. A circuit called a full adder takes the carry-in value into account.

We can use two half adders to make a full adder. How? Well, the input to the sum must be the carry-in and the sum from adding the two input values. That is, we add the sum from the half adder to the carry-in. Both of these additions have a carry-out. Could both of these carry-outs be 1, yielding yet another carry? Fortunately, no. Look at the truth table for the half adder. There is no case where the sum and the carry are both 1.

Figure 4.10 shows the logic diagram and the truth table for the full adder. This circuit has three inputs: the original two digits (A and B) and the carry-in value. Thus the truth table has eight rows. We leave the corresponding Boolean expression as an exercise.

To add two 8-bit values, we can duplicate a full-adder circuit eight times. The carry-out from one place value is used as the carry-in to the next highest place value. The value of the carry-in for the rightmost bit

> **Full adder** A circuit that computes the sum of two bits, taking an input carry bit into account

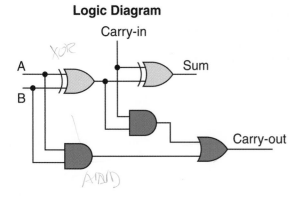

Logic Diagram

Truth Table

A	B	Carry-in	Sum	Carry-out
0	0	0	0	0
0	0	1	1	0
0	1	0	1	0
0	1	1	0	1
1	0	0	1	0
1	0	1	0	1
1	1	0	0	1
1	1	1	1	1

FIGURE 4.10 A full adder

position is assumed to be zero, and the carry-out of the leftmost bit position is discarded (potentially creating an overflow error).

There are various ways to improve on the design of these adder circuits, but we do not explore them in any more detail in this text.

■ Multiplexers

A multiplexer (often referred to as a *mux*) is a general circuit that produces a single output signal. This output is equal to one of several input signals to the circuit. The multiplexer selects which input signal to use as an output signal based on the value represented by a few more input signals, called *select signals* or *select control lines*.

Let's look at an example to clarify how a multiplexer works. Figure 4.11 shows a block diagram of a mux. The control lines S0, S1, and S2 determine which of eight other input lines (D0 through D7) are routed to the output (F).

The values of the three control lines, taken together, are interpreted as a binary number, which determines which input line to route to the output. Recall from Chapter 2 that three binary digits can represent eight different values: 000, 001, 010, 011, 100, 101, 110, and 111. These values, which simply count in binary from 0 to 7, correspond to our output values D0 through D7. Thus, if S0, S1, and S2 are all 0, the input line D0 would be the output from the mux. If S0 is 1, S1 is 0, and S2 is 1, then D5 would be output from the mux.

The following truth table shows how the input control lines determine the output for this multiplexer:

control lines

S0	S1	S2	F
0	0	0	D0
0	0	1	D1
0	1	0	D2
0	1	1	D3
1	0	0	D4
1	0	1	D5
1	1	0	D6
1	1	1	D7

> ❱❱ **Multiplexer** A circuit that uses a few input control signals to determine which of several input data lines is routed to its output

The digital archeologist
The work of modern archeology has been greatly assisted by digital technologies. For example, GIS (Geographic Information Systems) is used to georeference the vertical layers of an archeological site and can be used to produce a three-dimensional map. GPS (Global Positioning System)–currently a system of 24 orbiting satellites–is used to fix the geographical location of the site on the Earth. GPS data can be transferred to GIS, which makes the GIS representation of a site more powerful and precise. Archeologists, who were once reliant upon geographical survey maps, now use GPS to fix geographical points of their sites.

FIGURE 4.11 A block diagram of a multiplexer with three select control lines

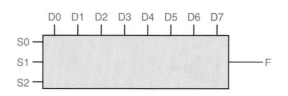

The block diagram in Figure 4.11 hides a fairly complicated circuit that carries out the logic of a multiplexer. Such a circuit could be shown using eight three-input AND gates and one eight-input OR gate. We won't get into the details of this circuit in this book.

A multiplexer can be designed with various numbers of input lines and corresponding control lines. In general, the binary values on n input control lines are used to determine which of 2^n other data lines are selected for output.

A circuit called a *demultiplexer* (*demux*) performs the opposite operation. That is, it takes a single input and routes it to one of 2^n outputs, depending on the values of the n control lines.

4.5 Circuits as Memory

Digital circuits play another important role: They can store information. These circuits form a sequential circuit, because the output of the circuit also serves as input to the circuit. That is, the existing state of the circuit is used in part to determine the next state.

Many types of memory circuits have been designed. We examine only one type in this book: the *S-R latch*. An S-R latch stores a single binary digit (1 or 0). An S-R latch circuit could be designed using a variety of gates. One such circuit, using NAND gates, is pictured in Figure 4.12.

The design of this circuit guarantees that the two outputs X and Y are always complements of each other. That is, when X is 0, Y is 1, and vice versa. The value of X at any point in time is considered to be the current state of the circuit. Therefore, if X is 1, the circuit is storing a 1; if X is 0, the circuit is storing a 0.

Recall that a NAND gate produces an output of 1 unless both of its input values are 1. Each gate in this circuit has one external input (S or R) and one input coming from the output of the other gate. Suppose the current state of the circuit is storing a 1 (that is, X is 1), and suppose both S and R are 1. Then Y remains 0 and X remains 1. Now suppose that the circuit is currently storing a 0 (X is 0) and that R and S are again 1. Then Y remains 1 and X remains 0. No matter which value is currently being

FIGURE 4.12 An S-R latch

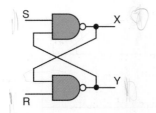

stored, if both input values S and R are 1, the circuit keeps its existing state.

This explanation demonstrates that the S-R latch maintains its value as long as S and R are 1. But how does a value get stored in the first place? We set the S-R latch to 1 by momentarily setting S to 0 while keeping R at 1. If S is 0, X becomes 1. As long as S is returned to 1 immediately, the S-R latch remains in a state of 1. We set the latch to 0 by momentarily setting R to 0 while keeping S at 1. If R is 0, Y becomes 0, and thus X becomes 0. As long as R is immediately reset to 1, the circuit state remains 0.

By carefully controlling the values of S and R, the circuit can be made to store either value. By scaling this idea to larger circuits, we can design memory devices with larger capacities.

4.6 Integrated Circuits

An integrated circuit (also called a chip) is a piece of silicon on which multiple gates have been embedded. These silicon pieces are mounted on a plastic or ceramic package with pins along the edges that can be soldered onto circuit boards or inserted into appropriate sockets. Each pin connects to the input or output of a gate, or to power or ground.

Integrated circuits (IC) are classified by the number of gates contained in them. These classifications also reflect the historical development of IC technology:

> » Integrated circuit (chip) A piece of silicon on which multiple gates have been embedded

Abbreviation	Name	Number of Gates
SSI	Small-Scale Integration	1 to 10
MSI	Medium-Scale Integration	10 to 100
LSI	Large-Scale Integration	100 to 100,000
VLSI	Very-Large-Scale Integration	more than 100,000

An SSI chip has a few independent gates, such as the one shown in Figure 4.13. This chip has 14 pins: eight for inputs to gates, four for output of the gates, one for ground, and one for power. Similar chips can be made with different gates.

How can a chip have more than 100,000 gates on it? That would imply the need for 300,000 pins! The key is that the gates on a VLSI chip are not independent, as they are in small-scale integration. VLSI chips embed circuits with a high gate-to-pin ratio. That is, many gates are combined to create complex circuits that require only a few input and output values. Multiplexers are an example of this type of circuit.

FIGURE 4.13 An SSI chip containing independent NAND gates

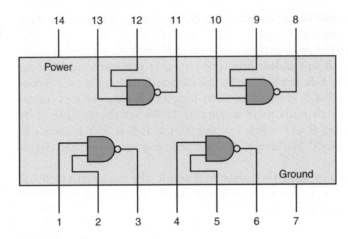

4.7 CPU Chips

The most important integrated circuit in any computer is the central processing unit (CPU). The processing of a CPU is discussed in the next chapter, but it is important to recognize at this point that the CPU is, in one sense, merely an advanced circuit with input and output lines.

Each CPU chip contains a large number of pins through which essentially all communication in a computer system occurs. This communication connects the CPU to memory and I/O devices, which are themselves, at fundamental levels, advanced circuits.

The explanation of CPU processing and its interaction with other devices takes us to another level of computer processing, sometimes referred to as *component architecture*. Although it is still primarily focused on hardware, computer component architecture applies the principle of abstraction yet again, allowing us to temporarily ignore the details of the gates and circuits discussed in this chapter and bringing us ever closer to a complete understanding of computer processing.

Summary

In this chapter we discussed how a computer operates at its lowest level by controlling the flow of electricity. Because we are dealing with digital computers that use binary information, we concern ourselves with only two voltage ranges, which we interpret as binary 1 or 0. The flow of electricity is guided by electronic devices called gates, which perform basic logical operations such as NOT, AND, and OR. A gate is created by using one or more transistors, an invention that revolutionized computing.

Gates can be combined into circuits, in which the output of one gate serves as an input to another gate. By designing these circuits carefully, we can create devices that perform more complex tasks such as adding, multiplexing, and storing data. Collections of gates, or complete circuits, are often embedded into a single integrated circuit, or chip, which leads to the concept of a central processing unit (CPU).

⚖ ETHICAL ISSUES ▸ Email Privacy

Have you ever written an important message, submitted your resume, or complained about your roommate through an email system? Would you have handled it differently if you knew that strangers, administrators, or your roommate could read your message? Once a tool for only the most computer literate, today email is a standard means of communication for millions of people. Many users, however, incorrectly assume that only those to whom the email is sent have access to its content. On its path from sender to recipient, email travels from server to server and can be read more easily than a postcard. Email security has become the center of many debates that search for a common ground between individual rights, corporate rights, and computer technology.

Many companies that rely on email for much of their communications now have policies that outline where workers' email privacy ends and email monitoring begins. Supporters of email monitoring state that all correspondence through a company's server belongs to the company. They argue that surveillance prevents employees from abusing their email access and allows the employer more control over correspondences for which the company could be held liable. Opponents explain that email monitoring creates an atmosphere of mistrust and disrespect, and suggest that surveillance is an unnecessary obstruction of employee autonomy.

The privacy issues that surround email extend beyond company policies. For example, in July 2000, the United Kingdom passed the Regulation of Investigatory Powers bill, giving the government access to all Internet correspondence. Internet service providers (ISPs) in that country must route all email through governmental headquarters, and government officials have access to all encryption keys that are used to protect and secure emails. Similarly, the USA Patriot Act allows for the monitoring of email in the United States.

Even after an email has reached its destination, an unintended audience can read its contents. The forwarding feature provided by most email services gives the recipient the ability to pass on email without the author's knowledge. Not only does forwarding the email allow the recipient to read the original sender's thoughts, but it also allows the recipient to see the name and contact information of the sender. Research shows that people consider reading someone else's email as less of an invasion of privacy than reading someone's ordinary mail. This belief, along with the ease of eavesdropping and monitoring, compromises the security of email correspondence.

🔑 Key Terms

Adder	Integrated circuit (also chip)
Boolean algebra	Logic diagram
Circuit	Multiplexer
Circuit equivalence	Semiconductor
Combinational circuit	Sequential circuit
Full adder	Transistor
Gate	Truth table
Half adder	

⌘   **Exercises**

For Exercises 1–17, mark the answers true or false as follows:
  A. True
  B. False

 1. Logic diagrams and truth tables are equally powerful in expressing the processing of gates and circuits.

 2. Boolean expressions are more powerful than logic diagrams in expressing the processing of gates and circuits.

 3. A NOT gate accepts two inputs.

 4. The output value of an AND gate is 1 when both inputs are 1.

 5. The AND and OR gates produce opposite results for the same input.

 6. The output value of an OR gate is 1 when both inputs are 1.

 7. The output of an OR gate when one input is 0 and one input is 1 is 0.

 8. The output value of an XOR gate is 0 unless both inputs are 1.

 9. The NOR gate produces the opposite results of the XOR gate.

10. A gate can be designed to accept more than two inputs.

11. A transistor is made of semiconductor material.

12. Inverting the output of an AND gate is equivalent to inverting the individual signals first, then passing them through an OR gate.

13. The sum of two binary digits (ignoring the carry) is expressed by an AND gate.

14. A full adder takes the carry-in value into account.

15. A multiplexer adds all of the bits on its input lines to produce its output.

16. Integrated circuits are classified by the number of gates contained in them.

17. A CPU is an integrated circuit.

For Exercises 18–29, match the gate with the description of the operation or the diagram.
  A. AND
  B. NAND
  C. XOR
  D. OR
  E. NOR
  F. NOT

18. Inverts its input.

19. Produces a 1 only if all its inputs are 1 and a 0 otherwise

20. Produces a 0 only if all its inputs are 0 and a 1 otherwise

21. Produces a 0 only if its inputs are the same and a 1 otherwise

22. Produces a 0 if all its inputs are 1 and a 1 otherwise

23. Produces a 1 if all its inputs are 0 and a 0 otherwise

24.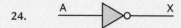

25.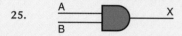

26.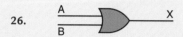

27.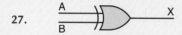

28.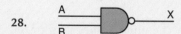

29.

Exercises 30–73 are short-answer or design questions.

30. How is voltage level used to distinguish between binary digits?

31. Distinguish between a gate and a circuit.

32. What are the three notational methods for describing the behavior of gates and circuits?

33. Characterize the notations asked for in Exercise 32.

34. How many input signals can a gate receive, and how many output signals can a gate produce?

35. Name six types of gates.

36. Give the three representations of a NOT gate and say in words what NOT means.

37. Give the three representations of an AND gate and say in words what AND means.

38. Give the three representations of an OR gate and say in words what OR means.

39. Give the three representations of an XOR gate and say in words what XOR means.

40. Give the three representations of a NAND gate and say in words what NAND means.

41. Give the three representations of a NOR gate and say in words what NOR means.

42. Compare and contrast the AND gate and the NAND gate.

43. Give the Boolean expression for a three-input AND gate, and then show its behavior with a truth table.

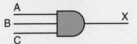

44. Give the Boolean expression for a three-input OR gate, and then show its behavior with a truth table.

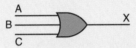

45. What is used in a gate to establish how the input values map to the output value?

46. How does a transistor behave?

47. Of what is a transistor made?

48. What happens when an electric signal is grounded?

49. What are the three terminals in a transistor, and how do they operate?

50. How many transistors does it take for each of these gates?
    a. NOT
    b. AND
    c. NOR
    d. OR
    e. XOR

51. Draw a transistor diagram for an AND gate. Explain the processing.

52. Draw a transistor diagram for an OR gate. Explain the processing.

53. How can gates be combined into circuits?

54. What are the two general categories of circuits, and how do they differ?

55. Draw a circuit diagram corresponding to the following Boolean expression:

    (A + B)(B + C)

56. Draw a circuit diagram corresponding to the following Boolean expression:

    (AB + C)D

57. Draw a circuit diagram corresponding to the following Boolean expression:

    A'B + (B + C)'

58. Draw a circuit diagram corresponding to the following Boolean expression:

    (AB)' + (CD)'

59. Show the behavior of the following circuit with a truth table:

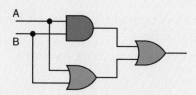

60. Show the behavior of the following circuit with a truth table:

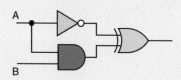

61. Show the behavior of the following circuit with a truth table:

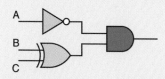

62. Show the behavior of the following circuit with a truth table:

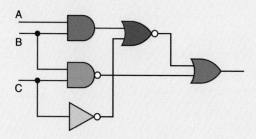

63. What is circuit equivalence?

64. Name six properties of Boolean algebra and explain what each means.

65. Differentiate between a half adder and a full adder.

66. What is the Boolean expression for a full adder?

67. What is a multiplexer?

68. a. Circuits used for memory are what type of circuits?
    b. How many digits does an S-R latch store?
    c. The design for an S-R latch shown in Figure 4.12 guarantees what about the outputs X and Y?

69. What is an integrated circuit or chip?

70. Define the abbreviations SSI, MSI, LSI, and VLSI.

71. In the chip shown in Figure 4.13, what are the pins used for?

72. Draw a circuit using two full adders that adds two two-bit binary values. Show its corresponding truth table.

73. How can the XOR operation be expressed using other operators?

??? Thought Questions

1. Throughout this chapter we have used Boolean expressions, truth tables, and logic diagrams to describe the same behavior. Is the relationship among these notational methods clear to you? Which do you find the most intuitive? Which do you find the least intuitive?

2. Many situations can be described by the ideas in this chapter—for example, the operation of a single light switch or a light that has two switches. Can you think of other everyday occurrences that can be described by the notational methods presented in this chapter?

3. Have you ever sent email to someone, only to regret it immediately? Do you find that you would say something in email that you would never say in person? Consider the following premise: "Email has lowered the civility of personal discourse." Do you agree or disagree?

4. If a person sends email from a school computer or a business computer, should that message be considered private? Does the institution or person that owns the computer from which email is sent have a right to inspect the message?

5. Do you consider reading someone else's email as less of an invasion of privacy than reading someone's ordinary mail?

The Hardware Layer

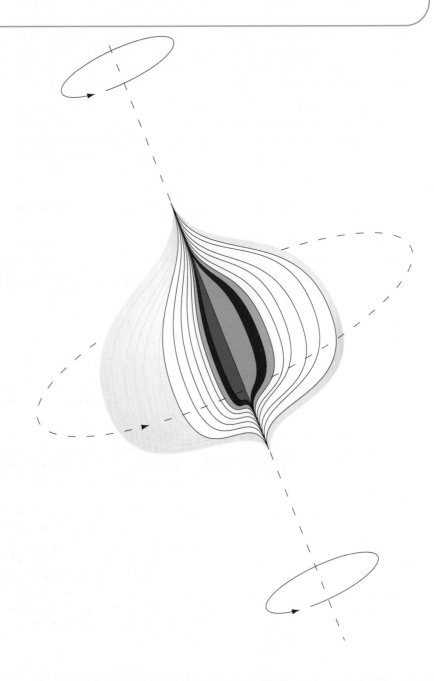

Computing Components

Chapter 2 described the binary number system in which all information is represented on a computer. Chapter 4 described how we control electricity at a fundamental level to manage binary values. Now we can describe the primary components of a computer that capitalize on these technologies. These primary components are like Lego pieces; they can be combined to build a variety of different computers, just as Legos can form a variety of buildings.

Although these components, such as main memory and the central processing unit (CPU), are often thought of as the most fundamental parts of a computer, we know that they are abstractions of even more fundamental concepts.

Goals

After studying this chapter, you should be able to:

- read an ad for a computer and understand the jargon.

- list the components and their function in a von Neumann machine.

- describe the fetch-decode-execute cycle of the von Neumann machine.

- describe how computer memory is organized and accessed.

- name and describe the various auxiliary storage devices.

- define three alternative parallel computer configurations.

- explain the concept of embedded systems and give examples from your own home.

5.1 Individual Computer Components

Computing, more than most fields, has its own special jargon and acronyms. We begin this chapter by translating an ad for a desktop computer. We then examine the components of a computer as a logical whole before looking at each component in some detail.

Consider the following ad for a laptop computer.

Insatavialion 640 Laptop
Exceptional Performance and Portability

- Intel® Core™ 2 Duo (2.66GHz/ 1066Mhz FSB/6MB cache)
- 15.6″ High Definition (1080p) LED Backlit LCD Display (1366 x 768)
- 512MB ATI Mobility Radeon Graphics
- Built-in 2.0MP Web Camera
- 4GB Shared Dual Channel DDR2 at 800MHz
- 500GB SATA Hard Drive at 5400RPM
- 8X Slot Load DL DVD+/- RW Drive
- 802.11 a/g/n and Bluetooth 3.0

- 85 WHr Lithium Ion Battery
- (2) USB 2.0, HDMI, 15-pin VGA, Ethernet 10/100/1000, IEEE 1394 Firewire, Express Card, Audio line-in, line-out, mic-in
- 14.8″W X 1.2″H X 10.1″D, 5.6 lbs
- Microsoft® Windows 7® Professional
- Microsoft® Office Home and Student 2007
- 36-Month subscription to McAfee Security Center Anti-virus

There are two important and interesting things about this ad: The average person hasn't the foggiest idea what it all means, and by the time you are reading it, the machine that it describes will be obsolete. In this chapter, we try to interpret the acronyms; we can't do anything about the speed at which computer hardware and software change.

Before we go on to describe computer components in the abstract, let's go through this specification and decipher the acronyms. After this exercise, we go through all of the material again in more depth, so don't be concerned if the terms seem confusing. You'll see all of them defined again later.

The first line describes the central processor inside the laptop. Core™ 2 is a type of processor, and Duo refers to the presence of two of these processors (called cores) on a single chip. The 2.66GHz tells how fast the processors are. The G in GHz is the abbreviation for giga, a metric prefix indicating one billion. Hz stands for hertz, a unit of frequency that measures cycles per second, named after Heinrich R. Hertz. In a computer, a centrally generated series of electrical pulses, called the clock, is used to ensure that all of its actions are coordinated. You can think of the clock like an orchestra conductor's waving baton, which keeps all of the musicians playing together at a particular tempo. The clock in this processor pulses 2.66 billion times per second.

Following the clock speed number we read: 1066MHz FSB. Knowing that M in the metric system stands for million, we can guess that something called FSB is pulsing 1066 million (or just over a billion) times per second.

What is the FSB? A processor needs to access memory and input/output devices and does so through a set of wires called a bus. A computer has many different buses, but the one that makes the primary connection between the processor and the outside world is called the front side bus (FSB). Thus, these processors can communicate with the outside world 1066 million times per second. But if each of the processors is performing 2.66 billion operations per second, how can the FSB keep up at only one billion accesses per second?

The answer is related to the "6MB cache." MB stands for megabytes. A byte is a unit of memory, and a megabyte is 2^{20} (a little more than a million) bytes. So 6MB refers to six megabytes of cache memory. Cache is a small, fast memory that is usually built into the processor chip. Thus, the two processors have direct access to 6MB of memory without using the FSB. Many of the processor's attempts to access memory will find what they need within the cache. They only activate the FSB when they need something that is not in cache. Thus, the FSB can be slower than the processors and still not get in their way.

In general, a faster clock, faster FSB, and more cache would seem to yield a more powerful computer. But as in all areas of engineering, there are trade-offs. If the processor runs faster it consumes more power, which can cause the circuitry to overheat and shut down. A faster FSB requires faster devices in the outside world, which means their circuitry is more expensive. As cache gets bigger, access to its data becomes slower, which slows down the processors.

The next part of the ad describes the screen. The number 15.6″ refers to the diagonal measurement of the display area. High Definition (1080p) says it is compatible with the high definition television standard with 1080 horizontal lines of display elements. As we'll see, this isn't completely true. The screen is described as an LED backlit LCD. LED stands for light emitting diode, just like those found in some flashlights. A strip of these lights shine up from the bottom to illuminate the display. LEDs are replacing the use of a miniature fluorescent light bulb. The advantages are that LEDs last longer without growing dim and do not contain the toxic metal mercury. Lastly, the numbers 1366 × 768 refer to the screen's resolution in picture elements (pixels). This screen is 1366 pixels wide and 768 pixels high. Note that the number of vertical pixels is less than the 1080 claimed earlier. The computer compresses the 1080 lines from a high definition source, such as a movie, to fit the 768 lines in its screen. It takes an informed consumer to recognize marketing exaggerations such as this.

Next the ad lists the brand and model of graphics processor unit (GPU). We also see that it has 512MB of memory. The GPU is a separate computer that can be even more powerful than the main processors. Games and other graphics software send commands to the GPU that cause it to manipulate the image on the screen very quickly. It thus relieves the main processors of this task. The GPU keeps the data for the screen image in its own memory. The more it has, the better it is able to work with complex images, support external displays, and so on.

The fourth line in the ad describes a built-in digital camera that faces the user from just above the screen. This camera can be used for video conferencing over the Internet or recording still images and videos. 2.0MP indicates that the camera has a resolution of 2 million pixels, which is sufficient for these tasks.

Next the ad lists the computer's random access memory (RAM), also called main memory. Random access means that each byte of memory can be accessed directly, rather than having to begin at the beginning and access each byte in turn until you get to the one you want. 4GB means that there are 4×2^{30} bytes of storage (2^{30} is just over one billion). Shared means that both processors have access to this memory. Dual-channel DDR2 is the type of memory. It provides two access paths (called channels), and DDR2 stands for second generation, double-data rate. Through clever use of circuitry, memory designers doubled the rate at which a memory could operate, compared with earlier designs. Their achievement is acknowledged in this acronym.

This laptop contains a hard disk drive, which is the common name for the computer's secondary (also called auxiliary) storage device. It is listed as having 500GB (500×2^{30} bytes) of storage. The disk uses an interface called SATA, which stands for Serial ATA. Serial means that its data is transmitted to and from the computer as a stream of individual bits, rather than the older approach of sending 16 bits at once over 16 wires (known as Parallel ATA). The ATA acronym has a long history, referring to a means of attaching a hard drive to the IBM® PC/AT—a computer that was introduced in 1984. Serial ATA is both faster and less costly to make, and it can transfer up to 300 MB per second, which is more than most hard disks can supply. The ad also mentions 5400 RPM (revolutions per minute), which is how fast the disk spins. Disks in laptops spin relatively slowly to conserve battery power. Disks are also available that spin at 7200 RPM and 15,000 RPM, enabling them to transfer data at a higher rate. Hard drives are gradually being replaced by all-electronic secondary storage, called solid-state disk (SSD). The technology of SSD is similar to RAM, except that data isn't lost when the power is turned off. Because it has no moving parts, it is faster and consumes less power than a hard drive. At this early stage in the transition, SSD is more expensive and has less storage capacity, but those factors can be expected to change as the technology advances.

A DVD drive comes with the machine. The ad describes it as being 8×, which means it can read data from a DVD as much as eight times faster than a DVD movie player. Slot load means that you insert a DVD into a narrow slit in the edge of the laptop, rather than pressing a button and having a drawer slide out to accept the disk. DL stands for dual layer, which means that the drive can work with second generation DVDs that store nearly twice as much data by using two layers of recording surface. Following the DVD acronym are the symbols +/-RW. The R indicates that the drive can record on special DVDs that are writeable. There are actually two standards for how these disks are made, called -R and +R, and the +/-

indicates that the drive is compatible with both standards. A DVD+/-R can have data written just once. After that, it can be read any number of times, but no more writing is allowed. Another type of DVD, called RW (for rewritable) can be written more than once. This laptop also supports RW disks. While DVD drives are still the most popular, laptops are starting to shift to the newer Blu-Ray format that has higher capacity and is being used to distribute high-definition movies.

The next line of the ad describes its wireless networking support. 802.11 is the number of a standard that has been defined by the Institute of Electrical and Electronics Engineers (IEEE), an engineering professional society. There are three accepted versions of the standard, a, g, and n. The original was 802.11a. The 802.11g version supports communication over longer distances, but at a slightly slower speed. With 802.11n, both greater speed and distance are achieved. This laptop is compatible with all three standards. Bluetooth is another form of wireless network, but it operates at much shorter ranges with a relatively weak signal. Typical uses for Bluetooth are to connect with a wireless keyboard, mouse, earphones, or for transferring data to and from a cell phone. There have been multiple versions of the Bluetooth® standard, each adding various features, and version 3.0 was adopted in 2009.

Of course, laptops run on batteries. Even so, they still consume quite a bit of power. When a laptop is idle, with the screen turned off, it will use just a few watts. But in playing a game that makes heavy use of both processors and the GPU it can draw 50 watts. That's far more energy than normal rechargeable batteries can supply, so special technology, based on the metal lithium, provides high electrical storage capacity. This laptop's battery can store 85 watt-hours of energy, which means that it could supply 85 watts for one hour, or 42.5 watts for two hours, etc. More capacity means a longer time without recharging, but it also adds size and weight to the laptop.

Next the ad has a long list of external connections (often called ports). USB, or universal serial bus, uses a cable to transfer data. As its name suggests, it can connect to just about anything, including an external hard drive, a digital camera, a printer, a scanner, a music player, and so on. This laptop has two second-generation USB ports, which transfer data faster than USB 1.0. HDMI stands for high definition multimedia interface, which can send digital video and audio to, for example, a home theater system. A 15-pin VGA port is used to connect the laptop to an external analog monitor or projector. An Ethernet cable connects to a router or cable modem for wired network access. There are three versions of Ethernet that provide 10, 100, and 1000 million bits per second of data transfer capacity, and this laptop handles all three. IEEE 1394 is another communication standard, also called Firewire. This port provides very fast digital data transfer and is commonly used for connecting high definition camcorders and high performance disk drives. The express card slot allows the user to insert a small circuit board to provide extra functionality, such as a solid-state disk or wireless communication with a cellular phone network. Lastly, we see that we can connect analog audio inputs and outputs, such as electronic musical instruments and headphones, plus an external microphone.

Physical size and weight are important parameters for a laptop that will be carried regularly. This is a mid-size, mid-weight model. At 5.6 pounds, it weighs over twice as much as this book. A lightweight laptop has roughly the same weight as this book, and heavier models, sometimes called desktop replacements, can weigh in at around 8 pounds. Generally, to reduce weight, the size shrinks and we give up features and battery life. However, it is also possible to reduce weight by replacing plastic in the case with aluminum, but for greater cost.

Lastly, the ad lists software that is preinstalled on the laptop. These include the operating system (Windows 7®), the Microsoft® Office suite of programs that includes a word processor, spreadsheet, and so on for performing common tasks, and a 3-year subscription to updates for a malware detection package. Malware is software that intends to do harm, and comes in many forms, such as viruses that can take over your computer when you open a downloaded file. Malware detection software constantly watches for such programs in files and web content to prevent them from running. But hackers are constantly creating new forms of malware, so it is necessary to regularly update the detection software to keep up with the latest threats.

Within this ad, multiple size measures have been used. Let's summarize the prefixes that are used frequently in computing.

> **Putting sizes in perspective**
> Admiral Grace Murray Hopper demonstrated the relative sizes of computer jargon by displaying a coil of wire nearly 1000 feet long, a short piece of wire about as long as your forearm, and a bag containing grains of pepper. She would point out that the wire coil was the distance traveled by an electron along the wire in the space of a microsecond. The short piece of wire was the distance traveled by an electron along the wire in the space of a nanosecond. The grains of pepper represented the distance traveled by an electron in a picosecond. She would admonish the members of her audience to remember their nanoseconds.

Power of 10	Power of 2	Value of Power of 2	Prefix	Abbreviation	Derivation
10^{-12}			pico	p	Italian for little
10^{-9}			nano	n	Greek for dwarf
10^{-6}			micro	μ	Greek for small
10^{-3}			milli	m	Latin for thousandth
10^{3}	2^{10}	1024	kilo	K	Greek for thousand
10^{6}	2^{20}	1,048,576	mega	M	Greek for large
10^{9}	2^{30}	1,073,741,824	giga	G	Greek for giant
10^{12}	2^{40}	not enough room	tera	T	Greek for monster
10^{15}	2^{50}	not enough room	peta	P	Greek prefix for five

Did you notice that we used powers of 10 when referring to time and powers of 2 when referring to storage? Time is expressed in multiples of seconds in decimal notation. Storage capacity is expressed in multiples of bytes in binary notation. If you keep this distinction in mind, it is clear that K is 1000 when referring to speed and 1024 when referring to storage.

We now move from the specific to the general. In the next several sections we look at each of the pieces of hardware that make up a computer from the logical level, rather than from a specific computer configuration.

5.2 Stored-Program Concept

A major defining point in the history of computing was the realization in 1944–1945 that data and instructions to manipulate the data were logically the same and could be stored in the same place. The computer design built upon this principle, which became known as the *von Neumann architecture*, is still the basis for computers today. Although the name honors John von Neumann, a brilliant mathematician who worked on the construction of the atomic bomb, the idea probably originated with J. Presper Eckert and John Mauchly, two other early pioneers who worked on the ENIAC at the Moore School at the University of Pennsylvania during the same time period.

■ von Neumann Architecture

Another major characteristic of the von Neumann architecture is that the units that process information are separate from the units that store information. This characteristic leads to the following five components of the von Neumann architecture, shown in Figure 5.1:

- The memory unit that holds both data and instructions
- The arithmetic/logic unit that is capable of performing arithmetic and logic operations on data
- The input unit that moves data from the outside world into the computer
- The output unit that moves results from inside the computer to the outside world
- The control unit that acts as the stage manager to ensure that all the other components act in concert

Memory

Recall from the discussion of number systems that each storage unit, called a bit, is capable of holding a 1 or a 0; these bits are grouped together into bytes (8 bits), and these bytes are in turn grouped together into words. Memory is a collection of cells, each with a unique physical address. We use the generic word *cell* here rather than byte or word, because the number of bits in each addressable location, called the memory's addressability, varies from one machine to another. Today, most computers are byte addressable.

> **?**
>
> Does it matter who was the father of the modern computer?
> All of the people involved in the research and development of electronic computing devices in the late 1930s and 1940s undoubtedly contributed to the computer as we know it. This list includes John Atanasoff, Clifford Berry, and Konrad Zuse, in addition to von Neumann, Eckert, and Mauchly.
> In 1951, Sperry Rand bought the patent for the ENIAC and its underlying concepts and began charging royalties to other computer manufacturers. Not wanting to pay royalties, Honeywell researched the history of modern computers and presented evidence that the work of John Atanasoff at Iowa State College had directly influenced Mauchly and Eckert. Because of this evidence, the patent for the ENIAC was invalidated in 1973.

>> Addressability The number of bits stored in each addressable location in memory

John Vincent Atanasoff

John Vincent Atanasoff was born in Hamilton, New York, on October 4, 1903, one of nine children. When he was about ten, his father bought a new slide rule. After reading the instructions, John Vincent became more interested in the mathematics involved than in the slide rule itself. His mother picked up on his interest and helped him study his father's old college algebra book. He continued his interest in mathematics and science and graduated from high school in two years. His family moved to Old Chicara, Florida, where John Vincent graduated from the University of Florida in 1925 with a degree in electrical engineering because the university didn't offer a degree in theoretical physics. A year later, he received a Master's degree in mathematics from Iowa State College. In 1930, after receiving his PhD in theoretical physics, he returned to Iowa State College as an assistant professor in mathematics and physics.

Courtesy of ISU Photo Service

Dr. Atanasoff became interested in finding a machine that could do the complex mathematical work he and his graduate students were doing. He examined computational devices in existence at that time, including the Monroe calculator and the IBM tabulator. Upon concluding that these machines were too slow and inaccurate, he became obsessed with finding a solution. He said that at night in a tavern after a drink of bourbon he began generating ideas of how to build this computing device. It would be electronically operated and would compute by direct logical action rather than enumeration, as in analog devices. It would use binary numbers rather than decimal numbers, condensers for memory, and a regenerative process to avoid lapses due to leakage of power.

In 1939, with a $650 grant from the school and a new graduate assistant named Clifford Berry, Dr. Atanasoff began work on the first prototype of the Atanasoff Berry Computer (ABC) in the basement of the physics building. The first working prototype was demonstrated that year.

In 1941, John Mauchly, a physicist at Ursinus College whom Dr. Atanasoff had met at a conference, came to Iowa State to visit the Atanasoffs and see a demonstration of the ABC machine. After extensive discussions, Mauchly left with papers describing its design. Mauchly and J. Presper Eckert continued their work on a computation device at the Moore School of Electrical Engineering at the University of Pennsylvania. Their machine, the ENIAC, completed in 1945, became known as the first computer.

Dr. Atanasoff went to Washington in 1942 to become director of the Underwater Acoustics Program at the Naval Ordnance Laboratory, leaving the patent application for the ABC computer in the hands of the Iowa State attorneys. The patent application was never filed and the ABC was eventually dismantled without either Atanasoff or Berry being notified. After the war, Dr. Atanasoff was chief scientist for the Army Field Forces and director of the Navy Fuse program at the Naval Ordnance Laboratory.

In 1952, Dr. Atanasoff established The Ordnance Engineering Corporation, a research and engineering firm, which was later sold to

» continued

John Vincent Atanasoff, continued

Aerojet General Corporation. He continued to work for Aerojet until he retired in 1961.

Meanwhile, in 1947 Mauchly and Eckert applied for the patent on their ENIAC computer. Sperry Rand brought suit. The subsequent trial lasted 135 working days and filled more than 20,000 pages of transcript from the testimony of 77 witnesses, including Dr. Atanasoff. Judge Larson found that Mauchly and Eckert "did not themselves first invent the automatic electronic digital computer, but instead derived that subject matter from one Dr. John Vincent Atanasoff."

In 1990, President George Bush acknowledged Dr. Atanasoff's pioneering work by awarding him the National Medal of Technology. Dr. Atanasoff died on June 15, 1995.

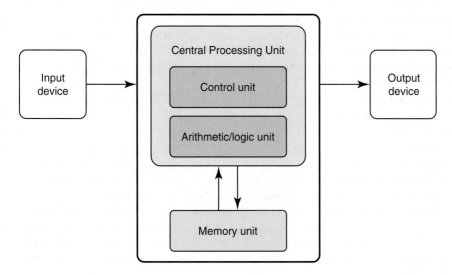

FIGURE 5.1 The von Neumann architecture

The ad in the previous section describes a memory of 4×2^{30} bytes. This means that each of the 4GB is uniquely addressable. Therefore, the addressability of the machine is 8 bits. The cells in memory are numbered consecutively beginning with 0. For example, if the addressability is 8, and there are 256 cells of memory, the cells would be addressed as follows:

Address	Contents
00000000	11100011
00000001	10101001
⋮	⋮
11111100	00000000
11111101	11111111
11111110	10101010
11111111	00110011

What are the contents of address 11111110? The bit pattern stored at that location is 10101010. What does it mean? We can't answer that question in the abstract. Does location 11111110 contain an instruction? An integer with a sign? A two's complement value? Part of an image? Without knowing what the contents represent, we cannot determine what it means: It is just a bit pattern. We must apply an interpretation on any bit pattern to determine the information it represents.

When referring to the bits in a byte or word, the bits are numbered from right to left beginning with zero. The bits in address 11111110 are numbered as follows:

7	6	5	4	3	2	1	0	← Bit position
1	0	1	0	1	0	1	0	← Contents

Arithmetic/Logic Unit

> **Arithmetic/logic unit (ALU)** The computer component that performs arithmetic operations (addition, subtraction, multiplication, division) and logical operations (comparison of two values)

> **Register** A small storage area in the CPU used to store intermediate values or special data

The arithmetic/logic unit (ALU) is capable of performing basic arithmetic operations such as adding, subtracting, multiplying, and dividing two numbers. This unit is also capable of performing logical operations such as AND, OR, and NOT. The ALU operates on words, a natural unit of data associated with a particular computer design. Historically the word length of a computer has been the number of bits processed at once by the ALU. However, the current Intel line of processors has blurred this definition by defining the word length to be 16 bits. The processor can work on words (16 bits), double words (32 bits), and quadwords (64 bits). In the rest of this discussion we continue to use "word" in its historical sense.

Most modern ALUs have a small number of special storage units called registers. These registers contain one word and are used to store information that is needed again immediately. For example, in the calculation of

One * (Two + Three)

Two is first added to Three and the result is then multiplied by One. Rather than storing the result of adding Two and Three in memory and then retrieving it to multiply it by One, the result is left in a register and

Who Was Herman Hollerith?

In 1889 the United States Census Bureau realized that unless it found a better way to count the 1890 census, the results might not be tabulated before the next required census in 1900. Herman Hollerith had designed a method of counting based on cards with holes

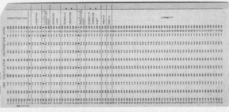

Courtesy of Douglas W. Jones

punched in them. This method was used for tabulating the census and the cards became known as Hollerith cards. Hollerith's electrical tabulating system led to the founding of the company known today as IBM.

the contents of the register are multiplied by One. Access to registers is much faster than access to memory locations.

Input/Output Units

All of the computing power in the world wouldn't be useful if we couldn't input values into the calculations from outside or report to the outside the results of those calculations. Input and output units are the channels through which the computer communicates with the outside world.

An input unit is a device through which data and programs from the outside world are entered into the computer. The first input units interpreted holes punched on paper tape or cards. Modern-day input devices include the keyboard, the mouse, and the scanning devices used at supermarkets.

An output unit is a device through which results stored in the computer memory are made available to the outside world. The most common output devices are printers and displays.

Control Unit

The control unit is the organizing force in the computer, for it is in charge of the fetch–execute cycle, discussed in the next section. There are two special registers in the control unit. The instruction register (IR) contains the instruction that is being executed, and the program counter (PC) contains the address of the next instruction to be executed. Because the ALU and the control unit work so closely together, they are often thought of as one unit called the central processing unit, or CPU.

Figure 5.2 shows a simplified view of the flow of information through the parts of a von Neumann machine. The parts are connected to one another by a collection of wires called a bus, through which data travels in

>> **Input unit** A device that accepts data to be stored in memory

>> **Output unit** A device that prints or otherwise displays data stored in memory or makes a permanent copy of information stored in memory or another device

>> **Control unit** The computer component that controls the actions of the other components so as to execute instructions in sequence

>> **Instruction register (IR)** The register that contains the instruction currently being executed

>> **Program counter (PC)** The register that contains the address of the next instruction to be executed

>> **CPU** The central processing unit, a combination of the arithmetic/logic unit and the control unit; the "brain" of a computer that interprets and executes instructions

FIGURE 5.2 Data flow through a von Neumann machine

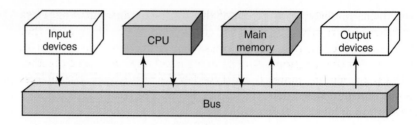

▶ **Bus width** The number of bits that can be transferred in parallel over the bus

▶ **Cache memory** A type of small, high-speed memory used to hold frequently used data

▶ **Pipelining** A technique that breaks an instruction into smaller steps that can be overlapped

▶ **Motherboard** The main circuit board of a personal computer

the computer. Each bus carries three kinds of information: address, data, and control. An address is used to select the memory location or device to which data will go, or from which it will be taken. Data then flows over the bus between the CPU, memory, and I/O devices. The control information is used to manage the flow of addresses and data. For example, a control signal will typically be used to determine the direction in which the data is flowing, either to or from the CPU. The bus width is the number of bits that it can transfer simultaneously. The wider the bus, the more address or data bits it can move at once.

Because memory accesses are very time consuming relative to the speed of the processor, many architectures provide cache memory. Cache memory is a small amount of fast-access memory into which copies of frequently used data are stored. Before a main memory access is made, the CPU checks whether the data is stored in the cache memory. Pipelining is another technique used to speed up the fetch–execute cycle. This technique splits an instruction into smaller steps that can be overlapped.

In a personal computer, the components in a von Neumann machine reside physically in a printed circuit board called the motherboard. The motherboard also has connections for attaching other devices to the bus, such as a mouse, a keyboard, or additional storage devices. (See the section on secondary storage devices later in this chapter.)

So just what does it mean to say that a machine is an *n*-bit processor? The variable *n* usually refers to the number of bits in the CPU general registers: Two *n*-bit numbers can be added with a single instruction. It also can refer to the width of the address bus, which is the size of the addressable memory—but not always. In addition, *n* can refer to the width of the data bus—but not always.

■ The Fetch-Execute Cycle

Before looking at *how* a computer does what it does, let's look at *what* it can do. The definition of a computer outlines its capabilities: A computer is a device that can store, retrieve, and process data. Therefore, all of the instructions that we give to the computer relate to storing, retrieving, and processing data. In Chapters 6 and 9, we look at various languages that we can use to give instructions to the computer. For our examples here, we use simple English-like instructions.

Recall the underlying principle of the von Neumann machine: Data and instructions are stored in memory and treated alike. This means that instructions and data are both addressable. Instructions are stored in contiguous memory locations; data to be manipulated are stored together in a different part of memory. To start the fetch–execute cycle, the address of the first instruction is loaded into the program counter.

The processing cycle includes four steps:

- Fetch the next instruction.
- Decode the instruction.
- Get data if needed.
- Execute the instruction.

Let's look at each of these steps in more detail. The process starts with the address in memory of the first instruction being stored in the program counter.

Fetch the Next Instruction

The program counter contains the address of the next instruction to be executed, so the control unit goes to the address in memory specified in the PC, makes a copy of the contents, and places the copy in the instruction register. At this point the IR contains the instruction to be executed. Before going on to the next step in the cycle, the PC must be updated to hold the address of the next instruction to be executed when the current instruction has been completed. Because the instructions are stored contiguously in memory, adding the number of bytes in the current instruction to the program counter should put the address of the next instruction into the PC. Thus the control unit increments the PC. It is possible that the PC may be changed later by the instruction being executed.

In the case of an instruction that must get additional data from memory, the ALU sends an address to the memory bus, and the memory responds by returning the value at that location. In some computers, data retrieved from memory may immediately participate in an arithmetic or logical operation. Other computers simply save the data returned by the memory into a register for processing by a subsequent instruction. At the end of execution, any result from the instruction may be saved either in registers or in memory.

Decode the Instruction

To execute the instruction in the instruction register, the control unit has to determine what instruction it is. It might be an instruction to access data from an input device, to send data to an output device, or to perform some operation on a data value. At this phase, the instruction is decoded into control signals. That is, the logic of the circuitry in the CPU determines which operation is to be executed. This step shows why a computer can execute only instructions that are expressed in its own machine language. The instructions themselves are literally built into the circuits.

FIGURE 5.3 The fetch–execute cycle

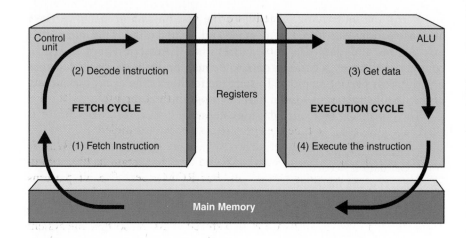

Get Data If Needed

The instruction to be executed may potentially require additional memory accesses to complete its task. For example, if the instruction says to add the contents of a memory location to a register, the control unit must get the contents of the memory location.

Execute the Instruction

Once an instruction has been decoded and any operands (data) fetched, the control unit is ready to execute the instruction. Execution involves sending signals to the arithmetic/logic unit to carry out the processing. In the case of adding a number to a register, the operand is sent to the ALU and added to the contents of the register.

When the execution is complete, the cycle begins again. If the last instruction was to add a value to the contents of a register, the next instruction probably says to store the results into a place in memory. However, the next instruction might be a control instruction—that is, an instruction that asks a question about the result of the last instruction and perhaps changes the contents of the program counter.

Figure 5.3 summarizes the fetch–execute cycle.

Hardware has changed dramatically in the last half-century, yet the von Neumann machine remains the basis of most computers today. As Alan Perlis, a well-known computer scientist, said in 1981, "Sometimes I think the only universal in the computing field is the fetch–execute cycle." [1] This statement is still true today, nearly three decades later.

■ RAM and ROM

As mentioned, RAM stands for random-access memory. RAM is memory in which each cell (usually a byte) can be directly accessed. Inherent in the idea of being able to access each location is the ability to *change* the contents of each location. That is, storing something else into that place can change the bit pattern in each cell.

In addition to RAM, most computers contain a second kind of memory, called ROM. ROM stands for read-only memory. The contents in locations in ROM cannot be changed. Their contents are permanent and cannot be altered by a stored operation. Placing the bit pattern in ROM is called *burning*. The bit pattern is burned either at the time the ROM is manufactured or at the time the computer parts are assembled.

RAM and ROM are differentiated by a very basic property: RAM is volatile; ROM is not. This means that RAM does not retain its bit configuration when the power is turned off, but ROM does. The bit patterns within ROM are permanent. Because ROM is stable and cannot be changed, it is used to store the instructions that the computer needs to start itself. Frequently used software is also stored in ROM so that the system does not have to read the software in each time the machine is turned on. Main memory usually contains some ROM along with the general-purpose RAM.

■ Secondary Storage Devices

As mentioned earlier, an input device is the means by which data and programs are entered into the computer and stored into memory. An output device is the means by which results are sent back to the user. Because most of main memory is volatile and limited, it is essential that there be other types of storage devices where programs and data can be stored when they are no longer being processed or when the machine is not turned on. These other types of storage devices (other than main memory) are called *secondary* or *auxiliary* storage devices. Because data must be read from them and written to them, each secondary storage device is also an input and an output device.

Secondary storage devices can be installed within the computer box at the factory or added later as needed. Because these devices can store large quantities of data, they are also known as mass storage devices. For example, the hard disk drive that comes with the laptop specified in the ad can store 500×2^{30} bytes as opposed to 4×2^{30} bytes in main memory.

The next sections describe some secondary storage devices.

Magnetic Tape

Card readers and card punches were among the first input/output devices. Paper tape readers and punches were the next input/output devices. Although paper tapes, like cards, are permanent, they cannot hold much data. The first truly mass auxiliary storage device was the *magnetic tape drive*. A magnetic tape drive is like a tape recorder and is most often used to back up (make a copy of) the data on a disk in case the disk is later damaged. Tapes come in several varieties, from small streaming-tape cartridges to large reel-to-reel models.

FIGURE 5.4 A magnetic tape

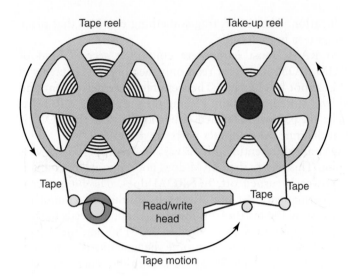

Tape drives have one serious drawback: To access data in the middle of the tape, all the data before the piece you want must be accessed and discarded. Although modern streaming-tape systems have the capability of skipping over segments of tape, the tape must physically move through the read/write heads. Any physical movement of this type is time-consuming. See Figure 5.4.

Magnetic Disks

A *disk drive* is a cross between a compact disk player and a tape recorder. A read/write head (similar to the record/playback head in a tape recorder) travels across a spinning magnetic disk, retrieving or recording data. As on a compact disk, the heads travel directly to the information desired; as on a tape, the information is stored magnetically.

Disks come in several varieties, but all of them consist of a thin disk made out of magnetic material. The surface of each disk is logically organized into tracks and sectors. Tracks are concentric circles around the surface of the disk. Each track is divided into sectors. Each sector holds a block of information as a continuous sequence of bits. [See Figure 5.5(a).] The figure depicts the original layout of data on a disk, in which each track has the same number of sectors, and each sector holds the same number of bits. The blocks of data nearer the center were more densely packed. On modern disks, there are fewer sectors near the middle and more toward the outside. The actual number of tracks per surface and the number of sectors per track vary, but 512 bytes or 1024 bytes is common. (The power of 2 strikes again.) The locations of the tracks and sectors are marked magnetically when a disk is formatted; they are not physically part of the disk.

The read/write head in a disk drive is positioned on an arm that moves from one track to another. [See Figure 5.5(b).] An input/output instruction

>> **Track** A concentric circle on the surface of a disk

>> **Sector** A section of a track

>> **Block** The information stored in a sector

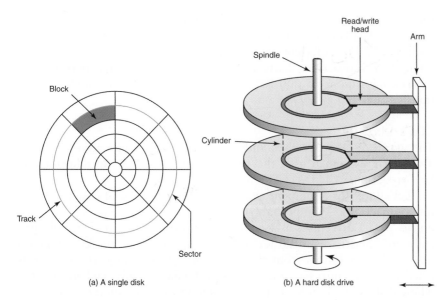

FIGURE 5.5 The organization of a magnetic disk

(a) A single disk

(b) A hard disk drive

specifies the track and sector. When the read/write head is over the proper track, it waits until the appropriate sector is beneath the head; it then accesses the block of information in that sector. This process gives rise to four measures of a disk drive's efficiency: seek time, latency, access time, and transfer rate. Seek time is the time it takes for the read/write head to get into position over the specified track. Latency is the time it takes for the specified sector to spin to the read/write head. The average latency is one-half the time for a full rotation of the disk. For this reason, latency is also called rotation delay. Access time is the sum of seek time and latency. Transfer rate is the rate at which data is transferred from the disk to memory.

Now let's look at some of the varieties of disks. One classification of disk is hard versus floppy. These terms refer to the flexibility of the disk itself. The original floppy disk, introduced in the 1970s, was 8″ in diameter and even its case was floppy. By the time of the rise in personal computers in the late 1970s, the floppy disk had been reduced in size to 5 1/2″ in diameter. Today's generic "floppy" disks are 3 1/2″ in diameter, encased in a hard plastic cover, and capable of storing 1.44MB of data. Newer machines do not automatically have built-in drives for these disks as they did a few years ago, but drives for them can be added.

Hard disks actually consist of several disks—this sounds strange, so let's explain. Let's call the individual disks platters. Hard disks consist of several platters attached to a spindle that rotates. Each platter has its own read/write head. All of the tracks that line up under one another are called a cylinder [see Figure 5.5(b)]. An address in a hard drive consists of the cylinder number, the surface number, and the sector. Hard drives rotate at much higher speeds

>> **Seek time** The time it takes for the read/write head to get positioned over the specified track

>> **Latency** The time it takes for the specified sector to be in position under the read/write head

>> **Access time** The time it takes for a block to start being read; the sum of seek time and latency

>> **Transfer rate** The rate at which data moves from the disk to memory

>> **Cylinder** The set of concentric tracks on all surfaces

than floppy drives do, and the read/write heads don't actually touch the surface of the platters but rather float above them. A typical hard disk drive rotates at 7200 revolutions per minute. Laptop hard disks usually spin at 5400 RPM, conserving battery power. The disks in high performance servers may run at 15,000 RPM, providing lower latency and a higher transfer rate.

CDs and DVDs

The world of compact discs and their drivers looks like acronym soup. The ad we examined used the acronym: DVD +/–/RW. In addition, we have to decipher CD-DA, CD-RW, and DVD.

Let's look for a moment at the acronym CD. CD, of course, stands for compact disk—you probably have a collection of them with recorded music. A CD drive uses a laser to read information that is stored optically on a plastic disk. Rather than having concentric tracks, a CD has one track that spirals from the inside out. As on magnetic disks, this track is broken into sectors. A CD has the data evenly packed over the whole disk, so more information is stored in the track on the outer edges and read in a single revolution. To make the transfer rate consistent throughout the disk, the rotation speed varies depending on the position of the laser beam.

The other letters attached to CD refer to various properties of the disk, such as formatting and whether the information on the disk can be changed. CD-DA is the format used in audio recordings; CD-DA stands for compact disk–digital audio. Certain fields in this format are used for timing information. A sector in a CD-DA contains 1/75 of a second of music.

CD-ROM is the same as CD-DA but the disk is formatted differently. Data is stored in the sectors reserved for timing information in CD-DA. ROM stands for read-only memory. As we said earlier, read-only memory means that the data is permanent and cannot be changed. A sector on a CD-ROM contains 2KB of data. CD-ROM capacity is in the neighborhood of 600MB.

CD-R stands for recordable, allowing data to be written after it is manufactured. The contents of a CD-R cannot be changed after data is recorded on it. A CD-RW is rewritable, meaning that it can have data recorded on it multiple times.

The most common format for distributing movies is now a DVD, which stands for digital versatile disk (although the acronym generally stands on its own these days). Because of its large storage capacity, a DVD is well suited to hold multimedia presentations that combine audio and video.

DVDs come in multiple forms: DVD+R, DVD-R, DVD+RW, and DVD-RW, and each of these may be preceded by DL. As we noted in describing the ad, the + and - refer to two competing formats. As with CD,

R means recordable and RW means rewritable. DL stands for dual layer, which nearly doubles the capacity of a DVD. DVD-R has a capacity of 4.7GB while DL DVD-R can hold 8.5GB. More recently, Blu-Ray disks with 25GB capacity and DL 50GB capacity have been introduced. Writable versions are also available. The name Blu-Ray refers to its use of a blue laser instead of the red laser in CD and DVD drives.

Note that the × used in rating CD and DVD speeds indicates the relative speed of access compared with a standard CD or DVD player. When evaluating these devices, be aware that the higher speeds listed represent maximums that are usually attainable only when retrieving data from certain parts of the disk. They are not averages. Therefore, faster may not be better in terms of the added cost.

Flash Drives

IBM introduced the flash drive in 1998 as an alternative to floppy disks. Figure 5.6 shows a flash drive (or thumb drive), which uses flash memory, a nonvolatile computer memory that can be erased and rewritten. The drive is integrated with a USB (universal serial bus). Most computers today do not come with floppy disks, but they do come with USB ports. In 2010, this little (thumb-sized) 8GB storage device could be bought for less than $20.

Flash memory is also being used to build solid state disks (SSD) that can directly replace a hard disk. Because SSD is all electronic and has no moving parts, it is faster and consumes less power than a hard disk. Even so, its storage elements can eventually wear out, meaning that it can suffer failures just as a hard disk can.

FIGURE 5.6 A flash drive
© Alex Kotlov/ShutterStock, Inc.

■ Touch Screens

We've seen how secondary memory devices provide locations in which to store programs and data used by the CPU. Other input/output (I/O) devices allow the human user to interact with an executing program. Many of these are commonplace—we often provide information through a keyboard and mouse, and we usually view information displayed on a monitor screen. Other input devices include bar code readers and image scanners; other output devices include printers and plotters.

Let's examine one particular type of I/O device in some detail. A *touch screen* displays text and graphics like a regular monitor, but it can also detect and respond to the user touching the screen with a finger or stylus. Usually, an I/O device serves either as an input device or an output device. A touch screen serves as both.

You've probably seen touch screens used in a variety of situations such as information kiosks, restaurants, and museums. Figure 5.7 shows someone using a touch screen. These devices are most helpful in situations in which complex input is not needed, and they have the added benefit of

FIGURE 5.7 A touch screen
© Randy Allbritton/Photodisc/Getty Images

Evolution of the BlackBerry®
The first BlackBerry device, known as the RIM Inter@ctive Pager 850, was introduced to the public in 1999 by Research in Motion, Ltd. The device appeared on the hit NBC television show *ER*, and is known as the first mobile email machine. Each year brought newer and better models. For example, 2006 saw the introduction of the BlackBerry Pearl™, which, with its smaller size, digital camera, enhanced software, and media player, appealed to the mass public in a way that the previous models hadn't. In 2008, the BlackBerry Storm™ was introduced as a sleek, touch screen handset built to compete with Apple's iPhone®. How popular is the BlackBerry? Even Barack Obama refused to give up his BlackBerry when he became president.

being fairly well protected. It's far better for a waiter at a restaurant to make a few choices using a touch screen than to have to deal with a keyboard, which has more keys than necessary (for the task) and may easily get damaged from food and drink.

A touch screen not only detects the touch, but also knows where on the screen it is being touched. Choices are often presented using graphical buttons that the user selects by touching the screen where the button is positioned. In this sense, using a touch screen is not much different from using a mouse. The mouse position is tracked as the mouse is moved; when the mouse button is clicked, the position of the mouse pointer determines which graphical button is pushed. In a touch screen, the location at which the screen is touched determines which button is pushed.

So how does a touch screen detect that it is being touched? Furthermore, how does it know where on the screen it is being touched? Several technologies are used today to implement touch screens. Let's briefly explore them.

A *resistive* touch screen is made up of two layers—one with vertical lines and one with horizontal lines of electrically conductive material. The two layers are separated by a very small amount of space. When the top layer is pressed, it comes in contact with the second layer, which allows electrical current to flow. The specific vertical and horizontal lines that make contact dictate the location on the screen that was touched.

A *capacitive* touch screen has a laminate applied over a glass screen. The laminate conducts electricity in all directions, and a very small current is applied equally on the four corners. When the screen is touched, current flows to the finger or stylus. The current is so low that the user doesn't even feel it. The location of the touch on the screen is determined by comparing the strength of the flow of electricity from each corner.

An *infrared* touch screen projects crisscrossing horizontal and vertical beams of infrared light just over the surface of the screen. Sensors on opposite sides of the screen detect the beams. When the user breaks the beams by touching the screen, the location of the break can be determined.

A *surface acoustic wave* (SAW) touch screen is similar to an infrared touch screen except that it projects high-frequency sound waves across the horizontal and vertical axes. When a finger touches the surface, the corresponding sensors detect the interruption and determine the location of the touch.

Note that a gloved hand could be used in resistive, infrared, and SAW touch screens, but cannot be used with capacitive screens, which rely on current flowing to the touch point.

5.3 Embedded Systems

Embedded systems are computers that are designed to perform a narrow range of functions as part of a larger system. Typically, an embedded system is housed on a single microprocessor chip with the programs stored in ROM. Virtually all appliances that have a digital interface—watches, microwaves, VCRs, cars—utilize embedded systems. In fact, embedded systems are everywhere: From consumer electronics, to kitchen appliances, to automobiles, to networking equipment, to industrial control systems, you find embedded systems lurking in the device. Some embedded systems include an operating system, but many are so specialized that the entire logic can be implemented as a single program.[2]

Early embedded systems were stand-alone 8-bit microprocessors with their own homegrown operating system. Today, they range from 8-bit controllers to 32-bit digital signal processors (DSPs) to 64-bit RISC (Reduced Instruction Set) chips. More and more embedded systems are based on networks of distributed microprocessors that communicate through wired and wireless buses, remotely monitored and controlled by regular network management communications protocols.

In fact, the term *embedded system* is nebulous because it encompasses just about everything except desktop PCs. The term originated because the first such computers were physically embedded within a product or device and could not be accessed. Now the term refers to any computer that is preprogrammed to perform a dedicated or narrow range of functions as part of a larger system. The implication is that there is only minimal end-user or operator intervention, if any.

Because the average person encounters an embedded system only in his or her kitchen, entertainment room, or car, we tend to equate these systems with hardware. In reality, programs must be written and burned into the read-only memory that comes with the system to make it accomplish its assigned function. Given that programs cannot be developed and tested on the embedded processor itself, how are they implemented? Programs are written on a PC and compiled for the target system, where the executable code is generated for the processor in the embedded system.

In early embedded systems, the size of the code and the speed at which it executed were very important. Because assembly-language programs provided the best opportunity to streamline and speed up the code, they were used almost exclusively for embedded systems. Even when the C language became popular and cross-compilers for C to embedded systems became available, many programmers continued to use assembly language for this purpose. C programs are approximately 25% larger and slower, but are easier to write than assembly-language programs. Even today, the size of the ROM may dictate that the code be as small as possible, leading to an assembly-language program.[3]

5.4 Parallel Architectures[4]

If a problem can be solved in n time units on a computer with one processor (von Neumann machine), can it be solved in $n/2$ time units on a computer with two processors, or $n/3$ on a computer with three processors? This question has led to the rise of parallel computing architectures.

■ Parallel Computing

There are four general forms of parallel computing: bit level, instruction level, data level, and task level.

Bit-level parallelism is based on increasing the word size of a computer. In an 8-bit processor, an operation on a 16-bit data value would require two operations: one for the upper 8 bits and one for the lower 8 bits. A 16-bit processor could do the operation in one instruction. Thus *increasing* the word size *reduces* the number of operations on data values larger than the word size. The current trend is to use 64-bit processors.

Instruction-level parallelism is based on the idea that some instructions in a program can be carried out independently in parallel. For example, if a program requires operations on unrelated data, these operations can be done at the same time. A superscalar is a processor that can recognize this situation and take advantage of it by sending instructions to different functional units of the processor. Note that a superscalar machine does not have multiple processors but does have multiple execution resources. For example, it might contain separate ALUs for working on integer and real numbers, enabling it to simultaneously compute the sum of two integers and the product of two real numbers. Such resources are called execution units.

Data-level parallelism is based on the idea that a single set of instructions can be run on different data sets at the same time. This type of parallelism is called SIMD (single instructions, multiple data) and relies on a control unit directing multiple ALUs to carry out the same operation, such as addition, on different sets of operands. This approach, which is also called synchronous processing, is effective when the same process needs to be applied to many data sets. For example, increasing the brightness of an image involves adding a value to every one of several million pixels. These additions can all be done in parallel. See Figure 5.8.

Task-level parallelism is based on the idea that different processors can execute different tasks on the same or different data sets. If the different processors are operating on the same data set, then it is analogous to pipelining in a von Neumann machine. When this organization is applied to data, the first processor does the first task. Then the second processor starts working on the output from the first processor, while the first processor applies its computation to the next data set. Eventually, each processor is working on one phase of the job, each getting material or data from the previous stage of processing, and each in turn handing over its work to the next stage. See Figure 5.9.

In a data-level environment, each processor is doing the same thing to a different data set. For example, each processor might be computing the

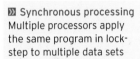

» Synchronous processing Multiple processors apply the same program in lock-step to multiple data sets

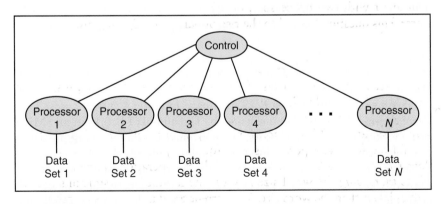

FIGURE 5.8 Processors in a synchronous computing environment

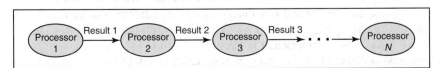

FIGURE 5.9 Processors in a pipeline

FIGURE 5.10 A shared-memory parallel processor

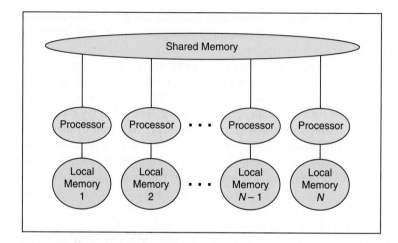

grades for a different class. In the pipelining task-level example, each processor is contributing to the grade for the same class. Another approach to task-level parallelism is to have different processors doing different things with different data. This configuration allows processors to work independently much of the time, but introduces problems of coordination among the processors. This leads to a configuration where each of the processors have both a local memory and a shared memory. The processors use the shared memory for communication, so the configuration is called a shared memory parallel processor. See Figure 5.10.

» **Shared memory parallel processor** The situation in which multiple processors share a global memory

■ Classes of Parallel Hardware

The classes of parallel hardware reflect the various types of parallel computing. Multicore processors have multiple independent cores, usually CPUs. Whereas a superscalar processor can issue multiple instructions to execution units, each multicore processor can issue multiple instructions to multiple execution units. That is, each independent core can have multiple execution units attached to it.

Symmetric multiprocessors (SMPs) have multiple identical cores. They share memory, and a bus connects them. The number of cores in an SMP is usually limited to 32 processors. A distributed computer is one in which multiple memory units are connected through a network. A cluster is a group of stand-alone machines connected through an off-the-shelf network. A massively parallel processor is a computer with many networked processors connected through a specialized network. This kind of device usually has more than 1000 processors.

The distinctions between the classes of parallel hardware are being blurred by modern systems. A typical processor chip today contains two to eight cores that operate as an SMP. These are then connected via a network to form a cluster. Thus, it is common to find a mix of shared and distributed memory in parallel processing. In addition, graphics processors that support general-purpose data-parallel processing may be connected to each of the multicore processors. Given that each of the cores is also applying instruction-level parallelism, you can see that modern parallel computers no longer fall into one or another specific classification. Instead, they typically embody all of the classes at once. They are distinguished by the particular balance that they strike among the different classes of parallel processing they support. A parallel computer that is used for science may emphasize data parallelism, whereas one that is running an Internet search engine may emphasize task-level parallelism.

Summary

The components that make up a computer cover a wide range of devices. Each component has characteristics that dictate how fast, large, and efficient it is. Furthermore, each component plays an integral role in the overall processing of the machine.

The world of computing is filled with jargon and acronyms. The speed of a processor is specified in GHz (gigahertz), the amount of memory is specified in MB (megabytes) and GB (gigabytes), and a display screen is specified in pixels.

The von Neumann architecture is the underlying architecture of most of today's computers. It has five main parts: memory, the arithmetic/logic (ALU) unit, input devices, output devices, and the control unit. The fetch–execute cycle, under the direction of the control unit, is the heart of the processing. In this cycle, instructions are fetched from memory, decoded, and executed.

RAM and ROM are acronyms for two types of computer memory. RAM stands for random-access memory; ROM stands for read-only memory. The values stored in RAM can be changed; those in ROM cannot.

Secondary storage devices are essential to a computer system. These devices save data when the computer is not running. Magnetic tape, magnetic disk, and flash drives are three common types of secondary storage.

Touch screens are peripheral devices that serve both input and output functions and are appropriate in specific situations such as restaurants and information kiosks. They respond to a human touching the screen with a finger or stylus, and can determine the location on the screen where the touch occurred. Several touch screen technologies exist, including resistive, capacitive, infrared, and surface acoustic wave (SAW) touch screens. They have varying characteristics that make them appropriate in particular situations.

Although von Neumann machines are by far the most common, other computer architectures have emerged. For example, there are machines with more than one processor so that calculations can be done in parallel, thereby speeding up the processing.

ETHICAL ISSUES ▸ Computer Hoaxes and Scams

As long as humans have known that other humans could be taken advantage of, there have been scammers, con artists, and hoaxers. The principal difference between a hoax and a scam is the financial purpose of the latter. The motives of a hoaxster are sometimes difficult to discern and may be as simple as the adolescent's impulse "to leave a mark" or "just for kicks." Hoaxes are annoying and time consuming. The ultimate motive of the con artist and scammer, however, is to trick the naive and unwary out of their money or possessions.

Before computers, these predators led difficult lives. They had to spend their own time and money to find individual victims. The amount taken from a victim could range from a few dollars—as would be the case in a typical "shell game"—to huge sums of money—as in "Brooklyn Bridge" schemes wherein victims thought they had purchased property that did

not exist or that was not for sale. The perpetrators of these crimes were limited in the number of potential victims they could reach at any one time.

Then came the Internet. With a few clicks of a mouse, a scammer can now reach thousands of potential victims through email. The gathering of email addresses can be automated, which creates an enormous population of potential victims. Websites can act as virtual spider webs, entrapping those who innocently wander in.

There was a time when the most common complaint of Internet users was the annoyance of commercial spam. Today, good email services provide filters that catch most commercial spam before it reaches the individual. According to the Federal Trade Commission (FTC), the most common complaints of computer users are now the following: Internet auctions, Internet access services, credit card fraud, international model dialing, Web cramming, multilevel marketing plans/pyramids, travel and vacation scams, bogus business opportunities/investments, healthcare products and services, and phishing scams.

Most serious are those crimes that steal financial information and passwords from Web surfers. Websites may be used to lull people into believing that they are responding to surveys or providing credit card information merely to prove they are 18. By stealing passwords, criminals can gain access to their victims' entire financial records. Identity theft is devastating to the victims and can take years to recover from. Perhaps the greatest threat comes from those who really want to wreak havoc. Today, airlines, banks, and municipal infrastructures are all tied into computer networks. The damage a determined cyber-criminal can cause is boundless.

The challenge of policing these schemes cannot be overstated. Perpetrators can disguise not only their identities, but also their geographical locations. For now, the best protection users have is skepticism. Refusing to give out credit card or other personal information to any request is mandatory. As computer use becomes even more widespread, chances are that the scammers, hoaxers, and con artists will keep pace. Until there is a viable way to stop their activities, surfers beware.

?

Scam email received by Nell Dale

IT Department Service,

You have exceeded the limit of your mailbox set by your IT Department service. And you will be having problems in sending and receiving new emails. To prevent this, you will have to contact the IT Department Service by email with your:

Current username:{   } and
Password:{   } *to help increase your storage limit.*

IT Department Service
E-mail:
<mailto:it.dept@administrativos.com>it.dept
@administrativos.com

Failure to do this, will result in limited access to your mailbox.

Regards,
IT Department Service

Would you have answered? What would have happened if you did?

🔑 Key Terms

Access time
Addressability
Arithmetic/logic unit (ALU)
Block
Bus width
Cache memory
Control unit
CPU
Cylinder
Input unit
Instruction register (IR)
Latency

Motherboard
Output unit
Pipelining
Program counter (PC)
Register
Sector
Seek time
Shared memory parallel processor
Synchronous processing
Track
Transfer rate

⌘ Exercises

For Exercises 1–16, match the power of 10 to its name or use.

    A. 10^{-12}
    B. 10^{-9}
    C. 10^{-6}
    D. 10^{-3}
    E. 10^{3}
    F. 10^{6}
    G. 10^{9}
    H. 10^{12}
    I. 10^{15}

1. Nano

2. Pico

3. Micro

4. Milli

5. Tera

6. Giga

7. Kilo

8. Mega

9. Often used to describe processor speed

10. Often used to describe size of memory

11. Used in relation to Internet speeds

12. Latin for "thousandth"

13. Italian for "little"

14. Peta

15. Roughly equivalent to 2^{10}

16. Roughly equivalent to 2^{50}

For Exercises 17–23, match the acronym with its most accurate definition.
- A. CD-ROM
- B. CD-DA
- C. CD-R
- D. DVD
- E. CD-RW
- F. DL DVD
- G. Blu-Ray

17. Format using two layers

18. Data is stored in the sectors reserved for timing information in another variant

19. Can be read many times, but written after its manufacture only once

20. Can be both read from and written to any number of times

21. Format used in audio recordings

22. A new technology storing up to 50 GB

23. The most popular format for distributing movies

Exercises 24–66 are problems or short-answer exercises.

24. Define the following terms:
    a. Core 2 processor
    b. Hertz
    c. Random access memory

25. What does FSB stand for?

26. What does it mean to say that a processor is 1.4 GHz?

27. What does it mean to say that memory is 133 MHz?

28. How many bytes of memory are there in the following machines?
    a. 512MB machine
    b. 2GB machine

29. Define RPM and discuss what it means in terms of speed of access to a disk.

30. What is the stored-program concept, and why is it important?

31. What does "units that process information are separate from the units that store information" mean in terms of computer architecture?

32. Name the components of a von Neumann machine.

33. What is the addressability of an 8-bit machine?

34. What is the function of the ALU?

35. Which component in the von Neumann architecture would you say acts as the stage manager? Explain.

36. Punched cards and paper tape were two early input/output media. Discuss their advantages and disadvantages.

37. What is an instruction register, and what is its function?

38. What is a program counter, and what is its function?

39. List the steps in the fetch–execute cycle.

40. Explain what is meant by "fetch an instruction."

41. Explain what is meant by "decode an instruction."

42. Explain what is meant by "execute an instruction."

43. Compare and contrast RAM and ROM.

44. What is a secondary storage device, and why are such devices important?

45. Discuss the pros and cons of using magnetic tape as a storage medium.

46. What are the four measures of a disk drive's efficiency?

47. Define what is meant by a block of data.

48. What is a cylinder?

49. Define the steps that a hard disk drive goes through to transfer a block of data from the disk to memory.

50. Distinguish between a compact disk and a magnetic disk.

51. Describe a parallel architecture that uses synchronous processing.

52. Describe a parallel architecture that uses pipeline processing.

53. How does a shared-memory parallel configuration work?

54. How many different memory locations can a 16-bit processor access?

55. Why is a faster clock not always better?

56. Why is a larger cache not necessarily better?

57. In the ad, why is the 1080p specification for the screen not entirely true?

58. Keep a diary for a week of how many times the terms *hardware* and *software* appear in television commercials.

59. Take a current ad for a laptop computer and compare that ad with the one shown at the beginning of this chapter.

60. What is the common name for the disk that is a secondary storage device?

61. To what does the expression *pixels* refer?

62. What is a GPU?

63. If a battery in a laptop is rated for 80 WHr, and the laptop draws 20 watts, how long will it run?

64. What is the difference between 1K of memory and a 1K transfer rate?

65. Compare and contrast a DVD-ROM and a flash drive.

66. "Giga" can mean both 10^9 and 2^{30}. Explain to which each refers. Can this cause confusion when reading a computer advertisement?

??? Thought Questions

1. Would octal or hexadecimal be a better way to refer to the addresses in a 16-bit processor? Justify your answer.

2. Relate the concept of a program to the fetch–execute cycle of the von Neumann machine.

3. Personal computers originally came equipped with one, then two floppy drives. After that, floppy drives became optional as CD drives became standard equipment. Now USB flash drives are the current medium for storage of data. What are the advantages of flash drives over other forms of disk storage? Do you think they will replace other media?

4. Why don't we just use powers of 10 when referring to storage? Aren't powers of 10 and powers of 2 close enough?

5. Walk through your kitchen and list the number of items that include embedded computers.

6. Have you ever been taken in by a hoax? Were you angry or just annoyed?

7. Have you or anyone you know been the victim of a scam artist?

The Programming Layer

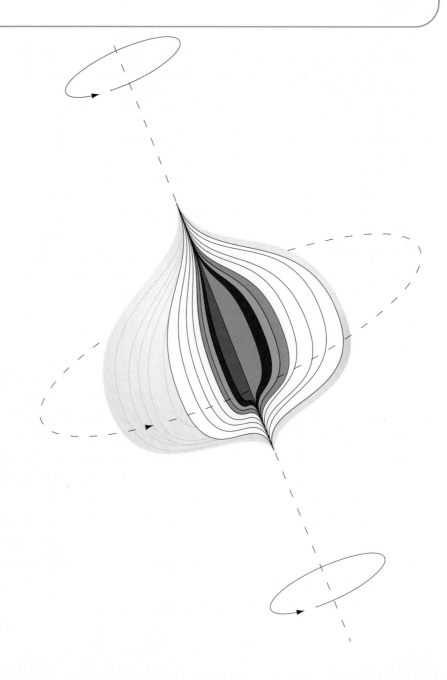

Low-Level Programming Languages and Pseudocode

6

Chapter 6 is the first chapter in the programming layer. In Chapters 2 and 3, we covered the basic information necessary for understanding a computing system, including number systems and ways to represent different types of information in a computer. In Chapters 4 and 5, we covered the hardware components of a computer. Now the emphasis changes from what a computer system is to how to use one.

We begin this chapter by looking at machine code, the lowest-level programming language of all—the language built into the machine. We then move up one level to assembly language, a language in which we can use a combination of letters to represent a machine-language instruction. Finally, we introduce the concept of pseudocode as a way to express algorithms.

Goals

After studying this chapter, you should be able to:

- list the operations that a computer can perform.
- describe the important features of the Pep/8 virtual machine.
- distinguish between immediate addressing mode and direct addressing mode.
- write a simple machine-language program.
- distinguish between machine language and assembly language.
- describe the steps in creating and running an assembly-language program.
- write a simple program in assembly language.

- distinguish between instructions to the assembler and instructions to be translated.
- distinguish between following an algorithm and developing one.
- describe the pseudocode constructs used in expressing an algorithm.
- use pseudocode to express an algorithm.
- describe two approaches to testing.
- design and implement a test plan for a simple assembly-language program.

6.1 Computer Operations

The programming languages we use must mirror the types of operations that a computer can perform. So let's begin our discussion by repeating the definition of a computer: A computer is a programmable electronic device that can store, retrieve, and process data.

The operational words here are *programmable*, *store*, *retrieve*, and *process*. In a previous chapter we pointed out the importance of the real-ization that data and instructions to manipulate the data are logically the same and could be stored in the same place. That is what the word *programmable* means in this context. The instructions that manipulate data are stored within the machine along with the data. To change what the computer does to the data, we change the instructions.

Store, *retrieve*, and *process* are actions that the computer can perform on data. That is, the instructions that the control unit executes can store data into the memory of the machine, retrieve data from the memory of the machine, and process the data in some way in the arithmetic/logic unit. The word *process* is very general. At the machine level, processing involves performing arithmetic and logical operations on data values.

Where does the data that gets stored in the computer memory come from? How does the human ever get to see what is stored there, such as the results of some calculation? There are other instructions that specify the interaction between an input device and the CPU and between the CPU and an output device.

6.2 Machine Language

As we pointed out in Chapter 1, the only programming instructions that a computer actually carries out are those written using machine language, the instructions built into the hardware of a particular computer. Initially humans had no choice except to write programs in machine language because other programming languages had not yet been invented.

So how are computer instructions represented? Recall that every processor type has its own set of specific machine instructions. These are the only instructions the processor can actually carry out. Because a finite number of instructions exist, the processor designers simply list the instructions and assign them a binary code that is used to represent them. This is similar to the approach taken when representing character data, as described in Chapter 3.

The relationship between the processor and the instructions it can carry out is completely integrated. The electronics of the CPU inherently recognize the binary representations of the specific commands, so there is

> ❱❱ Machine language The language made up of binary-coded instructions that is used directly by the computer

no actual list of commands the computer must consult. Instead, the CPU embodies the list in its design.

Each machine-language instruction performs only one very low-level task. Each small step in a process must be explicitly coded in machine language. Even the small task of adding two numbers together must be broken down into smaller steps: enter a number into the accumulator, add a number to it, save the result. Then these three instructions must be written in binary, and the programmer has to remember which combination of binary digits corresponds to which instruction. As we mentioned in Chapter 1, machine-language programmers have to be very good with numbers and very detail oriented.

However, we can't leave you with the impression that only mathematicians can write programs in machine language. It is true that very few programs are written in machine language today, primarily because they represent an inefficient use of a programmer's time. Although most programs are written in higher-level languages and then translated into machine language (a process we describe later in this chapter), every piece of software is actually implemented in machine code. Understanding even just a little about this level will make you a more informed user. In addition, this experience emphasizes the basic definition of a computer and makes you appreciate the ease with which people interact with computers today.

Managing endangered species
Zoos have established captive populations of endangered animals to save them from extinction, but they need to have a good distribution of ages and genetic diversity to protect the species against diseases and inbreeding. A computerized database of all captive animals that contains dates of births and deaths, gender, parentage, and location enables scientists to measure important factors governing the welfare of a species, such as reproductive and survival rates, degree of inbreeding, and loss of genetic diversity. For example, the Minnesota Zoological Garden coordinates the International Species Inventory System (ISIS). ISIS provides global information on many different species of animals, including more than 163,000 living animals, and many endangered animals are being bred in captivity due to its help.

■ Pep/8: A Virtual Computer

By definition, machine code differs from machine to machine. Recall that just as each lock has a specific key that opens it, each type of computer has a specific set of operations that it can execute, called the computer's machine language. That is, each type of CPU has its own machine language that it understands. So how can we give each of you the experience of using machine language when you may be working on different machines? We solve that problem by using a virtual computer. A virtual computer is a hypothetical machine—in this case, one that is designed to contain the important features of real computers that we want to illustrate. Pep/8, designed by Stanley Warford, is the virtual machine that we use here.[1]

Pep/8 has 39 machine-language instructions. This means that a program for Pep/8 must be a sequence consisting of a combination of these instructions. Don't panic: We will not ask you to understand and remember 39 sequences of binary bits! We merely plan to examine a few of these instructions, and we will not ask you to memorize any of them.

» Virtual computer (machine) A hypothetical machine designed to illustrate important features of a real machine

Important Features Reflected in Pep/8

The memory unit of the Pep/8 is made up of 65,536 bytes of storage. The bytes are numbered from 0 through 65,535 (decimal). Recall that each byte contains 8 bits, so we can describe the bit pattern in a byte using 2 hexadecimal digits. (Refer to Chapter 2 for more information on hexadecimal digits.) The word length in Pep/8 is 2 bytes, or 16 bits. Thus the information that flows into and out of the arithmetic/logic unit (ALU) is 16 bits in length.

Recall from Chapter 5 that a register is a small area of storage in the ALU of the CPU that holds special data and intermediate values. Pep/8 has seven registers, three of which we focus on at this point:

- The program counter (PC), which contains the address of the next instruction to be executed
- The instruction register (IR), which contains a copy of the instruction being executed
- The accumulator (A register)

The accumulator is used to hold data and the results of operations; it is the special storage register referred in Chapter 5 in the discussion of the ALU.

We realize that this is a lot of detailed information, but don't despair! Remember that our goal is to give you a feel for what is actually happening at the lowest level of computer processing. By necessity, that processing keeps track of many details.

Figure 6.1 shows a diagram of Pep8's CPU and memory. Notice that the addresses in memory appear in orange. This color is intended to

FIGURE 6.1   Pep/8's architecture

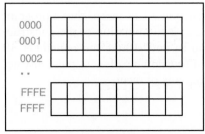

Pep/8's CPU (as discussed in this chapter)

A register (accumulator)

Program counter (PC)

Instruction register (IR)

Pep/8's Memory

0000
0001
0002
· ·
FFFE
FFFF

emphasize that the addresses themselves are not stored in memory, but rather that they *name* the individual bytes of memory. We refer to any particular byte in memory by its address.

Before we go on, let's review some aspects of binary and hexadecimal numbers. The largest decimal value that can be represented in a byte is 255. It occurs when all of the bits are 1s: 11111111 in binary is FF in hexadecimal and 255 in decimal. The largest decimal value that can be represented in a word (16 bits) is 65,535. It occurs when all 16 bits are 1s: 1111111111111111 in binary is FFFF in hexadecimal and 65,535 in decimal. If we represent both positive and negative numbers, we lose a bit in the magnitude (because one is used for the sign), so we can represent values ranging from −7FFF to +7FFF in hexadecimal, or −32,767 to +32,767 in decimal.

This information is important when working with the Pep/8 machine. The number of bits we have available determines the size of the numbers we can work with.

Instruction Format

We have talked about instructions going into the instruction register, being decoded, and being executed. Now we are ready to look at a set (or subset) of concrete instructions that a computer can execute. First, however, we need to examine the format of an instruction in Pep/8.

Figure 6.2(a) shows the format for an instruction in Pep/8. There are two parts to an instruction: the *instruction specifier* and (optionally) the 16-bit *operand specifier*. The instruction specifier indicates which operation is to be carried out, such as "add a number to a value already stored in a register," and how to interpret just where the operand is. The operand

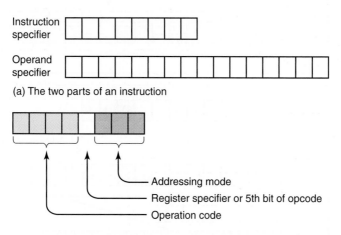

Instruction
specifier

Operand
specifier

(a) The two parts of an instruction

Addressing mode

Register specifier or 5th bit of opcode

Operation code

(b) The instruction specifier part of an instruction

FIGURE 6.2   Pep/8 instruction format

specifier (the second and third bytes of the instruction) holds either the operand itself or the address of where the operand is to be found. Some instructions do not use the operand specifier.

The format of the instruction specifier varies depending on the number of bits used to represent a particular operation. In Pep/8, *operation codes* (called opcodes) vary from 4 bits to 8 bits long. The opcodes that we cover are 4 or 5 bits long, with the fifth bit of 4-bit opcodes used to specify which register to use. The *register specifier* is 0 for register A (the accumulator), which is the only register that we will use. Thus the register specifier is only color coded in our diagrams when it is part of the opcode. [See Figure 6.2(b).]

The 3-bit *addressing mode specifier* (shaded green) indicates how to interpret the operand part of the instruction. If the addressing mode is 000, the operand is in the operand specifier of the instruction. This addressing mode is called immediate (i). If the addressing mode is 001, the operand is the memory address named in the operand specifier. This addressing mode is called direct (d). (Other addressing modes also exist, but we do not cover them here.) The distinction between the immediate addressing mode and the direct addressing mode is very important because it determines where the data involved in the operation is stored or is to be stored. See Figure 6.3. Locations that contain addresses are shaded in orange; operands are shaded in gray.

FIGURE 6.3 Difference between immediate addressing mode and direct addressing mode

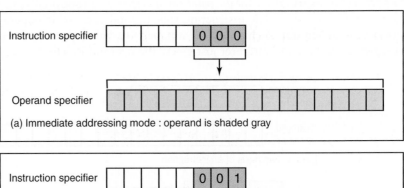

(a) Immediate addressing mode : operand is shaded gray

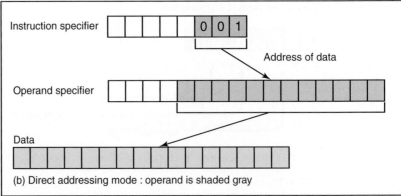

(b) Direct addressing mode : operand is shaded gray

Instructions that do not have an operand (data to be manipulated) are called *unary instructions*; they do not have an operand specifier. That is, unary instructions are only 1 byte long rather than 3 bytes long.

Some Sample Instructions

Let's look at some specific instructions in isolation and then put them together to write a program. Figure 6.4 contains the 4-bit operation code (or opcode) for the operations we are covering.

0000 Stop execution   During the fetch–execute cycle, when the operation code is all zeros, the program halts. Stop is a unary instruction, so it occupies only one byte. The three rightmost bits in the byte are ignored.

1100 Load the operand into the A register   This instruction loads one word (two bytes) into the A register. The mode specifier determines where the word is located. Thus the load opcode has different meanings depending on the addressing mode specifier. The mode specifier determines whether the value to be loaded is in the operand part of the instruction (the second and third bytes of the instruction) or is in the place named in the operand.

Let's look at concrete examples of each of these combinations. Here is the first 3-byte instruction:

The addressing mode is immediate, meaning that the value to be loaded into the A register is in the operand specifier. That is, the data is in the

Opcode	Meaning of Instruction
0000	Stop execution
1100	Load the operand into the A register
1110	Store the contents of the A register into the operand
0111	Add the operand to the A register
1000	Subtract the operand to the A register
01001	Character input to the operand
01010	Character output from the operand

FIGURE 6.4   Subset of Pep/8 instructions

operand specifier, so it is shaded gray. After execution of this instruction, the contents of the second and third bytes of the instruction (the operand specifier) would be loaded into the A register (the accumulator). That is, the A register would contain 0007 and the original contents of A would be lost.

Here is another load instruction:

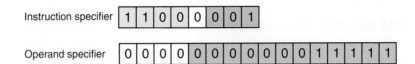

The addressing mode is direct, which means that the operand itself is not in the operand specifier (second and third bytes of the instruction); instead, the operand specifier holds the *address* (orange) of where the operand resides in memory. Thus, when this instruction is executed, the contents of *location* 001F would be loaded into the A register. Note that we have shaded the bits that represent a memory address in orange just as we have used orange for other addresses. The A register holds a word (2 bytes), so when an address is used to specify a word (rather than a single byte) as in this case, the address given is of the leftmost byte in the word. Thus the contents of adjacent locations 001F and 0020 are loaded into the A register. The contents of the operand (001F and 0020) are not changed.

1110 Store the A register to the operand   This instruction stores the contents of the A register into the location specified in the operand, which is either the operand itself or the place named in the operand.

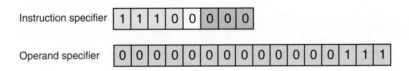

This instruction stores the value in the A register into the operand specifier of the instruction itself. The operand is gray to indicate that it consists of data.

Instruction specifier | 1 1 1 0 0 0 0 1

Operand specifier | 0 0 0 0 0 0 0 0 0 0 0 0 1 0 1 0

This instruction stores the contents of the A register into the word beginning at location 000A. It is invalid to use an immediate addressing mode with a store opcode; that is, we cannot try to store the contents of a register into the operand specifier.

0111 **Add the operand to the A register**   Like the load operation, the add operation uses the addressing mode specifier, giving alternative interpretations. The two alternatives for this instruction are shown below with the explanation following each instruction.

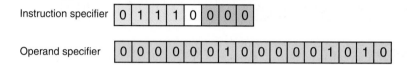

Instruction specifier `0 1 1 1 0 0 0 0`

Operand specifier `0 0 0 0 0 0 1 0 0 0 0 0 1 0 1 0`

The contents of the second and third bytes of the instruction (the operand specifier) are added to the contents of the A register (20A in hex). Thus we have shaded the operand specifier to show that it is data.

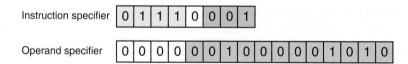

Instruction specifier `0 1 1 1 0 0 0 1`

Operand specifier `0 0 0 0 0 0 1 0 0 0 0 0 1 0 1 0`

Because the address mode specifier is direct, the contents of the operand specified in the second and third bytes of the instruction (location 020A) are added into the A register.

1000 **Subtract the operand** This instruction is just like the add operation except that the operand is subtracted from the A register rather than added. As with the load and add operations, there are variations of this instruction depending on the addressing mode.

0100 **Character input to the operand** This instruction allows the program to enter an ASCII character from the input device while the program is running. Only direct addressing is allowed, so the character is stored in the address shown in the operand specifier.

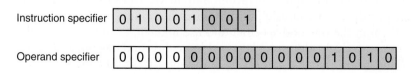

Instruction specifier `0 1 0 0 1 0 0 1`

Operand specifier `0 0 0 0 0 0 0 0 0 0 0 0 1 0 1 0`

This instruction reads an ASCII character from the input device and stores it into location 000A.

`0101` **Character output from the operand**　This instruction sends an ASCII character to the output device while the program is running. The addressing mode may be either immediate or direct.

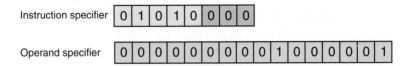

| Instruction specifier | 0 | 1 | 0 | 1 | 0 | 0 | 0 | 0 |

| Operand specifier | 0 | 0 | 0 | 0 | 0 | 0 | 0 | 0 | 0 | 1 | 0 | 0 | 0 | 0 | 0 | 1 |

Because immediate addressing is specified, this instruction writes out the ASCII character stored in the operand specifier. The operand specifier contains 1000001, which is 41 in hex and 65 in decimal. The ASCII character corresponding to that value is 'A', so the letter A is written to the screen.

| Instruction specifier | 0 | 1 | 0 | 1 | 0 | 0 | 0 | 1 |

| Operand specifier | 0 | 0 | 0 | 0 | 0 | 0 | 0 | 0 | 0 | 0 | 0 | 0 | 1 | 0 | 1 | 0 |

Because direct addressing is used, this instruction writes out the ASCII character stored in the location named in the operand specifier, location 000A. What is written? We cannot say unless we know the contents of location 000A. The ASCII character corresponding to whatever is stored at that location is printed.

6.3　A Program Example

We are now ready to write our first machine-language program: Let's write "Hello" on the screen. There are six instructions in this program: five to write out a character and one to indicate the end of the process. The instruction to write a character on the screen is 0101, the "Character output from the operand" operation. Should we store the characters in memory and write them using direct addressing mode, or should we just store them in the operand specifier and use immediate addressing mode? Let's use immediate addressing here and leave direct addressing as an exercise. This means that the addressing mode specifier is 000 and the ASCII code for the letter goes into the third byte of the instruction.

Action	Binary Instruction	Hex Instruction
Write "H"	01010000 0000000001001000	50 0048
Write "e"	01010000 0000000001100101	50 0065
Write "l"	01010000 0000000001101100	50 006C
Write "l"	01010000 0000000001101100	50 006C
Write "o"	01010000 0000000001101111	50 006F
Stop	00000000	00

The machine-language program is shown in binary in the second column and in hexadecimal in the third column. We must construct the operation specifier in binary because it is made up of a 4-bit opcode, a 1-bit register specifier, and a 3-bit addressing mode specifier. Once we have the complete 8 bits, we can convert the instruction to hexadecimal. Alternatively, we could construct the operand specifier directly in hexadecimal.

We used double quotes when referring to a collection of characters like "Hello" and single quotes when referring to a single character. This pattern is commonly used in programming languages, so we follow this convention here.

■ Hand Simulation

Let's simulate this program's execution by following the steps of the fetch–execute cycle. Such traces by hand really drive home the steps that the computer carries out.

Recall the four steps in the fetch–execute cycle:

1. Fetch the next instruction (from the place named in the program counter).
2. Decode the instruction (and update the program counter).
3. Get data (operand) if needed.
4. Execute the instruction.

There are six instructions in our program. Let's assume that they are in contiguous places in memory, with the first instruction stored in memory locations 0000–0002. Execution begins by loading 0000 into the program counter (PC). At each stage of execution, let's examine the PC (shown in yellow) and the instruction register (IR). The program does not access the A register, so we do not bother to show it. At the end of the first fetch, the PC and the IR look like the following diagram. (We continue to use color to emphasize the addresses, opcode, address mode specifier, and data.) Notice that the program counter is incremented as soon as the instruction has been accessed.

Program counter (PC): ` | | | 0 0 0 0 0 0 0 0 0 0 1 1`

Instruction register (IR):
- `0 1 0 1 0 0 0 0`
- `0 0 0 0 0 0 0 0 0 1 0 0 1 0 0 0`

This instruction is decoded as a "Write character to output" instruction using immediate addressing mode. Because this instruction takes 3 bytes, the PC is incremented by 3. The data is retrieved from the operand specifier in the IR, the instruction is executed, and 'H' is written on the screen.

The second fetch is executed and the PC and IR are as follows:

Program counter (PC): ` | | | 0 0 0 0 0 0 0 0 0 1 1 0`

Instruction register (IR):
- `0 1 0 1 0 0 0 0`
- `0 0 0 0 0 0 0 0 0 1 1 0 0 1 0 1`

This instruction is decoded as another "Write character to output" instruction using immediate addressing mode. The instruction takes 3 bytes, so the PC is again incremented by 3. The data is retrieved, the instruction is executed, and 'e' is written on the screen.

The next three instructions are executed exactly the same way. After the 'o' has been written, the PC and IR look as follows:

Program counter (PC): ` | | | 0 0 0 0 0 0 0 0 1 1 1 1`

Instruction register (IR):
- `0 0 0 0 0 0 0 0`
- (empty)

The opcode is decoded as a "Stop" instruction, so the contents of the addressing mode and the operand specifier are ignored. At this point, the fetch–execute cycle stops.

■ Pep/8 Simulator

Recall that the instructions are written in the Pep/8 machine language, which doesn't correspond to any particular CPU's machine language. We have just hand simulated the program. Can we execute it on the computer? Yes, we can. Pep/8 is a virtual (hypothetical) machine, but we have a *simulator* for the machine. That is, we have a program that behaves just like the Pep/8 virtual machine behaves. To run a program, we enter the hexadecimal code byte by byte, with exactly one blank between each byte, and end the program with zz. The simulator recognizes two z's as the end of the program. Here is a screen shot of the Pep/8 machine-language program:

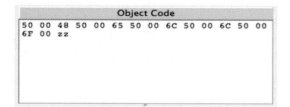

Let's go through the steps required to enter and execute a program. We assume that the Pep/8 simulator has been installed. To start the program, click on the Pep8 icon. One of several screens might appear, but each contains a section marked "Object Code." Enter your program in this window as described previously. You are now ready to run your program. Go to the menu bar. Here is a shot of the portion that you need:

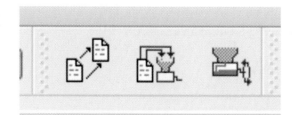

Click on the middle of these three icons, which calls the loader. After you click on this icon, your program is loaded into the Pep/8 memory.

Be sure the Terminal I/O button is darkened (pressed). Now click on the rightmost icon, which is the execute button. The program is executed and "Hello" appears in the output window. For everything that we do in this chapter, the Terminal I/O button should be darkened. This area is where you input and output values.

≫ **Loader** A piece of software that takes a machine-language program and places it into memory

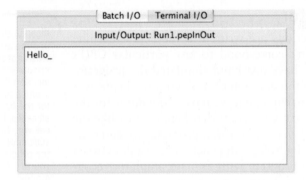

Pep/8 has a feature that lets you watch what is happening in the CPU as each instruction is executed. Here is a screen shot of the CPU after the program has been loaded. Notice that the "Trace Program" check box has been marked. This screen includes several boxes that we have not covered, but you can readily see the "Program Counter," "Instruction Register," and "OpCode" labels.

When the "Trace Program" option is checked, press the Single Step button and the first instruction will be executed. Continue pressing the Single Step button, and you can see the register values change.

Before we leave our machine code example, let's input two letters and print them out in reverse order. We can choose a place to put the input as it is read somewhere beyond the code. In this case we choose 0F and 12. We use direct addressing mode.

Action	Binary Instruction	Hex Instruction
Input a letter into location F	01001001 0000000000001000	49 000F
Input a letter into F + 1	01001001 0000000000010010	49 0010
Write out second letter	01010001 0000000000001000	51 0010
Write out first letter	01010001 0000000000001010	51 000F
Stop	00000000	00

Here is the object code and output window after entering 'A' and 'B':

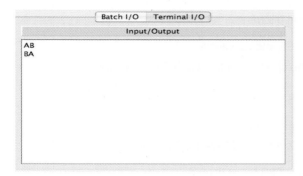

6.4 Assembly Language

As we pointed out in Chapter 1, the first tools developed to help the programmer were assembly languages. Assembly languages assign mnemonic letter codes to each machine-language instruction. The programmer uses these letter codes in place of binary digits. The instructions in an assembly language are much like those we would use to tell someone how to do a calculation on a hand-held calculator.

Because every program that is executed on a computer eventually must be in the form of the computer's machine language, a program called an assembler reads each of the instructions in mnemonic form and translates

>> **Assembly language** A low-level programming language in which a mnemonic represents each of the machine-language instructions for a particular computer

>> **Assembler** A program that translates an assembly-language program in machine code

it into the machine-language equivalent. Also, because each type of computer has a different machine language, there are as many assembly languages and translators as there are types of machines.

■ Pep/8 Assembly Language

The goal of this section is not to make you become an assembly-language programmer, but rather to make you appreciate the advantages of assembly-language programming over machine coding. With this goal in mind, we cover only a few of Pep/8's assembly-language features here. We begin by examining the same operations we looked at in the last sections plus three other useful operations. In Pep/8's assembly language, there is a different opcode for each register, the operand is specified by "0x" and the hexadecimal value, and the addressing mode specifier is indicated by the letters 'i' or 'd'.

Mnemonic	Operand, Mode Specifier	Meaning of Instruction
STOP		Stop execution
LDA	0x008B,i	Load 008B into register A
LDA	0x008B,d	Load the contents of location 8B into register A
STA	0x008B,d	Store the contents of register A into location 8B
ADDA	0x008B,i	Add 008B to register A
ADDA	0x008B,d	Add the contents of location 8B to register A
SUBA	0x008B,i	Subtract 008B for register A
SUBA	0x008B,d	Subtract the contents of location 8B from register A
BR		Branch to the location specified in the operand specifier
CHARI	0x008B,d	Read a character and store it into location 8B
CHARO	0x008B,i	Write the character 8B
	0x000B,d	Write the character stored in location 0B
DECI	0x008B,d	Read a decimal number and store it into location 8B
DECO	0x008B,i	Write the decimal number 139 (8B in hex)
DECO	0x008B,d	Write the decimal number stored in location 8B

Did you wonder why we didn't do any arithmetic in machine language? Well, the output was defined only for characters. If we had done arithmetic, we would have had to convert the numbers to character form to see the results, and this is more complex than we wished to get. The Pep/8 assembly language provides the mnemonics DECI and DECO, which allow us to do decimal input and output. This terminology is somewhat misleading, however, because these operations actually involve calls to a series of instructions behind the scenes.

■ Assembler Directives

In a machine-language program, every instruction is stored in memory and then executed. Beginning with assembly languages, most programming languages have two kinds of instructions: instructions to be translated and instructions to the translating program. Here are a few useful assembler directives for the Pep/8 assembler—that is, instructions to the assembler. These instructions to the assembler are also called pseudo-operations.

» Assembler directives Instructions to the translating program

Pseudo-op	Argument	Meaning
.ASCII	"Str\x00"	Represents a string of ASCII bytes
.BLOCK	Number of bytes	Creates a block of bytes
.WORD	Value	Creates a word and stores a value in it
.END		Signals the end of the assembly-language program

■ Assembly-Language Version of Program Hello

Let's take a look at the assembly-language program that writes "Hello" on the screen. Pep/8 assembly language allows us to directly specify the character to be output and to add a comment beside the instruction. A comment is text written for the human reader of the program that explains what is happening. Comments are an essential part of writing any program. The assembler ignores everything from the semicolon through the end of the line; it is a comment.

» Comment Explanatory text for the human reader

```
CHARO   0x0048,i; Output an 'H'
CHARO   0x0065,i; Output an 'e'
CHARO   0x006C,i; Output an 'l'
CHARO   0x006C,i; Output an 'l'
CHARO   0x006F,i; Output an 'o'
STOP
.END
```

FIGURE 6.5   Assembly process

This code is entered into the Source Code window. The icon to the left of the load icon is the assembler icon. Click this icon, and the object code into which the program is translated appears in the Object Code window. The Assembler Listing window shows the address to which an instruction has been assigned, the object code, and the assembly-language code; it is shown here:

	Addr	Code	Mnemon	Operand	Comment
☐	0000	500048	CHARO	0x0048,i	
☐	0003	500065	CHARO	0x0065,i	
☐	0006	50006C	CHARO	0x006C,i	
☐	0009	50006C	CHARO	0x006C,i	
☐	000C	50006F	CHARO	0x006F,i	
☐	000F	00	STOP		

Assembler Listing

The process of running a program coded in an assembly language is illustrated in Figure 6.5. The *input* to the assembler is a program written in assembly language. The *output* from the assembler is a program written in machine code. You can see why the creation of assembly language represented such an important step in the history of programming languages: It removed many of the details of machine-language programming by abstracting the instructions into words. Although it added a step to the process of executing a program (the translation of assembly to machine code), that extra step is well worth the effort to make the programmer's life easier.

■ A New Program

Let's make a step up in complexity and write a program to read in three numbers and write out their sum. How would we do this task by hand? If we had a calculator, we would first clear the total; that is, we would set the sum to zero. Then we would get the first number and add it to the total, get the second number and add it to the total, and finally get the third number and add it to the total. The result would be what is in the accumulator of the calculator. We can model our computer program on this by-hand solution.

The most complex problem is that that we must associate four identifiers with places in memory, and this requires knowing how many places the program itself takes—that is, if we put the data at the end of the program. Let's make this process easier by putting our data before the program. We can start associating identifiers with memory locations beginning with location 0001 and have the fetch–execute cycle skip over these places to continue with the program. In fact, we can assign identifiers to the memory locations and use these names later in the program. We set up space for the sum using the .WORD pseudo-op so that we can set the contents to 0. We set up space for the three numbers using the .BLOCK pseudo-op.

```
        BR         main      ; Branch around data
sum:    .WORD      0x0000    ; Set up word with zero
num1:   .BLOCK 2             ; Set up a two byte block for num1
num2:   .BLOCK 2             ; Set up a two byte block for num2
num3:   .BLOCK 2             ; Set up a two byte block for num3

main:   LDA        sum,d     ; Load zero into the accumulator
        DECI       num1,d    ; Read and store num1
        ADDA       num1,d    ; Add num1 to accumulator
        DECI       num2,d    ; Read and store num2
        ADDA       num2,d    ; Add num2 to accumulator
        DECI       num3,d    ; Read and store num3
        ADDA       num3,d    ; Add num3 to accumulator
        STA        sum,d     ; Store accumulator into sum
        DECO       sum,d     ; Output sum
        STOP                 ; Stop the processing
        .END                 ; End of the program
```

Here is the assembler listing for this program, followed by the Input/Output window after we execute the program. Note that the user keys in the three values, and the program prints their sum.

```
                                    Assembler Listing
      Addr   Code   Symbol   Mnemon   Operand   Comment
☐    0000   04000B            BR       main      ; Branch around data
☐    0003   0000   sum:       .WORD    0x0000    ; Set up word with zero
☐    0005   0000   num1:      .BLOCK   2         ; Set up a two byte block for num1
☐    0007   0000   num2:      .BLOCK   2         ; Set up a two byte block for num2
☐    0009   0000   num3:      .BLOCK   2         ; Set up a two byte block for num3

☐    000B   C10003 main:      LDA      sum,d     ; Load zero into the accumulator
☐    000E   310005            DECI     num1,d    ; Read and store num1
☐    0011   710005            ADDA     num1,d    ; Add num1 to accumulator
☐    0014   310007            DECI     num2,d    ; Read and store num2
☐    0017   710007            ADDA     num2,d    ; Add num2 to accumulator
☐    001A   310009            DECI     num3,d    ; Read and store num3
☐    001D   710009            ADDA     num3,d    ; Add num3 to accumulator
☐    0020   E10003            STA      sum,d     ; Store accumulator into sum
☐    0023   390003            DECO     sum,d     ; Output sum
☐    0026   00                STOP               ; Stop the processing
                              .END               ; End of the program


      Symbol   Value
☐    sum        0003
☐    num1       0005
☐    num2       0007
☐    num3       0009
☐    main       000B
```

```
                                    Input/Output
23
14
2
39
```

■ A Program with Branching

We have shown that the program counter can be changed with a BR
instruction that sets the program counter to the address of an instruction
to execute next. Are there other ways to change the flow of control of the
program? Can we ask a question and take one or another action on the
basis of the answer to our question? Sure—let's see how. Here are two
useful opcodes and their meaning:

Mnemonic	Operand, Mode Specifier	Meaning of Instruction
BRLT	i	Set the PC to the operand if the A register is less than zero
BREQ	i	Set the PC to the operand if the A register is equal to zero

For example:

```
LDA   num1,d      ; Load num1 into A register
BRLT lessThan     ; Branch to lessThan if num1 is less than 0
```

If the value stored in num1 is negative when it is loaded into the A register, the PC is set to location lessThan. If the value is not negative, the PC is unchanged.

Let's change the previous program so that it prints the sum if it is positive and displays an error message if the sum is negative. Where should the test go? Just before the contents of the answer is stored into location sum, we can test the A register and print 'E' if it is negative.

We can use the BRLT instruction to test whether the sum is negative. If the A register is negative, the operand beside the BRLT instruction replaces the contents of the program counter so that the next instruction comes from there. We need to give the instruction a name, so we can branch to it. Let's call the instruction that prints the error message negMsg. When the error message has been written, we must branch back to the line that says STOP, which means we must name that line. Let's name it finish.

Here is the source code of this changed program. Note that we have reduced the number of comments. If the comment just duplicates the instruction, it can be a distraction instead of a help.

```
            BR        main        ; Branch around data
sum:        .WORD     0x0000      ; Set up word with zero
num1:       .BLOCK 2              ; Set up a two byte block for num1
num2:       .BLOCK 2              ; Set up a two byte block for num2
num3:       .BLOCK 2              ; Set up a two byte block for num3

negMsg:  CHARO     0x0045,i  ; Print 'E'
            BR        finish      ; Branch to STOP instruction
main:    LDA       sum,d       ; Load zero into the accumulator
            DECI      num1,d      ; Read and add three numbers
            ADDA      num1,d
            DECI      num2,d
            ADDA      num2,d
            DECI      num3,d
            ADDA      num3,d
            BRLT      negMsg      ; Branch to negMsg of A < 0
            STA       sum,d       ; Store result into sum
            DECO      sum,d       ; Output sum
finish:  STOP                  ;
            .END                  ;
```

Here is the assembler listing, followed by a screen shot of the input and output:

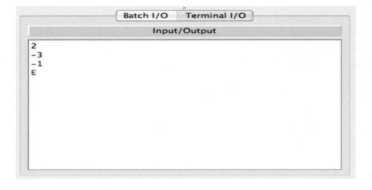

Addr	Code	Symbol	Mnemon	Operand	Comment
				Assembler Listing	
0000	040011		BR	main	; Branch around data
0003	0000	sum:	.WORD	0x0000	; Set up word with zero
0005	0000	num1:	.BLOCK	2	; Set up a two byte block for num1
0007	0000	num2:	.BLOCK	2	; Set up a two byte block for num2
0009	0000	num3:	.BLOCK	2	; Set up a two byte block for num3
000B	500045	negMsg:	CHARO	0x0045,i	; Print 'E'
000E	04002F		BR	finish	; Branch to STOP instruction
0011	C10003	main:	LDA	sum,d	; Load zero into the accumulator
0014	310005		DECI	num1,d	; Read and add three numbers
0017	710005		ADDA	num1,d	
001A	310007		DECI	num2,d	
001D	710007		ADDA	num2,d	
0020	310009		DECI	num3,d	
0023	710009		ADDA	num3,d	
0026	08000B		BRLT	negMsg	; Branch to negMsg of A < 0
0029	E10003		STA	sum,d	; Store result into sum
002C	390003		DECO	sum,d	; Output sum
002F	00	finish:	STOP		;
			.END		;

Symbol	Value
sum	0003
num1	0005
num2	0007
num3	0009
negMsg	000B
main	0011
finish	002F

Batch I/O	Terminal I/O
Input/Output	

```
2
-3
-1
E
```

■ A Program with a Loop

What if we wanted to read and sum four values? Five values? Any number of values? We can input how many values we want to sum (limit) and write the code to read and sum that many values. We do so by creating a counting loop—a section of code that repeats a specified number of times. Within the code of the loop, a value is read and summed. How can we keep track of how many values we have read? We can make a hash mark each time we repeat the loop and compare the sum of the hash marks to the number of times we wish to repeat the loop. Actually, our hash mark is a place in memory where we store a 0; let's call it counter. Each time the loop is repeated, we add a 1 to that place in memory. When counter equals limit, we are finished with the reading and counting.

In the next section we describe pseudocode, a less wordy way of explaining what we do in branching and looping situations. For now, here is the code that reads in the number of data values to read and sum, reads and sums them, and prints the result:

```
          BR      main         ; Branch around data
sum:      .WORD   0x0000       ; Set up word with zero
num:      .BLOCK  2            ; Set up a block for num
limit:    .BLOCK  2            ; Set up a block for limit
counter:  .WORD   0x0000       ; Set up counter

main:     DECI    limit,d      ; Input limit
loop:     DECI    num,d        ; Read and sum limit numbers
          LDA     num,d
          ADDA    sum,d
          STA     sum,d
          LDA     counter,d    ; Load counter into A register
          ADDA    1,i          ; Add one to counter
          STA     counter,d
          CPA     limit,d      ; Compare counter and limit
          BREQ    quit         ; Go to quit if equal
          BR      loop         ; Repeat loop
quit:     DECO    sum,d        ; Output sum
          STOP
          .END
```

Here is the assembler listing, followed by a screen shot of a run:

```
                                    Assembler Listing
Addr  Code    Symbol   Mnemon  Operand   Comment
0000  04000B           BR      main      ; Branch around data

0003  0000    sum:     .WORD   0x0000    ; Set up word with zero

0005  0000    num:     .BLOCK  2         ; Set up a block for num
0007  0000    limit:   .BLOCK  2
                       ; Set up a block for limit
0009  0000    counter: .WORD   0x0000    ; Set up counter

000B  310007  main:    DECI    limit,d   ; Input limit
000E  310005  loop:    DECI    num,d     ; Read and sum limit numbers
0011  C10005           LDA     num,d
0014  710003           ADDA    sum,d
0017  E10003           STA     sum,d
001A  C10009           LDA     counter,d ; Load counter into A register
001D  700001           ADDA    1,i       ; Add one to counter
0020  E10009           STA     counter,d
0023  B10007           CPA     limit,d   ; Compare counter and limit
0026  0A002C           BREQ    quit      ; Go to quit if equal
0029  04000E           BR      loop      ; Repeat loop
002C  390003  quit:    DECO    sum,d     ; Output sum
002F  00               STOP
                       .END


Symbol    Value
sum        0003
num        0005
limit      0007
counter    0009
main       000B
loop       000E
quit       002C


No errors. Successful assembly.
```

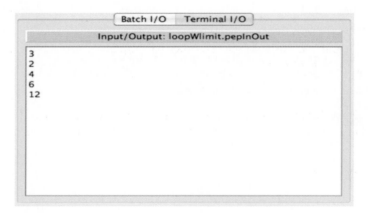

```
           Batch I/O   Terminal I/O
        Input/Output: loopWlimit.pepInOut

        3
        2
        4
        6
        12
```

6.5 Expressing Algorithms

In the previous sections, we have written programs to write out a greeting, read numbers in and write them out in reverse order, add three numbers together and print an error message if the sum is negative, and enter a value and read and sum that many numbers. We expressed the solution to each problem in paragraph form and then wrote the code. In computing, the plan for a solution is called an **algorithm**. As you saw, going from the problem in paragraph form to the code is not always a clear-cut process. **Pseudocode** is a language that allows us to express algorithms in a clearer form.

Pseudocode Functionality

In Chapter 1, we talked about the layers of language surrounding the actual machine. We didn't mention pseudocode at that time because it is not a computer language, but rather a shorthand-like language that people use to express actions. There are no special grammar rules for pseudocode, but to express actions we must be able to represent the following concepts.

Variables

Names that appear in pseudocode algorithms refer to places in memory where values are stored. The name should reflect the role of the content in the algorithm.

Assignment

If we have variables, we must have a way to put a value into one. We use the statement

Set sum to 0

to store a value into the variable sum. Another way of expressing the same concept uses a back arrow (<—):

sum <— 1

If we assign values to variables with the assignment statement, how do we access them later? We access values in sum and num in the following statement:

Set sum to sum + num

or

sum <— sum + num

The Music Genome Project
In 2002, Will Glaser, Jon Craft, and Tim Westergren founded the company Savage Beast Technologies and created the Music Genome Project. The project, which was created to capture "the essence of music at the most fundamental level," uses hundreds of musical attributes or "genes" to describe scores, as well as an intricate mathematical formula to analyze them. The project has analyzed tens of thousands of diverse scores and artists for attributes such as melody, harmony and rhythm, instrumentation, orchestration, arrangement, and lyrics. The results are incorporated in a program named Pandora and used to provide music recommendations for users listening on the Internet. When a user enters a song title into Pandora's search function, Pandora scans all of its analyzed song information to provide the most accurate and enjoyable playlist possible.

» **Algorithm** A plan or outline of a solution; a logical sequence of steps that solve a problem

» **Pseudocode** A language designed to express algorithms

The value stored in sum is added to the value in num and the result is stored back in sum. Thus, when a variable is used on the right side of the "to" or <—, the value of the variable is accessed. When a variable is used following "Set" or on the left side of <—, a value is stored into the variable.

The value being stored into a variable can be a single value (as in 0) or an *expression* made up of variables and operators (as in sum + num).

Input/Output

Most computer programs simply process data of some sort, so we must be able to input data values from the outside world and output the result on the screen. We can use the word "write" for output and the word "read" for input.

Write "Enter the number of values to read and sum"
Read num

The characters between the double quotation marks are called *strings* and tell the user what to enter or to describe what is written. It doesn't matter which exact words you use: Display or Print would be equivalent to Write; Get or Input would be synonyms for Read. Remember, pseudocode algorithms are written for a human to translate into some programming language at a later stage. Being consistent within a project is better style—both for you as you are working and for the person following you who may have to interpret what you have written.

The last two output statements demonstrate an important point:

Write "Err"
Write sum

The first writes the characters between the double quotation marks on the screen. The second writes the *contents* of the variable sum on the screen. The value in sum is not changed.

Selection

The selection construct allows a choice between performing an action or skipping it. Selection also allows a choice between two actions. The condition in parentheses determines which course of action to follow. For example, the following pseudocode segment prints the sum or an error message. (Sound familiar?)

// Read and sum three numbers
IF (sum < 0)
    Print error message
ELSE
    Print sum
// Stop or whatever comes next

We use indention to group statements (only one in this case). Control goes back to the statement that is not indented. The // introduces a comment to the reader, which is not part of the algorithm.

This version of the selection construct is called the *if-then-else* version because the algorithm chooses between two actions. The *if-then* version is the case where an action is executed or skipped. If we wanted to print the sum in any event, we could show the algorithm this way.

```
// Read and sum three numbers
IF(sum < 0)
      Print error message
Print sum
// Stop or whatever comes next
```

Repetition

The repetition construct allows instructions to be repeated. In the summing problem, for example, a counter is initialized, tested, and incremented. Pseudocode allows us to outline the algorithm so that the pattern becomes clear. Like the selection construct, the expression in parentheses beside the WHILE is a test. If the test is true, the indented code is executed. If the test is false, execution skips to the next non-indented statement.

```
Set limit to number of values to sum
WHILE (counter < limit)
      Read num
      Set sum to sum + num
      Set counter to counter + 1
// Rest of program
```

The expression in parentheses beside the WHILE and the IF is a **Boolean expression**, which evaluates to either true or false. In the IF, if the expression is true, the indented block is executed. If the expression is false, the indented block is skipped and the block below the ELSE is executed if it exists. In the WHILE, if the expression is true, the indented code is executed. If the expression is false, execution skips to the next non-indented statement. We are putting WHILE, IF, and ELSE in all capital letters because they are often used directly in various programming languages. They have special meanings in computing.

Table 6.1 summarizes these statements and shows examples or the words that each uses.

» **Boolean expression** An expression that when evaluated is either true or false

TABLE 6.1 Pseudocode Statements

Construct	What It Means	Words Used or Example
Variables	Represent named places into which values are stored and from which values are retrieved.	Names that represent the role of a value in a problem are just written in pseudocode
Assignment	Storing a value into a variable.	Set number to 1 number <—1
Input/output	Input: reading in a value, probably from the keyboard. Output: displaying the contents of a variable or a string, probably on the screen.	Read number Get number Write number Display number Write "Have a good day"
Repetition (iteration, looping)	Repeat one or more statements as long as a condition is true.	WHILE (condition) //Execute indented statement(s)

Selection: *if-then*	If a condition is true, execute the indented statements; if a condition is not true, skip the indented statements.	IF (newBase = 10)
		    Write "You are converting"
		    Write "to the same base."
		//Rest of code

Selection: *if-then-else*	If a condition is true, execute the indented statements; if a condition is not true, execute the indented statements below ELSE.	IF (newBase = 10)
		    Write "You are converting"
		    Write "to the same base."
		ELSE
		    Write "This base is not the"
		    Write "same."
		//Rest of code

Here is the pseudocode algorithm for the program that read and summed three values and printed an error message if the total was negative:

```
Set sum to 0
Read num1
Set sum to sum + num1
Read num2
Set sum to sum + num2
Read num3
Set sum to sum + num3
IF (sum < 0)
    Write 'E'
ELSE
    Write sum
```

Here is the pseudocode algorithm for the program that input the number of values to read, read them, and printed the sum:

```
Set counter to 0
Set sum to 0
Read limit
WHILE (counter < limit)
      Read num
      Set sum to sum + num
      Set counter to counter + 1
Print sum
```

A pseudocode description must eventually be translated into a program that can be run on a computer. A pseudocode statement might have to be translated into many assembly-language statements, but into only one statement in a high-level language. For example, go back and look at the last Pep/8 program. Here are the instructions needed to create the loop:

```
limit:        .BLOCK 2   ; Set up a block for limit
counter:      .BLOCK 2   ; Set up counter
...
loop:
...
      LDA     counter,d  ; Load limit into A register
      ADDA    1,i        ; Add one to counter
      STA     counter,d  ; Store counter
      CPA     limit,d    ; Compare counter and limit
      BREQ    quit       ; Go to quit if equal
      BR      loop       ; Repeat loop
```

In most high-level languages, a loop can be written in one statement. In the next sections, we explore more about pseudocode.

■ Following a Pseudocode Algorithm

In Chapter 2, we introduced an algorithm for converting from base 10 to other bases. We expressed this algorithm in pseudocode for a human to follow.

```
WHILE (the quotient is not zero)
      Divide the decimal number by the new base
      Set the next digit to the left in the answer to the remainder
      Set the decimal number to the quotient
```

To refresh our memories, we apply this algorithm to convert decimal number 93 to octal. We divide 93 by 8 (the new base), giving a quotient of 11 and a remainder of 5. This is the first division, so 5 becomes the digit in the units position of the answer. The original decimal number (93) is replaced by the quotient, 11. The quotient is not 0, so we divide 11 by 8, giving a quotient of 1 and a remainder of 3. The digit 3 becomes the digit to the left of 5, giving a temporary answer of 35. The current decimal number (11) is replaced by the quotient 1. The quotient is not 0, so we divide it by 8, giving a quotient of 0 and a remainder of 1. The digit 1 becomes the leftmost digit in the answer, giving a value of 135. The quotient is 0, so the process ends.

This paragraph again shows how confusing English descriptions can be! First let's summarize the calculations.

Division	Quotient	Remainder	Answer
93/8	11	5	5
11/8	1	3	35
1/8	0	1	135

Now let's start over again, giving names to the values that we need to keep: decimalNumber, newBase, quotient, remainder, and answer. We depict these items as named boxes in which we write a value. [See Figure 6.6(a)]. We have put a question mark in boxes for which we do not know the contents.

In following an algorithm, we draw boxes for variables and fill in the values. The algorithm begins by asking if the value in quotient is 0. Let's assume it is not, but we'll come back to this point later. Figure 6.6(b) shows the results after the first time through the loop, dividing 93 by 8.

FIGURE 6.6 Walk-through of conversion algorithm

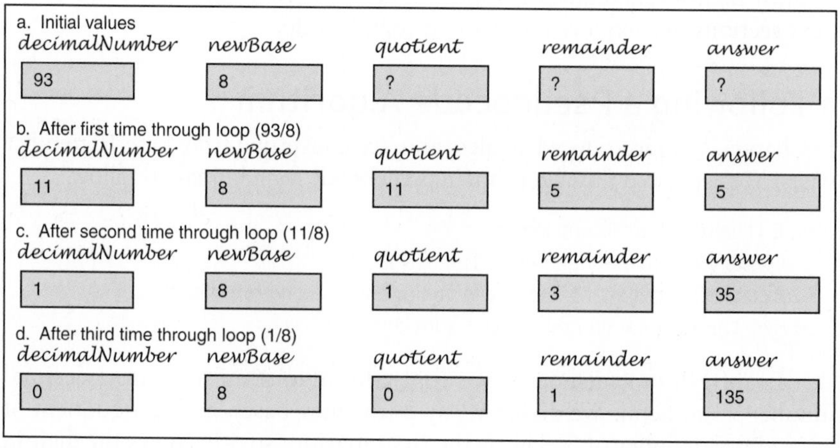

a. Initial values

decimalNumber	newBase	quotient	remainder	answer
93	8	?	?	?

b. After first time through loop (93/8)

decimalNumber	newBase	quotient	remainder	answer
11	8	11	5	5

c. After second time through loop (11/8)

decimalNumber	newBase	quotient	remainder	answer
1	8	1	3	35

d. After third time through loop (1/8)

decimalNumber	newBase	quotient	remainder	answer
0	8	0	1	135

The quotient is 11, so we repeat the process. Figure 6.6(c) displays the values after this repetition. The quotient is not 0, so we divide 1 by 8, giving the situation in Figure 6.6(d). Now quotient is 0, so the process stops.

One of our boxes, decimalNumber, originally contained the initial data value for the problem, the number to be converted. In a computer algorithm, we must give instructions to someone at the keyboard to input this value. Box newBase did not change throughout the process, but it, too, must be input from the keyboard because the algorithm is to change a decimal number into some other base, so the new base—base 8 in this case—must be input to the problem.

When we went through this algorithm, we knew that quotient had not been calculated yet, so we could assume it was not 0. In an algorithm for a computer to follow, we must make sure that quotient is not 0 by setting it to some nonzero value initially.

Here is the same algorithm rewritten in concrete steps from which a program could be written. DIV is an operator that returns the decimal quotient, and REM is an operator that returns the decimal remainder.

```
Write "Enter the new base"
Read newBase
Write "Enter the number to be converted"
Read decimalNumber
Set answer to 0
Set quotient to decimal number
WHILE (quotient is not zero)
    Set quotient to decimalNumber DIV newBase
    Set remainder to decimalNumber REM newBase
    Make the remainder the next digit to the left in the answer
    Set decimalNumber to quotient
Write "The answer is ",  answer
```

■ Writing a Pseudocode Algorithm

Here we will walk you through the algorithm development process on a small scale, pointing out strategies that we are using. In Chapter 7, we consider writing algorithms in more depth.

Let's read in pairs of positive numbers and print each pair in order. If there is more than one pair of numbers, we must have a loop. Here is a first approximation of the algorithm:

```
WHILE (not done)
    Write "Enter two values separated by a blank; press return"
    Read number1
    Read number2
    Print them in order
```

How do we know when to stop? That is, how do we break down *not done* into a question? We can ask the user to tell you how many pairs are to be entered. Here is the second pass:

```
Write "How many pairs of values are to be entered?"
Read numberOfPairs
Set pairsRead to 0
WHILE (pairsRead < numberOfPairs)
    Write "Enter two values separated by a blank; press return"
    Read number1
    Read number2
    Print them in order
```

How do we determine the order of the numbers? We compare the values using the conditional construct. If number1 is less than number2, we print number1 and then number2. Otherwise, we print number2 and then number1. Before we complete the algorithm, have we forgotten anything? numberRead never changes! We must increment numberRead.

```
Write "How many pairs of values are to be entered?"
Read numberOfPairs
Set numberRead to 0
WHILE (numberRead < numberOfPairs)
    Write "Enter two values separated by a blank; press return"
    Read number1
    Read number2
    IF (number1 < number2)
        Print number1 , " " , number2
    ELSE
        Print number2 , " " , number1
    Set numberRead to numberRead + 1
```

In going through the process of writing this algorithm, we used two major strategies. We *asked questions* and we *deferred details*. Asking questions is a strategy with which most of us are familiar. Deferring details means giving a task a name and then filling in the details of how to accomplish that task at a later time. That is, we first wrote the algorithm using *more pairs* and *print them in order*; then we filled in the details of how to accomplish these tasks at a later time. This strategy is known as *divide and conquer*.

An algorithm is not complete until it has been tested. We can use the same technique that we relied on to simulate the base conversion algorithm: We can choose data values and work through the code with paper and pencil. This algorithm has four variables that we must trace: numberOfPairs, numberRead, number1, and number2. Let's assume the user enters the following data when prompted:

3
10   20
20   10
10   10

Figure 6.7(a) shows the values of the variables at the beginning of the loop. numberRead is less than numberOfPairs, so the loop is entered. The prompt is issued and the two numbers are read. number1 is 10 and number2 is 20, so the *if* statement takes the *then* branch. number1 is printed, followed by number2. numberRead is incremented. Figure 6.7(b) shows the values at the end of the first repetition. numberRead is still less than numberOfPairs, so the code is repeated. The numbers are prompted for and read. number1 is 20 and number2 is 10, so the *else* branch is taken. number2 is printed, followed by number1. numberRead is incremented, resulting in the state of the variables at the end of the second iteration as shown in Figure 6.7(c).

numberRead is less than numberOfPairs, so the code is repeated. The inputs are prompted for and read, making number1 10 and number2 10. Because number1 is not less than number2, the *else* branch is taken. number2 is printed, followed by number1. Because the values are the same, it doesn't

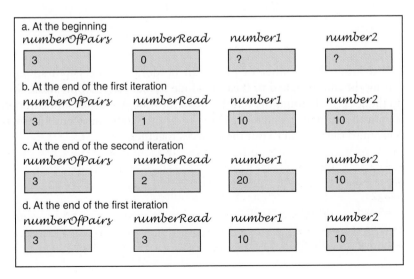

FIGURE 6.7   Walk-through of pairs algorithm

matter in which order they are printed. numberRead is incremented. numberRead is now not less than numberOfPairs, so the code is not repeated.

In this process, which is called desk checking, we sit at a desk with a pencil and paper and work through the design. It is useful to take actual data values and trace what happens to them as we reason about the design. This technique is simple but amazingly effective.

■ Translating a Pseudocode Algorithm

In Chapter 1, we described the layers of languages that were produced over time. In this chapter, we began with machine language (the lowest layer) and moved up one step to assembly language. How we translate a pseudocode algorithm depends on the language into which we are translating the algorithm. Here, where we are limited by the limits of an assembly language, one pseudocode statement requires several Pep/8 statements.

We have written our algorithm as an interactive program. That is, the program asks the user to do something. In this case, the first instruction was to write a request to the user to enter the number of pairs. This is exceptionally easy in a high-level language, but more complicated in Pep/8. First we have to set up the message using a .ASCII pseudo-operation and then set up the code to have it written out. Let's shorten the message to "Enter number." STRO, an instruction we have not seen before, is used to print the message.

```
mesg1:   .ASCII    "Enter number\x00"    ; First message
...
         STRO      mesg1                 ; Write message
```

Reading the number of pairs can be done in one Pep/8 statement. Setting the number read to 0 can be done in one pseudo-operation. We set up the loop by loading the number read into the A register and comparing it with the number to be read. Once within the loop, a second instruction is given to the user. Let's put these pieces together.

```
          Br        Main
mesg1:    .ASCII    "Enter number\x00"  ;
mesg2:    .ASCII    "Enter pairs\x00"   ;
numRead:  .WORD     0x00                ;
numPairs: .BLOCK    2                   ;
number1:  .BLOCK    2                   ;
```

```
number2:    .BLOCK    2               ;
Main:       STRO      mesg1,d         ;
            DECI      numPairs,d      ;
Begin:      STRO      mesg2,d         ;
            . . .
            BR        Begin           ;
```

Now we must translate the loop body, which requires writing a message, reading two values, and comparing them. The first two tasks require only one Pep/8 statement each, but the *if-then-else* statement will take more work. We must write the code to print each of the two statements, give names to the first instruction in each code block, and then determine which block should be executed.

Because you may never see assembly language again, we just present the source code listing. Note that we used one command that we have not covered: CPA, which compares the value in the accumulator to the value stored in a place in memory.

```
                                    Source Code
                    Br       Main        ; Branch to beginning of program
mesg1:      .ASCII  "Enter number\x00" ; Set up memory
mesg2:      .ASCII  "Enter pairs\x00"  ;
numRead:    .WORD   0x00               ;
numPairs:   .BLOCK  2                  ;
number1:    .BLOCK  2                  ;
number2:    .BLOCK  2                  ;
Main:               STRO     mesg1,d    ; Prompt for number of pairs
                    DECI     numPairs,d ; Read number of pairs
Begin:              STRO     mesg2,d    ; Prompt for pairs
                    DECI     number1,d  ;
                    DECI     number2,d  ;
                    LDA      number1,d  ; Load first number
                    CPA      number2,d  ; Compare to second number
                    BRLE     less       ; Branch to less if first less
                    BR       greater    ; Branch to greater if second less
test:               LDA      numRead,d  ; Increment counter
                    ADDA     1,i        ;
                    STA      numRead,d  ;
                    CPA      numPairs,d ; Compare with number to be read
                    BRLT     Begin      ; Repeat loop
                    BR       End        ; Branch to end
less:               DECO     number1,d  ; Output in order read
                    DECO     number2,d  ;
                    BR       test       ; Repeat loop
greater:            DECO     number2,d  ; Output in reverse order
                    DECO     number1,d  ;
                    BR       test       ; Repeat loop
End:                STOP                ; Stop execution
                    .END                ; Stop assembly
```

6.6 Testing

We briefly tested our programs by executing them to see if they produced the output we expected. However, there is far more to testing than just running the program once. Let's look at testing in more detail in the program that reads in three numbers and prints their sum. How do we test a specific program to determine its correctness? We design and implement a test plan. A test plan is a document that specifies how many times and with which data a program must be run to thoroughly test the program. Each set of input data values is called a test case. The test plan should list the reason for the choosing the data, the data values, and the expected output from each case.

The test cases should be chosen carefully. Several approaches to testing can be used to guide this process. Code coverage is an approach that designs test cases to ensure that each statement in the program is executed. Because the code is visible to the tester, this approach is also called clear-box testing. Data coverage, another approach, calls for designing test cases to ensure that the limits of the allowable data are covered. Because this approach is based solely on input data and not the code, it is also called black-box testing. Often testing entails a combination of these two approaches.

Test plan implementation involves running each of the test cases described in the test plan and recording the results. If the results are not as expected, you must go back to your design and find and correct the error(s). The process stops when each of the test cases gives the expected results. Note that an implemented test plan gives us a measure of confidence that the program is correct; however, all we know for sure is that our program works correctly on the test cases. Therefore, the quality of the test cases is extremely important.

In the case of the program that reads in three values and sums them, a clear-box test would include just three data values. There are no conditional statements in this program to test with alternate data. However, a clear-box test would not be sufficient here, because we need to try both negative and positive data values. The numbers that are being read in are stored in one word. The problem does not limit values to $\pm 2^{15} - 1$ but our implementation does. We should also try values at the limits of the size of the allowed input in the test plan, but because they are being summed, we need to be sure the sum does not exceed $\pm 2^{15} - 1$.

> **≫ Test plan** A document that specifies how a program is to be tested

> **≫ Code coverage (clear-box) testing** Testing a program or subprogram based on covering all the statements in the code

> **≫ Data coverage (black-box) testing** Testing a program or subprogram based on the possible input values, treating the code as a black box

> **≫ Test plan implementation** Using the test cases specified in a test plan to verify that a program outputs the predicted results

Reason for Test Case	Input Values	Expected Output	Observed Output
Assumption: Input values are no greater than 2^{15} or less than -2^{15}.			
Input three positive numbers	4, 6, 1	11	11
Input three negative numbers	−4, −6, −1	−11	−11
Input mixed numbers	4, 6, −1	9	9
	4, −6, −1	−1	−1
	−4, 6, 1	3	3
Input large numbers	32767, −1, + 1	32767	32767

To implement this test plan, we ran the program six times, once for each test case. The results were then written in the "Observed Output" column. They were what we predicted.

Summary

A computer can store, retrieve, and process data. A user can enter data into the machine, and the machine can display data so that the user can see it. At the lowest level of abstraction, instructions to the machine directly relate to these five operations.

A computer's machine language is the set of instructions that the machine's hardware is built to recognize and execute. Machine-language programs are written by entering a series of these instructions in their binary form. The Pep/8 is a virtual computer with an A register and two-part instructions. One part of the instruction tells which action the instruction performs, and the other part specifies where the data to be used (if any) can be found. Programs written using the Pep/8 instruction set can be run using a simulator, a program that behaves like the Pep/8 computer.

The Pep/8 assembly language is a language that allows the user to enter mnemonic codes for each instruction rather than binary numbers. Programs written in assembly language are translated into their machine-language equivalents, which are then executed using the Pep/8 simulator.

Pseudocode is a shorthand-like language that people use to express algorithms. It allows the user to name variables (places to put values), input values into variables, and print out the values stored in variables.

Pseudocode also allows us to describe algorithms that repeat actions and choose between alternative actions. Asking questions and deferring details are two problem-solving strategies used in algorithm design.

Programs, like algorithms, must be tested. Code coverage testing involves determining the input to the program by looking carefully at the program's code. Data coverage testing involves determining the input by considering all possible input values.

⚖ ETHICAL ISSUES ▶ Software Piracy and Copyrighting

Have you ever upgraded your operating system by borrowing the latest software from a friend? Or, when you spent only $50 to purchase sophisticated software, did you ignore your suspicion that this "steal" was too good to be true? The alarmingly casual attitude toward duplicating, downloading, and reselling software has made software piracy a critical issue for the computer industry. Research conducted by the Business Software Alliance indicated that, globally, $11.5 billion was lost in 2000 to pirated software. In 2003, the figure had risen to $29 billion. By 2007, the figure stood at $48 billion. The United States has the lowest piracy rate in the world, but lost revenues for U.S. software companies are still considerable.

Software piracy is the unlawful reproduction of copyrighted software or a violation of the terms of the agreement stated in the software's license. A software license is a document that outlines the terms by which the user may use the software purchased. When you lend software to a friend or download software onto multiple computers, you are failing to adhere to the license agreement and are, in fact, breaking the law.

Why is software copyrighted? Unlike an idea or written work, software has functionality. This unique quality distinguishes software from other forms of intellectual property and complicates its need for copyrighting. Richard Stallman, President of the Free Soft-

ware Foundation, argues that assigning copyrights to software hinders its development and that requiring licensing fees makes software cost-prohibitive for many people. Both of these negative consequences suggest to many people that standard copyrighting is not the best approach for software. Advocates of open-source code believe that a program's original source code should be in the public domain. Open-source code is code that anyone can download, enabling anyone to rewrite portions of the program, thereby participating in the software's evolution. While a number of programs, like the Linux operating system, have open-source code, companies such as Microsoft® have chosen to protect their code.

Respecting the copyrights of software, if it is not open code, is important from a number of perspectives. Research shows that in one year 107,000 jobs were lost in the United States because of pirated software. "Softlifting," or duplicating software from a friend's copy, contributes as much to this piracy problem as counterfeiting and "hard disk loading," which is the unauthorized installation of software into a computer's hard drive before it is sold. Using pirated software also puts the user at risk by exposing him or her to potential software viruses. The person who freely "borrows" software from a friend is actually stealing, and this action has significant ramifications.

🔑 Key Terms

Algorithm
Assembler
Assembler directives
Assembly language
Boolean expression
Code coverage (clear-box) testing
Comment
Desk checking

Data coverage (black-box) testing
Loader
Machine language
Pseudocode
Test plan
Test plan implementation
Virtual computer (machine)

⌘ Exercises

For Exercises 1–15, mark the answers true or false as follows:
  A. True
  B. False

1. Arithmetic can be performed in the instruction register.

2. Arithmetic can be performed in the A register.

3. Arithmetic can be performed in the accumulator.

4. LDA 0X008B,i loads 008B into register A.

5. ADDA 0x008B,i adds the contents of 008B to the A register.

6. The program counter and the instruction register are two names for the same place.

7. The A register and the accumulator are two names for the same place.

8. The instruction register is 3 bytes long.

9. The program counter is 3 bytes long.

10. The branch instruction, BR, branches to the location specified in the operand specifier.

11. The instruction specifier is 1 byte long.

12. If the data to be loaded into the accumulator is stored in the operand, the instruction specifier is 00.

13. If the data in the accumulator is to be stored in the place named in the operand, the instruction specifier is 00.

14. All Pep/8 instructions occupy 3 bytes.

15. At least one branching instruction is required in a loop.

Given the following state of memory (in hexadecimal), complete Exercises 16–20 by matching the problem to the solution shown.

```
0001   A2
0002   11
0003   00
0004   FF
```

    a. A2 11
    b. A2 12
    c. 00 02
    d. 11 00
    e. 00 FF

16. What are the contents of the A register after the execution of this instruction?

    C1 00 01

17. What are the contents of the A register after the execution of this instruction?

    C1 00 02

18. What are the contents of the A register after the execution of the following two instructions?

    C0 00 01

    70 00 01

19. What are the contents of the A register after the execution of the following two instructions?

    C1 00 01

    70 00 01

20. What are the contents of location 0001 after the execution of the following two instructions?

    C1 00 03

    E0 00 01

Exercises 21–60 are programs or short-answer questions.

21. What does it mean when we say that a computer is a *programmable* device?

22. List five operations that any machine language must include.

23. How many low-level tasks can each machine-language instruction perform?

24. What is a virtual machine? Discuss this definition in terms of the Pep/8 computer.

25. How many bits does an instruction take in Pep/8?

26. Describe the features of the Pep/8 CPU that we covered in this chapter.

27. Where is the data (operand) if the address mode specifier is
    a. 000?
    b. 001?

28. We discussed two mode specifiers. How many are there?

29. Distinguish between the IR (instruction register) and the PC (program counter).

30. How many bits are required to address the Pep/8 memory?

31. How many more cells could be added to memory without having to change the instruction format? Justify your answer.

32. Some Pep/8 instructions are unary, taking only 1 byte. Other instructions require 3 bytes. Given the instructions that we have covered in this chapter, would it be useful to define instructions that require only 2 bytes?

33. If the input character is A, what is the result of executing the following two instructions?

```
0001 49 00 06
0004 51 00 06
```

34. If the input number is 5, what is the contents of the A register after executing the following instructions?

```
0001   31 00 0F
0004   C1 00 0F
0007   70 00 02
```

35. Write the algorithm for writing out your name, given that the implementation language is Pep/8 machine code.

36. Write the machine-language program to implement the algorithm in Exercise 35.

37. Write the algorithm for writing out your name, given that the implementation language is Pep/8 assembly language.

38. Write the assembly-language program to implement the algorithm in Exercise 37.

39. Rewrite the example program in Section 6.3 using direct addressing.

40. Distinguish between the Pep/8 menu options *Assemble*, *Load*, and *Execute (run)*.

41. The following program seems to run, but does strange things with certain input values. Can you find the bug?

```
        BR      Main
sum:    .WORD   0x0000
num1:   .BLOCK  1
num2:   .BLOCK  1
num3:   .BLOCK  1
Main:   LDA     sum,d
        DECI    num1,d
        DECI    num2,d
        DECI    num3,d
        ADDA    num3,d
        ADDA    num2,d
        ADDA    num1,d
        STA     sum,d
        DECO    sum,d
        STOP
        .END
```

42. Correct the code in Exercise 41 and run the test plan outlined in the chapter.

43. Finish executing the test plan for the algorithm in the text that reads and sums three values.

44. Write a pseudocode algorithm that reads in three values and writes out the result of subtracting the second value from the sum of the first and third values.

45. Implement the algorithm in Exercise 44 as an assembly-language program.

46. Write and implement a test plan for the program in Exercise 45.

47. Design and implement, in assembly language, an algorithm that reads four values and prints the sum.

48. Is the test plan for a machine-language program valid for the same solution written in assembly language? Explain your answer.

49. Distinguish between the pseudo-operations .BLOCK and .WORD.

50. Distinguish between assembly-language pseudo-operations and mnemonic instructions.

51. Distinguish between test plans based on code coverage and data coverage.

52. Which button on the Pep/8 console must be clicked for keyboard input?

53. Write the Pep/8 assembly-language statement for the following instructions:
    a. Branch to location Branch1 if the accumulator is zero.
    b. Branch to location Branch1 if the accumulator is negative.
    c. Branch to location Branch1 if the accumulator is negative and to Branch2 if the accumulator is not negative.

54. Write a pseudocode algorithm to read in a name and write a "Good morning" message.

55. Write a pseudocode algorithm to get three integers from the user and print them in numeric order.

56. Enclose the design in Exercise 55 within a loop that reads in the three values until the user enters the first value of the trio as negative.

57. Rewrite the algorithm in Exercise 56 so that the user has to enter only one negative value to stop (that is, the second and third values are not entered).

58. Distinguish between pseudocode and pseudo-operations.

59. What are the constructs that pseudocode must be able to express?

60. Distinguish between the looping construct and the selection construct.

The Programming Layers

??? Thought Questions

1. Would you like to do assembly-language programming? Can you think of any personality types that would be well suited for such detail-oriented work?

2. The translation process has been demonstrated by showing the machine-language program that is the result of the assembly-language program. Look carefully at the solution in Exercise 45. Think about the steps that the assembler program must execute. Do you think that the translation can be made by looking at each assembly-language instruction once, or must each one be examined twice? Convince a friend that you are right.

3. If a person has two computers of the same kind, is it ethical to buy one copy of a software package and install it on both machines? What are the arguments on the yes side? What are the arguments on the no side?

4. Daniel Bricklin, whose biography appears in Chapter 12, did not patent (or copyright) his software, believing that software should not be proprietary. As a result, he lost a great deal of money in the form of possible royalties. Do you consider his actions to be visionary or naive?

5. The Free Software Foundation is a tax-exempt charity that raises funds for work on the GNU Project. GNU software is free. Go to the Web and read about its philosophy. Compare GNU products with those of manufacturers such as Microsoft and Sun.

6. If you were to continue with computing and become a programmer, which side of the argument would you take: Should software be copyrighted or should it be free?

The Programming Layer

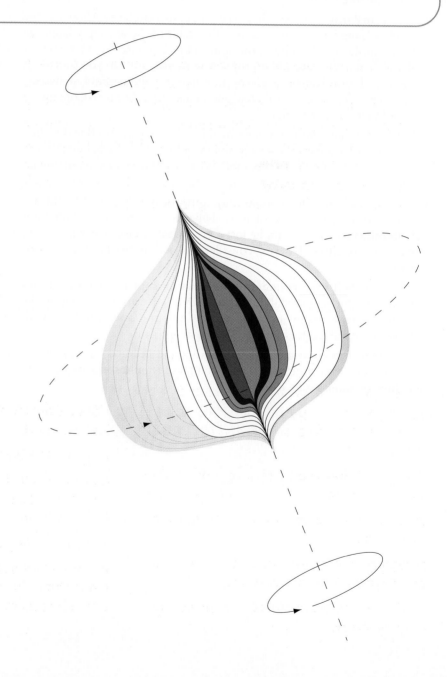

Problem Solving and Algorithms

7

In Chapter 6, we looked at machine code, which uses binary numbers to represent operations, and assembly language, which uses mnemonics to represent operations. Assembly languages are a step in the right direction, but the programmer still must think in terms of individual machine instructions. We also introduced pseudocode, an artificial language designed for expressing algorithms. We begin this chapter with a brief discussion of problem solving in general.

Goals

After studying this chapter, you should be able to:

- describe the computer problem-solving process and relate it to Polya's How to Solve It list.

- distinguish between a simple type and a composite type.

- describe three composite data-structuring mechanisms.

- recognize a recursive problem and write a recursive algorithm to solve it.

- distinguish between an unsorted array and a sorted array.

- distinguish between a selection sort and an insertion sort.

- describe the Quicksort algorithm.

- apply the selection sort, the bubble sort, insertion sort, and Quicksort to an array of items by hand.

- apply the binary search algorithm.

- demonstrate your understanding of the algorithms in this chapter by hand-simulating them with a sequence of items.

Computer science is sometimes defined as the study of algorithms and their efficient implementation in a computer. The focus of this chapter is on algorithms: their role in problem solving, strategies for developing them, techniques for following and testing them. We choose classic searching and sorting algorithms as the context for the discussion on algorithms.

Because algorithms operate on data, we examine ways to structure data so that it can be more efficiently processed.

7.1   How to Solve Problems

In 1945, George Polya wrote a little book entitled *How to Solve It: A New Aspect of Mathematical Method*.[1] Although this book was written more than 60 years ago, when computers were still experimental, it remains the classic description of the problem-solving process. The process is summarized in Figure 7.1.

What has made Polya's book a classic is that his How to Solve It list is quite general. Although it was written in the context of solving mathematical problems, we can replace the words *unknown* with *problem*, *data* with *information*, and *theorem* with *solution*, and the list becomes applicable to all types of problems. Of course, it is the second step—finding the connection between the information and the solution—that lies at the heart of problem solving. Let's look at several strategies suggested by Polya's list.

■ Ask Questions

If you are given a problem or task verbally, you typically ask questions until what you are to do is clear. You ask when, why, and where until your task is completely specified. If your instructions are written, you might put question marks in the margin; underline a word, a group of words, or a sentence; or in some other way indicate the parts of the task that are not clear. Perhaps your questions might be answered in a later paragraph, or you might have to discuss them with the person giving you the task. If the task is one that you set for yourself, this sort of questioning might not be verbal, but instead takes place on the subconscious level.

Some typical questions you should be asking are as follows:

- What do I know about the problem?
- What does the solution look like?
- What sort of special cases exist?
- How will I recognize that I have found the solution?

HOW TO SOLVE IT

UNDERSTANDING THE PROBLEM

First.
You have to *understand* the problem.

What is the unknown? What are the data? What is the condition?
Is it possible to satisfy the condition? Is the condition sufficient to determine the unknown? Or is it insufficient? Or redundant? Or contradictory?
Draw a figure. Introduce suitable notation.
Separate the various parts of the condition. Can you write them down?

DEVISING A PLAN

Second.
Find the connection between the data and the unknown. You may be obliged to consider auxiliary problems if an immediate connection cannot be found. You should obtain eventually a *plan* of the solution.

Have you seen it before? Or have you seen the same problem in a slightly different form?
Do you know a related problem? Do you know a theorem that could be useful?
Look at the unknown! And try to think of a familiar problem having the same or a similar unknown.
Here is a problem related to yours and solved before. Could you use it? Could you use its result? Could you use its method? Should you introduce some auxiliary element in order to make its use possible? Could you restate the problem? Could you restate it still differently? Go back to definitions.
If you cannot solve the proposed problem, try to solve first some related problem. Could you imagine a more accessible related problem? A more general problem? A more special problem? An analogous problem? Could you solve a part of the problem? Keep only a part of the condition, drop the other part; how far is the unknown then determined; how can it vary? Could you derive something useful from the data? Could you think of other data appropriate to determine the unknown? Could you change the unknown or the data, or both if necessary, so that the new unknown and the new data are nearer to each other? Did you use all the data? Did you use the whole condition? Have you taken into account all essential notions involved in the problem?

CARRYING OUT THE PLAN

Third.
Carry out your plan.

Carrying out your plan of the solution, *check each step.* Can you see clearly that the step is correct? Can you prove that it is correct?

LOOKING BACK

Fourth.
Examine the solution obtained.

Can you *check the result?* Can you check the argument? Can you derive the result differently? Can you see it at a glance? Can you use the result, or the method, for some other problem?

FIGURE 7.1   Polya's How to Solve It list. Source: Polya, G. *How to Solve It.* © 1945 Princeton University Press, 1973 renewed PUP. Reprinted by permission of Princeton University Press.

■ Look for Familiar Things

You should never reinvent the wheel. If a solution exists, use it. If you've solved the same or a similar problem before, just repeat the successful solution. We usually don't consciously think, "I have seen this before, and I know what to do"—we just do it. Humans are good at recognizing similar situations. We don't have to learn how to go to the store to buy milk, then to buy eggs, then to buy candy. We know that going to the store is always the same and only what we buy is different.

Recognizing familiar situations is particularly useful in computing. In computing, you see certain problems again and again in different guises. A good programmer sees a task, or perhaps part of a task (a subtask), that has been solved before and plugs in the solution. For example, finding the daily high and low temperatures in a list of temperatures is exactly the same problem as finding the highest and lowest grades in a list of test scores. You want the largest and smallest values in a set of numbers.

■ Divide and Conquer

We constantly break up a large problem into smaller units that we can handle. The task of cleaning the house or apartment, for example, may seem overwhelming. By contrast, the individual tasks of cleaning the living room, the dining room, the kitchen, the bedrooms, and the bathroom seem more manageable. This principle is especially relevant to computing: We break up a large problem into smaller pieces that we can solve individually.

This approach applies the concept of abstraction that we discussed in Chapter 1—cleaning the house is a large, abstract problem made up of the subtasks defined by cleaning the individual rooms. Cleaning a room can also be thought of as an abstraction of the details of straightening the dresser, making the bed, vacuuming the floor, and so on. Tasks are divided into subtasks, which can be divided further into sub-subtasks and so forth. The divide-and-conquer approach can be applied over and over again until each subtask is manageable.

We applied two of these strategies in the last chapter when we asked questions and deferred details in designing the algorithm to read in two numbers and output them in order.

■ Algorithms

The last sentence in the second step in Polya's list says that you should eventually obtain a plan of the solution. In computing, this plan is called an algorithm. We have used the term many times; here we define it in computing terms. Formally, an algorithm is set of instructions for solving a problem or subproblem in a finite amount of time using a finite amount of data. Implicit in this definition is the understanding that the instructions are unambiguous.

In computing, we must make certain conditions explicit that are implicit in human solutions. For example, in everyday life we would not consider a solution that takes forever to be much of a solution. We would also reject a solution that requires us to process more information than we

>> Algorithm Unambiguous instructions for solving a problem or subproblem in a finite amount of time using a finite amount of data

George Polya

George Polya was born in Budapest on December 13, 1887. Although he eventually became a world-famous mathematician, he did not show an early interest in mathematics. Polya's lack of interest might be explained by his memory of three high school mathematics teachers: "two were despicable and one was good."

In 1905, Polya entered the University of Budapest, where he studied law at the insistence of his mother. After one very boring semester, he decided to study languages and literature. He earned a teaching certificate in Latin and Hungarian—and never used it. He became interested in philosophy and took courses in math and physics as part of his philosophy studies. He settled on mathematics, commenting that "I am too good for philosophy and not good enough for physics. Mathematics is in between." He received his PhD in mathematics in 1912, which launched his career.

Polya did research and taught at the University of Göttingen, the University of Paris, and the Swiss Federation of Technology in Zurich. While in Zurich he interacted with John von Neumann, about whom he said, "Johnny was the only student I was ever afraid of. If, in the course of a lecture, I stated an unsolved problem, the chances were he'd come to me as soon as the lecture was over, with the complete solution in a few scribbles on a slip of paper."

Like many Europeans of that era, Polya moved to the United States in 1940 because of the political situation in Germany. After teaching at Brown University for two years, he moved to Palo Alto, California, to teach at Stanford University, where he remained for the rest of his career.

Polya's research and publications encompassed many areas of mathematics, including number theory, combinatorics, astronomy, probability, integral functions, and boundary value problems for partial differential equations. The George Polya Prize is given in his honor for notable application of combinatorial theory.

Yet, for all George Polya's contributions to mathematics, it is his contribution to mathematics education of which he was the most proud and for which he will be the most remembered. His book *How to Solve It*, published in 1945, sold more than 1 million copies and was translated into 17 languages. In this book, Polya outlines a problem-solving strategy designed for mathematical problems. The generality of the strategy makes it applicable to all problem solving, however. Polya's strategy is the basis of the computer problem-solving strategy outlined in this text. *Mathematics and Plausible Reasoning*, published in 1954, was another book dedicated to mathematics education. Polya not only wrote about mathematics education, but also took an active interest in the teaching of mathematics. He was a regular visitor to the schools in the Bay Area and visited most of the colleges in the western states. The Math Center at the University of Idaho is named for him.

On September 7, 1985, George Polya died in Palo Alto at the age of 97.

are capable of processing. These constraints must be explicit in a computer solution, so the definition of an algorithm includes them.

The third step in Polya's list is to carry out the plan—that is, to test the solution to see if it solves the problem. The fourth step is to examine the solution for future applicability.

■ Computer Problem-Solving Process

The computer problem-solving process includes four phases: the *analysis and specification phase*, the *algorithm development phase*, the *implementation phase*, and the *maintenance phase*. See Figure 7.2. The output from the first phase is a clearly written problem statement. The output from the algorithm development phase is a plan for a general solution to the problem specified in the first phase. The output from the third phase is a working computer program that implements the algorithm—that is, a specific solution to the problem. There is no output from the fourth phase, unless errors are detected or changes need to be made. If so, these errors or changes are sent back either to the first, second, or third phase, whichever is appropriate.

Figure 7.3 shows how these phases interact. The black lines show the general flow through the phase. The red lines represent paths that can be taken to backtrack to a previous phase if a problem occurs. For example, during the process of producing an algorithm, an error or contradiction in the specification may be found, in which case the analysis and specification must be corrected. Likewise, an error in the program may indicate that an algorithm must be corrected.

Analysis and Specification Phase
Analyze	Understand (define) the problem.
Specification	Specify the problem that the program is to solve.

Algorithm Development Phase
Develop algorithm	Develop a logical sequence of steps to be used to solve the problem.
Test algorithm	Follow the steps as outlined to see if the solution truly solves the problem.

Implementation Phase
Code	Translate the algorithm (the general solution) into a programming language.
Test	Have the computer follow the instructions. Check the results and make corrections until the answers are correct.

Maintenance Phase
Use	Use the program.
Maintain	Modify the program to meet changing requirements or to correct any errors.

FIGURE 7.2   The computer problem-solving process

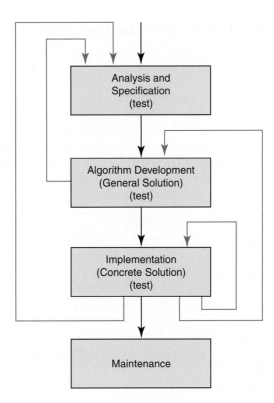

FIGURE 7.3   The interactions among the four problem-solving phases

All of Polya's phases are included in this outline of how we solve problems using the computer. The first step is always to understand the problem. You cannot write a computer solution to a problem you don't understand. The next step is to develop a plan—an algorithm—for the solution and express it in pseudocode. It is this phase on which we concentrate in this chapter.

The next step is to implement the plan in such a way that the computer can execute it and test the results. In Polya's list, the human executes the plan and evaluates the results. In a computer solution, a program is written expressing the plan in a language that the computer can execute. But it is the human who takes the results of the computer program and checks them to confirm that they are correct. The maintenance phase maps to Polya's last stage, where the results are examined and perhaps modified.

In this chapter we end the process at the pseudocode level. This text is language neutral; that is, we do not cover a high-level language in detail. However, some of you may be learning one in parallel with this text. In any case, remember that an algorithm must be written before any coding in a programming language can be done.

■ Summary of Methodology

The methodology for designing algorithms can be broken down into four major steps:

1. Analyze the Problem

Understand the problem! List the information you have to work with. This information will probably consist of the data in the problem. Specify what the solution will look like. If it is a report, specify the format. List any assumptions that you are making about the problem or the information. Think. How would you solve the problem by hand? Develop an overall algorithm or general plan of attack.

2. List the Main Tasks

The listing of the main tasks is called the *main module*. Use English or pseudocode to restate the problem in the main module. Use task names to divide the problem into functional areas. If the main module is too long, you are including too much detail for this level. Introduce any control structures that are needed at this point. Re-sequence the subparts logically, if needed. Postpone details to lower levels.

Don't worry if you don't know how to solve a task. Just pretend you have a "smart friend" who has the answer and postpone thinking about it until later. All you have to do in the main module is to give the names of lower-level modules that solve certain tasks. Use meaningful identifiers.

3. Write the Remaining Modules

There is no fixed number of levels. Modules at one level can specify more modules at lower levels. Each module must be complete, even if it references unwritten modules. Do successive refinements through each module until each statement is a concrete step.

4. Re-sequence and Revise as Necessary

Plan for change. Don't be afraid to start over. Several attempts and refinements may be necessary. Try to maintain clarity. Express yourself simply and directly.

The problem-solving strategy that parallels Polya's outline is known as *top-down design*. It produces a hierarchy of tasks to be solved. In Chapter 9, we introduce a strategy called *object-oriented design*, which produces a hierarchy of data objects.

■ Testing the Algorithm

The goal of mathematical problem solving is to produce a specific answer to a problem, so checking the results is the equivalent of testing the process by which the answer was derived. If the answer is correct, the process is correct. However, the goal of computer problem solving is to create the right *process*. The algorithm that embodies this process may be used again and again with different data, so the process itself must be tested or verified.

Testing an algorithm often involves running the program into which the algorithm is coded under various conditions and examining the results for problems. However, this type of testing can be done only when the program is complete, or at least partially complete, which is far too late to rely on just this kind of testing. The earlier problems are discovered and fixed, the cheaper and easier it is to address them.

Clearly, we need to perform testing at earlier stages in the development process. Specifically, the algorithms must be tested prior to implementing them. We demonstrated this process as we worked through the base-changing algorithm.

Rosetta Stone as a translation system
The Rosetta stone was unearthed by Napoleon's troops in 1799. Soldiers in Napoleon's army discovered the stone while digging the foundations of an addition to a fort near the town of el-Rashid, also known as Rosetta. The stone contained a proclamation marking the first anniversary of the coronation of Ptolemy V, inscribed in three languages: hieroglyphics, demotic (a cursive version of hieroglyphs), and Greek. Thomas Young, a British physicist, and Francois Champollion, a French Egyptologist, were able to decipher the ancient Egyptian languages using the Greek as a guide. Thus the Rosetta stone provided the key that unlocked the translation of Egyptian hieroglyphics.

7.2 Algorithms with Simple Variables

Simple (atomic) variables are those that cannot be divided. They are a value stored in a place. We used simple variables in the algorithms in Chapter 6. Numbers, for example, are simple variables.

■ An Algorithm with Selection

Suppose you want to write an algorithm to express what dress is appropriate for a given outside temperature. You would like to wear shorts if it is hot, short sleeves if it is nice but not too hot, a light jacket if the temperature is chilly, and a heavy coat if it is cold. If the temperature is below freezing, you stay inside.

The top-level (main) module just expresses the tasks.

```
Write "Enter the temperature"
Read temperature
Determine dress
```

The first two statements do not need further decomposing. However, Determine dress does. We need to associate temperatures with our descriptions. Let's define hot as anything above 90, nice as above 70, chilly as above 50, and cold as above 32. Now we can write the pseudocode for Determine dress.

Determine Dress

IF (temperature > 90)

    Write "Texas weather: wear shorts"

ELSE IF (temperature > 70)

    Write "Ideal weather: short sleeves are fine"

ELSE IF (temperature > 50)

    Write "A little chilly: wear a light jacket"

ELSE IF (temperature > 32)

    Write "Philadelphia weather: wear a heavy coat"

ELSE

    Write "Stay inside"

The only way to get to the second *if* statement is if the first expression is not true; thus, if the second expression is true, you know that the temperature is between 71 and 90. If the first and second expressions are not true and the third is, then the temperature is between 51 and 70. The same reasoning leads to the conclusion that Philadelphia weather is between 33 and 50, and "Stay inside" is written if the temperature is less than or equal to 32. Any one of the branches can contain a sequence of statements.

■ Algorithms with Repetition

There are two basic types of loops: count controlled and event controlled.

Count-Controlled Loops

A count-controlled loop is a loop that repeats a process a specified number of times. The looping mechanism simply counts each time the process is repeated and tests whether it has finished before beginning again. This was the type of loop we used in Chapter 6.

There are three distinct parts to this kind of loop, which makes use of a special variable called a *loop control variable*. The first part is initialization: The loop control variable is initialized to some starting value. The second part is testing: Has the loop control variable reached a predetermined value? The third part is incrementation: The loop control variable is incremented by 1. The following algorithm repeats a process limit times:

```
Set count to 0                 Initialize count to 0
WHILE (count < limit)          Test
    . . .                      Body of the loop
    Set count to count + 1     Increment
. . .                          Statement(s) following loop
```

The loop control variable, count, is set to 0 outside the loop. The expression count < limit is tested, and the loop is executed as long as the expression is true. The last statement in the loop increments the loop control variable, count. How many times does the loop execute? The loop executes when count is 0, 1, 2, . . ., limit − 1. Thus the loop executes limit times. The initial value of the loop control variable and the relational operator used in the Boolean expression determine the number of times the loop executes.

The *while* loop is called a pretest loop, because the testing takes place *before* the loop is executed. If the condition is false initially, the loop is not entered. What happens if the incrementation statement is omitted? The Boolean expression never changes. If the expression was false to begin with, nothing happens; the loop just is not executed. If the expression is true to begin with, the expression never changes, so the loop executes forever. Actually, most computing systems have a timer, so the program would not really run forever. Instead, the program would halt with an error message. A loop that never terminates is called an *infinite loop*.

This algorithm from Chapter 6 contains a count-controlled loop:

```
Write "How many pairs of values are to be entered?"
Read numberOfPairs
Set numberRead to 0
WHILE (numberRead < numberOfPairs)
    // Body of loop

    . . .
    Set numberRead to numberRead + 1
```

Pep/8 used a semicolon to indicate that what followed was a comment and not part of the program. In our pseudocode, we use two forward slashes to preface a comment.

Event-Controlled Loops

Loops in which the number of repetitions is controlled by an event that occurs within the body of the loop itself are called event-controlled loops. When implementing an event-controlled loop using a *while* statement, there are again three parts to the process: The event must be initialized, the event must be tested, and the event must be updated. The base conversion algorithm from Chapter 6 contains an event-controlled loop:

```
Write "Enter the new base"
Read newBase
Write "Enter the number to be converted"
Read decimalNumber
Set answer to 0
Set quotient to 1
WHILE (quotient is not zero)
    Set quotient to decimalNumber DIV newBase
    // Rest of loop body
Write "The answer is ", answer
```

A count-controlled loop is very straightforward: The process is repeated a specified number of times. The activity in an event-controlled loop is less clear-cut. It may not be immediately apparent what the event should be.

Let's look at a couple of examples. First, let's read and sum data values until we read a negative value. What is the event? Reading a positive value. How do we initialize the event? We read the first data value. We test the value to determine whether it is positive and enter the loop if it is. How do we update the event? We read the next data value. Here is the algorithm:

```
Read a value              Initialize event
WHILE (value >= 0)        Test event
    . . .                 Body of loop
    Read a value          Update event
. . .                     Statement(s) following loop
```

Now let's write the algorithm for reading and summing positive values until 10 have been counted. We will ignore zero or negative values. What is the event? The number of positive values read is less than 11. This means that we must keep a count of the number of positive values as we read them; let's call it *posCount*. How do we initialize the event? We set *posCount* to 0. We test *posCount* against 10, and exit the loop when *posCount* reaches 10. How do we update the event? We increment *posCount* each time we read a positive value.

```
Set sum to 0                            Initialize sum to zero
Set posCount to 0                       Initialize event
WHILE (posCount < 10)                   Test event
    Read a value
    IF (value > 0)                      Should count be updated?
        Set posCount to posCount + 1    Update event
        Set sum to sum + value          Add value into sum
    . . .                               Statement(s) following loop
```

This is not a count-controlled loop because we do not read 10 values: We read values until we have read 10.

Notice the selection control structure embedded within the loop. The statements to be executed or skipped in any control structure can be simple statements or compound statements (blocks of indented statements)—there is no constraint on what these statements can be. As a consequence, the statement to be skipped or repeated can contain a control structure. Selection statements can be nested within looping structures; looping structures can be nested within selection statements. Structures in which one control structure is embedded within another control structure are called **nested structures**.

Let's work through another example: finding the square root of a number.

>> Nested structure (nested logic) A structure in which one control structure is embedded within another

Square Root

Most students have to compute a square root in school. A rather complicated algorithm has been developed that works on integer values. We do not look at that algorithm here, but rather use a much simpler approximation that works on real numbers as well as integers.

Given the number of which you wish to find the square root, take the number and make a guess at the answer; then take the guess and square it. If your guess is correct, the guess squared is equal to the original value. If it is not, you adjust your guess and begin again. This process continues until the guess squared is close enough. Do you understand the problem? If not, reread this paragraph.

Now let's outline the major tasks:

```
Read in square
Calculate the square root
Write out square and the square root
```

Read in square does not need further expansion. Calculate the square root *does* need further expansion, because it is the heart of the algorithm. Clearly there is a loop: We keep refining the guess until the guess is good enough. Is it a count-controlled loop or an event-controlled loop? Because we have no idea how many iterations the process will take, it must be an event-controlled loop.

What do we mean by "good enough"? Let's say that if the difference between the guess squared and the original value is within plus or minus 0.001, the guess is good enough; we'll call this difference *epsilon*. How do we measure "plus or minus"? We take the absolute value of the difference. We indicate this by the expression *abs(epsilon)*, which stands for absolute value.

```
Calculate square root

Set epsilon to 1
WHILE (epsilon > 0.001)
    Calculate new guess
    Set epsilon to abs(square − guess * guess)
```

Now the only step that needs further expansion is Calculate new guess. Now we need to ask questions: What is the formula for calculating the new guess? We search online for "square root formula" and find the answer in Wikipedia. We replace the old guess by the average between the old guess and the square divided by the old guess.

```
Calculate new guess

Set newGuess to (guess + (square/guess)) / 2.0
```

In looking up the formula, we find that we had forgotten something: What is the original guess? Any positive value will work, but the solution is found with fewer iterations if the original guess is closer to the square

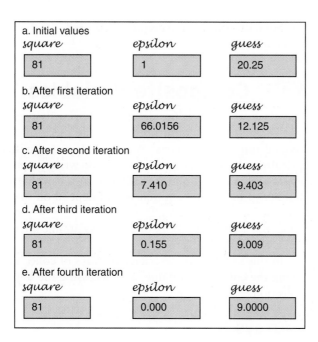

FIGURE 7.4   Walk-through of square root algorithm

root. A good approximation for the original guess is the square divided by 4. We do not need to have variables for old guess and new guess. We can call it *guess* and just keep changing its value. Here, then, is the completed algorithm:

```
Read in square
Set guess to square/4
Set epsilon to 1
WHILE (epsilon > 0.001)
      Calculate new guess
      Set epsilon to abs(square − guess * guess)
      Write out square and the guess
```

Let's desk check this algorithm with a value to which we know the answer: 81. Figure 7.4 shows the algorithm walk-through. It takes only four iterations to get the answer correct to five decimal places.

A step that needs to be expanded further is called an **abstract step**. A step that does not need to be expanded is called a **concrete step**. From here

> **»** **Abstract step** An algorithmic step for which some details remain unspecified
>
> **»** **Concrete step** A step for which the details are fully specified

on we will color the abstract steps red. Each abstract step must be expanded separately.

7.3 Composite Variables

The places to store values described previously were all atomic in nature; that is, each place could hold only one piece of data, which cannot be divided into smaller parts. We have also used a string of letters within quotations to represent a message to be written out. As you might expect, letters within quotations are called *strings*. If we were to store a string, the number of locations required would depend on the number of characters in the string. Thus a string is not atomic because it contains more than one value, but we tend to think of strings as atomic anyway because we do not access the individual letters.

In this section, we describe two ways of collecting data items together, giving the collection a name, and accessing the items individually or as a collection.

■ Arrays

An array is a named collection of *homogeneous* items in which individual items are accessed by their place within the collection. The place within the collection is called an *index*. Although people usually start counting at one, most programming languages start at zero—so that is what we will do here. Figure 7.5 shows an array with 10 items indexed from 0 through 9.

If the array is called numbers, we access each value by the expression

numbers[position]

where position, the index, is a value between 0 and 9.

FIGURE 7.5   An array of ten numbers

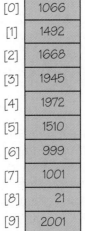

[0]	1066
[1]	1492
[2]	1668
[3]	1945
[4]	1972
[5]	1510
[6]	999
[7]	1001
[8]	21
[9]	2001

Here is the algorithm to put values into the places in an array:

```
integer numbers[10]
// Declares numbers to hold 10 integer values
Write "Enter 10 integer numbers, one per line"
Set position to 0 // Set variable position to 0
WHILE (position < 10)
     Read in numbers[position]
     Set position to position + 1
// Continue with processing
```

We indicate that numbers is an array that can hold integer values by listing integer followed by the array name with the number of slots in brackets beside the name. In our algorithms previously, we have not listed a variable; we have just assumed that when we use a variable name that the variable exists. Now that we are using composite structures, we need to say which kind of a structure we want.

Algorithms with arrays are classified into three categories: searching, sorting, and processing. *Searching* is just what it says—going through the items in the array one at a time looking for a particular value. *Sorting* is putting the items in the array into order. If the items are numbers, they would be put into numeric order; if the items are characters or strings, they would be put into alphabetic order. A sorted array is one in which the items are in order. *Processing* is a catch-all phrase the encompasses all other computing done to or with items in an array.

■ Records

A record is a named *heterogeneous* group of items in which individual items are accessed by name. "Heterogeneous" means that the elements in the collection do not have to be the same. The collection can contain integers, real values, strings, or any other type of data. Records are good choices for bundling items together that relate to the same object. For example, we might read in a name, an age, and an hourly wage. These three items could then be bound together into a record named Employee. This record is made up of three fields: name, age, and hourlyWage. We might draw them as seen in Figure 7.6.

If we declare a record variable employee of type Employee, each field of the record is accessed by the record variable, dot, and the field name. For example, employee.name refers to the name field of the record variable employee. There are no specific algorithms designed for records, because they are just a way of

Privacy of bloggers
Many Internet users see blogs as the perfect place to anonymously discuss their thoughts and feelings. Many bloggers post their uncensored thoughts regarding family, friends, and employment, believing that they are safe from any consequences. However, even bloggers who never give their real names or mention their places of employment are often discovered by their employers. Dozens of people have been fired for blogging, including workers at companies such as Delta® Airlines, Google™, and Microsoft®. While many believe that the First Amendment protects their right to free speech, it truly protects citizens only from lawful prosecution. Only California, New York, Colorado, Montana, and North Dakota have laws limiting the reasons an employer can fire someone for blogging.

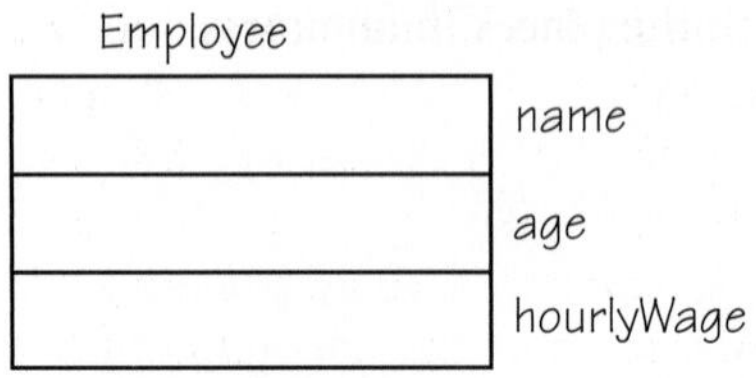

FIGURE 7.6   Record Employee

Employee

name

age

hourlyWage

grouping related items. However, they are very handy ways to refer to a group of related items.

The following algorithm stores values into the fields of the record:

```
Employee employee        // Declare an Employee variable
Set employee.name to "Frank Jones"
Set employee.age to 32
Set employee.hourlyWage to 27.50
```

A third composite data structure called a *class* characterizes object-oriented programming. We discuss this structure in Chapter 9.

7.4 Searching Algorithms

■ Sequential Search

You have an appointment with your English teacher. You get to the correct building and look for her name in the directory to find her office number. "Look for" is a synonym for searching—that is, you search the directory for her name.

Our first searching algorithm follows this definition of searching exactly. We look at each item in turn and compare it to the one for which we are searching. If it matches, we have found the item. If not, we look at the next item. When do we stop? We stop either when we have found the item or when we have looked at all the items and not found a match. This sounds like a loop with two ending conditions. Let's write the algorithm using the array numbers.

```
Set position to 0
Set found to FALSE
WHILE (position < 10 AND found is FALSE)
    IF (numbers[position] equals searchItem)
        Set found to TRUE
    ELSE
        Set position to position + 1
```

Because we have a compound condition in the *While* expression, we need to say a little more about Boolean variables. AND is a Boolean operator. The Boolean operators include the special operators AND, OR, and NOT. The AND operator returns TRUE if both expressions are TRUE, and FALSE otherwise. The OR operator returns FALSE if both expressions are FALSE, and TRUE otherwise. The NOT operator changes the value of the expression. These operations are consistent with the functionality of the gates described in Chapter 4. At that level, we were referring to the flow of electricity and the representation of individual bits. At this level, the logic is the same, but we can talk in terms of an expression as being either true or false.

We can simplify the second Boolean expression (found is FALSE) by using the NOT operator. NOT found is true when found is false. So we can say

WHILE (index < 10 AND NOT found)

Thus the loop will repeat as long as the index is less than 10 and we haven't found the matching item.

■ Sequential Search in a Sorted Array

If we know that the items in the array are sorted, we can stop looking when we pass the place where the item would be if it were present in the array. As we look at this algorithm, let's generalize our search somewhat. Rather than being specific about the number of items in the array, we use a variable length to tell us how many valid items are in the array. The length might be less than the size, which is the number of slots in the array. As data is being read into the array, a counter is updated so that we always know how many data items were stored. If the array is called data, the data with which we are working is from data[0] to data[length − 1]. Figures 7.7 and 7.8 show an unordered array and a sorted array, respectively.

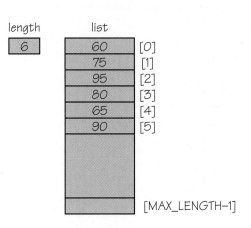

length   list

FIGURE 7.7   An unsorted array

FIGURE 7.8   A sorted array

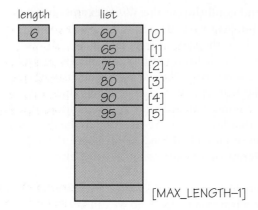

In the sorted array, if we are looking for 76, we know it is not in the array as soon as we examine data[3], because this position is where the number would be if it were there. Here is the algorithm for searching in a sorted array embedded in a complete program. We use the variable index rather than position in this algorithm. Programmers often use the mathematical identifier index rather than the intuitive identifier position or place when working with arrays.

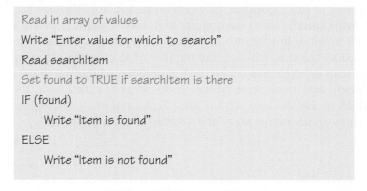

Read in array of values

Write "Enter value for which to search"

Read searchItem

Set found to TRUE if searchItem is there

IF (found)

    Write "Item is found"

ELSE

    Write "Item is not found"

Read in array of values

Write "How many values?"

Read length

Set index to 0

WHILE (index < length)

    Read data[index]

    Set index to index + 1

Set found to TRUE if searchItem is there
_____

Set index to 0

Set found to FALSE

WHILE (index < length AND NOT found)

    IF (data[index] equals searchItem)

        Set found to TRUE

    ELSE IF (data[index] > searchItem)

        Set index to length

    ELSE

        Set index to index + 1

■ Binary Search

How would you go about looking for a word in a dictionary? We certainly hope you wouldn't start on the first page and sequentially search for your word! A sequential search of an array begins at the beginning of the array and continues until the item is found or the entire array has been searched without finding the item.

A binary search looks for an item in an array using a different strategy: divide and conquer. This approach mimics what you probably do when you look up a word. You start in the middle and then decide whether your word is in the right-hand section or the left-hand section. You then look in the correct section and repeat the strategy.

The binary search algorithm assumes that the items in the array being searched are sorted, and it either finds the item or eliminates half of the array with one comparison. Rather than looking for the item starting at the beginning of the array and moving forward sequentially, the algorithm begins at the middle of the array in a binary search. If the item for which we are searching is less than the item in the middle, we know that the item won't be in the second half of the array. We then continue by searching the data in the first half of the array. See Figure 7.9.

Once again we examine the "middle" element (which is really the item 25% of the way into the array). If the item for which we are searching is greater than the item in the middle, we continue searching between the middle and the end of the array. If the middle item is equal to the one for which you are searching, the search stops. The process continues in this manner, with each comparison cutting in half the portion of the array where the item might be. It stops when the item is found or when the portion of the array where the item might be is empty.

>> Binary search Looking for an item in an already sorted list by eliminating large portions of the data on each comparison

FIGURE 7.9   Binary search example

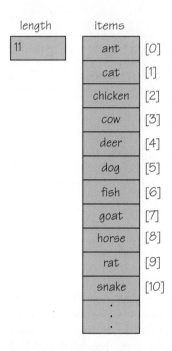

length	items	
11	ant	[0]
	cat	[1]
	chicken	[2]
	cow	[3]
	deer	[4]
	dog	[5]
	fish	[6]
	goat	[7]
	horse	[8]
	rat	[9]
	snake	[10]

Boolean Binary Search

```
Set first to 0
Set last to length–1
Set found to FALSE
WHILE (first <= last AND NOT found)
     Set middle to (first + last)/ 2
     IF (item equals data[middle])
          Set found to TRUE
     ELSE
          IF (item < data[middle])
               Set last to middle – 1
          ELSE
               Set first to middle + 1
Return found
```

Let's desk check (walk through) the algorithm searching for cat, fish, and zebra. Rather than boxes, we use a tabular form in Figure 7.10 to save space.

Searching for cat

First	Last	Middle	Comparison	
0	10	5	cat < dog	
0	4	2	cat < chicken	
0	1	0	cat < ant	
1	1	1	cat = cat	**Return: true**

Searching for fish

First	Last	Middle	Comparison	
0	10	5	fish > dog	
6	10	8	fish < horse	
6	7	6	fish = fish	**Return: true**

Searching for zebra

First	Last	Middle	Comparison	
0	10	5	zebra > dog	
6	10	8	zebra > horse	
9	10	9	zebra > rat	
10	10	10	zebra > snake	
11	10		first > last	**Return: false**

FIGURE 7.10 Trace of the binary search

Is the binary search algorithm really faster than the sequential search algorithm? Table 7.1 shows the number of comparisons required on average to find an item using a sequential search and using a binary search. If the binary search is so much faster, why don't we always use it? More computations are required for each comparison in a binary search because we must calculate the middle index. Also, the array must already be sorted. If the array is already sorted and the number of items is more than 20, a binary search algorithm is the better choice.

TABLE 7.1 Average Number of Comparisons

Length	Sequential Search	Binary Search
10	5.5	2.9
100	50.5	5.8
1000	500.5	9.0
10000	5000.5	12.0

7.5 Sorting

We all know what sorting is. We sort our music playlist, our bookshelves, even our priorities. Sorting is putting things in order. In computing, transforming an unsorted array into a sorted array is a common and useful operation. Entire books have been written about sorting algorithms. The goal is to come up with better, more efficient sorts. Because sorting a large number of elements can be extremely time-consuming, a good sorting algorithm is considered highly desirable. In fact, this is one area in which programmers are sometimes encouraged to sacrifice clarity in favor of speed of execution.

In this section, we present several diverse sorting algorithms to give you a flavor of how many different ways there are to solve the same problem.

▪ Selection Sort

If we handed you a set of index cards with names and asked you to put them in order by name, you would probably go through the cards looking for the name that comes first in the alphabet. You would then put that card as the first in a new stack. How would you determine which card comes first? You might turn the first card sideways to remember it. If you found one that comes before the turned card, you could turn the first card back and turn the new "first" card to remember it. When you have examined all the cards, the one that is turned up is the first one. You pull it out to start the sorted deck of cards. This process would continue until all the index cards have been moved to the new stack.

```
WHILE more cards in first deck
    Find smallest left in first deck
    Move to new deck
```

The selection sort algorithm is probably the easiest because it mirrors how we would sort a list of values if we had to do it by hand. Our deck of index cards is an array of names. The new deck is an array of sorted names. We remove items from the first and put them into successive places in the second. We remember the smallest so far by saving its position in a temporary variable.

This algorithm is simple, but it has one drawback: It requires space for two complete decks (arrays). Although we have not talked about memory space considerations, this duplication is clearly wasteful. A slight adjustment to this by-hand approach does away with the need to duplicate space,

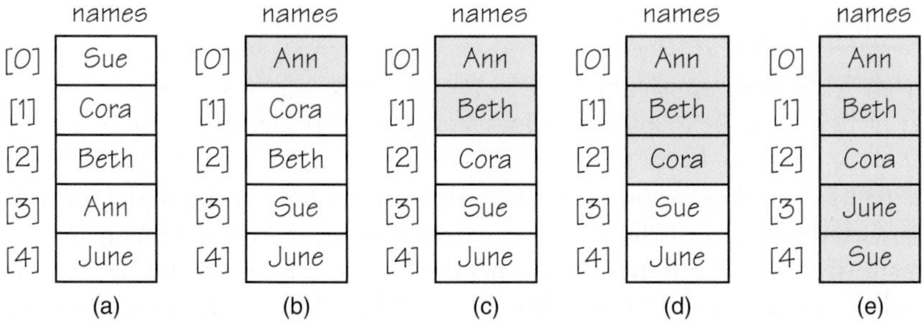

	names		names		names		names		names
[0]	Sue	[0]	Ann	[0]	Ann	[0]	Ann	[0]	Ann
[1]	Cora	[1]	Cora	[1]	Beth	[1]	Beth	[1]	Beth
[2]	Beth	[2]	Beth	[2]	Cora	[2]	Cora	[2]	Cora
[3]	Ann	[3]	Sue	[3]	Sue	[3]	Sue	[3]	June
[4]	June	[4]	June	[4]	June	[4]	June	[4]	Sue
	(a)		(b)		(c)		(d)		(e)

FIGURE 7.11   Example of selection sort (sorted elements are shaded)

however. As you move the smallest item to the new array, a free space opens up where it used to be. Instead of writing this name on a second list, we can exchange it with the name currently in the position where the new name should go. This "by-hand list" is represented in an array.

Let's look at an example—sorting the five-element array shown in Figure 7.11. Because of this algorithm's simplicity, it is usually the first sorting method that students learn.

Let's visualize the array as containing two parts: the unsorted part (not shaded) and the sorted part (shaded). Each time we add an item into its proper place, we are shrinking the unsorted part and extending the sorted part. Sorting begins with all of the items in the unsorted part and ends with all of the items in the sorted part. Here is the algorithm written to mirror this visualization:

Selection Sort

Set firstUnsorted to 0

WHILE (not sorted yet)

    Find smallest unsorted item

    Swap firstUnsorted item with the smallest

    Set firstUnsorted to firstUnsorted + 1

This algorithm includes only three abstract steps (colored in red): determining when the array is sorted, finding the index of the smallest element, and swapping the contents of two places. In moving from Figure 7.11(d) to 7.11(e), we added the last two items to the shaded part of the array. This is always the case because when the smaller of the last two items is put into its proper place, the last item is also in its proper place. Thus the loop continues as long as firstUnsorted is less than the length of array − 1.

Not sorted yet

firstUnsorted < length − 1

How would you find the name that comes first in the alphabet in the unsorted portion of the list if you were sorting it by hand? You see (and mentally record) the first one, and then you scan down the list (turning index cards) until you see one that comes before the first one. You remember this smaller one and continue scanning the list for a name that comes before this one in the alphabet. The process of remembering the smallest so far until you find a smaller one is repeated until you reach the end of the list. This by-hand algorithm is exactly the one we use here, except that we must remember the index of the smallest item because we will swap it with the item in the firstUnsorted position. Stated in terms of our list, we look for the smallest item in the unsorted portion, which runs from firstUnsorted through length − 1.

Find smallest unsorted item

Set indexOfSmallest to firstUnsorted
Set index to firstUnsorted + 1
WHILE (index <= length − 1)
    IF (data[index] < data[indexOfSmallest])
        Set indexOfSmallest to index
    Set index to index + 1

How many glasses does it take to swap the contents of two glasses? Three. You need a glass to temporarily hold the contents of one glass while you pour the contents of the other glass into the first. Swapping the contents of two places in memory is exactly the same problem. The swap algorithm must have the indexes of the two items to be swapped.

Swap firstUnsorted with smallest

Set tempItem to data[firstUnsorted]
Set data[firstUnsorted] to data[indexOfSmallest]
Set data[indexOfSmallest] to tempItem

■ Bubble Sort

The bubble sort is a selection sort that uses a different scheme for finding the minimum value. Starting with the last array element, we compare successive pairs of elements, swapping them whenever the bottom element of the pair is smaller than the one above it [Figure 7.12(a)]. In this way, the smallest element "bubbles up" to the top of the array. Each iteration puts the smallest unsorted item into its correct place using the same technique, but it also changes the locations of the other elements in the array [Figure 7.12(b)].

Before we write this algorithm, we must make an observation: The bubble sort is a very slow sorting algorithm. Sorting algorithms are usually compared based on the number of iterations it takes to sort an array, and this approach takes one iteration for every item in the array except the last. In addition, during each algorithm a lot of swapping goes on. Why, then, do we bother to mention the bubble sort if it is so inefficient? Because a very slight change in the sorting algorithm makes it an excellent choice to use in certain circumstances. Let's apply the algorithm to an already sorted array. See the right-most column in Figure 7.12(b).

We compare Phil with John and do not swap them. We compare John with Jim and do not swap them. We compare Jim with Bob and do not swap them. We compare Bob with Al and do not swap them. If no values are swapped during an iteration, then the array is sorted. We set a Boolean

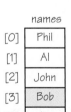

Free Wi-Fi
Borrowing a Wi-Fi connection, also known as piggybacking, has become a popular trend over the years as more and more households and business switch to wireless Internet service providers (ISPs). Approximately 54% of computer users admit that they've used someone else's Wi-Fi connection without permission. While most people don't consider it to be stealing, piggybacking slows down the owner's Internet connection and deprives the ISP of revenue. In 2006, an Illinois man was cited for accessing a wireless Internet connection belonging to a not-for-profit agency and was punished with a $250 fine and a year of court supervision–despite the fact that the connection was left unsecured by the company.

FIGURE 7.12 Example of a bubble sort

names
[0]	Phil
[1]	Al
[2]	John
[3]	Jim
[4]	Bob

names
[0]	Phil
[1]	Al
[2]	John
[3]	Bob
[4]	Jim

names
[0]	Phil
[1]	Al
[2]	Bob
[3]	John
[4]	Jim

names
[0]	Phil
[1]	Al
[2]	Bob
[3]	John
[4]	Jim

names
[0]	Al
[1]	Phil
[2]	Bob
[3]	John
[4]	Jim

a. First iteration (Sorted elements are shaded.)

names
[0]	Al
[1]	Phil
[2]	Bob
[3]	John
[4]	Jim

names
[0]	Al
[1]	Bob
[2]	Phil
[3]	Jim
[4]	John

names
[0]	Al
[1]	Bob
[2]	Jim
[3]	Phil
[4]	John

names
[0]	Al
[1]	Bob
[2]	Jim
[3]	John
[4]	Phil

b. Remaining iterations (Sorted elements are shaded.)

variable to FALSE before we enter the loop and set it to TRUE if a swap occurs. If the Boolean variable is still FALSE, then the array is sorted.

Compare the processing of the bubble sort to the selection sort on an already sorted array. The selection sort algorithm gives us no way to determine whether the array is sorted; therefore, we will go through the entire algorithm.

Bubble Sort

Set firstUnsorted to 0

Set swap to TRUE

WHILE (firstUnsorted < length − 1 AND swap)

    Set swap to FALSE

    "Bubble up" the smallest item in unsorted part

    Set firstUnsorted to firstUnsorted + 1

Bubble up

Set index to length − 1

WHILE (index > firstUnsorted + 1)

    IF (data[index] < data[index − 1])

        Swap data[index] and data[index − 1]

        Set swap to TRUE

    Set index to index − 1

■ Insertion Sort

If you have only one item in the array, it is sorted. If you have two items, you can compare and swap them if necessary. Now the first two are sorted with respect to themselves. Take the third item and put it into its place relative to the first two. Now the first three items are sorted with respect to one another. The item being added to the sorted portion can be bubbled up as in the bubble sort. When you find a place where the item being inserted is smaller than the item in the array, you store the item there. current is the item being inserted into the sorted portion. See Figure 7.13.

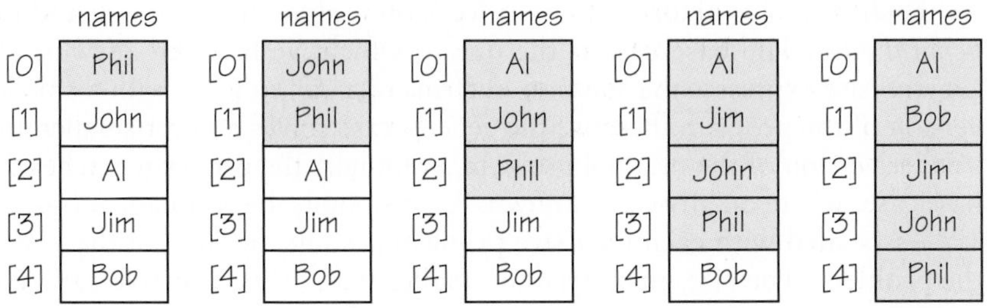

FIGURE 7.13   Insertion sort

	names			names			names			names			names
[0]	Phil		[0]	John		[0]	Al		[0]	Al		[0]	Al
[1]	John		[1]	Phil		[1]	John		[1]	Jim		[1]	Bob
[2]	Al		[2]	Al		[2]	Phil		[2]	John		[2]	Jim
[3]	Jim		[3]	Jim		[3]	Jim		[3]	Phil		[3]	John
[4]	Bob		[4]	Bob		[4]	Bob		[4]	Bob		[4]	Phil

Insertion Sort

```
Set current to 1
WHILE (current < length)
    Set index to current
    Set placeFound to FALSE
    WHILE (index > 0 AND NOT placeFound)
        IF (data[index] < data[index – 1])
            Swap data[index] and data[index – 1]
            Set index to index – 1
        ELSE
            Set placeFound to TRUE
    Set current to current + 1
```

At each iteration of a selection sort, one more item is put into its permanent place. At each iteration of an insertion sort, one more item is put into its proper place with respect to those above it.

7.6   Recursive Algorithms

When an algorithm uses its own name within itself, it is called a recursive algorithm. That is, if a task name at one level calls itself, the call is known as a *recursive* call. Recursion—the ability of an algorithm to call itself—is an alternative control structure to repetition (looping). Rather than use a looping statement to execute an algorithm segment, such an algorithm uses a selection statement to determine whether to repeat the algorithm by calling it again or to stop the process.

» Recursion The ability of an algorithm to call itself

Each recursive algorithm has at least two cases: the *base case* and the *general case*. The base case is the one to which we have an answer; the general case expresses the solution in terms of a call to itself with a smaller version of the problem. Because the general case solves an ever smaller and smaller version of the original problem, eventually the program reaches the base case, where an answer is known. At this point, the recursion stops.

Associated with each recursive problem is some measure of the size of the problem. The size must become smaller with each recursive call. The first step in any recursive solution is, therefore, to determine the *size factor*. If the problem involves a numerical value, the size factor might be the value itself. If the problem involves a structure, the size factor is probably the size of the structure.

So far, we have given a name to a task at one level and expanded the task at a lower level. Then we have collected all of the pieces into the final algorithm. With recursive algorithms, we must be able to give the algorithm data values that are different each time we execute the algorithm. Thus, before we continue with recursion, we must look at a new control structure: the *subprogram statement*. Although we are still at the algorithm level, this control structure uses the word *subprogram*.

■ Subprogram Statements

We can give a section of code a name and then use that name as a statement in another part of the program. When the name is encountered, the processing in the other part of the program halts while the named code executes. When the named code finishes executing, processing resumes with the statement just below where the name occurred. The place where the name of the code appears is known as the *calling unit*.

Two basic forms of subprograms exist: named code that does a particular task (void subprograms) and named code that also does a task but returns a single value to the calling unit (value-returning subprograms). The first form is used as a statement in the calling unit; the second form is used in an expression in the calling unit where the returned value is then used in the evaluation of the expression.

Subprograms are powerful tools for abstraction. The listing of a named subprogram allows the reader of the program to see that a task is being done without having to be bothered with the details of the task's implementation. If a subprogram needs information to execute its task, we place the name of the data value in parentheses by the subprogram heading. If the subprogram returns a value to the calling unit, it uses the word RETURN followed by the name of the data to be returned. See Figure 7.14.

a. Subprogram A does its task and calling unit continues with next statement

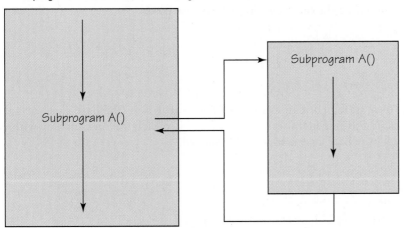

FIGURE 7.14   Subprogram flow of control

b. Subprogram B does its task and returns a value that is added to 5 and stored in x

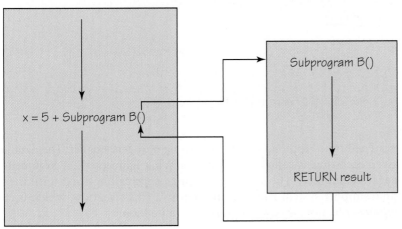

■ Recursive Factorial

The factorial of a number is defined as the number multiplied by the product of all the numbers between itself and 0:

$N! = N * (N - 1)!$

The factorial of 0 is 1. The size factor is the number for which we are calculating the factorial. We have a base case:

Factorial(0) is 1.

We also have a general case:

Factorial(N) is N * Factorial(N – 1).

An *if* statement can evaluate N to see if it is 0 (the base case) or greater than 0 (the general case). Because N is clearly getting smaller with each call, the base case is eventually reached.

```
Write "Enter N"
Read N
Set result to Factorial(N)
Write result + " is the factorial of " + N
```

```
Factorial(N)

IF (N equals 0)
     RETURN 1
ELSE
     RETURN N * Factorial(N–1)
```

Each time Factorial is called, the value of N gets smaller. The data being given each time is called the *argument*. What happens if the argument is a negative number? The subprogram just keeps calling itself until the run-time support system runs out of memory. This situation, which is called *infinite recursion*, is equivalent to an infinite loop.

■ Recursive Binary Search

Although we coded the binary search using a loop, the binary search algorithm sounds recursive. We stop when we find the item or when we know it isn't there (base cases). We continue to look for the item in the section of the array where it will be if it is present at all. A recursive algorithm must be called from a nonrecursive algorithm as we did with the factorial algorithm. Here the subprogram needs to know the first and last indices within which it is searching. Instead of resetting first or last as we did in the iterative version, we simply call the algorithm again with the new values for first and last.

BinarySearch (first, last)
_____

IF (first > last)

    RETURN FALSE

ELSE

    Set middle to (first + last)/ 2

    IF (item equals data[middle])

       RETURN TRUE

    ELSE

       IF (item < data[middle])

          BinarySearch (first, middle – 1)

       ELSE

          BinarySearch (middle + 1, last)

■ Quicksort

The Quicksort algorithm, developed by C. A. R. Hoare, is based on the idea that it is faster and easier to sort two small lists than one larger one. The name comes from the fact that, in general, Quicksort can sort a list of data elements quite rapidly. The basic strategy of this sort is "divide and conquer."

If you were given a large stack of final exams to sort by name, you might use the following approach: Pick a splitting value, say L, and divide the stack of tests into two piles, A–L and M–Z. (Note that the two piles do not necessarily contain the same number of tests.) Then take the first pile and subdivide it into two piles, A–F and G–L. The A–F pile can be further broken down into A–C and D–F. This division process goes on until the piles are small enough to be easily sorted by hand. The same process is applied to the M–Z pile.

Eventually, all of the small, sorted piles can be stacked one on top of the other to produce a sorted set of tests. See Figure 7.15.

This strategy is based on recursion—on each attempt to sort the stack of tests, the stack is divided, and then the same approach is used to sort each of the smaller stacks (a smaller case). This process continues until the small stacks do not need to be divided further (the base case). The variables first and last in the Quicksort algorithm reflect the part of the array data that is currently being processed.

FIGURE 7.15   Ordering a list using the Quicksort algorithm

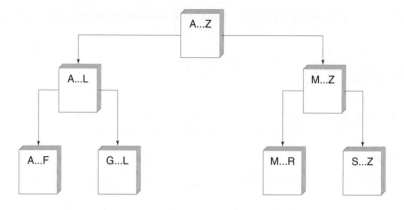

Quicksort(first, last)

IF (first < last)   // There is more than one item
   Select splitVal
   Split (splitVal)   // Array between first and
                     // splitPoint–1 <= splitVal
                     // data[splitPoint] = splitVal
                     // Array between splitPoint + 1
                     // and last > splitVal
   Quicksort (first, splitPoint − 1)
   Quicksort (splitPoint + 1, last)

How do we select splitVal? One simple solution is to use whatever value is in data[first] as the splitting value. Let's look at an example using data[first] as splitVal.

splitVal = 9

9	20	6	10	14	8	60	11

[first]   [last]

After the call to Split, all items less than or equal to splitVal are on the left side of the array and all items greater than splitVal are on the right side of the array.

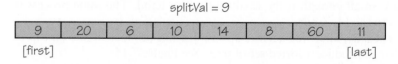

9	8	6	10	14	20	60	11

[first]   [splitPoint]   [last]

The two "halves" meet at splitPoint, the index of the last item that is less than or equal to splitVal. Note that we don't know the value of splitPoint until the splitting process is complete. We can then swap splitVal (data[first]) with the value at data[splitPoint].

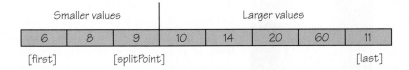

Our recursive calls to Quicksort use this index (splitPoint) to reduce the size of the problem in the general case.

Quicksort(first, splitPoint − 1) sorts the left "half" of the array. Quicksort(splitPoint + 1, last) sorts the right "half" of the array. (The "halves" are not necessarily the same size.) splitVal is already in its correct position in data[splitPoint].

What is the base case? When the segment being examined has only one item, we do not need to go on. That is represented in the algorithm by the missing *else* statement. If there is only one value in the segment being sorted, it is already in its place.

We must find a way to get all elements that are equal to or less than splitVal on one side of splitVal and all elements that are greater than splitVal on the other side. We do this by moving a pair of the indexes from the ends toward the middle of the array, looking for items that are on the wrong side of the split value. When we find pairs that are on the wrong side, we swap them and continue working our way into the middle of the array.

```
Split(splitVal)

Set left to first + 1
Set right to last
WHILE (left <= right)
    Increment left until data[left] > splitVal OR left > right
    Decrement right until data[right] < splitVal OR left > right
    IF(left < right)
        Swap data[left] and data[right]
Set splitPoint to right
Swap data[first] and data[splitPoint]
Return splitPoint
```

Tony Hoare[2]

Tony Hoare's interest in computing was awakened in the early 1950s, when he studied philosophy (together with Latin and Greek) at Oxford University under the tutelage of John Lucas. He was fascinated by the power of mathematical logic as an explanation of the apparent certainty of mathematical truth. During his National Service (1956–1958), he studied Russian in the Royal Navy. Then he took a qualification in statistics, and incidentally a course in programming given by Leslie Fox. In 1959, as a graduate student at Moscow State University, he studied the machine translation of languages (together with probability theory) in the school of Kolmogorov. To assist in efficient lookup of words in a dictionary, he discovered the well-known sorting algorithm Quicksort.

Courtesy of the Inamori Foundation

On return to England in 1960, he worked as a programmer for Elliott Brothers, a small scientific computer manufacturer. He led a team (including his later wife, Jill) in the design and delivery of the first commercial compiler for the programming language Algol 60. He attributes the success of the project to the use of Algol itself as the design language for the compiler, although the implementation used decimal machine code. Promoted to the rank of Chief Engineer, he then led a larger team on a disastrous project to implement an operating system. After managing a recovery from the failure, he moved as Chief Scientist to the computing research division, where he worked on the hardware and software architecture for future machines.

These machines were cancelled when the company merged with its rivals, and in 1968 Tony took a chance to apply for the Professorship of Computing Science at the Queen's University, Belfast. His research goal was to understand why operating systems were so much more difficult than compilers, and to see if advances in programming theory and languages could help with the problems of concurrency. In spite of civil disturbances, he built up a strong teaching and research department, and published a series of papers on the use of assertions to prove correctness of computer programs. He knew that this was long-term research, unlikely to achieve industrial application within the span of his academic career.

In 1977 he moved to Oxford University and undertook to build up the Programming Research Group, founded by Christopher Strachey. With the aid of external funding from government initiatives, industrial collaborations, and charitable donations, Oxford now teaches a range of degree courses in Computer Science, including an external Master's degree for software engineers from industry. The research of his teams at Oxford pursued an ideal that takes provable correctness as the driving force for the accurate specification, design, and development of computing systems, both critical and noncritical. Well-known results of the research include the Z specification language and the CSP concurrent programming model. A recent personal research goal has been the unification of a diverse range of theories applying to different programming languages, paradigms, and implementation technologies.

Throughout more than 30 years as an academic, Tony has maintained strong contacts with industry through consultation, teaching, and collaborative research projects. He took a particular interest in the sustenance of legacy code, where assertions are now playing a vital role, not for his original purpose of program proof, but rather in instrumentation of code for testing

» continued

Tony Hoare, continued

purposes. On reaching retirement age at Oxford, he welcomed an opportunity to return to industry as a senior researcher with Microsoft Research in Cambridge. He hopes to expand the opportunities for industrial application of good academic research, and to encourage academic researchers to continue the pursuit of deep and interesting questions in areas of long-term interest to the software industry and its customers.

Note: This biographical sketch was written by Sir Tony Hoare himself and reprinted with his permission. What he does not say is that he received the Turing Award in 1980 for his fundamental contributions to the definition and design of programming languages, and he was awarded a Knighthood in 1999 for his services to education and computer science.

Although we still have an abstract step, we can stop, because we have already expanded this abstract step in an earlier problem. This brings up a very important point: *Never reinvent the wheel.* An abstract step in one algorithm may have been solved previously either by you or by someone else. Figure 7.16 shows an example of this splitting algorithm.

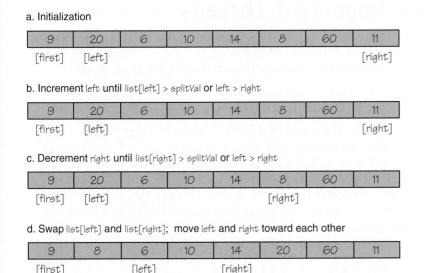

a. Initialization

b. Increment left until list[left] > splitVal or left > right

c. Decrement right until list[right] > splitVal or left > right

d. Swap list[left] and list[right]; move left and right toward each other

FIGURE 7.16 Splitting algorithm (continues on next page)

FIGURE 7.16   (continued)

e. Increment left until list[left] > splitVal or left > right
   Decrement right until list[right] <= splitVal or left > right

9	8	6	10	14	20	60	11

[first]   [right]   [left]

f. left > right so no swap occurs within the loop
   Swap list[first] and list[right]

6	8	9	10	14	20	60	11

[first]   [right]
                 (splitPoint)

Quicksort is an excellent sorting approach if the data to be sorted is in random order. If the data is already sorted, however, the algorithm degenerates so that each split has just one item in it.

Recursion is a very powerful and elegant tool. Nevertheless, not all problems can easily be solved recursively, and not all problems that have an obvious recursive solution should be solved recursively. Even so, a recursive solution is preferable for many problems. If the problem statement logically falls into two cases (a base case and a general case), recursion is a viable alternative.

7.7 Important Threads

In the last two chapters, we have mentioned several topics in passing that are important not only in problem solving but also in computing in general. Let's review some of the common threads discussed in these chapter.

■ Information Hiding

We have mentioned the idea of deferring the details several times. We have used it in the context of giving a name to a task and not worrying about how the task is to be implemented until later. Deferring the details in a design has distinct advantages. The designer sees just those details that are relevant at a particular level of the design. This practice, called information hiding, makes the details at a lower level inaccessible during the design of the higher levels.

This practice must seem very strange! Why shouldn't the details be accessible while the algorithm is being designed? Shouldn't the designer know everything? No. If the designer knows the low-level details of a module, he or she is more likely to base the module's algorithm on these

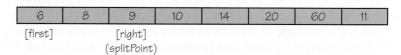

>> Information hiding The practice of hiding the details of a module with the goal of controlling access to the details of the module

details—and it is precisely these low-level details that are more likely to change. If they do, then the entire module has to be rewritten.

■ Abstraction

Abstraction and information hiding are two sides of the same coin. Information hiding is the practice of hiding details; abstraction is the result with the details hidden. As we said in Chapter 1, an abstraction is a model of a complex system that includes only the details that are essential for the viewer to know. Take, for example, Daisy, the English spaniel. To her owner, she is a household pet; to a hunter, she is a bird dog; and to the vet, she is a mammal. Her owner watches Daisy's wagging tail, hears her yelp when she gets left outside, and sees the hair she leaves everywhere. The hunter sees a finely trained helper who knows her job and does it well. The vet sees all of the organs, flesh, and bones of which she is composed. See Figure 7.17.

> ❯❯ **Abstraction** A model of a complex system that includes only the details essential to the viewer

FIGURE 7.17   Different views of the same concept

In computing, an algorithm is an abstraction of the steps needed to implement it. The casual user of a program that includes the algorithm, who sees only the description of how to run the program, is like the dog owner: He or she sees only the surface. The programmer, who incorporates another's algorithm in her program, is like the hunter who uses the well-trained dog: He or she uses the algorithm for a purpose. The implementer of the algorithm, who must understand it thoroughly, is like the vet: He or she must see the inner workings to implement the algorithm.

In computing, various kinds of abstraction are apparent. Data abstraction refers to the view of data; it is the separation of the logical view of data from its implementation. For example, your bank's computer may represent numbers in two's complement or one's complement, but this distinction is of no concern to you as long as your bank statements are accurate.

Procedural abstraction refers to the view of actions; it is the separation of the logical view of an action from its implementation. For example, when we gave a name to a subprogram, we were practicing procedural abstraction.

A third kind of abstraction in computing is called control abstraction. Control abstraction refers to the view of a control structure; it is the separation of the logical view of a control structure from its implementation. A control structure lets us alter this sequential flow of control of an algorithm. WHILE and IF are control structures. How these control structures are implemented in the languages into which we might translate an algorithm is immaterial to the design of the algorithms.

Abstraction is the most powerful tool people have for managing complexity. This statement is true in computing as well as real life.

> **Data abstraction** The separation of the logical view of data from its implementation
>
> **Procedural abstraction** The separation of the logical view of an action from its implementation
>
> **Control abstraction** The separation of the logical view of a control structure from its implementation
>
> **Control structure** A statement used to alter the normally sequential flow of control

■ Naming Things

When we write algorithms, we use shorthand phrases to stand for the tasks and data with which we are dealing. We give names to data and processes. These names are called *identifiers*. For example, we used newBase and decimalNumber in the base-changing algorithm. We also gave names to tasks. For example, we used Split to name the task of splitting an array in the Quicksort algorithm. Our identifiers for data values were created from a combination of the words, using uppercase to make the meaning clearer. We left the names of tasks as phrases. Eventually the task names must be converted to a single identifier.

When we get to the stage where we translate an algorithm into a program in a language that a computer can execute, we may have to modify the identifiers. Each language has its own rules about forming identifiers. So there is a two-stage process: Data and actions are given names in the algorithm, and then these names are translated into identifiers that meet the rules of the computer language. Notice that giving identifiers to data and actions is a form of abstraction.

■ Testing

We have demonstrated testing at the algorithm phase using algorithm walk-throughs. We have shown how to design test plans and implemented one in assembly language. Testing is important at every stage in programming. There are basically two types of testing: clear-box testing, which is based on the code itself, and black-box testing, which is based on testing all possible input values. Often, a test plan incorporates both types of testing.

Summary

Polya, in his classic book *How to Solve It*, outlined a problem-solving strategy for mathematical problems. This strategy can be applied to all problems, including those for which a computer program is to be written. These strategies include asking questions, looking for familiar things, and dividing and conquering; when these strategies are applied, they should lead to a plan for solving a problem. In computing, such a plan is called an algorithm.

Two categories of loops are distinguished: count controlled and event controlled. A count-controlled loop executes the loop a predetermined number of times. An event-controlled loop executes until an event within the loop changes.

Data comes in two forms: atomic (simple) and composite. An array is a homogeneous structure that gives a name to a collection of items and allows the user to access individual items by position within the structure.

Searching is the act of looking for a particular value in an array. In this chapter we examined the linear search in an unordered array, the linear search in a sorted array, and the binary search in a sorted array. Sorting is the act of putting the items in an array into some kind of order. The selection sort, bubble sort, insertion sort, and Quicksort are four commonly used sorting algorithms.

Recursive algorithms are algorithms for which the name of a subprogram appears in the subprogram itself. The factorial and binary search are naturally recursive algorithms.

ETHICAL ISSUES ▸ Open-Source Software Development

If an application you purchased from a proprietary software vendor breaks, you cannot pop open the hood, tinker with the source code, and continue working away. The source code is owned and copyrighted by the manufacturer, and modifying, copying, or reselling it to others is illegal.

Open-source software offers an alternative to this proprietary arrangement. Open-source applications allow users to modify the source code in any way they like. They can add to it, change it, or extend it. They can also copy it, give it away to others, or even sell it. The only proviso is that those to whom the revised code is further distributed have the same freedoms to access the source code, copy, or sell the software. This passing along of the freedoms of use is sometimes referred to as "copyleft" and is highly prized by open-source supporters. Perhaps the most famous example of open-source software is the Linux operating system, which is licensed under the Free Software Foundation's (FSF's) General Public License (GPL).

When proprietary software made its first appearance, some parties in the computing community saw it as a threat to the freedom of intellectual collaboration. They believed that software is essentially an intellectual product and, therefore, is best served by being treated as an idea: Anyone is welcome to join the debate, add an opinion, and bring friends into the conversation. Furthermore, if a person cannot gain access to software except by purchasing it from a proprietary vendor, then that individual is barred from joining the discussion until he or she hands over cash to the owner of the "idea."

In response to the changing landscape of computing in the 1980s, some MIT computer scientists formed FSF to promote the open use and sharing of software. The Boston-based group developed the GPL, which outlines the rules under which users can share, distribute, and collaborate on developing software products. For those who feel "free" might be an erroneous name, FSF points out it means "free as in free speech, not free as in free beer."

So what makes this seemingly simple idea so controversial? If anyone can upgrade or improve the product, doesn't this increase its value to users? Not according to opponents of the open-source ethic. Microsoft and other proprietary software producers view open-source code as a threat to their businesses. If people can fix and modify the source code on their own, they will not want to pay the sometimes enormous licensing fees required to use the proprietary products, nor will they want to purchase upgrades. Even more important, opponents claim, is the danger to intellectual property rights posed by the open-source model.

Open-source supporters point to the more cost-effective aspects of the model. Even if users initially pay for the software, the freedoms granted under the licensing agreement do not lock them into that choice. They can mix and match software to best suit the needs of their mission. Fans of the open-source model also note that such software tends to be more reliable, causing less downtime and requiring internal IT departments and engineers to spend less time fixing low-level problems that might otherwise cause great disruption. Those opposed to the use of software that allows anyone access to the source code claim that it poses much greater security risks than proprietary packages. If airlines, hospitals, and municipal infrastructures are using it, they leave themselves much more vulnerable to attack than if they use packages where only the maker has access to the source code.

The success of Linux has given great hope to the open-source community. This operating system is extremely popular and is even used, if somewhat sparingly, by government agencies. Versions of Linux are sold by a variety of vendors, including Red Hat, the best-known Linux distributor. Such examples serve as confirmation that the open-source model is commercially viable.

Proprietary producers have been working to block proposals that would require governments to shift to using open-source products. For now, patent and copy-

» continued

⚖️ ETHICAL ISSUES ▶ Open-Source Software Development, continued

right laws continue to favor proprietary software. Whether this will remain the case will become known in the future. Microsoft has suggested limiting open-source software in various ways, but so far has not proved successful in its quest. For now, the debate continues over whether the open-source model is a benefit for all or a danger to business and property rights.

In 2008, the open-source software community reached a legal milestone. The case in question centered on free software used in developing commercial software products for model trains. The software's creator, open-source software group Java Model Railroad Inter-face, claimed that when Matthew Katzer used its software to create commercial products without following the terms of the software license associated with the software, he had infringed on copyright laws. The software license stated that anyone using the free code had to credit the author, emphasize the source of the files, and explain how the code had been adapted. After a lower court ruling sided with Katzer, a federal appeals court ruled that open-source artistic licensing agreements could be upheld by copyright laws, enforcing the rights of companies using open-source software to protect their ideas.

🔑 Key Terms

Abstract step
Abstraction
Algorithm
Binary search
Concrete step
Control abstraction

Control structure
Data abstraction
Information hiding
Nested structure (nested logic)
Procedural abstraction
Recursion

⌘ Exercises

For Exercises 1–6, match the problem-solving strategy with the definition or example.
    A. Ask questions
    B. Look for familiar things
    C. Divide and conquer

1. The first strategy to use when given a problem.
2. Don't reinvent the wheel.
3. Strategy used in the binary search algorithms
4. Is a solution to a previous problem appropriate for the current one?
5. Strategy used in the Quicksort algorithm
6. There is an apparent contradiction in the problem statement.

For Exercises 7–10, match the following phase with its output.
- A. Analysis and specification phase
- B. Algorithm development phase
- C. Implementation phase
- D. Maintenance phase

7. Working program
8. None
9. Problem statement
10. General solution

For Exercises 11–15, match the term with the definition.
- A. Information hiding
- B. Abstraction
- C. Data abstraction
- D. Procedural abstraction
- E. Control abstraction

11. The practice of hiding the details of a module with the goal of controlling access to the details of the module
12. A model of a complex system that includes only those details essential to the viewer
13. The separation of the logical view of an action from its implementation
14. The separation of the logical view of a control structure from its implementation
15. The separation of the logical view of data from its implementation

For Exercises 16–36, mark the answers true or false as follows:
- A. True
- B. False

16. Count-controlled loops repeat a specific number of times.
17. Event-controlled loops repeat a specific number of times.
18. Count-controlled loops are controlled by a counter.
19. Event-controlled loops are controlled by an event.
20. An infinite loop is a loop that never terminates.
21. Loops can be nested, but selection structures cannot.
22. Selection structures can be nested, but loops cannot.
23. All control structures can be nested.
24. The square root algorithm uses a count-controlled loop.
25. An array is a homogeneous structure, but a record is not.
26. A record is a heterogeneous structure, but an array is not.

27. A record is a homogeneous structure; an array is a heterogeneous structure.

28. The bubble sort algorithm involves finding the smallest item in the unsorted portion of the array and swapping it with the first unsorted item.

29. Quicksort is not always quick.

30. A binary search can be applied to both a sorted array and an unsorted array.

31. A binary search is always faster than a linear search.

32. A selection sort puts one more item into its permanent place at each iteration.

33. An insertion sort puts one more item into its place with respect to the already sorted portion.

34. Recursion is another name for iteration.

35. Recursive algorithms use IF statements.

36. Iterative algorithms use WHILE statements.

Exercises 37–67 are short-answer questions.

37. List the four steps in Polya's How to Solve It list.

38. Describe the four steps listed in Exercise 37 in your own words.

39. List the problem-solving strategies discussed in this chapter.

40. Apply the problem-solving strategies to the following situations.
    a. Buying a toy for your four-year-old cousin
    b. Organizing an awards banquet four your soccer team
    c. Buying a dress or suit for an awards banquet at which you are being honored

41. Examine the solutions in Exercise 40 and determine three things they have in common.

42. What is an algorithm?

43. Write an algorithm for the following tasks.
    a. Making a peanut butter and jelly sandwich
    b. Getting up in the morning
    c. Doing your homework
    d. Driving home in the afternoon

44. List the phases of the computer problem-solving model.

45. How does the computer problem-solving model differ from Polya's problem-solving model?

46. Describe the steps in the algorithm development phase.

47. Describe the steps in the implementation phase.

48. Describe the steps in the maintenance phase.

49. Look up a recipe for chocolate brownies in a cookbook and answer the following questions.
    a. Is the recipe an algorithm? Justify your answer.
    b. Organize the recipe as an algorithm, using pseudocode.
    c. List the words that have meaning in computing.
    d. List the words that have meaning in cooking.
    e. Make the brownies and take them to your professor.

50. We said that following a recipe is easier than developing one. Go to the supermarket and buy a vegetable that you have not cooked (or eaten) before. Take it home and develop a recipe. Write up your recipe and your critique of the process. (If it is good, send it to the authors.)

51. Describe the top-down design process.

52. Differentiate between a concrete step and an abstract step.

53. Write a top-down design for the following tasks.
    a. Buying a toy for your four-year-old cousin
    b. Organizing an awards banquet four your soccer team
    c. Buying a dress or suit for an awards banquet at which you are being honored

54. Write a top-down design for the following tasks.
    a. Calculating the average of ten test scores
    b. Calculating the average of an unknown number of test scores
    c. Describe the differences in the two designs.

55. Write a top-down design for the following tasks.
    a. Finding a telephone number in the phone book
    b. Finding a telephone number on the Internet
    c. Finding a telephone number on a scrap of paper that you have lost
    d. Describe the differences among these designs.

56. Distinguish between information and data.

57. Write a top-down design for sorting a list of names into alphabetical order.

58. a. Why is information hiding important?
    b. Name three examples of information hiding that you encounter every day.

59. An airplane is a complex system.
    a. Give an abstraction of an airplane from the view of a pilot.
    b. Give an abstraction of an airplane from the view of a passenger.
    c. Give an abstraction of an airplane from the view of the cabin crew.

d. Give an abstraction of an airplane from the view of a maintenance mechanic.

e. Give an abstraction of an airplane from the view of the airline's corporate office.

60. List the identifiers and indicate whether they named data or actions for the designs in Exercise 53.

61. List the identifiers and indicate whether they named data or actions for the designs in Exercise 54.

62. List the identifiers and whether they named data or actions for the designs in Exercise 55.

Exercises 63–65 use the following array of values.

length   list

11		[0]	[1]	[2]	[3]	[4]	[5]	[6]	[7]	[8]	[9]	[10]
		23	41	66	20	2	90	9	34	19	40	99

63. Show the state of the list when firstUnsorted is first set equal to the fourth item in the selection sort.

64. Show the state of the list when firstUnsorted is first set equal to the fifth item in the bubble sort algorithm.

65. Show the state of the list when the first recursive call is made in Quicksort using list[0] as split value.

Exercises 66 and 67 use the following array of values.

length   list

11		[0]	[1]	[2]	[3]	[4]	[5]	[6]	[7]	[8]	[9]	[10]
		5	7	20	33	44	46	48	99	101	102	105

66. How many comparisons does it take using a sequential search to find the following values or determine that the item is not in the list?
   a. 4
   b. 44
   c. 45
   d. 105
   e. 106

67. How many comparisons does it take using a binary search to find the following values or determine that the item is not in the list?
    a. 4
    b. 44
    c. 46
    d. 105
    e. 106

1. Distinguish between a program that the CPU can execute directly and a program that must be translated.

2. Top-down design creates scaffolding that is used to write a program. Is all of this scaffolding just a waste of effort? Is it ever used again? Of what value is it after the program is up and running?

3. Which of the problem-solving strategies do you use the most? Can you think of some others that you use? Would they be appropriate for computing problem solving?

4. There are several common examples of open-source software that many people use in their everyday lives. Can you name any?

5. Do you believe that the quality of an open-source software product is likely to be higher or lower than the quality of software produced by a large corporation? How do you think technical support for open-source software compares to that for proprietary software?

The Programming Layer

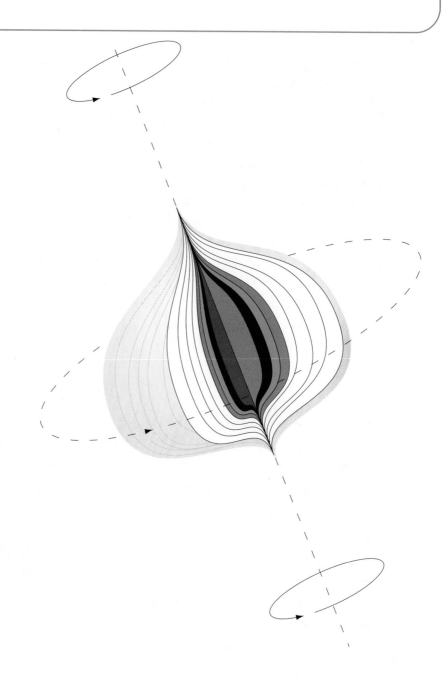

Abstract Data Types and Subprograms

8

In the programming layer, we have moved from the concreteness of machine language, to assembly language, to pseudocode, to expressing algorithms. We then went from algorithms using simple variables to algorithms using arrays.

Now we take a step up in abstraction and talk about abstract containers: composite structures for which we do not know the implementation. In computing circles, these abstract containers are called *abstract data types*. We know their properties and operations and we understand which types of values they can contain, but we have no information about their internal structure or implementation. That is, we know what the operations are and what they do, but we do not know how the operations are implemented.

The algorithm design we have been using is a top-down model, in which we break a task into smaller pieces. We

Goals

After studying this chapter, you should be able to:

- distinguish between an array-based visualization and a linked visualization.

- distinguish between an array and a list.

- distinguish between an unsorted list and a sorted list.

- distinguish between the behavior of a stack and the behavior of a queue.

- distinguish between a binary tree and a binary search tree.

- draw the binary search tree that is built from inserting a series of items.

- understand the difference between a tree and a graph.

- explain the concept of subprograms and parameters and distinguish between value and reference parameters.

conclude this chapter with more about subprogram statements, which are both a way to make the code mirror the design and the way that algorithms and subalgorithms communicate.

8.1 What Is an Abstract Data Type?

An abstract data type (ADT) is a container whose properties (data and operations) are specified independently of any particular implementation. Recall that the goal in design is to reduce complexity through abstraction. If we can define useful structures and the operations that manipulate those structures at the logical level, we can use them as if they exist when we need them in our designs.

To put the concept of an ADT into context, we need to look at how we view data. In computing, we view data from three perspectives: the application level, the logical level, and the implementation level.

The application (or user) level is the view of the data within a particular problem. The logical (or abstract) level is an abstract view of the data values (the domain) and the operations that manipulate them. The implementation level is a specific representation of the structure that holds the data items and the coding of the operations in a programming language. This view sees the properties represented as specific data fields and subprograms. It is concerned with data structures, the implementation of composite data field in an abstract data type.

The abstract data types that we examine in this chapter are those that history and experience have shown come up again and again in real-world problems. These ADTs are containers in which data items are stored, and each exhibits specific behaviors. They are called containers because their sole purpose is to hold other objects.

8.2 Stacks

Stacks and queues are abstract composite structures that are often thought of as a pair—like peanut butter and jelly, or motherhood and apple pie. Why this is so must be more for historical reasons than anything else, because these two structures have quite different behaviors.

A stack is an abstract composite structure in which accesses are made at only one end. You can insert an item as the first one and you can remove the first one. This design models many things in real life. Accountants call it LIFO, which stands for "last in, first out." The plate holder in a cafeteria has this property: We can take only the top plate. When we do so, the plate below rises to the top so the next person can take one. Canned

Abstract data type (ADT) A container whose properties (data and operations) are specified independently of any particular implementation

Data structure The implementation of a composite data field in an abstract data type

Containers Objects whose role is to hold and manipulate other objects

goods on a grocer's shelf exhibit this property. When we take the first can in a row, we are taking the last can put in that row.

Another way of stating the accessing behavior of a stack is to say that the item removed is the item that has been in the stack the shortest time. Viewing a stack from this perspective is more abstract. The insertion operation has no constraints; the entire LIFO behavior is specified through the removal operation.

The mental image of the cafeteria plates has left an imprint on the traditional names used for the insertion and removal operations. Adding an item to the stack is called Push; removing an item is called Pop. We Push an item onto the stack, and we Pop an item off the stack. A stack does not have the property of length, so there is no operation that returns the number of items on the stack. We do need operations that determine whether a stack is IsEmpty, however, because trying to Pop an item when the stack is empty is an error.

Here is an algorithm that reads in numbers and prints them in reverse order using a stack. We have not colored the stack operations in red because they have already been implemented by someone else; they are ours to use. Because the more data is not relevant to our discussion, we leave it unexpanded here and in the following algorithms.

```
WHILE (more data)
      Read value
      Push(myStack, value)
WHILE (NOT IsEmpty(myStack))
      Pop(myStack, value)
      Write value
```

Desk check this algorithm to convince yourself that the values are, indeed, written in reverse order.

8.3 Queues

A queue is an abstract structure in which items are entered at one end and removed from the other end. Accountants call this behavior FIFO, for "first in, first out." This ADT sounds like a waiting line in a bank or supermarket. Indeed, queues are used to simulate this type of situation. Insertions are made at the rear of the queue, and removals are made from the front of the queue.

Another way of stating the accessing behavior of a queue is to say that the item removed is the item that has been in the queue the longest time. Viewing a queue from this perspective is more abstract. Like the stack, the insert operation has no constraints; the entire FIFO behavior is specified in the removal operation. Unfortunately, there is no standard queue terminology relating to the insertion and deletion operations. Enqueue, Enque, Enq, Enter, and Insert are all names used for the insertion operation. Dequeue, Deque, Deq, Delete, and Remove are names used for the deletion operation.

Here is an algorithm that reads in data values and prints them in the order in which they were entered:

```
WHILE (more data)
    Read value
    Enque(myQueue, value)
WHILE (NOT IsEmpty(myQueue))
    Deque(myQueue, value)
    Write value
```

8.4 Lists

Lists occur as naturally in programming as they do in real life. We manipulate guest lists, grocery lists, class lists, and things-to-do lists. The list of lists is endless. Three properties characterize lists: The items are homogeneous, the items are linear, and lists have varying lengths. By *linear*, we mean that each item except the first has a unique component that comes before it, and each item except the last has a unique component that comes after it. For example, if there are at least three items in a list, the second item comes after the first and before the third.

Whereas stacks and queues have all the semantics in the deletion operation, lists usually provide operations to insert an item (Insert), delete an item (Delete), check whether an item is there (IsThere), and report the number of items in a list (GetLength). In addition, they have some mechanism for allowing the user to view each item in sequence (Reset, GetNext, MoreItems). Because items can be deleted and retrieved, the items in the list must be able to be compared.

Do not mistake a list for an array. An array is a built-in structure; a list is an abstract structure. However, a list may be implemented in an array, as shown in Figure 8.1.

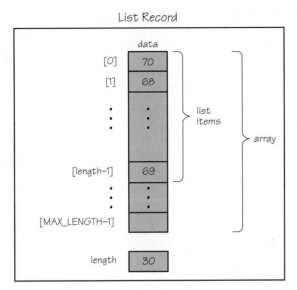

List Record

FIGURE 8.1   An unsorted list of integers

A list may also be visualized as a linked structure. A linked structure is based on the concept of a node. A node consists of two pieces of information: the user's data and a link or pointer that indicates where to find the next node. The end of the list is a link that contains null, which is indicated by a '/'. See Figure 8.2.

Unordered lists are those for which order is unimportant. Items are just haphazardly put into them. Sorted lists are those where there is a semantic relationship between items in the list. All items except the first come before the next item in this kind of list under some ordering relationship. All items except the last come after the one before it under the same relationship. Figures 8.3 and 8.4 visualize the array-based and linked versions of a sorted list.

> Linked structure An implementation of a container where the items are stored together with information on where the next item can be found

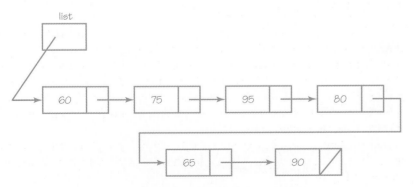

FIGURE 8.2   An unsorted linked list

FIGURE 8.3   A sorted list of integers

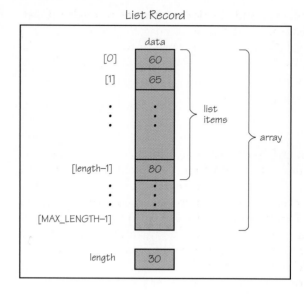

FIGURE 8.4   A sorted linked list

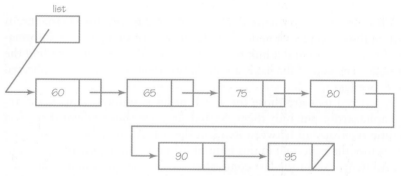

Here is an algorithm that reads values from a file and puts them into a list. The list is then printed.

```
WHILE (more data)
    Read value
    Insert(myList, value)
Reset(myList)
Write "Items in the list are "
WHILE (MoreItems(myList))
    GetNext(myList, nextItem)
    Write nextItem, ' '
```

We use Reset, MoreItems, and GetNext to iterate through the list, returning each item in sequence. If the list is an unsorted list, the items will be printed in the order in which they are inserted. If the list is sorted, the items will be printed in sorted order. This algorithm works regardless of the implementation of the list.

8.5 Trees

Abstract structures such as lists, stacks, and queues are linear in nature. Only one relationship in the data is being modeled. Items are next to each other in a list or are next to each other in terms of time in a stack or queue. Depicting more complex relationships requires more complex structures. Take, for example, family relationships. If we want to model family relationships in a program, we would need a hierarchical structure. The parents would appear at the top of the hierarchy, the children would be at the next level, the grandchildren at the next level, and so on (Figure 8.5).

Such hierarchical structures are called trees, and there is a rich mathematical theory relating to them. In computing, however, we often restrict our discussion to binary trees. In binary trees, each node in the tree can have no more than two children.

■ Binary Trees

A binary tree is an abstract structure in which each node is capable of having two successor nodes, called children. Each of the children, being nodes in the binary tree, can also have up to two child nodes, and these children can also have up to two children, and so on, giving the tree its branching structure. The beginning of the tree is a unique starting node called the root, which is not the child of any node. See Figure 8.6.

Each node in the tree may have zero, one, or two children. The node to the left of a node, if it exists, is called its *left child*. For example, in Figure 8.6, the left child of the root node contains the value 2. The node to the right of a node, if it exists, is its *right child*. The right child of the root node in Figure 8.6 contains the value 3. If a node has only one child, the

>> **Binary tree** An abstract composite structure with a unique starting node called the root, in which each node is capable of having two child nodes and in which a unique path exists from the root to every other node

>> **Root** The unique starting node in a tree

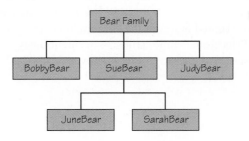

FIGURE 8.5   The Bear family tree

John von Neumann[1]

John von Neumann was a brilliant mathematician, physicist, logician, and computer scientist. Legends have been passed down about his astonishing memory and the phenomenal speed at which von Neumann solved problems. He used his talents not only for furthering his mathematical theories, but also for memorizing entire books and reciting them years after he had read them. But ask a highway patrolman about von Neumann's driving ability and he would be likely to throw up his hands in despair; behind the wheel, the mathematical genius was as reckless as a rebel teenager.

Courtesy of Los Alamos National Library

John von Neumann was born in Hungary in 1903, the oldest son of a wealthy Jewish banker. He was able to divide 8-digit numbers in his head by the age of 6. He entered high school by the time he was 11, and it wasn't long before his math teachers recommended he be tutored by university professors. He enrolled at the University of Berlin in 1921 to study chemistry as a compromise with his father, who wanted him to study something that would allow him to make money. He received his diploma in chemical engineering from the Technische Hochschule in Zürich in 1926. In the same year, he received his doctorate in mathematics from the University of Budapest, with a thesis on set theory. During the period from 1926 to 1929, von Neumann lectured at Berlin and at Hamburg while holding a Rockefeller fellowship for postdoctoral studies at the University of Göttingen.

von Neumann came to the United States in the early 1930s to teach at Princeton, while still keeping his academic posts in Germany. He resigned the German posts when the Nazis came to power; he was not, however, a political refugee as so many were at that time. While at Princeton, he worked with the talented and as-yet-unknown British student Alan Turing. He continued his brilliant mathematical career, becoming editor of *Annals of Mathematics* and co-editor of *Compositio Mathematica*. During World War II, von Neumann was hired as a consultant for the U.S. Armed Forces and related civilian agencies because of his knowledge of hydrodynamics. He was also called upon to participate in the construction of the atomic bomb in 1943. It was not surprising that, following this work, President Eisenhower appointed him to the Atomic Energy Commission in 1955.

Even though bombs and their performance fascinated von Neumann for many years, a fortuitous meeting in 1944 with Herbert Goldstine, a pioneer who developed one of the first operational electronic digital computers, introduced the mathematician to something more important than bombs—computers. von Neumann's chance conversation with Goldstine in a train station sparked a new fascination for him. He started working on the stored program concept and concluded that internally storing a program eliminated the hours of tedious labor required to reprogram computers (in those days). He also developed a new computer architecture to perform this storage task. In fact, today's computers are often referred to as von Neumann machines because the architectural principles he described have proven so tremendously successful. Changes in computers over the past 40 years have been primarily in terms

» continued

John von Neumann, continued

of the speed and composition of the fundamental circuits, but the basic architecture designed by von Neumann has persisted.

During the 1950s, von Neumann was a consultant for IBM, where he reviewed proposed and ongoing advanced technology projects. One such project was John Backus's FORTRAN, which von Neumann reportedly questioned, asking why anyone would want more than one machine language. In 1957, von Neumann died of bone cancer in Washington, D.C., at the age of 54. Perhaps his work with the atomic bomb resulted in the bone cancer that caused the death of one of the most brilliant and interesting minds of the twentieth century.

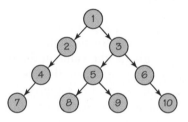

FIGURE 8.6   A binary tree

child could be on either side, but it is always on one particular side. In Figure 8.6, the root node is the parent of the nodes containing 2 and 3. (Earlier textbooks used the terms *left son*, *right son*, and *father* to describe these relationships.) If a node in the tree has no children, it is called a *leaf*. In Figure 8.6, the nodes containing 7, 8, 9, and 10 are leaf nodes.

In addition to specifying that a node may have up to two children, the definition of a binary tree states that a unique path exists from the root to every other node. In other words, every node (except the root) has a unique (single) parent.

Each of the root node's children is itself the root of a smaller binary tree, or subtree. In Figure 8.6, the root node's left child, containing 2, is the root of its left subtree, while the right child, containing 3, is the root of its right subtree. In fact, any node in the tree can be considered the root node of a subtree. The subtree whose root node has the value 2 also includes the nodes with values 4 and 7. These nodes are the descendants of the node containing 2. The descendants of the node containing 3 are the nodes with the values 5, 6, 8, 9, and 10. A node is the ancestor of another node if it is the parent of the node or the parent of some other ancestor of that node.

> **Leaf node** A tree node that has no children

(Yes, this is a recursive definition.) In Figure 8.6, the ancestors of the node with the value 9 are the nodes containing 5, 3, and 1. Obviously, the root of the tree is the ancestor of every other node in the tree.

■ Binary Search Trees

A tree is analogous to an unordered list. To find an item in the tree, we must examine every node until either we find the one we want or we discover that it isn't in the tree. A binary *search* tree is like a sorted list in that there is a semantic ordering in the nodes.

A binary search tree has the shape property of a binary tree; that is, a node in a binary search tree can have zero, one, or two children. In addition, a binary search tree has a semantic property that characterizes the values in the nodes in the tree: The value in any node is greater than the value in any node in its left subtree and less than the value in any node in its right subtree. See Figure 8.7.

Searching a Binary Search Tree

Let's search for the value 18 in the tree shown in Figure 8.7. We compare 18 with 15, the value in the root node. Because 18 is greater than 15, we know that if 18 is in the tree it will be in the right subtree of the root. Note the similarity of this approach to our binary search of a linear structure. As in the linear structure, we eliminate a large portion of the data with one comparison.

Next we compare 18 with 17, the value in the root of the right subtree. Because 18 is greater than 17, we know that if 18 is in the tree, it will be in the right subtree of the root. We compare 18 with 19, the value in the root of the right subtree. Because 18 is less than 19, we know that if 18 is in the tree, it will be in the left subtree of the root. We compare 18 with 18, the value in the root of the left subtree, and we have a match.

Now let's look at what happens when we search for a value that is not in the tree. Let's look for 4 in Figure 8.7. We compare 4 with 15. Because 4 is less than 15, if 4 is in the tree, it will be in the left subtree of the root. We compare 4 with 7, the value in the root of the left subtree. Because 4 is less than 7, if 4 is in the tree, it will be in 7's left subtree. We compare 4

FIGURE 8.7   A binary search tree

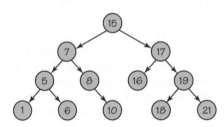

with 5. Because 4 is less than 5, if 4 is in the tree, it will be in 5's left subtree. We compare 4 with 1. Because 4 is greater than 1, if 4 is in the tree, it will be in 1's right subtree. But 1's left subtree is empty, so we know that 4 is not in the tree.

In looking at the algorithms that work with trees, we use the following conventions: If current points to a node, info(current) refers to the user's data in the node, left(current) points to the root of the left subtree of current, and right(current) points to the root of the right subtree of current. null is a special value that means that the pointer points to nothing. Thus, if a pointer contains null, the subtree is empty.

Using this notation, we can now write the search algorithm. We start at the root of the tree and move to the root of successive subtrees until either we find the item we are looking for or we find an empty subtree. The item to be searched for and the root of the tree (subtree) are parameters—the information that the subalgorithm needs to execute.

```
IsThere(tree, item)

IF (tree is null)
       RETURN FALSE
ELSE
     IF (item equals info(tree))
          RETURN TRUE
     ELSE
          IF (item < info(tree))
                IsThere(left(tree), item)
          ELSE
                IsThere(right(tree), item)
```

With each comparison, either we find the item or we cut the tree in half by moving to search in the left subtree or the right subtree. In half? Well, not exactly. The shape of a binary tree is not always well balanced. Clearly, the efficiency of a search in a binary search tree is directly related to the shape of the tree. How does the tree get its shape? The shape of the tree is determined by the order in which items are entered into the tree. Look at Figure 8.8. In part (a), the four-level tree is comparatively balanced. The nodes could have been entered in several different orders to get this tree. By comparison, the ten-level tree in part (b) could only have come from the values being entered in order.

FIGURE 8.8   Two variations of a
binary search tree

a. A four-level tree

b. A ten-level tree

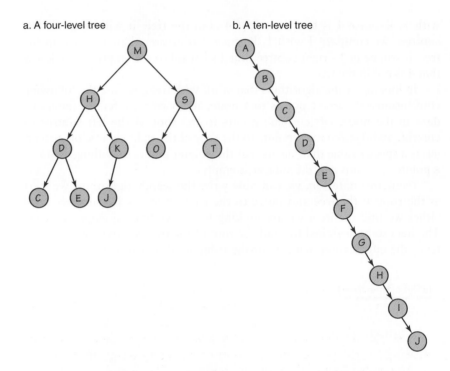

Building a Binary Search Tree

How do we build a binary search tree? One clue lies in the search algorithm we just used. If we follow the search path and do not find the item,
we end up at the place where the item would be if it were in the tree. Let's
now build a binary search tree using the following strings: john, phil, lila,
kate, becca, judy, june, mari, jim, sue.

Because john is the first value to be inserted, it goes into the root. The
second value, phil, is greater than john, so it goes into the root of the right
subtree. lila is greater than john but less than phil, so lila goes into the root of
the left subtree of phil. The tree now looks like this:

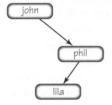

kate is greater than john, but less than phil and lila, so kate goes into the
root of the left subtree of lila. becca is less than john, so becca goes into the

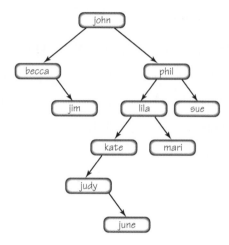

FIGURE 8.9   A binary search tree built from strings

root of the left subtree of john. judy is greater than john but less than phil, lila, and kate, so judy goes into the root of the left subtree of kate. We follow the same path for june as we did for judy. june is greater than judy, so june goes into the root of the right subtree of judy. mari becomes the root of lila's right subtree; jim becomes the root of the right subtree of becca; and sue becomes the root of the right subtree of phil. The final tree is shown in Figure 8.9.

```
Insert(tree, item)

IF (tree is null)
    Put item in tree
ELSE
    IF (item < info(tree))
        Insert (left(tree), item)
    ELSE
        Insert (right(tree), item)
```

Table 8.1 shows a trace of inserting nell into the tree shown in Figure 8.9. We use the contents of the info part of the node within parentheses to indicate the pointer to the subtree with that value as a root.

Although Put item in tree is abstract, we do not expand it. We would need to know more about the actual implementation of the tree to do so.

TABLE 8.1   Trace of Inserting *nell* into the Tree in Figure 8.9

Call to Insert	1st IF Statement	2nd IF Statement	Action or Call
Insert((john),nell)	(john)!=null	nell>john	Insert into the right subtree
Insert((phil),nell)	(phil)!=null	nell<phil	Insert into the left subtree
Insert((lila),nell)	(lila)!=null	nell>lila	Insert into the right subtree
Insert((mari),nell)	(mari)!=null	nell>mari	Insert into the right subtree
Insert((null),nell)	null=null		Store *nell* as root of the right subtree of (mari)

Printing the Data in a Binary Search Tree

To print the value in the root, we must first print all the values in its left subtree, which by definition are smaller than the value in the root. Once we print the value in the root, we must print all the values in the root's right subtree, which by definition are greater than the value in the root. We are then finished. Finished? But what about the values in the left and right subtrees? How do we print them? Why, the same way, of course. They are, after all, just binary search trees.

This algorithm sounds too easy. That's the beauty of recursive algorithms: They are often short and elegant (although sometimes they take some thought to trace). Let's write and trace this algorithm using the tree shown below the algorithm. We number the calls in our trace because there are two recursive calls. See Table 8.2.

```
Print (tree)

IF (tree is NOT null)
      Print (left(tree))        // Recursive call R1
      Write info(tree)
      Print(right(tree))        // Recursive call R2
```

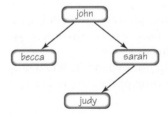

TABLE 8.2   Trace of Printing the Previous Tree

Calls	Which Call	IF Statement	Action or Call
Print((john))	R1	(john)!=null	Print(left(john))
Print((becca))	R1	(becca)!=null	Print(left(becca))
Print(null)	R1	null=null	Return
Print((becca))			Print becca, Print(right(becca))
Print(null)	R2	null=null	Return, Return
Print((john))			Print john, Print(right(john))
Print((sarah))	R2	(sarah)!=null	Print(left(sarah))
Print((judy))	R1	(judy)!=null	Print(left(judy))
Print(null)	R1	null=null	Return
Print((judy))			Print judy, Print(right(judy))
Print(null)	R2	null=null	Return, Return
Print((sarah))			Print sarah, Print(right(sarah))
Print(null)	R2	null=null	Return, Return

This algorithm prints the items in the binary search tree in ascending value order. Other traversals of the tree print the items in other orders. We explore them in the exercises.

■ Other Operations

By now, you should realize that a binary search tree is an object with the same functionality as a list. The characteristic that separates a binary search tree from a simple list is the efficiency of the operations; the other behaviors are the same. We have not shown the Remove algorithm, because it is too complex for this text. We have also ignored the concept length that must accompany the tree if it is to be used to implement a list. Rather than keep track of the number of items in the tree as we build it, let's write an algorithm that counts the number of nodes in the tree.

How many nodes are in an empty tree? Zero. How many nodes are in any tree? There are one plus the number of nodes in the left subtree and the number of nodes in the right subtree. This definition leads to a recursive definition of the Length operation:

Length(tree)

IF (tree is null)
    RETURN 0
ELSE
    RETURN Length(left(tree)) + Length(right(tree)) + 1

8.6 Graphs

The Bear family as shown in Figure 8.5 depicts only parent and child relationships. There is no way to determine that BobbyBear, JuneBear, and JudyBear are siblings. Wouldn't it be nice to be able to represent other types of relationships such as sibling, cousin, aunt, and so on?

Trees are a useful way to represent relationships in which a hierarchy exists. That is, a node is pointed to by at most one other node (its parent). If we remove the restriction that each node may have only one parent node, we have a data structure called a graph. A graph is made up of a set of nodes called vertices and a set of lines called edges (or arcs) that connect the nodes.

The vertices in the graph represent objects, and the edges describe relationships among the vertices. For instance, if the graph is representing a map, the vertices might be the names of cities, and the edges that link the vertices could represent roads between pairs of cities. Because the roads that run between cities are two-way paths, the edges in this graph have no direction. Such a graph is called an undirected graph. However, if the edges that link the vertices represent flights from one city to another, the direction of each edge is important. The existence of a flight (edge) from Houston to Austin does not assure the existence of a flight from Austin to Houston. A graph whose edges are directed from one vertex to another is called a directed graph (or digraph). A weighted graph is one in which there are values attached to the edges in the graph.

Look at the graphs in Figure 8.10. The relationships among siblings are undirected. For example, June is Sarah's sibling and Sarah is June's sibling; see Figure 8.10(a). The prerequisite chart in Figure 8.10(c) is directed: Computer Science I must come before Computer Science II. The flight schedule is both directed and weighted; see Figure 8.10(b). There is a flight from Dallas to Denver that covers a distance of 780 miles, but there is not a direct flight from Denver to Dallas.

≫ **Graph** A data structure that consists of a set of nodes and a set of edges that relate the nodes to each other

≫ **Vertex** A node in a graph

≫ **Edge (arc)** A pair of vertices representing a connection between two nodes in a graph

≫ **Undirected graph** A graph in which the edges have no direction

≫ **Directed graph (digraph)** A graph in which each edge is directed from one vertex to another (or the same) vertex

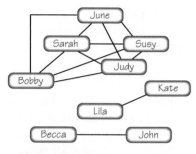

a. Vertices: People
   Edges: Siblings

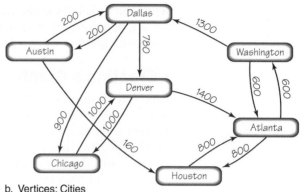

b. Vertices: Cities
   Edges: Direct Flights

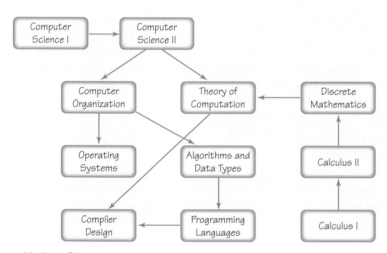

c. Vertices: Courses
   Edges: Prerequisites

FIGURE 8.10   Examples of graphs

If two vertices are connected by an edge, we say they are **adjacent vertices**. In Figure 8.10, June is adjacent to Bobby, Sarah, Judy, and Susy. A **path** from one vertex to another consists of a sequence of vertices that connect them. For example, there is a path from Austin to Dallas to Denver to Chicago. There is not a path from June to Lila, Kate, Becca, or John.

Vertices represent whatever objects are being modeled: people, houses, cities, courses, concepts, and so on. The edges represent relationships between those objects. For example, people are related to other people, houses are on the same street, cities are linked by direct flights, courses have prerequisites, and concepts are derived from other concepts. (See

» **Adjacent vertices** Two vertices that are connected by an edge

» **Path** A sequence of vertices that connects two nodes in a graph

Figure 8.10.) Mathematically, vertices are the undefined concept upon which graph theory rests. There is a great deal of formal mathematics associated with graphs, which is beyond the scope of this book.

■ Creating a Graph

Lists, stacks, queues, and trees are all just holding containers. The user chooses which is most appropriate for a particular problem. There are no inherent semantics other than those built into the retrieval process: A stack returns the item that has been in the stack the least amount of time; a queue returns the item that has been in the queue the longest amount of time. Lists and trees return the information that is requested. A graph, in contrast, has algorithms defined upon it that actually solve classic problems. First we talk about building a graph; then we discuss problems that are solvable using a graph.

A lot of information is represented in a graph: the vertices, the edges, and the weights. Let's visualize the structure as a table using the flight connection data. The rows and columns in Table 8.3 are labeled with the city names. A zero in a cell indicates that there is no flight from the row city to the column city. The values in the table represent the number of miles from the row city to the column city.

To build such a table we must have the following operations:

- Add a vertex to the table
- Add an edge to the table
- Add a weight to the table

We find a position in the table by stating the row name and the column name. That is, (Atlanta, Houston) has a flight of 800 miles. (Houston, Austin) contains a zero, so there is no direct flight from Houston to Austin.

TABLE 8.3   Data for the Flight Graph

	Atlanta	Austin	Chicago	Dallas	Denver	Houston	Washington
Atlanta	0	0	0	0	0	800	600
Austin	0	0	0	200	0	160	0
Chicago	0	0	0	0	1000	0	0
Dallas	0	200	900	0	780	0	0
Denver	1400	0	1000	0	0	0	0
Houston	800	0	0	0	0	0	0
Washington	600	0	0	1300	0	0	0

▪ Graph Algorithms

There are three classic searching algorithms defined on a graph, each of which answers a different question.

- ▪ Can I get from City X to City Y on my favorite airline?
- ▪ How can I fly from City X to City Y with the fewest number of stops?
- ▪ What is the shortest flight (in miles) from City X to City Y?

The answers to these three questions involve a depth-first search, a breadth-first search, and single-source shortest-path search.

Depth-First Search

Can I get from City X to City Y on my favorite airline? Given a starting vertex and an ending vertex, let's develop an algorithm that finds a path from startVertex to endVertex. We need a systematic way to keep track of the cities as we investigate them. Let's use a stack to store vertices as we encounter them in trying to find a path between the two vertices. With a depth-first search, we examine the first vertex that is adjacent with startVertex; if this is endVertex, the search is over. Otherwise, we examine all the vertices that can be reached in one step from this first vertex.

Meanwhile, we need to store the other vertices that are adjacent with startVertex to use later if we need them. If a path does not exist from the first vertex adjacent with startVertex, we come back and try the second vertex, third vertex, and so on. Because we want to travel as far as we can down one path, backtracking if endVertex is not found, a stack is the appropriate structure for storing the vertices.

```
Depth First Search(startVertex, endVertex)

Set found to FALSE
Push(myStack, startVertex)
WHILE (NOT IsEmpty(myStack) AND NOT found)
    Pop(myStack, tempVertex)
    IF (tempVertex equals endVertex)
        Write endVertex
        Set found to TRUE
    ELSE IF (tempVertex not visited)
        Write tempVertex
        Push all unvisited vertexes adjacent with tempVertex
        Mark tempVertex as visited
IF (found)
    Write "Path has been printed"
ELSE
    Write "Path does not exist"
```

We mark a vertex as visited once we have put all its adjacent vertices on the stack. If we process a vertex that has already been visited, we keep putting the same vertices on the stack over and over again. Then the algorithm isn't an algorithm at all because it might never end. So we must not process a vertex more than once.

Let's apply this algorithm to the sample airline-route graph in Figure 8.10(b). We want to fly from Austin to Washington. We initialize our search by pushing our starting city onto the stack [Figure 8.11(a)]. At the beginning of the loop, we pop the current city, Austin, from the stack. The places we can reach directly from Austin are Dallas and Houston; we push both these vertices onto the stack [Figure 8.11(b)]. At the beginning of the second iteration, we pop the top vertex from the stack— Houston. Houston is not our destination, so we resume our search from there. There is only one flight out of Houston, to Atlanta; we push Atlanta onto the stack [Figure 8.11(c)]. Again we pop the top vertex from the stack. Atlanta is not our destination, so we continue searching from there. Atlanta has flights to two cities: Houston and Washington.

But we just came from Houston! We don't want to fly back to cities that we have already visited; this could cause an infinite loop. But we have already taken care of this problem: Houston has already been visited, so we continue without putting anything on the stack. The second adjacent vertex, Washington, has not been visited, so we push it onto the stack [Figure 8.11(d)]. Again we pop the top vertex from the stack. Washington is our destination, so the search is complete.

Figure 8.12 shows the result of asking if we can reach Washington from Austin.

This search is called a depth-first search because we go to the deepest branch, examining all the paths beginning at Houston before we come back to search from Dallas. When you have to backtrack, you take the branch closest to where you dead-ended. That is, you go as far as you can down one path before you take alternative choices at earlier branches.

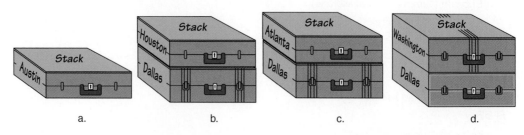

a.   b.   c.   d.

FIGURE 8.11   Using a stack to store the routes

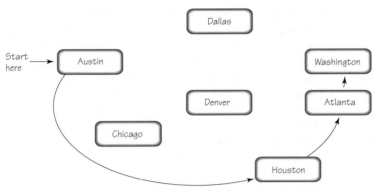

FIGURE 8.12 The depth-first search

Breadth-First Search

How can I get from City X to City Y in the fewest number of stops? The breadth-first traversal answers this question. When we come to a dead end in a depth-first search, we back up as *little* as possible. We try another route from the most recent vertex—the route on top of our stack. In a breadth-first search, we want to back up as *far* as possible to find a route originating from the earliest vertices. The stack is not the right structure for finding an early route. It keeps track of things in the order opposite of their occurrence—that is, the latest route is on top. To keep track of things in the order in which they happen, we use a queue. The route at the front of the queue is a route from an earlier vertex; the route at the back of the queue is from a later vertex. Thus, if we substitute a queue for a stack, we get the answer to our question.

Breadth First Search(startVertex, endVertex)

Set found to FALSE
Enque(myQueue, startVertex)
WHILE (NOT IsEmpty(myQueue) AND NOT found)
    Deque(myQueue, tempVertex)
    IF (tempVertex equals endVertex)
        Write endVertex
        Set found to TRUE
    ELSE IF (tempVertex not visited)
        Write tempVertex
        Enque all unvisited vertexes adjacent with tempVertex
        Mark tempVertex as visited
IF (found)
    Write "Path has been printed"
ELSE
    Write "Path does not exist"

Let's apply this algorithm to the same airline-route graph in Figure 8.10(b). Which path gives us the route from Austin to Washington with the fewest stops? Austin is in the queue to start the process [Figure 8.13(a)]. We deque Austin and enqueue all the cities that can be reached directly from Austin: Dallas and Houston [Figure 8.13(b)]. Then we dequeue the front queue element. Dallas is not the destination we seek, so we enqueue all the adjacent cities that have not yet been visited: Chicago and Denver [Figure 8.13(c)]. (Austin has been visited already, so it is not enqueued.) Again we dequeue the front element from the queue. This element is the other "one-stop" city— Houston. Houston is not the desired destination, so we continue the search. There is only one flight out of Houston, and it is to Atlanta. Because we haven't visited Atlanta before, it is enqueued [Figure 8.13(d)].

Now we know that we cannot reach Washington with one stop, so we start examining the two-stop connections. We dequeue Chicago; this is not our destination, so we put its adjacent city, Denver, into the queue [Figure 8.13(e)]. Now this is an interesting situation: Denver is in the queue twice. We have put Denver into the queue in one step and removed its previous

FIGURE 8.13   Using a queue to store the routes

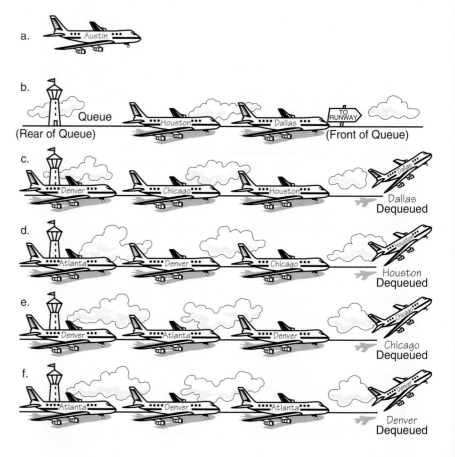

a.   Austin

b.
    Queue
(Rear of Queue)   Houston   Dallas   TO RUNWAY
                                            (Front of Queue)

c.
    Denver   Chicago   Houston   Dallas
                                                    Dallas
                                                    Dequeued

d.
    Atlanta   Denver   Chicago   Houston
                                                    Houston
                                                    Dequeued

e.
    Denver   Atlanta   Denver   Chicago
                                                    Chicago
                                                    Dequeued

f.
    Atlanta   Denver   Atlanta   Denver
                                                    Denver
                                                    Dequeued

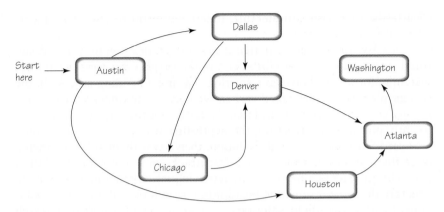

FIGURE 8.14 The breadth-first search

entry at the next step. Denver is not our destination, so we put its adjacent cities that haven't been visited (only Atlanta) into the queue [Figure 8.13(f)]. This processing continues until Washington is put into the queue (from Atlanta), and is finally dequeued. We have found the desired city, and the search is complete (Figure 8.14).

As you can see from these two algorithms, a depth-first search goes as far down a path from startVertex as it can before looking for a path beginning at the second vertex adjacent with startVertex. In contrast, a breadth-first search examines all of the vertices adjacent with startVertex before looking at those adjacent with these vertices.

Single-Source Shortest-Path Search

What is the shortest flight (in miles) from Austin to some other city? We know from the two search operations just discussed that there may be multiple paths from one vertex to another. Suppose that we want to find the *shortest path* from Austin to each of the other cities that your favorite airline serves. By "shortest path," we mean the path whose edge values (weights), when added together, have the smallest sum. Consider the following two paths from Austin to Washington:

Austin	
	160 miles
Houston	
	800 miles
Atlanta	
	600 miles
Washington	
Total miles 1560 miles	

Austin	
	200 miles
Dallas	
	780 miles
Denver	
	1400 miles
Atlanta	
	600 miles
Washington	
Total miles 2980 miles	

Clearly the first path is preferable, unless you want to collect frequent-flyer miles.

Let's develop an algorithm that displays the shortest path from a designated starting city to *every other city* in the graph—this time we are not searching for a path between a starting city and an ending city. As in the two graph searches described earlier, we need an auxiliary structure for storing cities that we process later. By retrieving the city that was most recently put into the structure, the depth-first search tries to keep going "forward." It tries a one-flight solution, then a two-flight solution, then a three-flight solution, and so on. It backtracks to a fewer-flight solution only when it reaches a dead end. By retrieving the city that had been in the structure the longest time, the breadth-first search tries all one-flight solutions, then all two-flight solutions, and so on. The breadth-first search finds a path with a minimum number of flights.

Of course, the minimum *number* of flights does not necessarily mean the minimum *total distance*. Unlike the depth-first and breadth-first searches, the shortest-path traversal must account for the number of miles (edge weights) between cities in its search. We want to retrieve the vertex that is *closest* to the current vertex—that is, the vertex connected with the minimum edge weight. In the abstract container called a *priority queue*, the item that is retrieved is the item in the queue with the highest priority. If we let miles be the priority, we can enqueue items made up of a record that contains two vertices and the distance between them.

This algorithm is far more complex than we have seen before, so we stop at this point. However, the mathematically adventurous reader may continue to pursue this solution.

8.7   Subprograms

At the time we examined recursion, we introduced the concept of a named subalgorithm. Here we look at them in the nonrecursive context and discuss how we pass information back and forth between algorithm and subalgorithm. Because we are talking about actual language constructs, we call these structures subprograms rather than subalgorithms.

Many subprograms are available as part of a high-level language or as part of the library that comes with the language. For example, mathematical problems often need to calculate trigonometric functions. Subprograms that calculate these values are available in most high-level languages in one way or another. When a program needs to calculate one of these values, the programmer looks up the name of the subprogram that calculates the value and just calls the subprogram to perform the calculation.

If one of these subprograms needs to have information passed to it, the calling unit sends over the values for the subprogram to use. For example,

---

the following two statements set x to m times the sine function of t and y to the absolute value of z. The sine function and the absolute value function are built into many languages. The information sent to the sine function is t; the information sent to the absolute value function is z. Both of these functions are value-returning subprograms.

```
Set x to m*sin(t)
Set y to abs(z)
```

The same is true when you write your own subprograms. We now look at the mechanism used for passing information back and forth between the calling program and subprogram.

We have assumed these capabilities in the algorithms relating to the abstract data types we have examined. Take, for example, the following list algorithm:

```
WHILE (more data)
     Read value
     Insert(myList, value)
Reset(myList)
Write "Items in the list are "
WHILE (MoreItems(myList))
     GetNext(myList, nextItem)
     Write nextItem, ' '
```

Insert needs a list and a value to insert into it. Reset needs the list to reset. MoreItems needs the list to see if more items remain to be returned. GetNext needs the list as input and returns the next item in the list. This communication is done through the concept of a *parameter list*.

■ Parameter Passing

A parameter list is a list of the identifiers or values with which the subprogram is to work; it appears in parentheses beside the subprogram name. Because a subprogram is defined before it is called, it does not know with which variables from the calling unit it is to work. To solve this dilemma, we specify a list of variable names in parentheses beside the subprogram name. These identifiers are called parameters. When the subprogram is called, the calling unit lists the subprogram name, followed by a list of

> **Parameter list** A mechanism for communicating between two parts of a program

> **Parameters** The identifiers listed in parentheses beside the subprogram name; sometimes called *formal parameters*

> **Arguments** The identifiers listed in parentheses on the subprogram call; sometimes called *actual parameters*

identifiers in parentheses. These identifiers are called arguments. The arguments represent actual variables in the calling unit with which the subprogram is to work.

You can think of a parameter as being a temporary identifier that is used within a subprogram. When a subprogram is called, the calling unit sends the names of the actual identifiers the subprogram is to use. The action in the subprogram is defined using the parameters; the action is executed using the arguments. When the action takes place, the arguments are substituted one-by-one for the parameters. This substitution can be done in several ways, but the most common practice is by position. The first argument substitutes for the first parameter, the second argument substitutes for the second parameter, and so on.

We have promised not to look at too many implementations, but this one is easy. We can implement a list using an array and a length field. When we add an item to the list, we store it in the array (values) at the length − 1 position and increment length. We bind the values and the length together into a record called list, which we pass to the subprogram that needs it.

Insert(list, item)   // Subprogram definition

Set list.values[list.length − 1] to item

Set list.length to list.length + 1

Insert(myList, value)   // Calling statement

list is the parameter and mylist is the argument. When Insert is executed, myList replaces list.

The substitution mechanism acts much like a message board. When a subprogram is called, a list of the arguments is given to the subprogram (put on the subprogram's message board). These arguments tell the subprogram where to find the values to use. When a parameter is used in the body of the subprogram, the subprogram accesses the argument through its relative position on the message board. That is, the subprogram looks for its first parameter in the first position on the message board and for its second parameter in the second position on the message board. See Figure 8.15.

The number of arguments in the call must match the number of parameters in the subprogram heading. Because the arguments and parameters are matched by position, their names don't have to be the same. This is very helpful when a subprogram is called more than once, with different arguments in each call. Parameters passed in this fashion are often called *positional parameters*.

Hackers funding hackers
Hardware hackers are well known for modifying hardware so as to improve its function and expand its capabilities. Two open-source hardware hackers, Justin Huynh and Matt Stack, have started the Open Source Hardware Bank (OSHB), using money pooled from hardware hackers to fund other open-source hardware hacking projects. The peer-to-peer lender is not yet considered a federally regulated lending institution, as the regulations governing this activity are not 100% clear. However, nearly 70 people have signed up to be lenders for OSHB, with the promise of a 5% to 15% return on their investment should the project succeed.

FIGURE 8.15   Passing parameters

List

Parameter
List

■ Value and Reference Parameters

There are two basic ways of passing parameters: by value and by reference (or address). If a parameter is a value parameter, the calling unit gives a *copy* of the argument to the subprogram. If a parameter is a reference parameter, the calling unit gives the *address* of the argument to the subprogram. This very fundamental difference means that a subprogram cannot change the content of a value argument because it receives only a copy of the argument. The subprogram can modify the copy, but the original variable will not be changed. In contrast, any argument passed by the calling unit to a reference parameter can be changed by the subprogram because the subprogram manipulates the actual variable, not a copy of it. In the previous example, the record being passed as list must be a reference parameter. If it is not, items would be inserted into the copy, not the original.

Think of the difference this way: To access a reference parameter, the subprogram accesses the contents of the *address* listed on the message board. To access a value parameter, the subprogram accesses the *contents* of the message board. Clearly, both the calling unit and the subprogram must know which parameter/argument is to be passed by value and which is to be passed by reference. Not all high-level languages allow both kinds of parameters, but those that do have some syntactic schemes to label parameters as value or reference.

Before we leave subprograms, let's look at an example that illustrates the difference between value and reference parameters. We have already

> ❱❱ Value parameter A parameter that expects a copy of its argument to be passed by the calling unit (put on the message board)

> ❱❱ Reference parameter A parameter that expects the address of its argument to be passed by the calling unit (put on the message board)

written an algorithm that swaps the contents of two places in memory. Here is the solution without problem-dependent variable names:

```
Swap (item1, item2)

Set temp to item2
Set item2 to item1
Set item1 to temp
```

Now suppose that the calling unit (the part of the program that wants the contents of the two places exchanged) calls Swap with data1 and data2 as parameters.

```
Swap(data1, data2)
```

Now let's say that data1 is stored in location 0002 and data2 is stored in location 0003. These locations contain the values 30 and 40, respectively. Figure 8.16 shows the content of the message board when the parameters are passed by value and passed by reference. When a parameter is a value parameter, the subprogram knows to manipulate the value on the message board. When a parameter is a reference parameter, the subprogram knows to manipulate the contents of the address on the message board. Should the parameters for subprogram Swap be value or reference parameters?

Before we leave the topic of subprograms and parameters, let's implement three more of the list subprograms: getLength, IsThere, and Delete. If

FIGURE 8.16 Difference between value parameters and reference parameters

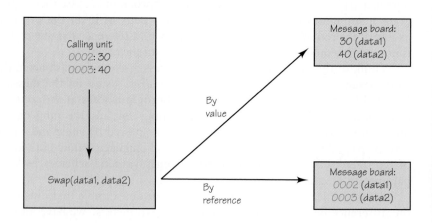

the list items are not to be kept in sorted order, we can just put the first one in the length position and increment length. For this example, let's assume that only one copy of item can be in the list.

```
getLength(list)

RETURN list.length
```

```
IsThere(list, item)

Set position to 0
WHILE (position < list.length AND list.values[position] != item)
    Set position to position + 1
RETURN position < list.length
```

IsThere is a subprogram that returns a value—in this case a Boolean value. Thus it would be used in an expression such as

```
IF (IsThere(myList, item))
    Write item "is in the list"
```

This type of subprogram is called a *value-returning* subprogram. Delete and Insert, in contrast, do not return a specific value. However, they do return the changed list through its parameters. If we assume that the item to be deleted is in the list, the implementation is simple: When we find the item to be deleted, we just exchange it with the last item in the list and decrement length.

```
Delete(list, item)

Set position to 1
WHILE (list.values[position] != item)
    Set position to position + 1
Swap(list.values[list.length – 1], list.values[position])
Set list.length to list.length – 1
```

IsThere can be used to make sure that the item to be deleted is in the list.

```
IF (IsThere(myList, item))
    Delete(myList, item)
```

Value-returning subprograms include the RETURN statement followed by a value to be returned. Non-value-returning subprograms may have a RETURN statement, but it is unnecessary. To conclude this section, here is a code segment that read values into the list and then deletes some values:

```
WHILE (more values)
    Read aValue
    IF (NOT IsThere(list, aValue)
        Insert(list, aValue)
Write "Input values to delete or "Quit" to quit"
Read aValue
IF (aValue != "Quit")
    IF (IsThere(list, aValue))
        Delete(list, aValue)
```

Summary

Lists, stacks, queues, trees, and graphs are all useful abstract composite structures. Each has its own defining property and the operations that guarantee that property. All of these abstract structures include operations to insert items and to remove items. Lists and trees also have operations to find items within the structure.

Lists and trees have the same properties: Items can be inserted, deleted, and retrieved. Items can be inserted in a stack, but the item removed and returned is the last item inserted into the stack—that is, the item that has been in the stack the shortest time. Items can be inserted into a queue, but the item removed and returned is the first item put into the queue—that is, the item that has been in the queue the longest time.

Lists, stack, queues, and trees are merely holding structures, but graphs are more complex. A wealth of mathematical algorithms can be applied to information in a graph. We examined three of these: the breadth-first search, the depth-first search, and the single-source shortest-path search.

Subprogram statements allow subalgorithms to be implemented independently. A subprogram may be value returning, in which case it is called by placing its name and arguments within an expression. Alternatively, a subprogram may be non-value returning (void), in which case the subprogram name is used as a statement in the calling program. Data sent to and from subprograms are transmitted by the use of parameter lists. Parameters may be either reference or value parameters. An argument is passed to a value parameter by sending a copy of the argument to the subprogram. An argument is passed to a reference parameter by sending the address of the argument to the subprogram.

⚖ ETHICAL ISSUES ▸ Influence of Internet on the 2008 Presidential Election

It cannot be debated that the Internet changed the way that presidential campaigns are run. Barack Obama is not the first or only candidate to use the Internet in his campaign. A single-day record for raising campaign contributions was set by Ron Paul (Republican), who collected $6 million in one day in 2007 through Internet donations. More notable was Howard Dean (Democrat), who used the Internet as a fundamental tool in his "50-state strategy" primary run in 2004. Although ultimately defeated in the election, none could deny Dean's success at raising funds through his pioneering Internet campaign of a "$100 revolution" in which 2 million Americans would give $100 to compete with the Republican candidate George W. Bush. Taking a lead from Dean's emphasis on small donors and the Internet, almost half of Obama's $639 million in funds was raised from 3 million donors who gave $300 or less. Understanding that a successful campaign was run on its cash flow, much of Obama's social networking and Internet time was directed toward raising campaign funds.

There were many similarities in the way that Obama and the Republican candidate John McCain used the Internet. Both men created an entire social media platform that pushed information and ideals to the masses, both online and off. The websites of both men became focal points where their supporters campaigned for them and the undecided went to get information. Both men used other Internet tools, such

as Facebook, MySpace™, Twitter, and YouTube, along with thousands of personal blogging sites and forums. On sites such as YouTube, more than 14.5 million hours of election coverage were available that pushed opinions and the campaign agenda—and those were cost-free hours to the candidates. The Internet allowed candidates to increase their visibility to larger audiences of potential voters at costs substantially less than those incurred for television campaign commercials that might reach fewer people. Moreover, the Internet allows candidates to quickly respond to negative feedback by simply editing text and video, whereas a television spot that is run cannot be undone.

Even those who argue that television is still "the" influential medium for reaching potential voters admit the influence of the Internet. An issue might start as a blogging buzz between hardcore followers. If the blogging buzz becomes loud enough, mainstream media pick up the issue in their articles and broadcasts. From there, the issue enters general discussions in day-to-day life.

It has been observed that the then relatively recent invention of television was responsible for getting John F. Kennedy elected in 1960. In a presidential debate with the Republican candidate, Richard Nixon, Kennedy was seen by television audiences as handsome, erudite, and relaxed, whereas Nixon was seen as ill at ease and sporting a 5 o'clock shadow. The debate, it is said, swayed just enough

» continued

voters to give Kennedy the election. Some disgruntled analysts suggested that had television existed in 1860, the great but physically unattractive Abraham Lincoln would not have been elected. Television, it is argued, robbed something from the democratic process. The Internet, we might now argue, has given some of it back.

🔑 Key Terms

Abstract data type (ADT)
Adjacent vertices
Arguments
Binary tree
Containers
Data structure
Directed graph (digraph)
Edge (arc)
Graph
Leaf node

Linked structure
Parameter list
Parameters
Path
Reference parameter
Root
Undirected graph
Value parameter
Vertex

⌘   Exercises

For Exercises 1–10, indicate which structure would be a more suitable choice for each of the following applications by marking them as follows:

    A. Stack
    B. Queue
    C. Tree
    D. Binary search tree
    E. Graph

1. A bank simulation of its teller operation to see how waiting times would be affected by adding another teller.

2. A program to receive data that is to be saved and processed in the reverse order.

3. An electronic address book, kept ordered by name.

4. A word processor to have a PF key that causes the preceding command to be redisplayed. Every time the PF key is pressed, the program is to show the command that preceded the one currently displayed.

5. A dictionary of words used by a spelling checker to be built and maintained.

6. A program to keep track of patients as they check into a medical clinic, assigning patients to doctors on a first-come, first-served basis.

7. A program keeping track of where canned goods are located on a shelf.

8. A program to keep track of the soccer teams in a city tournament.

9. A program to keep track of family relationships.

10. A program to maintain the routes in an airline.

For Exercises 11–30, mark the answers true or false as follows:
   A. True
   B. False

11. A binary search cannot be applied to a tree.

12. A stack and a queue are different names for the same ADT.

13. A stack displays FIFO behavior.

14. A queue displays LIFO behavior.

15. A leaf in a tree is a node with no children.

16. A binary tree is a tree in which each node can have zero, one, or two children.

17. A binary search tree is another name for a binary tree.

18. The value in the right child of a node (if it exists) in a binary search tree will be greater than the value in the node itself.

19. The value in the left child of a node (if it exists) in a binary search tree will be greater than the value in the node itself.

20. In a graph, the vertices represent the items being modeled.

21. Algorithms that use a list must know whether the list is array based or linked.

22. An list may be linear or nonlinear, depending on its implementation.

23. The root of a tree is the node that has no ancestors.

24. Binary search trees are ordered.

25. On average, searching in a binary search tree is faster than searching in an array-based list.

26. On average, searching in a binary search tree is faster than searching in a list.

27. A binary search tree is always balanced.

28. Given the number of nodes and the number of levels in a binary search tree, you can determine the relative efficiency of a search in the tree.

29. Insertion in a binary search tree is always into a leaf node.

30. A binary search tree is another implementation of a sorted list.

The following algorithm (used for Exercises 31–33) is a count-controlled loop going from 1 through 5. At each iteration, the loop counter is either printed or put on a stack depending on the result of Boolean function RanFun(). (The behavior of RanFun() is immaterial.) At the end of the loop, the items on the stack are popped and printed. Because of the logical properties of a stack, this algorithm cannot print certain sequences of the values of the loop counter. You are given an output and asked if the algorithm could generate the output. Respond as follows:

    A. True

    B. False

    C. Not enough information

```
Set count to 0
WHILE (count < 5)
        Set count to count + 1
        IF (RanFun())
              Write count, ' '
        ELSE
              Push(myStack, count)
WHILE (NOT IsEmpty(myStack))
        Pop(myStack, number)
        Write number, ' '
```

31. The following output is possible using a stack: 1 3 5 2 4.

32. The following output is possible using a stack: 1 3 5 4 2.

33. The following output is possible using a stack: 1 3 5 1 3.

The following algorithm (used for Exercises 34–36) is a count-controlled loop going from 1 through 5. At each iteration, the loop counter is either printed or put on a queue depending on the result of Boolean function RanFun(). (The behavior of RanFun() is immaterial.) At the end of the loop, the items on the queue are dequeued and printed. Because of the logical properties of a queue, this algorithm cannot print certain sequences of the values of the loop counter. You are given an output and asked if the algorithm could generate the output. Respond as follows:

    A. True

    B. False

    C. Not enough information

```
Set count to 0
WHILE (count < 5)
    Set count to count + 1
    IF (RanFun())
        Write count, ' '
    ELSE
        Enqueue(myQueue, count)
WHILE (NOT IsEmpty(myQueue))
    Dequeue(myQueue, number)
    Write number, ' '
```

34. The following output is possible using a queue: 1 3 5 2 4.
35. The following output is possible using a queue: 1 3 5 4 2.
36. The following output is possible using a queue: 1 3 5 1 3.

Exercises 37–50 are short-answer questions.

37. What is written by the following algorithm?

```
Push(myStack, 5)
Push(myStack, 4)
Push(myStack, 4)
Pop(myStack, item)
Pop(myStack, item)
Push(myStack, item)
WHILE (NOT IsEmpty(myStack))
    Pop(myStack, item)
    Write item, ' '
```

38. What is written by the following algorithm?

    ```
    Enqueue(myQueue, 5)
    Enqueue(myQueue, 4)
    Enqueue(myQueue, 4)
    Dequeue(myQueue, item)
    Dequeue(myQueue, item)
    Enqueue(myQueue, item)
    WHILE (NOT IsEmtpy(myQueue))
        Dequeue(myQueue, item)
        Write item, ' '
    ```

39. Write an algorithm that sets *bottom* equal to the last element in the stack, leaving the stack empty.

40. Write an algorithm that sets *bottom* equal to the last element in the stack, leaving the stack unchanged.

41. Write an algorithm to create a copy of myStack, leaving myStack unchanged.

42. Write an algorithm that sets *last* equal to the last element in a queue, leaving the queue empty.

43. Write an algorithm that sets *last* equal to the last element in a queue, leaving the queue unchanged.

44. Write an algorithm to create a copy of myQueue, leaving myQueue unchanged.

45. Write an algorithm *replace* that takes a stack and two items. If the first item is in the stack, replace it with the second item, leaving the rest of the stack unchanged.

46. Write an algorithm *replace* that takes a queue and two items. If the first item is in the queue, replace it with the second item, leaving the rest of the queue unchanged.

47. Draw the binary search tree whose elements are inserted in the following order:

    50   72   96   107   26   12   11   9   2   10   25   51   16   17   95

48. If Print is applied to the tree formed in Exercise 47, in which order would the elements be printed?

49. Examine the following algorithm and apply it to the tree formed in Exercise 47. In which order would the elements be printed?

Print2 (tree)

IF (tree is NOT null)
    Print (right(tree))   // Recursive call R1
    Write info(tree)
    Print(left(tree))   // Recursive call R2

50. Examine the following algorithm and apply it to the tree formed in Exercise 47. In which order would the elements be printed?

Print3 (tree)

IF (tree is NOT null)
    Print (right(tree))   // Recursive call R1
    Print(left(tree))   // Recursive call R2
    Write info(tree)

Exercises 51–55 are short-answer questions based on the following directed graph.

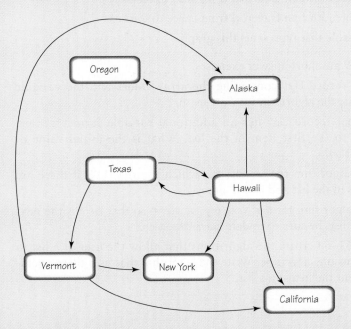

51. Is there a path from Oregon to any other state in the graph?
52. Is there a path from Hawaii to every other state in the graph?
53. From which state(s) in the graph is there a path to Hawaii?
54. Show the table that represents this graph.
55. Can you get from Vermont to Hawaii?

Exercises 56–60 are short-answer questions based on the following directed graph.

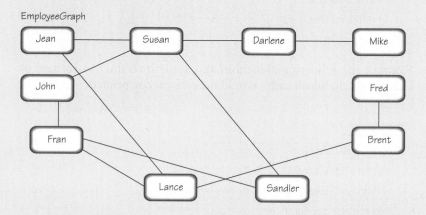

EmployeeGraph

56. Show the depth-first traversal from Jean to Sandler.
57. Show the depth-first traversal from Lance to Darlene.
58. Show the breadth-first traversal from Jean to Sandler.
59. Show the breadth-first traversal from Lance to Darlene.
60. Show the table that represents this graph.

Exercises 61–69 are short-answer exercises.

61. Given the record List containing the array values and the variable length, write the algorithm for GetLength.
62. Assume that record List has an additional variable currentPosition, initialized to the first item in the list. What is the initial value of currentPosition?
63. Write the algorithm for MoreItems, which returns TRUE if there are more items in the list and FALSE otherwise.
64. Write the algorithm for GetNext(myList, item) so that item is the next item in the list. Be sure to update currentPosition.
65. Exercises 61–64 create the algorithms that allow the user of a list to see the items one at a time. Write the algorithm that uses these operations to print the items in a list.

66. What happens if an insertion or deletion occurs in the middle of an iteration through the list? Explain.

67. Can you think of a way to keep the user from doing an insertion or deletion during an iteration?

68. Distinguish between value and reference parameters.

69. How are arguments and parameters matched?

??? Thought Questions

1. A spreadsheet is a table with rows and columns. Think about an ADT spreadsheet. Which operations would you need to construct the table? Which operations would you need to manipulate the values in the table?

2. Binary trees, binary search trees, and graphs are visualized as nodes and arrows (pointers) that represent the relationships between nodes. Compare these structures in terms of the operations that are allowed. Can a list ever be a tree? Can a tree ever be a list? Can a tree ever be a graph? Can a graph ever be a tree? How do the structures all relate to one another?

3. Were you actively involved in the 2008 presidential election? From where did you get your information—print media, television, friends, or the Internet?

4. One of the reasons that U.S. elections are so costly is that they cover such a large span of time. The United Kingdom has only about six weeks in which the candidates campaign. Would shortening the election cycle be a good idea? Does the use of the Internet to disseminate information affect your answer?

5. Is the Internet helping or hurting the democratic process?

The Programming Layer

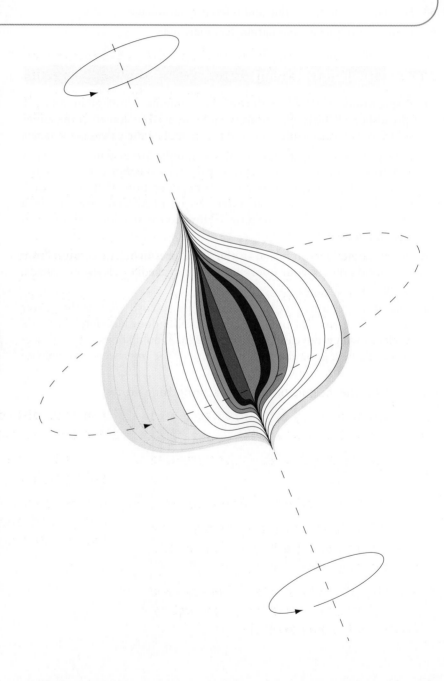

Object-Oriented Design and High-Level Programming Languages

9

In Chapter 1, we examined how the layers of languages were built up over time around the hardware to make computing easier for the applications programmer. In Chapter 6, we looked at machine code and then at an assembly language that allows the programmer to use mnemonics to represent instructions rather than numbers.

Assembly languages are a step in the right direction, but the programmer still must think in terms of individual machine instructions. To overcome this obstacle, we introduced pseudocode as an informal way to describe algorithms; pseudocode is closer to how humans think and communicate. High-level programming languages are a very formal way of accomplishing the same thing. Because computers can execute only machine code, translators were developed to translate programs written in these high-level languages into machine code.

Goals

After studying this chapter, you should be able to:

- distinguish between functional design and object-oriented design.

- describe the stages of the object-oriented design process.

- apply the object-oriented design process.

- name, describe, and give examples of the three essential ingredients of an object-oriented language.

- describe the translation process and distinguish between assembly, compilation, interpretation, and execution.

- name four distinct programming paradigms and give a language characteristic of each.

- define the concepts of a data type and strong typing.

- understand how the constructs of top-down design and object-oriented design are implemented in programming languages.

Before we look at high-level languages, we make a detour to look at object-oriented design. Object-oriented design is another way of looking at the design process, which views a program from the standpoint of data rather than tasks. Because the functionality associated with this design process is often incorporated into high-level programming languages, we need to understand this design process before looking as specific high-level languages.

9.1 Object-Oriented Methodology

We cover top-down design first because it more closely mirrors the way humans solve problems. As you saw earlier in this book, a top-down solution produces a hierarchy of tasks. Each task or named action operates on the data passed to it through its parameter list to produce the desired output. The tasks are the focus of a top-down design. Object-oriented design, by contrast, is a problem-solving methodology that produces a solution to a problem in terms of self-contained entities called *objects*, which are composed of both data and operations that manipulate the data. Object-oriented design focuses on the objects and their interactions within a problem. Once all of the objects within the problem are collected together, they constitute the solution to the problem.

In this process, Polya's principles of problem solving are applied to the data rather than to the tasks.

? It's in! No, it's out!

Have you ever watched a tennis match on television in which a player asks for confirmation of a line call? On a big screen you can see the path of the ball and the point of impact that shows whether the ball was in or out. How do they do it? By computer, of course. One system uses four high-speed digital cameras with computer software that can track a ball, determine its trajectory, and map its impact point. These cameras are connected to one another and to a main computer using wireless technology.

■ Object Orientation

Data and the algorithms that manipulate the data are bundled together in the object-oriented view, thus making each object responsible for its own manipulation (behavior). Underlying object-oriented design (OOD) are the concepts of *classes* and *objects*.

An object is a thing or entity that makes sense within the context of the problem. For example, if the problem relates to information about students, a student would be a reasonable object in the solution. A group of similar objects is described by an object class (or class for short). Although no two students are identical, students do have properties (data) and behaviors (actions) in common. Students are male or female humans who attend courses at a school (at least most of the time). Therefore, students would be a class. The word *class* refers to the idea of classifying objects

>> Object An entity or thing that is relevant in the context of a problem

>> Object class (class) A description of a group of objects with similar properties and behaviors

into related groups and describing their common characteristics. That is, a class describes the properties and behaviors that objects of the class exhibit. Any particular object is an *instance* (concrete example) of the class.

Object-oriented problem solving involves isolating the classes within the problem. Objects communicate with one another by sending messages (invoking one another's subprograms). A class contains fields that represent the properties and behaviors of the class. A field can contain data values and/or methods (subprograms). A method is a named algorithm that manipulates the data values in the object. A class in the general sense is a pattern for what an object looks like (data) and how it behaves (methods).

> **Fields** Named items in a class; can be data or subprograms

> **Method** A named algorithm that defines one aspect of the behavior of a class

■ Design Methodology

The decomposition process that we present involves four stages. *Brainstorming* is the stage in which we make a first pass at determining the classes in the problem. *Filtering* is the stage in which we go back over the proposed classes determined in the brainstorming stage to see if any can be combined or if any are missing. Each class that survives the filtering stage is examined more carefully in the next stage.

Scenarios is the stage in which the behavior of each class is determined. Because each class is responsible for its own behavior, we call these behaviors *responsibilities*. In this stage, "what if" questions are explored to be sure that all situations are examined. When all of the responsibilities of each class have been determined, they are recorded, along with the names of any other classes with which the class must collaborate (interact) to complete its responsibility.

Responsibility algorithms is the last stage, in which the algorithms are written for the responsibilities for each of the classes. A notation device called a CRC card is a handy way to record the information about each class at this stage.

Let's look at each of these stages in a little more detail.

Brainstorming

What is brainstorming? The dictionary defines it as a group problem-solving technique that involves the spontaneous contribution of ideas from all members of the group.[1] Brainstorming brings to mind a movie or TV show where a group of bright young people tosses around ideas about an advertising slogan for the latest revolutionary product. This picture seems at odds with the traditional picture of a computer analyst working alone in a closed, windowless office for days who finally jumps up shouting, "Ah ha!" As computers have gotten more powerful, the problems that can be solved have become more complex, and the picture of the genius locked in a windowless room has become obsolete. Solutions to complex problems need new and innovative solutions based on collective "Ah ha!"s—not the work of a single person.

In the context of object-oriented problem solving, brainstorming is a group activity designed to produce a list of possible classes to be used to solve a particular problem. Just as the people brainstorming for an advertising slogan know something about the product before the session begins, so brainstorming for classes requires that the participants know something about the problem. Each team member should enter the brainstorming session with a clear understanding of the problem to be solved. No doubt during the preparation, each team member will have generated his or her own preliminary list of classes.

Although brainstorming is usually a group activity, you can practice it by yourself on smaller problems.

Filtering

Brainstorming produces a tentative list of classes. The next phase is to take this list and determine which are the core classes in the problem solution. Perhaps two classes on the list are actually the same thing. These duplicate classes usually arise because people within different parts of an organization use different names for the same concept or entity. Also, two classes in the list may have many common attributes and behaviors that can be combined.

Some classes might not actually belong in the problem solution. For example, if we are simulating a calculator, we might list the user as a possible class. In reality, the user is not part of the internal workings of the simulation as a class; the user is an entity outside the problem that provides input to the simulation. Another possible class might be the *on* button. A little thought, however, shows that the *on* button is not part of the simulation; rather, it is what starts the simulation program running.

As the filtering is completed, the surviving list of classes is passed onto the next stage.

Scenarios

The goal of the scenarios phase is to assign responsibilities to each class. Responsibilities are eventually implemented as subprograms. At this stage we are interested only in *what* the tasks are, not in how they might be carried out.

Two types of responsibilities exist: what a class must know about itself (knowledge) and what a class must be able to do (behavior). A class *encapsulates* its data (knowledge), such that objects in one class cannot directly access data in another class. Encapsulation is the bundling of data and actions so that the logical properties of the data and actions are separated from the implementation details. Encapsulation is a key to abstraction. At the same time, each class has the responsibility of making data (knowledge) available to other classes that need it. Therefore, each class has a responsibility to know the things about itself that others need to be able to

>> Encapsulation Bundling data and actions so that the logical properties of data and actions are separated from the implementation details

get. For example, a student class should "know" its name and address, and a class that uses the student class should be able to "get" this information. These responsibilities are usually named "get" appended to the name of the data—for example, GetName or GetEmailAddress. Whether the email address is kept in the student class or whether the student class must ask some other class to access the address is irrelevant at this stage: The important fact is that the student class knows its own email address and can return it to a class that needs it.

The responsibilities for behavior look more like the tasks we described in top-down design. For example, a responsibility might be for the student class to calculate its grade-point average (GPA). In top-down design, we would say that a task is to calculate the GPA given the data. In object-oriented design, we say that the student class is responsible for calculating its own GPA. The distinction is both subtle and profound. The final code for the calculation may look the same, but it is executed in different ways. In a program based on a top-down design, the program calls the subprogram that calculates the GPA, passing the student object as a parameter. In an object-oriented program, a message is sent to the object of the class to calculate its GPA. There are no parameters because the object to which the message is sent knows its own data.

The name for this phase gives a clue about how you go about assigning responsibilities to classes. The team (or an individual) describes different processing scenarios involving the classes. Scenarios are "what if" scripts that allow participants to act out different situations or an individual to think through them.

The output from this phase is a set of classes with each class's responsibilities assigned, perhaps written on a CRC card. The responsibilities for each class are listed on the card, along with the classes with which a responsibility must collaborate.

Responsibility Algorithms

Eventually, algorithms must be written for the responsibilities. Because the problem-solving process focuses on data rather than actions in the object-oriented view of design, the algorithms for carrying out responsibilities tend to be fairly short. For example, the knowledge responsibilities usually just return the contents of one of an object's variables or send a message to another object to retrieve it. Action responsibilities are a little more complicated, often involving calculations. Thus the top-down method of designing an algorithm is usually appropriate for designing action responsibility algorithms.

Final Word

To summarize, top-down design methods focus on the *process* of transforming the input into the output, resulting in a hierarchy of tasks. Object-oriented design focuses on the *data objects* that are to be transformed, resulting in a hierarchy of objects. Grady Booch puts it this way: "Read the specification of the software you want to build. Underline the verbs if you are after procedural code, the nouns if you aim for an object-oriented program."[2]

We propose that you circle the nouns and underline the verbs as a way to begin. The nouns become objects; the verbs become operations. In a top-down design, the verbs are the primary focus; in an object-oriented design, the nouns are the primary focus.

Now, let's work through an example.

■ Example

Problem

Create a list that includes each person's name, telephone number, and email address. This list should then be printed in alphabetical order. The names to be included in the list are on scraps of paper and business cards.

Brainstorming and Filtering

Let's try circling the nouns and underlining the verbs.

Create a list that includes each person's name, telephone number, email, and address. This list should then be printed in alphabetical order. The names to be included in the list are on scraps of paper and business cards.

The first pass at a list of classes would include the following:

list
name
telephone number
email
address
list
order
names
list
scraps
paper
cards

Three of these classes are the same: The three references to *list* all refer to the container being created. *Order* is a noun, but what is an *order class*? It actually describes how the list class should print its items. Therefore, we discard it as a class. *Name* and *names* should be combined into one class. *Scraps*, *paper*, and *cards* describe objects that contain the data in the real world. They have no counterpart within the design. Our filtered list is shown below:

```
list
name
telephone number
email
address
```

The verbs in the problem statement give us a headstart on the responsibilities: *create*, *print*, and *include*. Like *scraps*, *paper*, and *cards*, *include* is an instruction to someone preparing the data and has no counterpart within the design. However, it does indicate that we must have an object that inputs the data to be put on the list. Exactly what is this data? It is the name, telephone number, email, and address of each person on the list. But this train of thought leads to the discovery that we have missed a major clue in the problem statement. A possessive adjective, *person's*, actually names a major class; name, telephone number, email, and address are classes that help define (are contained within) a person class.

Now we have a design choice. Should the person class have a responsibility to input its own data to initialize itself, or should we create another class that does the input and sends the data to initialize the person class? Let's have the person class be responsible for initializing itself. The person class should also be responsible for printing itself.

Does the person class collaborate with any other class? The answer to this question depends on how we decide to represent the data in the person class. Do we represent name, telephone number, email, and address as simple data items within the person class, or do we represent each as its own class? Let's represent name as a class with two data items, firstName and lastName, and have the others be string variables in class person. Both classes person and name must have knowledge responsibilities for their data values. Here are the CRC cards for these classes.

Class Name: *Person*		Superclass:		Subclasses:
Responsibilities			**Collaborations**	
Initialize itself (name, address, telephone, email)			Name, String	
Print			Name, String	
GetEmail			String	
GetName			Name, String	
GetAddress			String	
GetTelephone			String	

Class Name: *Name*		Superclass:		Subclasses:
Responsibilities			**Collaborations**	
Initialize itself (firstName, lastName)			String	
Print itself			String	
GetFirstName			String	
GetLastName			String	

What about the list object? Should the list keep the items in alphabetical order, or should it sort the items before printing them? Each language in which we might implement this design has a library of container classes available for use. Let's use one of these classes, which keeps the list in alphabetical order. This library class should also print the list. We can create a CRC card for this class, but mark that it most likely will be implemented using a library class.

Class Name: SortedList (from library)		Superclass:		Subclasses:
Responsibilities			**Collaborations**	
Insert (person)			Person	
Print itself			Person	

By convention, when a class reaches the CRC stage, we begin its itentifier with an uppercase letter.

Responsibility Algorithms

Person Class   There are two responsibilities to be decomposed: initialize and print. Because Name is a class, we can just let it initialize and print itself. We apply a subprogram (method) to an object by placing the object name before the method name with a period in between.

Initialize

name.initialize()

Write "Enter phone number; press return."

Get telephone number

Write "Enter email address; press return."

Get email address

Print

name.print()

Write "Telephone number: ", telephoneNumber

Write "Email address: ", emailAddress

Name Class   This class has the same two responsibilities: initialize and print. However, the algorithms are different. For the initialize responsibility, the user must be prompted to enter the name and the algorithm must read the name. For the print responsibility, the first and last names must be output with appropriate labels.

Initialize

"Enter the first name; press return."

Read firstName

"Enter the last name; press return."

Read lastName

Print

Print "First name: ", firstName

Print "Last name: ", lastName

We stop the design at this point. Reread the beginning of Chapter 7, where we discuss problem solving and the top-down design process. A top-down design produces a hierarchical tree with tasks in the nodes of the tree. The object-oriented design produces a set of classes, each of which has responsibilities for its own behavior. Is one better than the other? Well, the object-oriented design creates classes that might be useful in other contexts. Reusability is one of the great advantages of an object-oriented design. Classes designed for one problem can be used in another problem, because each class is self-contained; that is, each class is responsible for its own behavior.

You can think of the object-oriented problem-solving phase as mapping the objects in the real world into classes, which are descriptions of the categories of objects. The implementation phase takes the descriptions of the categories (classes) and creates instances of the classes that simulate the objects in the problem. The interactions of the objects in the program simulate the interaction of the objects in the real world of the problem. Figure 9.1 summarizes this process.

FIGURE 9.1   Mapping of problem into solution

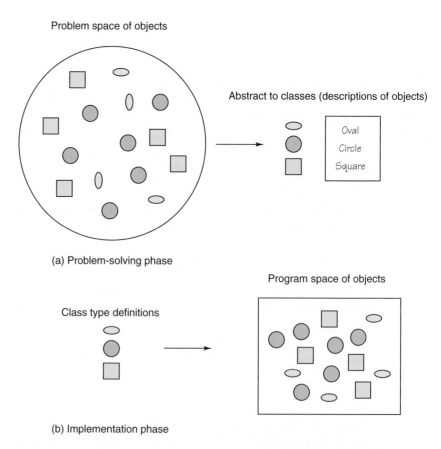

Problem space of objects

Abstract to classes (descriptions of objects)

Oval
Circle
Square

(a) Problem-solving phase

Class type definitions

Program space of objects

(b) Implementation phase

FIGURE 9.2   Compilation process

9.2   Translation Process

Recall from Chapter 6 that a program written in assembly language is input to the *assembler*, which translates the assembly-language instructions into machine code. The machine code, which is the output from the assembler, is then executed. With high-level languages, we employ other software tools to help with the translation process. Let's look at the basic function of these tools before examining high-level languages.

■ Compilers

The algorithms that translate assembly-language instructions into machine code are very simple because assembly languages are very simple. By "simple," we mean that each instruction carries out a fundamental operation. High-level languages provide a richer set of instructions that makes the programmer's life even easier, but because the constructs are more abstract, the translation process is more difficult. Programs that translate programs written in a high-level language are called compilers. In the early days of computer programming, the output of a compiler was an assembly-language version of the program, which then had to be run through an assembler to finally get the machine-language program to execute. As computer scientists began to have a deeper understanding of the translation process, compilers became more sophisticated and the assembly-language phase was often eliminated. See Figure 9.2.

A program written in a high-level language can run on any computer that has an appropriate compiler for the language. A compiler is a program; therefore, a machine-code version of the compiler must be available for a particular machine to be able to compile a program. Thus, to be used on multiple types of machines, each high-level language must have many compilers for that language.

>> **Compiler** A program that translates a high-level language program into machine code

>> **Interpreter** A program that inputs a program in a high-level language and directs the computer to perform the actions specified in each statement

■ Interpreters

An interpreter is a program that translates and executes the statements in sequence. Unlike an assembler or compiler that produces machine code as output, which is then executed in a separate step, an interpreter translates a statement and then immediately executes the statement. Interpreters can be viewed as *simulators* or *virtual machines* that understand the language in which a program is written. As Terry Pratt points out in his classic text on programming languages, both a translator and a simulator accept programs in a high-level language as input. The translator (assembler or compiler) simply produces an equivalent program in the appropriate machine language, which must then be run. The simulator executes the input program directly.[3]

Second-generation high-level languages came in two varieties: those that were compiled and those that were interpreted. FORTRAN, COBOL, and ALGOL were compiled; Lisp, SNOBOL4, and APL were interpreted. Because of the complexity of the software interpreters, programs in interpreted languages usually ran much more slowly than compiled programs. As a result, the trend was toward compiled languages—until the advent of Java.

Java was introduced in 1996 and took the computing community by storm. In the design of Java, portability was of primary importance. To achieve optimal portability, Java is compiled into a standard machine language called `Bytecode`. But how can there be a *standard machine language*? A software interpreter called the JVM (Java Virtual Machine) takes the Bytecode program and executes it. That is, Bytecode is not the machine language for any particular hardware processor. Any machine that has a JVM can run the compiled Java program.

Bytecode A standard machine language into which Java source code is compiled

The portability achieved by standardized high-level languages is not the same as the portability achieved by translating Java into Bytecode and then interpreting it on a JVM. A program written in a high-level language can be compiled and run on any machine that has the appropriate compiler; the program is translated into machine code that is directly executed by a computer. A Java program is compiled into Bytecode, and the compiled Bytecode program can run on any machine that has a JVM interpreter. That is, the output from the Java compiler is interpreted, not directly executed. (See Figure 9.3.) Java is always translated into Bytecode. In addition, there are compilers for other languages that translate the language into Bytecode rather than machine code. For example, there are versions of Ada compilers that translate Ada into Bytecode.

The JVM is a virtual machine, just like the Pep/8 system discussed in Chapter 6. In that chapter, we defined a virtual machine as a hypothetical machine designed to illustrate important features of a real machine. The JVM is a hypothetical machine designed to execute Bytecode.

UCSD's p-system predates Bytecode
In the 1970s, the University of California at San Diego had a system that executed p-code, a language very similar to Bytecode. Programs written in Pascal and FORTRAN were translated into p-code, which could be executed on any hardware with a p-code interpreter.

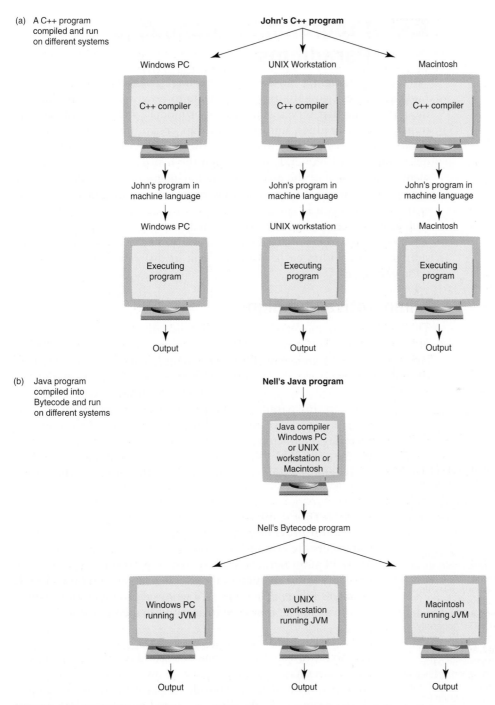

(a) A C++ program compiled and run on different systems

(b) Java program compiled into Bytecode and run on different systems

FIGURE 9.3 Portability provided by standardized languages versus interpretation by Bytecode

9.3 Programming Language Paradigms

What is a *paradigm*? The *American Heritage Dictionary of the English Language* gives two definitions that relate to how we, in computing, use the term: "one that serves as a pattern or model" and "a set of assumptions, concepts, values, and practices that constitute a way of viewing reality for the community that shares them, especially in an intellectual discipline."[4] In Chapter 1, we outlined the history of software development, listing some of the programming languages that were developed in each generation. Another way to view programming languages is to look at the ways different languages reflect differing views of reality—that is, to look at the different paradigms represented.

There are two main paradigms, imperative and declarative, and many subparadigms within each. We later look at different languages within these paradigms.

■ Imperative Paradigm

The von Neumann model of sequential instructions that operates on values in memory greatly influenced the most common model of a programming language: the *imperative* model. The dominant languages used in industry throughout the history of computing software come from this paradigm. These languages include FORTRAN, BASIC, C, Pascal, and C++. In this paradigm, the program describes the processing necessary to solve the problem. The imperative paradigm is, therefore, characterized by sequential execution of instructions, the use of variables that represent memory locations, and the use of assignment statements that change the values of these variables.[8]

The word *paradigm* has changed over the years The 1977 *Webster's New Collegiate Dictionary* defines *paradigm* as "an example or pattern, an outstanding example of an archetype, or an example of a conjugation or declension of a word." A search of the Internet in 2006 found many relevant definitions, including "a pattern or an example of something." The word also connotes the ideas of a mental picture and pattern of thought. Thomas Kuhn uses the word to mean the model that scientists hold about a particular area of knowledge. Kuhn's famous book, *The Structure of Scientific Revolutions*, presents his view of the stages through which a science goes in getting from one paradigm to the next.[5] The generally accepted perspective of a particular discipline at a given time: "He framed the problem within the psychoanalytic paradigm."[6] "*Paradigm* has also been defined as a model or frame of reference. Radical transformation in the way of looking at an issue or problem."[7]

Procedural Paradigm

Procedural programming is an imperative model in which the statements are grouped into subprograms. A program is a hierarchy of subprograms, each of which performs a specific task necessary to the solution of the overall program. Our pseudocode examples follow this model. We write subprograms and pass the data to them that they need to accomplish their function.

Object-Oriented Paradigm

The object-oriented view is one of a world of interacting objects. Each object has responsibility for its own actions. In the procedural paradigm, data are considered passive and are acted upon by the program. In the object-oriented paradigm, data objects are active. Objects and the code that manipulates them are bundled together, making each object responsible for its own manipulation. SIMULA and Smalltalk were the first two object-oriented programming languages. Java and Python are two modern object-oriented languages.

C++ and Java are imperative languages that are somewhat mixed in terms of their paradigm. Although Java is considered object-oriented, it has some procedural features. C++ is considered procedural, but it has some object-oriented features.

■ Declarative Paradigm

The *declarative* paradigm is a model in which the results are described, but the steps to accomplish the results are not stated. There are two basic models within this paradigm, functional and logic.

Functional Model

The *functional* model is based on the mathematical concept of the function. Computation is expressed in terms of the evaluation of functions; the solution to a problem is expressed in terms of function calls. Thus the basic mechanism is the evaluation of functions, and there are no variables and no assignment statements. For example, the addition of two values would be expressed this way:

(+ 30 40)

where the parentheses represent an expression to be evaluated by applying the first item (which must be a function) to the rest of the list. This expression is evaluated by applying the addition function to the next two numbers, which returns the value 70. There is no looping construct; repetition is expressed in terms of recursive function calls. The most well-known languages in the functional paradigm are Lisp, Scheme (a derivative of Lisp), and ML.

Let's examine a series of Scheme expressions that illustrate the flavor of the language. Scheme is interpreted, so the result immediately follows the statement. One interpreter uses #;> as a prompt to enter an expression; we shall use that here.[9] The lines without the prompt are what the system returns.

```
#;> (* 3 4)
12
#;> (+ (* 5 4) (+ 1 4))
25
#;> (length '(2 4 6 8 10))
5
#;> (max 2 5 1 3)
5
```

In the first expression, 3 is multiplied by 4, giving the result 12. In the second expression, the results of multiplying 5 times 4 and adding 1 and 4 are summed, giving 25. The third expression asks for the number of items in the list following the list indicated by the ' mark. In the fourth expression, the maximum of the following values is returned.

In Chapter 7, we wrote a recursive algorithm to compute the factorial of a number. lambda is the word for defining a function. Here is the corresponding Scheme code—compare it with the first algorithm:

```
#;> (define factorial
#;> (lambda(n)
#;>    (if
#;>    (= n 0)
#;>    1
#;>    (* n (factorial (- n 1))))))
#;> (factorial 7)
5040
```

After the factorial function is defined, giving the name and argument within parentheses executes the function, returning the value 5040.

Logic Programming

Logic programming is based on the principles of symbolic logic. This model comprises a set of facts about objects and a set of rules about the relationships among the objects. A program consists of asking questions about these objects and their relationships, which can be deduced from the facts and the rules. The underlying problem-solving algorithm uses the rules of logic to deduce the answer from the facts and rules.

PROLOG is a third-generation logic programming language that was developed in France in 1970. It rose to prominence in 1981, when Japanese researchers announced that logic programming would play a major role in their fifth-generation computer. A PROLOG program consists of three types of statements: One type declares facts about objects and their relationships with and to each other; another type defines rules about objects and their relationships; and a third type asks questions about the objects and their relationships.[10]

For example, the following code defines a set of facts relating pets to owners:

```
owns(mary,bo).
owns(ann,kitty).
owns(bob,riley).
owns(susy,charlie).
```

Here owns is the relationship name, the objects are within parentheses, and the period ends the statement of the fact. Does this mean that mary owns `bo` or `bo` owns `mary`? That is up to the programmer. He or she must be consistent in his or her interpretation.

When you have a database of facts, PROLOG allows you to ask question about the database. Look at these three PROLOG statements:

```
?-owns(mary,bo)
?-owns(bo,mary)
?-owns(susy,bo)
```

The PROLOG system replies `yes` to the first, `no` to the second, and `no` to the third.

In PROLOG, a constant begins with a lowercase letter and a variable begins with an uppercase letter. We ask questions about facts by substituting a variable for a constant in a fact.

```
?-owns(ann,Cat).
?-owns(Name,charlie).
```

In this example, the first statement returns `Cat` = `kitty`. The second returns `Name` = `susy`.

Both Lisp and PROLOG are used in artificial intelligence applications (described in Chapter 13). As you can see, programs in these languages bear little resemblance to the von Neumann architecture reflected in languages in the imperative paradigm as represented in our pseudocode.

9.4 Functionality in High-Level Languages

Two pseudocode constructs—selection and repetition (looping)—are hallmarks of imperative languages. In Chapter 6, we implemented these constructions in assembly language, showing how detailed the instructions had to be. We also examined these constructs along with subprograms in pseudocode. In high-level languages, selection and repetition are very easy. Subprograms and parameter passing, however, are more complicated.

First, we review the concept of a Boolean expression, which is the construct that high-level languages use to make choices. We then examine other constructs that high-level languages provide to make programming easier and safer.

■ Boolean Expressions

In Chapter 6, we wrote an algorithm to read in pairs of numbers and print them in order. It contained a selection statement within a loop. Here is the outline of the loop with the selection statement:

```
. . .
WHILE (numberRead < numberOfPairs)

    . . .

    IF (number1 < number2)
        Print number1, " ", number2
    ELSE
        Print number2, " ", number1
```

Each of these statements asks a question. Notice how these questions are phrased:

```
(numberRead < numberOfPairs)
(number1 < number2)
```

Each phrase is actually a statement. If the statement is true, the answer to the question is true. If the statement is not true, the answer to the question is false. Making statements and then testing whether they are true or false is how programming languages ask questions. These statements are called *assertions* or *conditions*. When we write algorithms, we make assertions in English-like statements. When the algorithms are translated into a high-level programming language, the English-like statements are rewritten as Boolean expressions.

What is a Boolean expression? In Chapter 4, we introduced the concept of Boolean operations when we discussed gates and circuits. Here we are using them at the logical level rather than the hardware level. A Boolean expression is a sequence of identifiers, separated by compatible operators, that evaluates to either true or false. A Boolean expression can be any of the following.

> ▶▶ Boolean expression A sequence of identifiers, separated by compatible operators, that evaluates to either true or false

- A Boolean variable
- An arithmetic expression followed by a relational operator followed by an arithmetic expression
- A Boolean expression followed by a Boolean operator followed by a Boolean expression

So far in our examples, variables have contained numeric values. A Boolean variable is a location in memory that is referenced by an identifier that can contain either true or false.[11]

A relational operator is one that compares two values. The six relational operators are summarized in the following chart, along with the symbols that various high-level languages use to represent the relation.

Symbol	Meaning	Example	Evaluation
<	Less than	Number1 < Number2	True if Number1 is less than Number2; false otherwise
<=	Less than or equal	Number1 <= Number2	True if Number1 is less than or equal to Number2; false otherwise
>	Greater than	Number1 > Number2	True if Number1 is greater than Number2; false otherwise
>=	Greater than or equal	Number1 >= Number2	True if Number1 is greater than or equal to Number2; false otherwise
!= or <> or /=	Not equal	Number1 != Number2	True if Number1 is not equal to Number2; false otherwise
= or ==	Equal	Number1 == Number2	True if Number1 is equal to Number2; false otherwise

A relational operator between two arithmetic expressions is asking if the relationship exists between the two expressions. For example,

xValue < yValue

is making the assertion that xValue is less than yValue. If xValue is less than yValue, then the result of the expression is true; if xValue is not less than yValue, then the result is false.

To avoid the confusion over the use of = and == to mean equality in different programming languages, we have used the word "equal" rather than choosing one of the symbols in our algorithms.

Recall that the three Boolean operators are the special operators AND, OR, and NOT. The AND operator returns true if both expressions are true and false otherwise. The OR operator returns false if both expressions are false and true otherwise. The NOT operator changes the value of the expression.

■ Data Typing

When working in an assembly language, we assign identifiers to memory locations with no regard as to what is to be stored into the locations. Many widely used, high-level languages (including both C++ and Java), require you to state what can be stored in a place when you associate it with an identifier. If a statement in a program tries to store a value into a variable that is not the proper type, an error message is issued. The requirement that only a value of the proper type can be stored into a variable is called strong typing.

>> Strong typing Each variable is assigned a type, and only values of that type can be stored in the variable

For example, look at the following eight bits: 00110001. What does it represent? It is a byte in memory. Yes, but what does it *mean*? Well, it could be the binary representation of the decimal number 49. It could also be the extended ASCII representation of the character '1'. Could it mean anything else? Yes, it could be the Pep/8 instruction specifier for the DCI direct mode trap instruction. Thus, when a program is executing, it must know how to interpret the contents of a place in memory.

In the next sections we look at common types of data values and explore how high-level languages allow you to associate locations with identifiers. Each of these data types has certain operations that legally can be applied to values of the type. A **data type** is a description of the set of values and the basic set of operations that can be applied to values of the type.

Of the languages that we explore, C++, Java, and VB .NET are strongly typed; Python is not.

> ❯❯ **Data type** A description of the set of values and the basic set of operations that can be applied to values of the type

Data Types

Data are the physical symbols that represent information. Inside a computer, both data and instructions are just binary bit patterns. The computer executes an instruction because the address of the instruction is loaded into the program counter and the instruction is then loaded into the instruction register. That same bit pattern that is executed can also represent an integer number, a real number, a character, or a Boolean value. The key is that the computer interprets the bit pattern to be what it expects it to be.

For example, in Pep/8 the instruction for Stop is a byte of all zero bits. When this instruction is loaded into the instruction register, the program halts. A byte of all zero bits can also be interpreted as an eight-bit binary number containing the value 0 (zero). If the location containing all zero bits is added to the contents of a register, the value is interpreted as a number.

Most high-level languages have four distinct data types built into the language: integer numbers, real numbers, characters, and Boolean values.

Consider the word *bow*
A word is a sequence of symbols taken from the alphabet. Some sequence or patterns of symbols have been assigned meanings; others have not (for example, the symbols *ceba* don't form a meaningful word in the English language). But *bow* is an English word. However, it can mean different things: part of a ship, something a little girl wears in her hair, something you play the violin with, or the act of bending from the waist. We can differentiate between the meanings based on the context of the word, just as a compiler can differentiate based on the surrounding syntax.

Integers   The integer data type represents a range of integer values, from the smallest to the largest. The range varies depending on how many bytes are assigned to represent an integer value. Some high-level languages provide several integer types of different sizes, which allows the user to choose the one that best fits the data in a particular problem.

The operations that can be applied to integers are the standard arithmetic and relational operators. Addition and subtraction are represented by the standard symbols + and -. Multiplication and division are usually represented by * and /. Depending on the language, integer division may return a real number or the integer quotient. Some languages have two symbols for division: one that returns a real result and one that returns the integer quotient. Most languages also have an operator that returns the integer remainder from division. This operator is called the *modulus operator*, but it may or may not act as the mathematical modulus operator. The relational operators are represented by the symbols shown in the table in the previous section.

Reals The real data type also represents a range from the smallest to the largest value with a given precision. Like the integer data type, the range varies depending on the number of bytes assigned to represent a real number. Many high-level languages have two sizes of real numbers. The operations that can be applied to real numbers are the same as those that can be applied to integer numbers. However, you must be careful when applying the relational operators to real values, because real numbers are often not exact. For example, 1/3 + 1/3 + 1/3 in computer arithmetic is not necessarily 1.0. In fact, 1/10 * 10 is *not* 1.0 in computer arithmetic.

Characters In Chapter 3, we said that a mapping of the ASCII character set to code requires only one byte. One commonly used mapping for the Unicode character set uses two bytes. In this mapping, our English alphabet is represented in ASCII, which is a subset of Unicode. Applying arithmetic operations to characters doesn't make much sense, and many strongly typed languages will not allow you to do so. However, comparing characters does make sense, so the relational operators can be applied to characters. The meanings of "less than" and "greater than" when applied to characters are "comes before" and "comes after," respectively, in the character set. Thus the character 'A' is less than 'B', 'B' is less than 'C', and so forth. Likewise, the character '1' (not the number) is less than '2', '2' is less than '3', and so forth. If you want to compare 'A' to '1', you must look up the relationship between these two characters in the character set you are using.

Boolean As we said in the previous section, the Boolean data type consists of two values: `true` and `false`. We can also assign a Boolean expression to a Boolean variable. Here is the pairs program using Boolean variables:

```
Write "How many pairs of values are to be entered?"
Read numberOfPairs
Set numberRead to 0
Set Stop to (numberRead equals numberOfPairs)
WHILE (NOT Stop)
    Write "Enter two values separated by a blank; press return"
    Read number1
    Read number2
    Set OneSmallest to number1 < number2
    IF (OneSmallest)
        Print number1 , " " , number2
    ELSE
        Print number2 , " " , number1
    Set numberRead to numberRead + 1
    Set Stop to (numberRead equals numberOfPairs)
```

Integers, reals, characters, and Booleans are called simple or atomic data types, because each value is distinct and cannot be subdivided into parts. In the last chapter, we discussed composite data types—that is, data types made up of a collection of values. The *string* data type has some of the properties of a composite type but is often considered a simple data type.

Strings   A string is a sequence of characters that in some languages can be considered as one data value. For example,

```
"This is a string."
```

is a string containing 17 characters: 1 uppercase letter, 12 lowercase letters, 3 blanks, and a period. The operations defined on strings vary from language to language, but often include concatenation of strings and comparison of strings in terms of lexicographic order. Other languages provide a complete array of operations, such as taking a substring of a given string or searching a given string for a substring.

Note that we have used single quotes to enclose characters and double quotes to enclose strings. Some high-level languages use the same symbol, thus not distinguishing between a character and a string with one character.

Declarations

A declaration is a language statement that associates an identifier with a variable, an action, or some other entity within the language that can be given a name so that the programmer can refer to that item by name. In this section we discuss how a variable is declared. Later we look at how actions are given names.

>> **Declaration** A statement that associates an identifier with a variable, an action, or some other entity within the language that can be given a name so that the programmer can refer to that item by name

Language	Variable Declaration
Python	None required

VB .NET	```Dim sum As Single = 0.0F ' set up word with 0 as contents```
	```Dim num1 As Integer ' set up a two byte block for num1```
	```Dim num2 As Integer ' set up a two byte block for num2```
	```Dim num3 As Integer ' set up a two byte block for num3```
	```...```
	```num1 = 1```

C++/Java	```float sum = 0.0; // set up word with 0 as contents```
	```int num1; // set up a two byte block for num1```
	```int num2; // set up a two byte block for num2```
	```int num3; // set up a two byte block for num3```
	```...```
	```num1 = 1;```

These examples illustrate some differences among high-level languages. For example, VB .NET uses a reserved word to signal a declaration. A reserved word is a word in a language that has special meaning; it cannot be used as an identifier. Dim is a reserved word in VB .NET used to declare variables. C++ and Java do not use a reserved word for this purpose.

C++ and Java use the semicolon to end a statement in the language. VB .NET uses the end of the line or the *comment symbol* to end the statement. Python programs do not require declarations because Python is not a strongly typed language. Python uses the pound sign (#) as the beginning of a comment that extends to the end of the line. Recall that Pep/8 uses a semicolon to signal that what follows is a comment.

C++, Java, Python, and VB .NET are case sensitive, which means that two copies of the same identifier, when capitalized differently, are considered different words. Thus Integer, INTEGER, InTeGeR, and INTeger are

>> **Reserved word** A word in a language that has special meaning; it cannot be used as an identifier

>> **Case sensitive** Uppercase and lowercase letters are not considered the same; two identifiers with the same spelling but different capitalization are considered to be two distinct identifiers

considered four different identifiers in case-sensitive languages. C++, Java, and VB .NET have a collection of type names for various sizes of integer and real numbers. Although Python does not declare identifiers, it does have the reserved words `long`, `int`, `float`, and `bool`.

Are these differences important? They are if you are writing a program in one of these languages. However, they are just syntactic issues—that is, different ways of doing the same thing. The important concept is that an identifier is associated with a place in memory and may or may not be associated with a data type. In the exercises, we ask you to compare the syntactic differences that surface in these examples.

The use of uppercase and lowercase in identifiers is part of the culture of a language. In our examples, we have tried to stick with the style that is common within the language's culture. For example, most C++ programmers begin variable names with lowercase and subprograms with uppercase, while VB .NET programmers tend to begin variable names with uppercase letters.

■ Input/Output Structures

In our pseudocode algorithms, we have used the expressions Read and Write or Print to indicate that we were interacting with the environment outside the program. Read was for getting a value from outside the program and storing it into a variable inside the program, and Write and Print were for displaying a message for the human to see.

High-level languages view text data as a stream of characters divided into lines. How the characters are interpreted depends on the data types of the places into which the values are to be stored. Any input statement has three parts: the declaration of the variables into which data are to be placed, the input statement with the names of the variables to be read, and the data stream itself. As an example, let's look at the pseudocode algorithm to input three values:

```
Read name, age, hourlyWage
```

In a strongly typed language, the variables name, age, and hourlyWage would have to be declared along with their respective data types. Let's assume the types are string, integer, and real. The input statement would list the three variables. Processing would proceed as follows. The first data item on the input stream would be assumed to be a string, because name is of type string. The string would be read and stored into name. The next variable is an integer, so the read operation expects to find an integer next in the input stream. This value is read and stored in *age*. The third variable is a real number, so the read operation expects to find a real value next on the input stream to be stored as *hourlyWage*.

The input stream may be from the keyboard or a data file, but the process is the same: The order in which the variables are listed in the input statement must be the same as the order in which the values occur in the input stream. The types of the variables being input determine how the characters in the input stream are interpreted. That is, the input stream is just a series of ASCII (or Unicode) characters. The type of the variable into which the next value is to be stored determines how a sequence of characters is interpreted. For simplicity, let's assume that the input statement believes that a blank separates each data value. For example, given the data stream

```
Maggie 10 12.50
```

"Maggie" would be stored in *name*, 10 would be stored in *age*, and 12.50 would be stored in *hourlyWage*. Both 10 and 12.50 are read in as characters and converted to type integer and real, respectively.

In a language that is not strongly typed, the format of the input determines the type. If the input appears between quotes, it is assumed to be a string and is stored that way. If the input is a number, it is stored that way.

Output statements create streams of characters. The items listed on the output statement can be literal values or variable names. Literal values are numbers or strings written explicitly in the output statement (or any statement, for that matter). The values to be output are processed one at a time by looking at the type of the identifier or literal. The type determines how the bit pattern is to be interpreted. If the type is a string, the characters are written into the output stream. If the bit pattern is a number, the number is converted to the characters that represent the digits and the characters are written out.

In a strongly typed language, regardless of the syntax of input/output statements or where the input/output streams are, the key to the processing lies in the data type that determines how characters are to be converted to a bit pattern (input) and how a bit pattern is to be converted to characters (output). In a language that is not strongly typed, the format of the input itself determines how the bit pattern is to be converted.

Here are input and output statements in the four languages we are using for demonstrations. The prompts are omitted. The input statements are in black; the output statements are in green.

Language	Input Statement
C++	`cin >> name >> age >> hourlyWage;` `cout << name << age << hourlyWage;`

Java	`Scanner inData;`
	`inData = new Scanner(system.in);`
	`name = inData.nextLine();`
	`age = inData.nextInt();`
	`hourlyWage = inData.nextFloat();`
	`System.out.println(name, ' ',`
	`    age, ' ', hourlyWage);`

Python	`name = input()`
	`age = input()`
	`hourlyWage = input()`
	`print name, age, hourlyWage`

VB .NET	`Uses windowing`

■ Control Structures

Our pseudocode provided three ways to alter the flow of control of the algorithm: repetition, selection, and subprogram. These constructs are called control structures because they determine the order in which other instructions in a program are executed.

» Control structure An instruction that determines the order in which other instructions in a program are executed

In a seminal article, "Notes on Structured Programming," published in 1972, Edsger W. Dijkstra pointed out that programmers should be precise and disciplined—in other words, they should use only selected control structures. This article and the others published with it introduced the era of *structured programming*.[12] According to this view, each logical unit of a program should have just one entry and one exit. The program should not jump randomly in and out of logical modules. Although programs could be designed in this way in assembly language using instructions that branch to other parts of the program, high-level languages introduced control constructs that made this discipline easy to follow. These constructs are selection statements, looping statements, and subprogram statements. With this approach, unrestricted branching statements are no longer necessary.

In our pseudocode algorithms, we used indention to group statements within the body of an *if* statement or a *while* statement. Python uses indention, but the other languages use actual markers. VB .NET uses `End If` and `End While` to end the corresponding statements. Java and C++ use braces (`{}`).

The following tables show code segments using *if* and *while* statements in the demonstration languages.

Language	*if* Statement
| Python | ```python
if temperature > 75:
    print "No jacket is necessary"
else:
    print "A light jacket is appropriate"
# Idention marks grouping
``` |
| VB .NET | ```
If (Temperature > 75) Then
    MsgBox("No jacket is necessary")
Else
    MsgBox("A light jacket is appropriate")
End If
``` |
| C++ | ```cpp
if (temperature > 75)
    cout << "No jacket is necessary";
else
    cout << "A light jacket is appropriate";
``` |
| Java | ```java
if (temperature > 75)
    System.out.print ("No jacket is necessary");
else
    System.out.print ("A light jacket is appropriate");
``` |

Language	Count-Controlled Loop with a *while* Statement
| Python | ```python
count = 0
while count < limit:
    ...
    count = count + 1
# Indention marks loop body
``` |
| VB .NET | ```
Count = 1
While (Count <= Limit)
    ...
    Count = Count + 1
End While
``` |
| C++/Java | ```cpp
count = 1;
while (count <= limit)
{
    ...
    count = count + 1;
}
``` |
```

Edsger Dijkstra[13]

Every field of human endeavor has its leading contributors who are acclaimed for their theoretical insights, extensions of fundamental ideas, or innovative changes that have redefined the subject. Just as Beethoven, Schubert, Mozart, and Hayden ring true in the world of classical music, and the Beatles, Rolling Stones, and the Who stand out in rock-'n-roll, so Edsger Dijkstra has a place reserved for him in the computer language hall of fame.

Courtesy of Dianne Driskell, UTCS, The University of Texas at Austin

Born to a Dutch chemist in Rotterdam in 1930, Dijkstra grew up with a formalist predilection toward the world. While studying at the University of Leiden in the Netherlands, he attended a summer course on programming in Cambridge, England, and became fascinated with programming. He took a part-time job at the Mathematical Centre in Amsterdam in 1952, and he continued to work there after his graduation. Dijkstra came to the United States in the early 1970s as a research fellow for Burroughs Corporation, and in September 1984 he came to the University of Texas at Austin, where he held the Schlumberger Centennial Chair in Computer Sciences. He retired in November 1999.

One of Dijkstra's most famous contributions to programming was his strong advocacy of structured programming principles. Dijkstra observed that programs written with *goto* statements often turned into a rat's nest of jumping back and forth among disorganized, ad hoc sections of programs, making the programs difficult to understand even for their authors—not to mention the colleagues who might later be asked to maintain the program. Dijkstra argued that the goto was not the be-all and end-all of control structures, and he strongly encouraged the use of iterative, or looping, constructs that clearly bracket the scope of branching in a program and effectively self-document the program. Dijkstra claimed that adhering to these structured programming principles would make programs far easier to understand and maintain and less likely to contain errors.

Beyond his clear theoretical contributions, Dijkstra is an interesting character in the computing world. He developed a reputation for speaking his mind, often in inflammatory or dramatic ways that most of us can't get away with. For example, Dijkstra once remarked that "the use of COBOL cripples the mind; its teaching should therefore be regarded as a criminal offense." Not a person to single out only one language for his criticism, he also said that "it is practically impossible to teach good programming to students [who] have had a prior exposure to BASIC; as potential programmers they are mentally mutilated beyond hope of regeneration." Some people find his message cogent and believe that his manner is politically necessary to make his point. Others, aware of the historical development of languages and the contexts in which they were designed, appreciate his message but find his manner a bit strident.

Besides his work in language design, Dijkstra is noted for his work in proofs of program correctness. The field of program correctness is an application of mathematics to computer programming. Researchers are trying to construct a language and

» continued

Edsger Dijkstra, continued

proof technique that might be used to certify unconditionally that a program will perform according to its specifications—entirely free of bugs. Needless to say, whether your application is customer billing or flight control systems, this claim would be extremely valuable.

In 1972, the Association for Computing Machinery acknowledged Dijkstra's rich contributions to the field by awarding him the distinguished Turing Award. The citation for the award read:

> Edsger Dijkstra was a principal contributor in the late 1950s to the development of ALGOL, a high-level programming language that has become a model of clarity and mathematical rigor. He is one of the principal exponents of the science and art of programming languages in general, and has greatly contributed to our understanding of their structure, representation, and implementation. His fifteen years of publications extend from theoretical articles on graph theory to basic manuals, expository texts, and philosophical contemplations in the field of programming languages.

In 1989, the Special Interest Group for Computer Science Education (SIGCSE) honored him with its award for Outstanding Contributions to Computer Science Education.

Dijkstra and his wife returned to the Netherlands when he found that he had only months to live. He had always said that he wanted to retire in Austin, Texas, but to die in the Netherlands. Dijkstra died on August 6, 2002.

In March 2003, the following email was sent to the distributed computing community:

> This is to announce that the award formerly known as the "PODC Influential-Paper Award" has been renamed the "Edsger W. Dijkstra Prize in Distributed Computing" after the late Edsger W. Dijkstra, a pioneer in the area of distributed computing. His foundational work on concurrency primitives (such as the semaphore), concurrency problems (such as mutual exclusion and deadlock), reasoning about concurrent systems, and self-stabilization comprises one of the most important supports upon which the field of distributed computing is built. No other individual has had a larger influence on research in principles of distributed computing.

The information on the award can be found at www.podc.org/dijkstra/.

Dijkstra was known for many concise and witty sayings. One that all who study computing should ponder is that "Computer science is no more about computers than astronomy is about telescopes."

The following table shows how VB .NET and C++ define a subprogram that does not return a single value. In this example, there are two integer value parameters and one real reference parameter. Again, this illustration is meant to give you a hint of the rich variety of syntax that abounds in high-level languages, not to make you competent in writing this construct in any of them. The ampersand (&) used in C++ is not a typographical error; it signals that three is a reference parameter.

Language	Subprogram declaration
VB .NET	```Public Sub Example(ByVal one As Integer, ByVal two As Integer, ByRef three As Single) . . . End Sub```
C++	```void Example(int one, int two, float& three) { . . . }```

We do not show a Java or Python example because they handle memory very differently, allowing only value parameters.

Nested Logic

The statements to be executed or skipped in any control statement can be simple statements or blocks (compound statements)—there is no constraint on what these statements can be. In fact, the statement to be skipped or repeated can contain a control structure. Selection statements can be nested within looping structures; looping structures can be nested within selection statements. Selection and looping statements can be nested within subprograms, and subprogram calls can be nested within looping or selection structures.

We have looked at nesting in our algorithms, but the topic is worth another look. Take, for example, the algorithm that counts and sums ten positive numbers in a file:

```
Set sum to 0                // Initialize sum
Set posCount to 0           // Initialize event
WHILE (posCount < 10)       // Test event
      Read a value
      IF (value > 0)            // Test to see if event should be updated
            Set posCount to posCount + 1   // Update event
            Set sum to sum + value         // Add value into sum
// Statement(s) following loop
```

The selection control structure is embedded within a looping control structure. If we wanted to sum and print weekly rainfall figures for a year, we would have the following nested looping structures:

```
Set weekCount to 1
WHILE (weekCount<= 52)
      Set weekSum to 0
      Set dayCount to 1
      WHILE (dayCount <= 7)
            Read rainfall
            Set weekSum to weekSum + rainfall
            Set dayCount to dayCount + 1
      Write "Week ", weekCount, " total: ", weekSum
      Set weekCount to weekCount + 1
```

Control structures within control structures within control structures . . . Theoretically, there is no limit to how deeply control structures can be nested! However, if the nesting becomes too difficult to follow, you should give the nested task a name and make it a subprogram, giving its implementation later. For example, examine the alternative version of the preceding pseudocode algorithm. Which is easier to follow?

```
Set weekCount to 1
WHILE (weekCount <= 52)
      Set weekSum to CalculateWeekSum(weekCount)
      Write "Week ", weekCount, " total: ", weekSum
      Set weekCount to weekCount + 1
```

```
CalculateWeekSum(weekCount)

Set weekSum to 0
Set dayCount to 1
WHILE (dayCount <= 7)
    Read rainfall
    Set weekSum to weekSum + rainfall
    Set dayCount to dayCount + 1
RETURN weekSum
```

Asynchronous Processing

You have likely grown up using a graphical user interface (GUI) that relies on the use of a mouse to manipulate multiple window frames on a screen. *Clicking* has become a major form of input to the computer. In fact, for many applications, filling in boxes and clicking buttons to say the input is ready has become the only form of input.

In traditional stream processing, an input statement is executed in the sequence in which it is encountered. Here are the first four statements in the algorithm shown earlier:

```
Write "How many pairs of values are to be entered?"
Read numberOfPairs
Set numberRead to 0
WHILE (numberRead < numberOfPairs)
    . . . .
```

We expect these statements to be executed in sequence. Output is written to a window, a value is read from the input stream, another value is stored, and the *while* loop is executed. Stream input and output is within the sequential flow of the program.

Mouse clicking, in contrast, does not occur within the sequence of the program. That is, a user can click a mouse at any time during the execution of a program. The program must recognize when a mouse click has occurred, process the mouse click, and then continue. This type of processing is called asynchronous, which means "not at the same time." The mouse can be clicked at any time; it is not synchronized with any other instructions.

>> Asynchronous Not occurring at the same moment in time as some specific operation of the computer; in other words, not synchronized with the program's actions

Asynchronous processing is also called *event-driven* processing. In other words, the processing is under the control of events happening outside the sequence of program instructions.

Asynchronous processing is used frequently in Java and VB .NET, but less often in the other languages.

9.5 Functionality of Object-Oriented Languages

As you might guess from the earlier discussion of object-oriented design, the basic construct in an object-oriented language is the *class*. In addition to looking at the class construct in this section, we examine the three essential ingredients in an object-oriented language: *encapsulation*, *inheritance*, and *polymorphism*. These ingredients foster reuse, thereby reducing the cost of building and maintaining software.

■ Encapsulation

In Chapter 7, we talked about important threads running through the discussion of problem solving. Two of these threads were *information hiding* and *abstraction*. Recall that information hiding is the practice of hiding the details of a module with the goal of controlling access to the details. We said in Chapter 7 that abstraction was a model of a complex system that includes only the details essential to the viewer. We defined three types of abstraction, but the definitions of each began and ended with the words "The separation of the logical view of . . . from its implementation details." Abstraction is the goal; information hiding is a technique used to achieve the goal.

In the discussion of object-oriented design, we said that encapsulation is the bundling of data and actions in such a way that the logical properties of the data and actions remain separate from the implementation details. Another way of saying this is that encapsulation is a language feature that enforces information hiding. A module's implementation is hidden in a separate block with a formally specified interface. An object knows things about itself, but not about any other object. If one object needs information about another object, it must request that information from that object.

》 **Encapsulation (second definition)** A language feature that enforces information hiding

The construct used to provide encapsulation is the class. Just as the concept of the class dominates object-oriented design, so the class concept is the major feature of Java and other object-oriented languages. Unfortunately, the related definitions are not standard across the phases of design

» Object (problem-solving phase) An entity or thing that is relevant in the context of a problem

» Class (implementation phase) A pattern for an object

» Object class (class) (problem-solving phase) A description of a group of objects with similar properties and behaviors

» Object (implementation phase) An instance of a class

and implementation. In the design (problem-solving) phase, an object is a thing or entity that makes sense within the context of the problem. In the implementation phase, a class is a language construct that is a pattern for an object and provides a mechanism for encapsulating the properties and actions of the object class.

▪ Classes

Syntactically, a class is like a record in that it is a heterogeneous composite data type. However, records have traditionally been considered passive structures; only in recent years have they had subprograms as fields. The class, by contrast, is an active structure and almost always has subprograms as fields. The only way to manipulate the data fields of a class is through the methods (subprograms) defined in the class.

Here is how we might define class Person, developed earlier:

```
public class Person
    // Class variables
    Name name
    String address
    String telephone
    String email
    // Class Methods
    Initialize()
        // Code for Initialize
    public Print()
        // Code for Print
    public Name GetName()
        RETURN Name
    public String GetAddress()
        RETURN address
    public String GetEmail()
        RETURN email
    public String GetTelephone()
        RETURN telephone
```

Figure 9.4 visualizes class Person. The variable fields are blank. The subprogram fields are orange to indicate that they do not contain values but are subprograms.

Person

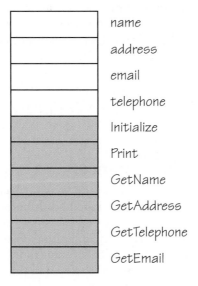

name

address

email

telephone

Initialize

Print

GetName

GetAddress

GetTelephone

GetEmail

FIGURE 9.4 Class Person

In our algorithms, we have used identifiers for simple variables and arrays without worrying about where they come from. If we use an identifier to represent a class, however, we must explicitly ask for the class to be created before we can use. That is, we have to instantiate the class by using the *new* operator to get an object that fits the pattern. This operator takes the class name and returns an instance of the class. This algorithm instantiates a class Person, gets an object aPerson of the class, and stores and retrieves values in the object. We first instantiate a Name object but assume that string variables email, telephone, and address already have values.

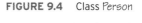 Instantiate To create an object from a class

```
Name aName = new Name()
aName.Initialize("Frank", "Jones")
Person aPerson = new Person()
aPerson.Initialize(aName, address, telephone, email)
aPerson.Print()
Write "Name: ", aPerson.GetName().Print()
Write "Address: ", aPerson.GetAddress()
Write " Telephone: ", aPerson.GetTelephone()
Write " Email: ", a Person.GetEmail()
```

The algorithms that declare class objects can access the fields of the class only through the subprograms (called methods) of the class.

The fields in a class are private by default. That is, none of the fields, either data or method, of an object of a particular class can be accessed by any other object unless the field is marked public. If a class needs to make a method available to be called by an object of another class, the class must explicitly specify that the method is public. The Person class methods are marked public so that a using program can call them.

■ Inheritance

> Inheritance A mechanism by which one class acquires the properties–data fields and methods–of another class

Inheritance is a property of object-oriented languages in which classes can inherit data and methods from other classes. This relationship is an "is-a" relationship. A *superclass* is a class being inherited from; a *derived class* is a class doing the inheriting. Classes form an inheritance hierarchy. In the hierarchy, objects become more specialized the lower in the hierarchy we go. Classes farther down in the hierarchy inherit all of the behaviors and data of their parent superclass.

In our latest example, we have been working with class Person. In an object-oriented language, we can define a class Student, which inherits all the properties of class Person and adds more data fields to hold the local address and telephone number. Objects of class Person have only one address and phone number, but objects of class Student have two: one inherited from class Person and one defined within class Student. We say that class Student is derived from class Person.

Here are the CRC card headings for Person and Student. Note that the Subclass and Superclass fields in the CRC cards have been filled in.

Class Name: *Person*	Superclass:	Subclasses: *Student*

Class Name: *Student*	Superclass: *Person*	Subclasses:

Let's assume that we have defined classes Person and Student. The following algorithm instantiates classes Person and Student and manipulates them:

```
Person myPerson = new Person()      // Instantiates myPerson
Student myStudent = new Student()   // Instantiates myStudent
myPerson.Initialize(...)            // myPerson initializes itself
myStudent.Initialize(...)           // myStudent initializes itself
myPerson.Print()                    // myPerson prints itself
myStudent.Print()                   // myStudent prints itself
```

Inheritance fosters reuse by allowing an application to take an already-tested class and derive a class from it that inherits the properties the application needs. Other necessary properties and methods can then be added to the derived class.

■ Polymorphism

In the previous section, classes Person and Student both have methods named Print and Initialize. The method in class Person prints the address defined in its class, and the method in class Student prints the address defined in its class. Here we have two methods with the same name but different implementations. The ability of a programming language to handle this apparent ambiguity is called polymorphism. How does the language know which method is meant when Initialize or Print is invoked by the calling unit? Methods that are part of a class are applied to an instance of the class by the calling unit. The class of object to which the method is applied determines which versions of the Initialize or Print method are used.

For example, if we had jane as an instance of class Person and jack as an instance of class Student, jane.Print would invoke the method defined in class Person to print jane's information. jack.Print would invoke the method defined in class Student to print jack's information. The Student class

》 **Polymorphism** The ability of a language to have duplicate method names in an inheritance hierarchy and to apply the method that is appropriate for the object to which the method is applied

could add a method PrintHomeAddress, which would then print the home address of a student.

The combination of inheritance and polymorphism allows the programmer to build useful hierarchies of classes that can be reused in different applications. Reuse does not apply only to object-oriented languages; however, the functionality of object-oriented languages makes writing general, reusable sections of code easier.

9.6 Comparison of Procedural and Object-Oriented Designs

At the end of Chapter 8, we used the implementation of ADT List algorithms to describe the process of value-returning and non-value-returning subprograms. The implementation of the List ADT was a record variable list, which contained an array values and a length field, that was passed to the List algorithms to be acted up. The calling program defined the implementation of the list and wrote the algorithms to manipulate it. The subprograms were tasks of the program that needed a list.

In an object-oriented design, the List data structure and subprograms would be bound together in a class as follows:

```
public class List
    // Class variables
    values[ ]
    length
    // Class methods
    public Boolean IsThere(item)
        Set position to 0
```

```
        WHILE (position < length AND
                values[position] != item)
            Set position to position + 1
        RETURN position < length
    public Delete(item)
        Set position to 1
        WHILE (values[position] != item)
            Set position to position + 1
        Swap(values[length – 1], values[position])
        Set length to length – 1
    // Rest of class operations
```

The code of the methods has direct access to the class variables; the user's code does not. The class would be compiled separately and the program that wanted to use the class would include it in its program. Here is a segment of pseudocode that would manipulate a List object:

```
List list = new List()                  // Instantiate List object
WHILE (more values)
    Read aValue
    IF (NOT list.IsThere(aValue))
        list.insert(aValue)
Write "Input value to delete or "Quit" to quit"
Read aValue
IF (aValue != "Quit")
    IF (list.IsThere(aValue))
        list.Delete(aValue)
```

In the procedural version, the list is represented by a record that is passed to the subprograms that operate on it. The data structure and the subprograms that manipulate it are part of the user's program. In the object-oriented version, the implementation of a class object is hidden from the user through encapsulation.

Summary

Object-oriented design focuses on determining the objects within a problem, and abstracting (grouping) those objects into classes based on like properties and behaviors. There are four stages to object-oriented decomposition:

- Brainstorming, in which we make a first pass at determining the classes in the problem
- Filtering, in which we review the proposed classes
- Scenarios, in which the responsibilities of each class are determined
- Responsibility algorithms, in which the algorithms are written for each of the responsibilities

An assembler translates an assembly-language program into machine code. A compiler translates a program written in a high-level language either into assembly language (to be later translated into machine code) or into machine code. An interpreter is a program that translates the instructions in a program and executes them immediately. An interpreter does not output machine-language code.

Various models of high-level programming languages exist, classified as either imperative (procedural and object-oriented) or declarative (functional and logic). The imperative model describes the processing to be done. The declarative model describes what is to be done, not how it is to be accomplished. The procedural model is based on the concept of a hierarchy of tasks to be completed; the object-oriented model is based on the concept of interacting objects. The functional model is based on the mathematical concept of a function; the logic model is based on mathematical logic.

A Boolean expression is an assertion about the state of a program. Boolean expressions are used to allow a program to execute one section of code or another (conditional statements) and to repeat a section of code (looping statements).

Each variable in a program is a certain data type. Strong typing means that variables are given a type and that only values of that data type can be stored into the variable. Storing a value into a variable is called assigning the value to the variable (assignment statements).

Object-oriented programs are characterized by the following constructs:

- *Encapsulation*, a language feature that enforces information hiding that is implemented using the class construct
- *Inheritance*, a language feature that allows one class to inherit the properties and behaviors of another class
- *Polymorphism*, the ability of a language to disambiguate between operations with the same name

⚖ ETHICAL ISSUES ▶ Gambling and the Internet

Most people think of gambling as sitting in front of a blackjack table or a slot machine in a Las Vegas casino, but more and more people are turning to the Internet for their gambling needs. Online gambling exploded onto the Internet in August 1995, when Internet Casinos, Inc., became the first online casino to accept real wagers. Since then, online gambling has grown into a multibillion-dollar a year business, with most of the businesses being run offshore. In 2008, Internet gambling sites earned revenues of $5.9 billion from players in the United States alone, and $21 billion worldwide.

With the growth of the online gambling industry, the issue of fraud has become a serious problem. The potential for fraud over an Internet gambling site is quite high. Gamblers provide credit card information and Social Security numbers to start an account, trusting that the games will be run fairly. All traditional casinos are regulated by the American Gaming Association to be sure that the games are run honestly. With the design of the Internet sites, however, it is impossible for the user to know whether the games are operated fairly; instead, gamblers must rely solely on the honesty of those operating the site.

Another problem with Internet gambling is that it has proved difficult for states to regulate. State govern-ments earn profits from any state-run gambling organizations, but they lose revenue from gamblers who use Internet gambling sites, as they are run offshore and are not subject to state taxation. Some states have been relying on state gambling laws to curb online gambling; Illinois, Indiana, Louisiana, Massachusetts, Nevada, Oregon, South Dakota, and Utah have all passed laws banning Internet gambling. This state regulation is for the most part ineffective, however, because the Internet goes beyond state and national restrictions.

Congress has been working to pass legislation that would ban all Internet gambling, but because such a ban would be so broad in scope, lawmakers have been largely unsuccessful. In 2006, the Unlawful Gambling Enforcement Act as attached to federal legislation created to increase U.S. port security. This legislation restricts the methods used to place bets on thousands of online gambling sites and makes it illegal for banks and credit card companies to collect on debts incurred on an online gambling site. The final regulations in the legislation were put into effect on January 19, 2009, but companies have until December 2009 to comply with the new laws.

🔑 Key Terms

Asynchronous
Boolean expression
Bytecode
Case sensitive
Class (implementation phase)
Compiler
Control structure
Data type
Declaration
Encapsulation
Fields
Inheritance

Instantiate
Interpreter
Method
Object
Object (implementation phase)
Object (problem-solving phase)
Object class (class)
Object class (class) (problem-solving
  phase)
Polymorphism
Reserved word
Strong typing

⌘ **Exercises**

For Exercises 1–10, match the activity with the phase of the object-oriented methodology.
   A. Brainstorming
   B. Filtering
   C. Scenarios
   D. Responsibility algorithms

1. Reviewing a list of possible classes, looking for duplicates or missing classes

2. Asking "what if" questions

3. Assigning responsibilities to classes

4. Generating a first approximation to the list of classes in a problem

5. Assigning collaborators to a responsibility

6. Developing algorithms for the responsibilities listed on a CRC card

7. Output from this phase is a fully developed CRC card for all classes

8. Output from this phase is the design ready to be translated into a program

9. During this phase, inheritance relationships are established

10. Phase in which functional programming techniques are appropriate

For Exercises 11–24, match the question with the appropriate translation or execution system.
   A. Interpreter
   B. Assembler
   C. Compiler
   D. Machine code

11. What translates a high-level language into machine code?

12. What translates a Java program into Bytecode?

13. What executes Bytecode?

14. What translates an assembly-language program?

15. What is the output of an assembler?

16. What takes input in a high-level language and directs the computer to perform the actions specified in each statement?

17. What executes the Java Virtual Machine?

18. What is used to translate a program in ALGOL?

19. What is used to translate a program in APL?

20. What is used to translate a program in COBOL?

21. What is used to translate a program in FORTRAN?

22. What is used to translate a program in Lisp?

23. What is used to translate a program in PROLOG?

24. Which translator runs the most slowly?

For Exercises 25–46, match the language paradigm and the language or the language description.
  A. Procedural
  B. Functional
  C. Logic
  D. Object oriented
  E. Procedural language with object-oriented features
  F. Object-oriented language with some procedural features

25. Which paradigm most accurately describes FORTRAN?

26. Which paradigm most accurately describes C++?

27. Which paradigm most accurately describes PASCAL?

28. Which paradigm most accurately describes Java?

29. Which paradigm most accurately describes Lisp?

30. Which paradigm most accurately describes BASIC?

31. Which paradigm most accurately describes PROLOG?

32. Which paradigm most accurately describes SIMULA?

33. Which paradigm most accurately describes ALGOL?

34. Which paradigm most accurately describes ML?

35. Which paradigm most accurately describes Scheme?

36. Which paradigm most accurately describes Python?

37. Which paradigm most accurately describes C?

38. Which paradigm most accurately describes Smalltalk?

39. The dominant languages used in industry throughout the history of computing software come from which paradigm?

40. Which paradigm did Japanese researchers choose for the fifth-generation computer?

41. Which paradigm allows the programmer to express algorithms as a hierarchy of objects?

42. Which paradigm allows the programmer to express algorithms as a hierarchy of tasks?

43. Which paradigm allows the programmer to express algorithms as mathematical functions?

44. Which paradigm has no assignment statement?

45. Which paradigm uses recursion exclusively to express repetition?

46. Which paradigm has no variables?

Exercises 47–84 are problems or short-answer questions.

47. What is the hallmark of an assembly language?

48. Distinguish between an assembler and a compiler.

49. Distinguish between a compiler and an interpreter.

50. Compare and contrast an assembler, a compiler, and an interpreter.

51. Describe the portability provided by a compiler.

52. Describe the portability provided by the use of Bytecode.

53. Describe the process of compiling and running a Java program.

54. Discuss the word *paradigm* as it relates to computing.

55. Distinguish between imperative and declarative paradigms.

56. What are the characteristics of the imperative paradigm?

57. What are the characteristics of the functional paradigm?

58. What are the characteristics of the logic paradigm?

59. What are the characteristics of a declarative paradigm?

60. How do you ask questions in a programming language?

61. What is a Boolean variable?

62. What is a Boolean expression?

63. Given variables one, two, and three, write an assertion for each of the following questions.
    a. Is one greater than both two and three?
    b. Is one greater than two, but less than three?
    c. Are all three variables greater than zero?
    d. Is one less than two or one less than three?
    e. Is two greater than one and three less than two?

64. Write the operation table for the Boolean operation AND.

65. Write the operation table for the Boolean operation OR.

66. Write the operation table for the Boolean operation NOT.

67. What is a data type?

68. What is strong typing?

69. Define the following data types.
    a. integer
    b. real
    c. character
    d. Boolean

70. Is the string data type an atomic data type? Justify your answer.
71. If the same symbol is used for both single characters and strings, how can you distinguish between a single character and a one-character string?
72. What is a declaration?
73. Fill in the following table showing the appropriate syntactic marker or reserved word for the language shown based on your observations of the tables in this chapter.

Language	Python	VB .NET	C++	Java
Comments				
End of statement				
Assignment statement				
Real data type				
Integer data type				
Beginning of declaration(s)				

74. How do the `.WORD` and `.BLOCK` assembler directives in the Pep/8 assembly language differ from the declarations in high-level languages?
75. Distinguish between instructions to be translated and instructions to the translating program.
76. Consider the following identifiers: Address, ADDRESS, AddRess, Name, NAME, NamE.
    a. How many different identifiers are represented if the language is Python?
    b. How many different identifiers are represented if the language is VB .NET?
    c. How many different identifiers are represented if the language is C++ or Java?

77. Distinguish between the definition of an object in the design phase and in the implementation phase.

78. Distinguish between the definition of a class in the design phase and in the implementation phase.

79. Distinguish between a field and a method.

80. How can objects relate to one another?

81. Discuss the differences between a top-down design and an object-oriented design.

82. In this chapter, we outlined a strategy for developing an object-oriented decomposition.
    a. List the four stages.
    b. Outline the characteristics of each stages.
    c. What is the output from each of the four stages?
    d. Are each of the stages independent? Explain.

83. Design the CRC cards for an inventory system for a car dealership, using brainstorming, filtering, and scenarios.

84. Design the CRC cards for a database for a zoo, using brainstorming, filtering, and scenarios.

??? Thought Questions

1. Distinguish between a program that the CPU can execute directly and a program that must be translated.

2. Top-down design and object-oriented design both create scaffolding that is used to write a program. Is all of this scaffolding just a waste of effort? Is it ever used again? Of what value is it after the program is up and running?

3. Which of the problem-solving strategies do you use the most? Can you think of some others that you use? Would they be appropriate for computing problem solving?

4. Have you ever visited an Internet gambling site?

5. Should Internet gambling be outlawed? Regulated? Taxed?

The Operating Systems Layer

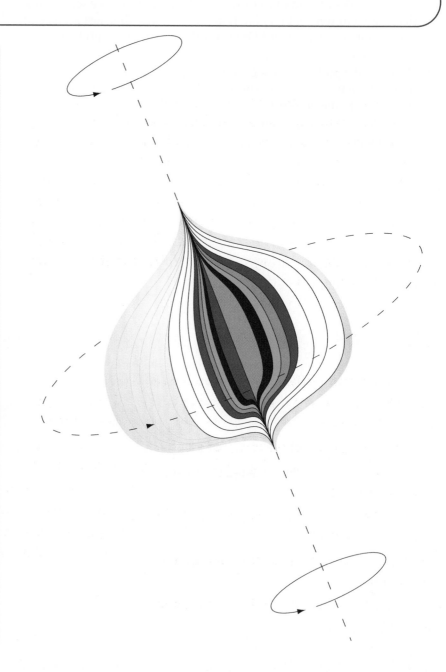

Operating Systems

10

To understand a computer system, you must understand the software that manages and coordinates its pieces. The operating system of a computer is the glue that holds the hardware and software together. It is the software foundation on which all other software rests, allowing us to write programs that interact with the machine. This chapter and the next one explore the way in which an operating system manages computer resources. Just as a policeman organizes the efficient flow of cars through an intersection, an operating system organizes the efficient flow of programs through a computer system.

Goals

After studying this chapter, you should be able to:

- describe the two main responsibilities of an operating system.

- define memory and process management.

- explain how timesharing creates the virtual machine illusion.

- explain the relationship between logical and physical addresses.

- compare and contrast memory management techniques.

- distinguish between fixed and dynamic partitions.

- define and apply partition selection algorithms.

- explain how demand paging creates the virtual memory illusion.

- explain the stages and transitions of the process life cycle.

- explain the processing of various CPU scheduling algorithms.

10.1 Roles of an Operating System

In Chapter 1, we talked about the changing role of the programmer. As early as the end of the first generation of software development, there was a split between those programmers who wrote tools to help other programmers and those who used the tools to solve problems. Modern software can be divided into two categories, application software and system software, reflecting this separation of goals. Application software is written to address specific needs—to solve problems in the real world. Word processing programs, games, inventory control systems, automobile diagnostic programs, and missile guidance programs are all application software. Chapters 12 through 14 discuss areas of computer science that relate to application software.

System software manages a computer system at a more fundamental level. It provides the tools and an environment in which application software can be created and run. System software often interacts directly with the hardware and provides more functionality than the hardware itself does.

The operating system of a computer is the core of its system software. An operating system manages computer resources, such as memory and input/output devices, and provides an interface through which a human can interact with the computer. Other system software supports specific application goals, such as a library of graphics software that renders images on a display. The operating system allows an application program to interact with these other system resources.

Figure 10.1 shows the operating system in its relative position among computer system elements. The operating system manages hardware resources. It allows application software to access system resources, either directly or through other system software. It provides a direct user interface to the computer system.

A computer generally has one operating system that becomes active and takes control when the system is turned on. Computer hardware is wired to initially load a small set of system instructions that is stored in permanent memory (ROM). These instructions load a larger portion of system software from secondary memory, usually a magnetic disk. Eventually all key elements of the operating system software are loaded, start-up programs are executed, the user interface is activated, and the system is ready for use. This activity is often called *booting* the computer. The term "boot" comes from the idea of "pulling yourself up by your own bootstraps," which is essentially what a computer does when it is turned on.

A computer could have two or more operating systems from which the user chooses when the computer is turned on. This configuration is often

> **Application software**
> Programs that help us solve real-world problems

> **System software**
> Programs that manage a computer system and interact with hardware

> **Operating system** System software that manages computer resources and provides an interface for system interaction

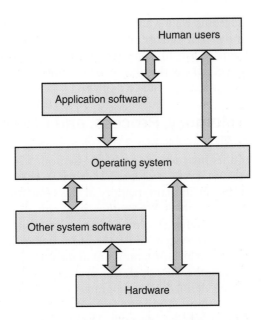

FIGURE 10.1 An operating system interacts with many aspects of a computer system.

called a *dual-boot* or *multi-boot* system. Only one operating system controls the computer at any given time, however.

You've likely used at least one operating system before. The various versions of Microsoft® Windows® (Windows NT, Windows XP, Windows Vista, Windows 7) are popular choices for personal computers. The different versions of these operating systems indicate how the software evolves over time as well as how changes occur in the way services are provided and managed. The Mac OS family is the operating system of choice for computers manufactured by Apple® Computer. UNIX has been a favorite of serious programmers for years, and a version of UNIX called Linux is popular for personal computer systems.

Any given operating system manages resources in its own particular way. Our goal in this chapter is not to nitpick about the differences among operating systems, but rather to discuss the ideas common to all of them. We occasionally refer to the methods that a specific OS (operating system) uses, and we discuss some of their individual philosophies. In general, however, we focus on the underlying concepts.

The various roles of an operating system generally revolve around the idea of "sharing nicely." An operating system manages resources, and these resources are often shared in one way or another among the various

Who is Blake Ross?
Blake Ross was designing Web pages by the age of 10. By 14, he was fixing bugs in Netscape's Web browser as a hobby. Before finishing high school, he helped develop Firefox®, an open-source Web browser. America Online® created a not-for-profit foundation to continue the development of Firefox®, which was officially released in November 2004. While in college, Ross continued fixing bugs in the browser. In 2005, he was nominated for *Wired* magazine's Renegade of the Year award. Ross joined up with another ex-Netscape employee to create Parakey, a new user interface designed to bridge the gap between the desktop and the Web. In 2007, Parakey was purchased by Facebook.

programs that want to use them. Multiple programs executing concurrently share the use of main memory. They take turns using the CPU. They compete for an opportunity to use input/output devices. The operating system acts as the playground monitor, making sure that everyone cooperates and gets a chance to play.

■ Memory, Process, and CPU Management

Recall from Chapter 5 that an executing program resides in main memory and its instructions are processed one after another in the fetch–decode–execute cycle. Multiprogramming is the technique of keeping multiple programs in main memory at the same time; these programs compete for access to the CPU so that they can do their work. All modern operating systems employ multiprogramming to one degree or another. An operating system must therefore perform memory management to keep track of which programs are in memory and where in memory they reside.

Another key operating system concept is the idea of a process, which can be defined as a program in execution. A program is a static set of instructions. A process is the dynamic entity that represents the program while it is being executed. Through multiprogramming, a computer system might have many active processes at once. The operating system must manage these processes carefully. At any point in time a specific instruction may be the next to be executed. Intermediate values have been calculated. A process might be interrupted during its execution, so the operating system performs process management to carefully track the progress of a process and all of its intermediate states.

Related to the ideas of memory management and process management is the need for CPU scheduling, which determines which process in memory is executed by the CPU at any given point.

Memory management, process management, and CPU scheduling are the three main topics discussed in this chapter. Other key operating system topics, such as file management and secondary storage, are covered in Chapter 11.

Keep in mind that the OS is itself just a program that must be executed. Operating system processes must be managed and maintained in main memory along with other system software and application programs. The OS executes on the same CPU as the other programs, and it must take its turn among them.

Before we delve into the details of managing resources such as main memory and the CPU, we need to explore a few more general concepts.

>> **Multiprogramming** The technique of keeping multiple programs in main memory at the same time, competing for the CPU

>> **Memory management** The act of keeping track of how and where programs are loaded in main memory

>> **Process** The dynamic representation of a program during execution

>> **Process management** The act of keeping track of information for active processes

>> **CPU scheduling** The act of determining which process in memory is given access to the CPU so that it may execute

Influential computing jobs
There were many influential jobs in computing in the 1960s, but none more so than the computer operator. In his or her hands rested the decision of whose computer jobs ran and when. Many a graduate student was known to have bribed a weary operator with coffee and cookies in the wee hours of the morning for just one more run.

■ Batch Processing

A typical computer in the 1960s and 1970s was a large machine stored in its own frigidly air-conditioned room. Its processing was managed by a human *operator*. A user would deliver his or her program, usually stored as a deck of punched cards, to the operator to be executed. The user would come back later—perhaps the next day—to retrieve the printed results.

When delivering the program, the user would also provide a set of separate instructions regarding the system software and other resources needed to execute the program. Together the program and the system instructions were called a *job*. The operator would make any necessary devices available and load any special system software required to satisfy the job. Obviously, the process of preparing a program for execution on these early machines was quite time-consuming.

To perform this procedure more efficiently, the operator would organize various jobs from multiple users into batches. A batch would contain a set of jobs that needed the same or similar resources. With batch processing, the operator did not have to reload and prepare the same resources over and over. Figure 10.2 depicts this procedure.

Batch systems could be executed in a multiprogramming environment. In that case, the operator would load multiple jobs from the same batch into memory, and these jobs would compete for the use of the CPU and other shared resources. As the resources became available, the jobs would be scheduled to use the CPU.

Although the original concept of batch processing is not a function of modern operating systems, the terminology persists. The term "batch" has come to mean a system in which programs and system resources are

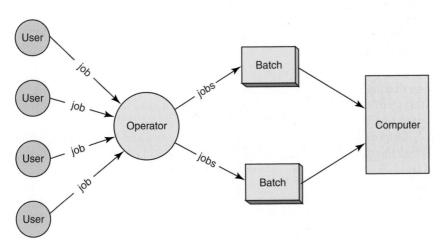

FIGURE 10.2 In early systems, human operators would organize jobs into batches

coordinated and executed without interaction between the user and the program. Modern operating systems incorporate batch-style processing by allowing the user to define a set of OS commands as a batch file to control the processing of a large program or a set of interacting programs. For example, files with the extension .bat in Microsoft Windows originated from the idea of batch control files; they contain system commands.

Although most of our computer use these days is interactive, some jobs still lend themselves to batch processing. For example, processing a corporation's monthly payroll is a large job that uses specific resources with essentially no human interaction.

Early batch processing allowed multiple users to share a single computer. Although the emphasis has changed over time, batch systems taught us valuable lessons about resource management. The human operator of early computer systems played many of the roles that modern operating system software handles now.

■ Timesharing

As we pointed out in Chapter 1, the problem of how to capitalize on computers' greater capabilities and speed led to the concept of *timesharing*. A timesharing system allows multiple users to interact with a computer at the same time. Multiprogramming allowed multiple processes to be active at once, which gave rise to the ability for programmers to interact with the computer system directly, while still sharing its resources.

Timesharing systems create the illusion that each user has exclusive access to the computer. That is, each user does not have to actively compete for resources, though that is exactly what is happening behind the scenes. One user may actually know he is sharing the machine with other users, but does not have to do anything special to allow it. The operating system manages the sharing of the resources, including the CPU, behind the scenes.

The word "virtual" means "in effect, though not in essence." In a timesharing system, each user has his or her own virtual machine, in which all system resources are (in effect) available for use. In essence, however, the resources are shared among many such users.

Originally, timesharing systems consisted of a single computer, often called the mainframe, and a set of dumb terminals connected to the mainframe. A dumb terminal is essentially just a monitor display and a keyboard. A user sits at a terminal and "logs in" to the mainframe. The dumb terminals might be spread throughout a building, with the mainframe residing in its own dedicated room. The operating system resides on the mainframe, and all processing occurs there.

Each user is represented by a *login process* that runs on the mainframe. When the user runs a program, another process is created (spawned

> **Timesharing** A system in which CPU time is shared among multiple interactive users at the same time

> **Virtual machine** The illusion created by a timesharing system that each user has a dedicated machine

> **Mainframe** A large, multiuser computer often associated with early timesharing systems

> **Dumb terminal** A monitor and keyboard that allowed the user to access the mainframe computer in early timesharing systems

by the user's login process). CPU time is shared among all of the processes created by all of the users. Each process is given a little bit of CPU time in turn. The premise is that the CPU is so fast that it can handle the needs of multiple users without any one user seeing any delay in processing. In truth, users of a timesharing system can sometimes see degradation in the system's responses, depending on the number of active users and the CPU capabilities. That is, each user's machine seems to slow down when the system becomes overburdened.

Although mainframe computers are interesting now mostly for historical reasons, the concept of timesharing remains highly relevant. Today, many desktop computers run operating systems that support multiple users in a timesharing fashion. Although only one user is actually sitting in front of the computer, other users can connect through other computers across a network connection.

■ Other OS Factors

As computing technology improved, the machines themselves got smaller. Mainframe computers gave rise to *minicomputers,* which no longer needed dedicated rooms in which to store them. Minicomputers became the basic hardware platform for timesharing systems. *Microcomputers,* which for the first time relied on a single integrated chip as the CPU, truly fit on an individual's desk. Their introduction gave rise to the idea of a *personal computer* (PC). As the name implies, a personal computer is not designed for multiperson use, and originally personal computer operating systems reflected this simplicity. Over time, personal computers evolved in functionality and incorporated many aspects of larger systems, such as timesharing. Although a desktop machine is still often referred to as a PC, the term "workstation" is sometimes used and is perhaps more appropriate, describing the machine as generally dedicated to an individual, but capable of supporting much more. Operating systems, in turn, evolved to support these changes in the use of computers.

Operating systems must also take into account the fact that computers are usually connected to networks. Today with the World Wide Web we take network communication for granted. Networks are discussed in detail in a later chapter, but we must acknowledge here the effect that network communication has on operating systems. Such communication is yet another resource that an OS must support.

An operating system is responsible for communicating with a variety of devices. Usually that communication is accomplished with the help of a device driver, a small program that "knows" the way a particular device expects to receive and deliver information. With device drivers, every operating system no longer needs to know about every device with which it might possibly be expected to communicate in the future. It's another beautiful example of abstraction. An appropriate device driver often comes with new hardware, and the most up-to-date drivers can often be downloaded for free from the manufacturing company's website.

One final aspect of operating systems is the need to support real-time systems. A real-time system is one that must provide a guaranteed minimum response time to the user. That is, the delay between receiving a stimulus and producing a response must be carefully controlled. Real-time responses are crucial in software that, for example, controls a robot, a nuclear reactor, or a missile. Although all operating systems acknowledge the importance of response time, a real-time operating system strives to optimize it.

>> **Real-time system** A system in which response time is crucial given the nature of the application domain

>> **Response time** The time delay between receiving a stimulus and producing a response

10.2 Memory Management

Let's review what we said about main memory in Chapter 5. All programs are stored in main memory when they are executed. All data referenced by those programs are also stored in main memory so that they can be accessed. Main memory can be thought of as a big, continuous chunk of space divided into groups of 8, 16, or 32 bits. Each byte or word of memory has a corresponding address, which is simply an integer that uniquely identifies that particular part of memory. See Figure 10.3. The first memory address is 0.

Earlier in this chapter we stated that in a multiprogramming environment, multiple programs (and their data) are stored in main memory at the same time. Thus operating systems must employ techniques to perform the following tasks:

- Track where and how a program resides in memory
- Convert logical program addresses into actual memory addresses

A program is filled with references to variables and to other parts of the program code. When the program is compiled, these references are changed into the addresses in memory where the data and code reside. But given that we don't know exactly where a program will be loaded into main memory, how can we know which address to use for anything?

The solution is to use two kinds of addresses: logical addresses and physical addresses. A logical address (sometimes called a virtual or relative address) is a value that specifies a generic location relative to the program but not to the reality of main memory. A physical address is an actual address in the main memory device, as shown in Figure 10.3.

When a program is compiled, a reference to an identifier (such as a variable name) is changed to a logical address. When the program is eventually loaded into memory, each logical address is translated into a specific physical address. The mapping of a logical address to a physical address is called address binding. The later we wait to bind a logical address to a

>> **Logical address** A reference to a stored value relative to the program making the reference

>> **Physical address** An actual address in the main memory device

>> **Address binding** The mapping from a logical address to a physical address

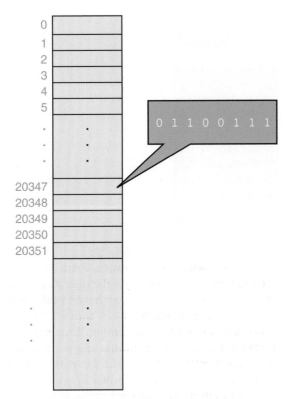

FIGURE 10.3 Memory is a continuous set of bits referenced by specific addresses

physical one, the more flexibility we have. Logical addresses allow a program to be moved around in memory or loaded in different places at different times. As long as we keep track of where the program is stored, we can always determine the physical address that corresponds to any given logical address. To simplify our examples in this chapter, we perform address-binding calculations in base 10.

The following sections examine the underlying principles of three techniques:

- Single contiguous memory management
- Partition memory management
- Paged memory management

■ Single Contiguous Memory Management

Let's initially keep things simple by assuming that there are only two programs in memory: the operating system and the application program we want to execute. We divide main memory up into two sections, one for each program, as shown in Figure 10.4. The operating system gets what space it needs, and the program is allocated the rest.

FIGURE 10.4 Main memory divided into two sections

Operating system

Application program

>> **Single contiguous memory management** The approach to memory management in which a program is loaded into one continuous area of memory

This approach is called single contiguous memory management because the entire application program is loaded into one large chunk of memory. Only one program other than the operating system can be processed at one time. To bind addresses, all we have to take into account is the location of the operating system.

In this memory management scheme, a logical address is simply an integer value relative to the starting point of the program. That is, logical addresses are created as if the program is loaded at location 0 of main memory. Therefore, to produce a physical address, we add a logical address to the starting address of the program in physical main memory.

Let's get a little more specific: If the program is loaded starting at address A, then the physical address corresponding to logical address L is A + L. See Figure 10.5. Let's plug in real numbers to make this example clearer. Suppose the program is loaded into memory beginning at address 555555. When a program uses relative address 222222, we know that it is actually referring to address 777777 in physical main memory.

FIGURE 10.5 Binding a logical address to a physical address

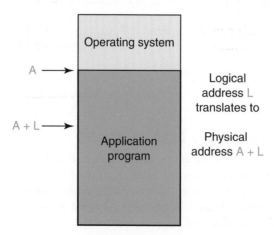

Operating system

A ⟶

A + L ⟶

Application program

Logical address L translates to

Physical address A + L

It doesn't really matter what address L is. As long as we keep track of A (the starting address of the program), we can always translate a logical address into a physical one.

You may be saying at this point, "If we switched the locations of the operating system and the program, then the logical and physical addresses for the program would be the same." That's true. But then you'd have other things to worry about. For example, a memory management scheme must always take security into account. In particular, in a multiprogramming environment, we must prevent a program from accessing any addresses beyond its allocated memory space. With the operating system loaded at location 0, all logical addresses for the program are valid unless they exceed the bounds of main memory itself. If we move the operating system below the program, we must make sure a logical address doesn't try to access the memory space devoted to the operating system. This wouldn't be difficult, but it would add to the complexity of the processing.

The advantage of the single contiguous memory management approach is that it is simple to implement and manage. However, it almost certainly wastes both memory space and CPU time. An application program is unlikely to need all of the memory not used by the operating system, and CPU time is wasted when the program has to wait for some resource.

> **Apple tracks DRM-free files**
> In January 2009, Apple announced that after six years, the iTunes® Store would soon completely stop selling music including DRM (Digital Rights Management) restrictions. For quite some time Apple has been selling select DRM-free tracks as iTunes Plus tracks. iTunes Plus originally included songs from only one major record label, EMI. Apple's new DMR-free library now includes tracks from Sony BMG, Warner Music, and Universal. While Amazon® has been selling DRM-free tracks from all four labels for quite some time, Amazon's audio files are in the MP3 format, while Apple's files use AAC (Advanced Audio Coding). AAC files generally have a better sound quality than MP3 files. By the end of March 2009, Apple had made all of its tracks available as DRM-free files.

■ Partition Memory Management

A more sophisticated approach is to have more than one application program in memory at the same time, sharing memory space and CPU time. In this case, memory must be divided into more than two partitions. Two strategies can be used to partition memory: fixed partitions and dynamic partitions. With the fixed-partition technique, main memory is divided into a particular number of partitions. The partitions do not have to be the same size, but their size is fixed when the operating system initially boots. A job is loaded into a partition large enough to hold it. The OS keeps a table of addresses at which each partition begins and the length of the partition.

With the dynamic-partition technique, the partitions are created to fit the unique needs of the programs. Main memory is initially viewed as one large empty partition. As programs are loaded, space is "carved out," using only the space needed to accommodate the program and leaving a new, smaller, empty partition, which may be used by another program later. The operating system maintains a table of partition information, but in dynamic partitions the address information changes as programs come and go.

At any point in time in both fixed and dynamic partitions, memory is divided into a set of partitions, some empty and some allocated to programs. See Figure 10.6.

>> **Fixed-partition technique** The memory management technique in which memory is divided into a specific number of partitions into which programs are loaded

>> **Dynamic-partition technique** The memory management technique in which memory is divided into partitions as needed to accommodate programs

FIGURE 10.6 Address resolution in partition memory management

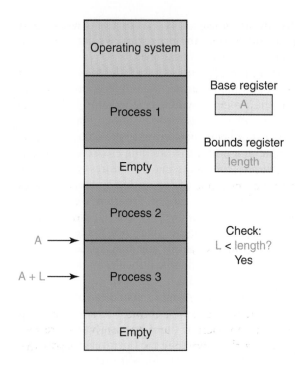

Address binding is basically the same for both fixed and dynamic partitions. As with the single contiguous memory management approach, a logical address is an integer relative to a starting point of 0. There are various ways an OS might handle the details of the address translation. One way is to use two special-purpose registers in the CPU to help manage addressing. When a program becomes active on the CPU, the OS stores the address of the beginning of that program's partition into the base register. Similarly, the length of the partition is stored in the bounds register. When a logical address is referenced, it is first compared to the value in the bounds register to make sure the reference is within that program's allocated memory space. If it is, the value of the logical address is added to the value in the base register to produce the physical address.

Which partition should we allocate to a new program? There are three general approaches to partition selection:

- *First fit,* in which the program is allocated to the first partition big enough to hold it
- *Best fit,* in which the program is allocated to the smallest partition big enough to hold it
- *Worst fit,* in which the program is allocated to the largest partition big enough to hold it

It doesn't make sense to use worst fit in fixed partitions because it would waste the larger partitions. First fit and best fit both work for fixed

» **Base register** A register that holds the beginning address of the current partition

» **Bounds register** A register that holds the length of the current partition

partitions. In dynamic partitions, however, worst fit often works best because it leaves the largest possible empty partition, which may accommodate another program later on.

When a program terminates, the partition table is updated to reflect the fact that the partition is now empty and available for a new program. In dynamic partitions, consecutive empty partitions are merged into one big empty partition.

Partition memory management makes efficient use of main memory by maintaining several programs in memory at one time. But keep in mind that a program must fit entirely into one partition. Fixed partitions are easier to manage than dynamic ones, but they restrict the opportunities available to incoming programs. The system may have enough free memory to accommodate the program, just not in one free partition. In dynamic partitions, the jobs could be shuffled around in memory to create one large free partition. This procedure is known as *compaction*.

■ Paged Memory Management

Paged memory management places more of the burden on the operating system to keep track of allocated memory and to resolve addresses. However, the benefits gained by this approach are generally worth the extra effort.

In the paged memory technique, main memory is divided into small fixed-size blocks of storage called frames. A process is divided into pages that (for the sake of our discussion) we assume are the same size as a frame. When a program is to be executed, the pages of the process are loaded into unused frames distributed through memory. Thus the pages of a process may be scattered around, out of order, and mixed among the pages of other processes. To keep track of these pages, the operating system maintains a separate page-map table (PMT) for each process in memory; it maps each page to the frame in which it is loaded. See Figure 10.7. Both pages and frames are numbered starting with zero, which makes the address calculations easier.

A logical address in a paged memory management system begins as a single integer value relative to the starting point of the program, as it was in a partitioned system. This address is modified into two values, a page number and an offset, by dividing the address by the page size. The page number is the number of times the page size divides the address, and the remainder is the offset. So a logical address of 2566, with a page size of 1024, corresponds to the 518th byte of page 2 of the process. A logical address is often written as <page, offset>, such as <2, 518>.

To produce a physical address, you first look up the page in the PMT to find the frame number in which it is stored. You then multiply the frame number by the frame size and add the offset to get the physical address. For example, given the situation shown in Figure 10.7, if process 1 is

>> **Paged memory technique** A memory management technique in which processes are divided into fixed-size pages and stored in memory frames when loaded

>> **Frame** A fixed-size portion of main memory that holds a process page

>> **Page** A fixed-size portion of a process that is stored into a memory frame

>> **Page-map table (PMT)** The table used by the operating system to keep track of page/frame relationships

FIGURE 10.7 A paged memory management approach

FIGURE 10.7 A paged memory management approach

P1 PMT

Page	Frame
0	5
1	12
2	15
3	7
4	22

P2 PMT

Page	Frame
0	10
1	18
2	1
3	11

Memory

Frame	Contents
0	
1	P2/Page2
2	
3	
4	
5	P1/Page0
6	
7	P1/Page3
8	
9	
10	P2/Page0
11	P2/Page3
12	P1/Page1
13	
14	
15	P1/Page2

active, a logical address of <1, 222> would be processed as follows: Page 1 of process 1 is in frame 12; therefore, the corresponding physical address is 12*1024 + 222 or 12510. Note that there are two ways in which a logical address could be invalid: The page number could be out of bounds for that process, or the offset could be larger than the size of a frame.

The advantage of paging is that a process no longer needs to be stored contiguously in memory. The ability to divide a process into pieces changes the challenge of loading a process from finding one large chunk of space to finding many small chunks.

An important extension to the idea of paged memory management is the idea of demand paging, which takes advantage of the fact that not all parts of a program actually have to be in memory at the same time. At any given point in time, the CPU is accessing one page of a process. At that point, it doesn't really matter whether the other pages of that process are even in memory.

>> **Demand paging** An extension to paged memory management in which pages are brought into memory only when referenced (on demand)

In demand paging, the pages are brought into memory on demand. That is, when a page is referenced, we first see whether it is in memory already and, if so, complete the access. If it is not already in memory, the page is brought in from secondary memory into an available frame, and then the access is completed. The act of bringing in a page from secondary memory, which often causes another page to be written back to secondary memory, is called a page swap.

The demand paging approach gives rise to the idea of virtual memory, the illusion that there are no restrictions on the size of a program (because the entire program is not necessarily in memory at the same time). In all of the memory management techniques we examined earlier, the entire process had to be brought into memory as a continuous whole. We therefore always had an upper bound on process size. Demand paging removes that restriction.

However, virtual memory comes with lots of overhead during the execution of a program. With other memory management techniques, once a program was loaded into memory, it was all there and ready to go. With the virtual memory approach, we constantly have to swap pages between main and secondary memory. This overhead is usually acceptable—while one program is waiting for a page to be swapped, another process can take control of the CPU and make progress. Excessive page swapping is called thrashing and can seriously degrade system performance.

>> **Page swap** Bringing in one page from secondary memory, possibly causing another to be removed

>> **Virtual memory** The illusion that there is no restriction on program size because an entire process need not be in memory at the same time

>> **Thrashing** Inefficient processing caused by constant page swapping

10.3 Process Management

Another important resource that an operating system must manage is the use of the CPU by individual processes. To understand how an operating system manages processes, we must recognize the stages that a process goes through during its computational life and understand the information that must be managed to keep a process working correctly in a computer system.

▪ The Process States

Processes move through specific states as they are managed in a computer system. That is, a process enters the system, is ready to be executed, is executing, is waiting for a resource, or is finished. Figure 10.8 depicts these process states. In the figure, each box represents a state a process might be in, and the arrows indicate how and why a process might move from one state to another.

Let's examine what is happing to a process in each state.

>> **Process states** The conceptual stages through which a process moves as it is managed by the operating system

- In the *new state,* a process is being created. It may, for instance, be a login process created by a user logging onto a timesharing system, an application process created when a user submits a program for execution, or a system process created by the operating system to accomplish a specific system task.

FIGURE 10.8 The process life cycle

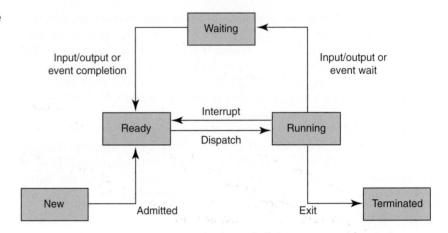

- A process that has no barriers to its execution is in the *ready state*. A process in the ready state is not waiting for an event to occur or for data to be brought in from secondary memory. Instead, it is waiting for its chance to use the CPU.
- A process in the *running state* is currently being executed by the CPU. Its instructions are being processed in the fetch–execute cycle.
- A process in the *waiting state* is currently waiting for resources (other than the CPU). For example, a process in the waiting state may be waiting for a page of its memory to be brought in from secondary memory or for another process to send it a signal that it may continue.
- A process in the *terminated state* has completed its execution and is no longer active. At this point the operating system no longer needs to maintain the information regarding the process.

Note that many processes may be in the ready state or the waiting state at the same time, but only one process can be in the running state.

After a process is created, the operating system admits it to the ready state. When the CPU scheduling algorithm dictates, a process is dispatched to the running state. (CPU scheduling is discussed in more detail later in Section 10.4.)

While running, the process might be interrupted by the operating system to allow another process to have its chance on the CPU. In that case, the process simply returns to the ready state. Alternatively, a running process might request a resource that is not available or require I/O to retrieve a newly referenced part of the process, in which case it is moved to the waiting state. A running process may finally get enough CPU time to complete its processing and terminate normally; otherwise, it may generate an unrecoverable error and terminate abnormally.

When a waiting process gets the resource it is waiting for, it moves to the ready state again.

■ The Process Control Block

The operating system must manage a large amount of data for each active process. Usually those data are stored in a data structure called a process control block (PCB). Generally, each state is represented by a list of PCBs, one for each process in that state. When a process moves from one state to another, its corresponding PCB moves from one state list to another in the operating system. A new PCB is created when a process is first created (the new state) and persists until the process terminates.

The PCB stores a variety of information about the process, including the current value of the program counter, which indicates the instruction in the process that is to be executed next. As the life cycle in Figure 10.8 indicates, a process may be interrupted many times during its execution. At each point, its program counter must be stored so that the next time the process gets into the running state it can pick up where it left off.

The PCB also stores the values of all other CPU registers for that process. Keep in mind that there is only one CPU and therefore only one set of CPU registers. These registers contain the values for the currently executing process (the one in the running state). Each time a process moves to the running state, the register values for the currently running process are stored into its PCB, and the register values of the new running state are loaded into the CPU. This exchange of information is called a context switch.

The PCB also maintains information about CPU scheduling, such as the priority that a process is given by the operating system. It contains memory management information as well, such as base and bound register values (for partitions) or page tables (for paged systems). Finally, the PCB holds accounting information, such as account numbers, time limits, and the amount of CPU time used so far.

>> **Process control block (PCB)** The data structure used by the operating system to manage information about a process

>> **Context switch** The exchange of register information that occurs when one process is removed from the CPU and another takes its place

10.4 CPU Scheduling

CPU scheduling is the act of determining which process in the ready state should be moved to the running state. That is, CPU scheduling algorithms decide which process should be given over to the CPU so that it can make computational progress.

CPU scheduling decisions are made when a process switches from the running state to the waiting state, or when a program terminates. This type of CPU scheduling is called nonpreemptive scheduling, because the need for a new CPU process results from the activity of the currently executing process.

CPU scheduling decisions may also be made when a process moves from the running state to the ready state or when a process moves from the waiting state to the ready state. These are examples of preemptive scheduling, because the currently running process (through no fault of its own) is preempted by the operating system.

>> **Nonpreemptive scheduling** CPU scheduling that occurs when the currently executing process gives up the CPU voluntarily

>> **Preemptive scheduling** CPU scheduling that occurs when the operating system decides to favor another process, preempting the currently executing process

» Turnaround time The
CPU scheduling metric that
measures the elapsed time
between a process's arrival
in the ready state and its
ultimate completion

Scheduling algorithms are often evaluated using metrics, such as the turnaround time for a process. This measure is the amount of time between when a process arrives in the ready state and when it exits the running state for the last time. We would like, on average, for the turnaround time for our processes to be small.

Several different approaches can be used to determine which process gets chosen first to move from the ready state to the running state. We examine three of them in the next sections.

■ First Come, First Served

In the first-come, first-served (FCFS) scheduling approach, processes are moved to the CPU in the order in which they arrive in the running state. FCFS scheduling is nonpreemptive. Once a process is given access to the CPU, it keeps that access unless it makes a request that forces it to wait, such as a request for a device in use by another process.

Suppose processes p1 through p5 arrive in the ready state at essentially the same time (to make our calculations simple) but in the following order and with the specified service time:

Process	Service time
p1	140
p2	75
p3	320
p4	280
p5	125

In the FCFS scheduling approach, each process receives access to the CPU in turn. For simplicity, we assume here that processes don't cause themselves to wait. The following Gantt chart shows the order and time of process completion:

0	140	215		535		815	940
p1	p2		p3		p4		p5

Because we are assuming the processes all arrived at the same time, the turnaround time for each process is the same as its completion time. The average turnaround time is (140 + 215 + 535 + 815 + 940) / 5 or 529.

In reality, processes do not arrive at exactly the same time. In this case, the calculation of the average turnaround time would be similar, but would take into account the arrival time of each process. The turnaround time for each process would be its completion time minus its arrival time.

The FCFS algorithm is easy to implement but suffers from its lack of attention to important factors such as service time requirements. Although we used the service times in our calculations of turnaround time, the algorithm didn't use that information to determine the best order in which to schedule the processes.

■ Shortest Job Next

The shortest-job-next (SJN) CPU scheduling algorithm looks at all processes in the ready state and dispatches the one with the smallest service time. Like FCFS, it is generally implemented as a nonpreemptive algorithm.

Below is the Gantt chart for the same set of processes we examined in the FCFS example. Because the selection criteria are different, the order in which the processes are scheduled and completed are different:

```
0    75     200    340              620             940
|----|------|------|----------------|---------------|
| p2 |  p5  |  p1  |       p4       |      p3       |
|----|------|------|----------------|---------------|
```

The average turnaround time for this example is (75 + 200 + 340 + 620 + 940) / 5 or 435.

Note that the SJN algorithm relies on knowledge of the future. That is, it gives access to the CPU to the job that runs for the shortest time when it is allowed to execute. That time is essentially impossible to determine. Thus, to run this algorithm, the service time value for a process is typically estimated by the operating system using various probability factors and taking the type of job into account. If these estimates are wrong, the premise of the algorithm breaks down and its efficiency deteriorates. The SJN algorithm is provably optimal, meaning that if we could know the service time of each job, the algorithm would produce the shortest turnaround time for all jobs compared to any other algorithm. However, because we can't know the future absolutely, we make guesses and hope those guesses are correct.

> **Tracking your workout**
> Nike® and Apple have created a product that enables a sneaker to talk to an iPod wirelessly. The Nike sensor is inserted into selected sneakers, together with a wireless rig. The system lets a runner record the distance, time, pace, and calories burned during each workout. Once a runner has completed his or her workout, data can be downloaded digitally using Apple's iTunes music software and stored and analyzed on a Nike-maintained website. The iTunes music store also features a sports section with special music and workout routines from famous athletes. In 2006, Marware® developed a solution for those consumers who do not happen to like Nike sneakers. The Marware Sportsuit Sensor Case is a neoprene case that attaches to the top of any pair of running sneakers, allowing the Nike sensor to work with non-Nike shoes.

■ Round Robin

Round-robin CPU scheduling distributes the processing time equitably among all ready processes. This algorithm establishes a particular time slice (or time quantum), which is the amount of time each process receives before it is preempted and returned to the ready state to allow another process to take its turn. Eventually the preempted process will be given

> **》 Time slice** The amount of time given to each process in the round-robin CPU scheduling algorithm

Steve Jobs

Born in 1955, Steve Jobs is probably best known for founding Apple Computers together with Steve Wozniak and Ronald Wayne in 1976. At the time, most computers were either mainframes (sometimes as large as a small room) or minicomputers (about the size of a refrigerator), often anything but user-friendly, and almost exclusively used by big businesses. Jobs had a vision of a personal computer that would be accessible to everyone. He is often credited with democratizing the computer.

© Christophe Ena/AP Photos

Jobs and Wozniak designed the Apple I in Jobs' bedroom and built it in the garage of his parents' house. Jobs and Wozniak sold their prize possessions (a Volkswagen microbus and Hewlett-Packard scientific calculator, respectively) to raise the $1300 capital with which they founded their company. Four years later, Apple went public. At the end of the first day of trading, the company had a market value of $1.2 billion.

Jobs headed the team that developed the Apple Macintosh® (named after the McIntosh apple), perhaps the most famous of the Apple computers. The Macintosh was the first commercially successful computer to be launched with a graphical user interface and a mouse. Shortly after the launch of the Macintosh, Jobs was forced out of Apple after a power struggle with John Sculley, Apple's CEO at the time.

Having been ousted from the company he founded, Jobs began another computer company, NeXT, which was purchased by Apple in 1996 for $402 million. Not only did the acquisition bring Jobs back to his original company, but it also made him CEO of Apple. Under his renewed leadership, Apple launched the iMac®, which has been described as the "gold standard of desktop computing."

In 1986, Jobs moved into the field of computer-generated animation when he bought a computer graphics company and renamed it Pixar®. Pixar has produced a number of box-office hits, including *A Bug's Life*, *Toy Story*, *Monsters, Inc.*, and *Finding Nemo*.

Jobs, himself a university dropout, gave the 2005 commencement address at Stanford University, in which he imparted the following piece of career advice to the graduates: "You've got to find what you love."

In 2007 Jobs was named the most powerful person in business by *Fortune* magazine and Governor Arnold Schwarzenegger inducted Jobs into the California Hall of Fame. Beginning in January 2009, Jobs took a six-month leave of absence from Apple due to concerns about his health, leaving former acting CEO Tim Cook in charge in his absence. Jobs, however, continued to be involved in major strategic decisions.

---

another time slice on the CPU. This procedure continues until the process gets all the time it needs to complete and terminates.

Note that the round-robin algorithm is preemptive. The expiration of a time slice is an arbitrary reason to remove a process from the CPU. This action is represented by the transition from the running state to the ready state.

Suppose the time slice used for a particular round-robin scheduling algorithm was 50 and we used the same set of processes as our previous examples. The Gantt chart results are:

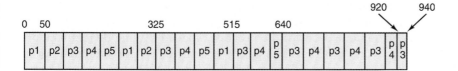

Each process is given a time slice of 50, unless it doesn't need a full slice. For example, process 2 originally needed 75 time units. It was given an initial time slice of 50. When its turn to use the CPU came around again, it needed only 25 time units. Therefore, process 2 terminates and gives up the CPU at time 325.

The average turnaround time for this example is (515 + 325 + 940 + 920 + 640) / 5, or 668. This turnaround time is larger than the times in the other examples. Does that mean the round-robin algorithm is not as good as the other options? No. We can't make such general claims based on one example. We can say only that one algorithm is better than another for that specific set of processes. General analysis of algorithm efficiencies is much more involved.

The round-robin CPU process scheduling algorithm is probably the most widely used. It generally supports all kinds of jobs and is considered the most fair.

Summary

An operating system is the part of the system software that manages resources on a computer. It serves as moderator among human users, application software, and the hardware devices in the system.

Multiprogramming is the technique for keeping multiple programs in memory at the same time, contending for time on the CPU. A process is a program in execution. The operating system must perform careful CPU scheduling, memory management, and process management to ensure fair access to the CPU.

Batch processing organizes jobs into batches that use the same or similar resources. Timesharing allows multiple users to interact with a computer at the same time, creating a virtual machine for each user.

An operating system must manage memory to control and monitor where processes are loaded into main memory. Any memory management technique must define the manner in which it binds a logical address to a physical one. Various strategies have been developed for memory management. The single contiguous approach allows only one program other than the operating system to be in main memory. The partition approach divides memory into several partitions into which processes are loaded. Fixed partitions have a set size, whereas dynamic partitions are created to satisfy the unique needs of the processes loaded. Paging divides memory into frames and programs into pages. The pages of a program need not be contiguous in memory. Demand paging allows for only a portion of a program to be in memory at any given time.

An operating system manages a process's life states, which are the stages a program goes through during its execution. The process control block stores the necessary information for any process.

CPU scheduling algorithms determine which process gets priority to use the CPU next. First-come, first-served CPU scheduling gives priority to the earliest-arriving job. The shortest-job-next algorithm gives priority to jobs with short running times. Round-robin scheduling rotates the CPU among active processes, giving a little time to each process.

⚖ ETHICAL ISSUES ▶ Digital Rights Management and the Sony® Rootkit Controversy

What is Digital Rights Management (DRM) technology? DRM refers to a cluster of technologies used by content owners to "control access to data (such as software, music, movies) and hardware" (*Wikipedia*, 2006). DRM technologies enable content providers and software manufacturers to embed code in digital media to control how their products are used.

Defenders of DRM systems argue that this technology is needed to prevent copyright violations on the part of users. But many of DRM's critics are concerned about the ways in which DRM can be used to enforce copyright law. For example, some law professors believe that DRM systems may violate the fair-use provision of copyright law. Other critics worry that DRM technology allows content owners to exercise considerably more control over uses of copyrighted works in digital media compared to the kind of control that was provided in traditional copyright protection schemes. For these reasons, Richard Stallman, founder of the Free Software Foundation (FSF), believes that DRM can be better understood as "digital restrictions management."

Other critics worry that DRM systems could be abused by content owners to control users' computers (behind the scenes) and could even be used by companies to "spy" on unsuspecting users. This concern recently became apparent in the case of Sony BMG Music Entertainment, which used a DRM system called Extended Copy Protection (XCP) to protect its music CDs.

The Sony incident drew considerable attention in October 2005, when a blogger wrote an article that identified flaws in the design of Sony's copy protection software—flaws in the form of security holes that could be exploited by malicious software programs, including viruses and worms. The blogger also noted that Sony did not provide users with an "uninstall" program to remove the XCP software. Shortly after this flaw had been made public, Sony released a utility intended to enable users to remove the controversial software. Unfortunately, Sony's removal utility exposed hidden files in the "rootkit" component of XCP (and did not remove the rootkit itself). The exposure or "unmasking" of the rootkit raised even more privacy and security concerns. Sony eventually released an updated version of the removal utility that enabled users to successfully uninstall the rootkit.

Some of Sony's critics argued that the company, through its XCP system, had violated the privacy of its customers by using code that created a "backdoor" into their machines. Others argued that Sony's DRM program had actually infringed on copyright law. In response to these and other criticisms, Sony decided to back away from its copy protection software; it recalled all unsold CDs from stores and it allowed customers to exchange their CDs for versions that did

» continued

⚖ **ETHICAL ISSUES ▶ Digital Rights Management and the Sony® Rootkit Controversy, cont'd.**

not include the XCP software. Sony's plan to remedy the situation, however, did not satisfy all of the companies' critics. A number of class-action lawsuits have since been filed against Sony BMG, including lawsuits by the states of California, New York, and Texas. These lawsuits were consolidated into one class-action lawsuit, which was settled in May 2006. The terms of the settlement stated that Sony BMG was required to refund people who purchased XCP-protected CDs either a cash payment of $7.50 plus a free album download, or three album downloads, whichever they preferred.

In January 2007, the final company producing audio CDs with DRM ceased production, and these CDs are no longer released by any music label. In February 2008, Wal-Mart made all of its music sales DRM free, and in January 2009, Steve Jobs called for Apple's iTunes Store to stop using DRM files.

The following kinds of questions arose in the Sony rootkit case: Do certain DRM systems infringe copyright law rather than protect it? Do they violate personal privacy? Can ordinary users trust content owners, such as Sony, which are easily able to spy on them and to control aspects of their computers via the use of DRM technology? Are the kinds of DRM systems used by Sony justifiable on grounds that content companies need DRM systems to protect their intellectual property rights?

🔑 Key Terms

Address binding
Application software
Base register
Bounds register
Context switch
CPU scheduling
Demand paging
Dumb terminal
Dynamic-partition technique
Fixed-partition technique
Frame
Logical address
Mainframe
Memory management
Multiprogramming
Nonpreemptive scheduling
Operating system
Page
Page-map table (PMT)

Page swap
Paged memory technique
Physical address
Preemptive scheduling
Process
Process control block (PCB)
Process management
Process states
Real-time system
Response time
Single contiguous memory
   management
System software
Thrashing
Time slice
Timesharing
Turnaround time
Virtual machine
Virtual memory

⌘ Exercises

For Exercises 1–18, mark the answers true or false as follows:
   A. True
   B. False

1. An operating system is an example of application software.

2. An operating system provides a basic user interface that allows the user to use the computer.

3. A computer can have more than one operating system, but only one OS is in control at any given time.

4. Multiprogramming is the technique of using multiple CPUs to run programs.

5. In the 1960s and 1970s, a human operator would organize similar computer jobs into batches to be run.

6. Batch processing implies a high level of interaction between the user and the program.

7. A timesharing system allows multiple users to interact with a computer at the same time.

8. A dumb terminal is an I/O device that connects to a mainframe computer.

9. A logical address specifies an actual location in main memory.

10. An address in a single contiguous memory management system is made up of a page and an offset.

11. In a fixed-partition system, main memory is divided into several partitions of the same size.

12. The bounds register contains the last address of a partition.

13. The first page in a paged memory system is page 0.

14. A process in the running state is currently being executed by the CPU.

15. The process control block (PCB) is a data structure that stores all information about a process.

16. CPU scheduling determines which programs are in memory.

17. The first-come, first-served scheduling algorithm is probably optimal.

18. A time slice is the amount of time each process is given before being preempted in a round-robin scheduler.

For Exercises 19–23, match the operating system with information about it.
   A. Mac OS
   B. UNIX
   C. Linux
   D. DOS
   E. Windows

19. Which is the operating system of choice for Apple computers?

20. Historically, which is the operating system of choice for serious programmers?

21. Which is the PC version of UNIX?

22. What is the Microsoft operating system family provided on PCs called?

23. What is the original PC operating system called?

For Exercises 24–26, match the following software type with its definition.
- **A.** Systems software
- **B.** Operating system
- **C.** Application software

24. Programs that help us solve real-world problems

25. Programs that manage a computer system and interact with hardware

26. Programs that manage computer resources and provide interfaces for other programs

Exercises 27–72 are problems or short-answer questions.

27. Distinguish between application software and system software.

28. What is an operating system?

29. Explain the term *multiprogramming*.

30. The following terms relate to how the operating system manages multiprogramming. Describe the part each plays in this process.
    - a. Process
    - b. Process management
    - c. Memory management
    - d. CPU scheduling

31. What constitutes a batch job?

32. Describe the evolution of the concept of batch processing from the human operator in the 1960s and 1970s to the operating systems of today.

33. Define *timesharing*.

34. What is the relationship between multiprogramming and timesharing?

35. Why do we say that users in a timesharing system have their own virtual machine?

36. In Chapter 6, we defined a virtual machine as a hypothetical machine designed to illustrate important features of a real machine. In this chapter, we define a virtual machine as the illusion created by a timesharing system that each user has a dedicated machine. Relate these two definitions.

37. How does the timesharing concept work?

38. What is a *real-time system*?

39. What is *response time*?

40. What is the relationship between real-time systems and response time?

41. In a multiprogramming environment, many processes may be active. What are the tasks that the operating system must accomplish to manage the memory requirements of active processes?

42. Distinguish between logical addresses and physical addresses.

43. What is *address binding*?

44. Name three memory management techniques and describe the general approach taken in each.

45. When is a logical address assigned to a variable?

46. When does address binding occur?

47. How is memory divided in the single contiguous memory management approach?

48. When a program is compiled, where is it assumed that the program will be loaded into memory? That is, where are logical addresses assumed to begin?

49. If, in a single contiguous memory management system, the program is loaded at address 30215, compute the physical addresses (in decimal) that correspond to the following logical addresses:
   a. 9223
   b. 2302
   c. 7044

50. In a single contiguous memory management approach, if the logical address of a variable is L and the beginning of the application program is A, what is the formula for binding the logical address to the physical address?

51. If, in a fixed-partition memory management system, the current value of the base register is 42993 and the current value of the bounds register is 2031, compute the physical addresses that correspond to the following logical addresses:
   a. 104
   b. 1755
   c. 3041

52. If more than one partition is being used (either fixed or dynamic), what does the base register contain?

53. Why is the logical address compared to the bounds register before a physical address is calculated?

54. If, in a dynamic-partition memory management system, the current value of the base register is 42993 and the current value of the bounds register is 2031, compute the physical addresses that correspond to the following logical addresses:
   a. 104
   b. 1755
   c. 3041

Exercises 55 and 56 use the following state of memory.

Operating System
Process 1
Empty 60 blocks
Process 2
Process 3
Empty 52 blocks
Empty 100 blocks

55. If the partitions are fixed and a new job arrives requiring 52 blocks of main memory, show memory after using each of the following partition selection approaches:
   a. First fit
   b. Best fit
   c. Worst fit

56. If the partitions are dynamic and a new job arrives requiring 52 blocks of main memory, show memory after using each of the following partition selection approaches:
   a. First fit
   b. Best fit
   c. Worst fit

57. If a logical address in a paged memory management system is <2, 133>, what do the values mean?

Exercises 58–60 refer to the following PMT.

Page	0	1	2	3
Frame	5	2	7	3

58. If the frame size is 1024, what is the physical address associated with the logical address <2, 85>?

59. If the frame size is 1024, what is the physical address associated with the logical address <3, 555>?

60. If the frame size is 1024, what is the physical address associated with the logical address <3, 1555>?

61. What is virtual memory and how does it apply to demand paging?

62. What are the conceptual stages through which a process moves while being managed by the operating system?

63. Describe how a process might move through the various process states. Cite specific reasons why this process moves from one state to another.

64. What is a process control block?

65. How is each conceptual stage represented in the operating system?

66. What is a context switch?

67. Distinguish between preemptive scheduling and nonpreemptive scheduling.

68. Name and describe three CPU scheduling algorithms.

Use the following table of processes and service time for Exercises 69 through 72.

Process	P1	P2	P3	P4	P5
Service time	120	60	180	50	300

69. Draw a Gantt chart that shows the completion times for each process using first-come, first-served CPU scheduling.

70. Draw a Gantt chart that shows the completion times for each process using shortest-job-next CPU scheduling.

71. Draw a Gantt chart that shows the completion times for each process using round-robin CPU scheduling with a time slice of 60.

72. Distinguish between fixed partitions and dynamic partitions.

??? Thought Questions

1. In Chapter 5, we said that the control unit was like the stage manager who organized and managed the other parts of the von Neumann machine. Suppose we now say the operating system is also like a stage manager, but on a much grander scale: Does this analogy hold or does it break down?

2. The user interface that the operating system presents to the user is like a hallway with doors leading to rooms housing applications programs. To go from one room to another, you have to go back to the hallway. Continue with this analogy: What would files be? What would be analogous to a time slice?

3. Are DRM systems needed to protect copyright in digital media, as DRM's proponents suggest, or do these systems sometimes infringe copyright as critics suggest?

4. Because some DRM protection schemes affecting some media enable content owners to "spy" on users, do those DRM systems violate the privacy of users?

5. Can DRM systems like Sony BMG's XCP Copy Protection Scheme be justified on ethical grounds? Should they be legal?

The Operating Systems Layer

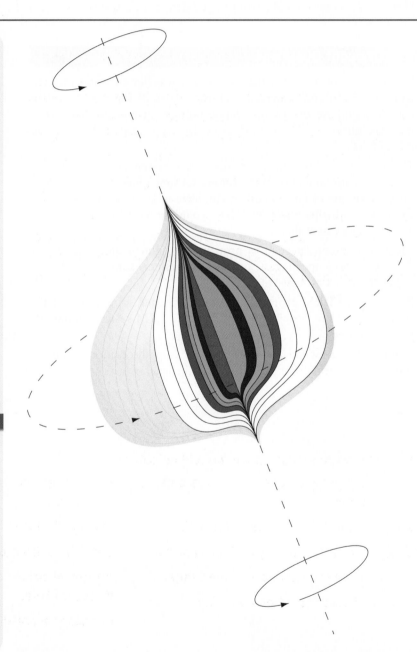

File Systems and Directories

The previous chapter examined some of the roles an operating system plays. In particular, it described the management of processes, the CPU, and main memory. Another key resource that the operating system manages is secondary memory—most importantly, magnetic disks. The organization of files and directories on disk plays a pivotal role in everyday computing. Like a card file on a desktop, the file system provides a way to access particular data in a well-organized manner. The directory structure organizes files into categories and subcategories. File systems and directory structures are explored in detail in this chapter.

Goals

After studying this chapter, you should be able to:

- describe the purpose of files, file systems, and directories.
- distinguish between text and binary files.
- identify various file types by their extensions.
- explain how file types improve file usage.
- define the basic operations on a file.
- compare and contrast sequential and direct file access.
- discuss the issues related to file protection.
- describe a directory tree.
- create absolute and relative paths for a directory tree.
- describe several disk-scheduling algorithms.

11.1 File Systems

In Chapter 5 we established the differences between main and secondary memory. Recall that main memory is where active programs and data are held while in use. Main memory is volatile, meaning that the data stored on it is lost if electric power is turned off. Secondary memory is nonvolatile—the data stored on it is maintained even when power is not on. Thus we use secondary memory for permanent storage of our data.

The most widely used secondary storage device is the magnetic disk drive. It includes both the hard drives that are found in the computer's main box and disks that are portable and can be moved easily between computers. The basic concepts underlying both types of disks are the same. Other secondary memory devices, such as tape drives, are used primarily for archival purposes. While many of the concepts that we explore in this chapter apply to all secondary storage devices, it's perhaps easiest to think about a standard disk drive.

We store data on a disk in files, a mechanism for organizing data on an electronic medium. A file is a named collection of related data. From the user's point of view, a file is the smallest amount of data that can be written to secondary memory. Organizing everything into files presents a uniform view for data storage. A file system is the logical view that an operating system provides so that users can manage data as a collection of files. A file system is often organized by grouping files into directories.

A file is a generic concept. Different types of files are managed in different ways. A file, in general, contains a program (in some form) or data (of one type or another). Some files have a very rigid format; others are more flexible.

A file may be considered a sequence of bits, bytes, lines, or records, depending on how you look at it. As with any data in memory, you have to apply an interpretation to the bits stored in a file before they have meaning. The creator of a file decides how the data in a file is organized, and any users of the file must understand that organization.

> **File** A named collection of data, used for organizing secondary memory

> **File system** The operating system's logical view of the files it manages

> **Directory** A named group of files

> **Text file** A file that contains characters

> **Binary file** A file that contains data in a specific format, requiring a special interpretation of its bits

■ Text and Binary Files

All files can be broadly classified as either text files or binary files. In a text file, the bytes of data are organized as characters from the ASCII or Unicode character sets. (Character sets are described in Chapter 3.) A binary file requires a specific interpretation of the bits based on the data in the file.

The terms "text file" and "binary file" are somewhat misleading. They seem to imply that the information in a text file is not stored as binary data. Ultimately, however, all data on a computer is stored as binary digits. These terms refer to how those bits are formatted: as chunks of 8 or 16 bits, interpreted as characters, or in some other special format.

Some information lends itself to a character representation, which often makes it easier for a human to read and modify the information. Though text files contain only characters, those characters can represent a variety of information. For example, an operating system may store much of its data as text files, such as information about user accounts. A program written in a high-level language is stored as a text file, which is sometimes referred to as a *source file*. Any text editor can be used to create, view, and change the contents of a text file, no matter what specific type of information it contains.

For other information types, it is more logical and efficient to represent data by defining a specific binary format and interpretation. Only programs set up to interpret that type of data can then be used to view or modify it. For example, many types of files store image information: bitmap, GIF, JPEG, and TIFF, to name a few. As we discussed in Chapter 3, even though each stores information about an image, all of these files store that information in different ways. Their internal formats are very specific. A program must be set up to view or modify a specific type of binary file. That's why a program that can handle a GIF image may not be able to handle a TIFF image, or vice versa.

Some files you might assume to be text files actually are not. Consider, for instance, a report that you type in a word processing program and save to disk. The document is actually stored as a binary file because, in addition to the characters in the document, it contains information about formatting, styles, borders, fonts, colors, and "extras" such as graphics or clip art. Some of the data (the characters themselves) are stored as text, but the additional information requires that each word processing program have its own format for storing the data in its document files.

■ File Types

Most files, whether they are in text or binary format, contain a specific type of information. For example, a file may contain a Java™ program, or a JPEG image, or an MP3 audio clip. Other files contain files created by specific applications, such as a Microsoft® Word document or a Visio drawing. The kind of information contained in a document is called the file type. Most operating systems recognize a list of specific file types.

A common mechanism for specifying a file type is to indicate the type as part of the file's name. File names are often separated, usually by a period, into two parts: the main name and the file extension. The extension indicates the type of the file. For example, the .java extension in the file name MyProg.java indicates that it is a Java source code program file. The .jpg extension in the file name family.jpg indicates that it is a JPEG image file. Figure 11.1 lists some common file extensions.

>> File type The specific kind of information contained in a file, such as a Java program or a Microsoft Word document

>> File extension Part of a file name that indicates the file type

Extensions	File type
txt	text data file
mp3, au, wav	audio file
gif, tiff, jpg	image file
doc, wp3	word processing document
java, c, cpp	program source files

File types allow the operating system to operate on the file in ways that make sense for that file. They also usually make life easier for the user. The operating system keeps a list of recognized file types and associates each type with a particular kind of application program. In an operating system with a graphical user interface (GUI), a particular icon is often associated with a file type as well. When you see a file in a folder, it is shown with the appropriate icon in the GUI. That makes it easier for the user to identify a file at a glance because now both the name of the file and its icon indicate which type of file it is. When you double-click on the icon to open the program, the operating system starts the program associated with that file type and loads the file.

For example, you might like a particular editor that you use when developing a Java program. You can register the .java file extension with the operating system and associate it with that editor. Then whenever you open a file with a .java extension, the operating system runs the appropriate editor. The details of how you associate an extension with an application program depend on the operating system you are using.

Some file extensions are associated with particular programs by default, which you may change if appropriate. In some cases, a file type could be associated with various types of applications, so you have some choice. For example, your system may currently associate the .gif extension with a particular Web browser, so that when you open a GIF image file, it is displayed in that browser window. You may choose to change the association so that when you open a GIF file, it is brought into your favorite image editor instead.

A file extension is merely an indication of what the file contains. You can name a file anything you want (as long as you use the characters that the operating system allows for file names). You could give any file a .gif extension, for instance, but that doesn't make it a GIF image file. Changing the extension does not change the data in the file or its internal format. If you attempt to open a misnamed file in a program that expects a particular format, you will get an error message.

■ File Operations

With the help of the operating system, you might perform any of several operations to and with a file:

- Create a file
- Delete a file
- Open a file
- Close a file
- Read data from a file
- Write data to a file
- Reposition the current file pointer in a file
- Append data to the end of a file
- Truncate a file (delete its contents)
- Rename a file
- Copy a file

Let's briefly examine how each of these operations is accomplished.

The operating system keeps track of secondary memory in two ways. It maintains a table indicating which blocks of memory are free (that is, available for use) and, for each directory, it maintains a table that records information about the files in that directory. To create a file, the operating system finds enough free space in the file system for the file content, puts an entry for the file in the appropriate directory table, and records the name and location of the file. To delete a file, the operating system indicates that the memory space previously used by the file is now free and removes the appropriate entry in the directory table.

Most operating systems require that a file be opened before read and write operations are performed on it. The operating system maintains a small table of all currently open files to avoid having to search for the file in the large file system every time a subsequent operation is performed. To close the file when it is no longer in active use, the operating system removes the entry in the open file table.

At any point in time, an open file has a current file pointer (an address) indicating the place where the next read or write operation should occur. Some systems keep a separate read pointer and a write pointer for a file. Reading a file means that the operating system delivers a copy of the data in the file, starting at the current file pointer. After the read occurs, the file pointer is updated. When data is written to a file, the data is stored at the location indicated by the current file pointer, and then the file pointer is updated. Often an operating system allows a file to be open for reading or writing, but not for both operations at the same time.

The current file pointer for an open file might be repositioned to another location in the file to prepare for the next read or write operation. Appending data to the end of a file requires that the file pointer be positioned to the end of a file; the appropriate data is then written at that location.

It is sometimes useful to "erase" the data in a file. Truncating a file means deleting the contents of the file without removing the administrative entries in the file tables. This operation avoids the need to delete a file and then recreate it. Sometimes the truncating operation is sophisticated enough to erase part of a file, from the current file pointer to the end of the file.

An operating system also provides an operation to change the name of a file, which is called renaming the file. Likewise, it provides the ability to create a complete copy of the contents of a file, giving the copy a new name.

▪ File Access

The data in a file can be accessed in several different ways. Some operating systems provide only one type of file access, whereas others provide a choice of access methods. The type of access available for a given file is established when the file is created.

Let's examine the two primary access techniques: sequential access and direct access. The differences between these two techniques are analogous to the differences between the sequential nature of magnetic tape and the direct access offered by a magnetic disk, as discussed in Chapter 5. However, both types of files can be stored on either type of medium. File access techniques define the ways that the current file pointer can be repositioned. They are independent of the physical restrictions of the devices on which the file is stored.

The most common access technique, and the simplest to implement, is sequential file access, which views the file as a linear structure. It requires that the data in the file be processed in order. Read and write operations move the current file pointer according to the amount of data that is read or written. Some systems allow the file pointer to be reset to the beginning of the file and/or to skip forward or backward by a certain number of records. See Figure 11.2.

Files with direct file access are conceptually divided into numbered logical records. Direct access allows the user to set the file pointer to any

> **Sequential file access** The technique in which data in a file is accessed in a linear fashion

> **Direct file access** The technique in which data in a file is accessed directly, by specifying logical record numbers

FIGURE 11.2 Sequential file access

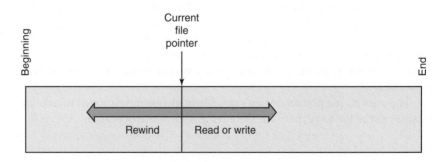

FIGURE 11.3 Direct file access

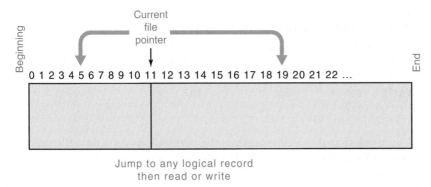

Jump to any logical record
then read or write

particular record by specifying the record number. Therefore, the user can read and write records in any particular order desired, as shown in Figure 11.3. Direct access files are more complicated to implement, but are helpful in situations where specific portions of large data stores must be available quickly, such as in a database.

■ File Protection

In multiuser systems, file protection is of primary importance. That is, we don't want one user to be able to access another user's files unless such access is specifically allowed. It is the operating system's responsibility to ensure valid file access. Different operating systems administer their file protection in different ways. In any case, a file protection mechanism determines who can use a file and for what general purpose.

For example, a file's protection settings in the UNIX operating system are divided into three categories: Owner, Group, and World. Under each category you can determine whether the file can be read, written, and/or executed. Under this mechanism, if you can write to a file, you can also delete the file.

Each file is "owned" by a particular user, who is often the creator of the file. The Owner usually has the strongest permissions regarding the file. A file may also have a group name associated with it—a group is simply a list of users. The Group permissions apply to all users in the associated group. You might create Group permissions, for instance, for all users who are working on a particular project. Finally, World permissions apply to anyone who has access to the system. Because these permissions give access to the largest number of users, they are usually the most restricted.

Using this technique, the permissions on a file can be shown in a 3 × 3 grid:

	Read	Write/Delete	Execute
Owner	Yes	Yes	No
Group	Yes	No	No
World	No	No	No

Suppose that this grid represents the permissions on a data file used in project Alpha. The owner of the file (perhaps the manager of the project) may read from or write to the file. Suppose also that the owner sets up a group (using the operating system) called TeamAlpha, which contains all members of the project team, and associates that group with this data file. The members of the TeamAlpha group may read the data in the file, but may not change it. No one else is given any permission to access the file. Note that no user is given execute privileges for the file because it is a data file, not an executable program.

Other operating systems set up their protection schemes in different ways, but the goal is the same: to control access so as to protect against deliberate attempts to gain inappropriate access as well as minimize inadvertent problems caused by well-intentioned but hazardous users.

11.2 Directories

As mentioned earlier, a directory is a named collection of files. It is a way to group files so that you can organize them in a logical manner. For example, you might place all of your papers and notes for a particular class in a directory created for that class. The operating system must carefully keep track of directories and the files they contain.

A directory, in most operating systems, is represented as a file. The directory file contains data about the other files in the directory. For any given file, the directory contains the file name, the file type, the address on disk where the file is stored, and the current size of the file. The directory also contains information about the protections set up for the file. In addition, it may hold information describing when the file was created and when it was last modified.

The internal structure of a directory file could be set up in a variety of ways, and we won't explore those details here. However, once it is set up, this structure must be able to support the common operations that are performed on directory files. For instance, the user must be able to list all of the files in the directory. Other common operations are creating,

RFID tags

As you leave a store after buying a pack of batteries, the batteries "tell" the store's inventory system to order batteries because stock is low. Radio-frequency identification (RFID) makes this type of communication possible. If the battery packaging has an RFID tag, it can tell a central radio-frequency transceiver where it is. In addition to items in retail stores, RFID technology is used to track shipping pallets, library books, vehicles, and animals. If you've ever used EZPass to go through a toll booth, or SpeedPass® to pay for your gas, you've used RFID technology. Researchers have even experimented with implanting RFID tags in people! In 2004, a club owner in Barcelona, Spain, and Rotterdam, the Netherlands, offered to implant his VIP customers with RFID tags. These chips identified the customers as VIPs, and the chips were used by the customers to pay for their drinks.

deleting, and renaming files within a directory. Furthermore, the directory is often searched to see whether a particular file is in the directory.

Another key issue when it comes to directory management is the need to reflect the relationships among directories, as discussed in the next section.

■ Directory Trees

A directory of files can be contained within another directory. The directory containing another directory is usually called the parent directory, and the one inside is called a subdirectory. You can set up such nested directories as often as needed to help organize the file system. One directory can contain many subdirectories. Furthermore, subdirectories can contain their own subdirectories, creating a hierarchy structure. To visualize this hierarchy, a file system is often viewed as a directory tree, showing directories and files within other directories. The directory at the highest level is called the root directory.

As an example, consider the directory tree shown in Figure 11.4. This tree represents a very small part of a file system that might be found on a computer using some flavor of the Microsoft® Windows® operating system. The root of the directory system is referred to using the drive letter C: followed by the backslash (\).

In this directory tree, the root directory contains three subdirectories: WINDOWS, My Documents, and Program Files. Within the WINDOWS directory, there is a file called calc.exe as well as two other subdirectories (Drivers and System). Those directories contain other files and subdirectories. Keep in mind that all of these directories in a real system would typically contain many more subdirectories and files.

Personal computers often use an analogy of folders to represent the directory structure, which promotes the idea of containment (folders inside other folders, with some folders ultimately containing documents or other data). The icon used to show a directory in the graphical user interface of an operating system is often a graphic of a manila file folder such as the kind you would use in a physical file drawer.

In Figure 11.4, two files have the name util.zip (in the My Documents directory, and in its subdirectory called downloads). The nested directory structure allows for multiple files to have the same name. All the files in any one directory must have unique names, but files in different directories or subdirectories can have the same name. These files may or may not contain the same data; all we know is that they have the same name.

At any point in time, you can be thought of as working in a particular location (that is, a particular subdirectory) of the file system. This subdirectory is referred to as the current working directory. As you "move" around in the file system, the current working directory changes.

> **»** Directory tree A structure showing the nested directory organization of the file system
>
> **»** Root directory The topmost directory, in which all others are contained
>
> **»** Working directory The currently active subdirectory

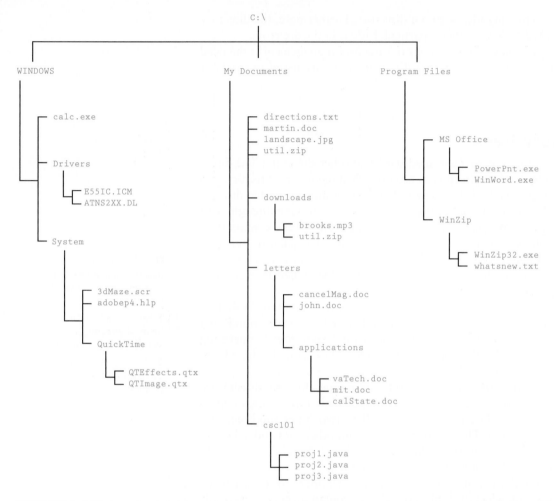

FIGURE 11.4 A Windows directory tree

The directory tree shown in Figure 11.5 is representative of one from a UNIX file system. Compare and contrast it to the directory tree in Figure 11.4. Both show the same concepts of subdirectory containment, but the naming conventions for files and directories are different. UNIX was developed as a programming and system-level environment, so it uses much more abbreviated and cryptic names for directories and files. Also, in a UNIX environment, the root is designated using a forward slash (/).

■ Path Names

How do we specify one particular file or subdirectory? Well, there are several ways to do it.

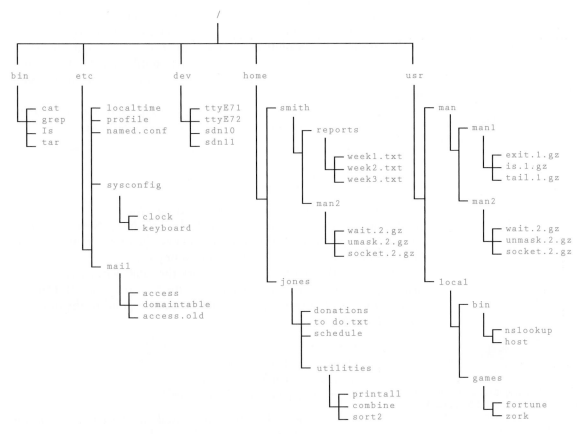

FIGURE 11.5 A UNIX directory tree

If you are working in a graphical user interface to the operating system, you can double-click with your mouse to open a directory and see its contents. The active directory window shows the contents of the current working directory. You can continue "moving" through the file system by using mouse clicks, thereby changing the current working directory, until you find the desired file or directory. To move up the directory structure, you can often use an icon on the window bar or a pop-up menu option to move to the parent directory.

Most operating systems also provide a nongraphical (text-based) interface to the operating system. Therefore, we must be able to specify file locations using text. This ability is very important for system instructions stored in operating system batch command files. Commands such as cd (which stands for "change directory") can be used in text mode to change the current working directory.

To indicate a particular file using text, we specify that file's path, which is the series of directories through which you must go to find the file. A path may be absolute or relative. An absolute path name begins at the root and specifies each step down the tree until it reaches the desired file or directory. A relative path name begins from the current working directory.

Let's look at examples of each type of path. The following are absolute path names based on the directory tree shown in Figure 11.4:

```
C:\Program Files\MS Office\WinWord.exe
C:\My Documents\letters\applications\vaTech.doc
C:\Windows\System\QuickTime
```

Each path name begins at the root and proceeds down the directory structure. Each subdirectory is separated by the backslash (\). Note that a path can specify a specific document (as it does in the first two examples) or an entire subdirectory (as it does in the third example).

Absolute paths in a UNIX system work the same way, except that the character used to separate subdirectories is the forward slash (/). Here are some examples of absolute path names that correspond to the directory tree in Figure 11.5:

```
/bin/tar
/etc/sysconfig/clock
/usr/local/games/fortune
/home/smith/reports/week1.txt
```

Relative path names are based on the current working directory. That is, they are relative to your current position (hence the name). Suppose the current working directory is C:\My Documents\letters (from Figure 11.4). Then the following relative path names could be used:

```
cancelMag.doc
applications\calState.doc
```

The first example specifies just the name of the file, which can be found in the current working directory. The second example specifies a file in the applications subdirectory. By definition, the first part of any valid relative path is located in the working directory.

Sometimes when using a relative path we need to work our way back up the tree. Note that this consideration was not an issue when we used absolute paths. In most operating systems, two dots (..) are used to specify the parent directory (a single dot is used to specify the current working directory). Therefore,

Soothing software
Chronic stress can lead to cardiovascular disease, diabetes, impaired cognitive function, and a weakened immune system. One measure of stress level is heart rate variability (HRV), the period in milliseconds between heartbeats that cardiologists study in at-risk patients. In a healthy person, HRV should be high but within a certain zone. One software package that measures HRV is supplied by HeartMath®. The emWave® (formerly Freeze-Framer Interactive Learning System) measures the subtle changes in your heart rhythms. It helps reduce stress by training the user to create more "cohearance," a term used to describe a physiological state in which the nervous, cardiovascular, hormonal, and immune systems are working efficiently and harmoniously. The emWave measures stress with a finger or ear sensor that detects the user's pulse. Just a few minutes of breathing with the emWave's pacer and thinking positive thoughts can bring HRV into the target zone. In this way, the user's response to stress can be slowly reprogrammed over several short sessions a day.

if the working directory is `C:\My Documents\letters`, the following relative path names are also valid:

```
..\landscape.jpg
..\csc111\proj2.java
..\..\WINDOWS\Drivers\E55IC.ICM
..\..\Program Files\WinZip
```

UNIX systems work essentially the same way. Using the directory tree in Figure 11.5, and assuming that the current working directory is `/home/jones`, the following are valid relative path names:

```
utilities/combine
../smith/reports
../../dev/ttyE71
../../usr/man/man1/ls.1.gz
```

Most operating systems allow the user to specify a set of paths that are searched (in a specific order) to help resolve references to executable programs. Often that set of paths is specified using an operating system variable called `PATH`, which holds a string that contains several absolute path names. Suppose, for instance, that user `jones` (from Figure 11.5) has a set of utility programs that he uses from time to time. They are stored in the directory `/home/jones/utilities`. When that path is added to the `PATH` variable, it becomes a standard location used to find programs that `jones` attempts to execute. Therefore, no matter what the current working directory is, when `jones` executes the `printall` program (just the name by itself), it is found in his utilities directory.

11.3 Disk Scheduling

The most important hardware device used as secondary memory is the magnetic disk drive. File systems stored on these drives must be accessed in an efficient manner. It turns out that transferring data to and from secondary memory is the worst bottleneck in a general computer system.

Recall from Chapter 10 that the speed of the CPU and the speed of main memory are much faster than the speed of data transfer to and from secondary memory such as a magnetic disk. That's why a process that must perform I/O to disk is made to wait while that data is transferred, to give another process a chance to use the CPU.

Because secondary I/O is the slowest aspect of a general computer system, the techniques for accessing data on a disk drive are of crucial importance to file systems. As a computer deals with multiple processes over a period of time, requests to access the disk accumulate. The technique that the operating

» Disk scheduling The act of deciding which outstanding requests for disk I/O to satisfy first

system uses to determine which requests to satisfy first is called disk scheduling. We examine several specific disk-scheduling algorithms in this section.

Recall from Chapter 5 that a magnetic disk drive is organized as a stack of platters, where each platter is divided into tracks, and each track is divided into sectors. The set of corresponding tracks on all platters is called a cylinder. Figure 11.6 revisits the disk drive depicted in Chapter 5 to remind you of this organization.

Of primary importance to us in this discussion is the fact that the set of read/write heads hovers over a particular cylinder along all platters at any given point in time. The *seek time* is the amount of time it takes for the heads to reach the appropriate cylinder. The *latency* is the additional time it takes the platter to rotate into the proper position so that the data can be read or written. Seek time is the more restrictive of these two parameters and, therefore, is the primary issue dealt with by the disk-scheduling algorithms.

At any point in time, a disk drive may have a set of outstanding requests that must be satisfied. For now, we consider only the cylinder (the parallel concentric circles) to which the requests refer. A disk may have thousands of cylinders. To keep things simple, let's also assume a range of 110 cylinders. Suppose at a particular time the following cylinder requests have been made, in this order:

49, 91, 22, 61, 7, 62, 33, 35

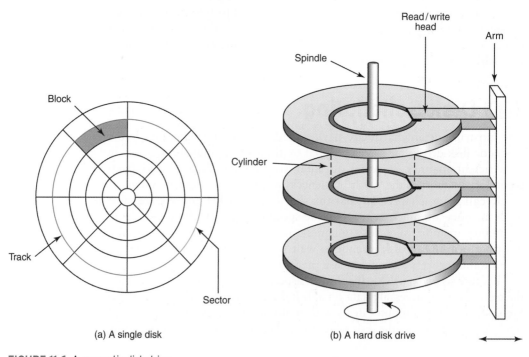

(a) A single disk

(b) A hard disk drive

FIGURE 11.6 A magnetic disk drive

Suppose also that the read/write heads are currently at cylinder 26. Now a question arises: To which cylinder should the disk heads move next? Different algorithms produce different answers to this question.

■ First-Come, First-Served Disk Scheduling

In Chapter 10 we examined a CPU scheduling algorithm called *first come, first served* (FCFS). An analogous algorithm can be used for disk scheduling. It is one of the easiest to implement, though not usually the most efficient.

In FCFS, we process the requests in the order they arrive, without regard to the current position of the heads. Therefore, under a FCFS algorithm, the heads move from cylinder 26 (the current position) to cylinder 49. After the request for cylinder 49 is satisfied (that is, the data is read or written), the heads move from 49 to 91. After processing the request at 91, the heads move to cylinder 22. Processing continues in this manner, satisfying requests in the order that they were received.

Note that at one point the heads move from cylinder 91 all the way back to cylinder 22, during which they pass over several cylinders whose requests are currently pending.

■ Shortest-Seek-Time-First Disk Scheduling

The *shortest-seek-time-first* (SSTF) disk-scheduling algorithm moves the heads by the minimum amount necessary to satisfy any pending request. This approach could potentially result in the heads changing directions after each request is satisfied.

Let's process our hypothetical situation using this algorithm. From our starting point at cylinder 26, the closest cylinder among all pending requests is 22. So, ignoring the order in which the requests came, the heads move to cylinder 22 to satisfy that request. From 22, the closest request is for cylinder 33, so the heads move there. The closest unsatisfied request to 33 is at cylinder 35. The distance to cylinder 49 is now the smallest, so the heads move there next. Continuing that approach, the rest of the cylinders are visited in the following order: 49, 61, 62, 91, 7.

This approach does not guarantee the smallest overall head movement, but it generally offers an improvement in performance over the FCFS algorithm. However, a major problem can arise with this approach. Suppose requests for cylinders continue to build up while existing ones are being satisfied. And suppose those new requests are always closer to the current position than an earlier request. It is theoretically possible that the early request never gets processed because requests keep arriving that take priority. This situation is called *starvation*. By contrast, FCFS disk scheduling cannot suffer from starvation.

■ SCAN Disk Scheduling

A classic example of algorithm analysis in computing comes from the way an elevator is designed to visit floors that have people waiting. In general, an elevator moves from one extreme to the other (say, the top of the building to the bottom), servicing requests as appropriate. It then travels from the bottom to the top, servicing those requests.

The *SCAN* disk-scheduling algorithm works in a similar way, except that instead of moving up and down, the read/write heads move in toward the spindle, then out toward the platter edge, then back toward the spindle, and so forth.

Let's use this algorithm to satisfy our set of requests. Unlike in the other approaches, though, we need to decide which way the heads are moving initially. Let's assume they are moving toward the lower cylinder values (and are currently at cylinder 26).

As the read/write heads move from cylinder 26 toward cylinder 1, they satisfy the requests at cylinders 22 and 7 (in that order). After reaching cylinder 1, the heads reverse direction and move all the way out to the other extreme. Along the way, they satisfy the following requests, in order: 33, 35, 49, 61, 62, 91.

New requests are not given any special treatment under this scheme. They may or may not be serviced before earlier requests—it depends on the current location of the heads and direction in which they are moving. If a new request arrives just before the heads reach that cylinder, it is processed right away. If it arrives just after the heads move past that cylinder, it must wait for the heads to return. There is no chance for starvation because each cylinder is processed in turn.

Some variations on this algorithm can improve its performance. For example, a request at the edge of the platter may have to wait for the heads to move almost all the way to the spindle and all the way back. To improve the average wait time, the Circular SCAN algorithm treats the disk as if it were a ring and not a disk. That is, when it reaches one extreme, the heads return all the way to the other extreme without processing requests.

Another variation is to minimize the extreme movements at the spindle and at the edge of the platter. Instead of going to the edge, the heads move only as far out (or in) as the outermost (or innermost) request. Before moving on to tackle the next request, the list of pending requests is examined to see whether movement in the current direction is warranted. This variation is referred to as the *LOOK* disk-scheduling algorithm, because it looks ahead to see whether the heads should continue in the current direction.

Keeping the elderly at home
Many new technologies are being developed to make it easier for the elderly to continue living independent lives at home. One example is the eNeighbor® system, a system with 12 kinds of sensors (e.g., bed, toilet flush, home away, open/closed) and an optional Web camera. Wireless sensors can detect changes in a person's habits (if a person falls down and does not move in his or her regular pattern, for example) and will relay that information to a central monitoring system. An operator then calls the house to ask if the patient is okay. If no response is received, more calls are made to family, neighbors, or the 911 emergency system. While the system is not covered under all insurance plans, the cost is still much less than that of a nursing home, and it allows the elderly the freedom to live at home.

Summary

A file system defines the way our secondary memory is organized. A file is a named collection of data with a particular internal structure. Text files are organized as a stream of characters; binary files have a particular format that is meaningful only to applications set up to handle that format.

File types are often indicated by the file extension of the file name. The operating system maintains a list of recognized file types so that it may open them in the correct kind of application and display the appropriate icons in the graphical user interface. The file extension can be associated with any particular kind of application that the user chooses.

The operations performed on files include creating, deleting, opening, and closing files. Of course, files must be able to be read from and written to as well. The operating system provides mechanisms to accomplish the various file operations. In a multiuser system, the operating system must also provide file protection to ensure only authorized users have access to files.

Directories are used to organize files on disk. They can be nested to form hierarchical tree structures. Path names that specify the location of a particular file or directory can be absolute, originating at the root of the directory tree, or relative, originating at the current working directory.

Disk-scheduling algorithms determine the order in which pending disk requests are processed. First-come, first-served disk scheduling takes all requests in order, but is not very efficient. Shortest-seek-time-first disk scheduling is more efficient, but could suffer from starvation. SCAN disk scheduling employs the same strategy as an elevator, sweeping from one end of the disk to the other.

⚖ ETHICAL ISSUES ▸ Spam

In 2004, Eric Idle developed a musical comedy for the Broadway stage by the name of *Spamalot*. The musical, a parody of both Arthurian legend and Broadway itself, comes from a line in the movie *Monty Python's Holy Grail*, which goes: "We eat ham, and jam and Spam a lot." *Monty Python's Flying Circus*, of which Eric Idle was one of the creators, is believed to be the origin of the word "spam." Beyond the Spam® (spiced ham food product) referenced in the title of this popular show, the word "spam" has now come to mean any unwanted, unsolicited, irrelevant, or inappropriate messages sent on the Internet to a large number of users.

In the past, the most common types of spam were the floods of advertising that came through the mail—circulars, catalogs, "special offers," and other third-class mail delivered to our mailboxes. Since the development of electronic advertising, marketers have sought new ways to make contact with potential customers. In addition to email spam, today there are many other forms of Internet spam: instant messaging, Usenet newsgroups, Web search engine, blogs, wikis, online classified ads, Internet forums, fax, and more.

For a time, spam was merely an annoyance. But as its use increased, the consequences increased, too. Unlike a home mailbox, spam has a cost attached to it,

» continued

⚖ ETHICAL ISSUES ▶ Spam, continued

both for the Internet service provider (ISP) and for the end user who pays for having an account with the ISP. The most recent estimates for the cost of spam in 2009 totaled $130 billion worldwide and $42 billion in the United States alone—figures that are up 30% from the 2007 costs, which in turn were up 100% from the 2005 costs. Broken down by employee, the average annual cost is in the thousands of dollars per year. By conservative estimates, spam accounts for 85% of emails and maybe even as much as 95%, according to some estimates.

Marketers say that any attempt to regulate spam is a restriction of free speech. They also say that spam is just another manifestation of the principles of capitalism, and that no good purpose is served by restricting businesses from using whatever means they have to let customers know about their products and services. The claim of the customer's right to know underpins many of the arguments advertisers cite to support their position. Without unsolicited bulk mailing, many business would have few good alternatives for finding customers.

Since the CAN-SPAM Act (Controlling the Assault of Non-solicited Pornography and Marketing Act) was enacted in January 2004, several major spammer offenders have been convicted and given harsh sentences. The law aims to protect the consumer by imposing regulations on commercial email. By law, all mass emails must now contain accurate routing information, a subject line that accurately reflects the content of the message, and an opt-out option to cancel future mailings. In addition, the message must be identified as an advertisement and include the sender's valid postal address. Failure to obey any of these laws can result in fines of as much as $11,000. Under the new law, states are also given the right to enforce much of their own spam legislation. Although the CAN-SPAM Act has not been completely effective in halting the transmission of spam email, legislators hope that it will aid in reducing the costs to the consumer.

⚷ Key Terms

Absolute path
Binary file
Direct file access
Directory
Directory tree
Disk scheduling
File
File extension

File system
File type
Path
Relative path
Root directory
Sequential file access
Text file
Working directory

⌘ Exercises

For Exercises 1–15, mark the answers true or false as follows:
  A. True
  B. False

1. A text file stores binary data that is organized into groups of 8 or 16 bits that are interpreted as characters.

2. A program written in a high-level language is stored in a text file that is also called a source file.

3. The type of a file determines which kinds of operations can be performed on it.

4. The current file pointer indicates the end of a file.

5. Sequential access and direct access take about the same amount of time to retrieve data.

6. Some operating systems maintain a separate read pointer and write pointer for a file.

7. UNIX file permissions allow a group of users to access a file in various ways.

8. In most operating systems, a directory is represented as a file.

9. Two files in a directory system can have the same name if they are in different directories.

10. A relative path is relative to the root of the directory hierarchy.

11. An absolute path and a relative path will always be the same length.

12. An operating system is responsible for managing the access to a disk drive.

13. The seek time is the amount of time it takes for the heads of a disk to reach a particular cylinder.

14. The shortest-seek-time-first disk scheduling algorithm moves the heads the minimum amount it can to satisfy a pending request.

15. The first-come, first-served disk scheduling algorithm moves the heads the minimum amount it can to satisfy a pending request.

For Exercises 16–20, match the file extensions with the appropriate file.
   A. txt
   B. mp3, au, and wav
   C. gif, tiff, and jpg
   D. doc and wp3
   E. java, c, and cpp

16. Audio file

17. Image file

18. Text data file

19. Program source file

20. Word processing file

For Exercises 21–23, match the symbol with its use.
   A. /
   B. \
   C. ..

21. Symbol used to separate the names in a path in a Windows environment
22. Symbol used to separate the names in a path in a UNIX environment
23. Symbol used to represent the parent directory in a relative path name

Exercises 24–57 are problems or short-answer questions.
24. What is a file?
25. Distinguish between a file and a directory.
26. Distinguish between a file and a file system.
27. Why is a file a generic concept and not a technical one?
28. Name and describe the two basic classifications of files.
29. Why is the term *binary file* a misnomer?
30. Distinguish between a file type and a file extension.
31. What would happen if you give the name `myFile.jpg` to a text file?
32. How can an operating system make use of the file types that it recognizes?
33. How does an operating system keep track of secondary memory?
34. What does it mean to open and close a file?
35. What does it mean to truncate a file?
36. Compare and contrast sequential and direct file access.
37. File access is independent of any physical medium.
    a. How could you implement sequential access on a disk?
    b. How could you implement direct access on a magnetic tape?
38. What is a file protection mechanism?
39. How does UNIX implement file protection?
40. Given the following file permission, answer these questions.

	Read	Write/Delete	Execute
Owner	Yes	Yes	Yes
Group	Yes	Yes	No
World	Yes	No	No

    a. Who can read the file?
    b. Who can write or delete the file?
    c. Who can execute the file?
    d. What do you know about the content of the file?
41. What is the minimum amount of information a directory must contain about each file?
42. How do most operating systems represent a directory?

43. Answer the following questions about directories.
   a. A directory that contains another directory is called what?
   b. A directory contained within another directory is called what?
   c. A directory that is not contained in any other directory is called what?
   d. The structure showing the nested directory organization is called what?
   e. Relate the structure in (d) to the binary tree data structure examined in Chapter 8.

44. What is the directory called in which you are working at any one moment?

45. What is a path?

46. Distinguish between an absolute path and a relative path.

47. Show the absolute path to each of the following files or directories using the directory tree shown in Figure 11.4:
   a. QTEffects.qtx
   b. brooks.mp3
   c. Program Files
   d. 3dMaze.scr
   e. Powerpnt.exe

48. Show the absolute path to each of the following files or directories using the directory tree shown in Figure 11.5:
   a. tar
   b. access.old
   c. named.conf
   d. smith
   e. week3.txt
   f. printall

49. Assuming the current working directory is C:\WINDOWS\System, give the relative path name to the following files or directories using the directory tree shown in Figure 11.4:
   a. QTImage.qtx
   b. calc.exe
   c. letters
   d. proj3.java
   e. adobep4.hlp
   f. WinWord.exe

50. Show the relative path to each of the following files or directories using the directory tree shown in Figure 11.5:
   a. localtime when working directory is the root directory
   b. localtime when the working directory is etc
   c. printall when the working directory is utilities
   d. week1.txt when the working directory is man2

51. What is the worst bottleneck in a computer system?

52. Why is disk scheduling concerned more with cylinders than with tracks and sectors?

53. Name and describe three disk scheduling algorithms.

Use the following list of cylinder requests in Exercises 54–56. They are listed in the order in which they were received.

40, 12, 22, 66, 67, 33, 80

54. List the order in which these requests are handled if the FCFS algorithm is used. Assume that the disk is positioned at cylinder 50.

55. List the order in which these requests are handled if the SSTF algorithm is used. Assume that the disk is positioned at cylinder 50.

56. List the order in which these requests are handled if the SCAN algorithm is used. Assume that the disk is positioned at cylinder 50 and the read/write heads are moving toward the higher cylinder numbers.

57. Explain the concept of starvation.

??? Thought Questions

1. The concept of a file permeates computing. Would the computer be useful if there were no secondary memory on which to store files?

2. The disk scheduling algorithms examined in this chapter sound familiar. In what other context have we discussed similar algorithms? How are these similar and how are they different?

3. Are there any analogies between files and directories and file folders and filing cabinets? Clearly, the name "file" came from this concept. Where does this analogy hold true and where does it not?

4. Spamming is the Internet equivalent of unsolicited telephone sales pitches. There are laws now that allow a telephone user to request that his or her name be removed from the solicitor's calling list. Should there be similar laws relating to spamming?

5. In your opinion, is "spamming" a reasonable business strategy, like regular direct or "junk" mail, or is it a form of electronic harassment? Why or why not?

6. Many critics of the CAN-SPAM Act say that the act is largely ineffective. Do you think that the government should have been more stringent in its efforts to eradicate spam, or do you think that this would violate the protection that the First Amendment provides to commercial free speech?

The Applications Layer

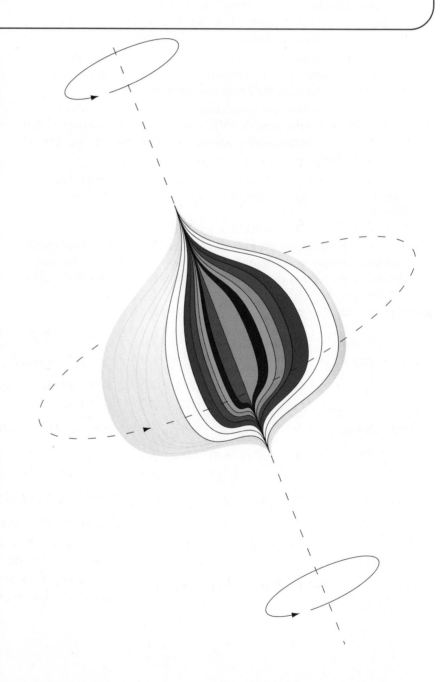

Information Systems

12

Most people interact with computers at the application level. That is, even if a person doesn't know anything about the details of the other underlying levels of computing, the chances are that he or she has used application software. Our goal at this level is to give you an appreciation for how various application systems work. Application software can be classified in several ways. In this chapter we focus

Goals

After studying this chapter, you should be able to:

- define the role of general information systems.
- explain how spreadsheets are organized.
- create spreadsheets for basic analysis of data.
- define appropriate spreadsheet formulas using built-in functions.
- design spreadsheets to be flexible and extensible.
- describe the elements of a database management system.
- describe the organization of a relational database.
- establish relationships among elements in a database.

- write basic SQL statements.
- describe an entity-relationship diagram.
- define and explain the role of e-commerce in society today.
- discuss the CIA triad.
- describe the role of cryptography in securing data.
- list three types of authentication credentials.
- define the following terms related to computer security: *malicious code, virus, worm, Trojan horse, logic bomb, spoofing, phishing, back door, buffer overflow, denial of service,* and *man-in-the-middle.*

on general information systems. In Chapter 13 we discuss applications in the realm of artificial intelligence, and in Chapter 14 we focus on simulations, graphics, and gaming.

Computers exist to manage and analyze data. Today they affect almost all aspects of our lives. We use general information systems to manage everything from sports statistics to payroll data. Likewise, cash registers and ATMs are supported by large information systems. In this chapter we examine general-purpose software, particularly spreadsheets and database management systems; these help us organize and analyze the huge amounts of data with which we must deal. We also examine the problems inherent in keeping the information in these systems secure.

12.1 Managing Information

In this book we've used the term *data* to describe raw facts, and *information* to mean data that has been organized to help us answer questions and solve problems. An information system can be generally defined as software that helps us organize and analyze data.

>> Information system Software that helps the user organize and analyze data

Any particular application program manages data, and some programs manage data in particular ways using particular structures. Other specialized applications use specific techniques that are geared toward the type of problems they are trying to solve. For example, as we discuss in the next chapter, data can be organized so as to support the analysis that typically occurs in the computing field of artificial intelligence.

Most situations, however, are more general. In fact, innumerable situations don't require any special consideration. We simply have data to manage and relationships among that data to capture. These situations don't necessarily require special organization or processing. What they do require, however, are flexible application software tools that allow the user to dictate and manage the organization of data, and that have basic processing capabilities to analyze the data in various ways.

Three of the most popular general application information systems are *electronic spreadsheets*, *database management systems*, and *e-commerce*. A spreadsheet is a convenient tool for basic data analysis based on extensible formulas that define relationships among the data. Database management systems are geared toward managing large amounts of data that are often searched and organized into appropriate subsections.

Entire books have been written about spreadsheets and how they are set up and used. The same can be said for database management systems. Our goal for this chapter is not to exhaustively explore either of these systems, but rather introduce the usefulness and versatility of both. After this discussion you should be able to create basic versions of either type of system, and you will have a foundation on which to explore them in more detail.

Spreadsheets and database management systems have been around since the 1970s. Electronic commerce, by comparison, is relatively new, coming about with the advent of the World Wide Web. These systems manage all aspects of buying and selling on the Internet.

Ellis Island database
Since its launch on April 17, 2001, the Ellis Island website (www.ellisisland.org) has received more than 12 billion hits. The site's searchable database includes the name, age, country of origin, and even the ship on which each of some 25 million passengers arrived in the Unites States. The website generates close to half a million new email addresses each year for its outreach database for donations. The Ellis Island Immigration Station processed arriving immigrants and visitors between 1892 and 1924, and the website includes a list of famous arrivals, such as Rudyard Kipling (1892), Sigmund Freud (1909), Harry Houdini (1914), and Albert Einstein (1921).

12.2 Spreadsheets

A variety of spreadsheet programs are available today. You may already have some experience with spreadsheets, though we don't assume any background knowledge in this discussion. Each spreadsheet program has its own particular nuances regarding its abilities and syntax, but all spreadsheets embrace a common set of concepts. Our discussion in this chapter focuses on these common concepts. The specific examples that we explore are consistent with the syntax and functionality of the Microsoft® Excel spreadsheet program.

A spreadsheet is a software application that allows the user to organize and analyze data using a grid of labeled cells. A cell can contain data or a formula that is used to calculate a value. Data stored in a cell can be text, numbers, or "special" data such as dates.

As shown in Figure 12.1, spreadsheet cells are referenced by their row and column designation, usually using letters to specify the column and numbers to specify the row. Thus we refer to cells such as A1, C7, and G45.

» **Spreadsheet** A program that allows the user to organize and analyze data using a grid of cells

» **Cell** An element of a spreadsheet that can contain data or a formula

	A	B	C	D
1				
2				
3				
4				
5				

FIGURE 12.1 A spreadsheet, made up of a grid of labeled cells

After the 26th column, spreadsheets begin to use two letters for the column designation, so some cells have designations such as AA19. There is usually some reasonably large maximum number of rows in a spreadsheet, such as 256. Furthermore, in most spreadsheet programs, multiple sheets can be combined into one large interacting system.

Spreadsheets are useful in many situations, and they are often designed to manage thousands of data values and calculations. Let's look at a small example that demonstrates fundamental spreadsheet principles. Suppose we have collected data on the number of students who came to get help from a set of tutors over a period of several weeks. We've kept track of how many students went to each of three tutors (Hal, Amy, and Frank) each week for a period of five weeks. Now we want to perform some basic analysis on that data. We might end up with the spreadsheet shown in Figure 12.2.

This spreadsheet contains, among other things, the raw data to be analyzed. Cell C4, for instance, contains the number of students whom Hal tutored in week 1. The column of data running from C4 to C8 contains the number of students tutored by Hal in each of the five weeks during which data was collected. Likewise, the data for Amy is stored in cells D4 through D8, and the data for Frank is stored in cells E4 through E8. This same data can be thought of in terms of the row it is in. Each row shows the number of students helped by each tutor in any given week.

In cells C9, D9, and E9, the spreadsheet computes and displays the total number of students helped by each tutor over all five weeks. In cells C10, D10, and E10, the spreadsheet also computes and displays the average number of students helped by each tutor each week. Likewise, the

FIGURE 12.2 A spreadsheet containing data and computations

	A	B	C	D	E	F	G	H	
1									
2				Tutor					
3			Hal	Amy	Frank	Total	Avg		
4		1	12	10	13	35	11.67		
5		2	14	16	16	46	15.33		
6	Week	3	10	18	13	41	13.67		
7		4	8	21	18	47	15.67		
8		5	15	18	12	45	15.00		
9		Total	59	83	72	214	71.33		
10		Avg	11.80	16.60	14.40	42.80	14.27		
11									
12									

total number of students helped each week (by all tutors) is shown in the column of cells running from F4 to F8. The average number of students helped per week is shown in cells G4 to G8.

In addition to the totals and averages per tutor and per week, the spreadsheet calculates some other overall statistics. Cell F9 shows the total number of students helped by all tutors in all weeks. The average per week (for all tutors) is shown in cell F10 and the average per tutor (for all weeks) is shown in cell G9. Finally, the average number of students helped by any tutor in any week is shown in cell G10.

The data stored in columns A and B and in rows 2 and 3 are simply used as labels to indicate what the values in the rest of the spreadsheet represent. These labels are meant to enhance the spreadsheet's human readability only and do not contribute to the calculations.

Note that the labels and some of the values in the spreadsheet in Figure 12.2 are shown in different colors. Most spreadsheet programs allow the user to control the look and format of the data in specific cells in various ways. The user can specify the font, style, and color of the data as well as the alignment of the data within the cell (such as centered or left justified). In the case of real numeric values, such as the averages computed in this example, the user can specify how many decimal places should be displayed. In most spreadsheet programs, the user can also dictate whether the grid lines for each cell are displayed or remain invisible (in this example they are all displayed) and what the background color or pattern of a cell should be. All of these user preferences are specified using menu options or buttons in the spreadsheet application software.

■ Spreadsheet Formulas

In our example spreadsheet, we performed several calculations that gave us insight into the overall situation regarding tutor support. It turns out that it is relatively easy to set up these calculations. You might say that it wouldn't take long to sit down with these numbers and produce the same statistics with a calculator, and you would be right. However, the beauty of a spreadsheet is that it is both easily modified and easily expanded.

If we've set up the spreadsheet correctly, we could add or remove tutors, add additional weeks of data, or change any of the data we have already stored—and the corresponding calculations would automatically be updated. For example, although we set up the tutor spreadsheet to use the data of three tutors, the same spreadsheet could be expanded to handle hundreds of tutors. Instead of five weeks of data, we could just as easily process a year's worth.

The power of spreadsheets comes from the formulas that we can create and store in cells. All of the totals and averages in the example in Figure 12.2 are computed using formulas. When a formula is stored in a cell, the result of the formula is displayed in the cell. Therefore, when we look at the values in a spreadsheet, it is sometimes challenging to tell whether the

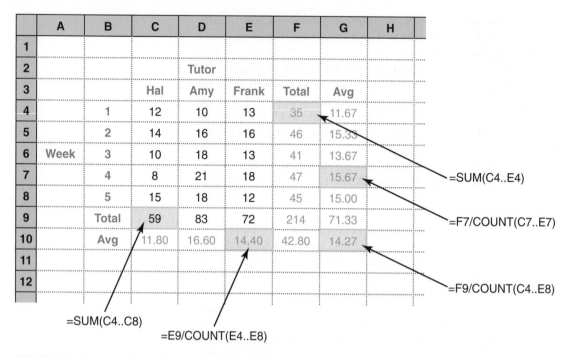

	A	B	C	D	E	F	G	H
1								
2				Tutor				
3			Hal	Amy	Frank	Total	Avg	
4		1	12	10	13	35	11.67	
5		2	14	16	16	46	15.33	
6	Week	3	10	18	13	41	13.67	
7		4	8	21	18	47	15.67	
8		5	15	18	12	45	15.00	
9		Total	59	83	72	214	71.33	
10		Avg	11.80	16.60	14.40	42.80	14.27	
11								
12								

=SUM(C4..E4)

=F7/COUNT(C7..E7)

=F9/COUNT(C4..E8)

=SUM(C4..C8)

=E9/COUNT(E4..E8)

FIGURE 12.3 The formulas behind some of the cells

data shown in a particular cell was entered directly or computed by an underlying formula.

Figure 12.3 shows the same spreadsheet as Figure 12.2, indicating the formulas underlying some of the cells. Formulas in our examples (as in many spreadsheet programs) begin with an equal sign (=). That's how the spreadsheet knows which cells contain formulas that must be evaluated.

The formulas in this example refer to particular cells (by their column and row designation). When a formula is evaluated, the values stored in the referenced cells are used to compute the result. Formulas in a spreadsheet are reevaluated whenever the spreadsheet changes; therefore, the results are always kept current. A spreadsheet is dynamic—it responds to changes immediately. If we changed the number of students whom Frank tutored in week 2, the totals and averages that use that value would be recalculated immediately to reflect the revised data.

Formulas can make use of basic arithmetic operations using the standard symbols (+, −, *, and /). They can also take advantage of spreadsheet functions that are built into the software. In the tutor example, the formula in cell C9 uses the SUM function to compute the sum of the values in the cells C4, C5, C6, C7, and C8.

Because functions often operate on a set of contiguous cells, spreadsheets provide a convenient way to specify a range of cells. Syntactically, a

>> **Spreadsheet function** A computation provided by the spreadsheet software that can be incorporated into formulas

>> **Range** A set of contiguous cells specified by the endpoints

range is specified with two dots (periods) between the two cell endpoints. A range can specify a set of cells along a row, such as C4..E4, or it can specify a set of cells down a column, such as C4..C8. A range can also specify a rectangular block of cells, ranging from the top left to the bottom right. For example, the range C4..E8 includes the cells C4 to C8, D4 to D8, and E4 to E8.

Several of the formulas shown in Figure 12.3 use the COUNT function, which computes the number of nonblank cells in the specified range. For example, the formula in cell G7 divides the value in cell F7 by the count of cells in the range C7..E7, which is 3.

The formula in cell G7 could have been written as follows:

=SUM(C7..E7)/3

Given the current status of the spreadsheet, this formula would compute the same result. However, this formula is not as good as the original, for two reasons. First, the sum of the values in C7 to E7 has already been computed (and stored in F7), so there is no need to recompute it. Any change to the data would affect the value of F7, and consequently change the value of G7 as well. Spreadsheets take all such relationships into account.

Second (and far more important), it is always a good idea to avoid using a constant in a formula unless it is specifically appropriate. In this case, using the value 3 as the predetermined number of tutors limits our ability to easily add or delete tutors from our analysis. Spreadsheet formulas respond to insertions and deletions just as they do to changes in raw data itself. If we insert a column for another tutor, the ranges in the original formulas in columns F and G (which would move to columns G and H due to the insertion) would automatically change to reflect the insertion. For example, if a new tutor column is inserted, the formula in cell F4 would be shifted to cell G4 and would now be

=SUM(C4..F4)

That is, the range of cells would increase to include the newly inserted data. Likewise, the ranges used by the COUNT function in other functions would change, resulting in a new—and correct—average. If we had used the constant 3 in the formula of cell G7, the calculation would be incorrect after the new column was inserted.

Usually a spreadsheet program provides a large number of functions that we can use in formulas. Some perform math or statistical calculations, common financial calculations, or special operations on text or dates. Others allow the user to set up logical relationships among cells. Examples of some common spreadsheet functions appear in Figure 12.4. A typical spreadsheet program provides dozens of functions that the user may incorporate into formulas.

Function	Computes
SUM(val1, val2, ...) SUM(range)	Sum of the specified set of values
COUNT(val1, val2, ...) COUNT(range)	Count of the number of cells that contain values
MAX(val1, val2, ...) MAX(range)	Largest value from the specified set of values
SIN(angle)	The sine of the specified angle
PI()	The value of PI
STDEV(val1, val2, ...) STDEV(range)	The standard deviation from the specified sample values
TODAY()	Today's date
LEFT(text, num_chars)	The leftmost characters from the specified text
IF(test, true_val, false_val)	If the test is true, it returns the true_val; otherwise, it returns the false_val
ISBLANK (value)	Returns true if the specified value refers to an empty cell

FIGURE 12.4 Some common spreadsheet functions

Another dynamic aspect of spreadsheets is the ability to copy values or formulas across a row or down a column. When formulas are copied, the relationships among cells are maintained. As a result, it becomes easy to set up a whole set of similar calculations. For instance, to enter the total calculations in our tutor example down the column from cell F4 to cell F8, we simply had to enter the formula in cell F4, and then copy that formula down the column. As the formula is copied, the references to the cells are automatically updated to reflect the row that the new formula is in. For our small example that tracks five weeks, the copy ability didn't save that much effort. But imagine if we were tracking this data for a whole year and had 52 summation formulas to create. The copy aspect of spreadsheets makes setting up that entire column a single operation.

Circular reference A set of formulas that ultimately, and erroneously, rely on each other to compute their results

■ Circular References

Spreadsheet formulas could be defined such that they create a circular reference—that is, a reference that can never be resolved because the result of

Daniel Bricklin

Many of the people whose biographies appear in this book have been winners of the ACM Turing Award, the highest award given in computer science. The ACM also gives an award for outstanding work done by someone younger than age 35, called the Grace Murray Hopper Award. The charge for this award reads:

Courtesy of Louis Fabian Bachrach/Dan Bricklin

> Awarded to the outstanding young computer professional of the year . . . selected on the basis of a single recent major technical or service contribution. . . . The candidate must have been 35 years of age or less at the time the qualifying contribution was made.

Daniel Bricklin won the Hopper Award in 1981, with the following citation:

> For his contributions to personal computing and, in particular, to the design of VisiCalc. Bricklin's efforts in the development of the "Visual Calculator" provide the excellence and elegance that ACM seeks to sustain through such activities as the Awards program.

Daniel Bricklin, born in 1951, is a member of the computer generation. He began his college career at the Massachusetts Institute of Technology in 1969 as a math major, but quickly changed to computer science. He worked in MIT's Laboratory for Computer Science, where he worked on interactive systems and met his future business partner, Bob Franksten. After graduation, he was employed by Digital Equipment Corporation, where he worked with computerized typeset-

ting and helped to design the WPS-8 word processing product.

After a very short stint with FasFax Corporation, a cash register manufacturer, Bricklin enrolled in the MBA program at the Harvard Business School in 1977. While there, he began to envision a program that could manipulate numbers much in the same way that word processors manipulate text. As Bricklin realized, such a program would have an immense impact on the business world. He teamed up with his MIT buddy Franksten and turned the dream into a reality. With Bricklin doing the design and Franksten doing the programming, the pair created VisiCalc, the first spreadsheet program. In 1978, they formed Software Arts to produce and market VisiCalc. In the fall of 1979, a version was made available for the Apple II for $100 per copy. A version for the IBM® PC became available in 1981.

Bricklin made the decision not to patent Visi-Calc, believing that software should not be proprietary. Although it didn't own a patent on its product, the company grew to 125 employees in four years. Soon, however, another start-up named Lotus® came out with a spreadsheet package called Lotus 1-2-3, which was both more powerful and more user-friendly than VisiCalc. Software Arts' sales suffered. After a long expensive court battle between Software Arts and VisiCorp (the company marketing VisiCalc), Bricklin was forced to sell to Lotus Software. In turn, Lotus 1-2-3 was surpassed by Microsoft's Excel spreadsheet program. Both Lotus 1-2-3 and Excel were based on VisiCalc.

After working for a short time as a consultant with Lotus Software, Bricklin again formed a new

» continued

Daniel Bricklin, continued

company. As president of Software Garden®, he developed a program for prototyping and simulating other pieces of software, which won the 1986 Software Publishers Association Award for "Best Programming Tool." In 1990, he cofounded Slate Corporation to develop applications software for pen computers—that is—small computers that use a pen rather than a keyboard for input. After four years, Slate closed its doors, and Bricklin went back to Software Garden.

In 1995, Bricklin founded Trellix Corporation, a leading provider of private-label website publishing technology. Trellix was acquired by Interland, Inc., in 2003. In early 2004, Bricklin returned to Software Garden as president.

When Bricklin was asked to share his view of the Internet, here is his reply as captured by the interviewer: "Most people don't understand it. They fail to grasp the capabilities of its underpinnings." He likens the Net to a primitive road during the early days of the automobile, when few saw the potential that a massive interstate highway system might one day provide. "We need to understand not so much the technology," he explains, "but the progression of technology and what might be built with it. E-commerce, like electricity or the telephone, simply enables us to use technology to do what we now do, only better."

one formula is ultimately based on another, and vice versa. For instance, if cell B15 contains the formula

=D22+D23

and cell D22 contains the formula

=B15+B16

there is a circular reference. Cell B15 uses the value in cell D22 for its result, but cell D22 relies on B15 for its result.

Circular references are not usually this blatant and may involve many cells. A more complicated situation is presented in Figure 12.5. Ultimately, cell A1 relies on cell D13 for its value, and vice versa. Spreadsheet software usually detects such a problem and indicates the error.

FIGURE 12.5 A circular reference situation that cannot be resolved

Cell	Contents
A1	=B7*COUNT(F8..K8)
B7	=A14+SUM(E40..E50)
E45	=G18+G19–D13
D13	=D12/A1

Spreadsheet Analysis

One reason spreadsheets are so useful is their versatility. The user of a spreadsheet determines what the data represents and how it is related to other data. Therefore, spreadsheet analysis can be applied to just about any topic area. We might, for instance, use a spreadsheet to perform the following tasks:

- Track sales
- Analyze sport statistics
- Maintain student grades
- Keep a car maintenance log
- Record and summarize travel expenses
- Track project activities and schedules
- Plan stock purchases

The list of potential applications is virtually endless. Business, in general, has a huge number of specific situations in which spreadsheet calculations are essential. It makes you wonder how we got along without them.

Their dynamic nature also makes spreadsheets highly useful. If we set up the spreadsheet formulas correctly, then our changes, additions, and deletions to the data are automatically taken into account by the appropriate calculations.

The dynamic nature of spreadsheets also provides the powerful ability to carry out what-if analysis. We can set up spreadsheets that take into account certain assumptions, and then challenge those assumptions by changing the appropriate values.

> » What-if analysis Modifying spreadsheet values that represent assumptions to see how changes in those assumptions affect related data

As an example, suppose we are setting up a spreadsheet to estimate the costs and potential profits for a seminar we are considering holding. We can enter values for the number of attendees, ticket prices, costs of materials, room rental, and other data that affects the final results. Then we can ask ourselves some what-if questions to see how our scenario changes as the situation changes:

What if the number of attendees decreased by 10%?

What if we increase the ticket price by $5?

What if we could reduce the cost of materials by half?

As we ask these questions, we change the data accordingly. If we've set up the relationships among all of the formulas correctly, then each change immediately shows us how it affects the other data.

Business analysts have formalized this process in various ways, and spreadsheets have become an essential tool in their daily work. Cost–benefit analysis, break-even calculations, and projected sales estimates all become a matter of organizing the spreadsheet data and formulas to take the appropriate relationships into account.

12.3 Database Management Systems

Almost all sophisticated data management situations rely on an underlying database and the support structure that allows the user (either a human or a program) to interact with it. A database can simply be defined as a structured set of data. A database management system (DBMS) is a combination of software and data made up of three components:

- The physical database—a collection of files that contain the data
- The database engine—software that supports access to and modification of the database contents
- The database schema—a specification of the logical structure of the data stored in the database

The database engine software interacts with specialized database languages that allow the user to specify the structure of data; add, modify, and delete data; and query the database to retrieve specific stored data.

The database schema provides the logical view of the data in the database, independent of how it is physically stored. Assuming that the underlying physical structure of the database is implemented in an efficient way, the logical schema is the more important point of view from the database user's perspective because it shows how the data items relate to each other.

Figure 12.6 depicts the relationships among the various elements of a database management system. The user interacts with the database engine software to determine and/or modify the schema for the database. The user then interacts with the engine software to access and possibly modify the contents of the database stored on disk.

■ The Relational Model

Several popular database management models have been proposed, but the one that has dominated for many years is the relational model. In a relational DBMS, the data items and the relationships among them are organized into tables. A table is a collection of records. A record is a collection of related fields. Each field of a database table contains a single data value. Each record in a table contains the same fields.

Sidebar definitions:

» Database A structured set of data

» Database management system A combination of software and data made up of the physical database, the database engine, and the database schema

» Query A request to retrieve data from a database

» Schema A specification of the logical structure of data in a database

» Relational model A database model in which data and the relationships among them are organized into tables

» Table A collection of database records

» Record (or object, or entity) A collection of related fields that make up a single database entry

» Field (or attribute) A single value in a database record

FIGURE 12.6 The elements of a database management system

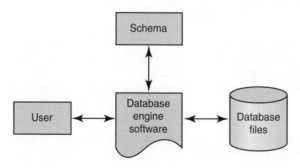

A record in a database table is also called a *database object* or an *entity*. The fields of a record are sometimes called the *attributes* of a database object.

As an example, consider the database table shown in Figure 12.7, which contains information about movies. Each row in the table corresponds to a record. Each record in the table is made up of the same fields in which particular values are stored. That is, each movie record has a Movield, a Title, a Genre, and a Rating that contain the specific data for each record. A database table is given a name, such as Movie in this case.

Usually, one or more fields of a table are identified as key fields. The key field(s) uniquely identifies a record among all other records in the table. That is, the value stored in the key field(s) for each record in a table must be unique. In the Movie table, the Movield field would be the logical choice for a key. That way, two movies could have the same title. Certainly the Genre and Rating fields are not appropriate key fields in this case.

Each value in the key field Movield must be unique. Most DBMSs allow such fields to be automatically generated to guarantee unique entries. The key values do not have to be consecutive, however. The last three entries of the table contain radically different movie identification numbers. As long as they are unique values, the Movield field can serve as the key.

The Movie table in Figure 12.7 happens to be presented in the order of increasing Movield value, but it could have been displayed in other ways, such as alphabetical by movie title. In this case, there is no inherent relationship among the rows of data in the table. Relational database tables present a logical view of the data and have nothing to do with the underlying physical organization (how the records are stored on disk). Ordering records becomes important only when we query the database for particular

>> **Key** One or more fields of a database record that uniquely identifies it among all other records in the table

Movield	Title	Genre	Rating
101	Sixth Sense, The	thriller horror	PG-13
102	Back to the Future	comedy adventure	PG
103	Monsters, Inc.	animation comedy	G
104	Field of Dreams	fantasy drama	PG
105	Alien	sci-fi horror	R
106	Unbreakable	thriller	PG-13
107	X-Men	action sci-fi	PG-13
5022	Elizabeth	drama period	R
5793	Independence Day	action sci-fi	PG-13
7442	Platoon	action drama war	R

FIGURE 12.7 Database table Movie, made up of records and fields

values, such as all movies that are rated PG. At that point we might want to sort the results of the query by title.

The structure of the table corresponds to the schema it represents. That is, a schema is an expression of the attributes of the records in a table. We can express the schema for this part of the database as follows:

Movie (Movield:key, Title, Genre, Rating)

Sometimes a schema representation indicates the type of data that is stored in individual fields, such as numeric or text. It may also indicate the specific set of values that are appropriate for a given field. For instance, the schema could indicate in this example that the Rating field can be only G, PG, PG-13, R, or NC-17. The schema for an entire database is made up of the individual schema that corresponds to individual tables.

Suppose we wanted to create a movie rental business. In addition to the list of movies for rent, we must create a database table to hold information about our customers. The Customer table in Figure 12.8 could represent this information.

Similar to what we did with our Movie table, the Customer table contains a CustomerId field to serve as a key. The fact that some CustomerId values correspond to some Movield values is irrelevant. Key values must be unique only within a table.

In a real database, we would be better off subdividing the Name field of our Customer table into FirstName and LastName fields. Also, we would probably use separate fields to hold various parts of a complete address, such as City and State. For our examples we are keeping things simple.

The Movie table and the Customer table show how data can be organized as records within isolated tables. The real power of relational database management systems, though, lies in the ability to create tables that conceptually link various tables together, as discussed in the next section.

FIGURE 12.8 Database table Customer containing customer data

CustomerId	Name	Address	CreditCardNumber
101	Dennis Cook	123 Main Street	2736 2371 2344 0382
102	Doug Nickle	456 Second Ave	7362 7486 5957 3638
103	Randy Wolf	789 Elm Street	4253 4773 6252 4436
104	Amy Stevens	321 Yellow Brick Road	9876 5432 1234 5678
105	Robert Person	654 Lois Lane	1122 3344 5566 7788
106	David Coggin	987 Broadway	8473 9687 4847 3784
107	Susan Klaton	345 Easy Street	2435 4332 1567 3232

■ Relationships

Recall that records represent individual database objects, and that fields of a record are the attributes of these objects. We can create a record to represent a relationship among objects and include attributes about the relationship in that record. In this way, we can use a table to represent a collection of relationships among objects.

Continuing our movie rental example, we need to be able to represent the situation in which a particular customer rents a particular movie. Because "rents" is a relationship between a customer and a movie, we can represent it as a record. The date rented and the date due are attributes of the relationship that should be in the record. The Rents table in Figure 12.9 contains a collection of these relationship records that represents the movies that are currently rented.

The Rents table contains information about the objects in the relationship (customers and movies), as well as the attributes of the relationship. It does not hold all of the data about a customer or a movie, however. In a relational database, we avoid duplicating data as much as possible. For instance, there is no need to store the customer's name and address in the rental table—that data is already stored in the Customer table. When we need that data, we use the CustomerId stored in the Rents table to look up the customer's detailed data in the Customer table. Likewise, when we need data about the movie that was rented, we look it up in the Movie table using the MovieId.

Note that the CustomerId value 103 is shown in two records in the Rents table. Its two appearances indicate that the same customer rented two different movies.

Data is modified in, added to, and deleted from our various database tables as needed. When movies are added or removed from the available stock, we update the records of the Movie table. As people become new customers of our store, we add them to the Customer table. On an ongoing basis we add and remove records from the Rents table as customers rent and return videos.

CustomerId	MovieId	DateRented	DateDue
103	104	3-12-2010	3-13-2010
103	5022	3-12-2010	3-13-2010
105	107	3-12-2010	3-15-2010

FIGURE 12.9 Database table Rents storing current movie rentals

Universal Product Code

When you look on the packaging of most products, you will find a Universal Product Code (UPC) and its associated bar code, such as the one shown at right. UPC codes were created to speed up the process of purchasing a product at a store and to help keep better track of inventory.

A UPC symbol

A UPC symbol is made up of the machine-readable bar code and the corresponding human-readable 12-digit UPC number. The first six digits of the UPC number are the *manufacturer identification number*. For example, General Mills has a manufacturer ID number of 016000. The next five digits are the *item number*. Each type of product, and each different packaging of the same product, is assigned a unique item number. For example, a 2-liter bottle of Coke has a different item number than a 2-liter bottle of Diet Coke, and a 10-ounce bottle of Heinz ketchup has a different item number than a 14-ounce bottle of Heinz ketchup.

The last digit of the UPC code is the *check digit*, which allows the scanner to determine whether it scanned the number correctly. After reading the number, a calculation is performed on the rest of the digits of the number to determine the check digit. The result is then verified against the actual check digit. (See Chapter 17 for more information on check digits.)

For some products, particularly small ones, a technique has been developed to create UPC numbers that can be shortened by eliminating certain digits (all zeros). In this way, the entire UPC symbol can be reduced in size.

Note that a product's price is not stored in the UPC number. When a product is scanned at a cash register—more formally called a point of sale (POS)—the manufacturer and item numbers are used to look up that item in a database. The database might contain a great deal of product information, including its price. Keeping only basic information in the UPC number makes it easy to change other information, such as the price, without having to relabel the products. Unfortunately, this flexibility also makes it easy to create situations of "scanner fraud" in which the database price of an item does not match the price on the store shelf, whether intentionally or not.

■ Structured Query Language

>> Structured Query Language (SQL) A comprehensive relational database language for data management and queries

The Structured Query Language (SQL) is a comprehensive database language for managing relational databases. It includes statements that specify database schemas as well as statements that add, modify, and delete database content. In addition, as its name implies, SQL provides the ability to query the database to retrieve specific data.

The original version of SQL was Sequal, developed by IBM in the early 1970s. In 1986, the American National Standards Institute (ANSI) published the SQL standard, which serves as the basis for commercial database languages for accessing relational databases.

SQL is not case sensitive, so keywords, table names, and attribute names can be uppercase, lowercase, or mixed case. Spaces are used as separators in a statement. Because this is a specific programming language, we use a monospaced code font.

Queries

Let's first focus on simple queries. The *select* statement is the primary tool for this purpose. The basic select statement includes a select clause, a from clause, and a where clause:

```
select attribute-list from table-list where condition
```

The select clause determines which attributes are returned. The from clause determines which tables are used in the query. The where clause restricts the data that is returned. For example:

```
select Title from Movie where Rating = 'PG'
```

The result of this query is a list of all titles from the Movie table that have a PG rating. The where clause can be eliminated if no special restrictions are necessary:

```
select Name, Address from Customer
```

This query returns the name and address of all customers in the Customer table. An asterisk (*) can be used in the select clause to denote that all attributes in the selected records should be returned:

```
select * from Movie where Genre like '%action%'
```

This query returns all attributes of records from the Movie table in which the Genre attribute contains the word "action." The like operator in SQL performs some simple pattern matching on strings, and the % symbol matches any string.

Select statements can also dictate how the results of the query should be sorted using the order by clause:

```
select * from Movie where Rating = 'R' order by Title
```

This query returns all attributes of R-rated movies sorted by the movie title.

SQL supports many more variations of select statements than are shown here. Our goal is simply to introduce the database concepts to you—you would require much more detail to become truly proficient at SQL queries.

Modifying Database Content

SQL's *insert, update,* and *delete* statements allow the data in a table to be changed. The insert statement adds a new record

?

Mathematical basis of SQL

SQL incorporates operations in an algebra that is defined for accessing and manipulating data represented in relational tables. E. F. Codd of IBM defined this algebra in the late 1960s; in 1981, he won the Turing Award for his work. SQL's fundamental operations include these:

- *Select* operation, to identify records in a table
- *Project* operation, to produce a subset of the columns in a table
- *Cartesian product* operation, to concatenate rows from two tables

Other operations include the set operations *union, difference, intersection, natural join* (a subset of the Cartesian product), and *division.*

to a table. Each insert statement specifies the values of the attributes for the new record. For example:

```
insert into Customer values (9876, 'John Smith',
'602 Greenbriar Court', '2938 3212 3402 0299')
```

This statement inserts a new record into the Customer table with the specified attributes.

The update statement changes the values in one or more records of a table. For example:

```
update Movie set Genre = 'thriller drama' where title =
'Unbreakable'
```

This statement changes the Genre attribute of the movie *Unbreakable* to "thriller drama."

The delete statement removes all records from a table matching the specified condition. For example, if we wanted to remove all R-rated movies from the Movie table, we could use the following delete statement:

```
delete from Movie where Rating = 'R'
```

As with the select statement, there are many variations of the insert, update, and delete statements.

■ Database Design

A database must be carefully designed from the outset if it hopes to fulfill its role. Poor planning in the early stages can lead to a database that does not support the required relationships.

One popular technique for designing relational databases is called entity-relationship (ER) modeling. Chief among the tools used for ER modeling is the ER diagram. An ER diagram captures the important record types, attributes, and relationships in a graphical form. From an ER diagram, a database manager can define the necessary schema and create the appropriate tables to support the database specified by the diagram.

Figure 12.10 presents an ER diagram showing various aspects of the movie rental example. Specific shapes are used in ER diagrams to differentiate among the various parts of the database. Types of records (which can also be thought of as classes for the database objects) are shown in rectangles. Fields (or attributes) of those records are shown in attached ovals. Relationships are shown in diamonds.

The positions of the various elements of an ER diagram are not particularly important, though giving some thought to them will make the diagram easier to read. Note that a relationship such as Rents can have its own associated attributes.

Also note that the relationship connectors are labeled, one side with a 1 and the other side with an M. These designations show the cardinality constraint of the relationship. A cardinality constraint puts restrictions on

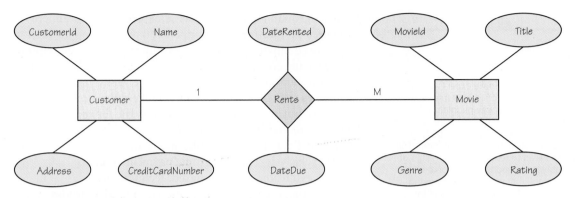

FIGURE 12.10 An ER diagram for the movie rental database

the number of relationships that may exist at one time. Three general cardinality relationships are possible:

- One-to-one
- One-to-many
- Many-to-many

The relationship between a customer and a movie is one-to-many. That is, one customer is allowed to rent many movies, but a movie can be rented by only a single customer (at any given time). Cardinality constraints help the database designer convey the details of a relationship.

12.4 E-Commerce

A growing area of computer applications is occurring in the realm of electronic commerce, or e-commerce, which deals with purchases made through the World Wide Web. It includes all aspects of the marketing, sales, and buying of both products and services. These days, more and more people are turning to the Web as their first option when making a purchase.

» Electronic commerce The process of buying and selling products and services using the World Wide Web

When the Web burst into public view in 1994, many people predicted that it would have a large impact on the way we do business. In fact, it took several years for e-commerce to begin to be trusted enough, and become functional enough, to take root in our culture. The "dot-com" collapse of 2001, instead of diminishing e-commerce, seemed to promote it by clearing the way for organizations with legitimate business models to make a place for themselves online. During this period, in addition to new, purely online businesses cropping up, traditional "bricks and mortar" businesses developed a significant online presence.

Amazon.com®, one of the oldest e-commerce sites on the Web, did not make a profit for many years. But by persevering through (sometimes-

Secondhand shopping

Websites such as eBay.com, craigslist.com, and i-soldit.com make it easy for people to sell unwanted goods. Some experts predict that the secondary auction industry may eventually change the way people think about what they buy. As it becomes easier to resell items, people may take this factor into consideration when purchasing an item. This trend could lead to temporary ownership of increasingly more goods, with people effectively "leasing" things rather than buying items and later discarding them. And for those items that would have been discarded, websites are popping up that offer freebies, such as Freecycle.com, which is a network built from the philosophy of going green by forming a worldwide gifting movement that reduces waste, saves resources, and eases the burden on landfills. There are even websites that allow consumers to swap old items with other consumers. Sites such as swapaDVD.com, bookmooch.com, and swaptree.com allow consumers to barter with one another to exchange anything from movies and music to books or clothes.

painful) growth spurts, it has emerged as a premiere e-commerce destination for shoppers. eBay®, a popular auction site, allowed anyone to sell their products online, even without an underlying formal business; today, many retailers conduct their transactions purely through the eBay environment. Companies such as PayPal®, which make the process of online purchases much easier by abstracting the buyer's financial details, were also key in the e-commerce success. In fact, eBay purchased PayPal in 2002; like many online sites, eBay uses PayPal exclusively as its electronic payment system.

The evolution of Web-based technologies was a major factor in the success of e-commerce, and the driving force behind some of it. The ability for an online application to provide enhanced user interaction was critical in this growth, as was the development of secure protocols and other factors that permit the secure transfer of electronic funds.

Electronic shopping carts are a key part of the e-commerce process, allowing users to maintain an ongoing collection of items and purchase those items in a single transaction. Many e-commerce sites track a user's purchases and make suggestions for other items that user might find interesting. This is an aspect of e-commerce that is not easily replicated with traditional store purchases.

Another important aspect to the success of e-commerce is the evolution of sellers' understanding of how shoppers shop. That is, the best e-commerce sites now have facilities that allow a user to search for and compare items in various ways. Again, these functional aspects often surpass the user's experience when visiting a physical store.

One of the biggest challenges that remains for e-commerce is the need to ensure security in the financial transactions inherent in the process. Many people still have strong misgivings about conducting business online, but trust in online transactions is growing rapidly. Indeed, the need for computer security is greater than ever.

12.5 Information Security

» Information security The techniques and policies used to ensure proper access to data

Any system used to manage information must address the security of that information to one level or another. Information security is the set of techniques and policies enforced by an organization or individual to ensure proper access to protected data. It makes certain that data cannot be read or modified by anyone without the proper authorization, and that the data will be available when needed to those who do. This is a challenging task to accomplish well.

■ Confidentiality, Integrity, and Availability

Information security can be described as the synthesis of confidentiality, integrity, and availability—the so-called CIA triad, depicted in Figure 12.11. Although these aspects of information security overlap and interact, they define three specific ways to look at the problem. Any good solution to the information security problem must adequately address each of these issues.

Confidentiality is ensuring that key data remains protected from unauthorized access. For example, you don't want just anyone to be able to learn how much money you have in your savings account.

Integrity is ensuring that data can be modified only by appropriate mechanisms. It defines the level of trust you can have in the information. You don't want a hacker to be able to modify your bank balance, of course, but you also don't want a teller (who has authorized access) to modify your balance in inappropriate ways and without your approval. Furthermore, you don't want your balance to be changed by a power surge or compromised during an electronic transmission of the data.

Availability is the degree to which authorized users can access appropriate information for legitimate purposes when needed. Even if the data is protected, it isn't useful if you can't get to it. A hardware problem such as a disk crash can cause an availability problem if precautions aren't taken to back up data and maintain redundant access mechanisms. Also, a hacker could launch a *denial-of-service* (DoS) attack, "flooding" a network with useless transmissions and thereby keeping legitimate users from connecting to remote systems.

From a business point of view, planning for information security requires risk analysis, which is the process of determining which data needs protecting, identifying the risks to that data, and calculating the likelihood that a risk may become reality. Once a risk analysis is complete, plans can be implemented to manage the risks accordingly. A risk is the pairing of a threat and a vulnerability. We want to minimize our vulnerability to threats that put us at the most risk. These threats

> » Confidentiality Ensuring that data is protected from unauthorized access
>
> » Integrity Ensuring that data can be modified only by appropriate mechanisms
>
> » Availability The degree to which authorized users can access information for legitimate purposes
>
> » Risk analysis Determining the nature and likelihood of the risks to key data

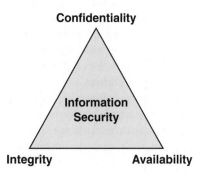

FIGURE 12.11 The CIA triad of information security

can be either malicious, such as a hacker, or accidental, such as a system crash.

Another principle embraced by information security experts is the concept of separating the available data management privileges so that no single individual has the authority to have a significant impact on the system. This principle is often implemented by having redundant checks and/or approvals needed for key activities. For instance, large financial transactions often require a separate authorization process. Administrators should assign to an individual only those privileges needed to carry out his or her job functions.

A variety of technological solutions exist at each layer of a computer system that support the goal of information security. In Chapters 10 and 11, we discussed security issues related to an operating system, such as keeping programs and users from accessing areas of memory that they shouldn't and using protection schemes to control access to particular files. Here we discuss computer security in general, including the common types of attacks a computer system must defend against. Chapter 15 discusses network-related security, such as the use of a *firewall*.

At this point, let's take a look at a technological approach that is particularly pertinent to the security of information: cryptography.

■ Cryptography

> **Cryptography** The field of study related to encoded information

> **Encryption** The process of converting plaintext into ciphertext

> **Decryption** The process of converting ciphertext into plaintext

> **Cipher** An algorithm used to encrypt and decrypt text

> **Key** The set of parameters that guide a cipher

> **Substitution cipher** A cipher that substitutes one character with another

> **Caesar cipher** A substitution cipher that shifts characters a certain number of positions in the alphabet

Cryptography is the field of study related to encoded information. The word *cryptography* comes from the Greek for "secret writing." The basic concepts of cryptography have been used in one form or another for thousands of years to help people keep secrets from falling into the wrong hands.

Encryption is the process of converting ordinary text, referred to as *plaintext* in cryptography terminology, into a form that is unreadable, called *ciphertext*. Decryption reverses this process, translating ciphertext into plaintext. A cipher is an algorithm used to perform a particular type of encryption and decryption. The key to a cipher is the set of particular parameters that guide the algorithm.

You might have played with ciphers of various kinds in the past. Substitution ciphers, as the name implies, substitute one character in the plaintext message with another character. To decode the message, the receiver performs the opposite substitution.

Perhaps the most famous substitution cipher is the Caesar cipher, used by Julius Caesar to communicate with his generals. The Caesar cipher simply shifts the characters of a message by a certain number of positions down the alphabet. For example, shifting the characters five positions to the right would result in the following substitutions:

Original: A B C D E F G H I J K L M N O P Q R S T U V W X Y Z
Substitute: F G H I J K L M N O P Q R S T U V W X Y Z A B C D E

Using this approach, the message "MEET ME AT THE OLD BARN" would be encrypted as

RJJY RJ FY YMJ TQI GFWS

The key to this cipher consists of the number of characters shifted and the direction (right or left). Of course, the space character could be left out of the encrypted version or substituted with another character, and punctuation could be included. Many other variations of substitution ciphers exist as well, such as those in which groups of letters are substituted as a unit, or those that perform different substitutions at different points in the message.

Transposition ciphers rearrange the order of the existing characters in a message in a certain way. For example, a route cipher is a transposition cipher that lays out the message as a grid of characters and specifies a route through the grid to encrypt the information. To encrypt the message "MEET ME AT THE OLD BARN," we could write the letters in columns as follows:

```
M T A H L A
E M T E D R
E E T O B N
```

We could encrypt this message by spiraling inward from the top right of the grid moving clockwise, yielding

ARNBOTEEEMTAHLDETM

After being delivered, the message would be decrypted by recreating the grid and reading the letters down the columns. The key in this cipher is composed of the dimensions of the grid and the route used to encrypt the data. When making the grid, extra characters could be used as placeholders if the number of characters didn't work out perfectly for a particular grid dimension.

Cryptanalysis is the process of "breaking" a cryptographic code. That is, it is the attempt to figure out the plaintext version of a message without knowing the cipher or its key. Older approaches to cryptography such as transposition and substitution ciphers don't pose much of a challenge for modern

» Transposition cipher A cipher that rearranges the order of characters in a message

» Route cipher A transposition cipher that lays out a message in a grid and traverses it in a particular way

» Cryptanalysis The process of decrypting a message without knowing the cipher or key used to encrypt it

Encryption
The debate regarding encryption has been going on for decades. In the 1990s, the FBI began supporting a policy that required citizens to surrender deciphering keys upon request. The government also wanted the ability to gain access to secure information through "back doors," bypassing the need for a deciphering key to access secure data. Privacy advocates protest against such encryption restrictions, arguing that the government's attempt to monitor encryption technology is Orwellian in nature. They also feel that back doors open up secure sites for hackers, and that powerful encryption helps keep confidential information out of the hands of criminals. These days, with more and more people turning to online shopping and telecommuting, online security is essential.

computers. Programs have been written that can fairly easily determine which of these types of encryption methods are used and produce the corresponding plaintext messages. For modern computing, more sophisticated approaches are needed.

Another drawback to these approaches is that both the sender and the receiver must share the cipher key, yet it must be kept secret otherwise. This shared key is a weakness in the process because it must be communicated between the two parties and could be intercepted. If the key is compromised, all future encrypted messages are at risk.

Let's look at a modern approach to cryptography that minimizes these weaknesses. In public-key cryptography, each user has a pair of keys that are related mathematically. This relationship is so complex that a message encrypted with one key can be decrypted only with the corresponding partner key. One key is designated as the *public key*, which can be freely distributed, and the other key is the *private key*.

Suppose two users (say, Alice and Bob) want to communicate securely with each other. Keep in mind that they each have their own public and private key pair. To send a message to Bob, Alice first obtains Bob's public key, which he makes readily available, and uses it to encrypt the message. Now no one—not even Alice—can decrypt the message except Bob. Alice then sends the message safely to Bob, who decrypts it with his private key.

Likewise, Bob sends a message to Alice only after encrypting it with Alice's public key. Alice decrypts the message with her own private key. As long as both Alice and Bob keep their private keys to themselves, it doesn't matter who has their public keys.

Public-key encryption has also given rise to the use of digital signatures, which offer a way to "sign" a document by appending extra data to the message that is both unique to the sender and very difficult to forge. The digital signature allows the recipient to verify that the message truly originates from the stated sender and has not been altered by a third party during transmission. The signature is created using software that compresses the message into a form called a *message digest*, and then encrypts the message digest with the sender's private key. The receiver uses the sender's public key to decrypt the message digest, and then compares it to the digest created from the message itself. If they match, the message is probably genuine and unaltered.

At the heart of public-key encryption is the fact that the public key can be made generally available and be freely distributed. But what if someone else creates a key pair using someone else's name? How can a receiver be sure that a public key is authentic? Organizations are handling this risk by creating a certificate authority center, which creates a digital certificate for each trusted sender. The certificate is made using the sender's personal data and authenticated public key. Then, when a new message arrives, it is verified using that digital certificate. If the message comes from someone for

Public-key cryptography An approach to cryptography in which each user has two related keys, one public and one private

Digital signature Data that is appended to a message, made from the message itself and the sender's private key, to ensure the authenticity of the message

Digital certificate A representation of a sender's authenticated public key used to minimize malicious forgeries

whom you don't have a digital certificate, you then have to decide whether to trust the message.

12.6 Computer Security

Computer security focuses on the availability and correct operation of the computer system.

Access control techniques are often the first things that come to mind when people think of computer security. Access control usually involves forcing users to identify themselves using particular authentication credentials before permitting access to programs and data. A user's privileges are usually restricted to a particular set of functions.

Three general types of authentication credentials are used for access control. The first, and most common, is based on something that the user knows, such as a username and password, a personal identification number (PIN), or a combination of these items. The second type is based on something that the user has, such as an identification card with a magnetic strip or a smart card that contains an embedded memory chip. This approach is more complex to administer, but is generally considered more secure than the first. The third type of authentication credentials is based on biometrics, such as a fingerprint, retina pattern, or voice pattern. This approach is the most expensive to implement and must deal with the problems of false rejection (rejecting an authorized individual) and false acceptance (accepting an unauthorized individual).

> **Authentication credentials** Information users provide to identify themselves for computer access
>
> **Smart card** A card with an embedded memory chip used to identify users and control access
>
> **Biometrics** Using human characteristics such as fingerprints, retina patterns, or voice patterns to identify users and control access
>
> **Malicious code** A computer program that attempts to bypass appropriate authorization and/or perform unauthorized functions

Because authentication using usernames and passwords is very common, it is important that users follow certain guidelines when creating a password. A password should be at least eight characters in length and include a mixture of alphabetic characters (both uppercase and lowercase), numbers, and special characters. The characters should not spell a word in the dictionary, no matter how obscure the word may be. A particular authorization system may force you to obey some of these (or similar) rules when creating your password.

Keeping unauthorized users out of a computer system is fundamental to maintaining the system's safety, but there are other ways to compromise security. Let's look at the types of programs that are written with exactly that purpose in mind, and then at the various ways attacks on a computer system can occur.

■ Malicious Code

Malicious code can be defined as any program code that explicitly attempts to bypass appropriate authorization and/or perform unauthorized functions. Such code is transferred to a computer across a network or from removable media such as memory sticks or floppy disks. Malicious code may cause serious damage, such as the destruction of data, or it may merely create a nuisance, such as popping up unwanted messages.

Computer virus is the term most often used to describe malicious code, even though sometimes the particular offender is a different type of problem. A virus is a program that embeds a copy of itself in another program. This "infected" file is the virus host. When the host is executed, the virus code runs as well.

A worm is self-replicating, like a virus, but does not require a host program to infect. The worm runs as a stand-alone program. A worm tends to cause problems on the networks it uses to send copies of itself to other systems, often by consuming bandwidth. In contrast, a virus tends to cause problems on a particular computer by corrupting or deleting files.

A Trojan horse, as the name implies, is a program that appears to be helpful in some way, but actually causes some kind of problem when executed. Even while the program is running, it may appear to the user as a benevolent resource, which makes it difficult to track down. Like a worm, a Trojan horse is a stand-alone program; like a virus, it tends to cause problems on the computer on which it is executing.

A logic bomb is malicious code that executes when a specific system-oriented event occurs. It is often set to execute on a certain date and time, but it could be triggered by many kinds of events.

■ Security Attacks

A computer system can be attacked in many different ways. Some attacks attempt to gain inappropriate access, others exploit development flaws, and still others rely on the vulnerabilities of digital communication. Let's examine the general characteristics of each type.

Earlier in this section we discussed the importance of picking good passwords and keeping them well guarded. Some attacks perform password guessing by repeatedly trying to log in to a system or application using different passwords. It would be impractical for a human to type in many different passwords, but a computer program can attempt thousands of possibilities each second in a "brute force" fashion. These programs will often try every word in an online dictionary, and combinations of words, and various other character combinations, to see if they can eventually find your password. To partially address this problem, some authentication systems will allow a user to attempt to enter a password only a few times without success, and then will terminate the session.

Instead of guessing a password, other attacks will attempt to trick you into divulging that information willingly. Phishing uses a Web page that looks like an official part of some trusted environment, but is actually a page designed to collect key information such as usernames and passwords. For example, you might receive an email, supposedly from eBay,

» Virus A malicious, self-replicating program that embeds itself into other code

» Worm A malicious stand-alone program that often targets network resources

» Trojan horse A malicious program disguised as a benevolent resource

» Logic bomb A malicious program that is set up to execute when a specific system event occurs

» Password guessing An attempt to gain access to a computer system by methodically trying to determine a user's password

» Phishing Using a Web page to masquerade as part of an authoritative system and trick users into revealing security information

suggesting that there is business you need to take care of and presenting a link for you to follow. The resulting Web page would ask you to log in. Instead of giving you access to your eBay account, however, the page simply transmits that information to a malicious user who will use it to gain inappropriate access to your account. Some of these schemes are very clever and look very official. Beware of any situation in which you are contacted (instead of you initiating the contact) and requested to provide security information.

Both password guessing and phishing are ways for a hacker to "spoof" a computer system. Spoofing, in general, is an attack that allows one user to masquerade as another.

A back door is an aspect of a program that allows special access to a computer system or application, usually granting high levels of functional privileges. A programmer explicitly puts a back door into a system, perhaps for benign testing purposes or perhaps for the unscrupulous intent to bypass the system security at a later point. In either case, a back door is a vulnerability that is deliberately integrated into a program and, therefore, might not raise any security flags. The key to protecting against back door attacks is a high-quality development process, in which careful code reviews by multiple participants minimize such abuses.

The development process can be the source of other security problems as well. A system defect, though unintentional, might allow a clever attacker to exploit the weakness. One such flaw allows a user to create a buffer overflow, which causes a program to crash and could leave the user in a state with increased authority levels—and thus with the ability to do things he or she couldn't do otherwise. A buffer is simply an area of memory of a particular size. If a program attempts to store more information than a buffer can accommodate, a system crash could occur. This problem is another issue related to the quality of the development process. Programmers should carefully guard against the potential for buffer overflows. As a user, you should also make a point of staying current with updates to your programs. Often these updates contain fixes that eliminate potential security risks that eluded the initial quality assurance process during development.

A denial of service (DoS) attack does not directly corrupt data or give inappropriate access. Instead, it renders a system essentially useless by keeping a valid user from being able to access the resource. Usually a DoS attack is network based, caused by flooding a website or other network resource with communication packets that keep it so busy it cannot deal with authorized users. It may even cause the system itself to crash due to the sheer volume of requests for its attention.

Another network-based security problem is called the man-in-the-middle attack. Network communication goes through many locations and devices as it moves from its source to its destination. Usually such communication is passed along as appropriate without a problem. A man-in-the-middle attack

> **Spoofing** An attack on a computer system in which a malicious user masquerades as an authorized user

> **Back door** A program feature that gives special and unauthorized access to a computer system to anyone who knows it exists

> **Buffer overflow** A defect in a computer program that could cause a system to crash and leave the user with heightened privileges

> **Denial of service** An attack on a network resource that prevents authorized users from accessing the system

> **Man-in-the-middle** A security attack in which network communication is intercepted in an attempt to obtain key data

occurs when someone has access to the communication path at some point in the network and "listens," usually with the help of a program, to the traffic as it goes by. The goal is to intercept key information, such as a password being transmitted as part of an email message. The encryption methods discussed in the previous section can guard against these problems. Network security issues are revisited in Chapter 15.

Summary

An information system is application software that allows the user to organize and manage data. General information system software includes spreadsheets and database management systems. Other domain areas, such as artificial intelligence, have their own specific techniques and support for data management.

A spreadsheet is a software application that sets up a grid of cells to organize data and the formulas used to compute new values. Cells are referenced by their row and column designations, such as A5 or B7. Formulas usually refer to the values in other cells and may rely on built-in functions to compute their result. In addition, formulas may use data across a range of cells. When a formula is stored in a spreadsheet cell, the value computed by the formula is actually shown in the cell. It is important that formulas in a spreadsheet avoid circular references, in which two or more cells rely on one another to compute their results.

Spreadsheets are both versatile and extensible. They can be used in many different situations, and they respond dynamically to change. As values in the spreadsheet change, affected formulas are automatically recalculated to produce updated results. If spreadsheet rows or columns are added, the ranges in spreadsheet formulas are adjusted immediately. Spreadsheets are particularly appropriate for what-if analysis, in which assumptions are modified to see their effect on the rest of the system.

A database management system includes the physical files in which the data are stored, the software that supports access to and modification of that data, and the database schema that specifies the logical layout of the database. The relational model is the most popular database approach today. It is based on organizing data into tables of records (or objects) with particular fields (or attributes). A key field, whose value uniquely identifies individual records in the table, is usually designated for each table.

Relationships among database elements are represented in new tables that may have their own attributes. Relationship tables do not duplicate data in other tables. Instead they store the key values of the appropriate database records so that the detailed data can be looked up when needed.

The Structured Query Language (SQL) is the language used for querying and manipulating relational databases. The select statement is used to formulate queries and has many variations so that particular data can be accessed from the database. Other SQL statements allow data to be added, updated, and deleted from a database.

A database should be carefully designed. Entity-relationship modeling, with its associated ER diagrams, is a popular technique for database design. ER diagrams graphically depict the relationships among database objects and show their attributes and cardinality constraints.

E-commerce is the process of buying and selling services over the Internet. As e-commerce has become increasingly more popular, more stringent security measures have had to be employed to ensure the integrity of sales over the Internet.

Security of information has become a major problem. It is important that the data entered be accurate, that people who have a right to access the information can do so, and that unauthorized access be prevented.

Computer security focuses on the correct operation of a computer system without regard to the information.

ETHICAL ISSUES ▸ Big Brother in the Workplace

Many people don't know that the same privacy rights they enjoy at home or in the marketplace do not extend to the workplace. Employees think conversations around the water cooler or on the phone at work are private. Usually, they're wrong. While they may know how to secure their Internet connections and phones at home, there is little they can do to provide themselves with the same privacy at work. An increasing number of employers are now using technology to monitor the workplace. Keystroke programs can gather and record every keystroke typed on a computer. Phones can be monitored and calls recorded. Some employers have installed cameras and audio devices that record conversations. There is even software that triggers a video scan of a cubicle if the keyboard has been idle for a certain length of time.

A 2005 survey reported that 76% of employers used technology to watch, listen in, and access email and computer files. Some 65% of companies used software to block connections to inappropriate websites—a 27% increase since 2001. The number of employers

that monitored the amount of time employees spent on the phone and tracked the numbers called also increased from 9% in 2001 to 51% in 2005.

Advocates of these practices hail these results as good news. The computers, phones, and physical space belong to the employer, after all, and are provided to the employees for use in their jobs. After discovering workers surfing the Internet, downloading pornography, and using email to harass others or chat with friends, businesses realized that the same technology that allows such behavior can be used to monitor how employees are spending their time. Employee Internet monitoring (EIM) has become big business. For example, a convenience store chain installed audio-equipped cameras to cut down on employee theft; the cameras are controlled from a central location so employees never know when they're being watched. Even municipalities are finding uses for surveillance technology. A neighborhood in Cincinnati has installed a Webcam in an area frequented by drug dealers and prostitutes. Residents claim that illegal activity has

» continued

ETHICAL ISSUES ▸ Big Brother in the Workplace, continued

fallen sharply on the four street corners that fall under the camera's eye.

Privacy advocates say the trend has gone too far. Approximately 26% of the employers surveyed in 2005 had fired workers for misuse of the Internet, while 25% had fired employees for email misuse; 6% of employers had even fired workers for misuse of the office phone.

Opponents of the monitoring technologies point out that people are not machines. They must take breaks and feel that they have some control over their environment to be productive, satisfied employees. Knowing that personal phone calls, hallway conversations, and email are monitored injects feeling of resent and apathy into the workplace. Who wants Big Brother for an office mate?

More than 80% of employers disclose their monitoring practices to their employees. However, relying on management fairness does not ease the qualms some feel about the practice of workplace monitoring. If only business-related emails can be accessed, someone still has to read the message to make the determination. The same is true of recorded phone calls and non-business-related conversations. Among the safeguards called for by privacy advocates are federal regulations, notification and training of employees on the various monitoring methods used, and limits of monitoring to cases where employers have cause to be suspicious of an employee. Up to now, lawmakers have chosen not to intervene. They point to the very real considerations of company security and the right of employers to monitor what goes on at the workplace. As technology continues to be used in new ways, the issues may perhaps become clearer.

Key Terms

Authentication credentials
Availability
Back door
Biometrics
Buffer overflow
Caesar cipher
Cardinality constraint
Cell
Cipher
Circular reference
Confidentiality
Cryptanalysis
Cryptography
Database
Database management system
Decryption
Denial of service
Digital certificate
Digital signature
Electronic commerce
Encryption
Entity-relationship (ER) modeling

ER diagram
Field (or attribute)
Information security
Information system
Integrity
Key (database)
Key (encryption)
Logic bomb
Malicious code
Man-in-the-middle
Password guessing
Phishing
Public-key cryptography
Query
Range
Record (or object, or entity)
Relational model
Risk analysis
Route cipher
Schema
Smart card
Spoofing

Spreadsheet
Spreadsheet function
Structured Query Language (SQL)
Substitution cipher
Table

Transposition cipher
Trojan horse
Virus
What-if analysis
Worm

⌘   **Exercises**

For Exercises 1–31, mark the answers true or false as follows:

A. True
B. False

1. A cell in a spreadsheet can contain only raw data.

2. The values in a spreadsheet can be formatted in a variety of ways.

3. A spreadsheet should be set up so that changes to the data are automatically reflected in any cells affected by that data.

4. A spreadsheet function is a program that the user writes to compute a value.

5. A range of cells can be specified that go horizontally or vertically, but not both.

6. A circular reference in a spreadsheet is a powerful and useful tool.

7. A spreadsheet is useful for performing what-if analysis.

8. What-if analysis can affect only one value at a time in a spreadsheet.

9. A database engine is software that supports access to the database contents.

10. The physical database represents the logical structure of the data in the database.

11. A query is a request to a database for information.

12. The results of a query can be structured in many ways.

13. The hierarchical model is the most popular database management model today.

14. A database table is a collection of records, and a record is a collection of fields.

15. The values in the key fields of a table uniquely identify a record among all other records in the table.

16. A database engine often interacts with a particular language for accessing and modifying the database.

17. An entity-relationship (ER) diagram represents primary database elements in a graphical form.

18. The cardinality of a relationship puts restrictions on the number of relationships that can exist at one time.

19. E-commerce is the process of keeping financial records, such as accounts payable, online.

20. The dot-com collapse promoted electronic commerce.

21. Information integrity ensures that data can be modified only by the appropriate mechanisms.

22. Pairing threats with vulnerabilities is a part of risk analysis.

23. Decryption is the process of converting plaintext into ciphertext.

24. A transposition cipher is an example of modern cryptography that is difficult for a computer to break.

25. A digital signature allows the recipient to verify that the message truly originates from the stated sender.

26. Using biometrics is one of the most expensive ways to collect authentication credentials.

27. A computer virus "infects" another program by embedding itself into that program.

28. A logic bomb is set to go off when a particular system event occurs, such as a particular date and time.

29. Phishing is a form of password guessing.

30. A back door threat is implemented by a programmer of the system under attack.

31. A denial-of-service attack does not directly corrupt data.

For Exercises 32–36, match the solution to the question.

A. dynamic	D. range
B. function	E. schema
C. circular	F. field

32. A spreadsheet is ____ in that it responds to changes in the data by immediately updating all affected values.

33. A spreadsheet formula may operate on a ____ of cells, such as C4..C18.

34. The database ____ is the specification of the logical structure of the data in the database.

35. A ____ reference occurs when the result of one formula is ultimately based on another, and vice versa.

36. A _____ contains a single data value.

Exercises 37–87 are problems or short-answer questions.

Use the following spreadsheet containing student grades for Exercises 37–45.

	A	B	C	D	E	F	G	H
1					Grades			
2				Exam 1	Exam 2	Exam 3	Average	
3								
4			Bill	89	33	80	67.3333	
5			Bob	90	50	75	71.6666	
6			Chris	66	60	70	65.3333	
7			Jim	50	75	77	67.3333	
8		Students	Judy	80	80	80	80	
9			June	83	84	85	84	
10			Mari	87	89	90	88.6666	
11			Mary	99	98	90	95.6666	
12			Phil	89	90	85	88	
13			Sarah	75	90	85	83.3333	
14			Suzy	86	90	95	90	
15		Total		893	839	912	881.333	
16		Average		81.1818	76.2727	82.9090	80.1212	

37. Specify the grades for Exam 2.
38. Specify the average for Exam 1.
39. Specify the average for Sarah.
40. Specify the third exam grade for Mari.
41. Specify the exam grades for Susy.
42. What formula is stored in F15?
43. D16 contains the formula D15/COUNT(D4..D14). What is another formula that would yield the same value?
44. What formula is stored in E13?
45. Which values would change if Phil's Exam 2 score was corrected to 87?
46. What is a spreadsheet circular reference? Why is it a problem?

47. Give a specific example of an indirect circular reference similar to the one shown in Figure 12.5.

48. What is what-if analysis?

49. Name some what-if analysis questions that you might ask if you were using a spreadsheet to plan and track some stock purchases. Explain how you might set up a spreadsheet to help answer those questions.

For Exercises 50–53, use the paper spreadsheet form supplied on the textbook's website or use an actual spreadsheet application program to design the spreadsheets. Your instructor may provide more specific instructions regarding these questions.

50. Design a spreadsheet to track the statistics of your favorite major league baseball team. Include data regarding runs, hits, errors, and runs batted in (RBIs). Compute appropriate statistics for individual players and the team as a whole.

51. Design a spreadsheet to maintain a grade sheet for a set of students. Include tests and projects, giving various weights to each in the calculation of the final grade for each student. Compute the average grade per test and project for the whole class.

52. Assume you are going on a business trip. Design a spreadsheet to keep track of your expenses and create a summary of your totals. Include various aspects of travel such as car mileage, flight costs, hotel costs, and miscellaneous expenses (such as taxis and tips).

53. Design a spreadsheet to estimate and then keep track of a particular project's activities. List the activities, the estimated and actual dates for those activities, and schedule slippage or gain. Add other data as appropriate for your project.

54. Compare a database with a database management system.

55. What is a database schema?

56. Describe the general organization of a relational database.

57. What is a field (attribute) in a database?

58. Which other fields (attributes) might we include in the database table of Figure 12.7?

59. Which other fields (attributes) might we include in the database table of Figure 12.8?

60. What is a key in a relational database table?

61. Specify the schema for the database table of Figure 12.8.

62. How are relationships represented in a relational database?

63. Define an SQL query that returns all attributes of all records in the Customer table.

64. Define an SQL query that returns the Movield number and title of all movies that have an R rating.

65. Define an SQL query that returns the address of every customer in the Customer table who lives on Lois Lane.

66. Define an SQL statement that inserts the movie *Armageddon* into the Movie table.

67. Define an SQL statement that changes the address of Amy Stevens in the Customer table.

68. Define an SQL statement that deletes the customer with a Customerld of 103.

69. What is an ER diagram?

70. How are entities and relationships represented in an ER diagram?

71. How are attributes represented in an ER diagram?

72. What are cardinality constraints, and how are they shown in ER diagrams?

73. What are the three general cardinality constraints?

74. Design a database that stores data about the books in a library, the students who use them, and the ability to check out books for a period of time. Create an ER diagram and sample tables.

75. Design a database that stores data about the courses taught at a university, the professors who teach those courses, and the students who take those courses. Create an ER diagram and sample tables.

76. What were some of the Web-based technologies that allowed e-commerce to become viable?

77. What is the CIA triad of information security?

78. Other than those presented in this chapter, give three examples of data integrity violations.

79. Using a Caesar cipher, shifting three letters to the right, encrypt the message "WE ESCAPE TONIGHT."

80. Using the Caesar cipher described in this chapter, decrypt the message "WJNSKTWHJRJSYX FWWNAJ RTSIFD."

81. Using the same transposition cipher technique used in this chapter, encrypt the message "WHO IS THE TRAITOR."

82. Describe how Claire would send a message to David using public-key encryption.

83. What are the three general approaches to presenting authorization credentials?

84. Describe how a Trojan horse attacks a computer system.

85. Describe a hypothetical scenario, other than the one described in this chapter, of a phishing attack.

86. How might a buffer overflow make a computer system vulnerable?

87. How does a man-in-the-middle attack work?

??? Thought Questions

1. Other than the examples given in this chapter, think of five situations for which you might set up a spreadsheet.

2. Other than the examples given in this chapter, think of five situations for which you might set up a database.

3. Does the use of computerized databases mean that we can do away with paper files? What sorts of paper files might still be needed?

4. What is encryption, and how does it relate to you as a student?

5. The word "hacker" used to be complimentary, describing a programmer who buried his or her head in the code, only coming up for air in the morning. A hacker would write very sophisticated programs almost overnight. Now the term has come to refer to someone with malicious intent. What connotations does the word have for you?

6. Before computers, water-cooler conversations were thought to be private. How has computer technology changed this assumption?

7. How do the rights of employees collide with privacy rights in the workplace?

The Applications Layer

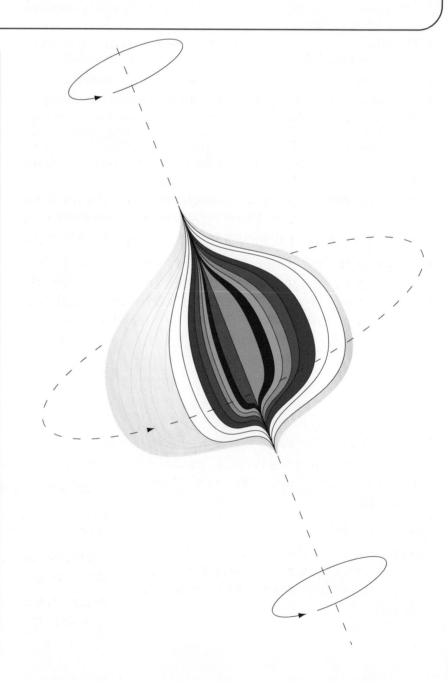

Artificial Intelligence

13

The subdiscipline of computing called artificial intelligence (AI) is important in many ways. To many people it represents the future of computing—the evolution of a machine to make it more like a human. To others it is an avenue for applying new and different technologies to problem solving.

The term *artificial intelligence* probably conjures up various images in your mind, such as a computer playing chess or a robot doing household chores. These are certainly aspects of AI, but it goes far beyond that. AI techniques affect the way we develop many types of application programs, from the mundane to the fantastic. The world of artificial intelligence opens doors that no other aspect of computing does. Its role in the development of state-of-the-art application programs is crucial.

Goals

After studying this chapter, you should be able to:

- distinguish between the types of problems that humans do best and those that computers do best.

- explain the Turing test.

- define what is meant by knowledge representation and demonstrate how knowledge is represented in a semantic network.

- develop a search tree for simple scenarios.

- explain the processing of an expert system.

- explain the processing of biological and artificial neural networks.

- list the various aspects of natural language processing.

- explain the types of ambiguities in natural language comprehension.

13.1 Thinking Machines

Computers are amazing devices. They can draw complex three-dimensional images, process the payroll of an entire corporation, and determine whether the bridge you're building will stand up to the pressure of the traffic expected. Yet they have trouble understanding a simple conversation and might not be able to distinguish between a table and a chair.

Certainly a computer can do some things better than a human can. For example, if you are given the task of adding 1000 four-digit numbers together using pencil and paper, you could do it. But the task would take you quite a long time, and you might very likely make an error while performing the calculations. A computer could perform the same calculation in a fraction of a second without error.

However, if you are asked to point out the cat in the picture shown in Figure 13.1, you could do it without hesitation. A computer, by contrast, would have difficulty making that identification and might very well get it

FIGURE 13.1 A computer might have trouble identifying the cat in this picture. *Courtesy of Amy Rose*

wrong. Humans bring a great deal of knowledge and reasoning capability to these types of problems; we are still struggling with ways to perform human-like reasoning using a computer.

In our modern state of technology, computers are good at computation, but less adept at things that require intelligence. The field of artificial intelligence (AI) is the study of computer systems that attempt to model and apply the intelligence of the human mind.

■ The Turing Test

In 1950, English mathematician Alan Turing wrote a landmark paper that asked the question: Can machines think? After carefully defining terms such as "intelligence" and "thinking," he ultimately concluded that we would eventually be able to create a computer that thinks. But then he asked another question: How will we know when we've succeeded?

His answer to that question came to be called the Turing test, which is used to empirically determine whether a computer has achieved intelligence. The test is based on whether a computer could fool a human into believing that the computer is another human.

Variations on Turing tests have been defined over the years, but we focus on the basic concept here. The test is set up as follows: A human interrogator sits in a room and uses a computer terminal to communicate with two respondents, A and B. The interrogator knows that one respondent is human and the other is a computer, but doesn't know which is which. (See Figure 13.2.) After holding conversations with both A and B, the interrogator must decide which respondent is the computer. This procedure is repeated with numerous human subjects. The premise is that if the computer could fool enough interrogators, then it could be considered intelligent.

Some people argue that the Turing test is a good test for intelligence because it requires that a computer possess a wide range of knowledge and have the flexibility necessary to deal with changes in conversation. To fool a human interrogator, the knowledge required by the computer goes beyond facts; it includes an awareness of human behavior and emotions.

Others argue that the Turing test doesn't really demonstrate that a computer understands language discourse, which is necessary for true intelligence. They suggest that a program could simulate language comprehension, perhaps enough to pass the Turing test, but that alone does not make the computer intelligent.

A computer that passes the Turing test would demonstrate weak equivalence, meaning that the two systems (human and computer) are equivalent in results (output) but do not arrive at those results in the same way. Strong equivalence indicates that two systems use the same internal

> ⟩⟩ **Artificial intelligence (AI)** The study of computer systems that model and apply the intelligence of the human mind

> ⟩⟩ **Turing test** A behavioral approach to determining whether a computer system is intelligent

> ⟩⟩ **Weak equivalence** The equality of two systems based on their results

> ⟩⟩ **Strong equivalence** The equality of two systems based on their results and the process by which they arrive at those results

FIGURE 13.2 In a Turing test, the interrogator must determine which respondent is the computer and which is the human

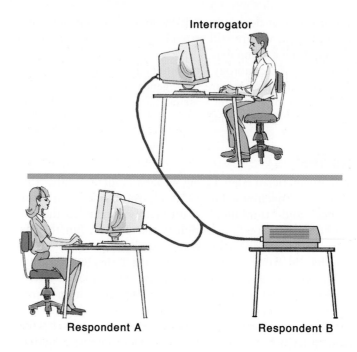

Interrogator

Respondent A

Respondent B

processes to produce results. Some AI researchers assert that true artificial intelligence will not exist until we have achieved strong equivalence—that is, until we create a machine that processes information as the human mind does.

New York philanthropist Hugh Loebner organized the first formal instantiation of the Turing test. This competition has been run annually since 1991. A grand prize of $100,000 and a solid gold medal will be awarded for the first computer whose responses are indistinguishable from a human's. So far the grand prize remains up for grabs. A prize of $2000 and a bronze medal is awarded each year for the computer that is determined to be the most human-like, relative to the rest of the competition that year. The Loebner prize contest has become an important annual event for computing enthusiasts interested in artificial intelligence.

Various programs, often referred to as chatbots, have been developed to perform this kind of conversational interaction between a computer and a person. Many are available through the World Wide Web and focus on a particular topic. Depending on how well they are designed, these programs can carry on a reasonable conversation. In most cases, though, it doesn't take long for the user to discover awkward moments in the conversation that betray the fact that a human mind is not determining the responses.

>> Loebner prize The first formal instantiation of the Turing test, held annually

>> Chatbot A program designed to carry on a conversation with a human user

■ Aspects of AI

The field of artificial intelligence has many branches. Our overall goal in this chapter is to give you some insight into the primary issues involved and the challenges yet to be overcome. In the remaining sections of this chapter, we explore the following issues in the world of AI:

- Knowledge representation—the techniques used to represent knowledge so that a computer system can apply it to intelligent problem solving
- Expert systems—computer systems that embody the knowledge of human experts
- Neural networks—computer systems that mimic the processing of the human brain
- Natural language processing—the challenge of processing languages that humans use to communicate
- Robotics—the study of robots

13.2 Knowledge Representation

The knowledge we need to represent an object or event varies based on the situation. Depending on the problem we are trying to solve, we need specific information. For example, if we are trying to analyze family relationships, it's important to know that Fred is Cathy's father, but not that Fred is a plumber or that Cathy owns a pickup truck. Furthermore, not only do we need particular information, but we also need it in a form that allows us to search and process that information efficiently.

There are many ways to represent knowledge. For example, we could describe it in natural language. That is, we could write an English paragraph describing, for instance, a student and the ways in which the student relates to the world. However, although natural language is very descriptive, it doesn't lend itself to efficient processing. Alternatively, we could formalize the language, by describing a student using an almost mathematical notation. This formalization lends itself to more rigorous computer processing, but it is difficult to learn and use correctly.

In general, we want to create a logical view of the data, independent of its actual underlying implementation, so that it can be processed in specific ways. In the world of artificial intelligence, the information we want to capture often leads to new and interesting data representations. We want to capture not only facts, but also relationships. The kind of problem we are trying to solve may dictate the structure we impose on the data.

As specific problem areas have been investigated, new techniques for representing knowledge have been developed. We examine two in this section: semantic networks and search trees.

Herbert A. Simon

Herbert A. Simon was a Renaissance man of our generation. His home pages included sections on Computer Science, Psychology, and Philosophy, yet his PhD was in Political Science and his Nobel Prize was in economics.

Simon was born in Milwaukee in 1916. His father was an engineer who became a patent attorney, and his mother was an accomplished pianist. Simon received his undergraduate degree in 1936 from the University of Chicago and worked for several years

Courtesy of Carnegie Mellon University

as an editor and administrator. He completed his PhD in political science at the University of Chicago in 1943 and then began a 58-year academic career, the last 52 years of which were at Carnegie Mellon.

In 1955, Simon, Allen Newell, and J. C. Shaw (a programmer) created Logic Theorist, a program that could discover geometric theorem proofs. At about the same time, Simon was working with E. A. Feigenbaum on EPAM, a program that modeled their theory of human perception and memory. These programs and the subsequent series of papers on the simulation of human thinking, problem solving, and verbal learning marked the beginning of the field of artificial intelligence. In 1988, Simon and Newell received the Turing Award of the Association for

Computing Machinery for their work in human problem solving. In 1995, Simon received the Research Excellence Award of the International Joint Conference on Artificial Intelligence.

Simon's interest in information processing and decision making led him to develop his economic theory of "bounded rationality," for which he received the 1978 Nobel Prize in economics. Classical economics had argued that people make rational choices so as to get the best item at the best price. Simon reasoned that determining the "best" choice was impossible because there are too many choices and too little time to analyze them. Instead, he argued, people choose the first option that is good enough to meet their needs. His Nobel Prize citation read "for his pioneering research into the decision-making process within economic organizations."

Simon remained extraordinarily productive throughout his long career. His bibliography contains 173 entries before 1960, 168 in the 1960s, 154 in the 1970s, 207 in the 1980s, and 236 in the 1990s. Outside of his professional life, Simon enjoyed playing the piano, especially with friends who played violin, viola, and other instruments. He died in February 2001, having continued his research and interactions with students until just a few weeks before his death.

■ Semantic Networks

>> Semantic network A knowledge representation technique that represents the relationships among objects

A semantic network is a knowledge representation technique that focuses on the relationships between objects. A directed graph is used to represent a semantic network or net. The nodes of the graph represent objects, and the arrows between nodes represent relationships. The arrows are labeled to indicate the types of relationships that exist.

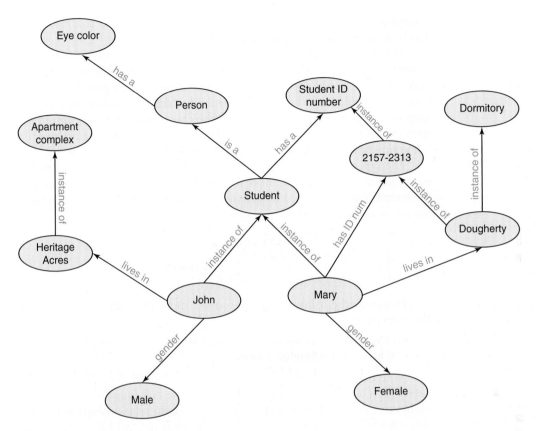

FIGURE 13.3 A semantic network

Semantic nets borrow many object-oriented concepts, which were discussed in Chapters 9, including inheritance and instantiation. An inheritance relationship indicates that one object *is-a* more specific version of another object. Instantiation is the relationship between an actual object and something that describes it (like a class).

Examine the semantic network shown in Figure 13.3. It has several *is-a* relationships and several *instance-of* relationships. But it also has several other types of relationships, such as *lives-in* (John lives in Heritage Acres). There are essentially no restrictions on the types of relationships that can be modeled in a semantic network.

Many more relationships could be represented in this semantic net. For instance, we could have indicated that any person is either left- or right-handed, that John owns a car that is a Honda, or that every student has a grade-point average. The relationships that we represent are completely our choice, based on the information we need to answer the kinds of questions that we will face.

The way in which we establish the relationships can vary as well. For example, instead of showing that individual students live in particular dwellings, we could show that dwellings house certain people. In other words, we could turn those arrows around, changing the *lives-in* relationship to a *houses* relationship. Again, the choice is ours as we design the network. Which approach best describes the kind of issues we address? In some situations we may choose to represent both relationships.

The types of relationships represented determine which questions are easily answered, which are more difficult to answer, and which cannot be answered. For example, the semantic net in Figure 13.3 makes it fairly simple to answer the following questions:

- Is Mary a student?
- What is the gender of John?
- Does Mary live in a dorm or an apartment?
- What is Mary's student ID number?

However, the following questions are more difficult to answer with this network:

- How many students are female and how many are male?
- Who lives in Dougherty Hall?

Note that the information to answer these questions is present in the network; it's just not as easy to process. These last questions require the ability to easily find all students, and there are no relationships that make this information easy to obtain. This network is designed more for representing the relationships that individual students have to the world at large.

This network cannot be used to answer the following questions, because the knowledge required is simply not represented:

- What kind of car does John drive?
- What color are Mary's eyes?

We know that Mary has an eye color, because she is a student, all students are people, and all people have a particular eye color. We just don't know what Mary's particular eye color is, given the information stored in this network.

A semantic network is a powerful, versatile way to represent a lot of information. The challenge is to model the right relationships and to populate (fill in) the network with accurate and complete data.

■ Search Trees

In Chapter 8, we mentioned the use of tree structures to organize data. Such structures play an important role in artificial intelligence. For example, we can use a tree to represent possible alternatives in adversarial situations, such as game playing.

A `search tree` is a structure that represents all possible moves in a game, for both you and your opponent. You can create a game program that maximizes its chances to win. In some cases it may even be able to guarantee a win.

In search trees, the paths down a tree represent the series of decisions made by the players. A decision made at one level dictates the options left to the next player. Each node of the tree represents a move based on all other moves that have occurred thus far in the game.

Let's define a simplified variation of a game called Nim to use as an example. In our version, there are a certain number of spaces in a row. The first player may place one, two, or three Xs in the leftmost spaces. The second player may then place one, two, or three Os immediately adjacent to the Xs. Play continues back and forth. The goal is to place your mark in the last (rightmost) space.

> **Search tree** A structure that represents alternatives in adversarial situations, such as game playing

Here is an example of a play of our version of Nim using nine spaces:

```
Initial:     _ _ _ _ _ _ _ _ _
Player 1:    X X X _ _ _ _ _ _
Player 2:    X X X O _ _ _ _ _
Player 1:    X X X O X _ _ _ _
Player 2:    X X X O X O O _ _
Player 1:    X X X O X O O X X      Player 1 wins.
```

The search tree in Figure 13.4 shows all possible moves in our version of the game using only five spaces (rather than the nine spaces used in the preceding example). At the root of the tree, all spaces are initially empty. The next level shows the three options the first player has (to place one, two, or three Xs). At the third level, the tree shows all options that Player 2 has, given the move that Player 1 already made.

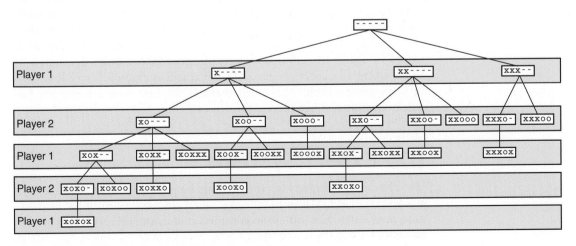

FIGURE 13.4 A search tree for a simplified version of Nim

Note that when a large number of marks are made in one turn, fewer options may be available to the next player, and the paths down the tree tend to be shorter. Follow the various paths down from the root, noting the different options taken by each player. Every single option in our simplified game is represented in this tree.

We've deliberately simplified the game of Nim so that we can show a simple search tree. The real game of Nim has some important differences—for example, there are multiple rows, and items are removed instead of added. However, even our simplified version demonstrates several interesting mathematical ideas.

The concepts of search tree analysis can be applied nicely to other, more complicated games such as chess. In such complex games the search trees are far more complicated, having many more nodes and paths. Think about all the possible moves you might initially make in a chess game. Then consider all possible moves your opponent might make in response. A full chess search tree contains all possible moves at each level, given the current status of the board. Because these trees are so large, only a fraction of the tree can be analyzed in a reasonable time limit, even with modern computing power.

As machines have become faster, more of the search tree can be analyzed, but still not all of the branches. Programmers have come up with ways to "prune" the search trees, eliminating paths that no human player would consider reasonable. Even so, the trees are too large to completely analyze for each move.

This leaves us with a question: Do we choose a depth-first approach, analyzing selective paths all the way down the tree that we hope will result in successful moves? Or do we choose a breadth-first approach, analyzing all possible paths but only for a short distance down the tree? Both approaches, shown in Figure 13.5, may miss key possibilities. While this issue has been debated among AI programmers for many years, a breadth-first approach tends to yield the best results. It seems that it's better to make consistently error-free conservative moves than to occasionally make spectacular moves.

Programs that play chess at the master level have become commonplace. In 1997, the computer chess program Deep Blue, developed by IBM® using an expert system, defeated world champion Garry Kasparov in a six-game match. This event marked the first time a computer had defeated a human champion at master-level play.

>> Depth-first approach
Searching down the paths of a tree prior to searching across levels

>> Breadth-first approach
Searching across levels of a tree prior to searching down specific paths

13.3 Expert Systems

We often rely on experts for their unique knowledge and understanding of a particular field. We go to a doctor when we have a health problem, an auto mechanic when our car won't start, and an engineer when we need to build something.

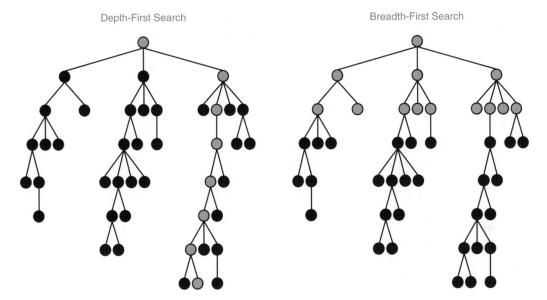

FIGURE 13.5 Depth-first and breadth-first searches

A **knowledge-based system** is a software system that embodies and uses a specific set of information (organized data) from which it extracts and processes particular pieces. The terms **expert system** and "knowledge-based system" are often used interchangeably, although expert systems usually embody the knowledge of a specialized field, modeling the expertise of a professional in that field. A user consults an expert system when confronted with a particular problem, and the system uses its expertise to advise the user how to proceed.

An expert system uses a set of rules to guide its processing, so it is called a **rule-based system**. The set of rules in an expert system is referred to as its knowledge base. The **inference engine** is the part of the software that determines how the rules are followed and, therefore, which conclusions can be drawn.

A doctor is the living equivalent of an expert system. He or she gathers data by asking you questions and running tests. Your initial answers and the test results may lead to more questions and more tests. The rules embodied by the doctor's knowledge allow him or her to know which questions to ask next. The doctor then uses the information to rule out various possibilities and eventually narrows the alternatives to a specific diagnosis. Once the problem is identified, that specific knowledge allows the doctor to suggest the appropriate treatment.

Let's walk through an example of expert-system processing. Suppose you wanted to answer this question: What type of treatment should I put on my lawn?

>> **Knowledge-based system** Software that uses a specific set of information

>> **Expert system** A software system based on the knowledge of human experts

>> **Rule-based system** A software system based on a set of *if-then* rules

>> **Inference engine** The software that processes rules to draw conclusions

An expert system that embodies the knowledge of a gardener would be able to guide you in this decision. Let's define a few variables so that we can abbreviate the rules in our gardening system:

NONE—apply no treatment at this time
TURF—apply a turf-building treatment
WEED—apply a weed-killing treatment
BUG—apply a bug-killing treatment
FEED—apply a basic fertilizer treatment
WEEDFEED—apply a weed-killing and fertilizer combination treatment

These values represent various conclusions that the expert system might draw after analyzing the situation. The following Boolean variables represent the current state of the lawn:

BARE—the lawn has large, bare areas
SPARSE—the lawn is generally thin
WEEDS—the lawn contains many weeds
BUGS—the lawn shows evidence of bugs

We assume that initially the system has no direct data regarding the status of the lawn. The user would have to be questioned to determine, for instance, if the lawn has large, bare areas. Other data may be available directly to the system through some calculation or in some type of database:

LAST—the last date a lawn treatment was applied
CURRENT—the current date
SEASON—the current season

Now we can formulate some rules that our system can use to draw a conclusion. Rules take the form of *if-then* statements.

if (CURRENT - LAST < 30) then NONE
if (SEASON = winter) then not BUGS
if (BARE) then TURF
if (SPARSE and not WEEDS) then FEED
if (BUGS and not SPARSE) then BUG
if (WEEDS and not SPARSE) then WEED
if (WEEDS and SPARSE) then WEEDFEED

Note that this is only a sample of the types of rules that may exist in such a system. Real expert systems may incorporate thousands of rules to help analyze a situation. The rules presented here do not cover all situations, even in our small example.

When executed, the inference engine selects a rule to determine whether it is applicable. That determination may be made only by ques-

> ### ? LISP is the language for AI
> LISP (*LISt* Processor) is one of the most popular programming languages for AI. John McCarthy created LISP for programming AI applications in the late 1950s. LISP's essential data structure is an ordered sequence of elements called a *list*. The elements in this list may be indivisible entities or they may be other lists. A list can be used to represent an almost limitless number of things, from expert rules to computer programs to thought processes to system components. To make decisions, LISP programs rely on recursion rather than looping. LISP and its dialects belong to the functional paradigm of languages.[1] LISP even has its own wiki; Cliki is a wiki that provides common LISP information.

tioning the user. If it is applicable, that rule may affect the applicability of other rules. The inference engine continues to apply rules until no applicable rules remain. Don't think of the rules as being a linear path (followed in sequence); instead, the inference engine applies whichever rules it can and continually loops until it reaches a conclusion.

An execution of our inference engine may result in the following interaction:

System: Does the lawn have large, bare areas?

User: No

System: Does the lawn show evidence of bugs?

User: No

System: Is the lawn generally thin?

User: Yes

System: Does the lawn contain significant weeds?

User: Yes

System: You should apply a weed-killing and fertilizer combination treatment.

Note that the system doesn't ask about things it can look up, such as the date of the last treatment. And apparently our scenario didn't take place in winter, because the system asked about a potential bug problem. If it had been winter, the bug issue would have already been eliminated.

An expert system has many advantages over other advising techniques. First, it is goal oriented: It doesn't focus on abstract or theoretical information, but rather focuses on solving a specific problem. Second, it is efficient: It records previous responses and doesn't ask irrelevant questions. Third, a real expert system, through a carefully constructed set of rules, can usually provide useful guidance even if you don't know the answers to some questions.

?

Is there a PKC in the house?
The Problem Knowledge Coupler (PKC) Corporation (www.pkc.org) has developed an expert system for medical diagnosis across the Internet. Users are led through a series of questions about themselves, their health, and their medical history. The questions collect relevant information about specific medical conditions. PKC has a staff of 25 full-time medical researchers who comb through the latest medical literature to write Coupler questions and match patient information with the latest medical information to produce patient-specific advice, including potential causes, treatments, and management strategies.

13.4 Neural Networks

As mentioned earlier, some artificial intelligence researchers focus on how the human brain actually works and try to construct computing devices that work in similar ways. An artificial neural network in a computer attempts to mimic the actions of the neural networks of the human body. Let's first look at how a biological neural network works.

》 **Artificial neural network**
A computer representation of knowledge that attempts to mimic the neural networks of the human body

■ Biological Neural Networks

A neuron is a single cell that conducts a chemically based electronic signal. The human brain contains billions of neurons connected into a network.

At any point in time a neuron is in either an *excited* state or an *inhibited* state. An excited neuron conducts a strong signal; an inhibited neuron conducts a weak signal. A series of connected neurons forms a pathway. The signal along a particular pathway is strengthened or weakened according to the state of the neurons it passes through. A series of excited neurons creates a strong pathway.

A biological neuron has multiple input tentacles called *dendrites* and one primary output tentacle called an *axon*. The dendrites of one neuron pick up the signals from the axons of other neurons to form the neural network. The gap between an axon and a dendrite is called a *synapse*. (See Figure 13.6.) The chemical composition of a synapse tempers the strength of its input signal. The output of a neuron on its axon is a function of all of its input signals.

A neuron accepts multiple input signals and then controls the contribution of each signal based on the "importance" the corresponding synapse assigns to it. If enough of these weighted input signals are strong, the neuron enters an excited state and produces a strong output signal. If enough of the input signals are weak or are weakened by the weighting factor of that signal's synapse, the neuron enters an inhibited state and produces a weak output signal.

Neurons fire, or pulsate, up to 1000 times per second, so the pathways along the neural nets are in a constant state of flux. The activity of our brain causes some pathways to strengthen and others to weaken. As we learn new things, new strong neural pathways form in our brain.

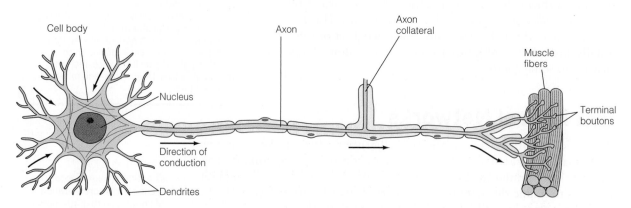

FIGURE 13.6 A biological neuron

Artificial Neural Networks

Each processing element in an artificial neural network is analogous to a biological neuron. An element accepts a certain number of input values and produces a single output value of either 0 or 1. These input values come from the output of other elements in the network, so each input value is either 0 or 1. Associated with each input value is a numeric weight. The **effective weight** of the element is defined as the sum of the weights multiplied by their respective input values.

» **Effective weight** In an artificial neuron, the sum of the weights multiplied by the corresponding input values

Suppose an artificial neuron accepts three input values: v1, v2, and v3. Associated with each input value is a weight: w1, w2, and w3. The effective weight is therefore

v1 * w1 + v2 * w2 + v3 * w3

Each element has a numeric threshold value. The element compares the effective weight to this threshold value. If the effective weight exceeds the threshold, the unit produces an output value of 1. If it does not exceed the threshold, it produces an output value of 0.

This processing closely mirrors the activity of a biological neuron. The input values correspond to the signals passed in by the dendrites. The weight values correspond to the controlling effect of the synapse for each input signal. The computation and use of the threshold value correspond to the neuron producing a strong signal if "enough" of the weighted input signals are strong.

Let's look at an actual example. In this case, we assume there are four inputs to the processing element. There are, therefore, four corresponding weight factors. Suppose the input values are 1, 1, 0, and 0; the corresponding weights are 4, −2, −5, and −2; and the threshold value for the element is 4. The effective weight is

1(4) + 1(−2) + 0(−5) + 0(−2)

or 2. Because the effective weight does not exceed the threshold value, the output of this element is 0.

Although the input values are either 0 or 1, the weights can be any value at all. They can even be negative. We've used integers for the weights and threshold values in our example, but they can be real numbers as well.

The output of each element is truly a function of all pieces of the puzzle. If the input signal is 0, its weight is irrelevant. If the input signal is 1, the magnitude of the weight, and whether it is positive or negative, greatly affects the effective weight. And no matter what effective weight is computed, it's viewed relative to the threshold value of that element. That is, an effective weight of 15 may be enough for one element to produce an output of 1, but for another element it results in an output of 0.

The pathways established in an artificial neural net are a function of its individual processing elements. And the output of each processing element changes on the basis of the input signals, the weights, and/or the threshold values. But the input signals are really just output signals from other elements. Therefore, we affect the processing of a neural net by changing the weights and threshold value in individual processing elements.

The process of adjusting the weights and threshold values in a neural net is called training. A neural net can be trained to produce whatever results are required. Initially, a neural net may be set up with random weights, threshold values, and initial inputs. The results are compared to the desired results and changes are made. This process continues until the desired results are achieved.

>> **Training** The process of adjusting the weights and threshold values in a neural net to get a desired outcome

Consider the problem we posed at the beginning of this chapter: Find a cat in a photograph. Suppose a neural net is used to address this problem, using one output value per pixel. Our goal is to produce an output value of 1 for every pixel that contributes to the image of the cat, and to produce a 0 if it does not. The input values for the network could come from some representation of the color of the pixels. We then train the network using multiple pictures containing cats, reinforcing weights and thresholds that lead to the desired (correct) output.

Think about how complicated this problem is! Cats come in all shapes, sizes, and colors. They can be oriented in a picture in thousands of ways. They might blend into their background (in the picture) or they might not. A neural net for this problem would be incredibly large, taking all kinds of situations into account. The more training we give the network, however, the more likely it will produce accurate results in the future.

What else are neural nets good for? They have been used successfully in thousands of application areas, in both business and scientific endeavors. They can be used to determine whether an applicant should be given a mortgage. They can be used in optical character recognition, allowing a computer to "read" a printed document. They can even be used to detect plastic explosives in luggage at airports.

The versatility of neural nets lies in the fact that there is no inherent meaning in the weights and threshold values of the network. Their meaning comes from the interpretation we apply to them.

13.5 Natural Language Processing

In a science fiction movie, it's not uncommon to have a human interact with a computer by simply talking to it. The captain of a spaceship might say, "Computer, what is the nearest starbase with medical facilities sufficient to handle Laharman's syndrome?" The computer might then respond, "Starbase 42 is 14.7 light-years away and has the necessary facilities."

How far is this science fiction from science fact? Ignoring space travel and advanced medicine for now, why don't we interact with computers just by talking to them? To a limited extent, we can. We don't tend to have free-flowing verbal conversations yet, but we've certainly made headway. Some computers can be set up to respond to specific verbal commands.

To probe this issue further, we must first realize that three basic types of processing occur during human/computer voice interaction:

- Voice recognition—recognizing human words
- Natural language comprehension—interpreting human communication
- Voice synthesis—recreating human speech

The computer must first recognize the distinct words that are being spoken to it, then understand the meaning of those words, and finally (after determining the answer) produce the words that make up the response.

Common to all of these problems is the fact that we are using a natural language, which can be any language that humans use to communicate, such as English, Farsi, or Russian. Natural languages have inherent grammatical irregularities and ambiguities that make some of this processing quite challenging.

Computing technology has made great strides in all of these areas, albeit in some areas more than others. Let's explore each one in more detail.

■ Voice Synthesis

Voice synthesis is generally a well-understood problem. There are two basic approaches to the solution: dynamic voice generation and recorded speech.

To generate voice output using dynamic voice generation, a computer examines the letters that make up a word and produces the sequence of sounds that correspond to those letters in an attempt to vocalize the word. Human speech has been categorized into specific sound units called phonemes. The phonemes for American English are shown in Figure 13.7.

After selecting the appropriate phonemes, the computer may modify the pitch of the phoneme based on the context in which it is used. The duration of each phoneme must also be determined. Finally, the phonemes are combined to form individual words. The sounds themselves are produced electronically, designed to mimic the way a human vocal track produces the sounds.

The challenges to this approach include the fact that the way we pronounce words varies greatly among humans, and the rules governing how letters contribute to the sound of a word are not consistent. Dynamic voice-generation systems often sound mechanical and stilted, though the words are usually recognizable.

>> **Voice recognition** Using a computer to recognize the words spoken by a human

>> **Natural language comprehension** Using a computer to apply a meaningful interpretation to human communication

>> **Voice synthesis** Using a computer to create the sound of human speech

>> **Natural language** Languages that humans use to communicate, such as English

>> **Phonemes** The set of fundamental sounds made in any given natural language

Consonants				Vowels	
Symbols	Examples	Symbols	Examples	Symbols	Examples
p	pipe	k	kick, cat	i	eel, sea, see
b	babe	g	get	I	ill, bill
m	maim	ŋ	sing	e	ale, aim, day
f	fee, phone, rough	š	shoe, ash, sugar	ɛ	elk, bet, bear
v	vie, love	ž	measure	æ	at, mat
θ	thin, bath	č	chat, batch	u	due, new, zoo
ð	the, bathe	ǰ	jaw, judge, gin	ʊ	book, sugar
t	tea, beat	d	day, bad	o	own, no, know
n	nine	ʔ	uh uh	ɔ	aw, crawl, law, dog
l	law, ball	s	see, less, city	a	hot, bar, dart
r	run, bar	z	zoo, booze	ə	sir, nerd, bird
				ʌ	cut, bun

Semi Vowels		Diphthongs	
w	we	aj	bite, fight
h	he	aw	out, cow
j	you, beyond	ɔj	boy, boil

FIGURE 13.7 Phonemes for American English

The other approach to voice synthesis is to play digital recordings of a human voice saying specific words. Sentences are constructed by playing the appropriate words in the appropriate order. Sometimes common phrases or groups of words that are always used together are recorded as one entity. Telephone voice mail systems often use this approach: "Press 1 to leave a message for Alex Wakefield."

Note that each word or phrase needed must be recorded separately. Furthermore, because words are pronounced differently in different contexts, some words may have to be recorded multiple times. For example, a word at the end of a question rises in pitch compared to its use in the middle of a sentence. As the need for flexibility increases, recorded solutions become problematic.

The dynamic voice-generation technique does not generally produce realistic human speech, but rather attempts to vocalize any words presented to it. Recorded playback is more realistic; it uses a real human voice but is limited in its vocabulary to the words that have been prerecorded, and it must have the memory capacity to store all the needed words. Generally, recorded playback is used when the number of words used is small.

■ Voice Recognition

When having a conversation, you might need to have something repeated because you didn't understand what the person said. It's not that you didn't understand the meaning of the words (you hadn't gotten that far); you simply didn't understand which words were being spoken. This might happen for several reasons.

First, the sounds that each person makes when speaking are unique. Every person has a unique shape to his or her mouth, tongue, throat, and nasal cavities that affect the pitch and resonance of the spoken voice. Thus we can say we "recognize" someone's voice, identifying him or her from the way the words sound when spoken by that person. But that also means that each person says any given word somewhat differently, complicating the task of recognizing the word in the first place. Speech impediments, mumbling, volume, regional accents, and the health of the speaker further complicate this problem.

Furthermore, humans speak in a continuous, flowing manner. Words are strung together into sentences. Sometimes we speak so quickly that two words may sound like one. Humans have great abilities to divide the series of sounds into words, but even we can become confused if a person speaks too rapidly.

Related to this issue are the sounds of words themselves. Sometimes it's difficult to distinguish between phrases like "ice cream" and "I scream." And homonyms such as "I" and "eye" or "see" and "sea" sound exactly the same but are unique words. Humans can often clarify these situations by considering the context of the sentence, but that processing requires another level of comprehension.

So, if we humans occasionally have trouble understanding the words we say to each other, imagine how difficult this problem is for a computer. Modern voice-recognition systems still do not do well with continuous, conversational speech. The best success has been with systems that assume disjointed speech, in which words are clearly separated.

Further success is obtained when voice-recognition systems are "trained" to recognize a particular human's voice and a set of vocabulary words. A spoken voice can be recorded as a voiceprint, which plots the frequency changes of the sound produced by the voice when speaking a specific word. A human trains a voice-recognition system by speaking a word several times so that the computer can record an average voiceprint for that word by that person. Later, when a word is spoken, the recorded voiceprints can be compared to determine which word was spoken.

>> **Voiceprint** The plot of frequency changes over time representing the sound of human speech

Voice-recognition systems that are not trained for specific voices and words do their best to recognize words by comparing generic voiceprints. While less accurate, using generic voiceprints avoids the time-consuming training process and allows anyone to use the system.

■ Natural Language Comprehension

Even if a computer recognizes the words that are spoken, it is another task entirely to understand the meaning of those words. This is the most challenging aspect of natural language processing. Natural language is inherently ambiguous, meaning that the same syntactic structure could have multiple valid interpretations. These ambiguities can arise for several reasons.

One problem is that a single word can have multiple definitions and can even represent multiple parts of speech. The word "light," for instance, is both a noun and a verb. This is referred to as a lexical ambiguity. A computer attempting to apply meaning to a sentence would have to determine how the word was being used. Consider the following sentence:

Time flies like an arrow.

This sentence might mean that time seems to move quickly, just like an arrow moves quickly. That's probably how you interpreted it when you read it. But note that the word *time* can also be a verb, such as when you time the runner of a race. The word *flies* can also be a noun. Therefore, you could interpret this sentence as a directive to time flies in the same manner in which an arrow times flies. Because an arrow doesn't time things, you probably wouldn't apply that interpretation. But it is no less valid than the other one! Given the definition of the words, a computer would not know which interpretation was appropriate. We could even interpret this sentence a third way, indicating the preferences of that rare species we'll call a "time fly." After all, fruit flies like a banana. That interpretation probably sounds ridiculous to you, but such ambiguities cause huge problems when it comes to a computer understanding natural language.

A natural language sentence can also have a syntactic ambiguity because phrases can be put together in various ways. For example:

I saw the Grand Canyon flying to New York.

Because canyons don't fly, there is one logical interpretation. But because the sentence can be constructed that way, there are two valid interpretations. To reach the desired conclusion, a computer would have to "know" that canyons don't fly and take that fact into account.

Referential ambiguity can occur with the use of pronouns. Consider the following:

The brick fell on the computer but it is not broken.

What is not broken, the brick or the computer? We might assume the pronoun "it" refers to the computer in this case, but that is not necessarily the correct interpretation. In fact, if a vase had fallen on the computer, even we humans wouldn't know what "it" referred to without more information.

Natural language comprehension is a huge area of study and goes well beyond the scope of this book, but it's important to understand the reasons why this issue is so challenging.

> ≫ Lexical ambiguity The ambiguity created when words have multiple meanings
>
> ≫ Syntactic ambiguity The ambiguity created when sentences can be constructed in various ways
>
> ≫ Referential ambiguity The ambiguity created when pronouns could be applied to multiple objects

13.6 Robotics

Robots are familiar to all of us. From television commercials about robotic dogs to the nightly news about space exploration to assembly lines producing beer, cars, or widgets, robots are a part of modern society. *Robotics*—the study of robots—breaks down into two main categories: *fixed* robots and *mobile* robots. Fixed robots are what you see on assembly lines. The machines stay put and the products move. Because the world of a fixed robot is circumscribed, its tasks can be built into the hardware. Thus fixed robots belong mostly in the area of industrial engineering. Mobile robots, by contrast, move about and must interact with their environment. Modeling the world of the mobile robot requires the techniques of artificial intelligence.

■ The Sense-Plan-Act Paradigm

Mobile robotics is the study of robots that move relative to their environment, while exhibiting a degree of autonomy. The original approach to modeling the world surrounding a mobile robot made use of *plans*. Planning systems are large software systems that, given a goal, a starting position, and an ending situation, can generate a finite set of actions (a plan) that, if followed (usually by a human), brings about the desired ending situation. These planning systems solve general problems by incorporating large amounts of domain knowledge. In the case of a mobile robot, the domain knowledge is the input from the robot's sensors. In this approach, the world of the robot is represented in a complex semantic net in which the sensors on the robot capture the data used to build up the net. Populating the net is time-consuming even for simple sensors; if the sensor is a camera, the process is *very* time-consuming. This approach is called the *sense–plan–act (SPA) paradigm*[2] and is shown in Figure 13.8.

The sensor data are interpreted by the world model, which in turn generates a plan of action. The robot's control system (the hardware) executes the steps in the plan. Once the robot moves, its sensors get new data, and the cycle repeats with the new data being incorporated into the semantic net. Problems occur when the new sensory data cannot be processed fast enough to be used. (Perhaps the robot falls into a hole before the world model recognizes that the change in light is a hole rather than a shadow.) The flaw in this approach is that the representation of the robot's world as domain knowledge in a general system is too general, too broad, and not tailored to the robot's task.

Sensing → World modeling → Planning → Control → Execution

FIGURE 13.8 The sense-plan-act (SPA) paradigm

Early Promise of Machine Translation Not Realized

Both the National Science Foundation and the U.S. military funded large machine translation projects in the late 1950s and early 1960s. The vision of using a computer to translate from one natural language to another seemed immediately realizable. But the approach of using large bilingual dictionaries and word-by-word translation soon proved inadequate. This inadequacy is demonstrated in the classic story of the translation of the English expression "The spirit is willing, but the flesh is weak" into Russian. The result was "The vodka is acceptable, but the meat has spoiled."

Researchers realized that they needed to do more fundamental research into language understanding before tackling automatic language translation.

ELIZA

ELIZA was an early natural-language program. In the following script, the program plays the role of a neutral psychotherapist. The computer's responses are in all uppercase.

Men are all alike.

IN WHAT WAY?

They're always bugging us about something or another.

CAN YOU THINK OF A SPECIFIC EXAMPLE?

Well, my boyfriend made me come here.

YOUR BOYFRIEND MADE YOU COME HERE?

He says I'm depressed much of the time.

I AM SORRY TO HEAR YOU ARE DEPRESSED.

It's true. I am unhappy.

DO YOU THINK COMING HERE WILL HELP YOU NOT TO BE UNHAPPY?

I need some help, that much seems certain.

. . .

WHAT ELSE COMES TO MIND WHEN YOU THINK OF YOUR FATHER?

Bullies.

DOES THAT HAVE ANYTHING TO DO WITH THE FACT THAT YOUR BOYFRIEND MADE YOU COME HERE?[3]

What is the *Sojourner* rover?
The *Sojourner* was human's first attempt to operate a remote control vehicle on another planet. After landing, *Sojourner* drove down one of the two ramps mounted to the lander petal. This exit and the subsequent exploration were watched by hundreds of millions of fascinated earth-bound viewers. The mission was conducted under the constraint of a once-per-sol (Martian day) opportunity for transmissions between the lander and earth operators. *Sojourner* was able to carry out her mission with a form of supervised autonomous control in which goal locations (called waypoints) or move commands were sent to the rover ahead of time, and Sojourner then navigated and safely traversed to these locations on her own.[4]

Courtesy of NASA/JPL-Caltech

Used by permission of Sony Electronics Inc.

Fans mourn the passing of Aibo
Sadly, Sony Corporation announced the demise of Aibo, the robot dog that could learn its owner's name, show anger (eyes became red), and express happiness (eyes became green). More than 150,000 of these machines, which were the size of a toy poodle, were sold.

NASA launches twin robots
In July 2003, NASA launched twin robots toward Mars. Since their safe arrival, *Spirit* and *Opportunity* have worked overtime to help scientists better understand the red planet's environment. The robots completed their original missions on Mars in April 2004 and continue to explore opposite sides of the planet through numerous mission extensions. As of April 2009, both robots were still sending data back to the team of scientists on the ground.

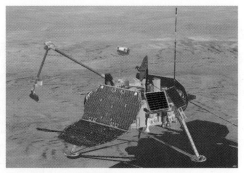

Courtesy of NASA/JPL-Caltech

■ Subsumption Architecture

In 1986, a paradigm shift occurred within the robotics community with Brooks's introduction of *subsumption architecture*.[5] Rather than trying to model the entire world all the time, the robot is given a simple set of behaviors, each of which is associated with the part of the world necessary for that behavior. The behaviors run in parallel unless they came in conflict, in which case an ordering of the goals of the behaviors determines which behavior should be executed next. The idea that the goals of behaviors can be ordered, or that the goal of one behavior can be subsumed by another, led to the name of the architecture.

In the model shown in Figure 13.9, *Keep going to the left* takes precedence over *Avoid obstacles* unless an object gets too close, in which case the *Avoid obstacles* behavior takes precedence. As a result of this approach, robots were built that could wander around a room for hours without running into objects or into moving people.

The three laws of robotics defined by Isaac Asimov fit neatly into this subsumption architecture.[6] See Figure 13.10.

FIGURE 13.9 The new control paradigm

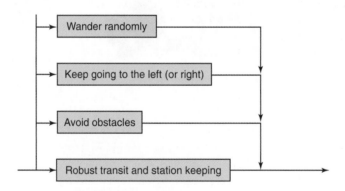

FIGURE 13.10 Asimov's laws of robotics are ordered.

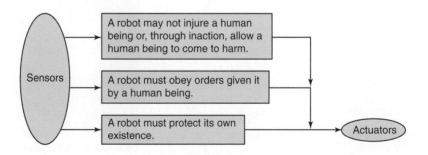

Another shift in robotics moved away from viewing the world as a uniform grid with each cell representing the same amount of real space and toward viewing the world as a topological map. Topological maps view space as a graph of places connected by arcs, giving the notion of proximity and order but not of distance. The robot navigates from place to place locally, which minimizes errors. Also, topological maps can be represented in memory much more efficiently than can uniform grids.

In the 1990s, a modified approach called hybrid deliberate/reactive, in which plans were used in conjunction with a set of behaviors with distributed world views, became popular.

▪ Physical Components

We have been discussing the various approaches to try to get a robot to exhibit human-like behavior and have ignored the physical components of a robot. A robot is made up of sensors, actuators, and computational elements (a microprocessor). The sensors take in data about the surroundings, the actuators move the robot, and the computational elements send instructions to the actuators. Sensors are transducers that convert some physical phenomena into electrical signals that the microprocessor can read as data. Some sensors register the presence, absence, or intensity of light. Near-infrared proximity detectors, motion detectors, and force detectors can all be used as sensors. Cameras and microphones can be sensors. The three most common systems on which robots move are wheels, tracks, and legs.

Into the wild red yonder
Think it's hard to hit a bull's eye with a dart or an arrow? Try sending a two-ton spacecraft 310 million miles to orbit around Mars. In March 2006, NASA's Mars Reconnaissance Orbiter began its orbit around Mars in what was hailed as a "picture-perfect" arrival just above the Martian atmosphere. The spacecraft sends data back to NASA from approximately 200 miles above the planet's surface. Its task is to find new landing sites for future missions.

Summary

Artificial intelligence deals with the attempts to model and apply the intelligence of the human mind. The Turing test is one measure to determine whether a machine can think like a human by mimicking human conversation.

The discipline of AI has numerous facets. Underlying all of them is the need to represent knowledge in a form that can be processed efficiently. Semantic networks are a graphical representation that captures the relationships among objects in the real world. Questions can be answered based on an analysis of the network graph. Search trees are a valuable way to represent the knowledge of adversarial moves, such as in a competitive game. For complicated games like chess, search trees are enormous, so we still have to come up with strategies for efficient analysis of these structures.

An expert system embodies the knowledge of a human expert. It uses a set of rules to define the conditions under which certain conclusions can be drawn. It is useful in many types of decision-making processes, such as medical diagnosis.

Artificial neural networks mimic the processing of the neural networks of the human brain. An artificial neuron produces an output signal based on multiple input signals and the importance we assign to those signals via a weighting system. This mirrors the activity of the human neuron, in which synapses temper the input signals from one neuron to the next.

Natural language processing deals with languages that humans use to communicate, such as English. Synthesizing a spoken voice can be accomplished by mimicking the phonemes of human speech or by replying with prerecorded words. Voice recognition is best accomplished when the spoken words are disjoint, and is even more effective when the system is trained to recognize a particular person's voiceprint. Comprehending natural language—that is, applying an interpretation to the conversational discourse—lies at the heart of natural language processing. It is complicated by various types of ambiguities that allow one specific sentence to be interpreted in multiple ways.

Robotics, the study of robots, focuses on two categories: fixed robots and mobile robots. Fixed robots stay put and have whatever they are working on come to them. Mobile robots are capable of moving and require the techniques of artificial intelligence to model the environment in which they navigate.

ETHICAL ISSUES ▸ HIPAA: Health Insurance Portability and Accountability Act

Whatever, in connection with my professional practice or not, in connection with it, I see or hear, in the life of men, which ought not to be spoken of abroad, I will not divulge, as reckoning that all such should be kept secret.

—From the Hippocratic Oath

Patients have the right to communicate with health care providers in confidence and to have the confidentiality of their individually identifiable health care information protected. Patients also have the right to review and copy their own medical records and request amendments to their records.

—From the Patient Bill of Rights

The Health Insurance Portability and Accountability Act (HIPAA) of 1996 took effect in 2003. The law was introduced to encourage and codify the electronic use and distribution of confidential patient information. The law allows access to medical records without patient consent. In addition to information about physical health, medical records may include information about family relationships, sexual behavior, substance abuse, and even the private thoughts and feelings that are discussed during psychotherapy. This information is often keyed to a Social Security number, making it easily accessible. Information from your medical records may influence your credit rating, admission to educational institutions, employment, and ability to obtain health insurance.

» continued

⚖ ETHICAL ISSUES ▶ HIPAA: Health Insurance Portability and Accountability Act, cont.

Proponents of the law claim current technology that allows collecting and sharing previously confidential information can help doctors diagnose patients, researchers develop new drugs, and governments track and combat public health threats like the 2003 outbreak of severe acute respiratory syndrome (SARS).

While opponents admit that these benefits do exist, they claim that unrestricted access to all information contained in medical records is neither necessary nor beneficial. They cite instances of psychiatrists being forced to allow insurance company personnel access to all patient records under threat of being dropped from the insurer's pool of care providers; hospitals sending entire records to third-party billing companies; and health maintenance organizations (HMOs) providing personal information to employers.

Another technological twist on health care is the use of medical identity cards. Although a plan to implement them has been on hold in the United States, one recently took effect in the United Kingdom. Citizens are assigned cards with magnetic strips. Every time a prescription is filled or a doctor's office is visited, the card is swiped and data is collected. An individual's entire medical history is available electronically. Another plan in the works in the United States

would include genetic information, such as the genetic markers for breast cancer and heart disease. This information could follow you regardless of whether you ever have had the actual disease.

The American Recovery and Reinvestment Act of 2009, adopted by Congress and signed by President Barack Obama, includes strong provisions for privacy in the proposed U.S. medical health network, including a ban on the sale of health information, audit trails, encryption, rights of access, improved enforcement mechanisms, and support for advocacy groups to participate in the regulatory process.

Do the benefits of tracking diseases and selling drugs more effectively outweigh the benefits of maintaining medical privacy? Privacy advocates claim that such "Big Brother" technological applications could have a chilling effect. Knowing that their relationships with their doctors are no longer private, patients might either avoid seeking medical attention or not divulge sensitive information, thereby reducing the effectiveness of the care they do receive. The battles over privacy and the HIPAA provisions continue, and it may be some time before their consequences are fully known. In the meantime, it is a fact of life that medical privacy is a thing of the past.

🔑 Key Terms

Artificial intelligence (AI)
Artificial neural network
Breadth-first approach
Chatbot
Depth-first approach
Effective weight
Expert system
Inference engine
Knowledge-based system
Lexical ambiguity
Loebner prize
Natural language
Natural language comprehension

Phonemes
Referential ambiguity
Rule-based system
Search tree
Semantic network
Strong equivalence
Syntactic ambiguity
Training
Turing test
Voice recognition
Voice synthesis
Voiceprint
Weak equivalence

⌘   **Exercises**

For Exercises 1–5, match the type of ambiguity with an example.
   A. Lexical
   B. Referential
   C. Syntactic

1. "Stand up for your flag."

2. "Go down the street on the left."

3. "He drove the car over the lawn mower, but it wasn't hurt."

4. "I saw the movie flying to Houston."

5. "Mary and Kay were playing until she came inside."

For Exercises 6–21, mark the answers true or false as follows:
   A. True
   B. False

6. A computer does some tasks much better than a human being.

7. A human being does some tasks much better than a computer.

8. A computer system that can pass the Turing test is considered to be intelligent.

9. Some AI researchers don't think we can achieve true artificial intelligence until a computer processes information in the same way the human mind does.

10. A semantic network is used to model relationships.

11. If information is stored in a semantic network, it is easy to answer questions about it.

12. A computer has never beaten a human at chess in master-level play.

13. An inference engine is part of a rule-based expert system.

14. A biological neuron accepts a single input signal and produces multiple output signals.

15. Each element in an artificial neural network is affected by a numeric weight.

16. Voice synthesis is the most difficult part of natural language processing.

17. Each human has a unique voiceprint that can be used to train voice recognition systems.

18. The word "light" can be interpreted in many ways by a computer.

19. Syntactic ambiguity is no longer a problem for natural language comprehension.

20. A robot may follow the sense–plan–act paradigm to control its movements.

21. Isaac Asimov created three fundamental laws of robotics.

For Exercises 22–30, match the task with who can solve it most easily.
 A. Computer
 B. Human

22. Identify a dog in a picture

23. Add a column of 100 four-digit numbers

24. Interpret a poem

25. Match a fingerprint

26. Paint a landscape

27. Carry on a conversation

28. Learn to speak

29. Judge guilt or innocence

30. Give affection

Exercises 31–76 are problems or short-answer questions.

31. What is the Turing test?

32. How is the Turing test organized and administered?

33. What is weak equivalence, and how does it apply to the Turing test?

34. What is strong equivalence?

35. What is the Loebner prize?

36. Name and briefly describe five issues in the world of AI covered in this chapter.

37. Name and define two knowledge-representation techniques.

38. Which data structure defined in Chapter 8 is used to represent a semantic network?

39. Create a semantic network for the relationships among your family members. List five questions that your semantic network could easily be used to answer and five questions that would be more of a challenge to answer.

40. Create a semantic network that captures the information in a small section of a newspaper article.

41. Which object-oriented properties do semantic networks borrow?

42. What is a search tree?

43. Why are trees for complex games like chess too large?

44. Distinguish between depth-first searching and breadth-first searching.

45. What does it mean to "prune a tree"?
46. Distinguish between knowledge-based systems and expert systems.
47. Distinguish between rule-based systems and inference engines.
48. What is an example of a human expert system?
49. What do we call a knowledge-based system that models the expertise of professionals in the field?
50. Why is an expert system called a rule-based system?
51. Which part of the software in an expert system determines how the rules are followed and what conclusions can be drawn?
52. How are the rules expressed in an expert system?
53. What are the advantages of an expert system?
54. What do we call a single cell that conducts a chemically based electronic signal?
55. What do a series of connected neurons form?
56. Upon what does the signal along a particular pathway depend?
57. What are the multiple input tentacles in a biological neuron?
58. What is the primary output tentacle in a biological neuron?
59. From where do dendrites of one neuron pick up the signals from other neurons to form a network?
60. What do we call the gap between an axon and a dendrite?
61. What tempers the strength of a synapse?
62. What is the role of a synapse?
63. How is a synapse modeled in an artificial neural network?
64. What is an effective weight in an artificial neuron?
65. How is the output value from an artificial neuron calculated?
66. If the processing element in an artificial neural net accepted five input signals with values of 0, 0, 1, 1, and 0 and corresponding weights of 5, −2, 3, 3, and 6, what is the output if the threshold is 5?
67. If the processing element in an artificial neural net accepted five input signals with values of 0, 0, 1, 1, and 0 and corresponding weights of 5, −2, 3, 3, and 6, what is the output if the threshold is 7?
68. What is a phoneme?
69. Describe the two distinct ways that voice synthesis can be accomplished.
70. Which issues affect the ability to recognize the words spoken by a human voice?

71. How can a voice recognition system be trained?

72. Why are personalized voice-recognition systems so much better than generic systems?

73. Name and describe two categories of robots.

74. What are planning systems?

75. What defines subsumption architecture?

76. Of what is a robot composed?

??? Thought Questions

1. Think of five questions that you might issue as the interrogator of a Turing test. Why would a computer have difficulty answering them well?

2. Do you think that strong equivalence is possible? How could it be proven?

3. When you think of robots, what comes to mind? Do you see a human-like machine scampering around the floor? An assembly line producing soft drinks or beer?

4. Would you withhold sensitive personal and medical information from your doctor if you knew there was a possibility that it might not remain private?

5. Should medical identity cards contain genetic marker information if they ever become widely used in the United States?

The Applications Layer

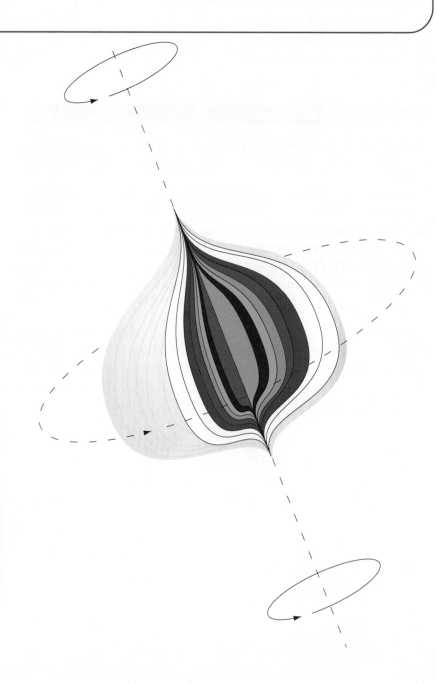

Simulation, Graphics, Gaming, and Other Applications

14

The technique of using a model to represent phenomena, objects, or situations is called *simulation*. Airplane manufacturers build wind tunnels to study airflow around an airfoil on a new aircraft design. Pilots spend countless hours in a flight simulator, a model that recreates the responses of an aircraft to actions the pilot might take, thus allowing a pilot to learn to control the aircraft before he or she ever gets into the cockpit of a real plane. Before the plans of a new supermarket are finalized, a computer program is run to help determine how many checkout stations are needed for the expected number of customers.

In this chapter, we look at the theory behind simulations and examine some concrete examples, including models that predict the weather. Then we cover three other application types—computer graphics, computational biology, and gaming—to round out the discussion of the applications layer.

Goals

After studying this chapter, you should be able to:

- define simulation.

- give examples of complex systems.

- distinguish between continuous and discrete event simulation.

- explain how object-oriented design principles can be used in building models.

- name and discuss the four parts of a queuing system.

- explain the complexity of weather and seismic models.

- describe the important issues in graphics image generation.

- explain the additional concerns for animation versus single images.

14.1 What Is Simulation?

>> Simulation Developing a model of a complex system and experimenting with the model to observe the results

A simulation is a powerful tool used to study complex systems. Simulation is the development of a *model* of a *complex system* and the experimental manipulation of that model to observe the results. Models may be purely physical, such as a wind tunnel; a combination of physical objects under software control, such as a spaceship or flight simulator; or logical, as represented in a computer program.

Computer simulations have been used to help in decision making since the mid-1950s. Building computer models of complex systems has allowed decision makers to develop an understanding of the performance of the systems over time. How many tellers should a bank have? Would the materials flow faster through the manufacturing line if there were more space between stations? What is the weather going to be tomorrow? Where is the optimal place to put the new fire station? We can gain considerable insight into all of these questions through simulation.

■ Complex Systems

System is one of those words that we all intuitively understand but have difficulty defining. The dictionary gives several definitions with the common theme of groups (collections) of objects interacting in some way. The objects can be animate or inanimate. A collection of hardware and software form a computer system. A collection of tracks and railway cars form a railroad system. A collection of teachers and students form a school system.

Systems that are best suited to being simulated are *dynamic, interactive,* and *complicated.*[1] That is, they should be complex. The behaviors of dynamic systems vary over time. The way that the behavior varies may be understood and captured in mathematical equations, such as the flight of a missile through nonturbulent atmosphere. Alternatively, the behavior may be only partially understood but amenable to statistical representation, such as the arrival of people at a traffic light. Although the definition of systems implies that the objects interact, the more interactions that exist in the system, the better a candidate the system is for simulation. Take, for example, the behavior of a plane under air traffic control. The performance characteristics of the individual plane, the interaction with the air traffic controller, the weather, and any routing changes due to problems on the ground all contribute to the plane's behavior. Finally, the system should be made up of many objects. If it weren't, simulating it would be a waste of time.

■ Models

Model is another of those words that we all understand but might have a difficult time defining. There are two dictionary definitions that relate to the use of the word in simulation: an analogy used to help visualize something that cannot be directly observed; and a set of postulates, data, and inferences presented as a mathematical description of an entity or state of affairs. Although these two definitions seem very different, they share one major thread: In both cases, a model is an abstraction of something else. In the first case, the model represents something that is not completely understood, so we are forced to say it is like something else. In the second case, the system is understood well enough to be described by a set of mathematical rules.

For our purposes, a model is an abstraction of a real system. It is a representation of the objects within the system and the rules that govern the interactions of those objects. The representation may be concrete, as in the case of the spaceship or flight simulator, or it may be abstract, as in the case of the computer program that examines the number of checkout stations needed. In the rest of the discussion of simulation, the models we refer to are abstract. Their realization comes only within a computer program.

>> Model An abstraction of a real system; a representation of objects within a system and the rules that govern the behavior of the objects

■ Constructing Models

The essence of constructing a model is to identify a small subset of characteristics or features that are sufficient to describe the behavior under investigation. Remember, a model is an abstraction of a real system; it is not the system itself. Therefore, there is a fine line between having too few characteristics to accurately describe the behavior of the system and having more characteristics than you need to accurately describe the system. The goal is to build the simplest model that describes the relevant behavior.

Models are built for two distinct types of simulation, and the process of choosing the subset of characteristics or features is different for each. The distinction between the two types is based on how time is represented: as a continuous variable or as a discrete event.

Continuous Simulation

Continuous simulations treat time as continuous and express changes in terms of a set of differential equations that reflect the relationships among the set of characteristics. Thus the characteristics or features chosen to model the system must be those whose behavior is understood mathematically. For example, meteorological modeling falls into this category. The characteristics of weather models are wind components, temperature, water vapor, cloud formation, precipitation, and so on. The interactions of these components over time can be modeled by a set of partial differential equations, which measure the rate of change of each component over some three-dimensional region.

Because of the technical nature of the characteristics in continuous simulations, engineers and economists frequently use this technique. The sets of possible characteristics and their interactions are well known in these fields. In a later section we look more closely at meteorological simulation.

Discrete-Event Simulation

Discrete-event models are made up of *entities*, *attributes*, and *events*. An entity represents some object in the real system that must be explicitly defined. That is, the characteristic or feature of the system is an object. For example, if we were modeling a manufacturing plant, the different machines and the product being created would be entities. An attribute is some characteristic of a particular entity. The identification number, the purchase date, and the maintenance history would be attributes of a particular machine. An event is an interaction between entities. For example, sending the output from one machine as input to the next machine would be an event.

An object that flows through a system is usually represented as an entity. For example, the output from one machine is an object that is passed on to the next machine. Thus a raw widget flows from one machine to another (a series of events) and ends up as a lovely doodad. An entity can also represent a resource that other entities need. For example, a cashier is a resource in a model of a bank. If a cashier is not available, the customer entity must enter a waiting line (a queue) until a cashier is available.

The keys to constructing a good model are choosing the entities to represent the system and correctly determining the rules that define the results of the events. Pareto's law says that in every set of entities, there exist a vital few and a trivial many. Approximately 80% of the behavior of an average system can be explained by the action of 20% of the components.[2] The second part of the definition of simulation gives us a clue where to begin: "experimental manipulation of that model to observe the results." Which results are to be observed? The answers to this question give a good starting point to the determination of the entities in the real system that must be present in the model. The entities and the rules that define the interactions of the entities must be sufficient to produce the results to be observed.

Because a computer program implements an abstract model, we can apply object-oriented design to the problem of building the model. The entities in the model are object classes. The attributes of the entities are properties of a class. Where do the events fall into this analogy? The events are the responsibilities of an entity. The rules that define the interactions of the entities in the system are represented by the collaborations of the classes.

14.2 Specific Models

In this section, we examine three types of simulation models.

■ Queuing Systems

Let's look at a very useful type of simulation called a *queuing system*. A queuing system is a discrete-event model that uses random numbers to represent the arrival and duration of events. A queuing system is made up of servers and queues of objects to be served. Recall from Chapter 8 that a queue is a first-in, first-out (FIFO) structure. We deal with queuing systems all the time in our daily lives. When you stand in line to check out at the grocery store or to cash a check at the bank, you are dealing with a queuing system. When you submit a "batch job" (such as a compilation) on a mainframe computer, your job must wait in line until the CPU finishes the jobs scheduled ahead of it. When you make a phone call to reserve an airline ticket and get a recording—"Thank you for calling Air Busters. Your call will be answered by the next available operator."—you are dealing with a queuing system.

Please Wait

Waiting is the critical element. The objective of a queuing system is to utilize the servers (the tellers, checkers, CPU, operators, and so on) as fully as possible while keeping the wait time within a reasonable limit. These goals usually require a compromise between cost and customer satisfaction.

To put this on a personal level, no one likes to stand in line. If there were one checkout counter for each customer in a supermarket, the customers would be delighted. The supermarket, however, would not be in business very long. So a compromise is made: The number of cashiers is kept within the limits set by the store's budget, and the average customer is not kept waiting *too* long.

How does a company determine the optimal compromise between the number of servers and the wait time? One way is by experience—the company tries out different numbers of servers and sees how things work out. There are two problems with this approach: It takes too long and it is too expensive. Another way of examining this problem is to use a computer simulation.

To construct a queuing model, we must know the following four things:

1. The number of events and how they affect the system so we can determine the rules of entity interaction
2. The number of servers
3. The distribution of arrival times so we can determine if an entity enters the system
4. The expected service time so we can determine the duration of an event

The simulation uses these characteristics to predict the average wait time. The number of servers, the distribution of arrival times, and the duration of service can be changed. The average wait times are then examined to determine what a reasonable compromise would be.

An Example

Consider the case of a drive-through bank with one teller. How long does the average car have to wait? If business gets better and cars start to arrive more frequently, what would be the effect on the average wait time? When would the bank need to open a second drive-through window?

This problem has the characteristics of a queuing model. The entities are a *server* (the teller), the *objects being served* (the customers in cars), and a queue to hold the objects waiting to be served (customers in cars). The *average wait time* is what we are interested in observing. The events in this system are the arrivals and the departures of customers.

Let's look at how we can solve this problem as a time-driven simulation. A *time-driven simulation* is one in which the model is viewed at uniform time intervals—say, every minute. To simulate the passing of a unit of time (a minute, for example), we increment a clock. We run the simulation for a predetermined amount of time—say, 100 minutes. (Of course, simulated time usually passes much more quickly than real time; 100 simulated minutes passes in a flash on the computer.)

Think of the simulation as a big loop that executes a set of rules for each value of the clock—from 1 to 100, in our example. Here are the rules that are processed in the loop body:

Rule 1. If a customer arrives, he or she gets in line.
Rule 2. If the teller is free and if there is anyone waiting, the first customer in line leaves the line and advances to the teller's window. The service time is set for that customer.

> **?**
>
> **SIMULA is designed for simulation**
> The SIMULA programming language, designed and built by Ole-Johan Dahl and Kristen Nygaard at the Norwegian Computing Centre (NCC) in Oslo between 1962 and 1967, was intended to be a language for discrete-event simulation. SIMULA was later expanded and reimplemented as a full-scale general-purpose programming language. Although SIMULA was never widely used, the language has greatly influenced modern programming methodology. SIMULA introduced such important object-oriented language constructs as classes and objects, inheritance, and polymorphism.[3]

Rule 3. If a customer is at the teller's window, the time remaining for that customer to be serviced is decremented.

Rule 4. If there are customers in line, the additional minute that they have remained in the queue (their wait time) is recorded.

The output from the simulation is the average wait time. We calculate this value using the following formula:

Average wait time = total wait time for all customers ÷ number of customers

Given this output, the bank can see whether its customers have an unreasonable wait in a one-teller system. If so, the bank can repeat the simulation with two tellers.

Not so fast! There are still two unanswered questions. How do we know if a customer arrived? How do we know when a customer has finished being serviced? We must provide the simulation with data about the arrival times and the service times, both of which are variables (parameters) in the simulation. We can never predict exactly when a customer will arrive or how long each individual customer will take. We can, however, make educated guesses, such as a customer arrives about every five minutes and most customers take about three minutes to service.

How do we know whether a job has arrived in this particular clock unit? The answer is a function of two factors: the number of minutes between arrivals (five in this case) and chance. *Chance?* Queuing models are based on chance? Well, not exactly. Let's express the number of minutes between arrivals another way—as the *probability* that a job arrives in any given clock unit. Probabilities range from 0.0 (no chance) to 1.0 (a sure thing). If on average a new job arrives every five minutes, then the chance of a customer arriving in any given minute is 0.2 (1 chance in 5). Therefore, the probability of a new customer arriving in a particular minute is 1.0 divided by the number of minutes between arrivals.

Now what about luck? In computer terms, luck can be represented by the use of a *random-number generator*. We simulate the arrival of a customer by writing a function that generates a random number between 0.0 and 1.0 and applies the following rules:

1. If the random number is between 0.0 and the arrival probability, a job has arrived.
2. If the random number is greater than the arrival probability, no job arrived in this clock unit.

By changing the rate of arrival, we simulate what happens with a one-teller system where each transaction takes about three minutes as more and more cars arrive. We can also have the duration of service time based on probability. For example, we could simulate a situation where 60% of the people require three minutes, 30% of the people require five minutes, and 10% of the people require ten minutes.

Simulation doesn't give us *the* answer or even *an* answer. Simulation is a technique for trying out "what if" questions. We build the model and run the simulation many times, trying various combinations of the parameters and observing the average wait time. What happens if the cars arrive more quickly? What happens if the service time is reduced by 10%? What happens if we add a second teller?

Other Types of Queues

The queue in the previous example was a FIFO queue: The entity that receives service is the entity that has been in the queue the longest time. Another type of queue is a *priority queue*. In a priority queue, each item in the queue is associated with a priority. When an item is dequeued, the item returned is the one with the highest priority. A priority queue operates like triage on the television show *M*A*S*H*. When the wounded arrive, the doctors put tags on each patient labeling the severity of his or her injuries. Those with the most severe wounds go into the operating room first.

Another scheme for ordering events is to have two FIFO queues: one for short service times and one for longer service times. This scheme is similar to the express lane at the supermarket. If you have fewer than ten items, you can go into the queue for the express lane; otherwise, you must enter the queue for one of the regular lanes.

■ Meteorological Models

In the last section we looked at a fairly simple simulation with discrete inputs and outputs. We now jump to a discussion of a continuous simulation: predicting the weather. The details of weather prediction are over the heads of all but professional meteorologists. In general, meteorological models are based on the time-dependent partial differential equations of fluid mechanics and thermodynamics. Equations exist for two horizontal wind velocity components, the vertical velocity, temperature, pressure, and water vapor concentration. A few such equations are shown in Figure 14.1. Don't worry, working with these equations is beyond the scope of this book—we just want to convey some of the complex processing that occurs in these types of models.

To predict the weather, initial values for the variables are entered from observation, and then the equations are solved to identify the values of the variables at some later time.[4] These results are then reintegrated using the predicted values as the initial conditions. This process of reintegrating using the predicted values from that last integration as the observed values for the current integration continues, giving the predictions over time. Because these equations describe rates of change of entities in the model, the answers after each solution give values that can be used to predict the next set of values.

Horizontal momentum:

$$\frac{\partial p^* u}{\partial t} = -m^2 \left[\frac{\partial p^* uu / m}{\partial x} + \frac{\partial p^* vu / m}{\partial y} \right] - \frac{\partial p^* u\sigma}{\partial \sigma} + uDIV$$

$$-\frac{mp^*}{\rho} \left[\frac{\partial p'}{\partial x} - \frac{\sigma}{p^*} \frac{\partial p^*}{\partial x} \frac{\partial p'}{\partial \sigma} \right] - p^* fv + D_u$$

$$\frac{\partial p^* v}{\partial t} = -m^2 \left[\frac{\partial p^* uv / m}{\partial x} + \frac{\partial p^* vv / m}{\partial y} \right] - \frac{\partial p^* v\sigma}{\partial \sigma} + vDIV$$

$$-\frac{mp^*}{\rho} \left[\frac{\partial p'}{\partial y} - \frac{\sigma}{p^*} \frac{\partial p^*}{\partial y} \frac{\partial p'}{\partial \sigma} \right] - p^* fu + D_v$$

Vertical momentum:

$$\frac{\partial p^* w}{\partial t} = -m^2 \left[\frac{\partial p^* uv / m}{\partial x} + \frac{\partial p^* vw / m}{\partial y} \right] - \frac{\partial p^* w\sigma}{\partial \sigma} + wDIV$$

$$+p^* g \frac{p_0}{\rho} \left[\frac{1}{p^*} \frac{\partial p'}{\partial \sigma} + \frac{T'_v}{T} - \frac{T_0 p'}{T p_0} \right] - p^* g \left[(q_c + q_r) \right] + D_w$$

Pressure:

$$\frac{\partial p^* p'}{\partial t} = -m^2 \left[\frac{\partial p^* up' / m}{\partial x} + \frac{\partial p^* vp' / m}{\partial y} \right] - \frac{\partial p^* p'\sigma}{\partial \sigma} + p'DIV$$

$$-m^2 p^* \gamma p \left[\frac{\partial u / m}{\partial x} - \frac{\sigma}{mp^*} \frac{\partial p^*}{\partial x} \frac{\partial u}{\partial \sigma} + \frac{\partial v / m}{\partial y} - \frac{\sigma}{mp^*} \frac{\partial p^*}{\partial y} \frac{\partial v}{\partial \sigma} \right]$$

$$+p_0 g \gamma p \frac{\partial w}{\partial \sigma} + p^* p_{0gw}$$

Temperature:

$$\frac{\partial p^* T}{\partial t} = -m^2 \left[\frac{\partial p^* uT / m}{\partial x} + \frac{\partial p^* vT / m}{\partial y} \right] - \frac{\partial p^* T\sigma}{\partial \sigma} + T DIV$$

$$+\frac{1}{\rho c_p} \left[p^* \frac{Dp'}{Dt} - p_0 g p^* w - D_{p'} \right] + p^* \frac{Q}{c_p} + D_T,$$

where

$$DIV = m^2 \left[\frac{\partial p^* u / m}{\partial x} + \frac{\partial p^* v / m}{\partial y} \right] + \frac{\partial p^* \sigma}{\partial \sigma},$$

and

$$\sigma = -\frac{p_0 g}{p^*} w - \frac{m\sigma}{p^*} \frac{\partial p^*}{\partial x} u - \frac{m\sigma}{p^*} \frac{\partial p^*}{\partial y} v.$$

FIGURE 14.1 Some of the complex equations used in meteorological models

These types of simulation models are computationally expensive. Given the complexity of the equations and the fact that they must hold true at each point in the atmosphere, high-speed parallel computers are needed to solve them in a reasonable amount of time.

Weather Forecasting

"Red sky in the morning, sailor take warning" is an often-quoted weather prediction. Before the advent of computers, weather forecasting was based on folklore and observations. In the early 1950s, the first computer models were developed for weather forecasting. These models took the form of very complex sets of partial differential equations. As computers grew in size, the weather forecasting models grew even more complex.

Ivan Sutherland

Ivan Sutherland has credentials in academia, industrial research, and in business. On his Web page, Sutherland lists his profession as Engineer, Entrepreneur, Capitalist, Professor. He has won the ACM's prestigious Turing Award, the Smithsonian Computer World Award, the First Zworykin Award from the National Academy of Engineering, and the Price Waterhouse Information Technology Leadership Award for Lifetime Achievement.

Reproduced by permission of Sun Microsystems

Sutherland received a BS from Carnegie Institute of Technology, an MS from the California Institute of Technology, and a PhD from the Massachusetts Institute of Technology. His PhD thesis, "Sketchpad: A Man–Machine Graphical Communications System," pioneered the use of the lightpen to create graphic images directly on a display screen. The graphic patterns could be stored in memory and later retrieved and manipulated just like any other data. Sketchpad was the first graphical user interface (GUI), arriving on the scene long before the term was invented, and opened up the field of computer-aided design (CAD).

The U.S. Department of Defense and the National Security Agency (NSA) spearheaded computing research in the early 1960s. When Sutherland graduated, he was inducted into the Army and assigned to the NSA. In 1964, he was transferred to the Defense Department's Advanced Research Projects Agency (ARPA, later DARPA), where he commissioned and managed computer science research projects as director of ARPA's Information Processing Techniques Office. After his stint with the military, Sutherland went to Harvard as an associate professor.

Sketchpad, which allowed people to interact with the computer in terms of images, was the logical predecessor to Sutherland's work in virtual reality. His goal was the "ultimate display," which would include a full-color, stereoscopic display that filled the user's entire field of vision. Turning the theory into practice was more difficult than first imagined because of the weight of the head-mounted display (HMD). In fact, the first implementation was mounted on the wall or ceiling rather than the head, earning it the nickname "Sword of Damocles."

In 1968, Sutherland moved to the University of Utah, where he continued his research into HMD systems. Sutherland and David Evans, another faculty member at Utah, founded Evans & Sutherland, a company specializing in hardware and software for visual systems for simulation, training, and virtual reality applications. In 1975, Sutherland returned to the California Institute of Technology as chairman of the Computer Sciences Department, where he helped to introduce circuit design into the curriculum.

Sutherland left Caltech in 1980 and established Sutherland, Sproull, and Associates, a consulting and venture capital firm. He now holds eight patents in computer graphics and hardware and continues his research into hardware technology. He is currently Vice President and Sun Fellow at Sun Microsystems.

Surtherland was awarded the Turing Award in 1988. The citation reads:

> For his pioneering and visionary contributions to computer graphics, starting with Sketchpad, and continuing after. Sketchpad, though written twenty-five years ago,

» continued

Ivan Sutherland, continued

introduced many techniques still important today. These include a display file for screen refresh, a recursively traversed hierarchical structure for modeling graphical objects, recursive methods for geometric transformations, and an object oriented programming style. Later innovations include a "Lorgnette" for viewing stereo or colored images, and elegant algorithms for registering digitized views, clipping polygons, and representing surfaces with hidden lines.

Despite all the honors Sutherland has received, he once cited his proudest accomplishment as his four grandchildren.

If weathercasters use computer models to predict the weather, why are TV or radio weathercasts in the same city different? Why are they sometimes wrong? Computer models are designed to aid the weathercaster, not replace him or her. The outputs from the computer models are predictions of the values of variables in the future. It is up to the weathercaster to determine what the values *mean*.

Note that in the last paragraph we referred to multiple models. Different models exist because they make different assumptions. However, all computer models approximate the earth's surface and the atmosphere above the surface using evenly spaced grid points. The distance between these points determines the size of the grid boxes, or resolution. The larger the grid boxes, the poorer the model's resolution becomes. The Nested Grid model (NGM) has a horizontal resolution of 80 km and 18 vertical levels, and views the atmosphere as divided into squares for various levels of the atmosphere. Grids with smaller squares are nested inside larger ones to focus on particular geographic areas. The NGM forecasts 0–48 hours into the future every 6 hours.

The Model Output Statistics (MOS) model consists of a set of statistical equations tailored to various cities in the United States. The ETA model, named after the ETA coordinate system that takes topographical features such as mountains into account, is a newer model that closely resembles to the NGM but has better resolution (29 km).[5] WRF is an extension of ETA, which uses a variable-size grid of 4 to 12.5, and 25 to 37 levels.

Tsunami detection

Tsunami experts are developing better ways to let people know when a tsunami is coming. In the past, tsunami warning systems were based on the seismometer. Unfortunately, this method is plagued by false alarms because not every earthquake triggers a tsunami. Scientists are now using sensors laid on cables on the sea floor to detect the very light disturbance of a tsunami passing overhead on the ocean surface. When the sensors pick up a tsunami, a buoy anchored nearby sends the signal to land via satellite. The National Oceanic and Atmospheric Administration's (NOAA) Pacific Marine Environmental Laboratory (PMEL), based in Seattle, designed the deep ocean assessment and reporting of tsunami (DART) buoys. These systems are able to detect sea-level changes of less than a millimeter in the ocean.

The output from weather models can be in text form or graphical form. The weathercaster's job is to interpret all of the output. But any good weathercaster knows that the output from any of these models is only as good as the input used as a starting point for the differential equations. These data come from a variety of sources, including radiosondes (to measure humidity, temperature, and pressure at high altitudes), rawinsondes (to measure wind velocity aloft), aircraft observations, surface observations, satellites, and other remote sensing sources. A small error in any of the input variables can cause an increasing error in the values as the equations are reintegrated over time. Another problem is that of scale. The resolution of a model may be too coarse for the weathercaster to accurately interpret the results within his or her immediate area.

Different weathercasters may believe the predictions or may decide that other factors indicate that the predictions are in error. In addition, the various models may give conflicting results. It is up the weathercaster to make a judgment as to which, if any, is correct.

Hurricane Tracking

The modules for hurricane tracking are called *relocatable models*, because they are applied to a moving target. That is, the geographical location of the model's forecast varies from run to run (that is, from hurricane to hurricane). The Geophysical and Fluid Dynamics Laboratory (GFDL) developed the most recent hurricane model in an effort to improve the prediction of where a hurricane would make landfall.

The GFDL hurricane model became operational in 1995. The equations were such that the forecasts couldn't be made fast enough to be useful until the National Weather Service's high-performance supercomputers were used in parallel operation, which increased the running time over the serial implementation by 18%. Figure 14.2 shows the improvement of this model over the previous ones used to track hurricanes.

GFDL is being replaced by a specialized version of WRF, called HWRF. HWRF uses 27- and 9-km grid cells with 42 levels. It also takes information from a second simulation called the Princeton Ocean Model, which provides data on ocean currents and temperatures.

Some researchers are producing models that combine the outputs of other models. Such combined models, which have been called "super-ensembles," give better results than individual models. The longer this kind of model runs, the better its results are. In one study focusing on a forecast of hurricane winds three days into the future, a combined model had an error of 21.5 mph as compared to the individual model errors that ranged from 31.3 mph to 32.4 mph.

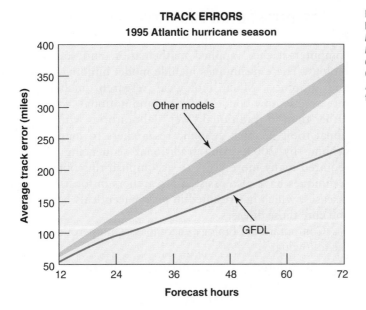

TRACK ERRORS
1995 Atlantic hurricane season

Other models

GFDL

Forecast hours

FIGURE 14.2 Improvements in hurricane models
Reprinted, by permission, from the National Science and Technology Council, High Performance Computing and Communications: Advancing the Frontiers of Information Technology

Specialized Models

Meteorological models can be adapted and specialized for research purposes. For example, numeric-model simulations of atmospheric process are being combined with air-chemistry models to diagnose atmospheric transport and diffusion for a variety of air-quality applications. One such study analyzed the part played by the topography of the Grand Canyon region of Arizona in the movement of air pollution.

Another study showed that by assimilating or ingesting observed data within the model solution as the model was running forward in time, rather than using observations at only the initial time, the model's performance increased significantly. This allows for improved numerical representations of the atmosphere for input into other specialized models.[6]

Advanced meteorological modeling systems can be used to provide guidance for other complex systems in the military or aviation industry. For example, the weather has an impact on projectile motions and must be taken into consideration in battlefield situations. In the aviation industry, meteorological data is used in diverse ways, from determining how much fuel to carry to deciding when to move planes to avoid hail damage.

?

Communication through touch
Haptics is the field of science and technology dedicated to tactile sensation, meaning touch. Haptic devices simulate touch-related sensations such as pressure, temperature, and texture. Force-feedback steering wheels and joysticks are examples of simple haptic devices. More sophisticated applications include force-feedback exoskeleton gloves, remote-control surgical robots, touch-screens, and video games that touch back. Today, for example, haptic devices are used as surgical-simulation tools to train doctors. Before such systems became available, trainee surgeons practiced on oranges! Haptic devices may even enable a surgeon to perform multiple surgeries at the same time from a single location. These advances in haptic technology have made it possible to explore how humans' sense of touch works—a great advancement, especially in the field of robotics.

Computational Biology

Computational biology is an interdisciplinary field that applies techniques of computer science, applied mathematics, and statistics to problems in biology. These techniques include model building, computer simulation, and graphics. Much biological research, including genetic/genomic research, is now conducted via computational techniques and modeling rather than in traditional "wet" laboratories with chemicals. Computational tools enabled genomic researchers to map the complete human genome by 2003; using traditional sequencing methods would have required many more years to accomplish this objective. Computational techniques have also assisted researchers in locating the genes for many diseases, which has resulted in pharmaceuticals being developed to treat and cure those diseases.

Computational biology encompasses numerous other fields, including the following:

> **Computational biology**
> An interdisciplinary field that applies techniques of computer science, applied mathematics, and statistics to problems in biology

- **Bioinformatics**, the application of information technology to molecular biology. It involves the acquisition, storage, manipulation, analyses, visualization, and sharing of biological information on computers and computer networks.
- **Computational biomodeling**, the building of computational models of biological systems.
- **Computational genomics**, the deciphering of genome sequences.
- **Molecular modeling**, the modeling of molecules.
- **Protein structure prediction**, the attempt to produce models of three-dimensional protein structures that have yet to be found experimentally.

Other Models

In a sense, every computer program is a simulation, because a program represents the model of the solution that was designed in the problem-solving phase. When the program is executed, the model is simulated. We do not wish to go down this path, however, for this section would become infinite. There are, however, several disciplines that explicitly make use of simulation.

Will the stock market go higher? Will consumer prices rise? If we increase the money spent on advertising, will sales go up? Forecasting models help to answer these questions. However, these forecasting models are different from those used in weather forecasting. Weather models are based on factors whose interactions are mostly known and can be modeled using partial differential equations of fluid mechanics and thermodynamics. Business and economic forecasting models are based on past history of the variables involved, so they use regression analysis as the basis for prediction.

Seismic models depict the propagation of seismic waves through the earth's medium. These seismic waves can come from natural events, such as earthquakes and volcanic eruptions, or from human-made events, such as controlled explosions, reservoir-induced earthquakes, or cultural noise (industry or traffic). For natural events, sensors pick up the waves. Models, using these observations as input, can then determine the cause and magnitude of the source causing the waves. For human-made events, given the size of the event and the sensor data, models can map the earth's subsurface. Such models may be used to explore for oil and gas. The seismic data is used to provide geologists with highly detailed three-dimensional maps of hidden oil and gas reservoirs before drilling begins, thereby minimizing the possibility of drilling a dry well.

■ Computing Power Necessary

Many of the equations necessary to construct the continuous models discussed here were developed many years ago. That is, the partial differential equations that defined the interactions of the entities in the model were known. However, the models based on them could not be simulated in time for the answers to be useful. The introduction of parallel high-performance computing in the mid-1990s changed all that. Newer, bigger, faster machines allow scientists to solve more complex mathematical systems over larger domains and ever-finer grids with even shorter wall clock times. The new machines are able to solve the complex equations fast enough to provide timely answers. Numerical weather forecasting, unlike some other applications, must beat the clock. After all, yesterday's weather prediction is not very useful if it is not received until today.

14.3 Computer Graphics

Computer graphics can be very generally described as the setting of pixel values on the computer screen. Recall that we talked about computer images in Chapter 3. At that time, we said that an image is a collection of pixel values specified as the red, green, and blue values. Although that earlier discussion referred to pictures we could scan and display on a computer screen, it also applies to everything we display on a computer screen.

Computer graphics plays a role in many aspects of computer science. The most common application is in the graphical user interface (GUI) of modern operating systems. Files and folders are represented as icons on the screen, with the icon indicating the file type. Interacting with the computer involves pointing, clicking, and dragging, which change the appearance of the screen. Computer graphics determines how to set the pixel colors to display the icons and how to change the pixel values as an icon is dragged across the screen.

Word processors and desktop publishing software are other applications of computer graphics. Their ability to show how the document will appear when printed is made possible by the way pixels are set on the screen. Although you might not think about black-and-white text on the screen when you think of computer graphics, it is still involved in the display. Illustrations in user's manuals are also generated with computer graphics. In this application, special techniques are used to produce images that highlight the feature or part being discussed instead of creating fully realistic images.

Companies also use computer graphics in the design and manufacturing of products. Computer-aided design (CAD) systems let engineers create the specification of new components using geometric modeling techniques (as in Figure 14.3). These parts can be displayed on the screen and can even be tested for stress points that could potentially break. These drawings can eventually be used to give instructions to assembly-line machines that create the parts.

Artists use computer graphics in many ways. Some artists use a computer as a high-tech canvas. Paint programs allow artists to create works using the computer instead of brushes and canvas. Image manipulation software allows photographers to touch up pictures or to combine multiple images to create unique effects. Artists also use the computer as an integral part of the artwork. For example, as far back as 1982, Jane Veeder created the WARPITOUT computer installation, which allowed users to take their pictures digitally and then manipulate them before they became part of a rotating gallery of recent images.

Scientific experimentation and simulations inevitably produce large amounts of data. A scientist who examines data as numbers on a page might miss a trend or pattern in those data. An alternative means of analysis is scientific visualization with data presented in a graphical format. Scientific visualization systems allow the user to change the colors associated with different values and create cross sections through the data to help discover patterns or trends. A related application is in medical imaging. Results of tests using technologies such as computerized tomography (CT), ultrasound, and magnetic resonance imaging

FIGURE 14.3 Geometric modeling techniques

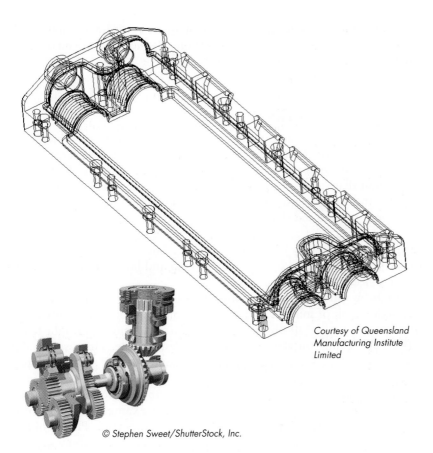

Courtesy of Queensland Manufacturing Institute Limited

© *Stephen Sweet/ShutterStock, Inc.*

(MRI) are presented in a graphical form, which a doctor or technician can then use to make a diagnosis.

Even though numerous applications of computer graphics exist, it is likely that when you think about computer graphics, you imagine computer games, animated films, or special effects on television and movies. These are the most "fun" of the applications—but also the most complex. The complexity comes from the need to simulate very complex processes—the interaction of light and objects, modeling of the shapes of simple and complex objects, the natural movement of characters and objects. The rest of this section will look at some of these issues in more detail. As you will see, there are a lot of details in computer graphics, which makes it a complex as well as a fun area of study. Because computer graphics is broad enough to be the subject of entire textbooks, this section can merely give you a hint of what's involved.

■ How Light Works

The human visual system works because light reflects off objects and enters our eyes. The lens of the eye focuses the light as it strikes the back of the eye. The back of the eye is composed of cone and rod cells that react to the light that strikes them. The cone cells come in three varieties—long, middle, and short—based on the wavelength of light they react to. The long cones react to red shades; the middle cones react to green shades; and the short cones react to blue shades. The rod cells react only to the intensity of the light, so they lack color sensitivity. The reactions in the cone and rod cells are interpreted by our visual system and brain, which ensure that we see objects in front of us.

Light in our world strikes objects, reflecting off of them. Although we might think of mirrors and polished objects as being the only reflective ones, in reality all objects reflect light. The amount of light that is reflected depends on the amount of light available. On a sunny day, many more objects are visible than on a cloudy day or at a time late in the evening.

In addition to the amount of light, the appearance of an object is influenced by what the object is made of. For example, plastic, wood, and metal all look different because of their properties. Plastic objects have color particles embedded in them but they have very shiny surfaces. Highlights on plastic objects are the same color as the light, no matter what color the object is. Wood objects are influenced by the grains in the wood, which reflect light unevenly. Metal objects have microscopically rough surfaces, so they have highlights, albeit not as sharp as those on plastic.

Consider a flat mirror. The direction in which the mirror points can be specified by its normal vector (**N**), which is perpendicular to the mirror surface (Figure 14.4). The angle that light reflects off the mirror (θ) will be the same relative to the normal vector as the angle from which the light arrives. If you are in the direction of a view vector (**V**), what you see will be influenced by the directions of all of these vectors. The entire process is complex because light can strike the mirror from many of different directions. When you look at yourself in a mirror, light reflects off your face and clothes from different directions before entering your eye.

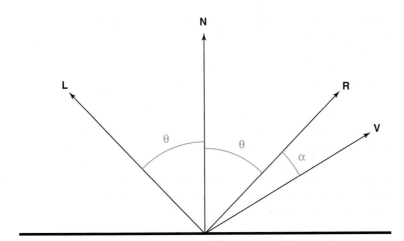

FIGURE 14.4 The normal (**N**), light (**L**), view (**V**), and reflection (**R**) vectors

Shadows are an important component of our world. They give us visual cues about the locations of objects and light sources. They also give us cues about the relative locations of two objects. If two objects are touching, for example, the shadow cast by one of the objects will be very close to that object. As the objects move apart, the shadow will change and, depending on the lighting conditions, could even disappear. This explains why some early hand-drawn cartoons seem odd: Some include shadows for the characters and some don't. Mickey Mouse casts a shadow but Fred Flintstone doesn't. The result is that Mickey seems to be walking on the ground, whereas Fred seems to be floating in air.

To produce realistic images, computer programs must do calculations that simulate the interaction between light and an object, the irregular surface of a textured object, and the change in light intensity in locations in shadows. These calculations can take a lot of time. Animated films and movie special effects look better than computer games because simplifications and shortcuts are needed so that a game can generate images in real time. Another important component of this process is the representation of the shape of objects in the image, which is discussed next.

■ Object Shape Matters

The shape of an object also influences the appearance of the object. When an object is flat, like a mirror, there is one normal vector direction for every location on the object. If an object is not flat, the normal vector direction can be different at various locations. This change in normal vector direction alters the highlight shape, which gives us visual cues as to the shape of the object.

Recall from your math classes that we use equations to describe lines, planes, spheres, cylinders, and other objects. These equations are used in computer graphics to specify the shapes of objects. If you look around, you will see that objects have a wide variety of shapes. Many are much more complex than these simple mathematical objects. Computer graphics also offers ways to mathematically describe the shapes of curved surfaces. Complex objects are then defined by a collection of individual curves.

Even though objects in our world are solid, computer graphics deals only with the surface of objects, because that is all we see. Additionally, these mathematical equations define smooth surfaces, even though real objects may have irregular surfaces. For example, bricks and concrete have a rough surface that will scatter light differently than a smooth surface does. Graphics software uses texture mapping techniques to simulate these rough surfaces.

■ Simulating Light

A number of techniques are used to simulate the interaction of light and objects in graphics. Some techniques are simple; others are very computationally complex. In general, the simulation of light interacting at one point on an object is called an *illumination model*, while the process of using an illumination model to determine the appearance of an entire object is called a *shading model* or just *shading*. The process of creating an entire image is called *rendering*.

One of the earliest illumination models from 1971 uses three different components: ambient light, diffuse reflections, and specular reflections. Ambient light is a general light that doesn't have a direction. This sort of light makes it possible for us to see objects that don't have light directed at them. Diffuse reflections occur because light strikes an object directly. These reflections occur in every direction and are based on the angle between the light direction and the surface normal (θ in Figure 14.4). The closer the light direction and the surface normal, the larger the diffuse reflection contribution will be. Specular highlights are the bright spots that appear on objects because of the mirror reflection direction. The specular reflection is based on the angle between the reflection direction and the viewer direction (α in Figure 14.4). The closer they are, the larger the specular reflection contribution will be. An object's appearance is determined by adding the ambient light, diffuse reflection, and specular reflection together. Although it was developed a long time ago, this illumination model is still commonly used in today's graphics software.

This illumination model does have a notable problem: It makes everything look like it is made of plastic. For this reason, adjustments have to be made to the results it produces to handle metal objects and objects with textures. The illumination model also cannot handle transparent objects or objects with mirror-like surfaces.

A second shading method is called ray tracing. In this method, a point in space is identified where the viewer is located. Then the location of the screen (where the image is to be drawn) is determined. Now a line can be drawn from the viewer location through each pixel location of the image. That line or ray is followed into the scene. If it doesn't hit any of the objects, that pixel is colored to match the background color. If it does hit an object, the illumination calculation is performed for that point and the result becomes the pixel color. If the object that is hit is reflective, like a mirror, the direction the ray reflects off the object is calculated and this new direction is followed to determine the pixel color. If the object that is hit is transparent, the direction the ray refracts into the object is calculated and this new direction is followed. Highly complex objects could be both reflective and transparent, so both of these calculations might be done and their results combined. Because the rays are followed as they bounce around a scene, ray tracing can handle both transparent and reflective objects.

You may have noticed that sometimes the color of your shirt reflects onto your face or arms. This phenomenon is called color bleeding. Another example occurs when someone wearing a bright red shirt stands near a white wall. The wall near the person can look pink because light reflects off the red shirt before striking the wall. None of the shading methods discussed so far can simulate this type of light interaction, but a technique called *radiosity* can handle color bleeding. In radiosity, light is treated as energy. Complex calculations look at how much energy is transferred from every object to every other object in a scene. Because the amount of energy received by a large object such as a wall will be different for different parts of the wall, large objects are subdivided into much smaller pieces before the energy interaction is calculated.

The amount of energy transferred between two patches in the scene depends on how far apart the two patches are and in which direction the patches are pointing. The farther apart two patches are, the less energy they will transfer. The closer the patches are to facing each other, the more energy they will transfer. This process is further complicated by the fact that patch A can transfer energy to patch B and, conversely, patch B can transfer energy to patch A. Additionally, the amount of energy patch A has available to transfer to patch B depends in part on how much energy patch

A gets from patch B. Likewise, the amount of energy patch B transfers to patch A depends on the amount of energy patch A transfers to it.

Radiosity is highly complex not only because of all of the potential combinations of energy transfer, but also because a scene can have more than 100,000 patches for which this energy transfer must be determined.

■ Modeling Complex Objects

Earlier we said that the shapes of simple objects could be modeled with simple mathematical objects and curved surfaces. Many objects in our world are much more complex in terms of their shapes and the ways that they interact with light. This is one area where graphics researchers are working to produce realistic simulations of natural phenomena that can be rendered in a reasonable amount of time. This section looks at some of these issues in a general way.

Natural landscapes provide a mixture of graphics challenges: realistic-looking terrain, reasonable-looking streams, and natural-looking plants. Figure 14.5 shows a natural-looking computer-generated landscape. Terrain can be modeled with fractal or erosion models. One *fractal model* uses a technique called midpoint subdivision. With this technique, you begin with a triangular patch. Each side of the triangle is subdivided at the midpoint, and extra edges are added between these points to give four triangular patches.

FIGURE 14.5 A natural computer-generated landscape
Reproduced from Oliver Deussen, et. al., "Realistic Modeling and Rendering of Plant Ecosystems." SIGGRAPH *(1998): 275-286. © 1998 ACM, Inc. Reprinted by permission. [http://doi.acm.org/10.1145/280814 .280898]*

The process is repeated again for each of the four patches, which produces sixteen triangular patches. This result isn't all that interesting by itself. However, if each of the midpoints is randomly moved up or down when subdivided, it generates an irregular terrain shape (Figure 14.6). *Erosion models* can be used to place streams and form the terrain around them. In an erosion model, the starting or ending point of the stream is chosen and then the stream is randomly moved through the terrain. The stream location sets the terrain height at those locations, and the areas around the stream can then be raised to irregular levels.

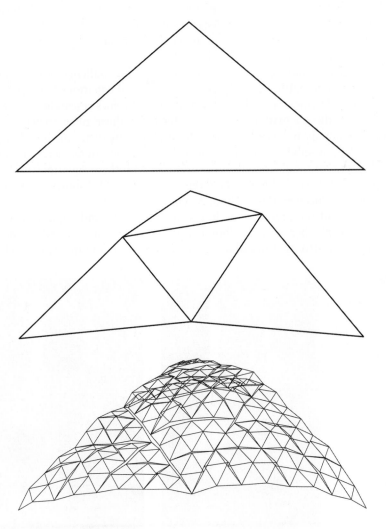

FIGURE 14.6 Midpoint subdivision for creating fractal terrains

Plant growth has been modeled through both grammar and probabilistic methods. In grammar-based tree models, rules much like those in English grammar specify how components of a plant change. For example, one rule might specify that a bud becomes a flower, while another rule specifies that a bud becomes a branch section with a new bud at its end. Different sets of rules will create different types of plants. Making choices among one set of rules will produce different examples of one plant type. Plant growth can be specified with as few as five to ten rules depending on the complexity of the plant. In probabilistic models, actual plants are studied to see how they grow. The probabilities of events—for example, that a bud on a plant will stay dormant, become a flower and die, become a new branch or set of branches, or just die—are measured. The lengths of branches and their relative positioning are also measured. The computer then uses all of these probabilities to generate plant shapes for rendering.

Liquids, clouds, smoke, and fire pose special challenges for graphics applications. Scientific researchers have developed equations that approximate the behavior of liquids, gases, and fire. Graphics researchers have, in turn, used these equations to create images of those phenomena. When modeling liquids and gases for computer graphics, the space the liquid or gas will occupy is subdivided into cubic cells. Data on atmospheric pressure, density, gravity, and external forces are used with these equations to determine how the material moves between cells. Figure 14.7 shows an example of water produced by this method. A cell-based model of clouds looks at the humidity and the presence of clouds in the current and adjacent cells to determine whether a cloud should appear in the current cell. Random numbers are also used to influence cloud formation and movement. These

FIGURE 14.7 Water pouring into a glass
Reproduced from Douglas Enright, et. al., "Animation and Rendering of Complex Water Surfaces." SIGGRAPH 21 (2002): 275-286. © 2002 ACM, Inc. Reprinted by permission. [http://doi.acm.org/10 .1145/566654.566645]

techniques can produce realistic clouds, as seen in Figure 14.8. Because smoke and fire are the results of the combustion of a material, heat contributes to the turbulence of the flame and smoke. Equations are also used to model the velocity of fire and smoke particles for the production of images such as those shown in Figures 14.9 and 14.10.

FIGURE 14.8 Cellular automata-based clouds
Reproduced from Yoshinori Dobashi, et. al., "A Simple, Efficient Method for Realistic Animation of Clouds". SIGGRAPH *(2000): 19-28.* © ACM, Inc. Reprinted by permission. [http://doi.acm.org/10.1145/344779.344795]

FIGURE 14.9 A campfire
Reproduced Duc Quang Nguye, et. al., "Physically Based Modeling and Animation of Fire". SIGGRAPH *(2002): 721-728.* © 2002 ACM, Inc. Reprinted by permission. [http://doi.acm.org/10.1145/566570.566643]

FIGURE 14.10 Blowing smoke *Reproduced Ronald Fedkiw, et. al., "Visual Simulation of Smoke."* SIGGRAPH (2001): 15-22. © 2001 ACM, Inc. Reprinted by permission. [http://doi.acm.org/10.1145/383259 .383260]

Cloth comes in two main types—woven and knit. Woven cloth has two sets of threads that are perpendicular. When cloth is woven, some of the vertical threads are up and some are down when a horizontal thread is passed between them. The set of threads that are up and down are changed before the next horizontal thread is added. The colors of the threads and the identities of which are up and down combine to create a pattern in the resulting fabric. Woven cloth can stretch, but only a little, depending on the threads and weaving pattern used. In contrast, knit cloth is created with one long thread or yarn that is interlocked using a series of loops. A pattern is created in knit cloth by the way that the yarn twists and turns within the loops. Knit cloth is very stretchy and easily deforms around objects.

Cloth that is laying flat isn't very interesting, but the way that cloth moves and drapes is interesting from a graphics standpoint. Modeling the drape of woven cloth can be done simply by looking at the shapes of the threads that make up the cloth. Because of gravity, a rope hanging between two posts takes on a shape known as a *catenary curve*. Modeling a cloth lying over two posts can be done by having the underlying threads form a catenary curve. The challenge is to make sure the cloth doesn't intersect with itself or with other objects—a challenge handled by using constraint techniques to make sure that in the calculations the cloth doesn't intersect something. Other techniques are used to untangle the cloth in situations where the first set of calculations can't prevent the intersection. Figure 14.11 shows an example of cloth that is draping and folded.

Knit cloth poses an entirely different set of problems because as it drapes, the cloth will stretch. This stretch deforms the loops that form the cloth. Furthermore, because knit cloth uses larger yarns, shadows will form in the fabric as the yarn blocks light from another part of the cloth. The thickness and fuzziness of the yarn also influence the cloth's appearance. One graphics technique for depicting knit cloth treats the path of the

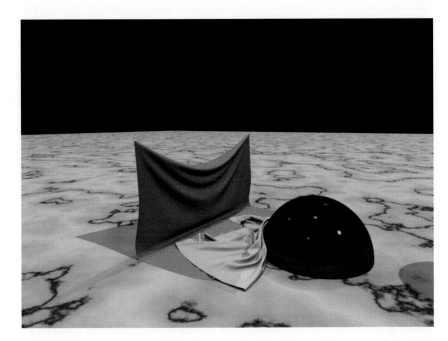

FIGURE 14.11 A simulation of cloth showing bending and draping *Courtesy of Robert Bridson. © 2004 Robert Bridson*

yarn in the cloth as a long curve. Points on the curve are associated with points on a plane to model the knit fabric at rest. To place the fabric on an object, the plane is deformed to the shape of the object. The deformation of the plane changes the locations of the points on the curve. The new locations of these points reflect where the knit fabric stretches and bends. Rendering the fabric then becomes a matter of rendering the yarn as it travels along the now deformed curve.

Skin requires special graphics techniques to handle both its shape and its appearance. Skin is soft and has a shape that depends on the underlying muscles and bone. As muscles contract and relax, our body shape changes and thus our skin will deform. Skin also stretches, wrinkles, and creases as our joints move. In graphics, an advanced technique called implicit surfaces can be used to model the shape of skin. For example, the equation for a sphere ($x^2 + y^2 + z^2 = r^2$) does not explicitly give the x, y, and z values that are on the surface of the sphere. Rather, we can try different values for x, y, and z until we find the ones that satisfy this equation for a given radius. Thus we implicitly find the points on the surface of the sphere. For skin, an even more complex set of equations is used to specify the implicit surface.

Once the shape of the skin is determined, skin must be rendered differently than most other objects. When light strikes the skin, some of the light reflects off the oils on the skin and the rest of the light actually penetrates the top layers of skin. The light that penetrates the skin will reflect off lower layers, pigment particles, and blood before emerging from the skin. If you look at your hand, you will probably notice that you clearly see the outer surface but that you also see underlying blood vessels and maybe even freckles. To accurately render skin, the graphics application must account for this subsurface scattering of light. Subsurface scattering must also be handled to accurately render marble and food products such as milk.

■ Getting Things to Move

So far, we have been talking about graphics from the perspective of a single image, but games and animated films require many images. A film uses 24 images per second and video uses 30 images per second. These images are shown rapidly, so that we perceive the changes between images as continuous motion. A 60-minute animated film requires 86,400 images and a 60-minute video requires 108,000 images. The work done for each individual image is the same even though that image is now part of a sequence of images.

Animation does pose a new challenge, however, if we want to create believable movement of objects. Deciding how to change the positions of objects between the images must be done carefully if the movement is to look realistic. In some cases, realistic movement can be generated based on physical properties. For example, if a ball is thrown into the air, we can predict how it will slow down and stop before falling to the ground based on the laws of gravity.

Having an object move from point A to point B in 10 seconds is not as simple as dividing the distance into 299 equal changes for the 300 images needed for the 10-second video. That result will not look realistic because when objects move there is a period during which their speed is increasing, called the "ease-in" in animation. During the ease-in, the object will move in smaller but increasing amounts between each frame. Also, the object will not come to a sudden stop, but rather will slow down until stopped, which is called the "ease-out" in animation. As a consequence, the change in distance for the ending images will get smaller with each additional image.

Animating figures is even more complex. We are very familiar with the movements of humans and animals, so even small problems in motion will obviously look unnatural. We are so good at recognizing motion of figures that we can recognize that someone in the distance is a friend by the way the person walks, even if he or she is not close enough for us to recognize the face. We can also sometimes identify someone approaching us, even if we merely hear the sounds of their footsteps.

Consider the process of having a character reach for an object. When we reach for something, the entire arm moves. If the object is just out of reach, the shoulder will move and the upper body will either bend at the waist or twist around the waist. To do this, the positioning of all of the arm segments and joints changes. Animating a character to reach could be done by determining where the hand needs to be and then determining what angles the joints should be for the hand to get to its destination. Over the length of the animation, we can change the joint angles from their starting values to the final values. Although this approach would deliver the motion needed, the result might not look realistic. This process becomes even more complex if we have to calculate a path of motion to avoid other objects in the scene.

Graphics researchers are using information gleaned through the study of human and animal motion to develop systems that can automatically generate more natural motion. There is, however, a way to cheat—motion capture. In motion capture, sensors are placed at significant locations on a person's body. The human then moves the way that the character is supposed to move. The location of the sensors is tracked during the entire motion. The sensor locations indicate where the equivalent part of the character should be during the movement. In this way, the sensor locations tell the graphics application where the character should be positioned for each of the images of the animation. This technique works well for film animation because the character movement is known. It doesn't work for computer games where the movement of the character depends on what is occurring in the game.

In our day-to-day lives, we do many things without thinking about them. We see objects without thinking about the way they are illuminated by light. We move ourselves and objects without thinking about the locations of our joints or how to avoid hitting other objects. But when it comes to computer graphics, we have to think about all of these concerns because we have to write computer programs to create images showing just these sorts of things.

14.4 Gaming

Computer gaming is a computer simulation of a virtual world, which draws players into the world as participants. Although computer games can be used as teaching tools, their primary function is to entertain.

A virtual world, which is also known as a digital or simulated world, is an interactive, computer-generated environment. Such worlds are often designed to resemble reality, where real-world rules and laws would still be applicable (to the character you are playing, of course), but they can also be built as deep fantasy worlds where such rules do not apply. Although there are many different types of virtual worlds, they all tend to share the same basic features. Virtual worlds are usually active all day, every day, barring any downtime for maintenance; the game continues to be played, whether individual players are logged in or not. Multiple players can participate in the games at the same time, with the entire interaction taking place in real time.

Virtual worlds are highly social places, encouraging players to form teams, guilds, neighborhoods, and clubs within the game. Unlike flat, one-

» Computer gaming   A computer simulation of a virtual world

dimensional games such as Solitaire, many of today's virtual worlds encompass 3D environments that are designed to immerse the player in the world in which he or she is playing.

Creativity and technological savvy are both required to create the virtual world of a computer game. Designers must be cognizant of aspects of computer science such as computer graphics, artificial intelligence, human-computer interaction, simulation, software engineering, and computer security, in addition to the fundamentals of mathematics. To make people, objects, and environments behave realistically in a virtual environment, programmers and designers also need to be aware of the laws of physics relating to gravity, elasticity, light, and sound.

■ History of Gaming

The general meaning of "gaming" has evolved over the past few decades. The first electronic games were developed in the 1940s, using a device that allowed a user to control a vector-drawn dot on the screen to simulate a missile being fired at targets. In 1971, the first coin-operated video game was sold on the commercial market. Gaming didn't really start to take off until the invention of the Atari 2600 and *Pong*, its wildly popular game, in 1977. The success of Atari's game console opened the doors for companies such as Nintendo® and Sony®, which have since released many popular game consoles, such as Nintendo 64, Nintendo Wii™, and Sony Playstation®.

One way of classifying games is by the type of platform they use: hand-held games such as Nintendo's Game Boy, consoles such as Nintendo 64 and Microsoft's Xbox® that plug into a television, or computer games that are either self-contained or offered over the Internet. Regardless of the platform, there is always a computer in the background running the simulation.

>> **Gameplay** The type of interactions and experiences a player has during the game

Another way of classifying games is by game genres, based on the gameplay. Gameplay is the type of interactions and experiences a player has during the interaction within the game. *Action* games require a player to use quick reflexes and timing to overcome obstacles. There are many subgenres of action games, such as *beat 'em up* and *hack-and-slash* games, which include one-on-many close combat situations. In contrast, *fighting* games emphasize one-on-one combat. Another subgenre of action games places the virtual world entirely within a maze.

Shooter games focus on using projectile weapons in combat. *Action-adventure* games present both short-term and long-term obstacles that must be overcome to succeed. *Life-simulation* games allow the player to control one or more artificial lives. *Role-playing* games allow the player to become a character in the story line of the game. *Strategy* games require careful problem solving and planning to achieve victory within the confines of the game.

■ Creating the Virtual World

A game engine is a software system within which games can be created. A game engine provides tools with the following functionality:

- A rendering engine for graphics
- A physics engine to provide a collision detection system and dynamics simulation to solve the problems related to forces affecting the simulated objects
- A sound-generating component
- A scripting language apart from the code driving the game
- Animation
- Artificial intelligence algorithms (e.g., path-finding algorithms)
- A scene graph, which is a general data structure to hold the spatial representation in a graphical scene

Collectively, these tools enable the game developer to create the virtual world of a game. All game engines need to include a renderer, which uses 50% of the CPU's processing. The renderer actually visualizes the scene, putting the environment up on the screen for the user to view. In addition, 3D objects are kept as vertices in a 3D world, showing the computer where to fill in images on the screen. This is all part of the renderer's functions.

A physics engine simulates models based on Newtonian physics, using mass, velocity, friction, and wind resistance calculations to determine which effects would occur in the real world, so that those effects can then be duplicated in the game engine. The accuracy of the simulation depends on the processing power of the system being used to create the content. High-precision physics engines use more processing power to determine exact calculations, so they are usually applied to animated movies. The physics engine used for computer gaming simplifies the calculations in the game to make sure that a real-time response to an action is achieved.

Collision detection algorithms check the accuracy of collision points or the intersection of two solids. For example, in a game of bowling, a collision detection algorithm would be used to determine the accuracy of the collision that occurs when the bowling ball intersects with the pins. These calculations can apply to solid objects, liquids, and even "human" characters. Rag-doll physics is a type of simulation used to accurately animate a "dying" character's movements or the movements of characters who are fighting. Rather than having characters drop limply to the ground, rag-doll physics essentially connects a character's "bones" through a series of joints (just as an actual human has) to simulate realistic movement.

>> Game engine A software system within which computer games are created

Artificial intelligence provides the illusion of intelligence in the behavior and actions of nonplayer characters. Essentially, it gives nonhuman entities algorithmic and mathematical solutions for problem solving, simulation of human thought, and decision making. While that might not sound terribly complicated, each idea must be expressed through mathematical expression or a script that calculates the odds and anticipates possible actions of the other human players. These nonplayer characters also need to have "knowledge" of language, planning, recognition, and the ability to learn from the actions of those human players around them.

■ Game Design and Development

The game design process begins with a concept, preferably one that nobody has seen before. After much brainstorming, the designer completes a game design document, outlining the many different aspects of the game, including its story line, art, characters, and environment. After the initial team is assigned to the project, the technical ideas for the game really start to flow, as designers, programmers, and artists seek to ensure that the most cutting-edge technology that they have at their fingertips is included in the game.

Once the game technology is at the point where actual gameplay can be developed, the game design is often broken down into fundamental tasks, such as construction of a small game segment, with subsequently developed segments then building on that part. For example, when working on character movement, designers would first develop each movement individually. They might start by making the characters move backward and forward and turn in multiple directions, thereby ensuring that basic navigation through the game is functioning. They would then build on that movement by adding options such as running, jumping, or crouching. After each new section of the game is introduced, the team must verify that the parts of the game developed previously still function with the new aspects of the game.

The development of a new virtual environment requires decisions about how advanced the graphics and simulations in the game should be. Developers may need to decide between a 2D and a 3D game, or even whether artificial intelligence technology will be included in the game. 3D images are created through the process of rendering—that is, using computer programs to generate an image from a model. Much like an artist's rendering of a scene, the computer model would contain geometry, viewpoint, texture, lighting, and shading information, all of which would allow the 3D image to be created with as much detail as possible.

Designers need to develop their ideas beyond the story line, character descriptions, and environmental specifications. Put simply, they have to think about *how* the characters and the environment will interact. These very visual aspects of the game may need a great deal of fine-tuning before designers, programmers, and artists are satisfied with the results. Inevitably, some elements will be missing from the design and will need to be added in later. For example, do the characters walk or stroll when they move? Does the clothing move with the characters' movements? If the game is set outside, are all the true elements of nature included? Does the wind blow? Are there birds and clouds in the sky? Do players design their characters' history themselves, or is that information written into the script? If the game is a fantasy, which powers will the characters have? The list of elements that designers need to think about is endless.

Although the first level of development sets the basic parameters for the design of the game, the design constantly evolves and changes throughout the development and production process. It is nearly impossible to stick to the original design, as the development of a game involves too many different aspects, such as mechanics, art, programming, audio, video, and scripting. All of these aspects depend on one another, and all of them need to remain flexible as other features of the game advance. A big part of the game design process is being willing to abandon much of the work that has been completed when it becomes evident that the game needs to go in a new direction. The game's content may need to change as the game evolves, features and levels may be removed or added, art may advance, and the entire backstory of the game may change.

■ Game Programming

When all the design decisions have been made, programmers produce the code to create the virtual world of the game. The coding process is the single biggest endeavor in game production, as it essentially runs all aspects of the game. C++ is one of the more popular languages used in game development, along with Java and C. Some prominent engine developers have created custom languages for games based on their engines, such as Epic Game®'s UnrealScript for the Unreal engine.

A variety of application programming interfaces (APIs) and libraries are available to assist developers with key programming tasks in the game. The choice of API determines which vocabulary and calling conventions the programmer should employ to use the services. The target game platform determines which service the programmer will use. Some libraries allow for cross-platform development, which streamlines the development pipeline and allows the programmer to program a game in a single language that will run on several platforms (such as Microsoft Windows [for PCs], Nintendo Wii, and Playstation). Also, because graphics are such an important feature in today's gaming industry, graphic APIs (such as Direct3D) are available to render 3D graphics in advanced applications.

The coding begins with creation of the "game loop." The game loop is responsible for managing the game world, regardless of whether the user has provided any input. For example, the game loop might update the enemy movement in the game, check for victory/loss conditions, update the game elements throughout the game world, and process input if provided. In short, the game loop manages the simulation.

Often, large design teams will have different programmers who focus on different aspects of the game. For example, the senior engine programmer may write and maintain the code for the game loop, design in-game engine editors, and make sure that the file formats are acceptable for importing and exporting 2D and 3D art packages and audio/video files. The 3D software programmer may design and implement the 3D graphics component, while the user-interface programmer works on the APIs in the game engine. The programmers work together to create a streamlined, working game.

Despite beta testing and demoing, new computer games often have bugs. The beauty of online games is that any "fixes," maintenance, or addition of new features and upgrades can be performed without interrupting the ongoing action.

Summary

Simulation is a major area of computing that involves building computer models of complex systems and experimenting with those models to observe their results. A model is an abstraction of the real system in which the system is represented by a set of objects or characteristics and the rules that govern their behavior.

There are two major types of simulation: continuous and discrete event. In continuous simulation, changes are expressed in terms of partial differential equations that reflect the relationships among the set of objects or characteristics. In discrete-event simulation, behavior is expressed in terms of entities, attributes, and events, where entities are objects, attributes are characteristics of an entity, and events are interactions among the entities.

Queuing systems are discrete-event simulations in which waiting time is the factor being examined. Random numbers are used to simulate the arrival and duration of events, such as cars at a drive-through bank or customers in a supermarket. Meteorological and seismic models are examples of continuous simulation.

Computer graphics is a fascinating area that combines computers, science, and art. Much of graphics depends on mathematical equations that simulate the natural phenomena presented in the image. Computer graphics combines light interactions, object properties such as transparency and surface texture, object shape, and physical properties to produce images that approach the realism of an actual photograph.

Computer gaming is the simulation of a virtual world within which the players can interact with the system and with each other. A game engine is a software system within which game developers, designers, and programmers create a game's virtual world.

⚖️ ETHICAL ISSUES ▶ Gaming as an Addiction   W

The term *addiction* refers to an obsession, compulsion, or excessive psychological dependence on things such as drugs, alcohol, pornography, gambling, and food. Experts have also been exploring a growing addition to video gaming. Video game addiction, while not yet included in the American Psychological Association's *Diagnostic and Statistical Manual of Mental Disorders* (*DSM*), shows the same symptoms as other impulse control disorders. These symptoms include problems at work or school, lying to family and friends, decreased attention to personal health, carpal tunnel syndrome, dry eyes, failure to stop playing games, and sleep disturbances.

Studies conducted at Stanford University School of Medicine have found evidence that video gaming does, indeed, have addictive characteristics. Dr. Maressa Hecht Orzack, a clinical psychologist at McLean Hospital in Massachusetts and founder of Computer Addiction Service, claims that as many as 40% of World of Warcraft (a wildly popular MMORPG—massively multiplayer online role-playing game) players are addicted, and states that these games should come with warning labels, much like cigarette packages do. Experts believe that these addictions are caused by individuals' needs to form human connections, which they may be unable to achieve in the real world, but can so easily achieve in a virtual fantasy world.

A 2007 Harris Interactive poll of 8- to 18-year-olds in the United States showed that the average time spent playing video games varies by age and sex, with teenage males averaging about 5 hours more per week than females. The Harris poll claimed that 8.5% of the teens surveyed could be "classified as pathological or clinically 'addicted' to playing video games." An MRI study conducted as part of the research at Stanford University showed that the region of the brain that produces satisfying feelings is more active in males than females during video game play.

Some countries have issued restrictions on the length of time that users can play online games. China, for example, issued a rule in 2005 that limited online game play to 3 hours per day. However, in 2007 the rule was changed, allowing players younger than age 18 to play for an unlimited length of time, but cutting off any experience their characters might gain after 5 hours of play.

Many countries, including China, the Netherlands, the United States, and Canada, have opened treatment centers, allowing people who are "addicted" to video games to go through a form of detoxification (detox). However, treatment for video game users is quite different from detoxing from an alcohol or drug addiction. Because computers are such an important part of a person's everyday routine at school or work, video game addicts have to learn to use computers responsibly, rather than avoiding them all together.

Key Terms

Computational biology	Game play
Computer gaming	Model
Game engine	Simulation

⌘ Exercises

For Exercises 1–8, match the kind of simulation with the example.
   A. Continuous simulation
   B. Discrete-event simulation

1. Weather forecasting

2. Stock portfolio modeling

3. Seismic exploration

4. Hurricane tracking

5. Predicting number of tellers a new bank needs

6. Determining the number of waiting rooms necessary for a doctor's office

7. Gas exploration

8. Air-chemistry propagation

For Exercises 9–24, mark the answers true or false as follows:
   A. True
   B. False

9. Simple systems are best suited to being simulated.

10. Complex systems are dynamic, interactive, and complicated.

11. A model is an abstraction of a real system.

12. The representation of a model may be concrete or abstract.

13. In computer simulations, the models are concrete.

14. The more characteristics or features represented in a model, the better.

15. Continuous simulations are represented by entities, attributes, and events.

16. Discrete-event simulations are represented by partial differential equations.

17. CAD stands for computer-aided drafting.

18. A time-driven simulation can be thought of as a big loop that executes a set of rules for each value of the clock.

19. A model whose realization is within a computer program is an abstract model.

20. A concrete model can be realized within a computer program.

21. Red is the specular highlight on a green plastic ball if the light source is red.

22. A commonly used illumination model in computer graphics was developed in the 1970s.

23. Ambient light, diffuse reflection, and specular reflection are three components of a common shading model for computer graphics.

24. Computer graphics relies on research from other scientific fields for equations used in image creation.

Exercises 25–52 are problems or short-answer questions.

25. Define simulation, and give five examples from everyday life.

26. What is the essence of constructing a model?

27. Name two types of simulations and distinguish between them.

28. What are the keys to constructing a good model?

29. What defines the interactions among entities in a discrete-event simulation?

30. What is the relationship between object-oriented design and model building?

31. Define the goal of a queuing system.

32. What are the four pieces of information needed to build a queuing system?

33. What part does a random number generator play in queuing simulations?

34. Write the rules for a queuing simulation of a one-pump gas station, where a car arrives every three minutes and the service time is four minutes.

35. Do you think the gas station in Exercise 34 will be in business very long? Explain.

36. Rewrite the simulation in Exercise 34 such that a car arrives every two minutes and the service time is two minutes.

37. Write the rules for a queuing system for an airline reservation counter. There are one queue and two reservation clerks. People arrive every three minutes and take three minutes to be processed.

38. Distinguish between a FIFO queue and a priority queue.

39. What did SIMULA contribute to object-oriented programming methodology?

40. In general, meteorological models are based on the time-dependent equations of what fields?

41. How much mathematics is necessary to be a meteorologist?

42. Why is there more than one weather prediction model?

43. Why do different meteorologists give different forecasts if they are using the same models?

44. What are specialized meteorological models, and how are they used?

45. What are seismic models used for?

46. A random-number generator can be used to vary service times as well as determine arrivals. For example, assume that 20% of customers take eight minutes and 80% of customers take three minutes. How might you use a random-number generator to reflect this distribution?

47. Why do we say that simulation doesn't give an answer?

48. What do simulations and spreadsheet programs have in common?

49. Explain why shadows are important in graphics applications.

50. What type of mathematical objects would you need to use to create a model of a table?

51. Explain why it is so difficult to get objects to move in computer animation.

52. Name five areas encompassed by computational biology.

??? Thought Questions

1. Priority queues (PQs) are very interesting structures. They can be used to simulate a stack. How might you use a PQ as a stack?

2. Priority queues can also be used to simulate a FIFO queue. How might you use a PQ as a FIFO queue?

3. In Chapter 8, we described the graph data structure. A depth-first traversal of a graph uses a stack, and a breadth-first traversal of a graph uses a FIFO queue. Can you explain why?

4. In this chapter we described queuing systems where there is a queue for each server. Other types of queuing systems exist as well. For example, in the airport there is usually one queue for many servers. When a server is free, the person at the front of the queue goes to that server. Could you represent this type of system in a simulation?

5. What other real-life situations can be modeled using a priority queue?

6. CAD systems are now available for everyday use. Go to your local computer store and see how many programs are available to help you design anything from a kitchen to a guitar.

7. Do you see video gaming as a problem for you or your friends? Has it affected your own or a friend's schoolwork?

The Communications Layer

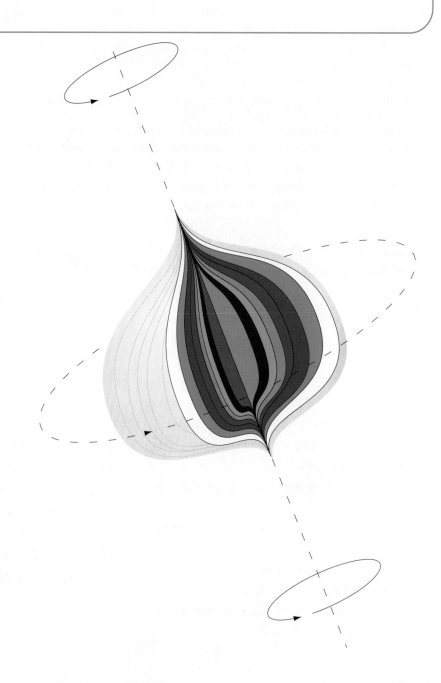

Networks

For many years, computers have played as important a role in communication as they do in computation. This communication is accomplished using computer networks. Like complex highway systems that connect roads in various ways to allow cars to travel from their origin to their destination, computer networks form an infrastructure that allows data to travel from some source computer to a destination. The computer receiving the data may be around the corner or around the world. This chapter explores some of the details of computer networks.

Goals

After studying this chapter, you should be able to:

- describe the core issues related to computer networks.
- list various types of networks and their characteristics.
- explain various topologies of local-area networks.
- explain why network technologies are best implemented as open systems.
- compare and contrast various technologies for home Internet connections.
- explain packet switching.
- describe the basic roles of network protocols.
- explain the role of a firewall.
- compare and contrast network hostnames and IP addresses.
- explain the domain name system.
- understand social networking as a model.

15.1 Networking

>> **Computer network** A collection of computing devices connected so that they can communicate and share resources

>> **Wireless** A network connection made without physical wires

>> **Node (host)** Any addressable device attached to a network

>> **Data transfer rate (bandwidth)** The speed with which data is moved from one place to another on a network

>> **Protocol** A set of rules that defines how data is formatted and processed on a network

>> **Client/server model** A distributed approach in which a client makes requests of a server and the server responds

>> **File server** A computer dedicated to storing and managing files for network users

A computer network is a collection of computing devices that are connected in various ways to communicate and share resources. Email, instant messaging, and Web pages all rely on communication that occurs across an underlying computer network. We use networks to share both intangible resources, such as files, and tangible resources, such as printers.

Usually, the connections between computers in a network are made using physical wires or cables. However, some connections are wireless, using radio waves or infrared signals to convey data. Networks are not defined only by physical connections; they are defined by the ability to communicate.

Computer networks contain devices other than computers. Printers, for instance, can be connected directly to a network so that anyone on the network can print to them. Networks also contain a variety of devices for handling network traffic. We use the generic term node or host to refer to any device on a network.

A key issue related to computer networks is the data transfer rate, the speed with which data is moved from one place on a network to another. We are constantly increasing our demand on networks as we rely on them to transfer more data in general, as well as data that is inherently more complex (and therefore larger). Multimedia components such as audio and video are large contributors to this increased traffic. Sometimes the data transfer rate is referred to as the bandwidth of a network. (Recall that we discussed bandwidth in Chapter 3 in the discussion of data compression.)

Another key issue in computer networks is the protocols they use. As we've mentioned at other points in this book, a protocol is a set of rules describing how two things interact. In networking, we use well-defined protocols to describe how transferred data is formatted and processed.

Computer networks have opened up an entire frontier in the world of computing called the client/server model. No longer do you have to think of computers solely in terms of the capabilities of the machine sitting in front of you. Instead, software systems are often distributed across a network, in which a client sends a request to a server for information or action, and the server responds, as shown in Figure 15.1.

For example, a file server is a computer that stores and manages files for multiple users on a network. That way every user doesn't need to have

FIGURE 15.1 Client/server interaction

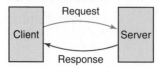

his or her own copy of the files. A web server is a computer dedicated to responding to requests (from the browser client) for Web pages. Client/server relationships have become more complex as we rely heavily on networks in our everyday lives. Therefore, the client/server model has become increasingly important in the world of computing.

The client/server model has also grown beyond the basic request/response approach. Increasingly, it is being used to support parallel processing, in which multiple computers are used to solve a problem by breaking it into pieces as discussed in Chapter 5. Using networks and the client/server model, parallel processing can be accomplished by the client requesting that multiple machines perform specific, separate parts of the same problem. The client then gathers their responses to form a complete solution to the problem.

■ Types of Networks

Computer networks can be classified in various ways. A local-area network (LAN) connects a relatively small number of machines in a relatively close geographical area. LANs are usually confined to a single room or building. They may sometimes span a few close buildings.

Various configurations, called topologies, have been used to administer LANs. A ring topology connects all nodes in a closed loop on which messages travel in one direction. The nodes of a ring network pass along messages until they reach their destination. A star topology centers on one node to which all others are connected and through which all messages are sent. A star network puts a huge burden on the central node; if it is not working, communication on the network is not possible. In a bus topology, all nodes are connected to a single communication line that carries messages in both directions. The nodes on the bus check any message sent on the bus, but ignore any that are not addressed to them. These topologies are pictured in Figure 15.2. A bus technology called Ethernet has become the industry standard for local-area networks.

A wide-area network (WAN) connects two or more local-area networks over a potentially large geographic distance. A WAN permits communication among smaller networks. Often one particular node on a LAN is set up to serve as a gateway to handle all communication going between that LAN and other networks. See Figure 15.3.

Communication between networks is called internetworking. The Internet, as we know it today, is essentially the ultimate wide-area network, spanning the entire globe. The Internet is a vast collection of smaller networks that have all agreed to communicate using the same protocols and to pass along messages so that they can reach their final destination.

▷▷ Web server A computer dedicated to responding to requests for Web pages

▷▷ Local-area network (LAN) A network connecting a small number of nodes in a close geographic area

▷▷ Ring topology A LAN configuration in which all nodes are connected in a closed loop

▷▷ Star topology A LAN configuration in which a central node controls all message traffic

▷▷ Bus topology A LAN configuration in which all nodes share a common line

▷▷ Ethernet The industry standard for local-area networks, based on a bus topology

▷▷ Wide-area network (WAN) A network connecting two or more local-area networks

▷▷ Gateway A node that handles communication between its LAN and other networks

▷▷ Internet A wide-area network that spans the planet

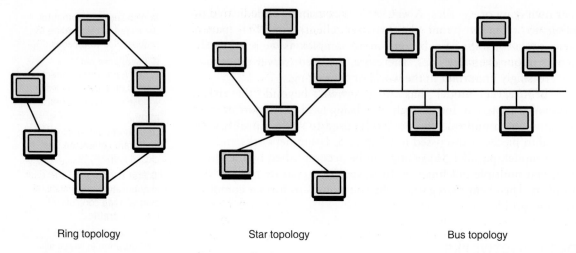

Ring topology   Star topology   Bus topology

FIGURE 15.2 Network topologies

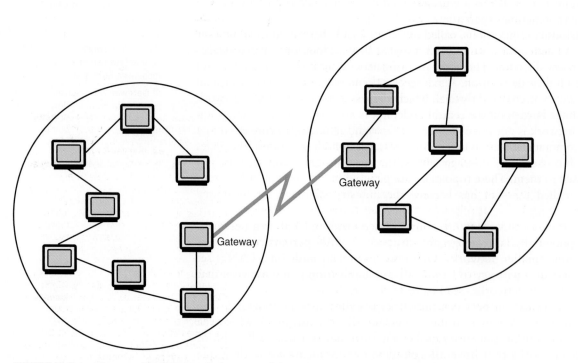

FIGURE 15.3 Local-area networks connected across a distance to create a wide-area network

The term metropolitan-area network (MAN) is sometimes used to refer to a large network that covers a campus or a city. Compared to a general wide-area network, a MAN is more narrowly focused on a particular organization or geographic area. A MAN that services a college or business campus typically interconnects the local-area networks used by various buildings and departments. Some cities have formed a MAN in their geographical area to service the general populace. Metropolitan-area networks are often implemented using wireless or optical fiber connections.

■ Internet Connections

So who owns the Internet? Well, no one. No single person or company owns the Internet or even controls it entirely. As a wide-area network, the Internet is made up of many smaller networks. These smaller networks are often owned and managed by a person or organization. The Internet, then, is defined by how connections can be made among these networks.

The Internet backbone refers to a set of high-capacity data routes that carry Internet traffic. These routes are provided by various companies such as AT&T, Verizon, and British Telecom, as well as by several government and academic sources. The backbone networks all operate using connections that have high data transfer rates, ranging from 1.5 megabits per second to more than 600 megabits per second (using special optical cables). Keep in mind, though, that Internet routes, including the backbone networks, employ a large amount of redundancy, so there is really no central network.

An Internet service provider (ISP) is a company that provides other companies or individuals with access to the Internet. ISPs connect directly to the Internet backbone, or they connect to a larger ISP with a connection to the backbone. America Online® and Prodigy® are examples of Internet service providers.

You can use any of several technologies to connect a home computer to the Internet. The three most popular techniques for home connections are a phone modem, a digital subscriber line, or a cable modem. Let's examine each in turn.

The telephone system had already connected homes throughout the world long before the desire for Internet connections came along. Therefore, it makes sense that the first technique for home-based network communication was a phone modem. The word *modem* stands for modulator/demodulator. A phone modem converts computer data into an analog audio signal for transfer over a telephone line, and then a modem at the destination converts it back into data again. One audio frequency is used to represent binary 0 and another to represent binary 1.

> ≫ Metropolitan-area network (MAN) A network infrastructure developed for a large city

> ≫ Internet backbone A set of high-speed networks carrying Internet traffic

> ≫ Internet service provider (ISP) A company providing access to the Internet

> ≫ Phone modem A device that converts computer data into an analog audio signal and back again

SETI at Home

SETI@Home (SETI at home) is a distributed computing experiment that uses Internet-connected computers in the Search for Extraterrestrial Intelligence (SETI). It is hosted by the Space Sciences Laboratory at the University of California, Berkeley. SETI@home uses spare computing capacity on users' computers to analyze data collected by the Arecibo radio telescope, which is searching for possible evidence of radio transmissions from extraterrestrial intelligence. The project has millions of participants worldwide, and it is acknowledged by the *Guinness Book of Records* as the largest computation in history. BOINC (Berkeley Open Infrastructure for Network Computing) is a middleware system for volunteer and grid computing originally developed to support SETI@home. BOINC lets users donate their idle computer time to projects such as SETI@home. It is now being used for other applications as well, such as mathematics, medicine, molecular biology, climatology, and astrophysics. BOINC has 565,000 active computers worldwide.

To use a phone modem, you must first establish a telephone connection between your home computer and a computer that is permanently connected to the Internet. That's where your Internet service provider comes in. You pay your ISP a monthly fee for the right to call one of several (preferably local) computers that it has set up for this purpose. Once that connection is made, you can transfer data via your phone lines to your ISP, which then sends it on its way through the Internet backbone. Incoming traffic is routed through your ISP to your home computer.

This approach was fairly simple to implement because it does not require any special effort on the part of the telephone company. Because the data is treated as if it were a voice conversation, no special translation is needed except at either end. But that convenience comes at a price. The data transfer rate available with this approach is limited to that of analog voice communication, usually 64 kilobits per second at most.

A phone line can provide a much higher transfer rate if the data is treated as digital rather than analog. A digital subscriber line (DSL) uses regular copper phone lines to transfer digital data to and from the phone company's central office. Because DSL and voice communication use different frequencies, it is even possible to use the same phone line for both purposes.

To set up a DSL connection, your phone company may become your Internet service provider, or it may sell the use of its lines to a third-party ISP. To offer DSL service, the phone company must set up special computers to handle the data traffic. Although not all phone companies support DSL yet, it is becoming an increasingly popular approach.

With DSL, there is no need to "dial in" to create the network connection, unlike with a phone modem. The DSL line maintains an active connection between your home and a computer at the ISP. However, to take advantage of DSL technology, your home must be within a certain distance from the central office; otherwise, the digital signal degrades too much while traveling between those two points.

A third option for home connections is a cable modem. In this approach, data is transferred on the same line that your cable TV signals come in on. Several leading cable TV companies in North America have pooled their resources to create Internet service providers for cable modem service.

Both DSL connections and cable modems fall into the category of broadband connections. Depending on the location and whether access is by satellite, phone wire, video cable, or fiber optics, it is possible to obtain broadband transfer speeds that range from 384 kilobits per second to 50 megabits per second or more. Increasingly more households are moving away from the use of phone modems to a broadband solution for their computing network needs. Debate between the DSL and cable modem communities continues to rage to see who can claim the dominant market share. Both generally provide data transfer speeds in the range of 1.5 to 3 megabits per second.

For both DSL and cable modems, the speed for downloads (getting data from the Internet to your home computer) may not be the same as the speed

Digital subscriber line (DSL) An Internet connection made using a digital signal on regular phone lines

Cable modem A device that allows computer network communication using the cable TV hookup in a home

Broadband Network technologies that generally provide data transfer speeds greater than 128K bps

Download Receiving data on your home computer from the Internet

Doug Engelbart

"Build a better mousetrap, and the world will beat a path to your door. Invent the computer mouse, and the world will all but forget your name." This was the lead paragraph in an article celebrating the twentieth birthday of the computer mouse.[1]

Designed by Doug Engelbart—the name that was forgotten—and a group of young scientists and engineers at Stanford Research Institute, the computer mouse debuted in 1968 at the Fall Joint Computer conference as part of a demonstration later called "The Mother of All Demos" by Andy van Dam. The historic demonstration foreshadowed human–computer interaction and networking. It wasn't until 1981 that the first commercial computer with a mouse was introduced, however. In 1984, the Apple® Macintosh® brought the mouse into the mainstream. To this day no one seems to know where the term "mouse" came from.

Engelbart grew up on a farm near Portland, Oregon, during the Depression. He served in the Navy in the Philippines during World War II as an electronics technician. Engelbart completed his electrical engineering degree in 1948 from Oregon State University and moved to the San Francisco Bay Area. In 1955 he received a PhD from the University of California at Berkeley and joined the Stanford Research Institute.

Engelbart's vision of the computer as an extension of human communication capabilities and a resource for the augmentation of human intellect was outlined in a seminal paper, "Augmenting Human Intellect: A Conceptual Framework," published in 1962. He has never lost this vision. Ever since, he has been developing models to improve the co-evolution of computers

Courtesy of Bootstrap Institute

with human organizations to boost collaboration, and to create what he calls "high-performance organizations."[2]

During the 1970s and 1980s, Engelbart was Senior Scientist at Tymshare, which was bought by McDonnell-Douglas. He founded the Bootstrap Institute in 1988 and remains involved as Founder Emeritus, while his daughter, Christina Engelbart, is now executive director. In 2005 he received a National Science Foundation grant to fund the open-source Hyper-Scope project. Since its inception in 2006, he has been on the board of advisors of the Hyperwords Company in the United Kingdom.

Engelbart feels encouraged by the open-source movement, in which programmers collaborate to create advanced and complicated software. He is currently planning a system of open software that can be distributed for free over the Internet.

Recognition may have been long in coming, but Englebart received 32 awards between 1987 and 2001, including the Turing Award in 1997 and the National Medal of Technology in 2000. The citations for these two prestigious awards read as follows:

(Turing Award) For an inspiring vision of the future of interactive computing and the invention of key technologies to help realize this vision.

(National Medal of Technology) For creating the foundations of personal computing including continuous real-time interaction based on cathode-ray tube displays and the mouse, hypertext linking, text editing, online journals, shared-screen teleconferencing, and remote collaborative work.

for uploads (sending data from your home computer to the Internet). Most traffic for home Internet users consists of downloads: receiving Web pages to view and retrieving data (such as programs and audio and video clips) stored somewhere else on the network. You perform an upload when you send an email message, submit a Web-based form, or request a new Web page. Because download traffic dominates upload traffic, many DSL and cable modem suppliers use technology that devotes more speed to downloads.

■ Packet Switching

To improve the efficiency of transferring data over a shared communication line, messages are divided into fixed-size, numbered packets. These packets are sent over the network individually to their destination, where they are collected and reassembled into the original message. This approach is referred to as packet switching.

The packets of a message may take different routes on their way to the final destination. Therefore, they may arrive in a different order than the way they were sent. The packets must be put into the proper order once again, and then combined to form the original message. Figure 15.4 illustrates this process.

A packet may make several intermediate hops between computers on various networks before it reaches its final destination. Network devices called routers direct the packets as they move between networks. Intermediate routers don't plan out the packet's entire course; each router merely knows the best next step to get it closer to its destination. Eventually a message reaches a router that knows where the destination machine is. If a path is blocked due to a down machine, or if a path currently has a lot of network traffic, a router might send a packet along an alternative route.

If a communication line spans a long distance, such as across an ocean, devices called repeaters are installed periodically along the line to strengthen and propagate the signal. Recall from Chapter 3 that a digital signal loses information only if it is allowed to degrade too much. A repeater keeps that from happening.

>> **Upload** Sending data from your home computer to a destination on the Internet

>> **Packet** A unit of data sent across a network

>> **Packet switching** The approach to network communication in which packets are individually routed to their destination, then reassembled

>> **Router** A network device that directs a packet between networks toward its final destination

>> **Repeater** A network device that strengthens and propagates a signal along a long communication line

FIGURE 15.4 Messages sent by packet switching

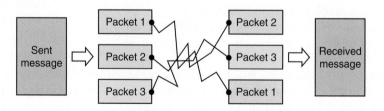

Message is divided into packets   Packets are sent over the Internet by the most expedient route   Packets are reordered and then reassembled

15.2 Open Systems and Protocols

Many protocols have been defined to assist in network communication. Some have gained a stronger foothold than others because of many reasons, often historical in nature. This section focuses on the protocols used for general Internet traffic. Before we discuss the details of particular protocols, however, it is important to put them in context by discussing the concept of an open system.

What is a protocol?
Protocol is defined as a code prescribing strict adherence to correct etiquette and procedure (as in a diplomatic exchange). Computing terminology has borrowed the word to describe the correct etiquette for computers to use when communicating with one another.

■ Open Systems

Early in the development of computer networks, commercial vendors came out with a variety of technologies that they hoped businesses would adopt. The trouble was that these proprietary systems were developed with their own particular nuances and did not permit communication between networks of differing types. As network technologies grew, the need for interoperability became clear; we needed a way for computing systems made by different vendors to communicate.

An open system is one based on a common model of network architecture and a suite of protocols used in its implementation. Open-system architectures maximize the opportunity for interoperability.

The International Organization for Standardization (ISO) established the Open Systems Interconnection (OSI) Reference Model to facilitate the development of network technologies. It defines a series of layers of network interaction. Figure 15.5 shows the seven layers of the OSI Reference Model.

Each layer deals with a particular aspect of network communication. The highest level deals with issues that relate most specifically to the application program in question. The lowest layer deals with the most basic electrical and mechanical issues of the physical transmission medium (such as types of wiring). The other layers fill in all other aspects. The network layer, for example, deals with the routing and addressing of packets.

>> **Proprietary system** A system that uses technologies kept private by a particular commercial vendor

>> **Interoperability** The ability of software and hardware on multiple machines and from multiple commercial vendors to communicate

>> **Open system** A system that is based on a common model of network architecture and an accompanying suite of protocols

>> **Open Systems Interconnection (OSI) Reference Model** A seven-layer logical breakdown of network interaction to facilitate communication standards

Number	Layer
7	Application layer
6	Presentation layer
5	Session layer
4	Transport layer
3	Network layer
2	Data Link layer
1	Physical layer

FIGURE 15.5 The layers of the OSI Reference Model

The details of these layers are beyond the scope of this book, but it is important to know that networking technology as we know it today is possible only through the use of open-system technology and approaches such as the OSI Reference Model.

■ Network Protocols

Following the general concepts of the OSI Reference Model, network protocols are layered such that each one relies on the protocols that underlie it, as shown in Figure 15.6. This layering is sometimes referred to as a protocol stack. The layered approach allows new protocols to be developed without abandoning fundamental aspects of lower levels. It also provides more opportunity for their use, in that the impact of new protocols on other aspects of network processing is minimized. Sometimes protocols at the same level provide the same service as another protocol at that level, but do so in a different way.

A protocol is, in one sense, nothing more than an agreement that a particular type of data will be formatted in a particular manner. The details of file formats and the sizes of data fields are important to software developers who are creating networking programs, but we do not explore those details here. The importance of these protocols is simple to understand: They provide a standard way to interact among networked computers.

The lower two layers in Figure 15.6 form the foundation of Internet communication. Other protocols, sometimes referred to as high-level protocols, deal with specific types of network communication. These layers are essentially one particular implementation of the OSI Reference Model and correspond in various ways to the levels described in that model. Let's explore these levels in more detail.

■ TCP/IP

TCP stands for Transmission Control Protocol and IP stands for Internet Protocol. The name TCP/IP (pronounced by saying the letters T-C-P-I-P) refers to a suite of protocols and utility programs that support low-level network communication. The name TCP/IP is written to reflect the nature of the protocols' relationship: TCP rests on top of the IP foundation.

>> **Protocol stack** Layers of protocols that build and rely on each other

>> **Transmission Control Protocol (TCP)** The network protocol that breaks messages into packets, reassembles them at the destination, and takes care of errors

>> **Internet Protocol (IP)** The network protocol that deals with the routing of packets through interconnected networks to the final destination

>> **TCP/IP** A suite of protocols and programs that support low-level network communication

FIGURE 15.6 Layering of key network protocols

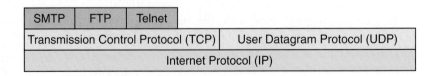

SMTP	FTP	Telnet	
Transmission Control Protocol (TCP)			User Datagram Protocol (UDP)
Internet Protocol (IP)			

IP software deals with the routing of packets through the maze of interconnected networks to their final destination. TCP software breaks messages into packets, hands them off to the IP software for delivery, and then orders and reassembles the packets at their destination. TCP software also deals with any errors that occur, such as if a packet never arrives at the destination.

UDP stands for User Datagram Protocol. It is an alternative to TCP. That is, UDP software plays the same role as TCP software. The main difference is that TCP is highly reliable, at the cost of decreased performance, whereas UDP is less reliable, but generally faster. UDP is part of the TCP/IP suite of protocols. Because of the heavy reliance on TCP, and for historical reasons, the entire suite is referred to as TCP/IP.

An IP program called ping can be used to test the reachability of network designations. Every computer running IP software "echoes" ping requests, which makes ping a convenient way to test whether a particular computer is running and can be reached across the network. Ping officially stands for Packet InterNet Groper, but the name was contrived to match the term used when submarines send out a sonar pulse and listen for the returned echo. Because ping works at the IP level, it often responds even when higher-level protocols might not. The term *ping* is often used as a verb among network administrators: "Ping computer X to see if it is alive."

Another TCP/IP utility program called traceroute shows the route that a packet takes to arrive at a particular destination node. The output of traceroute is a list of the computers that serve as the intermediate stopping points along the way.

>> User Datagram Protocol (UDP) An alternative to TCP that achieves higher transmission speeds at the cost of reliability

>> Ping A program used to test whether a particular network computer is active and reachable

>> Traceroute A program that shows the route a packet takes across the Internet

■ High-Level Protocols

Other protocols build on the foundation established by the TCP/IP protocol suite. Here are some of the key high-level protocols:

- Simple Mail Transfer Protocol (SMTP)—A protocol used to specify the transfer of electronic mail.
- File Transfer Protocol (FTP)—A protocol that allows a user on one computer to transfer files to and from another computer.
- Telnet—A protocol used to log into a computer system from a remote computer. If you have an account on a particular computer that allows telnet connections, you can run a program that uses the telnet protocol to connect and log in to that computer as if you were seated in front of it.
- Hypertext Transfer Protocol (HTTP)—A protocol defining the exchange of World Wide Web documents,

Sir Bill?
Bill Gates, co-founder of the Microsoft® Corporation with Paul Allen, is one of the best-known innovators of the PC revolution. He is consistently ranked as one of the world's wealthiest people and, as of March 2009, was ranked as "the" wealthiest. After his last full-time day at Microsoft in June 2008, he turned his attention to the Bill and Melinda Gates Foundation—the philanthropic institution he co-founded with his wife—which is currently the largest transparently operated charitable foundation in the world. In 2005, Gates received an honorary knighthood from Queen Elizabeth II in a private ceremony. He was honored for his charitable activities around the world and his contribution to the high-tech enterprise in Great Britain. Gates has received many honorary doctorate degrees, including one from Harvard University (2007), the university from which he dropped out in 1975 to found Microsoft.

which are typically written using the Hypertext Markup Language (HTML). HTML is discussed further in Chapter 16.

These protocols all build on TCP. Some high-level protocols have also been defined that build on top of UDP to capitalize on the speed it provides. However, because UDP does not provide the reliability that TCP does, UDP protocols are less popular.

Several high-level protocols have been assigned a particular *port* number. A port is a numeric designation that corresponds to a particular high-level protocol. Servers and routers use the port number to help control and process network traffic. Figure 15.7 lists common protocols and their ports. Some protocols, such as HTTP, have default ports but can use other ports as well.

> ▶ **Port** A numeric designation corresponding to a particular high-level protocol
>
> ▶ **MIME type** A standard for defining the format of files that are included as email attachments or on websites

■ MIME Types

Related to the idea of network protocols and standardization is the concept of a file's MIME type. MIME stands for Multipurpose Internet Mail Extension. Although MIME types do not define a network protocol, they define a standard for attaching or including multimedia or otherwise specially formatted data with other documents, such as email.

Based on a document's MIME type, an application program can decide how to deal with the data it is given. For example, the program you use to read email may examine the MIME type of an email attachment to determine how to display it (if it can).

MIME types have been defined for the documents created by many common application programs, as well as for data from particular content areas. Chemists and chemical engineers, for example, have defined a large set of MIME types for various types of chemical-related data.

FIGURE 15.7 Some protocols and the ports they use

Protocol	Port
Echo	7
File Transfer Protocol (FTP)	21
Telnet	23
Simple Mail Transfer Protocol (SMTP)	25
Domain Name Service (DNS)	53
Gopher	70
Finger	79
Hypertext Transfer Protocol (HTTP)	80
Post Office Protocol (POP3)	110
Network News Transfer Protocol (NNTP)	119
Internet Relay Chat (IRC)	6667

Protected LAN

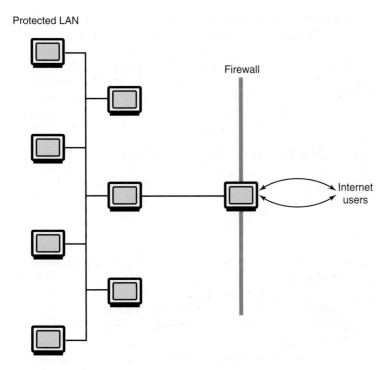

FIGURE 15.8 A firewall protecting a LAN

■ Firewalls

A firewall is a machine and its software that serve as a special gateway to a network, protecting it from inappropriate access. A firewall filters the network traffic that comes in, checking the validity of the messages as much as possible and perhaps denying some messages altogether. The main goal of a firewall is to protect (and, to some extent, hide) a set of more loosely administered machines that reside "behind" it. This process is pictured in Figure 15.8.

A firewall enforces an organization's access control policy. For example, a particular organization may allow network communication only between its users and the "outside world" via email, but deny other types of communication, such as accessing websites. Another organization may allow its users to freely access the resources of the Internet, but may not want general Internet users to be able to infiltrate its systems or gain access to its data.

The system administrators of an organization set up a firewall for their LAN that permits "acceptable" types of communication and denies other types. This policy can be implemented in a variety of ways, although the most straightforward approach is to deny traffic on particular ports. For example, a firewall could be set up to deny a user outside the LAN the

» Firewall A gateway machine and its software that protects a network by filtering the traffic it allows

» Access control policy A set of rules established by an organization that specify which types of network communication are permitted and denied

ability to create a telnet connection to any machine inside the LAN by denying all traffic that comes in on port 23.

More sophisticated firewall systems may maintain internal information about the state of the traffic passing through them and/or the content of the data itself. The more a firewall can determine about the traffic, the more able it is to protect its users. Of course, this security comes at a price. Some sophisticated firewall approaches might create a noticeable delay in network traffic.

15.3 Network Addresses

When you communicate across a computer network, you ultimately communicate with one particular computer out of all possible computers in the world. There is a fairly sophisticated mechanism for identifying specific machines to establish that communication.

A hostname is a unique identification that specifies a particular computer on the Internet. Hostnames are generally readable words separated by dots. For example:

```
matisse.csc.villanova.edu
condor.develocorp.com
```

> **Hostname** A name made up of words separated by dots that uniquely identifies a computer on the Internet; each hostname corresponds to a particular IP address

> **IP address** An address made up of four numeric values separated by dots that uniquely identifies a computer on the Internet

We humans prefer to use hostnames when dealing with email addresses and websites because they are easy to use and remember. Behind the scenes, however, network software translates a hostname into its corresponding IP address, which is easier for a computer to use. An IP address is usually represented as a series of four decimal numbers separated by dots. For example:

```
205.39.155.18
193.133.20.4
```

An IP address is stored in 32 bits. Each number in an IP address corresponds to one byte in the IP address. Because one byte (8 bits) can represent 256 things, each number in an IP address is in the range 0 to 255. See Figure 15.9.

It's tempting to assume that because both hostnames and IP addresses are separated into sections by dots, there is a correspondence between the sections. That is not true. An IP address always has four values, but hostnames can have a variety of sections.

FIGURE 15.9 An IP address is stored in four bytes

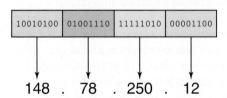

An IP address can be split into a network address, which specifies a specific network, and a host number, which specifies a particular machine in that network. How the IP address is split up depends on which network "class" it represents. The classes of networks (A, B, and C) provide for networks of various sizes.

Class A networks use the first byte for the network address and the remaining three bytes for the host number. Class B networks use the first and second bytes for the network address and the last two bytes for the host number. Class C networks use the first three bytes for the network number and the last byte for the host number.

Think about the range of values this addressing approach allows for the various network classes. There are relatively few class A networks, with potentially many hosts on each. Conversely, there are many class C networks, but only a few (maximum 256) hosts on each. Class C network addresses are assigned to most organizations, whereas class A and B networks are reserved for very large organizations and Internet service providers.

The entire Internet protocol is based on a 32-bit IP address. If the use of Internet-ready devices continues to grow, we will eventually run out of reasonable address space to use. Debate continues in networking circles about how to handle this dilemma.

>> **Network address** The part of an IP address that specifies a specific network

>> **Host number** The part of an IP address that specifies a particular host on the network

>> **Domain name** The part of a hostname that specifies a specific organization or group

>> **Top-level domain (TLD)** The last section of a domain name, specifying the type of organization or its country of origin

■ Domain Name System

A hostname consists of the computer name followed by the domain name. For example, in the hostname

matisse.csc.villanova.edu

matisse is the name of a particular computer, and csc.villanova.edu is the domain name. A domain name is separated into two or more sections that specify the organization, and possibly a subset of an organization, of which the computer is a part. In this example, matisse is a computer in the Department of Computing Sciences at Villanova University.

The domain names narrow in on a particular set of networks controlled by a particular organization. Note that two organizations (or even suborganizations) can have a computer named the same thing because the domain name makes it clear which one is being referred to.

The very last section of the domain is called its top-level domain (TLD) name. Figure 15.10 lists the primary top-level domains. Some TLDs (noted by asterisks in Figure 15.10) have been around since the Internet was first established; others are relatively recent additions.

CAPTCHA Codes
CAPTCHA codes are the distorted jumbles of letters and numbers that many websites require users to enter to deter automated computer programs such as those used by spammers. CAPTCHA is an acronym for "Completely Automated Public Turing Test to Tell Computers and Humans Apart." Approximately 200 million CAPTCHAs are solved by humans around the world every day. Programmers are trying to create new variations that will be easier for humans to enter but harder for computer programs to decipher. Most companies have added an audio version of a CAPTCHA code for visually impaired users, and other websites have developed CAPTCHAs that involve solving simple equations or answering simple questions. There are many programs available to create CAPTCHAs for websites. The reCAPTCHA Project is a program available online that will create CAPTCHAs for free for many different environments.

FIGURE 15.10 Some top-level
domains and their general purpose
(* indicates an original TLD)

Top-Level Domain	General Purpose
.aero	Aerospace industry
.biz	Business
.com*	U.S. commercial (unrestricted)
.coop	Cooperative
.edu*	U.S. educational
.gov*	U.S. government
.info	Information (unrestricted)
.int*	International organizations
.jobs	Employment
.mil*	U.S. military
.museum	Museums
.name	Individuals and families
.net*	Network (unrestricted)
.org*	Nonprofit organization (unrestricted)
.pro	Certain professions

FIGURE 15.10 Some top-level domains and their general purpose (* indicates an original TLD)

FIGURE 15.11 Some of the top-level domain names based on country codes

Country Code TLD	Country
.au	Australia
.br	Brazil
.ca	Canada
.gr	Greece
.in	India
.ru	Russian Federation
.uk	United Kingdom

A TLD generally indicates a particular type of organization, such as .com for commercial businesses and .edu for colleges and universities. Some TLDs (such as .edu) are carefully controlled, with registration restricted to only bona fide organizations of a particular type. Other TLDs are unrestricted in that sense. Organizations based in countries other than the United States often use a top-level domain that corresponds to their two-letter country codes. Some of these codes (there are hundreds of them) are listed in Figure 15.11.

The unrestricted nature of the .com, .org, and .net TLDs initially allowed anyone or any organization to register a domain name for its own use as long as that name hadn't already been taken. As the Internet expanded, this naming system became a problem. Newcomers to the Internet lamented that the best domain names had already been taken. Sometimes a name had already been claimed by another similar organization. In other cases people tried to claim as many popular names as possible, hoping to sell (some would say ransom) them to large corporations.

To alleviate this problem, additional top-level domains have been approved and made available over time. The ability to register a domain name using one of the newer TLDs has been somewhat controlled, giving preference to organizations that hold trademarks on particular names.

The domain name system (DNS) is chiefly used to translate hostnames into numeric IP addresses. Before the DNS system was established, a Stanford research group maintained a single file known as the *host table*. As new hostnames were established, the Stanford group would add them to the table (usually twice a week). System administrators would retrieve the revised host table occasionally to update their domain name servers, which are computers that translate (resolve) a hostname into its IP address.

As the number of hostnames grew, the single-table approach became unreasonable. It simply wasn't a practical way to update and distribute the information. In 1984, network engineers designed the more sophisticated domain name system that is in use today. DNS is an example of a distributed database; no one organization is responsible for updating the hostname/IP mappings.

When you specify a hostname in a browser window or email address, the browser or email software sends a request to a nearby domain name server. If that server can resolve the hostname, it does so. If not, that server asks another domain name server for help. If the second server can't resolve it, the request continues to propagate. Ultimately, either the request reaches a server that can resolve the name or the request expires because it took too much time to resolve.

> **Domain name system** A distributed system for managing hostname resolution

> **Domain name server** A computer that attempts to translate a hostname into an IP address

> **Social network** A model of how objects interact

15.4 Social Networks[3]

A social network is a model of how objects—individuals or organizations—interact. In this type of network, objects are represented as nodes that are tied together by some sort of interdependency such as friendship, kinship, religion, or socioeconomic background. Social network analysis views social relationships in terms of network theory about nodes and the ties between the nodes. Within a specific social network, nodes may be related by multiple ties. A network can be thought of as a map of all relevant interconnections among the objects being modeled.

Research in social networks began in the 1800s, long before the advent of the Internet. Networks have been used to model such diverse areas as the spread of new ideas and practices, the spread of diseases, and the forming of emotional clusters. One study showed that happiness tends to be correlated in social networks. When a person is happy, nearby friends have a 25% higher chance of being happy.[4] Clusters of unhappy people were also found.

Have you ever heard the expression "six degrees of separation"? The "small world phenomenon" is the hypothesis that the chain of social acquaintances necessary to connect any two arbitrary people is generally short. Stanley Milgram's social network study in 1967 showed the chain to be about six steps, leading to the famous phrase. Although his methods were later questioned, a recent study found that five to seven steps were sufficient to connect any two people through email.[5,6]

Social network services focus on building communities of people who share interests or activities. They form virtual communities in which the main form of communication is not face-to-face contact. If the mechanism is a computer network, they are called online communities. The first such community was formed in 1985 and began as a dial-up bulletin board system. Classmates.com began in 1995 to connect former schoolmates. In 1997, SixDegrees.com was formed as a website that focused on indirect relationships. Users were allowed to list family, friends, and acquaintances and post bulletin-board items and send messages to people in their first, second, and third degrees. This website was sold in 2000 for $125 million. A bevy of networking websites appeared in the early 2000s, with MySpace™ emerging as the biggest one by 2005.

Social networking services allow users to be classified into two general categories: *internal*, in which the participants are within a closed or private community such as a company, association, or organization; and *external*, in which there is no restriction on the participants. Both categories allow users to describe themselves, to set privacy settings, to block unwanted members, to have personal pages for pictures and/or blogging, and to form or be a member of a community within the network.

In January 2008, monthly visits to MySpace.com totaled more than 955 million, and those to Facebook.com exceeded 326 million. The relative order of these two changed in January 2009, with Facebook.com having 1.2 billion visits and MySpace.com having 810 million visits per month.[7]

Summary

A network is a collection of computers connected to share resources and data. Network technologies must concern themselves with underlying protocols and data transfer speeds. The client/server model has emerged as an important software technology given our ever-increasing reliance on networks.

Networks are often classified by their scope. A local-area network (LAN) covers a small geographic area and a relatively small number of connected devices. A wide-area network (WAN) embraces internet-working, connecting one network to another, and covers a large geographic area. A metropolitan-area network (MAN) is specially designed for large cities. LAN topologies include ring, star, and bus networks. Ethernet has become a standard topology for local-area networks.

Open systems are based on a common model of network architecture and protocols, allowing for interoperability. The OSI Reference Model is a seven-layer description of network processing based on open-system principles.

The Internet backbone is a set of high-speed networks provided by various companies. Internet service providers (ISPs) connect to the back-bone or to other ISPs and provide connections for both home and business computing. Popular home connection technologies include phone modems, digital subscriber lines (DSL), and cable modems. Phone modems transfer data as audio signals and, therefore, are quite slow. DSL uses the same phone lines but transfers data digitally. Cable modems are also digital but use cable TV wiring to transfer data.

Messages are transferred over the Internet by breaking them up into packets and sending those packets separately to their destination, where they are reassembled into the original message. Packets may make several intermediate hops between networks before arriving at their destination. Routers are network devices that guide a packet between networks. Repeaters strengthen digital signals before they degrade too much.

Network protocols are layered so that a high-level protocol relies on lower-level protocols that support it. The key lower-level protocol suite for Internet traffic is TCP/IP. IP protocols and software deal with the routing of packets. TCP protocols and software divide messages into packets, reassemble them at the destination, and handle any errors that occur. High-level protocols include SMTP for email traffic, FTP for file transfers, telnet for remote login sessions, and HTTP for Web traffic. Several high-level protocols have been assigned port numbers, which are used to help control and process network traffic. MIME types have been defined for many types of documents and special data formats.

A firewall protects a network from inappropriate access and enforces an organization's access control policy. Some firewalls simply block traffic on specific ports; other, more sophisticated firewalls analyze the content of network traffic.

An Internet network address must pinpoint a particular machine among all possible ones in the world. A hostname uses readable words separated by dots. A hostname is translated into an IP address, which is a numeric address separated into four sections. One part of the IP address identifies the network, and another part identifies the specific host on that network. How the IP address is broken down depends on the network class (A, B, or C) that the address references.

The domain name system (DNS) translates hostnames into IP addresses. DNS has evolved from using a single file containing all of the information into a distributed system dividing the responsibility among millions of domain name servers. Top-level domains, such as .com and .edu, have become crowded, so some new top-level domains, such as .info and .biz, have been approved.

Social networks are models of objects and their interactions. They can model human or corporate interactions. Social networking sites such as Facebook.com and MySpace.com allow users to describe themselves; list their family members, friends, and acquaintances; and send messages to those they have listed.

⚖ ETHICAL ISSUES ▸ Effects of Social Networking

Social networking sites such as Facebook, MySpace, LinkedIn, and Twitter have become wildly popular over the past few years. Students, parents, businesses, celebrities, and, yes, even Presidential candidates are using these sites. In some cases, the sites are used to help people keep in touch with family, friends, and colleagues, and keep people updated on what has been going on in their lives. According to a 2008 poll, 67% of 18- to 29-year-olds use social networking sites. While that percentage is reduced greatly for older age groups, more and more people in their 30s, 40s, and even 50s are joining these sites to keep in touch with old friends.

Celebrities, who primarily use Twitter as their preferred social networking site, use it not only to keep in touch with their own friends and family, but also as a way of reaching out to the general public. With a site like Twitter, celebrities can keep their fans updated on their current projects, hobbies, and family life, or even just let them know about a new favorite restaurant they might have. Oprah, Emeril Lagasse, and Martha Stewart use Twitter to update viewers about their television shows' current guest stars, topics for conversation, or favorite recipes. President Barack Obama and Senator John McCain even used social networking sites including Facebook and Twitter as major campaign tools during the 2008 Presidential race, advertising any debates, conventions, or meetings they were attending, and campaigning to get out the vote.

The popularity of these social networking sites has helped to bridge many social gaps, especially for teenagers. Teens who might normally be quite introverted can communicate through these social networking sites and reach out to more of their peers. Social networking has made a huge difference for college students as well, who can be in contact with more than just the students whom they happen to meet in class. These sites are also a great way to advertise any parties, meetings, concerts, or other events that are taking place, so more students are aware of campus events and social gatherings.

There are, of course, downsides to any social media, and networking sites are no exception. For example, a user has no way of confirming that the information put on the sites is accurate. Bullying is another major negative aspect that most notably affects teenagers, many of whom can be viciously competitive and vindictive without giving thought to the consequences of their actions. The sites can be prime avenues for humiliation and bullying, or *cyberbullying*, as it is now being referred to. Research conducted by the Pew Internet Project has shown that 39% of social networking users have been cyberbullied in some way. Some sites even have "security" patrolling the material posted on their sites for any items that might be considered bullying.

The real question is this: Do the benefits of social networking outweigh the potential costs? Society as a whole has a much easier way to communicate, keep in touch with friends, and get any important messages out to large groups of people, but the people who use these sites must be aware of the personal risks they are taking by putting themselves into such a forum.

🔑 Key Terms

Access control policy
Broadband
Bus topology
Cable modem
Client/server model
Computer network
Data transfer rate (bandwidth)
Digital subscriber line (DSL)
Domain name
Domain name server
Domain name system
Download
Ethernet
File server
Firewall
Gateway
Host number
Hostname
Internet
Internet backbone
Internet Protocol (IP)
Internet service provider (ISP)
Interoperability
IP address
Local-area network (LAN)
Metropolitan-area network (MAN)
MIME type

Network address
Node (host)
Open system
Open Systems Interconnection (OSI)
  Reference Model
Packet
Packet switching
Phone modem
Ping
Port
Proprietary system
Protocol
Protocol stack
Repeater
Ring topology
Router
Social network
Star topology
TCP/IP
Top-level domain (TLD)
Traceroute
Transmission Control Protocol (TCP)
Upload
User Datagram Protocol (UDP)
Web server
Wide-area network (WAN)
Wireless

⌘ Exercises

For Exercises 1–6, match the word or acronym with the definition or the appropriate blank.

    A. LAN
    B. WAN
    C. Gateway
    D. Bus topology
    E. Ethernet
    F. Internet

1. The Internet is a _____.

2. The industry standard for LANs.

3. A node that handles communication between its LAN and other networks.

4. A network that connects other networks.

5. Star topology is a _____ configuration.

6. Ethernet uses _____.

For Exercises 7–15, match the word or acronym with the definition or the appropriate blank.
  A. DSL
  B. TCP/IP
  C. UDP
  D. IP
  E. TCP
  F. Broadband

7. _____ and voice communication can use the same phone line.

8. DSL and cable modems are _____ connections.

9. An Internet connection made using a digital signal on regular phone lines.

10. Network technologies that generally provide data transfer speeds greater than 128 Kbps.

11. The network protocol that breaks messages into packets, reassembles the packets at the destination, and takes care of errors.

12. The suite of protocols and programs that supports low-level network communication.

13. An alternative to TCP that achieves higher transmission speeds.

14. Software that deals with the routing of packets.

15. _____ has more reliability than UDP.

For Exercises 16–20, match the protocol or standard with what it specifies or defines.
  A. SMTP
  B. FTP
  C. Telnet
  D. HTTP
  E. MIME type

16. Transfer of electronic mail.

17. Log in to a remote computer system.

18. Transfer files to and from another computer.

19. Format of email attachments.

20. Exchange of World Wide Web documents.

For Exercises 21–25, mark the answers true or false as follows:
  A. True
  B. False

21. A port is a numeric designation that corresponds to a particular high-level protocol.

22. A firewall protects a local-area network from physical damage.

23. Each company can establish its own access control policy.

24. Some top-level domains are based on the country in which the registering organization is based.

25. Two organizations cannot have the same name for a computer.

Exercises 26–68 are problems or short-answer questions.

26. What is a computer network?

27. How are computers connected together?

28. To what does the word *node* (*host*) refer?

29. Name and describe two key issues related to computer networks.

30. What is a synonym for data transfer rate?

31. Describe the client/server model and discuss how it has changed how we think about computing.

32. Just how *local* is a local-area network?

33. Distinguish between the following LAN topologies: ring, star, and bus.

34. How does the shape of the topology influence message flow through a LAN?

35. What is a MAN, and what makes it different from a LAN and a WAN?

36. Distinguish between the Internet backbone and an Internet service provider (ISP).

37. Name at least two national ISPs.

38. Name and describe three technologies for connecting a home computer to the Internet.

39. What role do ISPs play with the three technologies in Exercise 38?

40. What are the advantages and disadvantages of each of the technologies in Exercise 38?

41. Phone modems and digital subscriber lines (DSL) use the same kind of phone line to transfer data. Why is DSL so much faster than phone modems?

42. Why do DSL and cable modem suppliers use technology that devotes more speed to downloads than to uploads?

43. Messages sent across the Internet are divided into packets. What is a packet, and why are messages divided into them?

44. Explain the term *packet switching*.

45. What is a router?

46. What is a repeater?

47. What problems arise due to packet switching?

48. What are proprietary systems, and why do they cause a problem?

49. What do we call the ability of software and hardware on multiple platforms from multiple commercial vendors to communicate?

50. What is an open system, and how does it foster interoperability?

51. Compare and contrast proprietary and open systems.

52. What is the seven-layer logical breakdown of network interaction called?

53. What is a protocol stack, and why is it layered?

54. What is a firewall, what does it accomplish, and how does it accomplish it?

55. What is a hostname, and how is it composed?

56. What is an IP address, and how is it composed?

57. What is the relationship between a hostname and an IP address?

58. Into what parts can an IP address be split?

59. What are the relative sizes of class A networks, class B networks, and class C networks?

60. How many hosts are possible in class C networks, in class B networks, and in class A networks?

61. What is a domain name?

62. What is a top-level domain name?

63. How does the current domain name system try to resolve a hostname?

64. What is the "small world phenomenon"?

65. What is the currently most-visited social networking site?

66. List three positive results from using online social networking sites.

67. List three possible negative outcomes from using social networking sites.

68. Is a social network the same as a semantic net? Explain.

The Communications Layer

??? Thought Questions

1. What is the computer system in your school like? Are all the computers networked? Is there more than one network? Are the dormitories networked?

2. If you wanted to register a domain name, how would you go about it? `.biz`, `.info`, `.pro`, `.museum`, `.aero`, and `.coop` are new top-level domain names. Are there any current restrictions on the use of these new top-level domain names?

3. Do you think that the name *Internet* is appropriate? Would *Intranet* be a better name?

4. How many social networking sites have you visited? How many do you use regularly?

5. In your opinion, does the good side of social networking sites outweigh the bad?

The Communications Layer

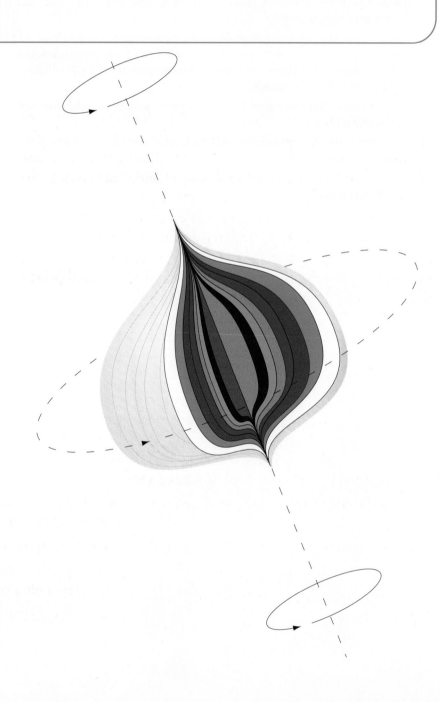

The World Wide Web

The evolution of the World Wide Web has made network communication a convenient reality for many users who would otherwise avoid computers completely. As the name implies, the Web has created spider-like connections across the entire planet, forming an infrastructure of information and resources, and making them available at the click of a mouse button. Several different underlying technologies make the Web the productive tool it is today. This chapter explores a few of them and establishes a foundation of Web-based principles on which all future technologies likely will rely.

Goals

After studying this chapter, you should be able to:

- compare and contrast the Internet and the World Wide Web.

- describe general Web processing.

- write basic HTML documents.

- describe several specific HTML tags and their purposes.

- describe the processing of Java applets and Java server pages.

- compare and contrast HTML and XML.

- define basic XML documents and their corresponding DTDs.

- explain how XML documents are viewed.

16.1 Spinning the Web

Many people use the words *Internet* and *Web* interchangeably, but in reality they are fundamentally different. The details of computer networks were discussed in Chapter 15. Networks have been used to connect computers since the 1950s. Communication via the Internet has been possible for many years, but in the early days that communication was almost exclusively accomplished via text-based email and basic file exchanges.

Compared to the Internet, the World Wide Web (or simply the Web) is a relatively new idea. The Web is an infrastructure of distributed information combined with software that uses networks as a vehicle to exchange that information. A Web page is a document that contains or references various kinds of data, such as text, images, graphics, and programs. Web pages also contain links to other Web pages so that the user can "move around" as desired using the point-and-click interface provided by a computer mouse. A website is a collection of related Web pages, usually designed and controlled by the same person or company.

The Internet makes the communication possible, but the Web makes that communication easy, more productive, and more enjoyable. Although universities and some high-tech companies had been using the Internet for years, it wasn't until the mid-1990s, when the World Wide Web was developed, that the Internet became a household name. Suddenly, Internet service providers (ISPs) began springing up everywhere, allowing people to connect to the Internet from their homes. The Internet, largely because of the World Wide Web, is now a primary vehicle for business. Electronic shopping, financial transactions, and group management are all common online activities. The Web has literally changed the way we conduct our personal and business lives.

When we use the Web, we often talk about "visiting" a website, as if we were going there. In truth, we actually specify the resource we want, and it is brought to us. The concept of visiting a site is understandable in that we often don't know what's at a particular site until we "go to it" and see.

We communicate on the Web using a Web browser, such as Firefox® or Microsoft's Internet Explorer®. A Web browser is a software tool that issues the request for the Web page we want and displays it when it arrives. Figure 16.1 depicts this process.

The requested Web page is usually stored on another computer, which may be down the hall or halfway around the world. That computer that is set up to respond to Web requests is called a web server.

In a browser, we specify the Web page we want by using a Web address such as

```
www.villanova.edu/academics.html
```

A Web address is the core part of a Uniform Resource Locator (URL), which uniquely identifies the page you want out of all of the pages stored anywhere in the world. Note that part of a URL is the hostname of the

≫ World Wide Web (Web) An infrastructure of information and the network software used to access it

≫ Web page A document that contains or references various kinds of data

≫ Link A connection between one Web page and another

≫ Website A collection of related Web pages, usually designed and controlled by the same person or company

≫ Web browser A software tool that retrieves and displays Web pages

≫ Web server A computer set up to respond to requests for Web pages

≫ Uniform Resource Locator (URL) A standard way of specifying the location of a Web page

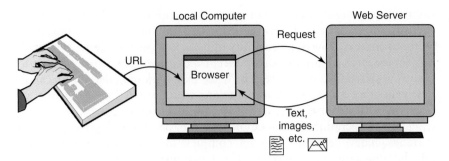

Local Computer

Web Server

URL

Browser

Request

Text, images, etc.

FIGURE 16.1 A browser retrieving a Web page

computer on which the information is stored. Chapter 15 discussed host-names and network addresses in detail.

In addition to text, a Web page often consists of separate elements such as images. All elements associated with a particular Web page are brought over when a request for that Web page is made.

Various technologies contribute to the design and implementation of a website. Our goal in this chapter is to introduce you to a few of these technologies. More detail about these topics can be found on this book's own website.

■ Search Engines

A Web *search engine* is a site that helps you find other websites. You've probably used a search engine, such as Google or Yahoo!®, many times. When you enter keywords that indicate the type of information you're looking for, the search engine provides a list of links to potential sites.

A search engine produces its list of candidate sites by searching a database containing information about millions of websites. A good search engine keeps its database up-to-date and has effective techniques for matching the keywords to the content of a Web page.

Most search engines compare the keywords entered by the search engine user to a set of keywords that have been indexed about each website. Some search engines index almost every word on every Web page in their databases, usually eliminating common words such as "a," "an," and "the." Other search engines index only part of a page, such as the document's title and headings. Some indexing techniques are case sensitive; others are not.

Keyword searching is challenging to do effectively because natural languages such as English are inherently ambiguous (this issue was discussed in Chapter 13 as well). For example, the terms *hard cider*, *hard brick*, *hard exam*, and *hard drive* all

The dancing spiders of Google™
A high search ranking on Google is essential for online businesses. Google updates its ranking two or three times per year using spider "bots"–search programs that "crawl" through more than 1 trillion unique URLs in sweeps known as "Google dances." Firms that specialize in search-engine optimization (SEO) help online businesses maintain high search rankings by making adjustments to their clients' websites that are valued by Google's spider bots. SEO firms simplify complicated Web page addresses, simplify text on Web pages, and add extra keywords to the invisible page descriptions (called "metatags") read by indexing software. The best SEOs can improve their clients' search rankings dramatically. In contrast, SEO companies that employ overly aggressive techniques, such as keyword stuffing, can get labeled as spamdexers or "black hat" SEOs (as opposed to "white hat") and get their clients' websites banned from the search results.

use the word "hard" in different ways. If enough keywords are provided, the search engines will ideally prioritize the matches appropriately. Without context, however, the utility of basic keyword matching is limited.

Some search engines perform *concept-based searches*, which attempt to figure out the context of your search. When they work well, they return candidate pages that contain content that relates to your search topic, whether or not the words in the page match the keywords in the query exactly.

Several techniques are employed for performing concept-based searches. They generally rely on complex linguistic theories that are beyond the scope of this book. The basic premise is called clustering, which compares words to other words found in close proximity. For example, the word *heart*, used in a medical sense, may be near words like *artery*, *cholesterol*, and *blood*.

Concept-based searches are far more complicated than keyword searches, and concept-based techniques have not been perfected. Nevertheless, they have far more potential to be effective once these techniques improve.

■ Instant Messaging

Instant messaging (IM) applications are among the most popular uses of the Web. As the name implies, they allow you to send messages to friends and coworkers in real time. If both the sender and the receiver have an active messaging application running, the messages pop up immediately upon arrival, allowing two people to have an ongoing "conversation" online. The leading IM application today is America Online® (AOL) Instant Messenger (AIM).

Today's IM applications are fairly sophisticated, allowing the user to tailor his or her list of contacts, set up default replies, and send standard and custom graphics as well as text. The IM model has become a routine method of communication for many Web users.

Most IM applications use a proprietary protocol that dictates the precise format and structure of the messages that are sent across the network to the receiver. AIM's protocol is proprietary as well, but it is not restricted to AOL users. That's one of the reasons that AIM has gained such popularity.

Instant messaging, though convenient, is not secure. The messages sent through the various IM protocols are not encrypted and could be intercepted at any intermediate point along the network communication path. Unencrypted email is similarly unsecure.

■ Weblogs

A *weblog*, or *blog* for short, is a mechanism for publishing periodic articles on a website. Depending on author, the topic, and the nature of the blog, these articles could range from one paragraph to extensive articles comparable to those you might find in a newspaper or magazine.

A website might be organized entirely as a blog, or a blog might be just one aspect of a site that contains many other elements. The tools and online services available for creating and publishing blogs have made it easy for many novices to get a website up and running.

Weblogs have evolved significantly since they first came on the scene in the late 1990s. Although you can still find many blogs that discuss the inconsequential thoughts and activities of their authors, many blogs serve as outlets for serious thought leaders on a variety of topics. Some blogs are a great source of information regarding particular issues, and as such have a devoted following. In 2004, the *Merriam-Webster Dictionary* declared the word "blog" to be the word of the year.

Some bloggers refer to themselves as "citizen journalists," promoting the idea that their blogs are as much a source of valid and valuable information as other media. One particular event is given credit for this change in status. In 2004, during the U.S. presidential campaign, CBS's Dan Rather reported on documents that criticized the military service of George Bush, supposedly written by Bush's former commander. Many bloggers challenged the authenticity of the documents based on numerous problems with the document's typography. CBS and Rather defended the authenticity of the documents for more than two weeks before finally admitting the documents were probably forgeries. This event is one of the clearest examples of the Web providing a voice for the "average person" loud enough to challenge the traditional information brokers.

Because blogs are online publications, they can respond to events much more quickly than conventional print media. For that reason, many established journalists have developed their own blogs to supplement their work available through other, more traditional outlets.

Save the trees
Environmentalists point out that to produce one week's Sunday newspapers, 500,000 trees must be cut down. Recycling a single run of the Sunday *New York Times* would save 75,000 trees. Each ton of recycled paper can save 17 trees; those 17 trees can absorb a total of 250 pounds of carbon dioxide from the air each year. Burning that same ton of paper would create 1500 pounds of carbon dioxide. Also driving the current "go green" trends are the changing habits of consumers who increasingly get their daily news from online news and weblogs. Today, sales of papers and advertising have dropped so low that most newspapers are in financial trouble and will need to reinvent themselves quickly if they are to survive. Two bailout tactics are online video marketing (video SEO) and subscription charges for viewing online newspapers.

■ Cookies

Cookies are another Web-based technology that has advanced the abilities and usefulness of Web to its users. A cookie is a small text file that a Web server stores on your local computer's hard disk. A website may store a cookie on a user's machine to capture key information about previous interactions that occurred between that machine and that website.

The pieces of information stored in a cookie are name–value pairs, plus the name of the site that stores the information. For example:

```
UserID    KDFH547FH398DFJ    www.goto.com
```

As in this example, a website might generate a unique ID number for each visiting computer and store it on the local machine. More sophisticated cookies may store timing information about how long a site was visited and what information was viewed.

Websites use cookies in many different ways. Some website use cookies to accurately determine how many unique visitors come to their site. Others store user preferences so that the website interaction is customized for that user. Cookies are also used to implement shopping carts that can be maintained from visit to visit.

One problem with using cookies is that people often share computers to use the Web. Because cookies are based on the machine that's making the connection (not the person), using cookies for personalizing the visit does not always work.

There are many misconceptions about cookies in general. A cookie is not a program, and it does not execute anything on your computer. It cannot collect personal information about you or your machine. Even so, cookies have not been embraced with open arms.

16.2 HTML

> **Hypertext Markup Language (HTML)** The language used to create or build a Web page

> **Markup language** A language that uses tags to annotate the information in a document

> **Tag** The syntactic element in a markup language that indicates how information should be displayed

Web pages are created (or built) using a language called the Hypertext Markup Language (HTML). The term *hypertext* refers to the fact that the information is not organized linearly, like a book. Instead, we can embed links to other information and jump from one place to another as needed. These days, the more accurate term would be *hypermedia*, because we deal with many types of information in addition to text, including images, audio, and video.

The term markup language comes from the fact that the primary elements of the language take the form of tags that we insert into a document to annotate the information stored there. In the case of HTML, the tags indicate how the information should be displayed. It's as if you took a printed document and marked it up with extra notation to specify other details, as shown in Figure 16.2.

HTML documents are regular text and can be created in any general-purpose editor or word processor. There are also special-purpose software tools designed to help us create Web pages, but these tools ultimately generate HTML documents. It is these HTML documents that are transported over the Web when a Web page is requested.

An HTML tag indicates the general nature of a piece of information (such as a paragraph, an image, or an itemized list) as well as how it should be displayed (such as the font style, size, and color). Think of tags as suggestions to the browser. Two different browsers may interpret the same tags in slightly different ways. Therefore, the same Web page may look different depending on which browser you use to view it.

Let's look at an example Web page as displayed by a browser and then examine the underlying HTML document with the various tags embedded

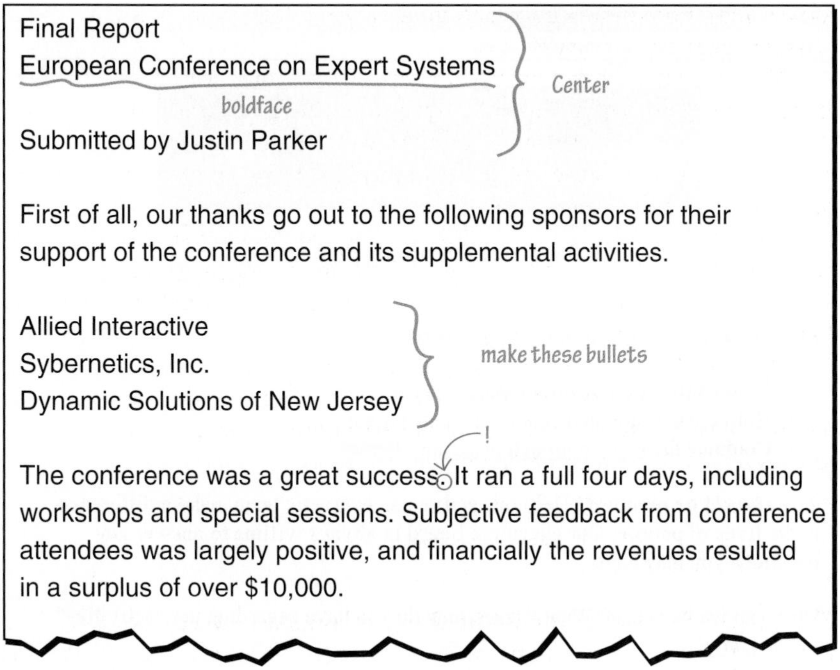

FIGURE 16.2 A marked-up document

in it. Figure 16.3 shows a Web page displayed in the Netscape Navigator® browser. The page contains information about a student organization called Student Dynamics.

This Web page contains an image at the top showing the name of the group. Below the image, offset by a pair of horizontal lines, is a single phrase in italics. Below that is some information about the organization, including a bulleted list of upcoming events followed by some short paragraphs. The small image at the end of one bulleted item indicates that this information has been recently updated. The blue, underlined text represents links that, when clicked using the mouse, open a new Web page. Some of the text has special styling, such as bold or italics, and some is centered.

Figure 16.4 shows the underlying HTML document for this Web page. It specifies all of the formatting seen in this Web page. The tags embedded among the main document contents are highlighted in blue.

Tags are enclosed in angle brackets (<. . . >). Words such as HEAD, TITLE, and BODY are called *elements* and specify the type of the tag. Tags are often used in pairs consisting of a start tag such as <BODY> and a corresponding end tag with a / before the element name, such as </BODY>. HTML is not case sensitive, so <body> and <BODY> are considered to be the same tag.

Every HTML file contains two main sections: the head of the document, followed by the body of the document. The head contains information about

FIGURE 16.3 The Student Dynamics Web page as displayed in Netscape Navigator

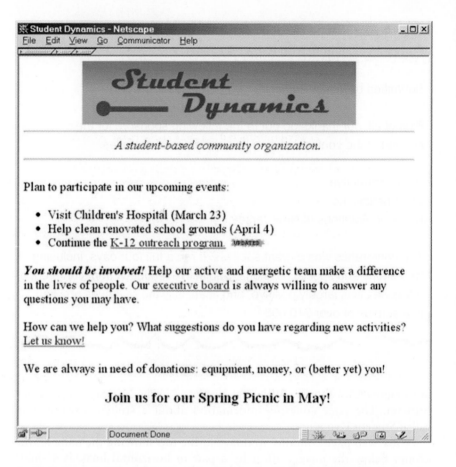

the document itself, such as its title. The body of the document contains the information to be displayed.

The entire HTML document is enclosed between `<HTML>` and `</HTML>` tags. The head and body sections of the document are similarly indicated. The text between the `<TITLE>` and `</TITLE>` tags appears in the title bar of the Web browser when the page is displayed.

The browser determines how the page should be displayed based on the tags. It ignores the way we format the HTML document using carriage returns, extra spaces, and blank lines. Indenting some lines of the document makes it easier for a human to read, but such formatting is irrelevant to the way it is finally displayed. A browser takes into account the width and height of the browser window. When you resize the browser window, the contents of the Web page are reformatted to fit the new size.

A browser does its best to make sense of the way a document is marked up with tags and displays the page accordingly. If HTML tags conflict, or if they are not properly ordered or nested, the results can be surprising—and unattractive.

```
<HTML>
   <HEAD>
      <TITLE>Student Dynamics</TITLE>
   </HEAD>
   <BODY>
      <CENTER><IMG SRC="stuDynamics.gif"></CENTER>
      <HR>
      <CENTER><I>A student-based community organization.</I></CENTER>
      <HR>
      <P>Plan to participate in our upcoming events:</P>
      <UL>
         <LI>Visit Children's Hospital (March 23)</LI>
         <LI>Help clean renovated school grounds (April 4)</LI>
         <LI>Continue the <a href="outreach.html">K-12 outreach
             program.</a> <IMG SRC="updated.gif"></LI>
      </UL>
      <P><B><I>You should be involved!</B></I> Help our active and
         energetic team make a difference in the lives of people. Our
         <a href="execBoard.html">executive board</a> is always willing
         to answer any questions you may have.</P>
      <P>How can we help you? What suggestions do you have regarding
         new activities? <a href="suggestions.html">Let us know!</a></P>
      <P>We are always in need of donations: equipment, money, or
         (better yet) you!</P>
      <CENTER><H3>Join us for our Spring Picnic in May!</H3></CENTER>
   </BODY>
</HTML>
```

FIGURE 16.4 The HTML document defining the Student Dynamics Web page

■ Basic HTML Formatting

The paragraph tags (`<P>` ... `</P>`) specify text that should be treated as a separate paragraph. In most browsers, the closing `</P>` tag is unnecessary, but we use it in Figure 16.4 for clarity. A browser usually begins each paragraph on a new line, with some space separating it from preceding and following paragraphs.

The center tags (`<CENTER>` ... `</CENTER>`) indicate that the enclosed information should be centered in the browser window.

The B, I, and U elements are used to indicate that the enclosed text should be bold, italic, or underlined, respectively. These elements can be nested, causing multiple effects to occur at the same time, although this is not the case with all tags. That is, not all tags make sense when they are nested.

The `<HR>` tag inserts a horizontal rule (that is, a line) across the page. Horizontal rules are often helpful in breaking up a Web page into sections.

>> **Attribute** Part of a tag that provides additional information about the element

We often have cause to display a list of items. The UL element stands for an unordered list, and the LI element represents a list item. In the Student Dynamics example, three list items are enclosed in the `<UL>` ... `</UL>` tags. Most browsers display an unordered list using bullets. If the ordered list element (OL) is used, the list items are numbered sequentially. Both unordered lists and ordered lists can be nested, creating a hierarchy of lists. Unordered nested lists use different bullet types for each level, and the numbering for each ordered list begins over again at each level.

Several elements are used to define headings in a document. HTML includes six predefined heading elements: H1, H2, H3, H4, H5, and H6. Text enclosed in `<H3>` ... `</H3>` tags, for instance, is treated as a level 3 heading, which is displayed in a larger font than level 4, but a smaller font than level 2. Heading tags don't have to specify text that introduces a section; they can be used anywhere you want to change the size of the font.

■ Images and Links

Many tags can contain **attributes** that indicate additional details about the information or describe how the enclosed information should be displayed.

Attributes take the following form:

```
attribute-name = value
```

For example, an image can be incorporated into a Web page using the IMG element, which takes an attribute that identifies the image file to display. The attribute name is SRC, which stands for the source of the image. There is no closing tag for the IMG element. For example,

```
<IMG SRC = "myPicture.gif">
```

inserts the image stored in file `myPicture.gif` into the HTML document. At least one space must separate IMG and SRC.

An image is used as a banner to the entire page in the Student Dynamics example. In another location, a small image is used to indicate information on the website that has been recently updated.

In HTML, a link is specified using the element A, which stands for anchor. The tag includes an attribute called HREF that specifies the URL of the destination document. For example,

```
<A HREF = "http://duke.csc.villanova.edu/docs/">
Documentation Central! </A>
```

shows the text "Documentation Central!" on the screen, usually underlined and in blue type. When the user clicks this link with the mouse, the

Tim Berners-Lee

Tim Berners-Lee is the first holder of the 3COM (Computer Communication Compatibility) Chair at the Computer Science and Artificial Intelligence Laboratory (CSAIL) at Massachusetts Institute of Technology. He is the 3COM Founders Professor of Engineering in the School of Engineering with a joint appointment in the Department of Electrical Engineering and CSAIL at MIT. Berners-Lee is a researcher, evangelist, and visionary rather than an academician. He is Director of the World Wide Web Consortium, which coordinates Web development worldwide. The Consortium, with teams at MIT, ERCIM in France, and Keio University in Japan, aims to help the Web achieve its full potential, ensuring its stability through rapid evolution and revolutionary transformations of its usage.

Courtesy of Le Fevre Communications/WC3

How did Tim Berners-Lee arrive at this very important position? He built his first computer while a student at Queen's College, Oxford, in the United Kingdom. After graduation, he worked for two years with Plessey Telecommunications Ltd., a major telecom equipment manufacturer in the United Kingdom; he then worked as an independent consultant for a year and a half, followed by three years at Image Computer Systems Ltd. His various projects during this time included real-time control firmware, graphics and communications software, and a generic macro language.

In 1984, Berners-Lee took up a fellowship at CERN, the European Organization for Nuclear Research in Geneva, Switzerland, where he worked on a heterogeneous remote procedure call system and a distributed real-time system for scientific data acquisition and system control. In 1989, he proposed a global hypertext project to be known as the World Wide Web. It was designed to allow people to work together by combining their knowledge in a web of hypertext documents. Berners-Lee wrote the first World Wide Web server, "httpd," and the first client, "World Wide Web," a what-you-see-is-what-you-get hypertext browser/editor. The work began in October 1990, and the program "World Wide Web" was made available within CERN in December 1990 and on the Internet at large in the summer of 1991.

Between 1991 and 1993, Berners-Lee continued working on the design of the Web, coordinating feedback from users across the Internet. His initial specifications of URLs, HTTP, and HTML were refined and discussed in larger circles as the Web technology spread. Eventually, it became apparent that the physics lab in Geneva was not the appropriate place for the task of developing and monitoring the Web. In October 1994, the World Wide Web Consortium was founded by Berners-Lee at the MIT Laboratory for Computer Science.

In a *New York Times* article in 1995, Berners-Lee was asked about private corporations trying to dominate Web standards for profit. He responded, "There's always the threat that a particular company would dominate the market and control the standards of the Web." But he feels strongly that this should not happen. "The essence of the Web is that it's a universe of information," he said. "And it wouldn't be universal if it was tied, in any way, to one company."

Michael Dertouzos, the director of the Computer Science Laboratory at MIT, has said that Berners-Lee seems to embody the "libertarian idealism" of the Internet culture. "He has a real commitment to keeping the Web open as a public good, in economic terms," Dertouzos said. "That's

» continued

his mission." Berners-Lee concludes: "Reasonable competition speeds the pace of innovation. Companies will promote the proprietary aspects of their browsers and applications, and they should. But the navigation of the Web has to be open. If the day comes when you need six browsers on your machine, the World Wide Web will no longer be the World Wide Web."

Berners-Lee was one of *Time* magazine's 100 most important people in the twentieth century. In recognition of his work on the World Wide Web, Queen Elizabeth II made Berners-Lee a Knight Commander, Order of the British Empire (KBE).

In June 2007, he received the Order of Merit from Queen Elizabeth II, which entitles him to use "OM" after his name. In September 2008, he was awarded the IEEE/RSE Wolfson James Clerk Maxwell Award for conceiving and further developing the World Wide Web, and in 2009 he was elected as a foreign associate of the National Academy of Sciences. Berners-Lee is currently serving as the Director of the World Wide Web Consortium; a Director of the Web Science Research Institute and the World Wide Web Foundation; the 3COM Founders Professor of Engineering in the School of Engineering, with a joint appointment in the Department of Electrical Engineering and Computer Science and MIT's Computer Science Artificial Intelligence Laboratory (CSAIL), leading the Decentralized Information Group (DIG); and as Professor of Computer Science at Southampton ECS.

Web page whose address is `duke.csc.villanova.edu/docs` is fetched and displayed in the browser, replacing the current page. Notice that both the name of a file and a URL are enclosed in quotes.

We have merely scratched the surface of HTML's capabilities in our discussion. Nevertheless, the few tags we've examined already give us the ability to create fairly versatile and useful Web pages.

16.3 Interactive Web Pages

When HTML was first developed, it was amazing in its ability to format network-based text and images in interesting ways. However, that information was static—there was no way to interact with the information and pictures presented in a Web page.

As users have clamored for a more dynamic Web, new technologies have been developed to accommodate these requests. These technologies take different approaches to solving the problem. Many of the new ideas are offshoots of the Java™ programming language, which is able to exploit the Web because of its platform independence. Let's look briefly at two of these technologies: *Java applets* and *Java Server Pages*.

■ Java Applets

A Java applet is a program that is designed to be embedded into an HTML document and transferred over the Web to someone who wants to

>> Java applet A Java program designed to be embedded into an HTML document, transferred over the Web, and executed in a browser

run the program. An applet is actually executed in the browser used to view the Web page.

An applet is embedded into an HTML document using the APPLET tag. For example:

```
<APPLET code="MyApplet.class" width=250 height=160>
</APPLET>
```

When a Web user references the page containing this tag, the applet program MyApplet.class is sent along with any text, images, and other data that the page contains. The browser knows how to handle each type of data—it formats text appropriately and displays images as needed. In the case of an applet, the browser has a built-in interpreter that executes the applet, allowing the user to interact with it. Thousands of Java applets are available on the Web, and most browsers are set up to execute them.

Consider the difficulties inherent in this situation. A program is written on one computer, but then may be transferred to any other computer on the Web to be executed. How can we execute a program that was written on one type of computer on possibly many other types of computers? The key, as briefly explained in Chapter 9, is that Java programs are compiled into Bytecode, a low-level representation of a program that is not the machine code for any particular type of CPU. This Bytecode can be executed by any valid Bytecode interpreter, no matter which type of machine it is running on.

The applet model puts the burden on the client's machine. That is, a Web user brings the program to his or her computer and executes it there. It may be frightening to think that, while you are casually surfing the Web, suddenly someone's program may begin executing on your computer. That would be a problem, except that Java applets are restricted as to what they can do. The Java language has a carefully constructed security model. An applet, for instance, cannot access any local files or change any system settings.

Depending on the nature of the applet, the client's computer may or may not be up to the job of executing the applet. For this reason, and because applets are transferred over a network, they tend to be relatively small. Although appropriate for some situations, applets do not resolve all of the interactive needs of Web users.

■ Java Server Pages

A Java Server Page (JSP) is a Web page that has JSP scriptlets embedded in it. A scriptlet is a small piece of executable code intertwined among regular HTML content. While not exactly the same as Java, JSP code resembles the general Java programming language.

A JSP scriptlet is encased in special tags beginning with <% and ending with %>. Special objects have been predefined to facilitate some processing. For example, the object called out can be used to produce output, which is

>> JSP scriptlet A portion of code embedded in an HTML document designed to dynamically contribute to the content of the Web page

integrated into the Web page wherever the scriptlet occurs. The following scriptlet produces the phrase "hello there" between the opening and closing tag of an H3 header:

```
<H3>
<%
out.println ("hello there");
%>
</H3>
```

In this particular case, the result is equivalent to

```
<H3>hello there</H3>
```

But imagine JSP scriptlets as having the expressive power of a full programming language (which they do). We can make use of almost all aspects of a regular Java program, such as variables, conditionals, loops, and objects. With that kind of processing power, a JSP page can make significant decisions resulting in truly dynamic results.

JSPs are executed on the server side, where the Web page resides. They help dynamically define the content of a Web page before it is shipped to the user. By the time it arrives at your computer, all active processing has taken place, producing a static (though dynamically created) Web page.

JSPs are particularly good for coordinating the interaction between a Web page and an underlying database. The details of this type of processing are beyond the scope of this book, but you've probably encountered this type of processing while surfing the Web. Electronic storefronts (sites that exist primarily to sell products), in particular, make extensive use of this type of processing. The data about available products are not stored in static HTML pages. Instead, those data are stored in a database. When you make a request for information about a particular product, a JSP may actually respond to you. The scriptlets in the page interact with the database and extract the needed information. Scriptlets and regular HTML format the data appropriately and then ship the page to your computer for viewing.

16.4 XML

HTML is fixed; that is, HTML has a predefined set of tags and each tag has its own semantics (meaning). HTML specifies how the information in a Web page should be formatted, but it doesn't really indicate what the information represents. For example, HTML may indicate that a piece of text should be formatted as a heading, but it doesn't specify what that heading describes. In fact, nothing about HTML tags describes the true content of a document. The

Extensible Markup Language (XML) allows the creator of a document to describe its contents by defining his or her own set of tags.

XML is a metalanguage. *Metalanguage* is the word *language* plus the prefix *meta*, which means "beyond" or "more comprehensive." A metalanguage goes beyond a normal language by allowing us to speak precisely about that language. It is a language for talking about, or defining, other languages. It is like an English grammar book describing the rules of English.

A metalanguage called the Standard Generalized Markup Language (SGML) was used by Tim Berners-Lee to define HTML. XML is a simplified version of SGML and is used to define other markup languages. XML has taken the Web in a new direction. It does not replace HTML—it enriches it.

Like HTML, an XML document is made up of tagged data. But when you write an XML document, you are not restricted to a predefined set of tags, because there are none. You can create any set of tags necessary to describe the data in your document. The focus is not on how the data should be formatted, but rather on what the data is.

For example, the XML document in Figure 16.5 describes a set of books. The tags in the document annotate data that represents a book's title, author(s), number of pages, publisher, ISBN number, and price.

> **» Extensible Markup Language (XML)** A language that allows the user to describe the content of a document
>
> **» Metalanguage** A language that is used to define other languages

```
<?xml version="1.0" ?>
<!DOCTYPE books SYSTEM "books.dtd">
<books>
<book>
<title>The Hobbit</title>
<authors>
   <author>J. R. R. Tolkien</author>
</authors>
<publisher>Ballantine</publisher>
<pages>287</pages>
<isbn>0-345-27257-9</isbn>
<price currency="USD">7.95</price>
</book>
<book>
<title>A Beginner's Guide to Bass Fishing</title>
<authors>
   <author>J. T. Angler</author>
   <author>Ross G. Clearwater</author>
</authors>
<publisher>Quantas Publishing</publisher>
<pages>750</pages>
<isbn>0-781-40211-7</isbn>
<price currency="USD">24.00</price>
</book>
</books>
```

FIGURE 16.5 An XML document containing data about books

>> **Document Type Definition (DTD)** A specification of the organization of an XML document

>> **Extensible Stylesheet Language (XSL)** A language for defining transformations from XML documents to other output formats

The first line of the document indicates the version of XML that is used. The second line indicates the file that contains the **Document Type Definition (DTD)** for the document. The DTD is a specification of the organization of the document. The rest of the document contains the data about two particular books.

The structure of a particular XML document is described by its corresponding DTD document. The contents of a DTD document not only define the tags, but also show how they can be nested. Figure 16.6 shows the DTD document that corresponds to the XML books example.

The ELEMENT tags in the DTD document describe the tags that make up the corresponding XML document. The first line of this DTD file indicates that the books tag is made up of zero or more book tags. The asterisk (*) beside the word book in parentheses stands for zero or more. The next line specifies that the book tag is made up of several other tags in a particular order: title, authors, publisher, pages, isbn, and price. The next line indicates that the authors tag is made up of one or more author tags. The plus sign (+) beside the word author indicates one or more authors are permitted. The other tags are specified to contain PCDATA (Parsed Character Data), which indicates that the tags are not further broken down into other tags.

The only tag in this set that has an attribute is the price tag. The last line of the DTD document indicates that the price tag has an attribute called currency and that it is required.

XML provides a standard format for organizing data without tying it to any particular type of output. A related technology called **Extensible Stylesheet Language (XSL)** can be used to transform an XML document into another format suitable for a particular user. For example, an XSL document

```
<!ELEMENT books (book*)>
<!ELEMENT book (title, authors, publisher, pages, isbn, price)>
<!ELEMENT authors (author+)>
<!ELEMENT title (#PCDATA)>
<!ELEMENT author (#PCDATA)>
<!ELEMENT publisher (#PCDATA)>
<!ELEMENT pages (#PCDATA)>
<!ELEMENT isbn (#PCDATA)>
<!ELEMENT price (#PCDATA)>
<!ATTLIST price currency CDATA #REQUIRED>
```

FIGURE 16.6 The DTD document corresponding to the XML books document

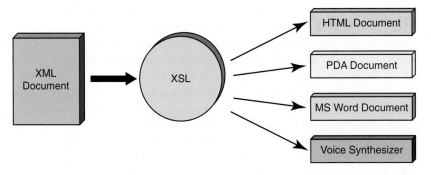

FIGURE 16.7 An XML document can be transformed into many output formats.

can be defined that specifies the transformation of an XML document into an HTML document so that it can be viewed on the Web. Another XSL document might be defined to transform the same XML document into a Microsoft Word document, into a format suitable for a personal data assistant (PDA) such as a Palm Pilot, or even into a format that can be used by a voice synthesizer. This process is depicted in Figure 16.7. We do not explore the details of XSL transformations in this book.

Another convenient characteristic of languages specified using XML is that documents in the language can be generated automatically with relative ease. A software system, usually with an underlying database, can be used to generate huge amounts of specific data formatted in a way that is easily conveyed and analyzed online. Once generated, the data can be transformed and viewed in whatever manner best serves individual users.

Several organizations have already developed XML languages for their particular topic areas. For example, chemists and chemical engineers have defined the Chemistry Markup Language (CML) to standardize the format of molecular data. CML includes a huge number of tags covering specific aspects of chemistry. It provides a common format by which chemistry professionals can share and analyze data.

Keep in mind that XML is a *markup specification language*, whereas XML files are *data*. The files just sit there until you run a program that displays them (like a browser), does some work with them (like a converter that writes the data in another format or a database that reads the data), or modifies them (like an editor). XML and its related technologies provide a powerful mechanism for information management and for communicating that information over the Web in a versatile and efficient manner. As these technologies evolve, new opportunities to capitalize on them will surely emerge.

Summary

Although the terms *Internet* and *Web* are often used interchangeably, they are not the same. The World Wide Web is an infrastructure of information distributed among thousands of computers across the world and the software by which that information is accessed. The Web relies on underlying networks, especially the Internet, as the vehicle to exchange the information among users.

A Web page contains information as well as references to other resources such as images. A collection of Web pages managed by a single person or company is called a website. Links are established among various Web pages across the globe, giving credence to the name World Wide Web.

Visiting a website is really the act of requesting that a Web page stored on a remote web server be brought to the local computer for viewing. A Uniform Resource Locator (URL) is used to specify the Web document the user wishes to view.

Some websites, such as that run by Google, serve as search engines, allowing the user to enter a word or phrase on which to base a search for information. The search engine responds with a list of candidate websites that the user hopes will match his or her needs. Some search engines are based solely on the keywords entered in the search; others try to interpret the concept underlying the search.

Instant messaging (IM) applications have given the Web another level of interaction, allowing users to conduct ongoing conversations online. IM programs are evolving to include graphics and even video.

Weblogs, or blogs, are Web-based publications that feature regularly updated articles. The more serious blogs serve as significant resources on particular topics. Others have given rise to "citizen journalists," whose work supplements that of the mainstream media.

Cookies are small text files that a website deposits on your hard drive, so that when you return to the site, information about you and your prior visit can be incorporated into your current visit. Cookies are often used to track the activities of users, and they are generally considered helpful for both the user and the sites using them. A cookie is not a program, so it cannot execute code on your computer.

Hypertext Markup Language (HTML) is the primary method of defining Web pages. An HTML document consists of information that is annotated by tags that specify how a particular element should be treated and formatted. A Web browser displays an HTML page without regard to extra spacing, blank lines, or indentation. The tags alone guide the browser, and a given Web page may look slightly different when viewed in different browsers.

HTML tags include those that specify the overall document structure as well as tags that perform basic formatting, such as for headings, paragraphs, and centered text. Font styles, such as bold and italics, are specified using tags as well. Unordered and ordered lists have their own sets of tags.

Some HTML tags include attributes that specify additional information. The source attribute of an image tag specifies the file in which the image is stored, for instance. Anchor tags define links and use an attribute to specify the location of the target Web page.

Additional opportunities to interact with and dynamically create the content of Web pages exist. Two technologies that support Web-based interaction are Java applets and Java Server Pages (JSPs). Java applets are Java programs designed to be embedded in HTML pages and executed in a Web browser. Their cross-platform nature is possible because applets are compiled into Java Bytecode, which is architecture neutral.

Java Server Pages embed scriptlets into HTML code that is executed by the web server to help dynamically define the content of a Web page. Scriptlets have all the expressive power of a full language. JSPs are particularly good at coordinating the interaction between a Web page and its underlying database.

Extensible Markup Language (XML) is a metalanguage, which means it is used to define other languages. Unlike HTML, whose tags focus on the format of displayed data, XML tags specify the nature of the data. The user is not constrained to use particular tags; he or she can define any tags that make sense for the data being described.

The format and relationships among XML tags are defined in a Document Type Definition (DTD) document. A set of Extensible Stylesheet Language (XSL) transformations define the way the content of an XML document is turned into another format suitable for the current needs of the user.

ETHICAL ISSUES ▶ Blogging

Like websites, *blogs* have become ubiquitous virtually overnight. A blog is a Weblog or online journal. Most blogs are interactive and provide for feedback from readers. Whereas most bloggers write about mundane matters, the *blogosphere* has also emerged as a viable alternative news medium. Blogs are having a growing impact, sometimes supplementing or correcting reporting of the mainstream media. In 2004, blogs quickly exposed the inauthenticity of the documents used in a *60 Minutes* story about President George W. Bush's National Guard service. Many other blogs consistently provide a unique and unconventional perspective on the local and national news.

According to the *Wall Street Journal*, the audience for alternative media is expanding: "The number of Americans reading blogs jumped 58% in 2004 to an estimated 32 million people . . . with about 11 million looking to political blogs for news during the [2004] presidential campaign."[1]

But blogs are not just for online journalists or political commentators. Their use has also grown among doctors, lawyers, and teachers. Blogs have even become popular in the classroom. Many students have their own blogs where they record their impressions about teachers or other school-related information in a diary-like format. The use of student blogs has led to a new debate about the amount of control educators should exert over online classroom activities.

Of course, the blogosphere is not without its share of controversies. One such controversy erupted in

» continued

⚖ ETHICAL ISSUES ▸ Blogging, continued

2005 after some bloggers posted confidential Apple® Computer documents about an unreleased Apple product. Apple demanded to know the source of this information but the bloggers argued that they were journalists, so they should be protected under federal and state laws from revealing their sources. A California judge disagreed, however, as he ruled that the bloggers must reveal their sources. Unfortunately, the judge in this case did not address the central question: Do bloggers deserve the same privileges to protect their sources that are accorded to journalists? On the one hand, these bloggers are acting just like journalists by reporting the news, so why shouldn't they have the same privileges as journalists? On the other hand, "the prospect of 10, 20, or 50 million bloggers claiming journalistic privilege terrifies judges and First Amendment lawyers alike, [since] they fear that anyone who has a Website, if called to testify by a grand jury, could claim the privilege and refuse to cooperate."[2]

Because blogging is such a new phenomenon, there has not been much debate about "blogging ethics." But such debate is surely needed. What are the responsibilities of bloggers, especially those who operate alternative news sites? Do they have the same obligations as the conventional media? Should they be held to the same standards of objectivity?

Although it may not be a good idea to put too many restrictions on bloggers, they are, of course, subject to the same ethical duties as anyone who communicates information. First and foremost, bloggers have an obligation to avoid lying. St. Thomas Aquinas defines a *lie* as the intentional saying of what is false.[3] In Aquinas's view, lying is odious because it is an offense against reason and it disrupts the harmony necessary for our common life. From a natural law perspective, lying and deception are wrong because they impede the intrinsic good of knowledge. Thus bloggers, like everyone else, must strive to be truthful at all times. They also have an obligation to check their sources and to identify those sources whenever possible so that readers are fully informed; in an online environment, this can often be done by providing links to other sites. Bloggers also have a duty to avoid unjust accusations and to retract erroneous information as quickly as possible. Finally, bloggers should consider disclosing any conflicts of interest in cases where their objectivity may be compromised. Sometimes it may be necessary for a blogger to disclose who pays his or her salary or who provides funding for the website's operating costs. As one blogger explained, "The audience should be able to come to your blog and assume you're not on the take."[4] If bloggers can follow these simple rules, they will engender trust among their readers and the weblog will continue to have a bright future.

Material used in this case description has been excerpted from R. Spinello, Cyberethics: Morality and Law in Cyberspace, *third edition (Sudbury, MA: Jones and Bartlett, 2006).*

🔑 Key Terms

Attribute
Document Type Definition (DTD)
Extensible Markup Language (XML)
Extensible Stylesheet Language (XSL)
Hypertext Markup Language (HTML)
Java applet
JSP scriptlet
Link
Markup language
Metalanguage

Tag
Uniform Resource Locator (URL)
Web browser
Web page
Web server
Website
World Wide Web (Web)

⌘ Exercises

For Exercises 1–12, mark the answers true or false as follows:

A. True
B. False

1. The Internet and the Web are essentially two names for the same thing.

2. The computer that is set up to respond to Web requests is a Web browser.

3. When we visit a website, we actually bring the site to us.

4. Most search engines use a context-based approach for finding candidate pages.

5. A Weblog is the same thing as a blog.

6. A Weblog can serve as an online publication for "citizen journalists."

7. A cookie is a program that is executed on your computer.

8. All elements associated with a particular Web page are brought over when a request for that Web page is made.

9. Networks have been used to connect computers since the 1950s.

10. Network communication was not possible until the advent of the Web.

11. The Web was developed in the mid-1990s.

12. You must have a Web browser to access the Web.

For Exercises 13–22, match the word or acronym with the definition or blank.

A. JSP scriptlet
B. URL
C. HTML
D. Tag
E. Java applet
F. XML

13. A program designed to be embedded into an HTML document.

14. Uniquely identifies every Web page.

15. _____ runs on the web server.

16. _____ runs on the Web browser.

17. Tags in _____ are fixed.

18. Tags in _____ are not predefined.

19. _____ is a metalanguage.

20. The structure of an _____ document is described by its corresponding Document Type Definition (DTD).

21. The syntactic element in a markup language that indicates how information should be displayed.

22. Part of a _____ is the hostname of the computer on which the information is stored.

Exercises 23–70 are problems or short-answer questions.

23. What is the Internet?

24. What is the Web?

25. What is a Web page?

26. What is a website?

27. What is a link?

28. Why is a spiderweb a good analogy for the World Wide Web?

29. What is the relationship between a Web page and a website?

30. What is the difference between the Internet and the Web?

31. Describe how a Web page is retrieved and viewed by a Web user.

32. What is a Uniform Resource Locator?

33. What is a markup language? Where does the name come from?

34. Compare and contrast hypertext and hypermedia.

35. Describe the syntax of an HTML tag.

36. What is a horizontal rule? What are these rules useful for?

37. Name five formatting specifications that can be established using HTML tags.

38. What is a tag attribute? Give an example.

39. Write the HTML statement that inputs the image on file `mine.gif` into the Web page.

40. Write the HTML statement that sets up a link to http://www.cs.utexas.edu/users/ndale/ and shows the text "Dale Home Page" on the screen.

41. What happens when a user clicks on "Dale Home Page" as set up in Exercise 40?

42. Design and implement an HTML document for an organization at your school.

43. Design and implement an HTML document describing one or more of your personal hobbies.

44. What is a Java applet?

45. How do you embed a Java applet in an HTML document?

46. Where does a Java applet get executed?

47. What kinds of restrictions are put on Java applets? Why?

48. What is a Java Server Page?

49. What is a scriptlet?

50. How do you embed a scriptlet in an HTML document?

51. How does JSP processing differ from applet processing?

52. What is a metalanguage?

53. What is XML?

54. How are HTML and XML alike, and how are they different?

55. How does an XML document relate to a Document Type Definition?

56. a. In a DTD, how do you indicate that an element is to be repeated zero or more times?
    b. In a DTD, how do you indicate that an element is to be repeated one or more times?
    c. In a DTD, how do you indicate that an element cannot be broken down into other tags?

57. What is XSL?

58. What is the relationship between XML and XSL?

59. How does an XML document get viewed?

60. Define an XML language (the DTD) for your school courses and produce a sample XML document.

61. Define an XML language (the DTD) for political offices and produce a sample XML document.

62. Define an XML language (the DTD) for zoo animals and produce a sample XML document.

63. This chapter is full of acronyms. Define each of the following ones:
    a. HTML
    b. XML
    c. DTD
    d. XSL

   e. SGML
   f. URL
   g. ISP

64. Create an HTML document for a Web page that has each of the following features:
   a. Centered title
   b. Unordered list
   c. Ordered list
   d. Link to another Web page
   e. A picture

65. Distinguish between an HTML tag and an attribute.

66. Why might the same Web page look different in different browsers?

67. What are the two sections of every HTML document?

68. What are the contents of the two parts of an HTML document?

69. What does the A stand for in the tag that specifies a URL for a page?

70. Create an HTML document for a Web page that has each of the following features:
   a. A right-justified title in large type font
   b. An applet class named `Exercise.class`
   c. Two different links
   d. Two different pictures

??? Thought Questions

1. How has the Web affected you personally?

2. Did you have a website before you started this class? How sophisticated was it? Did you use HTML or some other Web design language? If you used some other language, go to your website and view your pages as source pages. Look at the HTML tags that actually format your website. Are there any there that we have not discussed in this chapter? If so, look them up to see what they mean. (Where? On the Web, of course.)

3. Have you ever taken a Web-based course? Did you enjoy the experience? Did you feel that you learned less or more than you would have in a regular classroom-based course?

4. Give your vision of the future as it relates to the Web.

5. In your opinion, how many restrictions should be placed on bloggers? Should they be held to the same standards as journalists?

6. Is blogging an effective tool to communicate with the general public? Or does its individualistic stance and lack of an editor make it an unreliable source of information?

7. Is blogging only helpful in reporting news, or are there other valuable uses for Weblogs?

In Conclusion

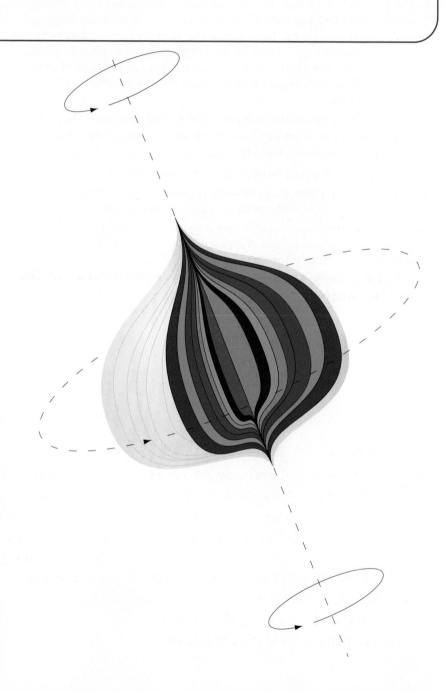

Limitations of Computing

17

In the last 16 chapters, we have looked at computers: what they are, what they can do, and how to use them to solve problems. In this chapter, we look at what computers *cannot* do. That is, we examine the limits imposed by the hardware, the software, and the problems themselves. The dictionary gives multiple meanings for the word *limit*, including "boundary" and "something that is exasperating or intolerable." We use both of these definitions of *limit* in this chapter.

Just as a roadblock stops traffic, the limits imposed by the hardware, software, and problems stop certain kinds of processing.

Goals

After studying this chapter, you should be able to:

- describe the limits that the hardware places on the solution to computing problems.

- discuss how the finiteness of the computer influences the solutions to numeric problems.

- discuss ways to ensure that errors in data transmission are detected.

- describe the limits that the software places on the solutions to computing problems.

- discuss ways to build better software.

- describe the limits inherent in computable problems themselves.

- discuss the continuum of problem complexity from problems in Class P to problems that are unsolvable.

17.1 Hardware

The limits on computing caused by hardware stem from several factors. One factor is that numbers are infinite, but the representation of them within the computer is not. Another problem with hardware is just the fact that it is hardware; that is, it is made up of mechanical and electronic components that can fail. Another set of problems occurs when data is transmitted from one internal device to another or from one computer to another. Let's look at each of these problems and some strategies to minimize their impact.

■ Limits on Arithmetic

We discussed numbers and their representation in the computer in Chapters 2 and 3. There are limitations imposed by computer hardware on the representations of both integer numbers and real numbers.

Integer Numbers

In the Pep/8 machine discussed in Chapter 6, the register that is used for arithmetic is 16 bits long. We said that the largest value we could store there is 65,535 if we represent only positive values and 32,767 if we represent both positive and negative values. Pep/8 is a virtual machine—but what about real machines? If the word length is 32 bits, the range of integer numbers that can be represented is −2,147,483,648 to 2,147,483,647. Some hardware systems support long-word arithmetic, where the range is −9,223,372,036,854,775,808 to 9,223,372,036,854,775,807: Surely this is large enough for any calculation. Or is it?

Henry Walker, in his book *The Limits of Computing*, tells the following fable.[1] When the king asked a bright young dot-com'er to undertake a task for him, she agreed if the pay was adequate. She offered the king two choices: The king could pay her 1/5 of the crops produced in the kingdom for the next five years or base her payment on a chess board as follows:

- One kernel of corn on the first square
- Two kernels of corn on the second square
- Four kernels of corn on the third square
- Eight kernels of corn on the fourth square
- The kernels of corn would double on each successive square until the 64th square had been reached.

After a moment's thought, the king chose the second option. (Which would you have chosen?)

When it came time to pay up, the king started placing kernels of corn on the squares. There were 255 kernels on the first row (1 + 2 + 4 + 8 + 17 + 32 + 64 + 128); not too bad, he thought. For the next row, there were 65,280 kernels; still not too bad. The third row, however, with its 963,040 kernels of corn, made the king uneasy. During the counting of the next row, the king thought ahead to the last square, for he now understood the pattern. The 64th square alone would have 2^{63} kernels of corn—roughly 8×10^{18} kernels or 110,000 billion bushels. The king abdicated his throne in light of such a staggering debt, and the mathematically sophisticated young lady became queen.

The moral of this story is that integer numbers can get very big very fast. If a computer word is 64 bits and we represent only positive numbers, we could just represent the number of kernels on the 64th square. If we tried to add up the kernels on the 64 squares, we could not do so. Overflow would occur.

The hardware of a particular machine determines the limits of the numbers, both real and integer, that can be represented. Some software solutions, however, allow programs to overcome these limitations. For example, we could represent a very large number as a list of smaller numbers. Figure 17.1 shows how integers could be presented by putting one or more digits in each word. The program that manipulates integers in these forms would have to add each pair of digits beginning at the rightmost and add any carry into the next addition to the left.

Real Numbers

In Chapter 3, we said that a real number is stored as an integer along with information about the position of the radix point. To better understand why real numbers pose a problem, let's look at a coding scheme that represents the digits and the *radix-point information*.

To simplify the following discussion, let's assume that we have a computer in which each memory location is the same size and is divided into a sign plus five decimal digits. When a variable or constant is defined, the location assigned to it consists of five digits and a sign. When an integral variable or constant is defined, the interpretation of the number stored in that place is straightforward. When a real variable is declared or a real constant is defined, the number stored there has both a whole-number part and a fractional part. The number must be coded to represent both parts.

Let's see what these coded numbers might look like and what this coding does to arithmetic values in programs. We begin with integers. The range of the numbers we can represent with five digits is $-99,999$ through $+99,999$:

| − | 9 | 9 | 9 | 9 | 9 | Largest negative number |

| + | 0 | 0 | 0 | 0 | 0 | Zero |

| + | 9 | 9 | 9 | 9 | 9 | Largest positive number |

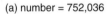

(a) number = 752,036

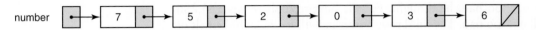

(b) number = 752,036

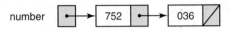

(c) sum = 83536 + 41

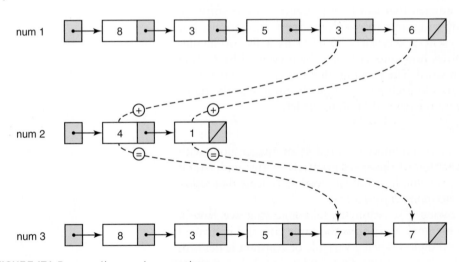

FIGURE 17.1 Representing very large numbers

>> Precision The maximum number of significant digits that can be represented

The precision (the maximum number of digits that can be represented) is five digits, and each number within that range can be represented exactly. What happens if we allow one of these digits (let's say the leftmost one, in red) to represent an exponent? For example,

+	3	2	3	4	5

represents the number $+2345 * 10^3$. The range of numbers we can now represent is much larger:

$-9999 * 10^9$ to $+9999 * 10^9$

or

$-9,999,000,000,000$ to $+9,999,000,000,000$

Now the precision is only four digits. That is, we can represent only four **significant digits** (nonzero digits or zero digits that are exact) of the number itself. This means we can represent only four-digit numbers exactly in our system. What happens to larger numbers? The four left-most digits are correct, and the balance of the digits are assumed to be zero. We lose the rightmost, or *least significant*, digits. The following example shows what happens.

> **Significant digits** Those digits that begin with the first nonzero digit on the left and end with the last nonzero digit on the right (or a zero digit that is exact)

Number	Sign	Exp.					Value
+99,999	+	1	9	9	9	9	+99,990
−999,999	−	2	9	9	9	9	−999,900
+1,000,000	+	3	1	0	0	0	+1,000,000
−4,932,416	−	3	4	9	3	2	−4,932,000

Notice that we can represent 1,000,000 exactly, but not −4,932,417. Our coding scheme is limited to four significant digits; the digits we cannot represent are assumed to be zero.

To extend our coding scheme to represent real numbers, we need to be able to represent negative exponents. For example,

$4394 * 10^{-2} = 43.94$

or

$22 * 10^{-4} = 0.0022$

Because our scheme does not allow for a sign for the exponent, we have to change the scheme slightly. Let's allow the sign that we have already been using to be the sign of the exponent and add a sign to the left of it to be the sign of the number itself.

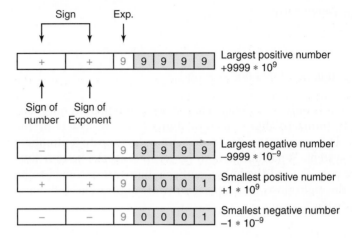

Now we can represent all of the numbers between $-9999 * 10^{-9}$ and $9999 * 10^9$ accurately to four digits, including all the fractional values.

Suppose we want to add three real numbers x, y, and z using this coding scheme. We could add x to y, then add z to the result. Or we could do it another way: add y to z, then add x to the result. The associative law of arithmetic says that the two answers should be the same—but are they?

The computer limits the precision (the number of significant digits) of a real number. Using our coding scheme of four significant digits and an exponent, let's add the following allowable values of x, y, and z:

$$x = -1324 * 10^3 \qquad y = 1325 * 10^3 \qquad z = 5424 * 10^0$$

First let's look at the result of adding z to the sum of x and y:

$$
\begin{array}{ll}
(x) & -1324 * 10^3 \\
(y) & \underline{1325 * 10^3} \\
& 1 * 10^3 = 1000 * 10^0
\end{array}
$$

$$
\begin{array}{ll}
(x + y) & 1000 * 10^0 \\
(z) & \underline{5424 * 10^0} \\
& 6424 * 10^0 = (x + y) + z
\end{array}
$$

Now let's see what happens when we add x to the sum of y and z:

$$
\begin{array}{ll}
(y) & 1325000 * 10^0 \\
(z) & \underline{5424 * 10^0} \\
& 1330424 * 10^0 = 1330 * 10^3 \text{ (truncated to four digits)}
\end{array}
$$

$$(y + z) \qquad 1330 * 10^3$$
$$(x) \qquad \underline{-1324 * 10^3}$$
$$6 * 10^3 = 6000 * 10^0 = x + (y + z)$$

Our answers are the same in the thousands place but are different in the hundreds, tens, and ones places. This is called representational error or round-off error. The result of adding y to z gives us a number with seven digits of precision, but only four digits can be stored.

In addition to representational errors, there are two other problems to watch out for in floating-point arithmetic: underflow and overflow. Underflow is the condition that arises when the absolute value of a calculation gets too small to be represented. Going back to our decimal representation, let's look at a calculation involving very small numbers:

$$4210 * 10^{-8}$$
$$\underline{* \ 2000 * 10^{-8}}$$
$$8420000 * 10^{-16} = 8420 * 10^{-13}$$

This value cannot be represented in our scheme because the exponent -13 is too small. Our minimum is -9. Therefore, the result of the calculation would be set to zero. Any value too small to be represented is set of zero, which is a reasonable thing to do under the circumstances.

Overflow is the condition that arises when the absolute value of a calculation gets too large to be represented. Overflow is a more serious problem because there is no logical thing to do when it occurs. For example, the result of the calculation

$$9999 * 10^9$$
$$\underline{* \ 1000 * 10^9}$$
$$9999000 * 10^{18} = 9999 * 10^{21}$$

cannot be stored. What should we do? To be consistent with our response to underflow, we could set the result to $9999 * 10^9$, the maximum real value allowed in our scheme. But this seems intuitively wrong. The alternative is to stop the computation and issue an error message.

Another type of error that can happen with floating-point numbers is cancellation error. This error happens when numbers of widely differing magnitudes are added or subtracted. Here's an example:

$$(1 + 0.00001234 - 1) = 0.00001234$$

>> **Representational (round-off) error** An arithmetic error caused by the fact that the precision of the result of an arithmetic operation is greater than the precision of our machine

>> **Underflow** The condition that occurs when the results of a calculation are too small to represent in a given machine

>> **Overflow** The condition that occurs when the results of a calculation are too large to represent in a given machine

>> **Cancellation error** A loss of accuracy during addition or subtraction of numbers of widely differing sizes, due to limits of precision

The laws of arithmetic say this equation should be true. But what happens when the computer is doing the arithmetic?

$$
\begin{array}{r}
100000000 \; * \; 10^{-8} \\
+ \; 1234 \; * \; 10^{-8} \\
\hline
100001234 \; * \; 10^{-8}
\end{array}
$$

With four-digit accuracy, this becomes $1000 * 10^{-3}$. Now the computer subtracts 1:

$$
\begin{array}{r}
1000 \; * \; 10^{-3} \\
- \; 1000 \; * \; 10^{-3} \\
\hline
0
\end{array}
$$

The result is 0, not 0.00001234.

We have been discussing problems with real numbers, but integer numbers can also overflow (both negatively and positively). The moral of this discussion is twofold. First, the results of real calculations often are not what you expect. Second, if you are working with very large numbers or very small numbers, you need to be very careful of the order in which you perform the calculations.

■ Limits on Components

"My hard disk crashed." "The file server was down." "My email went down last night." Any computing instructor has heard these tales of woe hundreds of time, as they are used to explain (excuse?) late assignments. Of course, if an assignment is started when it is handed out rather than the day it is due, these failures can be overcome. However, the problems of hardware failure do exist: Disks do crash, file servers do go down, and networks do fail. The *Titanic effect*, which states that "The severity with which a system fails is directly proportional to the intensity of the designer's belief that it cannot," was coined by J. A. N. Lee.[2] Hardware failures do occur: The best solution is preventive maintenance. In computing, this means periodic tests to detect problems and replacement of worn parts.

Preventive maintenance also means that the computer is housed in an appropriate physical environment. Large mainframe computers often require air-conditioned, dust-free rooms. PCs should not be set up under leak-prone plumbing. Alas, not all situations can be anticipated. One such situation occurred during the days prior to the advent of integrated circuits. A machine that had been working correctly started producing erratic results. The problem was finally traced to a moth that had gotten into the cabinet of the machine. This incident led to the computer term *bug* for a computer error. A more recent incident involved a DSL connection that intermittently disconnected itself. The trouble was finally traced to faulty telephone lines on which the local band of squirrels had enjoyed munching.

Of course, any discussion of component limits assumes that the computer hardware has been thoroughly tested at the design stage and during manufacturing. A major scandal in 1994 was the circuit flaw in Intel's Pentium® processor. The Pentium chip was installed in millions of computers manufactured by IBM, Compaq, Dell, Gateway 2000, and others. The circuit flaw was a design error in the floating-point unit that caused certain types of division problems involving more than five significant digits to give the wrong answer.

How often would the error affect a calculation? IBM predicted that spreadsheet users would experience an error every 24 days, Intel asserted that that it would occur every 27,000 years, and *PC Week*'s test suite placed the frequency once every 2 months to 10 years.[3] The chip's flaw was corrected, but Intel did not recall all of the already-released chips. The experience was a public relations disaster for Intel, but the company remains one of the leading chip manufacturers today.

■ Limits on Communications

The flow of data within a computer and between computers is the life's blood of computing. Therefore, it is extremely important that the data not be corrupted in any way. This realization leads to strategies known as *error-detecting* and *error-correcting codes*. Error-detecting codes determine that an error has occurred during the transmission of data and alert the system to this fact. Error-correcting codes not only determine that an error has occurred, but also try to determine what the correct value actually is.

Parity Bits

Parity bits are used to detect that an error has occurred between the storing and retrieving of a byte or the sending and receiving of a byte. A parity bit is an extra bit that is associated with each byte in the hardware that uses the scheme. This bit is used to ensure that the number of 1 bits in a 9-bit value (byte plus parity bit) is odd (or even) across all bytes.

Odd parity requires the number of 1s in a byte plus parity bit to be odd. For example, if a byte contains the pattern 11001100, the parity bit would be 1, giving an odd number of 1s. If the pattern were 11110001, the parity bit would be 0, giving an odd number of 1s. When a byte is retrieved from memory or received from a transmission, the number of 1 bits is counted (including the parity bit). If the number is even, an error has occurred. If this scheme is used in the hardware, each byte actually has an extra bit, accessible only by the hardware, that is used for error detection. *Even parity* uses the same scheme, but the number of 1 bits must be even.

Check Digits

A software variation of the same scheme is to sum the individual digits of a number, and then store the unit's digit of that sum with the number. For example, given the number 34376, the sum of the digits is 23, so the number would be stored as 34376–3. If the 4 became corrupted as a 3, the error would be detected. Of course, if the 7 were corrupted to a 6 and the 6 were corrupted to a 7, the sum would still be correct, but the number would not be.

This scheme could be expanded to carry an additional digit, perhaps the unit's digit of the sum of the odd digits. In this case, 34376 would be stored as 34376–23: 3 is the unit's digit, of the sum of all the digits, and 2 is the unit's digit of sum of the first, third, and fifth digits. This technique would catch a transposition error between adjacent digits, but would miss other transpositions. Of course, we could also carry the unit's digit of the sum of the even digits. You get the idea. The more important it is for errors to be detected, the more complex the algorithm used to detect them is.

Error-Correcting Codes

If we keep enough information about a byte or number, it becomes possible to deduce what an incorrect bit or digit must be. The ultimate redundancy would be to keep two separate copies of every value that is stored. If the parity is in error or there is an error in the check digits, we could look back at the extra copy to determine the correct value. Of course, both copies could be in error.

The major work in error-correcting codes relates to disk drives and CDs, where imperfections in the surface can corrupt data.

17.2 Software

We have all encountered horror stories about software that contained errors; they make for very interesting reading. Are software errors in running programs really common occurrences? Can't we do something to make software more error free? To answer the first question, a Web search for "software bugs" retrieved 261,000,000 hits. To answer the second, software developers are trying. In the next few sections, we examine why error-free software is difficult—if not impossible—to produce. We also discuss current approaches to software quality, and we end with a collection of interesting bugs.

■ Complexity of Software

If we accept the premise that commercial software contains errors, the logical question is "Why?" Don't software developers test their products? The problem is actually not a lack of diligence but rather our old nemesis *complexity*. As our machines have grown increasingly more powerful, the problems that can be tackled have become increasingly more complex. A single programmer with a problem moved to a programming team with a problem and finally graduated to a team of teams with a problem.

Software testing can demonstrate the presence of bugs but cannot prove their absence. We can test software, find errors and fix them, and then test the software some more. As we find problems and fix them, we raise our confidence that the software performs as it should. But we can never guarantee that we have removed all of the bugs. There is always the possibility of another bug lurking in the software that we haven't found yet.

Given that we can never know for sure if we have found all the problems, when do we stop testing? It becomes a question of risk. How much are you willing to risk that your software may hold yet another bug? If you're writing a game, you might take that risk a lot sooner than you would if you're writing airplane control software in which lives are on the line.

As Nancy Leveson points out in *Communications of the ACM*, a branch of computing known as *software engineering* emerged in the 1960s with the goal of introducing engineering discipline into the development of software.[4] Great strides toward this goal have been made in the last half-century, including a greater understanding of the role of abstraction, the introduction of modularity, and the notions of the software life cycle, which we discuss in detail later.

Most of these ideas come from engineering, but had to be adapted to the unique problems that arose when working with more abstract materials. Hardware designs are guided and limited by the nature of materials used to implement these designs. Software appears to have limits that are related more closely to human abilities than to physical limitations. Leveson continues, "Thus, the first 50 years may be characterized as our learning about the limits of our field, which are intimately bound up with the limits of complexity with which humans can cope."

Building software has changed. The early days were filled with the drive to write new software, but more and more the problems of maintaining and evolving existing software have taken center stage. As our

> **?**
>
> **Breaking into a university's computer system**
> In March 2005, Stanford University announced that 41 people who had applied for admission to the school's MBA program had gained unauthorized access to Stanford's admissions database. Similar "break-ins" have occurred at other graduate schools, including Dartmouth, Harvard, and MIT. The applicants were able to gain access to their electronic files, but were not able to gain knowledge about whether they were accepted; nor did they access any information about other applicants. The applicants argued that they were not guilty of privacy violations because they viewed only their own files, containing their own personal information. Some even argued that they were, in fact, the legal owners of the information. While it could be argued that no privacy violation occurred, the security of the university's computer system was breached. Due to the fact that Stanford's database is a proprietary system, it was clear that a security violation had occurred.

systems have grown bigger and required large teams of designers, we have started to examine the ways humans collaborate and to devise ways to assist them to work together more effectively.

■ Current Approaches to Software Quality

Although the complexity of large software systems makes error-free products almost an impossibility, it doesn't mean that we should just give up. There are strategies that we can adopt that, if used, improve the quality of software.

Software Engineering

In Chapter 7, we outlined four stages of computer problem solving: write the specification, develop the algorithm, implement the algorithm, and maintain the program. When we move from small, well-defined tasks to large software projects, we need to add two extra layers on top of these: software *requirements* and *specifications*. **Software requirements** are broad, but precise, statements outlining what is to be provided by the software product. **Software specifications** are a detailed description of the function, inputs, processing, outputs, and special features of a software product. The specifications tell *what* the program does, but not *how* it does it.

Leveson mentions the software life cycle as part of the contributions of software engineering. The *software life cycle* is the concept that software is developed, not just coded, and evolves over time. Thus the life cycle includes the following phases:

- Requirements
- Specifications
- Design (high-level and lower-level)
- Implementation
- Maintenance

> **Software requirements** A statement of what is to be provided by a computer system or software product

> **Software specification** A detailed description of the function, inputs, processing, outputs, and special features of a software product; it provides the information needed to design and implement the software

Verification activities must be carried out during all of these phases. Do the requirements accurately reflect what is needed? Do the specifications accurately reflect the functionality needed to meet the requirements? Does the high-level design accurately reflect the functionality of the specifications? Does each succeeding level of design accurately implement the level above? Does the implementation accurately code the designs? Do changes implemented during the maintenance phase accurately reflect the desired changes? Are the implementations of these changes correct?

In Chapters 6 and 7, we discussed the testing of the designs and code for the relatively small problems presented in this book. Clearly, as the problems get larger, verification activities become more important and more complex. (Yes, *that* word again.) Testing the design and finished code is only a small—albeit important—part of the process. Half the errors in a typical project occur in the design phase; only half occur in the implementation phase. This data is somewhat misleading. In terms of the cost to *fix* an error, the earlier in the design process an error is caught, the cheaper it is to correct the error.[5]

Teams of programmers produce large software products. Two verification techniques effectively used by programming teams are design or code walk-throughs and inspections. These are formal team activities, the intention of which is to move the responsibility for uncovering errors from the individual programmer to the group. Because testing is time-consuming and errors cost more the later they are discovered, the goal is to identify errors before testing begins.

In a walk-through, the team performs a manual simulation of the design or program with sample test inputs, keeping track of the program's data by hand on paper or a blackboard. Unlike thorough program testing, the walk-through is not intended to simulate all possible test cases. Instead, its purpose is to stimulate discussion about the way the programmer chose to design or implement the program's requirements.

At an inspection, a reader (never the program's author) goes through the requirements, design, or code line by line. The inspection participants are given the material in advance and are expected to have reviewed it carefully. During the inspection, the participants point out errors, which are recorded on an inspection report. Team members, during their pre-inspection preparation, will have noted many of the errors. Just the process of reading aloud will uncover other errors. As with the walk-through, the chief benefit of the team meeting is the discussion that takes place among team members. This interaction among programmers, testers, and other team members can uncover many program errors long before the testing stage begins.

At the high-level design stage, the design should be compared to the program requirements to make sure that all required functions have been included and that this program or module works correctly in conjunction with other software in the system. At the low-level design stage, when the design has been filled out with more details, it should be inspected yet again before it is implemented. When the coding has been completed, the compiled listings should be inspected again. This inspection (or walk-through) ensures that the implementation is consistent with both the requirements and the design. Successful completion of this inspection means that testing of the program can begin.

Walk-throughs and inspections should be carried out in as nonthreatening a way as possible. The focus of these group activities is on removing

» Walk-through A verification method in which a team performs a manual simulation of the program or design

» Inspection A verification method in which one member of a team reads the program or design aloud line by line and the others point out errors

defects in the product, not on criticizing the technical approach of the author of the design or the code. Because these activities are led by a moderator who is not the author, the focus is on the errors, not the people involved.

In the last 10 to 20 years, the Software Engineering Institute at Carnegie Mellon University has played a major role in supporting research into formalizing the inspection process in large software projects, including sponsoring workshops and conferences. A paper presented at the SEI Software Engineering Process Group (SEPG) Conference reported on a project that was able to reduce product defects by 86.6% using a two-tiered inspection process of group walk-throughs and formal inspections. The process was applied to packets of requirements, design, or code at every stage of the life cycle. Table 17.1 shows the defects per 1000 source lines of code (KSLOC) that were found in the different phases of the software life cycle in a maintenance project.[6] During the maintenance phase, 40,000 lines of source code were added to a program with more than half a million lines of code. The formal inspection process was used in all of the phases except testing activities.

We have talked about large software projects. Before we leave this section, let's quantify what we mean by "large." The Space Shuttle Ground Processing System has more than 500,000 lines of code; Vista® has 50 million lines of code. Most large projects fall somewhere in between.

We have pointed out that the complexity of large projects makes the goal of error-free code almost impossible to attain. The following is a guideline for the number of errors per lines of code that can be expected:[7]

Standard software: 25 bugs per 1000 lines of program

Good software: 2 errors per 1000 lines

Space Shuttle software: < 1 error per 10,000 lines

TABLE 17.1 Errors found during a maintenance project

Stage	Defects per KSLOC
System design	2
Software requirements	8
Design	12
Code inspection	34
Testing activities	3

Formal Verification

It would be nice if we could use a tool to automatically locate the errors in a design or code without our even having to run the program. That sounds unlikely, but consider an analogy from geometry. We wouldn't try to prove the Pythagorean theorem by proving that it worked on every triangle—that would simply demonstrate that the theorem works for every triangle *we tried*. We prove theorems in geometry mathematically. Why can't we do the same for computer programs?

The verification of program correctness, independent of data testing, is an important area of theoretical computer science research. The goal of this research is to establish a method for proving programs that is analogous to the method for proving theorems in geometry. The necessary techniques exist for proving that code meets its specifications, but the proofs are often more complicated than the programs themselves. Therefore, a major focus of verification research is the attempt to build automated program provers—verifiable programs that verify other programs.

Formal methods have been used successfully in verifying the correctness of computer chips. One notable example is the verification of a chip to perform real-number arithmetic, which won the Queen's Award for Technological Achievement. Formal verification to prove that the chip met its specifications was carried out by C. A. R. Hoare, head of the Programming Research Group of Oxford University, together with MOS Ltd. In parallel, a more traditional testing approach was taking place. As reported in *Computing Research News*:

> The race [between the two groups] was won by the formal development method—it was completed an estimated 12 months ahead of what otherwise would have been achievable. Moreover, the formal design pointed to a number of errors in the informal one that had not shown up in months of testing. The final design was of higher quality, cheaper, and was completed quicker.[8]

It is hoped that success with formal verification techniques at the hardware level will eventually lead to success at the software level. However, software is far more complex than hardware, so we do not anticipate any major breakthroughs within the near future.

Open-Source Movement[9]

In the early days of computing, software came bundled with the computer, including the source code for the software. Programmers adjusted and adapted the programs and happily shared the improvements they made. In the 1970s, firms began withholding the source code, and software became big business.

Dijkstra decried the term "bugs"
Ever since the first moth was found in the hardware, computer errors have been called *bugs*. Edsger Dijkstra chided us for the use of this terminology. He said that it can foster the image that errors are beyond the control of the programmer–that a bug might maliciously creep into a program when no one is looking. He contended that this perspective is intellectually dishonest because it disguises that the error is the programmer's own creation.[11]

With the advent of the Internet, programmers from all over the world can collaborate at almost no cost. A simple version of a software product can be made available via the Internet. Programmers interested in extending or improving the program can do so. A "benevolent dictator" who keeps track of what is going on governs most open-source projects. If a change or improvement passes the peer review of fellow developers and gets incorporated into the next version, it is a great coup.

Linux is the best-known open-source project. Linus Torvolds wrote the first simple version of the operating system using UNIX as a blueprint and continued to oversee its development. IBM spent $1 billion on Linux in 2001 with the objective of making it a computing standard. As *The Economist* says,

> Some people like to dismiss Linux as nothing more than a happy accident, but the program looks more like a textbook example of an emerging pattern. . . . Open source is certainly a mass phenomenon, with tens of thousands of volunteer programmers across the world already taking part, and more joining in all the time, particularly in countries such as China and India. SourceForge, a website for developers, now hosts more than 18,000 open-source projects that keep 145,000 programmers busy.[10]

Now, ten years later, open source is still going strong. Some companies consider it one of several design choices; others consider it critical to their operations. SourceForge now has more than 230,000 software projects registered and more than 2 million registered users. However, there is no evidence that the open-source movement has led to higher-quality software.

■ Notorious Software Errors

Everyone involved in computing has his or her favorite software horror story. We include only a small sample here.

AT&T Down for Nine Hours

In January 1990, AT&T's long-distance telephone network came to a screeching halt for nine hours because of a software error in the electronic switching systems. Of the 148 million long-distance and toll-free calls placed with AT&T that day, only 50% got through. This failure caused untold collateral damage:

- Hotels lost bookings.
- Rental car agencies lost rentals.
- American Airlines' reservation system traffic fell by two-thirds.
- A telemarketing company lost $75,000 in estimated sales.
- MasterCard didn't get to process its typical 200,000 credit approvals.
- AT&T lost some $60 million to $75 million.

As AT&T Chairman Robert Allen said, "It was the worst nightmare I've had in 32 years in the business." [12]

How did this happen? Earlier versions of the switching software worked correctly. The software error was in the code that upgraded the system to make it respond more quickly to a malfunctioning switch. The error involved a *break* statement in the C code.[13] As Henry Walker points out in *The Limits of Computing*, this breakdown illustrates several points common to many software failures. The software had been tested extensively before its release, and it worked correctly for about a month. In addition to testing, code reviews had been conducted during development. One programmer made the error, but many others reviewed the code without noticing the error. The failure was triggered by a relatively uncommon sequence of events, difficult to anticipate in advance. And the error occurred in code designed to improve a correctly working system—that is, it arose during the maintenance phase. E. N. Adams in the *IBM Journal of Research and Development* estimates that 15 to 50% of attempts to remove an error from a large program result in the introduction of additional errors.

Therac-25

One of the most widely cited software-related accidents involved a computerized radiation therapy machine called the Therac-25. Between June 1985 and January 1987, six known accidents involved massive overdoses by the Therac-25, leading to deaths and serious injuries. These accidents have been described as the worst series of radiation accidents in the 35-year history of medical accelerators.

It is beyond the scope of this book to go into a detailed analysis of the software failure. Suffice it to say there was only a single coding error, but tracking down the error exposed serious flaws in the whole design. Leveson and Turner, in their article in *IEEE Computer*, add this scathing comment:

> A lesson to be learned from the Therac-25 story is that focusing on particular software bugs is not the way to make a safe system. Virtually all complex software can be made to behave in an unexpected fashion under certain conditions. The basic mistakes here involved poor software-engineering practices and building a machine that relies on the software for safe operation. Furthermore, the particular

coding error is not as important as the general unsafe design of the software overall." [14]

Bugs in Government Projects

On February 25, 1991, during the first Gulf War, a Scud missile struck a U.S. Army barracks, killing 28 soldiers and injuring roughly 100 other people. A U.S. Patriot Missile battery in Dhahran, Saudi Arabia, failed to track and intercept the incoming Iraqi Scud missile because of a software error. This error, however, was not a coding error but a design error. A calculation involved a multiplication by 1/10, which is a nonterminating number in binary. The resulting arithmetic error accumulated over the 100 hours of the batteries' operation amounted to 0.34 second, enough for the missile to miss its target.[15]

The General Accounting Office concluded:

> The Patriot had never before been used to defend against Scud missiles nor was it expected to operate continuously for long periods of time. Two weeks before the incident, Army officials received Israeli data indicating some loss in accuracy after the system had been running for 8 consecutive hours. Consequently, Army officials modified the software to improve the system's accuracy. However, the modified software did not reach Dhahran until February 26, 1991— the day after the Scud incident." [16]

The Gemini V missed its expected landing point by about 100 miles. The reason? The design of the guidance system did not take into account the need to compensate for the motion of Earth around the Sun.[17]

In October 1999, the Mars Climate Orbiter entered the Martian atmosphere about 100 kilometers lower than expected, causing the craft to burn up. Arthur Stephenson, chairman of the Mars Climate Orbiter Mission Failure Investigation Board, concluded:

> The "root cause" of the loss of the spacecraft was the failed transla-tion of English units into metric units in a segment of ground-based, navigation-related mission software, as NASA has previously announced . . . The failure review board has identified other signifi-cant factors that allowed this error to be born, and then let it linger and propagate to the point where it resulted in a major error in our understanding of the spacecraft's path as it approached Mars.[18]

Launched in July 1962, the Mariner 1 Venus probe veered off course almost immediately and had to be destroyed. The problem was traced to the following line of FORTRAN code:

```
DO 5 K = 1. 3
```

The period should have been a comma. An $18.5 million space exploration vehicle was lost because of this typographical error.

Errors in software are not only the province of the U.S. government. An unmanned Ariane 5 rocket launched by the European Space Agency exploded on June 4, 1996, just 40 seconds after lift-off. The development cost for the rocket was $7 billion, spanning over a decade. The rocket and its cargo were valued at $500 million. What happened? A 64-bit floating-point number, relating to the horizontal velocity with respect to the platform, was converted to a 17-bit signed integer; the number was larger than 32,767. The resulting error caused the launcher to veer off its flight path, break up, and explode.

17.3 Problems

Life is full of all kinds of problems. There are problems for which it is easy to develop and implement computer solutions. There are problems for which we can implement computer solutions, but we wouldn't get the results in our lifetime. There are problems for which we can develop and implement computer solutions provided we have enough computer resources. There are problems for which we can prove there are no solutions. Before we can look at these categories of problems, we must introduce a way of comparing algorithms.

■ Comparing Algorithms

As we have shown in previous chapters, there is more than one way to solve most problems. If you were asked for directions to Joe's Diner (see Figure 17.2), you could give either of two equally correct answers:

1. "Go east on the big highway to the Y'all Come Inn, and turn left."

or

2. "Take the winding country road to Honeysuckle Lodge, and turn right."

The two answers are not the same, but because following either route gets the traveler to Joe's Diner, both answers are functionally correct.

If the request for directions contained special requirements, one solution might be preferable to the other. For instance, "I'm late for dinner. What's the quickest route to Joe's Diner?" calls for the first answer, whereas "Is there a scenic road that I can take to get to Joe's Diner?" suggests the second. If no special requirements are known, the choice is a matter of personal preference—which road do you like better?

FIGURE 17.2 Equally valid solutions to the same problem

Often the choice between algorithms comes down to a question of efficiency. Which one takes the least amount of computing time? Which one does the job with the least amount of work? Here we are interested in the amount of work that the computer does.

To compare the work done by competing algorithms, we must first define a set of objective measures that can be applied to each algorithm. The analysis of algorithms is an important area of theoretical computer science; in advanced computing courses, students see extensive work in this area. We cover only a small part of this topic in this book—just enough to allow you to compare two algorithms that do the same task and understand that the complexity of algorithms forms a continuum from easy to unsolvable.

How do programmers measure the work that two algorithms perform? The first solution that comes to mind is simply to code the algorithms and then compare the execution times for running the two programs. The one with the shorter execution time is clearly the better algorithm. Or is it? Using this technique, we really can determine only that program A is more efficient than program B on a particular computer. Execution times are specific to a *particular computer*. Of course, we could test the algorithms on all possible computers, but we want a more general measure.

A second possibility is to count the number of instructions or statements executed. This measure, however, varies with the programming language used as well as with the style of the individual programmer. To standardize this measure somewhat, we could count the number of passes through a critical loop in the algorithm. If each iteration involves a constant amount of work, this measure gives us a meaningful yardstick of efficiency.

Another idea is to isolate a particular operation fundamental to the algorithm and then count the number of times that this operation is performed. Suppose, for example, that we are summing the elements in an integer list. To measure the amount of work required, we could count the integer addition operations. For a list of 100 elements, there are 99 addition operations. Note that we do not actually have to count the number of addition operations; it is some *function* of the number of elements (N) in the list. Therefore, we can express the number of addition operations in terms of N: for a list of N elements, there are $N - 1$ addition operations. Now we can compare the algorithms for the general case, not just for a specific list size.

Big-O Analysis

We have been talking about work as a function of the size of the input to the operation (for instance, the number of elements in the list to be summed). We can express an approximation of this function using a mathematical notation called order of magnitude, or Big-O notation. (This is the letter O, not a zero.) The order of magnitude of a function is identified with the term in the function that increases fastest relative to the size of the problem. For instance, if

$$f(N) = N^4 + 100N^2 + 10N + 50$$

then $f(N)$ is of order N^4—or, in Big-O notation, $O(N^4)$. That is, for large values of N, some multiple of N^4 dominates the function for sufficiently large values of N. It isn't that $100N^2 + 10N + 50$ is not important, it is just that as N gets larger, all other factors become irrelevant because the N^4 term dominates.

How is it that we can just drop the low-order terms? Well, suppose you needed to buy an elephant and a goldfish from one of two pet suppliers. You really need only to compare the prices of elephants, because the cost of the goldfish is trivial in comparison. In analyzing algorithms, the term that increases most rapidly relative to the size of the problem dominates the function, effectively relegating the others to the "noise" level. The cost of an elephant is so much greater that we could just ignore the goldfish. Similarly,

>> Big-O notation A notation that expresses computing time (complexity) as the term in a function that increases most rapidly relative to the size of a problem

for large values of N, N^4 is so much larger than 50, $10N$, or even $100N^2$ that we can ignore these other terms. This doesn't mean that the other terms do not contribute to the computing time; it simply means that they are not significant in our approximation when N is "large."

What is this value N? N represents the size of the problem. Most problems involve manipulating data structures like those discussed in Chapter 8. As we already know, each structure is composed of elements. We develop algorithms to add an element to the structure and to modify or delete an element from the structure. We can describe the work done by these operations in terms of N, where N is the number of elements in the structure.

Suppose that we want to write all the elements in a list into a file. How much work does that task require? The answer depends on how many elements are in the list. Our algorithm is

```
Open the file
While (more elements)
    Get next element
    Write next element
```

Family Laundry: An Analogy

How long does it take to do a family's weekly laundry? We might describe the answer to this question with the function

$$f(N) = c * N$$

where N represents the number of family members and c is the average number of minutes that each person's laundry takes. We say that this function is $O(N)$ because the total laundry time depends on the number of people in the family. The "constant" c may vary a little for different families, depending on how big the washing machine is and how fast the family members can fold clothes, for instance. That is, the time to do the laundry for two different families might be represented with these functions:

$$f(N) = 100 * N$$
$$g(N) = 90 * N$$

Overall, we describe these functions as $O(N)$.

Now, what happens if Grandma and Grandpa come to visit the first family for a week or two? The laundry time function becomes

$$f(N) = 100 * (N + 2)$$

We still say that the function is $O(N)$. How can that be? Doesn't the laundry for two extra people take any time to wash, dry, and fold? Of course it does! If N is small (the family consists of Mother, Father, and Baby), the extra laundry for two people is significant. But as N grows large (the family consists of Mother, Father, 12 kids, and a live-in baby-sitter), the extra laundry for two

people doesn't make much difference. (The family's laundry is the elephant; the guests' laundry is the goldfish.) When we compare algorithms using Big-O complexity, we are concerned with what happens when N is "large."

If we are asking the question, "Can we finish the laundry in time to make the 7:05 train?", we want a precise answer. The Big-O analysis doesn't give us this information; it gives us an approximation. So, if $100 * N$, $90 * N$, and $100 * (N + 2)$ are all $O(N)$, how can we say which is "better"? We can't—in Big-O terms, they are all roughly equivalent for large values of N. Can we find a better algorithm for getting the laundry done? If the family wins the state lottery, they can drop all their dirty clothes at a professional laundry 15 minutes' drive from their house (30 minutes round trip). Now the function is

$$f(N) = 30$$

This function is $O(1)$. The answer does not depend on the number of people in the family. If they switch to a laundry 5 minutes from their house, the function becomes

$$f(N) = 10$$

This function is also $O(1)$. In Big-O terms, the two professional-laundry solutions are equivalent: No matter how many family members or house guests you have, it takes a constant amount of the family's time to do the laundry. (We aren't concerned with the professional laundry's time.)

If N is the number of elements in the list, the "time" required to do this task is

time-to-open-the-file + [N * (time-to-get-one-element +
time-to-write-one-element)]

This algorithm is O(N) because the time required to perform the task is proportional to the number of elements (N)—plus a little to open the file. How can we ignore the open time in determining the Big-O approximation? Assuming that the time necessary to open a file is constant, this part of the algorithm is our goldfish. If the list has only a few elements, the time needed to open the file may seem significant. For large values of N, however, writing the elements is an elephant in comparison with opening the file.

The order of magnitude of an algorithm does not tell us how long in microseconds the solution takes to run on our computer. Sometimes we may need that kind of information. For instance, suppose a word processor's requirements state that the program must be able to spell-check a 50-page document (on a particular computer) in less than 120 seconds. For this kind of information, we do not use Big-O analysis; we use other measurements. We can compare different implementations of a data structure by coding them and then running a test, recording the time on the computer's clock before and after we conduct the test. This kind of "benchmark" test tells us how long the operations take on a particular computer, using a particular compiler. The Big-O analysis, by contrast, allows us to compare algorithms without reference to these factors.

Common Orders of Magnitude

O(1) is called *bounded time*.   The amount of work is bounded by a constant and is not dependent on the size of the problem. Assigning a value to the ith element in an array of N elements is O(1), because an element in an array can be accessed directly through its index. Although bounded time is often called constant time, the amount of work is not necessarily constant. It is, however, bounded by a constant.

O($\log_2 N$) is called *logarithmic time*.   The amount of work depends on the log of the size of the problem. Algorithms that successively cut the amount of data to be processed in half at each step typically fall into this category. Finding a value in a list of sorted elements using the binary search algorithm is O($\log_2 N$).

O(N) is called *linear time*.   The amount of work is some constant times the size of the problem. Printing all of the elements in a list of N elements is O(N). Searching for a particular value in a list of unsorted elements is also O(N) because you (potentially) must search every element in the list to find it.

O($N \log_2 N$) is called (for lack of a better term) *$N \log_2 N$ time*.   Algorithms of this type typically involve applying a logarithmic algorithm N times.

The better sorting algorithms, such as Quicksort, Heapsort, and Merge-sort, have $N \log_2 N$ complexity. That is, these algorithms can transform an unsorted list into a sorted list in $O(N \log_2 N)$ time, although Quicksort degenerates to $O(N^2)$ under certain input data.

$O(N^2)$ **is called** *quadratic time.* Algorithms of this type typically involve applying a linear algorithm N times. Most simple sorting algorithms are $O(N^2)$ algorithms.

$O(2^N)$ **is called** *exponential time.* These algorithms are costly. As you can see in Table 17.2, exponential times increase dramatically in relation to the size of N. The fable of the King and the Corn demonstrates an exponential time algorithm, where the size of the problem is a kernel of corn. (The values in the last column of Table 17.2 grow so quickly that the computation time required for problems of this order may exceed the estimated life span of the universe!)

$O(N!)$ **is called** *factorial time.* These algorithms are even more costly than exponential algorithms. The traveling salesperson graph algorithm (see page 580) is a factorial time algorithm.

Algorithms whose order of magnitude can be expressed as a polynomial in the size of the problem are called polynomial-time algorithms. Recall from Chapter 2 that a polynomial is a sum of two or more algebraic terms, each of which consists of a constant multiplied by one or more variables raised to a nonnegative integral power. Thus polynomial algorithms are those whose order of magnitude can be expressed as the size of

» Polynomial-time algorithms Algorithms whose complexity can be expressed as a polynomial in the size of the problem

TABLE 17.2 Comparison of rates of growth

N	$\log_2 N$	$N \log_2 N$	N^2	N^3	2^N
1	0	1	1	1	2
2	1	2	4	8	4
4	2	8	16	64	16
8	3	24	64	512	256
16	4	64	256	4096	65,536
32	5	160	1024	32,768	4,294,967,296
64	6	384	4096	262,144	About 5 years' worth of instructions on a supercomputer
128	7	896	16,384	2,097,152	About 600,000 times greater than the age of the universe in nano-seconds (for a 6-billion-year estimate)
256	8	2048	65,536	16,777,216	Don't ask!

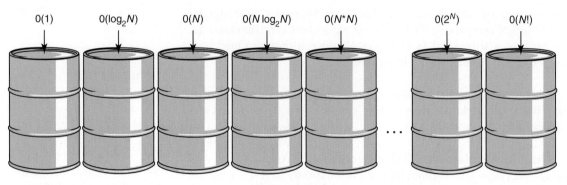

FIGURE 17.3 Orders of complexity

the problem to a power, and the Big-O complexity of the algorithm is the highest power in the polynomial. All polynomial-time algorithms are defined as being in Class P.

Think of common orders of complexity as being bins into which we sort algorithms (see Figure 17.3). For small values of the size of the problem, an algorithm in one bin may actually be faster than the equivalent algorithm in the next-more-efficient bin. As the size increases, the difference among algorithms in the different bins gets larger. When choosing between algorithms in the same bin, we look at the goldfish that we ignored earlier.

■ Turing Machines

We have mentioned the name of Alan Turing several times in this book. He developed the concept of a computing machine in the 1930s. He was not interested in implementing his machine; rather, he used it as a model to study the limits of what can be computed.

A Turing machine, as his model became known, consists of a control unit with a read/write head that can read and write symbols on an infinite tape. The tape is divided into cells. The model is based on a person doing a primitive calculation on a long strip of paper using a pencil with an eraser. Each line (cell) of the paper contains a symbol from a finite alphabet. Starting at one cell, the person examines the symbol and then either leaves the symbol alone or erases it and replaces it with another symbol from the alphabet. The person then moves to an adjacent cell and repeats the action.

The control unit simulates the person. The human's decision-making process is represented by a finite series of instructions that the control unit can execute. Each instruction causes

- A symbol to be read from a cell on the tape.
- A symbol to be written into the cell.

Alan Turing

Time magazine chose Alan Turing as one of its 100 most influential persons of the twentieth century. The biography of Turing said:

> For what this eccentric young Cambridge don did was to dream up an imaginary machine—a fairly simple typewriter-like contraption capable somehow of scanning, or reading, instructions encoded on a tape of theoretically infinite length. As the scanner moved from one square of the tape to the next—responding to the sequential commands and modifying its mechanical response if so ordered—the output of such a process, Turing demonstrated, could replicate logical human thought.
>
> The device in this inspired mind-experiment quickly acquired a name: the Turing machine, and so did another of Turing's insights. Since the instructions on the tape governed the behavior of the machine, by changing those instructions, one could induce the machine to perform the functions of all such machines. In other words, depending on the tape it scanned, the same machine could calculate numbers or play chess or do anything else of a comparable nature. Hence his device acquired a new and even grander name: the Universal Turing Machine.
>
> . . .

So many ideas and technological advances converged to create the modern computer that it is foolhardy to give one person the credit

© the Turing family <King's College Library, Cambridge, AMT/K/7/13>

for inventing it. But the fact remains that everyone who taps at a keyboard, opening a spreadsheet or a word-processing program, is working on an incarnation of a Turing machine.[19]

Alan Turing was born in June 1912 to Julius Mathison Turing, a member of the Indian Civil Service, and Ethel Sara Stoney, the daughter of the chief engineer of the Madras railway. His father and mother spent most of their time in India, while he and his older brother were in various foster homes in England until his father's retirement in 1926.

The British public (read *private* in American English) school system of the day did not foster original thinking, so Turing had trouble fitting in. He was criticized for his handwriting, struggled in English, and even in mathematics didn't produce the expected conventional answers. At Sherborne School, which he had entered at 13, the headmaster said that if he was solely a scientific specialist, he was wasting his time at a public school. Yet a public school education was terribly important to his mother, so Turing persisted. Two things sustained him during this period: his own independent study and the friendship of Christopher Morcom, who was a student a year ahead of him in school. Morcom provided vital intellectual companionship, which ended after two years with Morcom's sudden death.

In 1931, Turing entered King's College, Cambridge, to study mathematics. The atmosphere at King's College encouraged free-ranging thought, providing him with an intellectual home for the first time. He graduated in 1934 and was elected a fellow of King's College in 1935 for a

» continued

Alan Turing, continued

dissertation "On the Gaussian Error Function," which proved fundamental results in probability theory.

Turing then began to work on decidability questions, based on a course he had taken on the foundations of mathematics with Max Newman. In 1936, Turing published a paper in which he introduced the concept of what we now call a Turing machine. These concepts were introduced within the context of whether a definite method or process exists by which it could be decided whether any given mathematical assertion was provable. Alonzo Church's work at Princeton on the same subject became known at the same time, so Turing's paper was delayed until he could refer to Church's work. As a result, Turing spent two years as a student at Princeton working with Church and von Neumann.

At the outbreak of World War II, Turing went to work for the British government. Again we quote from the *Time* magazine text:

> Turing, on the basis of his published work, was recruited to serve in the Government Code and Cypher School, located in a Victorian mansion called Bletchley Park in Buckinghamshire. The task of all those so assembled—mathematicians, chess champions, Egyptologists, whoever might have something to contribute about the possible permutations of formal systems—was to break the Enigma codes used by the Nazis in communications between headquarters and troops. Because of secrecy restrictions, Turing's role in this enterprise was not acknowledged until long after his death. And like the invention of the computer, the work done by the Bletchley Park crew was

very much a team effort. But it is now known that Turing played a crucial role in designing a primitive, computer-like machine that could decipher at high speed Nazi codes to U-boats in the North Atlantic.[20]

Turing was awarded the Order of the British Empire in 1945 for his contributions to the war effort.

After a frustrating experience at the National Physical Laboratory in London, where he was to build a computer, Turing returned to Cambridge, where he continued to work and write. The wartime spirit of cooperation that had short-circuited bureaucracy had faded, and the ACE (Automatic Computing Engine) was never built. In 1948, Turing became a Deputy Director of the computing laboratory at Manchester University. The vague title reflected its meaninglessness, and Turing spent the next years working and writing on a variety of different subjects.

In 1950, he published an article reflecting one of his major interests: Can machines think? From this article came the well-known Turing test. Turing also became interested in morphogenesis, the development of pattern and form in living organisms. All the while he continued his research in decidability and quantum theory.

On June 7, 1954, Turing died of cyanide poisoning, a half-eaten apple laying beside his bed. His mother believed that he accidentally died while conducting an experiment; the coroner's verdict was suicide. A few years ago, the award-winning one-man play called *Breaking the Code* was performed in London's West End and on Broadway, giving audiences a brief glimpse of Turing's brilliant, complex character.

FIGURE 17.4 Turing machine processing

- The tape to be moved one cell left, to be moved one cell right, or to remain positioned as it was.

These actions do, indeed, model a person with a pencil, if we allow the person to replace a symbol with itself. See Figure 17.4.

Why is such a simple machine (model) of any importance? It is widely accepted that *anything that is intuitively computable can be computed by a Turing machine*. This statement is known as the Church–Turing thesis, named for Turing and Alonzo Church, another mathematician who developed a similar model known as the *lambda calculus* and with whom Turing worked at Princeton. The works of Turing and Church are covered in-depth in theoretical courses in computer science.

It follows from the Church–Turing thesis that if we can find a problem for which a Turing-machine solution can be proven *not* to exist, then that problem must be unsolvable. In the next section we describe such a problem.

■ Halting Problem

It is not always obvious that a computation (program) halts. In Chapter 6, we introduced the concept of repeating a process; in Chapter 7, we talked about different types of loops. Some loops clearly stop, some loops clearly do not (infinite loops), and some loops stop depending on input data or calculations that occur within the loop. When a program is running, it is difficult to know whether it is caught in an infinite loop or whether it just needs more time to run.

It would be very beneficial if we could predict that a program with a specified input would not go into an infinite loop. The **halting problem** restates the question this way: *Given a program and an input to the program, determine if the program will eventually stop with this input.*

The obvious approach is to run the program with the specified input and see what happens. If it stops, the answer is clear. What if it doesn't stop? How long do you run the program before you decide that it is in an infinite loop? Clearly, this approach has some flaws. Unfortunately, there are flaws in every other approach as well. This problem is unsolvable. Let's look at the outlines of a proof of this assertion, which can be rephrased as follows: "There is no Turing-machine program that can determine whether a program will halt given a particular input."

How can we prove that a problem is unsolvable or, rather, that we just haven't found the solution yet? We could try every proposed solution and show that every one contains an error. Because there are many known solutions and many yet unknown, this approach seems doomed to failure. Yet, this approach forms the basis of Turing's solution to this problem. In his proof, he starts with any proposed solution and then shows that it doesn't work.

Assume that there exists a Turing-machine program called SolvesHalt-ingProblem that determines for any program Example and input SampleData whether program Example halts given input SampleData. That is, Solves-HaltingProblem takes program Example and SampleData and prints "Halts" if the program halts and "Loops" if the program contains an infinite loop. This situation is depicted in Figure 17.5.

Recall that both programs (instructions) and data look alike in a computer; they are just bit patterns. What distinguishes programs from data is how the control unit interprets the bit pattern. So we could give program Example a copy of itself as data in place of SampleData. Thus SolvesHaltingProblem should be able to take program Example and a second copy of program Example as data and determine whether program Example halts with itself as data. See Figure 17.6.

» Halting problem The unsolvable problem of determining whether any program will eventually stop given a particular input

FIGURE 17.5 Proposed program for solving the halting problem

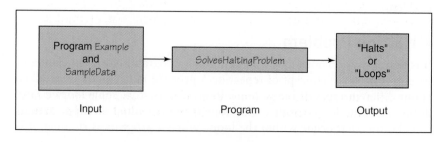

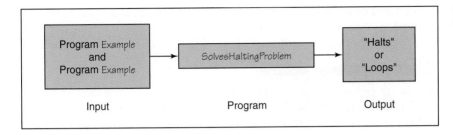

FIGURE 17.6 Proposed program for solving the halting problem

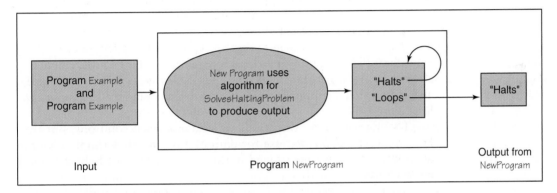

FIGURE 17.7 Construction of NewProgram

Now let's construct a new program, NewProgram, that takes program Example as both program and data and uses the algorithm from Solves-HaltingProblem to write "Halts" if Example halts and "Loops" if it does not halt. If "Halts" is written, NewProgram creates an infinite loop; if "Loops" is written, NewProgram writes "Halts." Figure 17.7 shows this situation.

Do you see where the proof is leading? Let's now apply program Solves-HaltingProblem to NewProgram, using NewProgram as data. If SolvesHalting-Problem prints "Halts," program NewProgram goes into an infinite loop. If SolvesHaltingProblem prints "Loops," program NewProgram prints "Halts" and stops. In either case, SolvesHaltingProblem gives the wrong answer. Because SolvesHaltingProblem gives the wrong answer in at least one case, it doesn't work on all cases. Therefore, any proposed solution must have a flaw.

■ Classification of Algorithms

Figure 17.3 showed the common orders of magnitude as bins. We now know that there is another bin to the right, which would contain

FIGURE 17.8 A reorganization of algorithm classifications

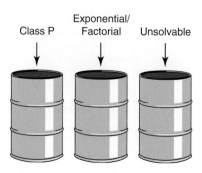

Class P   Exponential/
            Factorial   Unsolvable

>> **Class P problems** Problems that can be solved with one processor in polynomial time

>> **Class NP problems** Problems that can be solved in polynomial time with as many processors as desired

>> **NP-complete problems** A class of problems within Class NP that has the property that if a polynomial time solution with one processor can be found for any member of the class, such a solution exists for every member of the class

?

The Traveling Salesman problem
A classic NP problem is called the *Traveling Salesman problem*. A salesman is responsible for visiting all the cities in his sales district. To visit every one in an efficient manner, he wants to find a route of minimal cost that goes through each city once and only once before returning to the starting point. The cities can be represented in a graph with the edges representing highways between cities. Each edge is labeled with the distance between the cities. The solution then becomes a well-known graph algorithm whose solution with one processor is O(N!).

algorithms that are unsolvable. Let's reorganize our bins a little, combining all polynomial algorithms in a bin labeled Class P, combine exponential and factorial algorithms into one bin, and add a bin labeled *Unsolvable*. See Figure 17.8.

The algorithms in the middle bin have known solutions, but they are called *intractable* because for data of any size, they simply take too long to execute. We mentioned parallel computers in Chapter 1 when we reviewed the history of computer hardware. Could some of these problems be solved in a reasonable time (polynomial time) if enough processors worked on the problem at the same time? Yes, they could. A problem is said to be in Class NP if it can be solved with a sufficiently large number of processors in polynomial time.

Clearly, Class P problems are also in Class NP. An open question in theoretical computing is whether Class NP problems, whose only tractable solution is with many processors, are also in Class P. That is, do there exist polynomial-time algorithms for these problems that we just haven't discovered (invented) yet? We don't know, but the problem has been and is still keeping computer science theorists busy looking for the solution. *The* solution? Yes, the problem of determining whether Class P is equal to Class NP has been reduced to finding a solution for one of these algorithms. A special class called NP-complete problems is part of Class NP; these problems have the property that they can be mapped into one another. If a polynomial-time solution with one processor can be found for any one of the algorithms in this class, a solution can be found for each of them—that is, the solution can be mapped to all the others. How and why this is so is beyond the scope of this book. However, if the solution is found, you will know, because it will make headlines all over the computing world.

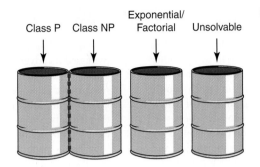

FIGURE 17.9 Adding Class NP

For now we picture our complexity bins with a new companion—a bin labeled *Class NP*. This bin and the Class P bin have dotted lines on their adjacent sides, because they may actually be just one bin. See Figure 17.9.

Summary

Limits are imposed on computer problem solving by the hardware, the software, and the nature of the problems to be solved. Numbers are infinite, but their representation within a computer is finite. This limitation can cause errors to creep into arithmetic calculations, giving incorrect results. Hardware components can wear out, and information can be lost during intercomputer and intracomputer data transfers.

The sheer size and complexity of large software projects almost guarantee that errors will occur. Testing a program can demonstrate errors, but it cannot prove the absence of errors. The best way to build good software is to pay attention to quality from the first day of the project, applying the principles of software engineering.

Problems vary from those that are very simple to solve to those that cannot be solved at all. Big-O analysis provides a metric that allows us to compare algorithms in terms of the growth rate of a size factor in the algorithm. Polynomial-time algorithms are those algorithms whose Big-O complexity can be expressed as a polynomial in the size factor. Class P problems can be solved with one processor in polynomial time. Class NP problems can be solved in polynomial time with an unlimited number of processors. As proved by Turing, the halting problem does not have a solution.

⚖ ETHICAL ISSUES ▶ Deep Linking   Ⓦ

The incredible impact that the World Wide Web has on society can undoubtedly be attributed to its ability to facilitate communication and information exchange. It is a revolutionary medium in which people can interact, conduct research, and post their thoughts and ideas almost instantaneously. Users surf from Web page to Web page with ease, following hyperlinks that direct them to relevant topics and points of interest. These hyperlinks, which can appear as text or images, respond to a mouse click and send the user a new page often from outside of the original website. By connecting pages, hyperlinks provide an important service to the user and are a defining feature of the Web.

In the early stages of Web development, linking was embraced as essential and recognized as an indispensable guide to mapping cyberspace. As the Web has matured, however, deep linking has become more controversial. Deep linking occurs when one Web page includes a hyperlink to a Web page that is buried deep within another site (i.e., not to the other site's home page). While many companies welcome visitors who stumble on one of their pages, regardless of whether it is their home page, other companies feel that deep linking is illegitimate—a technique that unfairly bypasses a site's "front door."

Ticketmaster.com brought the problem to public attention when it sued Microsoft® in 1997 for inappropriately linking to its site. Microsoft's city-guide "Sidewalk" provided links to ticketing for specific events on Ticketmaster.com that sent a wave of visitors to pages deep within that site. Despite the traffic this link created, Ticketmaster.com felt that it should have control over how others link to its site and that the deep link unfairly bypassed its advertising. Although this case was settled out of court, Ticketmaster.com has subsequently sued one of its rivals, Tickets.com, for a number of offenses including improper linking. Ticketmaster.com contended that Tickets.com was conducting unfair business practices by linking directly to pages within its site and not to its home page. Ticketmaster.com listed a number of specific complaints, among them that deep linking hurt its advertising. The court ruled that Tickets.com did not violate copyright law because it did not republish in a new format the page to which it linked, nor was the relationship between the two sites likely to be misconstrued.

This decision, however, does not mean that the issue of deep linking has been totally resolved. GateHouse Media, a New York company that publishes more than 100 local newspapers in Massachusetts, is suing the New York Times Company over the issue of deep linking. GateHouse Media claims that the New York Times Company violated copyright laws by allowing the *Boston Globe* online newspaper site to copy the headlines and leading sentences from newspaper articles posted on GateHouse's website. (The New York Times Company owns the *Boston Globe*.) GateHouse claims that it is losing advertising revenue because *Boston Globe* readers are able to bypass GateHouse's main pages and posted advertisements.

Most of the current issues with deep linking involve very specific cases. The practice of deep linking as a whole doesn't look to be in any danger of going away anytime soon, as most sites are happy to receive the exposure that deep linking provides them.

🔑 Key Terms

Big-O notation
Cancellation error
Class NP problems
Class P
Class P problems
Halting problem
Inspection
NP-complete problems
Overflow

Polynomial-time algorithms
Precision
Representational (round-off) error
Significant digits
Software requirements
Software specification
Underflow
Walk-through

⌘ Exercises

For Exercises 1–15, match the Big-O notation with its definition or use.

    A. $O(1)$
    B. $O(\log_2 N)$
    C. $O(N)$
    D. $O(N \log_2 N)$
    E. $O(N^2)$
    F. $O(2^N)$
    G. $O(N!)$

1. Factorial time

2. $N \log N$ time

3. Linear time

4. Quadratic time

5. Exponential time

6. Logarithmic time

7. Bounded time

8. Time not dependent on the size of the problem

9. Algorithms that successively cut the amount of data to be processed in half at each step

10. Mergesort and Heapsort

11. Selection sort and bubble sort

12. Adding a column of N numbers

13. Demonstrated by the fable of the King and the Corn

14. Traveling salesman problem

15. What Quicksort degenerates to if the data are already sorted

For Exercises 16–20, match the name of the technique with the algorithm.

    A. Even parity
    B. Odd parity
    C. Check digits
    D. Error-correcting codes
    E. Parity bit

16. An extra bit is associated with each byte in the hardware that ensures that the number of 1 bits is odd or even across all bytes.

17. Ultimate redundancy would be to keep two copies of every value.

18. The number of 1 bits plus the parity bit is odd.

19. The number of 1 bits plus the parity bit is even.

20. A scheme to sum the individual digits in a number and store the unit's digit of that sum with the number.

For Exercises 21–30, mark the answers true or false as follows:
   A. True
   B. False

21. $(1 + x - 1)$ is always equal to x.

22. Representational error is a synonym for round-off error.

23. Software verification activities are limited to the implementation phase.

24. Half the errors in a software project occur in the design phase.

25. Most large software projects are designed by a single genius and then given to teams of programmers to implement.

26. The later in the software life cycle that an error is detected, the cheaper it is to fix.

27. Formal verification of programs is of theoretical interest but has never really been useful.

28. Big-O notation tells us how long the solution takes to run in terms of microseconds.

29. Software engineering, a branch of computing, emerged in the 1960s.

30. Maintaining and evolving existing software has become more important than building new systems.

Exercises 31–61 are problems or short-answer questions.

31. Define *representational error*, *cancellation error*, *underflow*, and *overflow*. Discuss how these terms are interrelated.

32. Show the range of integer numbers that can be represented in each of following word sizes:
   a. 8 bits
   b. 16 bits
   c. 24 bits
   d. 32 bits
   e. 64 bits

33. There is a logical action to take when underflow occurs, but not when overflow occurs. Explain.

34. a. Show how the numbers 1066 and 1492 would be represented in a linked list with one digit per node.
   b. Use a linked list to represent the sum of these integers.
   c. Outline an algorithm to show how the calculation might be carried out in a computer.

35. Explain the *Titanic* effect in relation to hardware failure.

36. Have any hardware failures happened to you? Explain.

37. Given the following 8-bit code, what is the parity bit if odd parity is being used?
    a. 11100010
    b. 10101010
    c. 11111111
    d. 00000000
    e. 11101111

38. Given the following 8-bit code, what is the parity bit if even parity is being used?
    a. 11100010
    b. 10101010
    c. 11111111
    d. 00000000
    e. 11101111

39. Given the following numbers, what would be the check digit for each?
    a. 1066
    b. 1498
    c. 1668
    d. 2001
    e. 4040

40. What errors would be detected using the check bits in Exercise 39?

41. Given the following numbers, what would be the additional digits if the unit's digit of the sum of the even digits is used along with the check digit?
    a. 1066
    b. 1498
    c. 1668
    d. 2001
    e. 4040

42. Given the following numbers, what would be the additional digits if the unit's digit of the sum of the odd digits is used along with the check digit?
    a. 1066
    b. 1498
    c. 1668
    d. 2001
    e. 4040

43. How do the representations in Exercises 41 and 42 improve the error detection over a simple check digit?

44. Explain the concept of the software life cycle.

45. Where do most of the errors occur in a software project?

46. Why does the cost of fixing an error increase the longer the error remains undetected?

47. Compare and contrast the software verification activities of code or design walk-throughs and inspections.

48. How can a program be verified to be correct but still be worthless?

49. Name at least five places where a software error could be introduced.

50. How was the AT&T software failure typical of such failures?

51. What is formal verification?

52. Explain the analogy of the elephant and the goldfish.

53. Define polynomial time.

54. How is it possible to throw away all but the term with the largest exponent when assessing the Big-O complexity of a polynomial-time algorithm?

55. Give the Big-O complexity measure of the following polynomials:
    a. $4x^3 + 32x^2 + 2x + 1003$
    b. $x^5 + x$
    c. $x^2 + 124{,}578$
    d. $x + 1$

56. Explain the analogy of bins of complexity measures.

57. Who manufactures a Turing machine?

58. How does a Turing machine simulate a human with a paper and pencil?

59. Are there problems for which there are no solutions?

60. Describe the halting problem.

61. How is the fact that data and programs look alike inside a computer used in the proof that the halting problem is unsolvable?

???   Thought Questions

1. Go on the Web and perform a search for information on the Pentium chip error. Try different keywords and combinations of keywords, recording how many hits occur with each. Read at least three of the articles, and then write a description of the problem in your own words.

2. Search the Web for the answers to the following questions.
   a. Did the Russian *Phobos 1* spacecraft commit suicide?
   b. What caused the delay in the opening of the Denver airport?
   c. What was the cost of the software repair in London, England's ambulance dispatch system failure?
   d. The USS *Yorktown* was dead in the water for several hours in 1998. What software error caused the problem?

3. A professor was giving a lecture to a local service club about the limits of computing. A member of the audience said, "But I didn't think

there were any limits." If you were the professor, how would you have answered?

4. What do you think about deep linking? Should all access to another website occur only through the home page of that website? Would you feel uncomfortable if someone accessed pages on your site that are in the middle of your site? Isn't such a practice like taking comments out of context?

5. Many commercial websites make their money by advertising. Is bypassing the advertising through deep linking ethical? Should laws be passed to disallow deep linking?

6. If you have a website, do you have links? Are any of your links deep links? After reading about the issues surrounding deep linking, are you going to change them?

Glossary

Absolute path   A path that begins at the root and includes all successive subdirectories

Abstract data type (ADT)   A container whose properties (data and operations) are specified independently of any particular implementation

Abstract step   An algorithmic step for which some details remain unspecified

Abstraction   A mental model that removes complex details; a model of a complex system that includes only the details essential to the viewer

Access control policy   A set of rules established by an organization that specifies which types of network communication are permitted and denied

Access time   The time it takes for a block to start being read; the sum of seek time and latency

Adder   An electronic circuit that performs an addition operation on binary values

Addressability   The number of bits stored in each addressable location in memory

Address binding   The mapping from a logical address to a physical address

Adjacent vertices   Two vertices that are connected by an edge

Aggregate operation   An operation on a data structure as a whole, as opposed to an operation on an individual component of the data structure

Algorithm   Unambiguous instructions for solving a problem or subproblem in a finite amount of time using a finite amount of data; a plan or outline of a solution; a logical sequence of steps that solves a problem

ALU   See arithmetic/logic unit

Analog data   A continuous representation of data

Application software   Programs that help us solve real-world problems

Arguments   The identifiers listed in parentheses on the subprogram call; sometimes called *actual parameters*

Arithmetic/logic unit (ALU)   The computer component that performs arithmetic operations (addition, subtraction, multiplication, division) and logical operations (comparison of two values)

Artificial intelligence (AI)   The study of computer systems that model and apply the intelligence of the human mind

Artificial neural network   A computer representation of knowledge that attempts to mimic the neural networks of the human body

Assembler   A program that translates an assembly-language program into machine code

Assembler directives   Instructions to the translating program

Assembly language   A low-level programming language in which a mnemonic represents each of the machine-language instructions for a particular computer

Assignment statement   A statement that stores the value of an expression into a variable

Asynchronous   Not occurring at the same moment in time as some specific operation of the computer; in other words, not synchronized with the program's actions

Attribute   Part of a tag that provides additional information about the element

Authentication credentials   Information users provide to identify themselves for computer access

Availability   The degree to which authorized users can access information for legitimate purposes

Back door   A program feature that gives special and unauthorized access to a computer system to anyone who knows it exists

Bandwidth   The number of bits or bytes that can be transmitted from one place to another in a fixed amount of time

Base   The foundational value of a number system, which dictates the number of digits and the value of digit positions

Base register   A register that holds the beginning address of the current partition

Big-O notation   A notation that expresses computing time (complexity) as the term in a function that increases most rapidly relative to the size of a problem

Binary digit   A digit in the binary number system; a 0 or a 1

Binary file   A file that contains data in a specific format, requiring a special interpretation of its bits

Binary search   Looking for an item in an already sorted list by eliminating large portions of the data on each comparison

Binary tree An abstract composite structure with a unique starting node called the root, in which each node is capable of having two child nodes, and in which a unique path exists from the root to every other node

Biometrics Using human characteristics such as fingerprints, retina patterns, or voice patterns to identify users and control access

Bit Binary digit

Block The information stored in a sector on a disk

Boolean algebra A mathematical notation for expressing two-valued logical functions

Boolean expression A sequence of identifiers, separated by compatible operators, that evaluates to true or false; an expression that when evaluated is either true or false

Bounds register A register that holds the length of the current partition

Breadth-first approach Searching across levels of a tree prior to searching down specific paths

Broadband Network technologies that generally provide data transfer speeds greater than 128K bps

Buffer overflow A defect in a computer program that could cause a system to crash and leave the user with heightened privileges

Bus topology A LAN configuration in which all nodes share a common line

Bus width The number of bits that can be transferred in parallel over the bus

Byte Eight binary digits

Bytecode A standard machine language into which Java source code is compiled

Cable modem A device that allows computer network communication using the cable TV hookup in a home

Cache memory A type of small, high-speed memory used to hold frequently used data

Caesar cipher A substitution cipher that shifts characters a certain number of positions in the alphabet

Cancellation error A loss of accuracy during addition or subtraction of numbers of widely differing sizes due to limits of precision

Cardinality constraint The number of relationships that may exist at one time among entities in an ER diagram

Case sensitive Uppercase and lowercase letters are not considered the same; two identifiers with the same spelling but different capitalization are considered to be two distinct identifiers

Cell   An element of a spreadsheet that can contain data or a formula

Character set   A list of the characters and the codes used to represent each one

Chatbot   A program designed to carry on a conversation with a human user

Cipher   An algorithm used to encrypt and decrypt text

Circuit   A combination of interacting gates designed to accomplish a specific logical function

Circuit equivalence   The same output for each corresponding input-value combination for two circuits

Circular reference   A set of formulas that ultimately, and erroneously, rely on each other to compute their results

Class (implementation phase)   A pattern for an object

Class NP problems   Problems that can be solved in polynomial time with as many processors as desired

Class P   The class made up of all polynomial-time algorithms

Class P problems   Problems that can be solved with one processor in polynomial time

Client/server model   A distributed approach in which a client makes requests of a server and the server responds

Code-coverage (clear-box) testing   Testing a program or subprogram based on covering all the statements in the code

Combinational circuit   A circuit whose output is solely determined by its input values

Comment   Explanatory text for the human reader

Compiler   A program that translates a high-level language program into machine code

Compression ratio   The size of the compressed data divided by the size of the uncompressed data

Computational biology   An interdisciplinary field that applies techniques of computer science, applied mathematics, and statistics to problems in biology

Computer gaming   A computer simulation of a virtual world

Computer hardware   The physical elements of a computing system

Computer network   A collection of computing devices that are connected so that they can communicate and share resources

Computer software   The programs that provide the instructions that a computer executes

Computing system Computer hardware, software, and data, which interact to solve problems

Concrete step A step for which the details are fully specified

Confidentiality Ensuring that data is protected from unauthorized access

Constant time An algorithm whose Big-O work expression is a constant

Containers Objects whose role is to hold and manipulate other objects

Context switch The exchange of register information that occurs when one process is removed from the CPU and another takes its place

Control abstraction The separation of the logical view of a control structure from its implementation

Control structure A statement used to alter the normally sequential flow of control; an instruction that determines the order in which other instructions in a program are executed

Control unit The computer component that controls the actions of the other components so as to execute instructions in sequence

CPU The central processing unit, a combination of the arithmetic/logic unit and the control unit; the "brain" of a computer that interprets and executes instructions

CPU scheduling The act of determining which process in memory is given access to the CPU so that it may execute

Cryptanalysis The process of decrypting a message without knowing the cipher or the key used to encrypt it

Cryptography The field of study related to encoded information

Cylinder The set of concentric tracks on all surfaces

Data Basic values or facts

Data abstraction The separation of the logical view of data from its implementation

Data compression Reducing the amount of space needed to store a piece of data

Data coverage (black-box) testing Testing a program or subprogram based on the possible input values, treating the code as a black box

Data structure The implementation of a composite data field in an abstract data type

Data transfer rate (bandwidth) The speed with which data is moved from one place to another on a network

Data type A description of the set of values and the basic set of operations that can be applied to values of the type

Database A structured set of data

Database management system A combination of software and data made up of the physical database, the database engine, and the database schema

Declaration A statement that associates an identifier with a variable, an action, or some other entity within the language that can be given a name so that the programmer can refer to that item by name

Decryption The process of converting ciphertext into plaintext

Demand paging An extension to paged memory management in which pages are brought into memory only when referenced (on demand)

Denial of service An attack on a network resource that prevents authorized users from accessing the system

Depth-first approach Searching down the paths of a tree prior to searching across levels

Desk checking Tracing the execution of a design on paper

Digital certificate A representation of a sender's authenticated public key used to minimize malicious forgeries

Digital data A discrete representation of data

Digital signature Data that is appended to a message, made from the message itself and the sender's private key, to ensure the authenticity of the message

Digital subscriber line (DSL) An Internet connection made using a digital signal on regular phone lines

Digitize The act of breaking information down into discrete pieces

Direct file access The technique in which data in a file is accessed directly by specifying logical record numbers

Directed graph (digraph) A graph in which each edge is directed from one vertex to another (or the same) vertex

Directory A named group of files

Directory tree A structure showing the nested directory organization of the file system

Disk scheduling The act of deciding which outstanding requests for disk I/O to satisfy first

Document Type Definition (DTD) A specification of the organization of an XML document

Domain name The part of a hostname that specifies a specific organization or group

Domain name server A computer that attempts to translate a hostname into an IP address

Domain name system A distributed system for managing hostname resolution

Download Receiving data on your home computer from the Internet

Dumb terminal   A monitor and keyboard that allowed the user to access the mainframe computer in early timesharing systems

Dynamic-partition technique   The memory management technique in which memory is divided into partitions as needed to accommodate programs

Edge (arc)   A pair of vertices representing a connection between two nodes in a graph

Effective weight   In an artificial neuron, the sum of the weights multiplied by the corresponding input values

Electronic commerce   The process of buying and selling products and services using the World Wide Web

Encapsulation   A language feature that enforces information hiding; bundling data and actions so that the logical properties of data and actions are separated from the implementation details

Encryption   The process of converting plaintext into ciphertext

Entity-relationship (ER) modeling   A popular technique for designing relational databases

ER diagram   A graphical representation of an ER model

Ethernet   The industry standard for local-area networks, based on a bus topology

Expert system   A software system based on the knowledge of human experts

Extensible Markup Language (XML)   A language that allows the user to describe the content of a document

Extensible Stylesheet Language (XSL)   A language for defining transformations from XML documents to other output formats

Field (or **attribute**)   A single value in a database record

Fields   Named items in a class; can be data or subprograms

File   A named collection of data, used for organizing secondary memory

File extension   Part of a file name that indicates the file type

File server   A computer dedicated to storing and managing files for network users

File system   The operating system's logical view of the files it manages

File type   The specific kind of information contained in a file, such as a Java™ program or a Microsoft® Word document

Firewall   A gateway machine and its software that protects a network by filtering the traffic it allows

Fixed-partition technique   The memory management technique in which memory is divided into a specific number of partitions into which programs are loaded

Floating point　A representation of a real number that keeps track of the sign, mantissa, and exponent

Frame　A fixed-size portion of main memory that holds a process page

Full adder　A circuit that computes the sum of two bits, taking an input carry bit into account

Game engine　A software system within which computer games are created

Gameplay　The type of interactions and experiences a player has during the game

Gate　A device that performs a basic operation on electrical signals, accepting one or more input signals and producing a single output signal

Gateway　A node that handles communication between its LAN and other networks

Graph　A data structure that consists of a set of nodes and a set of edges that relate the nodes to each other

Half adder　A circuit that computes the sum of two bits and produces the appropriate carry bit

Halting problem　The unsolvable problem of determining whether any program will eventually stop given a particular input

Host number　The part of an IP address that specifies a particular host on the network

Hostname　A name made up of words separated by dots that uniquely identifies a computer on the Internet; each hostname corresponds to a particular IP address

Huffman encoding　Using a variable-length binary string to represent a character so that frequently used characters have short codes

Hypertext Markup Language (HTML)　The language used to create or build a Web page

Inference engine　The software that processes rules to draw conclusions

Information　Data that has been organized or processed in a useful manner

Information hiding　The practice of hiding the details of a module with the goal of controlling access to the details of the module

Information security　The techniques and policies used to ensure proper access to data

Information system　Software that helps the user organize and analyze data

Inheritance　A mechanism by which one class acquires the properties—data fields and methods—of another class

Input unit　A device that accepts data to be stored in memory

Inspection   A verification method in which one member of a team reads the program or design line by line and the others point out errors

Instantiate   To create an object from a class

Instruction register (IR)   The register that contains the instruction currently being executed

Integer   A natural number, a negative of a natural number, or zero

Integrated circuit (chip)   A piece of silicon on which multiple gates have been embedded

Integrity   Ensuring that data can be modified only by appropriate mechanisms

Interactive system   A system that allows direct communication between the user and the computer

Internet   A wide-area network that spans the planet

Internet backbone   A set of high-speed networks carrying Internet traffic

Internet Protocol (IP)   The network protocol that deals with the routing of packets through interconnected networks to the final destination

Internet service provider (ISP)   A company providing access to the Internet

Interoperability   The ability of software and hardware on multiple machines and from multiple commercial vendors to communicate

Interpreter   A program that inputs a program in a high-level language and directs the computer to perform the actions specified in each statement

IP address   An address made up of four numeric values separated by dots that uniquely identifies a computer on the Internet

Java applet   A Java program designed to be embedded into an HTML document, transferred over the Web, and executed in a browser

JSP scriptlet   A portion of code embedded in an HTML document designed to dynamically contribute to the content of the Web page

Key   One or more fields of a database record that uniquely identifies it among all other records in the table; the set of parameters that guide a cipher

Keyword encoding   Replacing a frequently used word with a single character

Knowledge-based system   Software that uses a specific set of information

Latency   The time it takes for the specified sector to be in position under the read/write head

Leaf node   A tree node that has no children

Lexical ambiguity   The ambiguity created when words have multiple meanings

Link   A connection between one Web page and another

Linked list   A list in which the order of the components is determined by an explicit link field in each node, rather than by the sequential order of the components in memory

Linked structure   An implementation of a container where the items are stored together with information on where the next item can be found

Loader   A piece of software that takes a machine-language program and places it into memory

Local-area network (LAN)   A network connecting a small number of nodes in a close geographic area

Loebner prize   The first formal instantiation of the Turing test, held annually

Logic bomb   A malicious program that is set up to execute when a specific system event occurs

Logic diagram   A graphical representation of a circuit; each type of gate has its own symbol

Logical address   A reference to a stored value relative to the program making the reference

Lossless compression   A data compression technique in which there is no loss of information

Lossy compression   A data compression technique in which there is loss of information

Machine language   The language made up of binary-coded instructions that is used directly by the computer

Mainframe   A large, multi-user computer often associated with early time-sharing systems

Malicious code   A computer program that attempts to bypass appropriate authorization and/or perform unauthorized functions

Man-in-the-middle   A security attack in which network communication is intercepted in an attempt to obtain key data

Markup language   A language that uses tags to annotate the information in a document

Memory management   The act of keeping track of how and where programs are loaded in main memory

Metalanguage   A language that is used to define other languages

Method   A named algorithm that defines one aspect of the behavior of a class

Metropolitan-area network (MAN)   A network infrastructure developed for a large city

MIME type   A standard for defining the format of files that are included as email attachments or on websites

Model   An abstraction of a real system; a representation of objects within a system and the rules that govern the behavior of the objects

Motherboard   The main circuit board of a personal computer

Multimedia   Several different media types

Multiplexer   A circuit that uses a few input control signals to determine which of several input data lines is routed to its output

Multiprogramming   The technique of keeping multiple programs in main memory at the same time, competing for the CPU

Natural language   Languages that human beings use to communicate, such as English

Natural language comprehension   Using a computer to apply a meaningful interpretation to human communication

Natural number   The number 0 and any number obtained by repeatedly adding 1 to it

Negative number   A value less than 0, with a sign opposite to its positive counterpart

Nested structure (nested logic)   A structure in which one control structure is embedded within another

Network address   The part of an IP address that specifies a specific network

Node (host)   Any addressable device attached to a network

Nonpreemptive scheduling   CPU scheduling that occurs when the currently executing process gives up the CPU voluntarily

NP-complete problems   A class of problems within Class NP that has the property that if a polynomial time solution with one processor can be found for any member of the class, such a solution exists for every member of the class

Number   A unit of an abstract mathematical system subject to the laws of arithmetic

Object   A collection of data values and associated operations

Object (implementation phase)   An instance of a class

Object (problem-solving phase)   An entity or thing that is relevant in the context of a problem

Object class (class problem-solving phase)   A description of a group of objects with similar properties and behaviors

Open system   A system that is based on a common model of network architecture and an accompanying suite of protocols

Open Systems Interconnection (OSI) Reference Model A seven-layer logical breakdown of network interaction to facilitate communication standards

Operating system System software that manages computer resources and provides an interface for system interaction

Output unit A device that prints or otherwise displays data stored in memory or makes a permanent copy of information stored in memory or another device

Overflow The condition that occurs when the results of a calculation are too large to represent in a given machine; a situation where a calculated value cannot fit into the number of digits reserved for it

Packet A unit of data sent across a network

Packet switching The approach to network communication in which packets are individually routed to their destination, then reassembled

Page A fixed-size portion of a process that is stored into a memory frame

Page-map table (PMT) The table used by the operating system to keep track of page/frame relationships

Page swap Bringing in one page from secondary memory, possibly causing another to be removed

Paged memory technique A memory management technique in which processes are divided into fixed-size pages and stored in memory frames when loaded

Parameter list A mechanism for communicating between two parts of a program

Parameters The identifiers listed in parentheses beside the subprogram name; sometimes called *formal parameters*

Password guessing An attempt to gain access to a computer system by methodically trying to determine a user's password

Path A text designation of the location of a file or subdirectory in a file system; a sequence of vertices that connects two nodes in a graph

Phishing Using a Web page to masquerade as part of an authoritative system and trick users into revealing security information

Phone modem A device that converts computer data into an analog audio signal and back again

Phonemes The set of fundamental sounds made in any given natural language

Physical address An actual address in the main memory device

Ping A program used to test whether a particular network computer is active and reachable

Pipelining A technique that breaks an instruction into smaller steps that can be overlapped

Pixels Individual dots used to represent a picture; stands for picture elements

Polymorphism The ability of a language to have duplicate method names in an inheritance hierarchy and to apply the method that is appropriate for the object to which the method is applied

Polynomial-time algorithms Algorithms whose complexity can be expressed as a polynomial in the size of the problem

Port A numeric designation corresponding to a particular high-level protocol

Positional notation A system of expressing numbers in which the digits are arranged in succession, the position of each digit has a place value, and the number is equal to the sum of the products of each digit by its place value

Precision The maximum number of significant digits that can be represented

Preemptive scheduling CPU scheduling that occurs when the operating system decides to favor another process, preempting the currently executing process

Procedural abstraction The separation of the logical view of an action from its implementation

Process The dynamic representation of a program during execution

Process control block (PCB) The data structure used by the operating system to manage information about a process

Process management The act of keeping track of information for active processes

Process states The conceptual stages through which a process moves as it is managed by the operating system

Program A sequence of instructions written to perform a specified task

Program counter (PC) The register that contains the address of the next instruction to be executed

Proprietary system A system that uses technologies kept private by a particular commercial vendor

Protocol A set of rules that defines how data is formatted and processed on a network

Protocol stack Layers of protocols that build and rely on each other

Pseudocode A language designed to express algorithms

Public-key cryptography An approach to cryptography in which each user has two related keys, one public and one private

Pulse-code modulation Variation in a signal that jumps sharply between two extremes

Query A request to retrieve data from a database

Radix point   The dot that separates the whole part from the fractional part in a real number in any base

Range   A set of contiguous cells specified by the endpoints

Raster-graphics format   Storing image information pixel by pixel

Rational number   An integer or the quotient of two integers (division by zero excluded)

Real-time system   A system in which response time is crucial given the nature of the application domain

Reclock   The act of reasserting an original digital signal before too much degradation occurs

Record (or **object,** or **entity**)   A collection of related fields that make up a single database entry

Recursion   The ability of a subprogram to call itself

Reference parameter   A parameter that expects the address of its argument to be passed by the calling unit (put on the message board)

Referential ambiguity   The ambiguity created when pronouns could be applied to multiple objects

Register   A small storage area in the CPU used to store intermediate values or special data

Relational model   A database model in which data and the relationships among them are organized into tables

Relative path   A path that begins at the current working directory

Repeater   A network device that strengthens and propagates a signal along a long communication line

Representational (round-off) error   An arithmetic error caused by the fact that the precision of the result of an arithmetic operation is greater than the precision of our machine

Reserved word   A word in a language that has special meaning; it cannot be used as an identifier

Resolution   The number of pixels used to represent a picture

Response time   The time delay between receiving a stimulus and producing a response

Ring topology   A LAN configuration in which all nodes are connected in a closed loop

Risk analysis   Determining the nature and likelihood of the risks to key data

Root   The unique starting node in a tree

Root directory   The topmost directory, in which all others are contained

Route cipher   A transposition cipher that lays out a message in a grid and traverses it in a particular way

Router   A network device that directs a packet between networks toward its final destination

Rule-based system   A software system based on a set of *if-then* rules

Run-length encoding   Replacing a long series of a repeated characters with a count of the repetition

Schema   A specification of the logical structure of data in a database

Scientific notation   An alternative floating-point representation

Search tree   A structure that represents alternatives in adversarial situations, such as game playing

Secondary storage device   See auxiliary storage device

Sector   A section of a track

Seek time   The time it takes for the read/write head to get positioned over the specified track

Semantic network   A knowledge representation technique that represents the relationships among objects

Semiconductor   Material such as silicon that is neither a good conductor nor a good insulator

Sequential circuit   A circuit whose output is a function of its input values and the current state of the circuit

Sequential file access   The technique in which data in a file is accessed in a linear fashion

Shared memory parallel processor   The situation in which multiple processors share a global memory

Signed-magnitude representation   Number representation in which the sign represents the ordering of the number (negative and positive) and the value represents the magnitude

Significant digits   Those digits that begin with the first nonzero digit on the left and end with the last nonzero digit on the right (or a zero digit that is exact)

Simulation   Developing a model of a complex system and experimenting with the model to observe the results

Single contiguous memory management   The approach to memory management in which a program is loaded into one continuous area of memory

Smart card   A card with an embedded memory chip used to identify users and control access

Social network   A model of how objects interact

Software requirements   A statement of what is to be provided by a computer system or software product

Software specification   A detailed description of the function, inputs, processing, outputs, and special features of a software product; it provides the information needed to design and implement the software

Spatial compression   Movie compression technique based on the same compression techniques used for still images

Spoofing   An attack on a computer system in which a malicious user masquerades as an authorized user

Spreadsheet   A program that allows the user to organize and analyze data using a grid of cells

Spreadsheet function   A computation provided by the spreadsheet software that can be incorporated into formulas

Star topology   A LAN configuration in which a central node controls all message traffic

Strong equivalence   The equality of two systems based on their results and the process by which they arrive at those results

Strong typing   Each variable is assigned a type, and only values of that type can be stored in the variable

Structured Query Language (SQL)   A comprehensive relational database language for data management and queries

Substitution cipher   A cipher that substitutes one character with another

Synchronous processing   Multiple processors apply the same program in lockstep to multiple data sets

Syntactic ambiguity   The ambiguity created when sentences can be constructed in various ways

System software   Programs that manage a computer system and interact with hardware

Table   A collection of database records

Tag   The syntactic element in a markup language that indicates how information should be displayed

TCP/IP   A suite of protocols and programs that support low-level network communication

Temporal compression   Movie compression technique based on differences between consecutive frames

Ten's complement   A representation of negative numbers such that the negative of I is 10 raised to k minus I

Test plan   A document that specifies how a program is to be tested

Test plan implementation   Using the test cases specified in a test plan to verify that a program outputs the predicted results

Text file   A file that contains characters

Thrashing   Inefficient processing caused by constant page swapping

Time slice   The amount of time given to each process in the round-robin CPU scheduling algorithm

Timesharing   A system in which CPU time is shared among multiple interactive users at the same time

Top-level domain (TLD)   The last section of a domain name, specifying the type of organization or its country of origin

Traceroute   A program that shows the route a packet takes across the Internet

Track   A concentric circle on the surface of a disk

Training   The process of adjusting the weights and threshold values in a neural net to get a desired outcome

Transfer rate   The rate at which data moves from the disk to memory

Transistor   A device that acts either as a wire or a resister, depending on the voltage level of an input signal

Transmission Control Protocol (TCP)   The network protocol that breaks messages into packets, reassembles them at the destination, and takes care of errors

Transposition cipher   A cipher that rearranges the order of characters in a message

Trojan horse   A malicious program disguised as a benevolent resource

Truth table   A table showing all possible input values and the associated output values

Turing test   A behavioral approach to determining whether a computer system is intelligent

Turnaround time   The CPU scheduling metric that measures the elapsed time between a process's arrival in the ready state and its ultimate completion

Underflow   The condition that occurs when the results of a calculation are too small to represent in a given machine

Undirected graph   A graph in which the edges have no direction

Uniform Resource Locator (URL)   A standard way of specifying the location of a Web page

Upload   Sending data from your home computer to a destination on the Internet

User Datagram Protocol (UDP)   An alternative to TCP that achieves higher transmission speeds at the cost of reliability

Value parameter   A parameter that expects a copy of its argument to be passed by the calling unit (put on the message board)

Variable   A location in memory, referenced by an identifier, that contains a data value

Vector graphics   Representation of an image in terms of lines and shapes

Vertex   A node in a graph

Video codec   Methods used to shrink the size of a movie

Virtual computer (machine)   A hypothetical machine designed to illustrate important features of a real machine

Virtual machine   The illusion created by a timesharing system that each user has a dedicated machine

Virtual memory   The illusion that there is no restriction on program size because an entire process need not be in memory at the same time

Virus   A malicious, self-replicating program that embeds itself into other code

Voice recognition   Using a computer to recognize the words spoken by a human

Voice synthesis   Using a computer to create the sound of human speech

Voiceprint   The plot of frequency changes over time representing the sound of human speech

Walk-through   A verification method in which a team performs a manual simulation of the program or design

Weak equivalence   The equality of two systems based on their results

Web browser   A software tool that retrieves and displays Web pages

Web page   A document that contains or references various kinds of data

Web server   A computer dedicated to responding to requests for Web pages

Website   A collection of related Web pages, usually designed and controlled by the same person or company

What-if analysis   Modifying spreadsheet values that represent assumptions to see how changes in those assumptions affect related data

Wide-area network (WAN)   A network connecting two or more local-area networks

Wireless   A network connection made without physical wires

Word   A group of one or more bytes; the number of bits in a word is the word length of the computer

Working directory   The currently active subdirectory

World Wide Web (Web)   An infrastructure of information and the network software used to access it

Worm   A malicious stand-alone program that often targets network resources

Endnotes

Chapter 1

1. G. A. Miller, "Reprint of the Magical Number Seven Plus or Minus Two: Some Limits on Our Capacity for Processing Information," *Psychological Review* 101, no. 2 (1994): 343352.

2. "Beyond All Dreams," http://www.mith.umd.edu/flare/lovelace/index.html

3. National Geographic News, (29 May 2008).

4. Written by Chip Weems, adapted from: N. Dale, C. Weems, and M. Headington, *Java and Software Design* (Sudbury, MA: Jones and Bartlett Publishers, Inc., 2001): 3523.

5. P. E. Grogono and S. H. Nelson, *Problem Solving and Computer Programming* (Reading, MA: Addison-Wesley, 1982): 92.

6. P. E. Cerruzzi, *A History of Modern Computing* (Cambridge, MA: The MIT Press, 1998): 217.

7. R. X. Gringely, "Be Absolute for Death: Life after Moore's Law," *Communications of the ACM* 44, no. 3 (2001): 94.

8. P. E. Cerruzzi, *A History of Modern Computing* (Cambridge, MA: The MIT Press, 1998): 291.

9. S. Levy, "Back to the Future," Newsweek (21 April 2003).

10. L. Kappelman, "The Future is Ours," *Communications of the ACM* 44, no. 3 (2001): 46.

11. http://wilk4.com/humor/humore10.htm (accessed April 10, 2009)

12. http://digg.com/d1LmM (accessed April 13, 2009)

13. P. Denning, "Computer Science the Discipline," *Encyclopedia of Computer Science*, ed. E. Reilly, A. Ralston, and D. Hemmendinger (Groves Dictionaries, Inc., 2000).

14. Andrew Tannenbaum. Keynote address at the Technical Symposium of the Special Interest Group on Computer Science Education, San Jose, California, February 1997.

15. P. Denning, D. Comer, D. Gries, et al., "Computing as a Discipline," *Communications of ACM 32*, no. 1(1989): 932.

Chapter 2

1. *Webster's New Collegiate Dictionary*, 1977, s.v. "positional notation."
2. G. Ifrah, *From the Abacus to the Quantum Computer: The Universal History of Computing* (John Wiley & Sons, Inc., 2001): 245.

Chapter 3

1. Character set maze from draft article by Bob Bemer.

Chapter 4

1. Written by Chip Weems, adapted from: N. Dale, C. Weems, and M. Headington, *Java and Software Design* (Sudbury, MA: Jones and Bartlett Publishers, Inc., 2001): 2423.
2. R. Siegel, "What Is a Nanosecond" (New York).
3. R. Orr, "Augustus DeMorgan," http://www.engr.iupui.edu/~orr/webpages/cpt120/mathbios/ademo.htm
4. B. Dart, Austin American-Statesman, (19 April 2003).

Chapter 5

1. A. Perlis, "Epigrams on Programming," *ACM Sigplan Notices* (October, 1981): 713.
2. Webopedia, s.v. "embedded systems," http://webopedia.com/TERM/E/embedded_system.htm
3. The Ganssle Group. *Microcontroller C Compilers*, http://www.ganssle.com/articles/acforuc.htm
4. http://en.wikipedia.org (accessed May 14, 2009)

Chapter 6

1. Pep/1 through Pep/8 are virtual machines designed by Stanley Warford for his textbook *Computer Systems* (Sudbury, MA: Jones and Bartlett, 2010).

Chapter 7

1. G. Polya, *How to Solve It: A New Aspect of Mathematical Method*, 2nd ed., (Princeton, NJ: Princeton University Press, 1945).

2. T. Hoare. Adapted from autobiography.

Chapter 8

1. S. Warford, *Computer Systems* (Sudbury, MA: Jones and Bartlett Publishers, Inc., 1999): 146.

Chapter 9

1. *Webster's New Collegiate Dictionary*, 1977, s.v. "brainstorming."

2. G. Booch, "What Is and Isn't Object Oriented Design," *American Programmer* 2, no. 78 (Summer 1989).

3. T. W. Pratt, *Programming Languages: Design and Implementation*, 2nd ed., (Englewood Cliffs, NJ: Prentice-Hall, Inc., 1984): 604.

4. Bartleby.com, "Great Books Online" http://www.bartleby.com

5. Techtarget.com (2001): http://WhatIs.techtarget.com

6. http://dictionary.babylon.com/paradigm

7. http://www.moneywords.com/glossary

8. K. C. Louden, *Programming Languages: Principles and Practice* (Boston: PWS-KENT Publishing Company, 1993).

9. SISC: Second Interpreter for Scheme Code, http://sisc-scheme.org/sisc-online.php (accessed June 9, 2009)

10. Rogers, Jean B. *A Prolog Primer.* Reading, MA: Addison-Wesley, 1986.

11. When referring to code in a specific language or to what is actually stored in memory, we use a monospace (code) font.

12. O. Dahl, E. W. Dijkstra, and C. A. R. Hoare, *Structured Programming* (New York: Academic Press, 1972).

13. S. Warford, *Computer Systems* (Sudbury, MA: Jones and Bartlett Publishers, Inc., 1999): 222.

Chapter 13

1. D. Kortenkamp, R. P. Bonasso, and R. Murphy, *Aritificial Intelligence and Mobile Robots* (Menlo Park, CA: AAAI Press/The MIT Press, 1998).

2. J. Weizenbaum, *Computer Power and Human Reason* (San Francisco: W. H. Freeman, 1976): 34.

3. Mars Now Team and the California Space Institute, 6 October 2001.

4. R. A. Brooks, "A Robust Layered Control System for a Mobile Robot," *IEEE Transactions on Robotics and Automation* 2, no. 1: 1423.

5. J. H. L. Jones and A. M. Flynn, *Mobile Robots: Inspiration to Implementation* (Wellesley, MA: A K Peters, 1993): 175.

Chapter 14

1. M. Pidd, "An Introduction to Computer Simulation," *Proceedings of the 1994 Winter Simulation Conference.*

2. R. E. Shannon, "Introduction to the Art and Science of Simulation," *Proceedings of the 1998 Winter Simulation Conference.*

3. http://heim.ifi.uio.no/~kristen/FORSKNINGSDOK_MAPPE/F_OO_start.html

4. D. R. Stauffer, N. L. Seaman, T. T. Warner, and A. M. Lario, "Application of an Atmospheric Simulation Model to Diagnose Air-Pollution Transport in the Grand Canyon Region of Arizona," *Chemical Engineering Communications* 121, (1993): 925.

5. "Some Operational Forecast Models," *USA Today Weather*, (8 November 2000), http://www.usatoday.com/weather/wmodlist.htm

6. D. R. Stauffer, N. L. Seaman, T. T. Warner, and A. M. Lario. "Application of an Atmospheric Simulation Model to Diagnose Air-Pollution Transport in the Grand Canyon Region of Arizona," *Chemical Engineering Communications* 121, (1993): 925.

Chapter 15

1. D. Sefton, Newhouse, News Service, *Austin American Statesman* (27 April 2001).

2. M. Softky, "Douglas Engelbart. Computer Visionary Seeks to Boost People's Collective Ability to Confront Complex Problems Coming at a Faster Pace," *The Almanac* (21 February 2001), http://www.almanacnews.com/morgue/2001/2001_02_21.cover21.html

3. http://en.wikipedia.org/wiki/social_networks (accessed July 25, 2009)

4. J. H. Fowler and N. A. Christakis, "Dynamic Spread of Happiness in a Large Social Network: Longitudinal Analysis over 20 years in the Framingham Heart Study." *British Medical Journal* (4 December 2008), doi:10.1136/bmj.a2338. Media account for those who cannot

retrieve the original: "Happiness: It Really Is Contagious." Retrieved December 5, 2008.

5. J. Kleinfeld, "Could It Be A Big World After All?"

6. D. Watts, "Six Degrees: The Science of a Connected Age."

7. http://blog.compete.com/2009/02/09/facebook-myspace-twitter-social-network/ (retrieved July 27, 2009)

Chapter 16

1. J. Mintz, "When Bloggers Make News," *The Wall Street Journal,* January 21, 2005, p. B1.

2. Editorial, "The Apple Case Isn't Just a Blow to Bloggers," *Business Week,* March 28, 2005, p. 128.

3. St. Thomas Aquinas, *Summa Theologiae,* (New York: Benziger Bros, 1947), IIa-IIa, 109–110.

4. J. Mintz, "When Bloggers Make News," *The Wall Street Journal,* January 21, 2005, p. B4.

Chapter 17

1. H. M. Walker, *The Limits of Computing* (Sudbury, MA: Jones and Bartlett Publishers, 1994). This fable and many of the ideas in this chapter come from Dr. Walker's thought-provoking little book. Thank you, Henry.

2. *Software Engineering Note* 11, no. 1 (January 1986): 14.

3. J. Markoff, "Circuit Flaw Causes Pentium Chip to Miscalculate, Intel Admits," *The New York Times* (24 November 1994), c. 1991, N.Y. Times News Service.

4. N. G. Leveson, "Software Engineering: Stretching the Limits of Complexity," *Communications of the ACM* 40, no. 2 (February 1997): 129.

5. D. Bell, I. Morrey, and J. Pugh, *Software Engineering, A Programming Approach*, 2nd ed. (Prentice Hall, 1992).

6. T. Huckle, *Collection of Software Bugs,* http://www5.in.tum.de/~huckle/bugse.html

7. Dennis Beeson, Manager, Naval Air Warfare Center, Weapons Division, F18 Software Development Team.

8. D. Gries, "Queen's Awards Go to Oxford University Computing and INMOS," *Computing Research News* 2, no. 3 (July 1990): 11.

9. "Out in the open," *The Economist,* (April 2001).

10. "Out in the open," *The Economist,* (April 2001).

11. E. Dijkstra, "On the Cruelty of Really Teaching Computing Science," *Communications of the ACM* 32, no. 12 (December 1989): 1402.

12. "Ghost in the Machine," *TIME—The Weekly Newsmagazine,* (29 January 1990): 59.

13. T. Huckle, *Collection of Software Bugs,* http://www5.in.tum.de/~huckle/bugse.html

14. N. G. Leveson and C. S. Turner, "An Investigation of the Therac25 Accidents," *IEEE Computer* 26, no. 7 (July 1993): 1841.

15. Douglas Arnold, *The Patriot Missile Failure,* http://www.ima.umn.edu/~arnold/disasters/patriot.html

16. United States General Accounting Office Information Management and Technology Division, B247094 (February 4, 1992).

17. J. Fox, *Software and Its Development* (Englewood Cliffs, NJ: Prentice-Hall, 1982): 187188.

18. Douglas Isbell and Don Savage, *Mars Polar Lander* (1999), http://mars.jpl.nasa.gov/msp98/news/mco991110.html

19. Paul Gray, "Computer Scientist Alan Turing," http://www.time.com/time/time100/scientist/profile/turing.html

20. Paul Gray, "Computer Scientist Alan Turing," *Time Magazine,* (29 March 1999).

Index

Italicized page locators indicate a figure; tables are noted with a *t*.